# The Rowman & Littlefield Handbook on Aging and Work

## The Rowman & Littlefield Handbook Series

This contemporary series of academic handbooks provides an authoritative guide to relevant and emerging topics across the humanities and social sciences. To encourage greater dialogue across disciplines, this series engages high-quality, original, and multi-disciplinary research on topics, themes, and key debates in academia today.

- Each handbook draws together newly commissioned work to provide a comprehensive benchmark for a field or subdiscipline
- The individual handbooks include an international team of contributors, with valuable expertise, knowledge, and perspective in their fields
- Handbooks in this series correspond to the latest topics on courses around the world

Each Handbook is available for purchase in both print and digital formats. For more information, see www.rowman.com.

*The Rowman & Littlefield Handbook of Christianity in the Middle East*
Edited by Mark A. Lamport and Mitri Raheb
*The Rowman & Littlefield Handbook of Media Management and Business*
Edited by L. Meghan Mahoney and Tang Tang
*The Rowman & Littlefield Handbook on Aging and Work*
Edited by Elizabeth F. Fideler

# The Rowman & Littlefield Handbook on Aging and Work

Edited by
ELIZABETH F. FIDELER

ROWMAN & LITTLEFIELD
*Lanham • Boulder • New York • London*

Published by Rowman & Littlefield
An imprint of The Rowman & Littlefield Publishing Group, Inc.
4501 Forbes Boulevard, Suite 200, Lanham, Maryland 20706
www.rowman.com

6 Tinworth Street, London SE11 5AL, United Kingdom



British Library Cataloguing in Publication Information Available

**Library of Congress Cataloging-in-Publication Data**

Names: Fideler, Elizabeth F., editor.

Title: The Rowman & Littlefield handbook on aging and work / edited by Elizabeth F. Fideler.

Description: Lanham : Rowman & Littlefield, 2021. | Series: The Rowman & Littlefield handbook series | Includes bibliographical references and index.

Identifiers: LCCN 2021005850 (print) | LCCN 2021005851 (ebook) | ISBN 9781538129944 (cloth) | ISBN 9781538129951 (epub)

Subjects: LCSH: Older people—Employment—United States. | Age and employment—United States. | Personnel management—United States. | Ageism—United States. | Employees—Rating of—United States.

Classification: LCC HD6280 .R69 2021 (print) | LCC HD6280 (ebook) | DDC 331.3/980973—dc23

LC record available at https://lccn.loc.gov/2021005850

LC ebook record available at https://lccn.loc.gov/2021005851

∞™ The paper used in this publication meets the minimum requirements of American National Standard for Information Sciences—Permanence of Paper for Printed Library Materials, ANSI/NISO Z39.48-1992.

# Contents

1 **The Aging Workforce: An Overview** *by Elizabeth F. Fideler, Editor* 1

PART I • **FISCAL CHALLENGES AND THE OLDER WORKER**

2 **The Growing Financial Imperative to Work Longer** *by Richard W. Johnson, Karen E. Smith, and Damir Cosic* 15

3 **Challenges and Opportunities to Living and Working Longer in the Twenty-First Century** *by Ernest Gonzales and Sarah Michelle Steeley* 35

4 **The Choices of (Low-Income) Aging Workers on the Margins: Expanding the Narrative** *by Christina Matz and Melissa Brown* 53

5 **Precariously and Securely Employed Older Women and Prospects for Extended Working Lives** *by Debra Street and Áine Ní Léime* 69

6 **Retirement Security and Timing among Hispanics: Is Working Longer a Fair Expectation for Everyone in the U.S.?** *by Antonia Díaz-Valdés I.* 87

PART II • **DEMOGRAPHIC SHIFTS AND WORKFORCE MANAGEMENT**

7 **Adapting to an Aging Workforce: Evolving Talent Strategies and HR Practices** *by Jennifer Schramm* 111

8 **Managing Aging and Age-Diverse Workforces** *by Hannes Zacher and Cort W. Rudolph* 131

9 **Collaborative Work in the Twenty-First Century: An Intergenerational, Age-Diverse Perspective** *by Jensine Paoletti, Ruilin Wu, and Eduardo Salas* 149

10 **The Role of Employers in Shaping the Lives of Experienced Employees: Moving from Awareness to Activity** *by Brian Kaskie and Hannah Rochford* 171

11 **Creating Age-Friendly Workplaces for Older Workers: Challenges and Opportunities** *by Amanda Sonnega* 191

12 **Tackling Ageism in the Workplace** *by Hannah J. Swift, Ben Steeden, and Georgina Randsley de Moura* 211

PART III · **FACTORS INFLUENCING LABOR FORCE PARTICIPATION AT OLDER AGES**

13 **Older Workers and Job Performance** *by Elora C. Voyles and Michael P. Robinson* 231

14 **Productive Engagement among Older Workers** *by Yi Wang, Takashi Amano, and Kara A. Carter* 249

15 **Self-Management of Career and Retirement: Issues of Competence and Dyscompetence** *by Harvey L. Sterns and Anthony A. Sterns* 267

16 **Older Workers' Self-Management and Sustainable Employability at Work: Lessons Learned from Science and Practice** *by Annet de Lange, Trude Furunes, and Anne-Marije Buckens* 285

17 **Emerging Technologies, the Aging Workforce, and the Future of Work** *by Margaret E. Beier and Meghan K. Davenport* 307

18 **Living Longer, Working Longer, Learning Longer** *by Phyllis A. Cummins, Peter Riley Bahr, and Takashi Yamashita* 327

PART IV · **DETERMINANTS OF EMPLOYEE WELL-BEING**

19 **Resilience, Need Fulfillment, and Well-Being in Older Workers** *by Katherine D. King and Christine Rutledge Smith* 351

20 **Aging, Work, and Caregiving: Current Knowledge and Directions for Future Research** *by Sarah E. Patterson and Andrew Arche* 371

PART V · **AS THE EXPERIENCE OF AGING CHANGES, SO TOO DOES RETIREMENT**

21 **The Changing Landscape of Retirement** *by Helen Dennis and Kelly Ann Marnfeldt* 393

22 **Bridge Employment** *by Karen Pak and Mo Wang* 411

23 **Senior Entrepreneurship: The Twenty-First Century's Most Underrated Economic Engine** *by Elizabeth Isele* 425

24 **Older Workers as Volunteers** *by Doug Dickson* 441

PART VI · **SUMMARY AND FUTURE OUTLOOK**

25 **Social Policy and the Older Worker: An International Perspective** *by Janet M. Hively and Moira Allan* 461

26 **A Portfolio Framework for Extended Work Pathways: Leveraging the Strengths of Older Workers** *by Dawn C. Carr, Brittany M. King, and Phyllis Moen* 481

INDEX 505

ABOUT THE CONTRIBUTORS 517

CHAPTER 1

# The Aging Workforce

## An Overview

Elizabeth F. Fideler, Editor

In 1922 G. Stanley Hall published *Senescence: The Last Half of Life*, in which he railed against the marginalization of the elderly. Hall was a major contributor to the then new field of psychology, the scientific study of human development.[1] While Hall is best known for his 1904 study of adolescence, his *Senescence* is far less familiar though similarly wide ranging and influential. It is considered to be "the first major work in gerontology by an American social scientist"[2] and "the first major analysis by an American social scientist of the changing experience of aging."[3] Written after Hall had retired, *Senescence* is "at once a personal document, an aging manual, and a call to scientific study and professional service."[4] In Hall's view, "the new aged" have "a vital yet unrecognized role to play in the modern world, a role requiring a greater knowledge of the last stage of life" in which they "use their matured powers of impartiality and synthesis to lead mankind safely into the future."[5] In addition, *Senescence* was an early call for a new "curriculum," led by scientists and helping professionals serving as "initiators" into the final phases of life, that specialized in gerontology.

However, the "reconstruction of old age" that ensued was not the response that Hall envisioned. Thereafter, and for too long, the aged continued to be "set off as a class apart" in "a society that simultaneously lengthens life and drains it of substance."[6] The crisis of old age had many manifestations but was above all psychological in nature, owing largely to what was deemed the "economic uselessness of men after 60." (Women apparently did not come into Hall's purview.) Feeling isolated, unnecessary, and displaced both personally and professionally (he passed away at age eighty in 1924), Hall decried stereotypical notions of aging and retirement (which meant being eased out of the workplace to "glide into a peaceful harbor") that spurred decline and thwarted one's ability to remain necessary, able to participate actively in public life, and achieve a new vitality.[7]

One hundred years after Hall's manifesto, the *Rowman & Littlefield Handbook on Aging and Work* sheds light on the multifaceted context in which the U.S. workforce is aging, explaining as well what extended work life looks like and the various forces driving its increase. What Hall decried as "economic uselessness"—being put on the shelf or out to pasture at a certain age—is no longer automatic in most fields. What he saw as the "changing experience of aging" continues to change today, though the results are far from uniformly positive. Later life means decline for some and, for the more fortunate, vitality plus active participation in public and private life.

Well before the COVID-19 pandemic struck and sent the labor market reeling, aging and work researchers described older workers navigating "a rocky path to a secure retirement."[8] So says the American Society on Aging (ASA) in an issue of its journal devoted entirely to "The Future of Work and Older Workers." Despite working longer, ASA's guest editors Ghilarducci and Radpour assert, older adults are seeing a "steady erosion of retirement income security," especially those in precarious, temporary, or part-time jobs who earn low wages and are not eligible for benefits, such as a workplace retirement savings plan or health insurance.[9] What's more, they point out, assumptions about the benefits of staying on the job to augment income can be trumped by workplace conditions, including ageist attitudes, age discrimination, lack of training opportunities, and withholding of job flexibility. And, because working longer is not "a perfect 'free lunch' policy solution,"[10] they propose that older workers have government protection via a strengthened Social Security system to help them stay out of poverty. In the same journal, other authors comment on a weakening of older workers' "experience premium" (long considered their greatest asset), a decline in older workers' earnings, their lack of financial preparedness,[11] and their vulnerability to long-term joblessness.[12]

If older workers were vulnerable before the novel coronavirus, its deleterious effects on our society in general and the economy in particular have only made things worse. The chair of the Federal Reserve, Jerome H. Powell, deemed the crisis "the biggest economic shock, in the U.S. and the world, really, in living memory. We went from the lowest level of unemployment in 50 years to the highest level in close to 90 years, and we did it in two months."[13] Getting to specifics, Rudolph and colleagues characterize the pandemic's impact on organizations and the people who work in them as presenting challenges (and sometimes opportunities), with particular regard to the following: occupational health and safety, work-family issues, telecommuting, virtual teamwork, job insecurity, precarious work, leadership, human resources policy, the aging workforce, and careers.[14]

Each of those topics and many others of particular relevance to mature workers are discussed in this volume. Most of the handbook authors submitted their chapters before the pandemic took hold and were completely unaware of the widespread health risks, loss of life, financial hardship, business closures, spikes in unemployment, and overall insecurity afflicting our country and the rest of the world. As of this writing, it is only fair to acknowledge there is no way to know whether and when the virus will be stopped in its tracks so that it cannot continue to upend the lives and livelihoods of not just older workers but all Americans for months or years to come.

Aging and work researchers will undoubtedly be attuned to changes in labor force participation rates triggered by the pandemic, changes such as older workers, the fastest-growing demographic in the American workforce, disproportionately losing employment.[15] And they will monitor any surge in retirements owing to laid-off older workers in a broad spectrum of industries giving up after repeated efforts to find reemployment during the recession.[16]

Readers will find the handbook's approach to be comprehensive, multidisciplinary, and focused on both employers and employees. Contributing authors represent the fields of sociology, industrial and organizational psychology, gerontology, social work, business management, economics, and journalism. There is a very healthy balance between senior scholars and early-career researchers chosen on the basis of their cutting-edge work regarding important aspects of aging and work. The majority of the authors are U.S. based; a smaller number are in the Netherlands, England, Ireland, France, Germany, Norway, Chile, and China. The volume's focus, however, is primarily on aging and work in the U.S.

Yet, because trends observed in this country are also occurring in many places around the globe, comparisons with other countries are usefully drawn. One forecast of worldwide developments during the coming decade comes from the Milken Institute's Center for the Future of Aging, which notes how closely the United Nations, the World Health Organization, the National Academy of Medicine, and other national and global organizations are focusing on this period and the stakes involved: "The next ten years will see the largest population of older adults in human history navigate changing environments, workplaces, health systems, technologies, and institutions of learning. Intergenerational relations will be tested, and pension, caregiving, and retirement norms will be disrupted."[17]

The extent to which government policy makers in the U.S. will attend to these trends and enact bipartisan legislation supportive of older workers is hard to predict. Aside from familiar and worrying prognostications about the sustainability of Social Security, Medicare, and Medicaid, Americans hear far less from their state and federal government leaders about social policy affecting older workers. Forward-thinking countries around the world—developed and developing, singly and in multinational alliances—are showing the way. This is clearly evident in chapter 25 of the handbook where Hively and Allan outline social policy and programs benefiting older workers in the U.S. and abroad.

Inevitably, within the broad framework of aging and work, various topics, such as economic conditions and demographic shifts, are raised in more than one chapter of the handbook. Where overlap occurs, the reader is directed to other chapters that will be of interest. What follows is a brief orientation to the handbook's contents.

## FISCAL CHALLENGES AND THE OLDER WORKER

Chapters in this section address fiscal realities causing older adults to extend work life. In "The Growing Financial Imperative to Work Longer," Johnson, Smith, and Cosic point to surging employment rates at older ages over the past quarter century, a phenomenon partly attributable to shrinking benefits that have made early retirement increasingly unaffordable. They argue that financial pressures on retirees will intensify in coming decades, fueling further increases in work at older ages. Whether or not Social Security benefits are fully paid in coming years, the prognosis for maintaining preretirement living standards is not good.

The next chapters in this cluster, "Challenges and Opportunities to Living and Working Longer in the Twenty-First Century" by Gonzales and Steeley and "The Choices of (Low-Income) Aging Workers on the Margins: Expanding the Narrative" by Matz and Brown, disentangle the plight of low-skilled, low-income older workers for whom a lifetime of cumulative disadvantage and constraints eliminates choices about retirement generally enjoyed by better-educated, healthier, longer-lived, and more affluent men and women.

Along similar lines, in chapter 5 Street and Ní Léime contrast precariously employed older women with older women who are securely employed. Older women, it is important to understand, face far more unsettling fiscal realities than older men, even after years in the workforce. These and other authors in this volume doubt that extended work life, with all its purported benefits, is a good option for precariously employed women. Chapter 6 by Díaz-Valdes I. then continues the discussion of retirement security and timing with a particular focus on Hispanic older workers, many of whom are in physically demanding jobs and cannot work from home. Laying out cultural norms that influence older Hispanics' family- and employment-related decision-making, the author asks whether extended work life is a good solution for everyone in the U.S.

## DEMOGRAPHIC SHIFTS AND WORKFORCE MANAGEMENT

In a second cluster of chapters researchers examine extended work life through the lens of workforce management. Schramm's "Adapting to an Aging Workforce: Evolving Talent Strategies and HR Practices" delineates the economic conditions, new technologies, and other factors that are sure to influence the workplace in the years ahead. Nonetheless, she foresees the aging population remaining an underlying and forceful driver of change, one requiring a strategic response by employers and workforce managers. Forward-thinking industry leaders will not ignore these demographic shifts; instead, she maintains, they will recognize both the value of older workers as a source of talent and the competitive advantage that building an age-diverse workforce will give them.

Complementing Schramm's overview of demographic shifts and changing HR practices, "Managing Aging and Age-Diverse Workforces" is based on theories and empirical evidence from lifespan and organizational psychology. In this chapter, coauthors Zacher and Rudolph provide guidance for human resource managers and for work organizations, more broadly, describing various individual age-related changes that influence work outcomes and reviewing the literature on negative age stereotypes toward older and younger workers. Evidence-based practices for attracting, hiring, retaining, and reemploying workers of different ages are summarized, particularly personnel recruitment, selection, and development; work design and performance and health management; and leadership and teamwork in the context of aging and age-diverse workforces.

Also in the realm of workforce management, Paoletti, Wu, and Salas focus on intergenerational teamwork in "Collaborative Work in the Twenty-First Century: An Intergenerational, Age-Diverse Perspective." They describe the affective and motivational components of collaborative work, explaining how affect and motivation change over the lifespan as put forward by organizational science and commonly held stereotypes. They examine the benefits and challenges for individuals, collaborative dyads, and teams attributable to age-related differences in people-oriented, task-oriented, and organization-oriented attitudes.

In the next chapter within this cluster, Kaskie and Rochford home in on the tendency for managers and human resource specialists to "talk the talk" without "walking the walk"—acknowledging how valuable their older workers are without taking steps to institute policies and programs that support extended work life. "The Role of Employers in Shaping the Lives of Experienced Employees: Moving from Awareness to Activity" explores the implications of age-based labor force changes and considers the roles individual employers, public policy, and academia can play in responding strategically. The authors identify nine areas in which employers can position themselves more effectively by moving beyond mere awareness to implementation of age-inclusive policies and programs. They also consider employer capacity to implement those approaches and the means by which public policy can support employers' efforts to adopt age-inclusive policies and programs.

Continuing with the theme of older workers and workplace management, Sonnega presents issues relevant to creating age-friendly workplaces for older workers in the twenty-first century. Her chapter gives fair treatment to demands from both the "firm side" and the "worker side" with respect to creating new workplace conditions. Acknowledging the global nature of changing demographics, Sonnega looks both within and beyond the U.S. to the experience of other nations grappling with similar challenges. She then reports on one particular feature of the age-friendly workplace—flexible work arrangements—presenting preliminary results of a qualitative study into the advantages and disadvantages of implementing flexibility from the point of view of line managers. Sloan Foundation initiatives on workplace flexibility and working longer come in for special mention, projects stemming from the belief that "adjusting U.S. labor market institutions for the new demographic realities is a tier-one challenge for the 21st century."[18]

Chapter 12, "Tackling Ageism in the Workplace," reveals the opposite of organizational age-friendliness by taking a close look at the often covert act of pitying, patronizing, or ignoring older workers or dismissing their concerns[19] and at workplace practices that force them to retire before they are ready.[20] Coauthors Swift, Steeden, and Randsley de Moura describe the ways in which ageism manifests in the workplace and in organizational settings. And while prejudice and discrimination can affect anyone at any age, the authors predominately focus on ageism experienced on the basis of perceived old age, whether directed toward others or *toward the self* when a worker internalizes negative age stereotypes. The chapter concludes with some promising social-psychological interventions to tackle ageism in the workplace.

## FACTORS INFLUENCING LABOR FORCE PARTICIPATION AT OLDER AGES

Shifting the emphasis from workforce management to the employee side of the equation, the next cluster of chapters explores what motivates and enables older adults to be productive and what discourages and deters them from remaining in the labor force. These chapters look at technological change and older workers, self-management skills, competence or lack thereof, training and development, and for-credit learning opportunities, plus two omnipresent topics of undeniable relevance for work satisfaction and extended work life—stereotypes and how they can affect job performance and age discrimination.

The Society for Human Resource Management (SHRM) Foundation reminds us that ageism in the workplace is counterproductive: "To reap the benefits of a productive age-diverse workforce, organizations need to move beyond outdated and limiting beliefs about older workers." Those beliefs might include assuming that they are less engaged than younger workers, that they avoid new challenges or are afraid of learning new technologies.[21] SHRM recommends removing the lens of age when viewing existing or potential employees, shifting the focus instead to their abilities, skills, experience, and knowledge, and in the process expanding the talent recruitment pool, to the ultimate benefit of the organization. In fact, "the productivity of both older and younger workers is higher in companies with mixed-age work teams."[22] Moreover, age diversity "consistently leads to better outcomes for solving complex problems."[23]

In chapter 13, "Older Workers and Job Performance," Voyles and Robinson discuss the influence of age-induced physical and cognitive changes on work performance before introducing general and performance-related stereotypes and metastereotypes targeting older workers that can have important implications for their performance and other outcomes in the workplace. To enhance performance, they urge organizations to adopt policies and practices that will motivate and accommodate a workforce that is growing older.

In a similar vein, chapter 14 from Wang, Amano, and Carter focuses on engagement in productive activities among older workers, activities that make economic and social contributions to society, such as working, volunteering, and caregiving. The coauthors review engagement prevalence and patterns, determinants and motives, and benefits and outcomes. Their chapter also explores gender and age differences in such engagement and sheds light on future directions for supporting those who want to or need to engage in productive activities outside of their employment.

In "Self-Management of Career and Retirement: Issues of Competence and Dyscompetence," Sterns and Sterns focus on another aspect of performance, positing that maintaining competence through self-management is the key determinant of worker success. Nonperformance, or dyscompetence, may be the reason a person needs to stop working, to choose less demanding employment, or to retire. The coauthors employ six definitions of older workers that cast light on how competence is understood, maintained, and appropriately assessed, and explain the different definitions' influence on work changes, opportunities, and incentives to remain in the workforce.

Self-management comes in for further treatment in chapter 16, "Older Workers' Self-Management and Sustainable Employability at Work: Lessons Learned from Science and Practice." De Lange, Furunes, and Buckens present an overview of relevant theory and empirical research on self-management skills and capabilities of older workers, and delineate practical intervention methods to prolong working lives. They employ an integrative perspective on multiple factors in the workplace to understand the dynamics between self-management of older workers in relation to person-environment fit and sustainable employability at work. Illustrative case reports are drawn from an agency that specializes in reskilling and retraining mature workers who want to change careers or are unemployed and searching for new work.

"Emerging Technologies, the Aging Workforce, and the Future of Work," by Beier and Davenport, examines two converging societal phenomena: the aging of the labor force and the proliferation of technology in the workplace, which, we are told, promise to change the landscape of work in the twenty-first century. (Indeed, numerous workers are performing their jobs remotely today, including 44 percent of workers over the age of fifty-five and 47 percent of workers over the age of sixty-five.)[24] This chapter describes the benefits and challenges associated with ubiquitous computing, automation, artificial intelligence, and other technological innovations, particularly their relationship to job demands and resources and their potential implications for older worker learning, training, and development.

Chapter 18 is an apt follow-on to Beier and Davenport's discussion of changing technologies and mature workers. In "Living Longer, Working Longer, Learning Longer," Cummins, Bahr, and Yamashita address changes in the age structure of the labor force, the need for continued skill upgrading over the life course to remain employable, and patterns of participation in adult learning and development activities, with close attention to the role community colleges play in providing education and skills training to middle-aged and older adults. Lifelong learning specifically for the purpose of *earning* comes to the fore.

## DETERMINANTS OF EMPLOYEE WELL-BEING

Continuing with the focus on older employees, the next two chapters center on factors that contribute to or detract from their well-being—psychosocial health especially, plus physical and financial well-being. Interest in person-environment fit ("a broad constellation of constructs related to an individual's congruence with their work environment")[25] and its importance for work satisfaction is strong among aging and work researchers as well as human resource managers. But when it comes to work-family balance and the ways that caregiving can upset that balance, researchers are miles ahead of HR managers and policy and program decision makers.

King and Smith's "Resilience, Need Fulfillment, and Well-Being in Older Workers" portrays employment in the later years as an essential consideration and key influence on psychological health. Despite general acknowledgment that work satisfaction is linked to life satisfaction, the workplace is frequently ignored as an important domain of life, these authors observe. Their chapter describes resilience, defines older workers, and emphasizes a variety of psychosocial aspects of resilience and well-being among older workers. Maslow's catalog of human needs serves as a useful framework for considering potential dimensions of well-being.

Patterson and Arche's "Aging, Work, and Caregiving: Current Knowledge and Directions for Future Research" depicts mid- and later-life adults (ages fifty and up) balancing work and caregiving duties as both life expectancy and labor force participation are elongated. The authors report that current findings on outcomes are mixed but generally indicate caregiving's negative impact on older workers' employment, mental health, and physical health. Their knowledge of the uneven impact among different demographic groups is still emerging; there remains much to learn about the balance of work and caregiving among various populations as well as differences in the effects of balancing both at mid- and later life for the caregiver's own well-being.

## AS THE EXPERIENCE OF AGING CHANGES, SO TOO DOES RETIREMENT

The handbook turns next to the various ways older workers can experience retirement—no longer do "work" and "retirement" constitute an oxymoron. Furthermore, the traditional "lockstep life-line" that dictated getting an education, raising a family, having a job, and "retiring full stop" is no longer valid, the Pass It On Network reminds us.[26] Instead, women and men are interweaving learning, work, leisure activities, and family across the lifespan. Thus, "a more fluid pattern" has emerged, says a RAND Corporation study, "often involving phased retirement, short-term jobs, and periods of nonemployment and returns to work."[27]

Likewise, in their overview of "The Changing Landscape of Retirement," Dennis and Marnfeldt observe that exiting the labor force to a life of leisure pursuits has morphed into a life stage with various options. The shape retirement takes depends in part on microlevel factors such as financial security, health, and family responsibilities, as well as personal resources, needs, and aspirations. Retirement is also influenced by public and corporate policies addressing systemic social and economic problems associated with health care, employment, housing, and transportation as well as age, gender, and race discrimination. The chapter concludes with the authors' recommendations for tackling systemic problems affecting older adults.

Pak and Wang's chapter on "Bridge Employment" illustrates one of the optional work arrangements in which workers gradually transition into retirement, an increasingly common practice. This chapter provides a definition of bridge employment, links research on bridge employment to research on major life events, discusses three important theories in relation to bridge employment, and describes its antecedents and outcomes.

Yet another alternative work option is presented in "Senior Entrepreneurship: The Twenty-First Century's Most Underrated Economic Engine." According to entrepreneurship expert Elizabeth Isele, major demographic shifts are creating unprecedented numbers of senior entrepreneurs in the U.S. and abroad. Isele addresses why this is happening and how older entrepreneurs are boosting economies locally and globally, drawing on their extensive experience, adaptable minds, and willingness to take risks to help solve some of society's most pressing challenges. The chapter also highlights what we need to do to harness the individual and collective wisdom, know-how, and experience of senior entrepreneurs.

Doug Dickson also writes about older adults contributing their accumulated wisdom and experience for the benefit of others, arguing in "Older Workers as Volunteers" that the demographic boom (or *boon*) can be tapped to generate an "experience dividend" for society. This chapter looks at who in the mature adult population is volunteering, what we know about them, their reasons for volunteering while working, and the impact of doing so. The chapter offers a brief history of programs organized to engage older volunteers, describes best practices for recruiting and retaining them, and concludes with an assessment of current challenges and prospects for the future.

## SUMMARIZING WHAT WE KNOW ABOUT OLDER WORKERS AND ANTICIPATING WHAT'S AHEAD FOR THEM

Tying together many of the themes highlighted in this volume, its final two chapters offer a broad view of later-life employment—the first through the powerful lens of social policy and the second via a unique "portfolio framework." In "Social Policy and the Older Worker: An International Perspective," Hively and Allan set social policy concerning older workers in the context of the worldwide longevity revolution. Their chapter first addresses productive aging, changing expectations for older workers, and the stakeholders involved in older workforce policy making, followed by a review of comprehensive policy planning in the United States and abroad. It next describes policy innovations that support older workers by assuring "bridges" to employment, preparing a welcoming workplace, and promoting economic security. A final section focuses on the future for older workers.

In "A Portfolio Framework for Extended Work Pathways: Leveraging the Strengths of Older Workers," Carr, King, and Moen lay out the components of a proposed new framework for later-life work. Their chapter has five parts. The first describes the financial and macrolevel forces shaping new work trajectories in later life. The second presents alternatives to full-time work in later life. The third enumerates current barriers facing those interested in extended work lives and alternative work arrangements in later life. The fourth suggests the benefits and limitations of longer work lives for older people. The fifth summarizes key components of a new portfolio framework for later-life work and retirement, with suggestions for businesses and policy makers as well as for older workers as they prepare for the latter phases of their work lives.

## SUGGESTIONS FOR FUTURE RESEARCH ON THE AGING WORKFORCE AND RETIREMENT

As G. Stanley Hall would have appreciated, not only does the lived experience of aging inevitably bring changes, social assumptions about aging and retirement—conventionally a period of decline and becoming *un*necessary—can also change. Were he alive today, Hall would no doubt be gratified to see so many older adults working in their later years, participating actively in public life, and remaining vital.

However, with the advent of COVID-19 in spring 2020 and the pandemic's devastating impact on health, education, social well-being, and the economy here and abroad, we simply do not know what the near term holds for older workers, let alone the coming decades. Researchers, practitioners, and policy makers will want answers to the following array of questions:

- To what extent has COVID-19 reinforced ageist attitudes, for example, categorizing the elderly as the most vulnerable as well as the most expendable?
- Which industries and occupations will not recover fully from the downturn, and what are the implications of their losses, particularly in terms of unemployment rates and reemployment possibilities? To what extent do educational attainment and experience buffer older workers from layoffs? What befalls the older worker's sense of control in the workplace?
- How will current and emerging technologies, such as automation and artificial intelligence, affect jobs and the ability of older workers to qualify for and retain those jobs?
- Will employer attitudes toward the older workforce become more supportive or less so? For example, will management install programs and allow practices that offer flexible work arrangements, such as working remotely (telework)? Will employers respond to the work-life balance challenges facing employees with caregiving responsibilities? Will employers be more willing to invest in training and retraining of older workers?
- Do older workers value lifelong learning for the purpose of enhanced employment opportunities as well as for quality-of-life purposes? Do they understand the importance of continuous learning and development (self-management) to job satisfaction and retention, especially in light of the effects of the pandemic, and will they act on that understanding?
- Do intergenerational teams function well even when team members are working remotely, and do older and younger workers differ in their response to the new situation?
- Is self-employment a desired option for older workers, and if so, what makes it appealing? What does it take to become a senior entrepreneur, especially when current economic conditions are unfavorable?
- Which older adults benefit from extended work life in terms of health and well-being? Does extended work life stave off feelings of isolation, loneliness, and depression?
- Do working men and women experience income inequality and cumulative disadvantage across the life course differently? Has the pandemic exacerbated racial and ethnic differences with respect to fiscal insecurity in the later years?
- Has the economic downturn caused by the pandemic altered retirement patterns, for example, by causing older workers to retire earlier than planned, and by making phased retirement and working in retirement harder to come by? Is extended work life the right goal for all older adults? What motivates older adults who are employed to undertake volunteer work?
- In the arena of social policy making, what changes to Social Security, Medicaid, Medicare, and other programs would be of greatest benefit to older workers, now

and in the future? What can the U.S. learn from other countries' policies, programs, and practices that address the questions on this list?

Let's conclude with the words of essayist Marilynne Robinson, who asks, "What Kind of Country Do We Want?"

> The assumption that things can get better, with the expectation that they should, creates the kind of social ferment that yields progress.[28]

## NOTES

1. Among other accomplishments, G. Stanley Hall was appointed to the first psychology professorship in America in 1884 at Johns Hopkins University, founded the *American Journal of Psychology* in 1887, established the American Psychological Association in 1892, and became first president of Clark University in Worcester, Massachusetts.
2. Thomas R. Cole. 1984. "The Prophecy of Senescence: G. Stanley Hall and the Reconstruction of Old Age in America." *The Gerontologist* 24(4):360.
3. Manon Parry. July 2006. "G. Stanley Hall: Psychologist and Early Gerontologist." *American Journal of Public Health* 96(7):1161.
4. Cole, "Prophecy of Senescence," 360.
5. Cole, "Prophecy of Senescence," 361.
6. Cole, "Prophecy of Senescence," 363.
7. G. Stanley Hall. 1922. *Senescence: The Last Half of Life*. New York: D. Appleton.
8. Teresa Ghilarducci and Siavash Radpour. Fall 2019. "Older Worker Exploitation: Magnitude, Causes, and Solutions." ASA, *Generations* 43(3):6.
9. Ghilarducci and Radpour, "Older Worker Exploitation," 8.
10. Ghilarducci and Radpour, "Older Worker Exploitation," 4.
11. Michael Papadopoulos. Fall 2019. "The Time Is Now to Focus on Older Workers: Trends in Employment and Wages." ASA, *Generations* 43(3):11.
12. Carl E. Van Horn and Maria Heidkamp. Fall 2019. "Older Workers, Precarious Jobs, and Unemployment: Challenges and Policy Recommendations." ASA, *Generations* 43(3):21.
13. Jeanna Smialek and Alan Rappeport. June 11, 2020. "Fed Chair Says Economic Pain May Last Years." *New York Times*:A1, A5.
14. Cort W. Rudolph et al. May 22, 2020. "Pandemics: Implications for Research and Practice in Industrial and Organizational Psychology." *PsyArXiv*. Center for Open Science. (https://doi.org/10.31234/osf.io/k8us2).
15. Madison Darbyshire. June 9, 2020. "Older Staff Most Likely to Benefit from Work from Home." *Financial Times*. (www.ft.com).
16. Mark Miller. June 28, 2020. "The Pandemic May Lead Many to Retire Early." *New York Times* Business:5.
17. Milken Institute. December 2019. Center for the Future of Aging. (www.milkeninstitute.org).
18. Alfred P. Sloan Foundation. "Working Longer" grant program. Retrieved March 28, 2020 (www.sloan.org).
19. Ben Steeden and Hannah J. Swift. March 23, 2020. "Wise, but Incompetent? The Effect of Ageist Attitudes in the UK." Centre for Ageing Better, Blog. (ageing-better.org.uk).
20. Richard Eisenberg. February 17, 2020. "The UN and AARP Team Up for Age-diverse Workforces." *Next Avenue, Money and Work*. (nextavenue.org/un-aarp-age-diverse-workforces).
21. Eisenberg, "UN and AARP Team Up."

22. Lori A. Trawinski. October 2016. "Leveraging the Value of an Age-diverse Workforce." SHRM Foundation Executive Briefing; based on AARP, "Disrupting Aging in the Workplace—Profiles in Intergenerational Diversity Leadership." Retrieved August 2, 2019 (shrmfoundation.org).

23. Eisenberg, "UN and AARP Team Up."

24. Darbyshire, "Older Staff."

25. Rachel S. Rauvola et al. November 7, 2019. "Person-environment Fit and Work Satisfaction: Exploring the Conditional Effects of Age." *Work, Aging and Retirement* 6(2):101–17.

26. Pass It On Network. April 7, 2020. "Lifelong Learning and Earning—Creating Support for Education & Work in the Longevity Economy." UN Open-ended Working Group on Aging Workshop. (www.passitonnetwork.org).

27. Miller, "Pandemic."

28. Marilynne Robinson. June 11, 2020. "What Kind of Country Do We Want?" *New York Review of Books* 67(10):43.

## REFERENCES

Alfred P. Sloan Foundation. "Working Longer" grant program. Retrieved March 28, 2020 (www.sloan.org).

Cole, Thomas R. 1984. "The Prophecy of Senescence: G. Stanley Hall and the Reconstruction of Old Age in America." *The Gerontologist* 24(4):360–66.

Darbyshire, Madison. June 9, 2020. "Older Staff Most Likely to Benefit from Work from Home." *Financial Times*. (www.ft.com).

Eisenberg, Richard. February 17, 2020. "The UN and AARP Team Up for Age-diverse Workforces." *Next Avenue, Money and Work*. (nextavenue.org/un-aarp-age-diverse-workforces).

Ghilarducci, Teresa and Siavash Radpour. Fall 2019. "Older Worker Exploitation: Magnitude, Causes, and Solutions." ASA, *Generations* 43(3):6–10.

Hall, G. Stanley. 1922. *Senescence: The Last Half of Life*. New York: D. Appleton.

Milken Institute. December 2019. Center for the Future of Aging. (www.milkeninstitute.org).

Miller, Mark. June 28, 2020. "The Pandemic May Lead Many to Retire Early." *New York Times* Business:5.

Papadopoulos, Michael. Fall 2019. "The Time Is Now to Focus on Older Workers: Trends in Employment and Wages." ASA, *Generations* 43(3):11.

Parry, Manon. July 2006. "G. Stanley Hall: Psychologist and Early Gerontologist." *American Journal of Public Health* 96(7):1161.

Pass It On Network. April 7, 2020. "Lifelong Learning and Earning—Creating Support for Education & Work in the Longevity Economy." UN Open-ended Working Group on Aging Workshop. (www.passitonnetwork.org).

Rauvola, Rachel S., et al. November 7, 2019. "Person-environment Fit and Work Satisfaction: Exploring the Conditional Effects of Age." *Work, Aging and Retirement* 6(2):101–17.

Robinson, Marilynne. June 11, 2020. "What Kind of Country Do We Want?" *New York Review of Books* 67(10):43.

Rudolph, Cort W., et al. May 22, 2020. "Pandemics: Implications for Research and Practice in Industrial and Organizational Psychology." *PsyArXiv*. Center for Open Science. (https://doi.org/10.31234/osf.io/k8us2).

Smialek, Jeanna and Alan Rappeport. June 11, 2020. "Fed Chair Says Economic Pain May Last Years." *New York Times*:A1, A5.

Steeden, Ben and Hannah J. Swift. March 23, 2020. "Wise, but Incompetent? The Effect of Ageist Attitudes in the UK." Centre for Ageing Better, Blog. (ageing-better.org.uk).

Trawinski, Lori A. October 2016. "Leveraging the Value of an Age-diverse Workforce." SHRM Foundation Executive Briefing; based on AARP, "Disrupting Aging in the Workplace—Profiles in Intergenerational Diversity Leadership." Retrieved August 2, 2019 (shrmfoundation.org).

Van Horn, Carl E. and Maria Heidkamp. Fall 2019. "Older Workers, Precarious Jobs, and Unemployment: Challenges and Policy Recommendations." ASA, *Generations* 43(3):21.

# PART I

# FISCAL CHALLENGES AND THE OLDER WORKER

CHAPTER 2

# The Growing Financial Imperative to Work Longer

Richard W. Johnson, Karen E. Smith, and Damir Cosic

The growth in employment at older ages is one of the most striking labor market developments of the past quarter century. Data from the Bureau of Labor Statistics show that from 1995 to 2018, the employment-to-population ratio at ages sixty-two to sixty-nine increased 12 percentage points for men and 13 percentage points for women.[1] This employment growth significantly benefits older adults. The earnings that older adults receive by continuing to work help them cover current living expenses and facilitate additional retirement savings. Working longer enables them to accumulate more Social Security credits and, if they participate in a 401(k) plan at work, retirement plan contributions from their employer, which augment future retirement incomes. And those savings do not have to last as long when people extend their careers and shrink their retirement period. One study estimates that older workers without disabilities can boost their future annual retirement income 9 percent, on average, by working one additional year.[2] There is also evidence that working longer improves emotional well-being and physical health.[3]

In addition, working longer pays important dividends for employers and the broader economy. When older adults extend their careers, they pay income taxes on their earnings that bolster federal and state government finances and help cover the cost of critical public services.[4] Older workers also expand the workforce, helping employers meet their staffing needs and fueling productivity gains and economic growth.

Several factors appear to drive this employment growth. Improvements over the past few decades in health status and educational attainment at older ages, along with declines in the physical demands of work, have made it easier for older adults to remain in the labor force and have encouraged employers to hire and retain them.[5] Changes in Social Security rules have increased work incentives at older ages, mostly by making early retirement less affordable.[6] For example, the full retirement age for Social Security is gradually increasing from sixty-five to sixty-seven, beginning with people who turned sixty-two in 2000. This change does not affect the age at which workers can begin collecting retirement benefits, but it reduces the monthly benefits they receive. The monthly Social Security payment to retirees born in 1960 who begin collecting at age sixty-five, for example, will be 13.33 percent less than it would have been if the retirement age had not increased. Employer-provided defined benefit (DB) pension coverage has also been steadily falling in the private sector, making it harder for retirees to replace their earnings without working longer.[7] In addition, fewer employers now offer retiree health insurance benefits, forcing many workers to remain on the job with their employer health benefits until they reach age sixty-five and quality for Medicare.[8]

Is the uncertainty about retirement security that fueled recent employment growth at older ages likely to persist and induce future generations to delay retirement? This chapter explores that question by showing how changing patterns of lifetime earnings, retirement plan participation, and wealth accumulation outside of retirement plans will combine to shape future economic well-being at age seventy, when most have retired and accrued all their retirement savings. We use the Urban Institute's Dynamic Simulation of Income Model 4 (DYNASIM4) to compare outcomes for five birth cohorts: pre-boomers, born between 1936 and 1945; early boomers, born between 1946 and 1955; late boomers, born between 1956 and 1965; early Gen Xers, born between 1966 and 1975; and late Gen Xers and early millennials, born between 1976 and 1985, a microgeneration that some have labeled Xennials. We use that term in this chapter. Our projected outcomes run from 2006, when the older pre-boomers turned seventy, to 2055, when the youngest Xennials turn seventy. These projections, which largely incorporate the assumptions adopted by the Social Security trustees for their long-term forecasting,[9] assume that the growth in older adults' employment rates observed over the past two decades will level off for men and continue at a slower pace for women. We report all dollar amounts in inflation-adjusted 2018 dollars.[10]

Despite some encouraging trends, our projections raise serious concerns about future retirement security. As economic growth boosts future earnings and retirement benefits, boomers, Gen Xers, and early millennials will receive more income at age seventy than pre-boomers. That income, however, will replace a smaller share of their preretirement earnings because of the increase in the Social Security retirement age and the loss of DB pensions. We project that if promised Social Security benefits are fully paid, 30 percent of early Gen Xers and 32 percent of Xennials will be unable to maintain their preretirement living standards at age seventy, compared with 26 percent of early boomers. Social Security's looming financial problems further threaten future retirement security. If policy makers do not raise Social Security revenues within the next fifteen years, benefits will need to be cut about 25 percent. Under that scenario, 38 percent of early Gen Xers and 40 percent of Xennials will be at risk of having their retirement resources fall short. Rising out-of-pocket expenditures on medical care and long-term services and supports could further undermine future retirement security. These financial pressures will raise the imperative of work at older ages, as more seniors will need to remain employed to secure a financially comfortable retirement.

## CHANGING DEMOGRAPHICS

Shifting demographics will shape future retirement income security. The older population will become much more racially and ethnically diverse over the coming decades, reflecting a surge of younger immigrants from Latin America and Asia since 1980 and relative high fertility rates among Latinxs. The Latinx and Asian shares of the age seventy population will be roughly twice as high among Xennials as pre-boomers (table 2.1). DYNASIM4 projects that at age seventy, Latinxs will account for 23 percent of all Xennials and Asians will account for 10 percent. Non-Hispanic whites will account for only 57 percent of the age seventy population for the Xennial generation, compared with 75 percent for pre-boomers. The non-Hispanic black share of the older population will not change much over time.

Older Americans are living longer. Between 1980 and 2015, life expectancy at age sixty-two increased four years for men and two years for women.[11] Reduced mortality is a significant achievement, although the gains have been concentrated among well-educated and high-income Americans.[12] Longer life expectancy has lengthened retirements, even though many people are working longer. Longer retirements in turn raise the cost of Social Security and DB pensions and mean that retirees' savings must last longer.

Lower mortality reflects better health at older ages and greater investments in health care. Between 1982 and 2017, the share of Americans ages sixty-five to seventy-four reporting fair or poor health fell from 35 to 18 percent.[13] Whether this trend will continue, however, is unclear. The gains occurred mostly before 2000, and disability rates are now increasing for people in their forties and fifties.[14] Nonetheless, the Social Security trustees project that age sixty-two life expectancy will increase another 2.8 years for men and 2.4 years for women by 2050.[15] Many other analysts predict that future generations will live even longer,[16] despite some recent setbacks in mortality gains at younger ages.[17]

Higher educational attainment by boomers and later generations will enhance their financial security. Education boosts earnings and helps qualify workers for less physically demanding jobs, promoting work at older ages. The rise in college attendance that began in the late 1960s[18] increases the projected share of seventy-year-old Xennial men

**TABLE 2.1.** Racial and Ethnic Composition of the Age 70 Population, by Birth Cohort (%)

| | *Pre-boomers (1936–1945)* | *Early Boomers (1946–1955)* | *Late Boomers (1956–1965)* | *Early Gen Xers (1966–1975)* | *Xennials (1976–1985)* |
|---|---|---|---|---|---|
| Non-Hispanic white | 75 | 72 | 68 | 60 | 57 |
| Non-Hispanic black | 10 | 10 | 11 | 11 | 11 |
| Latinx | 10 | 11 | 14 | 20 | 23 |
| Asian and other | 5 | 6 | 7 | 9 | 10 |

*Source:* Authors' estimates from DYNASIM4, ID963.

TABLE 2.2. Educational Attainment of the Age 70 Population by Gender and Birth Cohort (%)

| | Pre-boomers (1936–1945) | Early Boomers (1946–1955) | Late Boomers (1956–1965) | Early Gen Xers (1966–1975) | Xennials (1976–1985) |
|---|---|---|---|---|---|
| *Men* | | | | | |
| Did not complete high school | 18 | 11 | 12 | 12 | 12 |
| High school diploma, never attended college | 31 | 31 | 33 | 28 | 27 |
| Attended college but did not earn a four-year degree | 21 | 24 | 24 | 26 | 27 |
| Four-year college degree | 30 | 33 | 30 | 34 | 33 |
| *Women* | | | | | |
| Did not complete high school | 19 | 11 | 12 | 12 | 11 |
| High school diploma, never attended college | 39 | 33 | 31 | 25 | 20 |
| Attended college but did not earn a four-year degree | 20 | 26 | 28 | 26 | 27 |
| Four-year college degree | 23 | 30 | 29 | 36 | 43 |

*Source:* Authors' estimates from DYNASIM4, ID963.

with a bachelor's degree to 33 percent, up from 30 percent for their pre-boomer counterparts (table 2.2). The projected educational gains are more dramatic for women, with 43 percent of Xennial women projected to complete four years of college, up from 23 percent for pre-boomer women. We project that only 12 percent of Xennial men and 11 percent of Xennial women who survive to age seventy will fail to complete high school, compared with 18 percent for pre-boomer men and 19 percent for pre-boomer women.

Marriage, divorce, and widowhood patterns are changing and will influence financial security at older ages. Singles forgo the financial security of a second paycheck during working ages and the cost savings from shared expenses, and retirees often lose some of their spouse's Social Security and DB pension benefits when they become widowed or divorced. As a result, widowed, divorced, and never-married seniors have much higher poverty rates than married couples.[19]

As men's life expectancy rises, the gender gap in mortality will shrink and widowhood will become less common among older women. Our projections indicate that only 15 percent of Xennial women and 16 percent of late boomer and early Gen-X women will

**TABLE 2.3.** Marital Status of the Age 70 Population by Gender and Birth Cohort (%)

| | *Pre-boomers (1936–1945)* | *Early Boomers (1946–1955)* | *Late Boomers (1956–1965)* | *Early Gen Xers (1966–1975)* | *Xennials (1976–1985)* |
|---|---|---|---|---|---|
| ***Men*** | | | | | |
| Married | 69 | 63 | 60 | 61 | 55 |
| Widowed | 7 | 7 | 6 | 6 | 6 |
| Divorced | 18 | 22 | 23 | 22 | 23 |
| Never married | 6 | 8 | 11 | 10 | 16 |
| ***Women*** | | | | | |
| Married | 52 | 49 | 48 | 53 | 51 |
| Widowed | 23 | 18 | 16 | 16 | 15 |
| Divorced | 19 | 25 | 26 | 22 | 22 |
| Never married | 5 | 8 | 10 | 9 | 12 |

*Source:* Authors' estimates from DYNASIM4, ID963.

be widowed at age seventy, down from 23 percent among pre-boomer women (table 2.3). Falling marriage rates, especially among women born after 1955, will increase the share of women in recent generations who never marry by age seventy. Divorced women who did not remarry will make up a growing portion of the older female population through the late boomer generation, reflecting the 1970s surge in the divorce rate.[20] The subsequent decline in the divorce rate will reduce the share of early Gen-X and Xennial women who are divorced at older ages, although our projections show that divorced women will remain more common in those generations than in the pre-boomer generation. Combining these trends, we project that the share of seventy-year-old women who are married will fall as we move from the pre-boomers to the boomers and then will rebound for early Gen Xers and Xennials.

Trends in marital patterns are similar for men, except we do not project significant declines in the share of older men who are widowed. Our projections show that late boomer, early Gen-X, and Xennial men are more likely to be divorced or never married at age seventy than pre-boomer men. As a result, the share of men married at age seventy will be lower for late boomers, early Gen Xers, and Xennials than for pre-boomers.

## LIFETIME EARNINGS

Retirement incomes depend critically on how much people worked and earned when they were younger. Higher lifetime earnings mean more Social Security and—for those with coverage—larger pensions and retirement account balances. It also means the ability to save more outside of retirement accounts.

The employment rate for women grew dramatically over the past generation. Between 1972 and 2018, the share of women ages twenty-five to fifty-four participating in the labor force (either working or looking for work) increased from 52 percent to 75 percent. Over the same period, their male counterparts scaled back their work, with labor force participation rates falling from 95 percent to 90 percent as job opportunities for low-skilled men eroded.[21] As noted earlier, older men and women are both working more.

These trends will significantly boost lifetime employment for boomer, early Gen-X, and Xennial women. By age seventy, according to our projections, the median length of lifetime employment will reach thirty-nine years for Xennial women, compared with thirty-one years for pre-boomer women. By contrast, a typical Xennial man will have worked forty-one years by age seventy, two years less than a typical pre-boomer man.

More recent cohorts of employed women are also being paid more than their predecessors. Employed late boomer women ages thirty-five to thirty-nine earned 25 percent more a year in inflation-adjusted dollars than their pre-boomer counterparts ($29,900 versus $23,900); Xennial women earn 50 percent more ($35,900; figure 2.1). However, median earnings have been falling or stagnant for men. At ages thirty-five to thirty-nine, median earnings for employed men were 6 percent lower for late boomers than pre-boomers ($52,400 versus $56,000) and 13 percent lower for Xennials ($48,700; figure 2.2). The long-term stagnation in men's median earnings, which has been widely debated among scholars and policy makers, has been driven by the scarcity of well-paying jobs for men with no more than a high school diploma.

Xennial earnings projections after age forty depend on how fast we assume wages will grow in the future. The current analysis follows the Social Security trustees' assumptions, which set long-term average real wage growth at 1.2 percent a year and even higher for 2018 to 2028.[22] This growth rate seems optimistic because average wages grew only 0.6 percent a year over the past fifty years. Nonetheless, the trustees' assumed growth rate implies that at ages fifty to fifty-four, median earnings for employed Xennial men will exceed the median for pre-boomer men by 7 percent and the median late boomer men by 20 percent. For employed women ages fifty to fifty-four, our projections

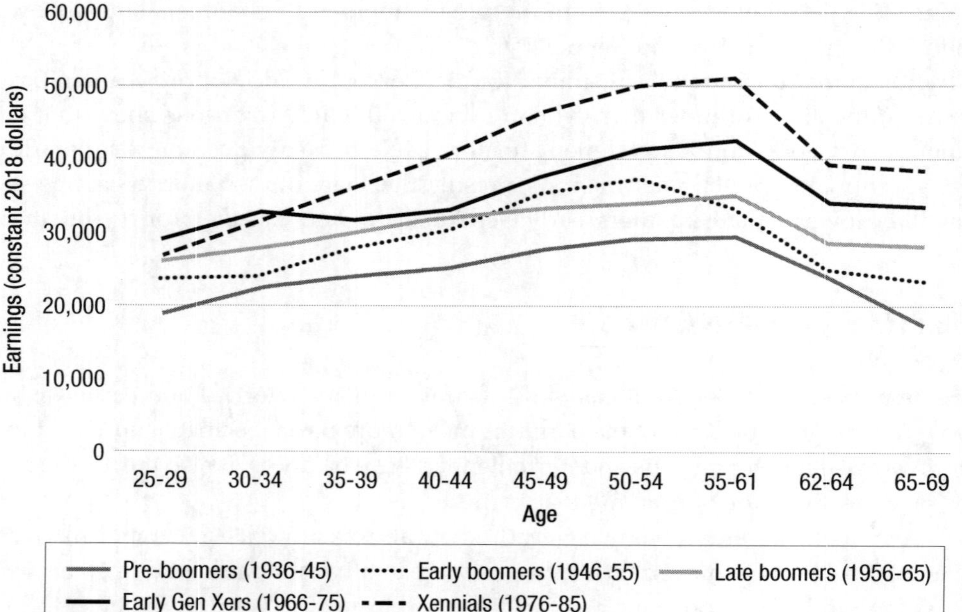


**FIGURE 2.1.** Median Annual Earnings for Employed Women, by Birth Cohort (constant 2018 dollars)

*Source:* Authors' estimates from DYNASIM4, ID963.

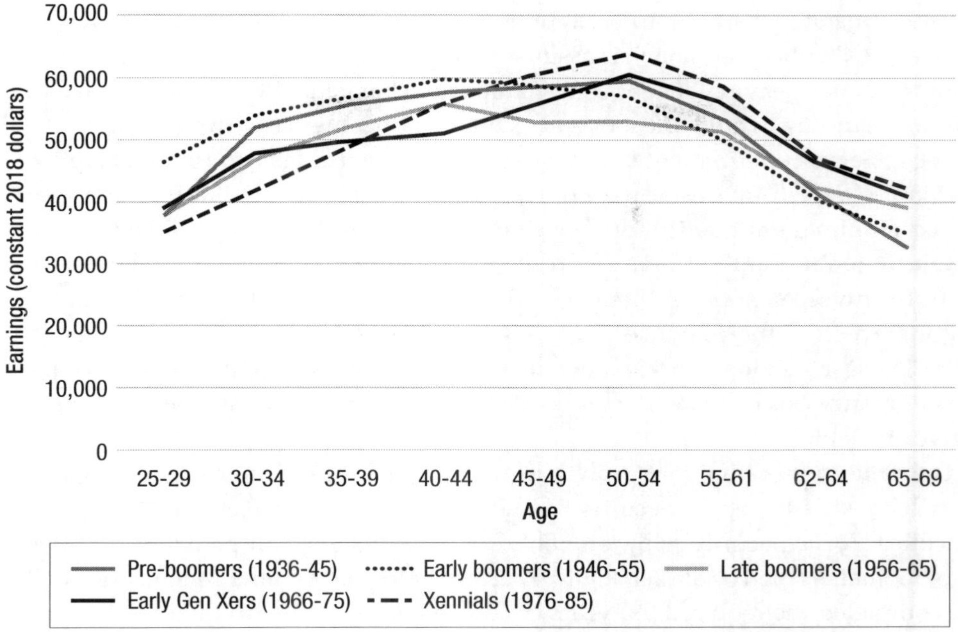


**FIGURE 2.2.** Median Annual Earnings for Employed Men, by Birth Cohort (constant 2018 dollars)
*Source:* Authors' estimates from DYNASIM4, ID963.

show that median earnings for Xennial women will exceed the median for pre-boomer women by 71 percent and the median for late boomer women by 47 percent.

## RETIREMENT INCOMES

Although more retirees will rely on earnings to augment their incomes at age seventy and beyond, most will still rely primarily on traditional sources of retirement income. Social Security historically has provided the bulk of retirement income,[23] at least for lower- and moderate-income retirees, and will continue to play this role for boomers, Gen Xers, and Xennials. Many will receive some income from employer retirement plans, although DB pensions are being replaced by riskier 401(k)-type plans. Most future retirees also will have some other financial assets and housing equity. Whether these income sources will adequately replace preretirement income, though, depends on how much retirees will spend, especially on medical care and long-term services and supports.

### Social Security

Social Security will continue to be the primary income source for retirees, despite the ongoing debate over its financing. The system now spends more than it collects in revenue, but benefits are paid for through the early 2030s—according to the Social Security trustees' projections—by a reserve fund built up mostly between 1988 and 2008, when tax revenues far outpaced benefit payments.[24] If nothing is done to close Social

Security's financing gap, the trustees project that benefits will have to be cut by about one-quarter. Our baseline analysis assumes Congress closes the financing gap solely by raising revenues, leaving benefit computations unchanged, although we see later how Social Security cuts would affect overall retirement income security.

Social Security retirement benefits are based on earnings (up to the taxable maximum) over a thirty-five-year period. Retirees who have worked at least ten years in covered employment qualify for these worker benefits. Those who have not worked enough to qualify on their own can receive a benefit equal to one-half their spouse's benefit (or divorced spouse's benefit, if they had been married for at least ten years). They may receive their spouse's (or divorced spouse's) full benefit after his or her death. Those receiving worker benefits smaller than their spouse's collect partial spousal or survivor benefits so that the combined payment equals the full spousal or survivor benefit.

The projections show that growth in women's labor force participation and earnings will boost future Social Security benefits. Seventy-seven percent of Xennial women who collect Social Security will claim only a worker benefit, compared with 53 percent of pre-boomer women (table 2.4). Only 4 percent of female Xennial beneficiaries will not have completed the required ten years of covered employment to qualify for a worker benefit and will receive only spousal or survivor benefits at age seventy, down from 13 percent among pre-boomer women.

The projections indicate that if promised Social Security benefits are paid, Xennial women will receive much more Social Security income than their predecessors. Median annual benefits for Xennial women will be 68 percent higher in inflation-adjusted dollars than those for pre-boomer women and 38 percent higher than those for late boomers ($22,000 compared with $13,100 and $16,000, respectively; table 2.5). Lifetime Social Security benefits will rise even more rapidly for Xennial women because they will live longer and collect more monthly benefit checks than their predecessors. Future benefits for boomers and later generations would be even higher if not for the scheduled increase in Social Security's full retirement age, which, as noted earlier, significantly cuts monthly benefits.

For men, the retirement-age change, combined with stagnant earnings, will dampen future growth in retirement benefits. If recent earnings patterns hold and promised

**TABLE 2.4.** Social Security Benefit Type at Age 70 for Female Beneficiaries, by Birth Cohort (%)

| | *Pre-boomers (1936–1945)* | *Early Boomers (1946–1955)* | *Late Boomers (1956–1965)* | *Early Gen Xers (1966–1975)* | *Xennials (1976–1985)* |
|---|---|---|---|---|---|
| Worker only | 53 | 64 | 69 | 74 | 77 |
| Worker supplemented by spousal or survivor | 34 | 30 | 27 | 23 | 19 |
| Spousal or survivor only | 13 | 5 | 4 | 4 | 4 |

*Source:* Authors' estimates from DYNASIM4, ID963.

**TABLE 2.5.** Median Annual Own Social Security Income among Beneficiaries at Age 70, by Birth Cohort ($)

| | *Pre-boomers (1936–1945)* | *Early Boomers (1946–1955)* | *Late Boomers (1956–1965)* | *Early Gen Xers (1966–1975)* | *Xennials (1976–1985)* |
|---|---|---|---|---|---|
| Men and women | 17,200 | 18,300 | 18,900 | 21,400 | 23,900 |
| Men | 20,800 | 21,800 | 22,200 | 24,600 | 26,000 |
| Women | 13,100 | 15,000 | 16,000 | 18,700 | 22,000 |

*Source:* Authors' estimates from DYNASIM4, ID963.

Social Security benefits are paid, inflation-adjusted Social Security benefits will inch up 7 percent for the late boomer cohort relative to the pre-boomer cohort ($22,200 compared with $20,800). The median age seventy Social Security benefit for male Xennial beneficiaries will exceed the median for pre-boomer men by 25 percent because Xennial men will earn more over their lifetimes than pre-boomer men. Of course, future retirees could end up with higher benefits if they wait more for unreduced benefits and work longer than current trends predict. On the other hand, future benefits could be lower if Social Security's financing gap leads to benefit cuts.

## Pensions

Employers offering retirement plans have moved away from DB pensions that pay a lifetime benefit typically based on earnings and years of service to defined contribution (DC) plans that build up account balances from employer and employee contributions over the years of coverage. In 2018, 13 percent of private-sector workers participated in employer-sponsored DB plans, and 47 percent participated in DC plans.[25] Nonetheless, many future retirees will receive a DB pension because many work in industries where DB plans are still common, especially the public sector.

The shift toward DC plans and away from DB plans will have mixed effects for boomers', Gen Xers', and Xennials' retirement income security. Workers who often change employers typically do not earn much of a DB benefit because these benefits typically accumulate most rapidly in the years immediately before retirement age. Benefits accrued early on erode with inflation. In contrast, DC balances earn investment returns even after workers change jobs, as long as they keep their funds in a DC plan or transfer them to an individual retirement account. The uncertainty of investment returns, however, makes DC plans riskier for workers. Prolonged market downturns, for example, can leave workers with a small account that generates little retirement income. Retirement account assets (DC plans and individual retirement accounts) dropped by $2.7 trillion (31 percent) from the third quarter of 2007 through the end of the first quarter of 2009 as the stock market collapsed, although most of this aggregate loss has since been recovered.[26] Another potential risk in DC plans relative to DB plans is the temptation they present for workers to withdraw assets before retirement.[27]

As employment rates for women have increased, more boomer, Gen-X, and Xennial women will qualify for a pension based on their own earnings, improving retirement income security for themselves and their families. Pension coverage among

**TABLE 2.6.** Own Expected Lifetime DB Pension Benefits and Retirement Account Balances at Age 70, by Birth Cohort

| | *Pre-boomers (1936–1945)* | *Early Boomers (1946–1955)* | *Late Boomers (1956–1965)* | *Early Gen Xers (1966–1975)* | *Xennials (1976–1985)* |
|---|---|---|---|---|---|
| ***DB pension*** | | | | | |
| Percentage with pension | 42 | 37 | 32 | 29 | 21 |
| Median expected lifetime value of benefits ($) | 282,800 | 294,200 | 183,700 | 122,900 | 98,200 |
| ***Retirement Account*** | | | | | |
| Percentage with account | 45 | 62 | 64 | 65 | 64 |
| Median account balance ($) | 81,100 | 117,500 | 132,900 | 145,000 | 155,800 |
| ***DB pension or retirement account*** | | | | | |
| Percentage with pension or account | 63 | 71 | 71 | 70 | 68 |
| Median value of lifetime benefits or account balance ($) | 275,700 | 263,700 | 197,400 | 183,200 | 183,300 |

*Source:* Authors' estimates from DYNASIM4, ID963.

women has steadily increased since the late 1980s so that it now approximates coverage for men.[28] Because future pension benefits are tied to earnings, these benefits grow as women earn more.

The shift away from DB pensions, increases in women's pension coverage, and assumptions about rates of return on account assets will substantially affect the projected lifetime value of future pension benefits. The share of seventy-year-olds with a DB pension will fall from 42 percent for pre-boomers to 21 percent for Xennials, while the median inflation-adjusted expected lifetime value of future DB pension benefits for those with DB pensions will drop 65 percent between the two generations ($282,800 to $98,200; table 2.6). In contrast, the share of seventy-year-olds with retirement account balances will increase from 45 to 64 percent from the pre-boomer generation to the Xennial generation, and the median projected retirement account balances for account holders will grow 92 percent in inflation-adjusted dollars (from $81,100 to $155,800). The combined pension picture shows that 68 percent of Xennials will have some retirement wealth at age seventy, 5 percentage points more than among pre-boomers. However, we project that age seventy median total retirement wealth among those with pensions or retirement accounts will be substantially lower for late boomers, Gen Xers, and Xennials than for earlier generations.

## Housing and Financial Wealth outside Retirement Accounts

Financial assets and housing equity are especially difficult to project. Recent stock market volatility shows that savings held in equities can dramatically fall (or grow) in any given year, and housing values plummeted from 2007 to 2009.[29] However, the history of market indexes suggests an eventual return to long-term average growth. Despite the 2008 stock market crash, the S&P 500 stock index reached an all-time high in 2019, and housing values began to rebound in 2012. Our simulations capture this decline and recovery in financial and housing wealth and assume that real rates of return will eventually stabilize at their historical levels. The projections also reflect how changes in individual characteristics likely will affect these accumulations.

Although most retirees do not tap into the equity in their homes, doing so can generate income through a reverse annuity mortgage, home equity loan, home equity line of credit, or cash-out refinance. The projections show that boomers, Gen Xers, and Xennials, like their predecessors, will have high rates of homeownership, with nearly eight in ten owning a home at age seventy (table 2.7). Boomers benefited from rising housing prices during their careers, while Gen Xers were affected more by the bust and stagnation in housing prices between 2007 and 2012. Projected median per capita housing wealth increases from $114,800 for pre-boomers to $141,600 for early Gen Xers and $154,000 for Xennials. The projected slow growth in home equity for late boomers and Gen Xers also reflects trends in increased borrowing against homes before retirement.[30]

Though quite low, projected median household financial wealth per person at age seventy grows over time. The median seventy-year-old Xennial with financial holdings outside of retirement accounts will have assets valued at $49,800, compared with $24,600 among pre-boomers.

**TABLE 2.7.** Median Per Capita Housing and Financial Wealth outside Retirement Accounts at Age 70, by Birth Cohort

| | *Pre-boomers (1936–1945)* | *Early Boomers (1946–1955)* | *Late Boomers (1956–1965)* | *Early Gen Xers (1966–1975)* | *Xennials (1976–1985)* |
|---|---|---|---|---|---|
| *Housing* | | | | | |
| Percentage with housing wealth | 78 | 76 | 76 | 77 | 75 |
| Median housing wealth ($) | 114,800 | 134,400 | 138,600 | 141,600 | 154,000 |
| *Financial wealth* | | | | | |
| Percentage with wealth | 85 | 90 | 93 | 93 | 94 |
| Median amount ($) | 24,600 | 26,100 | 32,000 | 34,900 | 49,800 |

*Source:* Authors' estimates from DYNASIM4, ID963.

## TOTAL RETIREMENT INCOME

Combining all income sources at age seventy, including Social Security, Supplemental Security, other government benefits, DB pensions, labor market earnings, interest, dividends, capital gains, and withdrawals from retirement accounts, we find that median per capita income increases significantly over time, under the assumption that all promised Social Security benefits are paid. Our projected values for men and women combined increase from $33,500 for pre-boomers to $39,800 for early Gen Xers, a 19 percent increase, and $42,400 for Xennials, a 27 percent increase (table 2.8).

**TABLE 2.8.** Median Annual Per Capita Family Income at Age 70, by Birth Cohort ($)

| | *Pre-boomers (1936–1945)* | *Early Boomers (1946–1955)* | *Late Boomers (1956–1965)* | *Early Gen Xers (1966–1975)* | *Xennials (1976–1985)* |
|---|---|---|---|---|---|
| Men and women | 33,500 | 37,800 | 37,100 | 39,800 | 42,400 |
| Men | 37,800 | 40,500 | 39,300 | 42,700 | 43,600 |
| Women | 30,900 | 35,700 | 35,500 | 37,600 | 41,200 |

*Source:* Authors' estimates from DYNASIM4, ID963.

## WILL THESE RESOURCES BE ADEQUATE?

Will boomers, Gen Xers, and early millennials have enough to retire comfortably? Some analysts unequivocally conclude that most boomers will have too little;[31] others argue many boomers are saving too much.[32] Some analyses conclude that retirement income security will gradually erode, and Gen Xers will be less likely than today's retirees to have enough retirement income to maintain their preretirement standard of living.[33]

The answer depends partly on assumptions about the amount needed to maintain preretirement living standards, which is often expressed as the ratio of income in old age to preretirement earnings, typically called a replacement rate. A 75 percent replacement rate is commonly used as an adequacy rule of thumb because spending typically declines in retirement; retirees do not pay payroll taxes or save in retirement accounts, their children have usually already left home, and they no longer incur employment-related expenses once they stop working. Others argue that as health care prices and use increase, retirees need at least as much income as they had before retiring to cover rising medical costs.[34] Comparing retirement income to a replacement rate threshold can provide some insight into financial security at older ages, but using a single threshold for all retirees is reductive because the appropriate threshold can vary by such factors as income, homeownership, and number and age of children.

We compute replacement rates by comparing resources available at age seventy to average annual earnings received from ages fifty to fifty-nine. Our age seventy resource measure includes all usual sources of retirement income, plus the income that could be generated by annuitizing 80 percent of retirement accounts and other financial assets. Including this annuity value provides a more complete accounting of the resources available to older adults, particularly for future generations of retirees who are more likely than past generations to save for retirement in a DC plan than receive a regular DB pension benefit that counts as monthly income. (We exclude the value of home equity from our resource measure because historically, relatively few retirees have tapped into their housing wealth.) We adjust our estimates for marital status. For people who are married at age seventy, we divide their retirement resources by two; for people who are married in their fifties, we add the annual earnings received each year by their spouse and divide the couple's earnings by two for each year they are married.

Our DYNASIM4 projections show that about three-quarters of pre-boomers, early boomers, and late boomers can replace at least 75 percent of their preretirement earnings at age seventy. We estimate that 26 percent of pre-boomers and early boomers and 25 percent of late boomers will fall short of this resources standard (table 2.9). However, the retirement outlook is more discouraging for later generations. Even if all promised Social Security benefits are paid after the program's trust fund is scheduled to run out in 2035, we estimate that 30 percent of early Gen Xers and 32 percent of Xennials will be unable to replace at least 75 percent of their preretirement earnings at age seventy and risk being unable to maintain their preretirement living standards. The outlook becomes more ominous if policy makers fail to close Social Security's long-term financing gap. If Social Security does not receive an infusion of additional revenues by 2035 and benefits instead fall across the board by 25 percent—the approximate benefit cut that the Social Security trustees estimate would be necessary if policy makers fail to address the financing gap[35]—38 percent of early Gen Xers and 40 percent of Xennials would be unable to replace at least 75 percent of their preretirement earnings. Any Social Security cuts that result from funding shortfalls would affect pre-boomers and early boomers after age seventy but not at age seventy, because they will reach seventy before the Social Security trust funds are projected to run out.

Of course, a 75 percent replacement rate may not be sufficient in the future. If out-of-pocket health care costs continue to grow rapidly, older adults will need more resources to finance an adequate retirement income. A recent study, for example, projects that median out-of-pocket health spending (point-of-care plus premiums) as a share of income will rise from 10 percent in 2012 to 14 percent in 2035 for adults ages

**TABLE 2.9.** Percentage of Adults Unable to Replace 75 Percent of Preretirement Earnings at Age 70, by Birth Cohort

| | *Pre-boomers (1936–1945)* | *Early Boomers (1946–1955)* | *Late Boomers (1956–1965)* | *Early Gen Xers (1966–1975)* | *Xennials (1976–1985)* |
|---|---|---|---|---|---|
| Promised Social Security benefits are paid | 26 | 26 | 25 | 30 | 32 |
| Only 75% of promised Social Security benefits are paid | 26 | 26 | 26 | 38 | 40 |

*Source:* Authors' estimates from DYNASIM4, ID963.

**TABLE 2.10.** Percentage of Adults with Incomes below the Federal Poverty Level at Age 70, by Birth Cohort

| | *Pre-boomers (1936–1945)* | *Early Boomers (1946–1955)* | *Late Boomers (1956–1965)* | *Early Gen Xers (1966–1975)* | *Xennials (1976–1985)* |
|---|---|---|---|---|---|
| Promised Social Security benefits are paid | 7.3 | 6.3 | 6.8 | 6.2 | 6.1 |
| Only 75% of promised Social Security benefits are paid | 7.3 | 6.3 | 7.4 | 8.8 | 8.1 |

*Source:* Authors' estimates from DYNASIM4, ID963.

sixty-five and older.[36] The rising needs for long-term services and supports as older people develop disabilities and require help with everyday activities create additional income needs in retirement.[37] Growing health care spending burdens suggest that late boomers and Gen Xers may need to have 80 percent or more of their preretirement income to achieve the same living standard as their pre-boomer predecessors.

If policy makers resolve Social Security's long-term financing problems by raising system revenues and maintaining existing benefit rules, old-age poverty rates are projected to fall slowly over time. We project that the share of seventy-year-olds with family income below the federal poverty level will fall from 7.3 percent for pre-boomers to 6.1 percent for the Xennials as earnings growth raises average Social Security benefit payments and other retirement income sources (table 2.10). However, if policy makers fail to act and Social Security benefits are cut about 25 percent across the board beginning in 2035, old-age poverty rates will rise significantly. Such a benefit cut would increase the number of retirees living in poverty about 42 percent for early Gen Xers and 33 percent for Xennials.

## SUMMARY AND IMPLICATIONS

The financial outlook for coming generations of retirees is uncertain. An encouraging trend is the growth in employment and earnings for boomer and later generations of women, which will raise women's future retirement incomes. The projections show that most boomer and Gen-X women will earn their own Social Security and will receive higher benefits than previous generations. Also, more women will have their own pensions or retirement accounts, which will generally be worth more than earlier generations' accounts. These gains will help offset anemic growth in benefits for boomer and later generations of men, who will have little more Social Security than their predecessors because of their stagnant wages and somewhat reduced labor market activity at earlier ages.

The shift in employer coverage from DB pensions to DC plans means that more men and women with coverage will retire on benefits subject to the volatility of stocks and bonds. Although risky for workers, these accounts will bolster retirement income security if workers participate, assets are invested prudently, and financial markets provide positive long-term rates of return.

Although projected median age seventy income will be higher for boomers, Gen Xers, and early millennials than for their predecessors, the picture of Gen Xers' and early millennials' retirement income security is worrisome. We estimate that, if promised Social Security benefits are fully paid, 30 percent of early Gen Xers and 32 percent of Xennials will lack sufficient income at age seventy to replace 75 percent of what they earned between ages fifty and fifty-nine. The retirement outlook becomes more discouraging if policy makers allow cuts to Social Security as the program runs out of funding. If Social Security benefits are cut across the board after 2035, the year Social Security's trustees project that the program's trust funds run out, our projections indicate that four in ten Xennials will be unable to live as comfortably in retirement as in their fifties. Under both scenarios, Gen Xers and early millennials face a significantly higher risk than boomers and pre-boomers of being unable to maintain their living standards when they retire.

How boomers, Gen Xers, and early millennials fare in retirement will hinge on several unknowns, including how wages grow over coming decades, how those gains will be distributed across the workforce, how much stocks and bonds earn, how many seniors dip into their housing wealth to fund retirement needs, and how much income future retirees will need. In particular, how much will boomers and Gen Xers need to spend on health and long-term services and supports? One estimate shows that out-of-pocket medical costs will consume 14 percent of income in 2035 for the median older adult, up from 10 percent in 2012,[38] suggesting that future generations will need more than their predecessors to enjoy a comfortable retirement. A benchmark of 75 percent of preretirement income may no longer be adequate. Moreover, using the same replacement rate threshold to assess financial security for all retirees is reductive. Retirees with limited lifetime earnings, for example, likely need to replace more of their preretirement earnings than retirees with higher lifetime earnings. Retirees who fully own their homes generally need less income than renters or those with outstanding mortgages. People who raised large families can generally tolerate larger income declines when they retire than those without children. Our future research will delve deeper into understanding how much income retirees need to maintain their preretirement living standards.

Perhaps the most important question regarding future retirement income security concerns whether future generations delay retirement and prolong their working lives. Our projections assume that current retirement patterns will persist. In light of the looming retirement income shortfalls we have uncovered, however, it seems likely that more older workers will choose to work longer than we assumed. Working longer is arguably the best way to improve retirement security. Extending one's working life boosts monthly Social Security benefits and helps people save more in retirement accounts and other savings vehicles. However, older adults can work longer only if they are physically and cognitively able to work and if employers are willing to retain or hire them. Policy makers may need to strengthen prohibitions against age discrimination in the workplace and provide additional supports for older people with health problems who cannot extend their working lives.

## NOTES

Acknowledgments: The research described in this chapter was funded by the Alfred P. Sloan Foundation. The views expressed are those of the authors and should not be attributed to the Urban Institute, its trustees, or its funders. Funders do not determine research findings or the insights and recommendations of Urban experts. Further information about the Urban Institute's funding principles is available at http://www.urban.org/aboutus/our-funding/funding-principles.

1. Authors' calculations.

2. Barbara A. Butrica, Karen E. Smith, and C. Eugene Steuerle. 2006. "Working for a Good Retirement." Washington, DC: Urban Institute.

3. Maria D. Fitzpatrick and Timothy J. Moore. January 2018. "The Mortality Effects of Retirement: Evidence from Social Security Eligibility at Age 62." *Journal of Public Economics* 157:121–37; Eleonora Patacchini and Gary V. Engelhardt. 2016. "Work, Retirement, and Social Networks at Older Ages." Chestnut Hill, MA: Center for Retirement Research, Boston College; Susann Rohwedder and Robert J. Willis. Winter 2010. "Mental Retirement." *Journal of Economic Perspectives* 24(1):119–38; Alice Zulkarnain and Matthew S. Rutledge. 2018. "How Does Delayed Retirement Affect Mortality and Health?" Chestnut Hill, MA: Center for Retirement Research, Boston College.

4. Gary Burtless and Henry J. Aaron, eds. 2013. *Closing the Deficit: How Much Can Later Retirement Help?* Washington, DC: Brookings Institution.

5. Eric French. April 2005. "The Effects of Health, Wealth, and Wages on Labour Supply and Retirement Behaviour." *Review of Economic Studies* 72(2):395–427; Richard W. Johnson. 2018. "Is It Time to Raise the Social Security Retirement Age?" Washington, DC: Urban Institute; Richard W. Johnson, Gordon B. T. Mermin, and Matthew Resseger. 2011. "Job Demands and Work Ability at Older Ages." *Journal of Aging and Social Policy* 23(2):101–18; Kathleen McGarry. Summer 2004. "Health and Retirement: Do Changes in Health Affect Retirement Expectations?" *Journal of Human Resources* 39(3):624–48.

6. Alan Gustman and Thomas Steinmeier. September 2015. "Effects of Social Security Policies on Benefit Claiming, Retirement and Saving," *Journal of Public Economics* 129:51–62; Gordon B. T. Mermin, Richard W. Johnson, and Dan Murphy. September 2007. "Why Do Boomers Plan to Work Longer?" *Journal of Gerontology: Social Sciences* 62B(5):S286–94; Jae Song and Joyce Manchester. 2007. "Have People Delayed Claiming Retirement Benefits? Responses to Changes in Social Security Rules." *Social Security Bulletin* 67(2):1–23.

7. Leora Friedberg and Anthony Webb. Spring 2005. "Retirement and the Evolution of Pension Structure." *Journal of Human Resources* 40(2):281–308.

8. Richard W. Johnson, Amy J. Davidoff, and Kevin Perese. July 2003. "Health Insurance Costs and Early Retirement Decisions." *Industrial and Labor Relations Review* 56(4):716–29.

9. Board of Trustees of the Federal Old-age and Survivors Insurance and Federal Disability Insurance Trust Funds. 2018. *The 2018 Annual Report*. Washington, DC: U.S. Government Printing Office.

10. For more information about DYNASIM, see Melissa M. Favreault, Karen E. Smith, and Richard W. Johnson. 2015. "The Dynamic Simulation of Income Model (DYNASIM): An Overview." Washington, DC: Urban Institute; Urban Institute. 2015. "DYNASIM: Projecting Older Americans' Future Well-being." Washington, DC: Urban Institute.

11. Social Security Administration. 2018. "Death Probabilities." Baltimore, MD: Social Security Administration, Office of the Chief Actuary. (https://www.ssa.gov/OACT/HistEst/Death/2018/DeathProbabilities2018.html).

12. Barry Bosworth, Gary Burtless, and Kan Zhang. 2016. *Later Retirement, Inequality in Old Age, and the Growing Gap in Longevity between Rich and Poor*. Washington, DC: Brookings Institution;

Ellen Meara, Seth Richards, and David M. Cutler. February 2008. "The Gap Gets Bigger: Changes in Mortality and Life Expectancy, by Education, 1981–2000." *Health Affairs* 27(2):350–60; National Academies of Sciences, Engineering, and Medicine. 2015. *The Growing Gap in Life Expectancy by Income: Implications for Federal Programs and Policy Responses* Washington, DC: National Academies Press; Hilary Waldron. 2007. "Trends in Mortality Differentials and Life Expectancy for Male Social Security–covered Workers, by Socioeconomic Status." *Social Security Bulletin* 67(3):1–28; Hilary Waldron. 2013. "Mortality Differentials by Lifetime Earnings Decile: Implications for Evaluations of Proposed Social Security Law Changes." *Social Security Bulletin* 73(1):1–37.

13. Authors' calculations of National Health Interview Survey data, retrieved through IPUMS.

14. Johnson, "Is it Time."

15. Authors' calculations of unpublished data from the Social Security Administration.

16. Social Security Advisory Board. 2015. *Report to the Social Security Advisory Board*. Washington, DC: Technical Panel on Assumptions and Methods. (http://www.ssab.gov/Details-Page/ArticleID/656/2015-Technical-Panel-on-Assumptions-and-Methods-A-Report-to-the-Board-September-2015).

17. Anne Case and Angus Deaton. December 8, 2015. "Rising Morbidity and Mortality in Midlife among White Non-Hispanic Americans in the 21st Century." *Proceedings of the National Academy of Sciences* 112(49):15078–83; Kenneth D. Kochanek et al. 2017. "Mortality in the United States, 2016." *Data Brief* 293. Hyattsville, MD: National Center for Health Statistics.

18. National Center for Education Statistics. 1994. *The Condition of Education 1994*. Washington, DC: U.S. Government Printing Office; National Center for Education Statistics. 2016. *The Condition of Education 2016*. Washington, DC: U.S. Department of Education.

19. Social Security Administration. 2016. *Income of the Population 55 or Older, 2014*. Washington, DC: Social Security Administration.

20. Rose M. Kreider and Renee Ellis. 2011. "Number, Timing, and Duration of Marriages and Divorces: 2009." Current Population Reports P70-125. Washington, DC: U.S. Census Bureau.

21. Authors' calculations of data from the Annual Social and Economic Supplement of the Current Population Survey, retrieved through IPUMS.

22. Board of Trustees of the Federal Old-age and Survivors Insurance and Federal Disability Insurance Trust Funds, *2018 Annual Report*.

23. Adam Bee and Joshua Mitchell. 2017. "Do Older Americans Have More Income Than We Think?" Working Paper 2017-39. Washington, DC: U.S. Census Bureau; Center for Economic Studies, Social, Economic, and Housing Statistics Division.

24. Board of Trustees of the Federal Old-age and Survivors Insurance and Federal Disability Insurance Trust Funds, *2018 Annual Report*.

25. Bureau of Labor Statistics. March 2018. *National Compensation Survey: Employee Benefits in the United States, March 2018*. Washington, DC: U.S. Department of Labor.

26. Barbara A. Butrica. 2013. "Retirement Plan Balances." Washington, DC: Urban Institute.

27. Robert Argento, Victoria L. Bryant, and John Sabelhaus. January 2015. "Early Withdrawals from Retirement Accounts during the Great Recession." *Contemporary Economic Policy* 33(1):1–16.

28. Barbara A. Butrica and Richard W. Johnson. June 30, 2010. "Racial, Ethnic, and Gender Differentials in Employer-Sponsored Pensions." Statement to the ERISA Advisory Council, US Department of Labor. (http://www.urban.org/research/publication/racial-ethnic-and-gender-differentials-employer-sponsored-pensions).

29. S&P Dow Jones Indices LLC. S&P/Case-Shiller 20-City Composite Home Price Index [SPCS20RSA] FRED, the Federal Reserve Bank of St. Louis. Retrieved November 20, 2018 (https://fred.stlouisfed.org/series/SPCS20RSA).

30. Barbara A. Butrica and Stipica Mudrazija. 2016. "Home Equity Patterns among Older American Households." Washington, DC: Urban Institute.

31. Alicia H. Munnell, Wenliang Hou, and Geoffrey T. Sanzenbacher. 2016. "National Retirement Risk Index Shows Modest Improvement in 2016." *Issue Brief* 18-1. Chestnut Hill, MA: Center for Retirement Research, Boston College; Jack VanDerhei. 2014. "What Causes EBRI Retirement Readiness Ratings to Vary: Results from the 2014 Retirement Security Projection Model." *Issue Brief* 396. Washington, DC: Employee Benefit Research Institute.

32. John Karl Scholz, Ananth Seshadri, and Surachai Khitatrakun. August 2006. "Are Americans Saving 'Optimally' for Retirement?" *Journal of Political Economy* 114(4):607–43.

33. Barbara A. Butrica, Karen E. Smith, and Howard Iams. 2012. "This Is Not Your Parents' Retirement: Comparing Retirement Income across Generations." *Social Security Bulletin* 72(1): 1–22.

34. Jack VanDerhei, 2015. "Retirement Savings Shortfalls: Evidence from EBRI's Retirement Security Projection Model." *Issue Brief* 410. Washington, DC: Employee Benefit Research Institute.

35. Board of Trustees of the Federal Old-age and Survivors Insurance and Federal Disability Insurance Trust Funds, *2018 Annual Report.*

36. Laura A. Hatfield et al. February 2018. "Modeling Health Care Spending Growth of Older Adults." *Health Services Research* 53(1):138–55.

37. Melissa M. Favreault and Judith Dey. 2016. "Long-term Services and Supports for Older Americans: Risks and Financing Research Brief." Washington, DC: U.S. Department of Health and Human Services, Office of the Assistant Secretary for Planning and Evaluation.

38. Hatfield et al. "Modeling Health Care Spending."

## REFERENCES


Argento, Robert, Victoria L. Bryant, and John Sabelhaus. January 2015. "Early Withdrawals from Retirement Accounts during the Great Recession." *Contemporary Economic Policy* 33(1):1–16.

Bee, Adam and Joshua Mitchell. 2017. "Do Older Americans Have More Income Than We Think?" Working Paper 2017-39. Washington, DC: U.S. Census Bureau, Center for Economic Studies, Social, Economic, and Housing Statistics Division.

Board of Trustees of the Federal Old-age and Survivors Insurance and Federal Disability Insurance Trust Funds. 2018. *The 2018 Annual Report.* Washington, DC: U.S. Government Printing Office.

Bosworth, Barry, Gary Burtless, and Kan Zhang. 2016. *Later Retirement, Inequality in Old Age, and the Growing Gap in Longevity between Rich and Poor.* Washington, DC: Brookings Institution.

Bureau of Labor Statistics. 2018. *National Compensation Survey: Employee Benefits in the United States, March 2018.* Washington, DC: U.S. Department of Labor.

Burtless, Gary and Henry J. Aaron, eds. 2013. *Closing the Deficit: How Much Can Later Retirement Help?* Washington, DC: Brookings Institution.

Butrica, Barbara A. 2013. "Retirement Plan Balances." Washington, DC: Urban Institute.

Butrica, Barbara A. and Richard W. Johnson. June 30, 2010. "Racial, Ethnic, and Gender Differentials in Employer-Sponsored Pensions." Statement to the ERISA Advisory Council, U.S. Department of Labor. (http://www.urban.org/research/publication/racial-ethnic-and-gender-differentials-employer-sponsored-pensions).

Butrica, Barbara A. and Stipica Mudrazija. 2016. "Home Equity Patterns among Older American Households." Washington, DC: Urban Institute.

Butrica, Barbara A., Karen E. Smith, and Howard Iams. 2012. "This Is Not Your Parents' Retirement: Comparing Retirement Income across Generations." *Social Security Bulletin,* 72(1):1–22.

Butrica, Barbara A., Karen E. Smith, and C. Eugene Steuerle. 2006. "Working for a Good Retirement." Washington, DC: Urban Institute.

Case, Anne and Angus Deaton. December 8, 2015. "Rising Morbidity and Mortality in Midlife among White Non-Hispanic Americans in the 21st Century." *Proceedings of the National Academy of Sciences* 112(49):15078–83.

Favreault, Melissa M. and Judith Dey. 2016. "Long-term Services and Supports for Older Americans: Risks and Financing Research Brief." Washington, DC: U.S. Department of Health and Human Services, Office of the Assistant Secretary for Planning and Evaluation.

Favreault, Melissa M., Karen E. Smith, and Richard W. Johnson. 2015. "The Dynamic Simulation of Income Model (DYNASIM): An Overview." Washington, DC: Urban Institute.

Fitzpatrick, Maria D. and Timothy J. Moore. January 2018. "The Mortality Effects of Retirement: Evidence from Social Security Eligibility at Age 62." *Journal of Public Economics* 157:121–37.

French, Eric. April 2005. "The Effects of Health, Wealth, and Wages on Labour Supply and Retirement Behaviour." *Review of Economic Studies* 72(2):395–427.

Friedberg, Leora and Anthony Webb. Spring 2005. "Retirement and the Evolution of Pension Structure." *Journal of Human Resources* 40(2):281–308.

Gustman, Alan and Thomas Steinmeier. September 2015. "Effects of Social Security Policies on Benefit Claiming, Retirement and Saving." *Journal of Public Economics* 129:51–62.

Hatfield, Laura A., et al. February 2018. "Modeling Health Care Spending Growth of Older Adults." *Health Services Research* 53(1):138–55.

Johnson, Richard W. 2018. "Is It Time to Raise the Social Security Retirement Age?" Washington, DC: Urban Institute.

Johnson, Richard W., Amy J. Davidoff, and Kevin Perese. July 2003. "Health Insurance Costs and Early Retirement Decisions." *Industrial and Labor Relations Review* 56(4):716–29.

Johnson, Richard W., Gordon B. T. Mermin, and Matthew Resseger. 2011. "Job Demands and Work Ability at Older Ages." *Journal of Aging and Social Policy* 23(2):101–18.

Kochanek, Kenneth D., et al. 2017. "Mortality in the United States, 2016." *Data Brief* 293. Hyattsville, MD: National Center for Health Statistics.

Kreider, Rose M. and Renee Ellis. 2011. "Number, Timing, and Duration of Marriages and Divorces: 2009." Current Population Reports P70-125. Washington, DC: U.S. Census Bureau.

McGarry, Kathleen. Summer 2004. "Health and Retirement: Do Changes in Health Affect Retirement Expectations?" *Journal of Human Resources* 39(3):624–48.

Meara, Ellen, Seth Richards, and David M. Cutler. February 2008. "The Gap Gets Bigger: Changes in Mortality and Life Expectancy, by Education, 1981–2000." *Health Affairs* 27(2):350–60.

Mermin, Gordon B. T., Richard W. Johnson, and Dan Murphy. September 2007. "Why Do Boomers Plan to Work Longer?" *Journal of Gerontology: Social Sciences* 62B(5):S286–94.

Munnell, Alicia H., Wenliang Hou, and Geoffrey T. Sanzenbacher. 2016. "National Retirement Risk Index Shows Modest Improvement in 2016." *Issue Brief* 18-1. Chestnut Hill, MA: Center for Retirement Research, Boston College.

National Academies of Sciences, Engineering, and Medicine. 2015. *The Growing Gap in Life Expectancy by Income: Implications for Federal Programs and Policy Responses.* Washington, DC: National Academies Press.

National Center for Education Statistics. 1994. *The Condition of Education 1994.* Washington, DC: U.S. Government Printing Office.

National Center for Education Statistics. 2016. *The Condition of Education 2016.* Washington, DC: U.S. Department of Education.

Patacchini, Eleonora and Gary V. Engelhardt. 2016. "Work, Retirement, and Social Networks at Older Ages." Chestnut Hill, MA: Center for Retirement Research, Boston College.

Rohwedder, Susann and Robert J. Willis. Winter 2010. "Mental Retirement." *Journal of Economic Perspectives* 24(1):119–38.

S&P Dow Jones Indices LLC. S&P/Case-Shiller 20-City Composite Home Price Index [SPCS20RSA] FRED, the Federal Reserve Bank of St. Louis. Retrieved November 20, 2018 (https://fred.stlouisfed.org/series/SPCS20RSA).

Scholz, John Karl, Ananth Seshadri, and Surachai Khitatrakun. August 2006. "Are Americans Saving 'Optimally' for Retirement?" *Journal of Political Economy* 114(4):607–43.

Social Security Administration. 2016. *Income of the Population 55 or Older, 2014.* Washington, DC: Social Security Administration.

Social Security Administration. 2018. "Death Probabilities." Baltimore, MD: Social Security Administration, Office of the Chief Actuary. (https://www.ssa.gov/OACT/HistEst/Death/2018/DeathProbabilities2018.html).

Social Security Advisory Board. 2015. *Report to the Social Security Advisory Board.* Washington, DC: Technical Panel on Assumptions and Methods. (http://www.ssab.gov/Details-Page/ArticleID/656/2015-Technical-Panel-on-Assumptions-and-Methods-A-Report-to-the-Board-September-2015).

Song, Jae and Joyce Manchester. 2007. "Have People Delayed Claiming Retirement Benefits? Responses to Changes in Social Security Rules." *Social Security Bulletin* 67(2):1–23.

Urban Institute. 2015. "DYNASIM: Projecting Older Americans' Future Well-being." Washington, DC: Urban Institute.

VanDerhei, Jack. 2014. "What Causes EBRI Retirement Readiness Ratings to Vary: Results from the 2014 Retirement Security Projection Model." *Issue Brief* 396. Washington, DC: Employee Benefit Research Institute.

VanDerhei, Jack. 2015. "Retirement Savings Shortfalls: Evidence from EBRI's Retirement Security Projection Model." *Issue Brief* 410. Washington, DC: Employee Benefit Research Institute.

Waldron, Hillary. 2007. "Trends in Mortality Differentials and Life Expectancy for Male Social Security–covered Workers, by Socioeconomic Status." *Social Security Bulletin* 67(3):1–28.

Waldron, Hillary. 2013. "Mortality Differentials by Lifetime Earnings Decile: Implications for Evaluations of Proposed Social Security Law Changes." *Social Security Bulletin* 73(1):1–37.

Zulkarnain, Alice and Matthew S. Rutledge. 2018. "How Does Delayed Retirement Affect Mortality and Health?" Chestnut Hill, MA: Center for Retirement Research, Boston College.

CHAPTER 3

# Challenges and Opportunities to Living and Working Longer in the Twenty-First Century

Ernest Gonzales and Sarah Michelle Steeley

## OVERVIEW

Population aging is not going as planned. Prior to the twenty-first century, life expectancy rose steadily with concurrent increases in education and health among the American population. Yet the first two decades of the twenty-first century have revealed growing health and economic inequities—recession, civil unrest, and a worldwide pandemic, to name a few. In this chapter, we review the many risks and challenges associated with working longer by a heterogeneous older adult population. We also review factors promoting and limiting choices and opportunities to work, including policies and practices related to informal caregiving, discrimination, and lifetime socioeconomic disadvantages and shocks. Economic, health, and psychosocial drivers to working longer will likely persist; that is, retirement income deficits and the desire to contribute to society through work will likely continue. Yet informal caregiving, discrimination, and socioeconomic disadvantages that start in early life will remain ongoing challenges to working in later life.

Rooted in a strengths-based and assets perspective, *productive engagement* exemplifies a logical and promising response to the demands of population aging. Through this alternative lens and under the right social conditions, productive activities by older adults can lead to multiple positive ends: offsetting the fiscal strains of a larger older population, contributing to the betterment of families and civil society, and promoting population health and economic well-being among older adults and their families. *Productive aging* is defined as any activity by an older individual that contributes to the production of goods or services, whether paid for or not.[1] While a number of activities can qualify as productive, we mainly focus on older adults' paid employment in this chapter, although we review how informal caregiving and volunteering interact with their employment.

Delaying retirement has become the national mantra among policy experts.[2,3] There has been a fundamental shift of saving for retirement from personal savings, employer contributions, and Social Security retirement income to individual responsibility.[4] Women, racial and ethnic minorities, and lower-educated individuals are less likely to have pensions from employers and more likely to experience pay inequities across their lifetime, have saved significantly less for retirement, and are at jeopardy of living in poverty in later life.[5,6] Individuals who are able to delay retirement to the normal retirement age (approximately sixty-six for baby boomers) can expect an increase in Social Security income by 33 percent or an additional 40 percent if they are able to wait until the age of seventy[7] rather than retiring early at age sixty-two. In addition, job demands that match employees' capacity can improve health, purpose, and meaning.[8,9,10] For a combination of these reasons, working in retirement is becoming more prevalent.[11,12,13] Yet not everyone can work longer, and there are many risks and protective factors that influence employment decisions by older adults.

In this chapter, we utilize a risk and protective framework to reveal the many challenges to working longer among a heterogeneous population. Specifically, section one reviews evidence of social systems that compromise individual capacity for and choices about work, such as informal caregiving, age discrimination and other forms of prejudice, and cumulative disadvantage and shocks. In section two, we review social policies that have the potential to bolster resilience and consequently leverage more choices for work among older adults. In section three, we emphasize that work should be meaningful and purposeful, rather than simply a job or a paycheck, in order to enhance health and well-being. We conclude by critiquing existing research and identifying gaps in the literature for future research.

## RISKS THAT COMPROMISE THE CAPACITY TO WORK LONGER

### Informal Caregiving

Family caregivers are the backbone of long-term services and supports.[14] (See also chapter 20.) Approximately forty million adults help their family members and friends with instrumental activities of daily living (IADLs, e.g., housekeeping, taking medications, managing finances) and other basic activities of daily living (ADLs) such as eating, bathing, dressing, toileting, mobility and grooming, meal preparation, and grocery shopping.[15] The economic value of these activities is approximately $470 billion, annually. Caregivers in the twenty-first century are very diverse. Typically, caregivers are aged seventy-five and older, white, unemployed, female, and providing care to one adult for approximately thirty-four hours a week without any other unpaid help.[16] However, one out of four of the forty million caregivers represents individuals within the millennial cohort—individuals born between 1981 and 1996. Among these caregivers, half are African American/black, Hispanic/Latinx, or Asian American/Pacific Islander.[17] And they offer more than twenty hours per week while balancing paid employment in full-time jobs that pay approximately less than $30,000 per year. Millennials also spend approximately $6,800 a year (or $566 per month) on caregiving expenses such as food, supplies, and home modifications.

Informal caregivers, most of whom are women, are more likely to be forced into retirement and to retire earlier when compared to non-caregivers.[18,19,20] And while there is a large body of research that examines bridge employment and phased retirement,[21,22,23] few studies focus on unretirement[24] (the term describing retirees going back to work) and there is a significant lack of attention to caregivers. Do caregivers *un*retire at the same rates as non-caregivers? And does the nature of informal caregiving have any effect on returning to work?

Informed by role theory,[25,26,27] survival analyses of 8,334 older adults in the United States from 1998 to 2008 revealed that when compared to non-caregivers, helping a spouse with ADLs or IADLs reduced the odds of returning to work in the subsequent wave by 78 percent and 55 percent, respectively, while controlling for economic, health, and household covariates. Results, which revealed role strain rather than role enhancement, informed several studies domestically and internationally.[28,29] Consequently, caregivers' overall weaker relationship with the labor force heightens the risk of living in poverty in later life.[30,31,32]

## Discrimination

Ageism affects all of us, young and old, across racial and ethnic groups, and socioeconomic status. Ageism is global and multidimensional, and spans from internalized perceptions of self (see chapter 12) to cultural scripts within and beyond the United States. Ageism intersects with other forms of minority social and economic positions in a racialized society.[33] Ageism is also costly: one study estimated that $850 billion is lost in the production of goods and services by individuals in later life simply because of their age.[34] And finally, ageism undermines aspects of our health[35] and mental health specifically,[36,37] with detriments to our health costing an additional $63 billion annually.[38] Ageism is one of the last forms of bigotry to be acknowledged and systematically dismantled.

Research in the twentieth century provided solid evidence of ageist views about older workers. Within the workplace, older workers were often perceived to be resistant to change, to bring a lower return on investments, to be unwilling or unable to learn and adapt, to lack creativity, and to perform poorly within workplace settings.[39,40] These stereotypes by employers, supervisors, and peers have led to biased assessments of older workers' performance and recommendations for recruitment, training, promotion, job transition, and retention.[41,42,43,44] Yet this large body of research neglected to examine the perspective of older workers themselves.

At the turn of the twenty-first century, the field was missing an instrument that captured the individual's perspective on age-based discrimination at work, thus limiting our knowledge of the linkages between ageism, health, and labor force participation. Through a collaborative process, Marchiondo, Gonzales, and Ran developed a unidimensional scale, the workplace age discrimination scale (WADS), that captured perceived age discrimination within the workplace.[45] The WADS is the only instrument with high validity and reliability that is applicable to individuals aged eighteen and older. Through three separate studies, the researchers revealed a U-shape distribution of discrimination across the working lifespan, where young and older workers perceive greater age discrimination than middle-aged workers. Researchers in this and another study also demonstrated how perceived age discrimination is negatively associated with mental health, stress, and job satisfaction, and how it heightens intentions to leave the organization and possibly retire early.[46,47] Aside from developing a new valid and reliable measure for the field, this study is important because it confirmed aspects of selective incivility theory and disrupts a long-standing assumption that older adults are the only targets of age discrimination within the workplace. This research urges scholars and policy makers to examine ageism across the entire working lifespan.

Sexism and racism, in addition to ageism, are also prevalent and have been linked with barriers to working longer.[48] Drawing from *cumulative inequality and dis/advantage theories*, it appears that ageism alone cannot explain the breadth and depth of social disadvantages experienced by diverse older adults. Multiple forms of perceived discrimination, as well as neighborhood conditions, were seen to have affected mental health and hastened retirement among a representative sample of older adults in the Health and Retirement Study (2006–2014; n=2,028).[49] This empirical study revealed how major lifetime discrimination, chronic work discrimination, everyday discrimination, neighborhood physical disorder and social incohesion, as well as a summative disadvantage index, were all associated with depressive symptomatology and hastened earlier retirement. Individuals who did not experience discrimination and resided in resourceful neighborhoods retired at age sixty-five, the age at which this sample was eligible for their full retirement benefits, whereas respondents with the highest level of discrimination and neighborhood disadvantage retired earlier, approximately at age 62.5, and consequently received a reduced monthly amount of Social Security retirement income. Mental health mediated the relationships.

Interestingly, whites, blacks/African Americans, and Hispanics/Latinxs retired at similar ages.[50] All racial and ethnic groups reported high levels of ageism, along with significant rates of sexism, racism, nativism, and ableism. This national study revealed that whites reported the highest levels of chronic work discrimination and everyday discrimination, whereas blacks reported the highest levels of major lifetime discrimination and neighborhood social incohesion, and Hispanics/Latinxs reported the highest levels of neighborhood physical disorder. Indeed, ageism was a common and pronounced experience across these racial and ethnic groups. This heterogeneity needs to be further explored, possibly with latent class analyses, to assess various dimensions of health. Discrimination and neighborhood disorder are physically, socially, and psychologically stressful.[51] Also of note, preliminary analyses reveal positive associations between social disadvantage and various aspects of decline in cognitive health, physical health, and other aspects of psychological well-being, which may weaken labor force attachment in later life. This warrants further study.

The aforementioned national study contributed to the field by offering a conceptual framework of cumulative disadvantage and a new construct with high reliability (summative disadvantage index).[52] It is also important because it explored the unique and compounded effects of discrimination and neighborhood conditions related to psychological well-being and *actual* retirement behavior. Two ways of strengthening federal, state, and private-sector employment policies and practices that would protect workers from work discrimination[53,54] are the Protecting Older Workers against Discrimination Act (S. 443, a bipartisan bill currently under review in Congress) and the Fair Employment Protection Act (S. 2019, which aims to protect individuals from modern and covert forms of discrimination based on age, race, gender, and other characteristics).

### Cumulative Disadvantages and Shocks

The longitudinal population-based studies reviewed above are important for a number of reasons—they helped to expand the conceptualization of productive aging with rigorous statistical techniques by exploring populations and issues that were counter to the normative white-male retirement model and evidence base. Yet, these secondary data analyses often missed the perspectives, voices, and experiences of low-income older adults trying to find employment. Moreover, the themes of resilience, and chains of risk and protective factors, were missing from the literature concerning this vulnerable population. Through an ongoing partnership with practitioners and with support from Senior Service America Inc. (now the Center for Workforce Inclusion) and the Peter T. Paul Career Development Award from Boston University, the senior author of this chapter explored themes of protective factors and risk to health and employment among low-income older adults engaged in the Senior Community Service Employment Program (SCSEP). SCSEP is authorized by Title V of the Older Americans Act and is under the auspices of the Department of Labor. The goals of the program are to provide job training and employment assistance to jobless low-income workers aged fifty-five and older who earn less than 125 percent of the federal poverty level. It is arguably the only federally funded program to help older adults gain employment and is often at jeopardy of losing federal support.

Qualitative results supported ecological systems theory with identifying themes of protective factors at the micro, mezzo, and macro levels. Cumulative dis/advantage theory revealed risk and protective factors at particularly sensitive life stages, affecting their lifespan.[55] While the presence and magnitude of risk factors cannot be overlooked,[56] respondents exhibited a great deal of grit and found support from a number of resources within their social systems. Respondents handled difficult situations well and tried to redirect their adversity to a stronger, healthier path. Importantly, this study revealed how work itself, under the right conditions, reversed negative wear and tear on health and led to improvements in physical, mental, and overall health. These qualitative studies were especially useful in that they contextualized systems, routines, psychosocial fears and hopes, and institutional characteristics that supported individuals with their health and work.

## PROTECTIVE FACTORS AS POTENTIAL SOLUTIONS

### Discrimination Laws and Practices and Unarming the Enemy Within

Overcoming discrimination will require multilevel and multimodal approaches. Centrally concerned with discrimination within the workplace, the Protecting Older

Workers against Discrimination Act (S. 443) has bipartisan support and can help expand and bolster protection of older workers from subtle and overt forms of discrimination. This legislation is important because it says that *age* can be *a factor*, rather than *the factor*, when pursuing discrimination claims via the Age Discrimination in Employment Act.[57] The Fair Employment Protection Act (S. 2019) also has bipartisan support and can protect individuals from not just age discrimination but also forms of bigotry and incivility.[58] It is also important for employers to create a "common in-group identity" within the workplace, while simultaneously raising awareness about biases large and small and attitudinal dispositions. The intergroup contact hypothesis[59,60] could be extended into the workplace to achieve these goals and research should document its effectiveness. Occupational social workers and other mental health counselors can also bolster individual resilience and assist clients with psychosocial education to help recognize discrimination, identify protective factors (e.g., meditation, spirituality, religiosity, physical exercise, social support, and federal protection). It is also important for occupational social workers to raise awareness about internalized ageism and other isms[61] and undo cognitive, physical, and emotional damage to health. Tackling stereotypes and discrimination is best addressed through a life course perspective. Cognitive schemas begin early in life: early childhood, adolescence, emerging adulthood, middle adulthood, and early late life are all sensitive psychosocial opportunities for critical reflection, undoing cognitive schemas, and becoming free from cultural scripts and internal forms of oppression.

## Employer, Federal, and State Policies for Work-Life Balance

Informal caregivers warrant our support for their health and to ensure they have opportunities to work should they want and/or need to be engaged in the paid labor force. The studies on role strain have clear implications for social policy: Family and Medical Leave Act (FMLA), Schedules That Work Act, and the Social Security Caregiver Credit Act. Under the current FMLA of 1993, 60 percent of the U.S. workforce can take twelve weeks of unpaid leave to handle emergencies and caregiving burdens.[62] Additionally, five states and the District of Columbia have enacted paid family leave (PFL) models that their residents can access. Qualifying family members tend to include children, parents, spouses, domestic partners, and grandparents, while some states include grandchildren, siblings, civil union partners, and parents-in-law. The time allowed by each state varies from four to twelve weeks, and payments range from 60 to 90 percent of weekly wages with caps ranging from $637 to $1,216 per week. While these policies have been found to provide family caregivers with financial security, lessen the strain of caregiving, decrease employer expenditure by increasing employment retention, and aid in maintaining a productive workforce, it was found that only half of the state populations in California, New Jersey, and Rhode Island knew their state had a PFL policy.[63,64] Older folks, lower-waged workers, and communities of color had the lowest level of awareness of these programs within their states.[65]

By March 2018, only 16 percent of the United States private industry workforce had access to PFL because it is a voluntary benefit from private-sector employers.[66] While a law passed in December 2017, H.R. 1 (P.L. 115-97) includes tax incentives to employers who offer voluntary PFL, rates of implementation are still low. Twenty-five of the United States' thirty-five contemporaries in the Organisation for Economic Co-operation and Development (OECD) offer some type of national PFL to those caring for the ill and/or elderly. The proposed Family and Medical Insurance Leave Act (FAMILY Act, S. 463/H.R. 1185) would create a national wage insurance program. There are many suggestions that ought to be considered to improve the United States' ability to provide a healthy work-life balance for its caregiving population. While some promote using the tax code to provide tax advantages to those who need to engage in caregiving, others recommend providing a national PFL program and/or direct supports and financial assistance to family members providing care.[67,68]

Many workers face unpredictable and unfair scheduling, causing a large percentage of the workforce to struggle to meet the needs of their families and hampering their ability to fully engage in economic opportunities.[69] The proposed Schedules That Work Act (H.R. 2941) would improve employees' control over their schedule as well as increase its predictability and stability.[70,71]

Because people usually must exit the workforce to provide care for children and other dependents, including the elderly, the Social Security Caregiver Credit Act (H.R. 4126), currently introduced in the House, would make strides toward compensating those folks.[72,73] The bill suggests that anyone providing more than eighty hours of care to someone under age twelve or to someone who is chronically dependent would qualify for credit calculated toward total deemed wages that would influence future Social Security benefits.[74] Those with the lowest wages during that time would accrue the most credit, with those earning regular salaries earning the least.

Flexible work is important for a variety of employees and households. (See also chapter 11.) Hewlett-Packard was the first company to introduce flexible work scheduling policies in 1972.[75] Federal employees have been allowed alternative work schedules since 1978 through the Federal Employees Flexible and Comparable Work Schedules Act. Since the 1970s, worker access to flexible work scheduling has steadily (albeit slowly) increased across the workforce.[76] Companies have the choice of implementing flexible work arrangements, including flexible scheduling, telecommuting, job sharing, workweek compression, part-time scheduling, and part-year scheduling.[77,78,79] One study that covered a wide range of professions, most of which were not highly skilled, found that 72 percent of workers had access to some sort of flexible work schedule.[80] Men and highly educated workers were more likely to have access to flexible work. Surprisingly, this study found that highly skilled workers were 25 percent less likely to have access to flexible work. Limitations of this study were that it excluded the poorest workers in the workforce and only focused on seven types of occupations. Another study found that women and African Americans have less access to flexible working arrangements.[81] Married men with children and women with pre-school-aged children have more access to working-at-home options. The American Academy of Social Work and Social Welfare's Grand Challenges Initiative has been endorsing these policies to help leverage choice among informal caregivers.[82,83,84]

### Formal Volunteering as a Mechanism for Social Capital

Another national study (supported by the John A. Hartford Foundation) explored how social capital (bonding, bridging, and linking) facilitated older adults returning to work after retirement.[85] Labor economists and sociologists had already demonstrated how formal education, health, and occupational characteristics were related to working longer and unretirement specifically. But how do different social resources inform these later-life transitions, above and beyond economic and human capital factors? Indeed, a number of economic and human capital factors are related to unretirement (e.g., pension, employer-sponsored health insurance, education, self-rated health, and occupations). This study revealed that social capital plays an important role. Aside from having a spouse or partner who was employed, high-intensity formal and informal volunteers were pulled back into paid work. These findings are important because participation in national volunteer programs can help bolster social ties and facilitate the acquisition of information and employment opportunities as well as maintain the health of older adults. Thus, federal programs such as Senior Corps (Retired and Senior Volunteer Program, Foster Grandparent Program, and Senior Companion), Senior Community Service Employment Program (SCSEP), and Experience Corps can all help to ensure that older adults have opportunities to give back to their communities through schools, religious organizations, and nonprofits, as well as to maintain an important resource—social capital—to help facilitate longer working lives.[86]

## POLICIES AND PRACTICES THAT BUFFER CUMULATIVE DISADVANTAGE AND SHOCKS

The challenges to working longer are clearly more acute and enduring for often-marginalized populations, namely, women, racial and ethnic minorities, and individuals with lower socioeconomic status. Most older adults, irrespective of their minority status, experience discrimination based on age. And consequently, their health and opportunities for work are diminished. Raising the retirement age across the board without consideration of these inequities and structural challenges will only add insult to injury. Because individuals with lower socioeconomic status tend to die earlier, raising the retirement age will in effect shorten their time in retirement when compared to individuals with higher socioeconomic status.[87]

Health and education are major predictors of work and longevity of work in the United States and abroad. Policies that address inequities in health, academic achievement, pay, and accessibility to pensions beginning in early life and throughout the adult life course will likely result in bolstering individual capacity and desire to engage in meaningful work. Federal policies, such as Title V of the Older Americans Act, the Affordable Care Act, and the Paycheck Fairness Act, as well as the establishment of standard minimum wages, can all increase individual capacity to work and have meaningful work. These policies are not without controversy. Each of them needs to be debated based on the latest science and evidence of the impact on human capital and labor force status. For instance, Title V of the Older Americans Act is widely considered to be an ineffective job training program for low-income older adults. The performance measures are narrow in scope, and practitioners often do not have the necessary resources to fully address their many challenges, such as homelessness, mental health (depression, isolation), poor physical health (cancer, emphysema), and a lifetime of missed opportunities for education and job training of quality. Many scholars continue to discuss whether this program would be best situated under the auspices of the Administration for Community Living, which focuses on health improvement, given that most participants experience significant improvements in cognitive and mental health as well as physical health when job training opportunities are carefully matched with their physical ability and personal desires.[88,89]

## THE MANY MEANINGS OF WORK

The meaning of work differs across generations and over time. Current research suggests that the search for meaning in work largely takes place during emerging adulthood.[90] Even so, many older workers still glean meaning from their paid work and volunteer activities long after they have retired.[91] Work in later life not only maintains health and fosters workers' personal development, but it also actively involves them in wider society and increases the sense of personal control over later life that many boomers are seeking.[92,93] Boomers want to find meaning in their postretirement activities and typically look for roles with more flexibility and less demanding tasks.[94,95] They desire to remain engaged, but the decision to work is shaped by physical health, finances, family circumstances, interests outside of work, and working conditions. While motivation for work changes throughout a worker's career, it does not uniformly decline over time.[96] The types of tasks workers are assigned, as well as their perceptions of those tasks, impact the motivation to work. While women and males with young second families are more likely to consider finances as an important factor in maintaining work in later life,[97] many workers keep working to add meaning to life and to stay intellectually alert.[98] Single men rely on the social value of work more than any other group.[99]

## LIMITATIONS AND FUTURE RESEARCH

The twenty-first century has become more heterogeneous than previous centuries. Research has yet to fully and carefully incorporate how intersecting identities are related to various dimensions of health, nor has it adequately explored how these factors are associated with working longer. Most of the literature on discrimination fails to query respondents on *why* they believe they were discriminated against—was it because of their age, race, ethnicity, or something else? Caregiving has clearly become a challenge for many adults, and how this impacts labor force status, poverty, and work preferences has yet to be fully addressed. Furthermore, research that examines multiple levels, such as public- and private-sector employment policies and how they intersect with neighborhood conditions, household structure, and across the diverse populations in the United States, has clearly not been accomplished. Qualitative research and longitudinal analyses will help tackle these remaining issues of sample bias and limited conceptualization.

## CONCLUSION

Working longer is a challenge for many, and the pressure to work in later life is more acute for women, racial and ethnic minorities, and individuals with lower levels of socioeconomic status. While we review a number of policies and practices that can bolster individual resilience, we should keep in mind that work is central to our identity and our place in society. And we must create policies and an environment that foster individual capacity to engage in meaningful work starting in early life and leading to productive aging. To feel satisfied with one's production of goods and services for a society that respects one's efforts is an important part of the recipe for health and human transcendence.

## NOTES

1. Scott Bass, Francis J. Caro, and Yung-Ping Chen. 1993. *Toward a Productive Aging Society.* Westport, CT: Auburn House.
2. Alicia H. Munnell. 2011. "What Is the Average Retirement Age?" Chestnut Hill, MA: Center for Retirement Research, Boston College. Brief No. 11:1–7.
3. Richard W. Johnson. November 12, 2018. "A Tale of Two Retirements: Working Longer Is Exacerbating Income Inequality among Older Adults." Washington, DC: Urban Institute blog. (https://www.urban.org/urban-wire/tale-two-retirements-working-longer-exacerbating-income-inequality-among-older-americans).
4. Alicia H. Munnell and Steven A. Sass. 2009. *Working Longer: The Solution to the Retirement Income Challenge*. Washington, DC: Brookings Institution.
5. Ernest Gonzales. 2015. "Workplace Policies and Practices: Opportunities for and Barriers to Accumulating Assets in Midlife and Later." In *Financial Capabilities across the Life Course*, edited by Nancy Morrow-Howell and Michael Sherraden. New York: Oxford University Press.
6. Ernest Gonzales. 2013. "An Examination on Un-retirement: Retirees Returning to Work." PhD dissertation. Washington University, St. Louis, MO. (https://openscholarship.wustl.edu/etd/1132).
7. Johnson, "Tale of Two Retirements."
8. Ernest Gonzales, Kathy Lee, and Robert Harootyan. Forthcoming. "Voices from the Field: Ecological Factors That Promote Employment and Health among Low-income Older Adults with Implications for Direct Social Work Practice." *Clinical Social Work Journal*. (https://doi.org/10.1007/s10615-019-00719-x).
9. Jacquelyn B. James and Marcie Pitt-Catsouphes. 2016. "Introduction to the Special Issue: Change in the Meaning and Experience of Work in Later Life." *Work, Aging, and Retirement* 2(3):281–85. (https://doi.org/10.1093/workar/waw020).
10. Michael A. Smyer and Marcie Pitt-Catsouphes. 2007. "The Meanings of Work for Older Workers." *Generations* 31(1):23–30.
11. Ernest Gonzales, Christina Matz-Costa, and Nancy Morrow-Howell. 2015. "White House Conference on Aging 2015. Increasing Opportunities for the Productive Engagement of Older Adults: A Response to Population Aging." *The Gerontologist* 55(2):252–61. (https://doi.org/10.1093/geront/gnu176).
12. Dawn Carr et al. Forthcoming. "Post-recession Retirement Transition Profiles in the United States: An Exploratory Analysis."
13. Nicole Maestas and Julie Zissimopoulos. 2010. "How Longer Work Lives Ease the Crunch of Population Aging." *Journal of Economic Perspectives* 24(1):139–60.
14. Robert L. Kane. 2015. "A New Long-term Care Manifesto." *The Gerontologist* 55:296–301.
15. Brendan Flinn. 2018. "Millennials: The Emerging Generation of Family Caregivers." Washington, DC: AARP Public Policy Institute. *Spotlight* 33:1–11.

16. AARP. 2015. "Caregiving in the U.S." *Research Report*. (https://www.aarp.org/content/dam/aarp/ppi/2015/caregiving-in-the-united-states-2015-report-revised.pdf).

17. Flinn, "Millennials."

18. Emma Dentinger and Marin Clarkberg. 2002. "Informal Caregiving and Retirement Timing among Men and Women: Gender and Caregiving Relationships in Late Midlife." *Journal of Family Issues* 23(7):857–79.

19. Eliza K. Pavalko and Julie E. Artis. 1997. "Women's Caregiving and Paid Work: Causal Relationships in Late Midlife." *Journals of Gerontology, Series B: Psychological Sciences and Social Sciences* 52(4):S170–79.

20. Maximiliane E. Szinovacz and Adam Davey. 2005. "Predictors of Perceptions of Involuntary Retirement." *The Gerontologist* 45(1):36–47.

21. Kevin E. Cahill, Michael D. Giandrea, and Joseph F. Quinn. 2015. "Evolving Patterns of Work and Retirement." Pp. 271–91 in *Handbook of Aging and the Social Sciences*, 8th ed., edited by Linda K. George and Kenneth F. Ferraro. London: Elsevier.

22. Esteban Calvo, Ignacio Madero-Cabib, and Ursula M. Staudinger. 2018. "Retirement Sequences of Older Americans: Moderately Destandardized and Highly Stratified across Gender, Class, and Race." *The Gerontologist*, 58(6):1166–76. (https://doi.org/10.1093/geront/gnx052).

23. Melissa Brown et al. 2014. "Returning to the Workforce after Retiring: Perceptions of Job Demands, Job Control, and Social Support." *International Journal of Human Resource Management* 25(22):3113–33. (https://doi.org/10.1080/09585192.2014.919951).

24. Nicole Maestas. 2010. "Back to Work: Expectations and Realizations of Work after Retirement." *Journal of Human Resources* 45(3):718–48.

25. Phyllis Moen, Julie Robison, and Donna Dempster-McClain. 1995. "Caregiving and Women's Well-being: A Life-course Approach." *Journal of Health and Social Behavior* 36(3):259–73.

26. Wagner A. Kamakura. 2009. "American Time-styles: A Finite-mixture Allocation Model for Time-use Analysis." *Multivariate Behavioral Research* 44(3):332–61.

27. Dale Southerton and Mark Tomlinson. 2005. "'Pressed for Time'—The Differential Impacts of a 'Time Squeeze.'" *Sociological Review* 53(2):215–39.

28. Sherry E. Sullivan and Akram Al Ariss. 2018. "Employment after Retirement: A Review and Framework for Future Research." *Journal of Management* 45(1):262–84.

29. Peter M. Smith et al. 2019. "Male/female Differences in the Impact of Caring for Elderly Relatives on Labor Market Attachment and Hours of Work: 1997–2015." *Journals of Gerontology: Social Sciences* 75(3):694–704. (https://doi.org/10.1093/geronb/gbz026).

30. Jennifer Crane Greenfield. 2013. "The Long-term Costs of Caring: How Caring for an Aging Parent Impacts Wealth Trajectories of Caregivers." PhD dissertation. Washington University, St. Louis, MO. (https://openscholarship.wustl.edu/etd/1108).

31. Yeonjung Lee et al. 2015. "The Vicious Cycle of Parental Caregiving and Financial Well-being: A Longitudinal Study of Women." *Journals of Gerontology, Series B: Psychological Sciences and Social Sciences* 70(3):425–31.

32. Chizuko Wakabayashi and Katharine M. Donato. 2006. "Does Caregiving Increase Poverty among Women in Later Life? Evidence from the Health and Retirement Survey." *Journal of Health and Social Behavior* 47(3):258–74.

33. Ernest Gonzales, Yeonjung Jane Lee, and Lisa A. Marchiondo. December 11, 2019. "Exploring the Consequences of Major Lifetime Discrimination, Neighborhood Conditions, Chronic Work, and Everyday Discrimination on Health and Retirement." *Journal of Applied Gerontology*. (https://doi.org/10.1177/0733464819892847).

34. AARP. 2020. "The Economic Impact of Age Discrimination." (https://www.aarp.org/content/dam/aarp/research/surveys_statistics/econ/2020/impact-of-age-discrimination.doi.10.26419-2Fint.00042.003.pdf).

35. Becca R. Levy et al. 2020. "Ageism Amplifies Cost and Prevalence of Health Conditions." *The Gerontologist* 60(1):174–81. (https://doi.org/10.1093/geront/gny131).

36. Lisa A. Marchiondo, Ernest Gonzales, and Shan Ran. 2015. "Development and Validation of the Workplace Age Discrimination Scale (WADS)." *Journal of Business and Psychology* 4. (https://doi.org/10.1007/s10869-015-9425-6).

37. Lisa A. Marchiondo, Ernest Gonzales, and Larry J. Williams. 2017. "Trajectories of Perceived Workplace Age Discrimination and Long-term Associations with Mental, Self-rated, and Occupational Health." *Journal of Gerontology: Social Sciences* 74(4):655–63. (https://doi.org/10.1093/geronb/gbx095).
38. Levy et al., "Ageism Amplifies Cost."
39. Warren C. K. Chiu et al. 2001. "Age Stereotypes and Discriminatory Attitudes towards Older Workers: An East–West Comparison." *Human Relations* 54(5):629–61.
40. Richard A. Posthuma and Michael A. Campion. 2009. "Age Stereotypes in the Workplace: Common Stereotypes, Moderators, and Future Research Directions." *Journal of Management* 35(1):158–88.
41. Chiu et al., "Age Stereotypes and Discriminatory Attitudes."
42. Lisa M. Finkelstein and Michael J. Burke. 1998. "Age Stereotyping at Work: The Role of Rater and Contextual Factors on Evaluations of Job Applicants." *Journal of General Psychology* 125(4):317–45.
43. Barbara Fritzsche and Justin Marcus. 2013. "The Senior Discount: Biases against Older Career Changers." *Journal of Applied Social Psychology* 43(2):350–62.
44. Franciska Krings, Sabine Sczesny, and Annette Kluge. 2011. "Stereotypical Inferences as Mediators of Age Discrimination: The Role of Competence and Warmth." *British Journal of Management* 22(2):187–201.
45. Marchiondo, Gonzales, and Ran, "Development and Validation of the Workplace Age Discrimination Scale."
46. Marchiondo, Gonzales, and Ran, "Development and Validation of the Workplace Age Discrimination Scale."
47. Marchiondo, Gonzales, and Williams, "Trajectories of Perceived Workplace Age Discrimination."
48. Gonzales, Lee, and Marchiondo, "Exploring the Consequences of Major Lifetime Discrimination."
49. Ernest Gonzales et al. 2018. "Exploring the Consequences of Discrimination and Health for Retirement by Race and Ethnicity: Results from the Health and Retirement Study." Chestnut Hill, MA: Center for Retirement Research, Boston College. *Working Paper* 6.
50. Ernest Gonzales et al. 2019. "Theoretical Orientations to Intergenerational Home Sharing: Implications for Direct Social Work Practice on Addressing Student Debt and Aging-in-community." *Clinical Social Work Journal*:1–10.
51. Marie-France Marin et al. 2011. "Chronic Stress, Cognitive Functioning and Mental Health." *Neurobiology of Learning and Memory* 96(4):583–95.
52. Marin, "Chronic Stress."
53. Gonzales, Lee, and Marchiondo, "Exploring the Consequences of Major Lifetime Discrimination."
54. Gonzales et al., "Exploring the Consequences of Discrimination and Health."
55. Gonzales, Lee, and Harootyan, "Voices from the Field."
56. Kelsi Carolan et al. 2018. "Institutional and Individual Factors Affecting Health and Employment among Low-income Women with Chronic Health Conditions." *Journals of Gerontology: Social Sciences*. (https://doi.org/10.1093/geronb/gby149).
57. See: https://www.congress.gov/bill/115th-congress/senate-bill/443.
58. See: https://www.congress.gov/bill/116th-congress/senate-bill/2287/text.
59. Thomas F. Pettigrew and Linda R. Troop. 2006. "A Meta-analytic Test of Intergroup Contact Theory." *Journal of Personality and Social Psychology* 90(5):751–83. (https://doi.org/10.1037/0022-3514.90.5.751).
60. Sadie E. Rubin et al. 2015. "Challenging Gerontophobia and Ageism through a Collaborative Intergenerational Art Program." *Journal of Intergenerational Relationships* 13(3):241–54. (https://doi.org/10.1080/15350770.2015.1058213).
61. Gonzales et al., "Theoretical Orientations to Intergenerational Home Sharing."
62. Lynn F. Feinberg. 2019. "Paid Family Leave: An Emerging Benefit for Employed Family Caregivers of Older Adults." *Journal of the American Geriatrics Society* 67(7):1336–41. (https://doi-org.proxy.library.nyu.edu/10.1111/jgs.15869).

63. Feinberg, "Paid Family Leave."
64. Seth K. Kornfeld. 2018. "A Need Not Being Met: Providing Paid Family and Medical Leave for All Americans." *Family Court Review* 56(1):165–79. (https://doi.org/10.1111/fcre.12329).
65. Feinberg, "Paid Family Leave."
66. Sarah A. Donovan. 2019. "Paid Family Leave in the United States." Congressional Research Service: *Report*:1–16.
67. Nancy Morrow-Howell et al. 2017. "Approaches, Policies, and Practices to Support the Productive Engagement of Older Adults." *Journal of Gerontological Social Work* 60(3):193–200. (https://doi.org/10.1080.01634372.2016.1275912).
68. Donovan, "Paid Family Leave in the United States."
69. National Partnership for Women & Families. 2017. "Schedules That Work" [Fact sheet]. (https://www.nationalpartnership.org/our-work/resources/economic-justice/equal-opportunity/schedules-that-work-act-fact-sheet.pdf).
70. Congressional Research Service. 2017. H.R. 2942—115th Congress (2017–2018): Schedules That Work Act. Congress.gov. (www.congress.gov/bill/115th-congress/house-bill/2942).
71. National Partnership for Women & Families, "Schedules That Work."
72. National Organization for Women. 2014. "Background on Rep. Lowey's Social Security Caregiver Credit Act." (https://now.org/wp-content/uploads/2014/08/Background-on-Rep.-Nita-Loweys-Social-Security-Caregiver-Credit-Act.pdf).
73. Congressional Research Service. July 31, 2019. H.R. 4126—116th Congress (2019–2020). Social Security Caregiver Credit Act of 2019. Congress.gov. (www.congress.gov/bill/116th-congress/house-bill/4126?q=%7B%22search%22%3A%5B%22social+security+caregiver+credit+act%22%5D%7D).
74. National Organization for Women, "Background on Rep. Lowey's Social Security Caregiver Credit Act."
75. Mark Wilson and Rebecca Lukens. 1997. "Flex-time for Families: What Works for the Government Can Work for the Private Sector." Washington, DC: Heritage Foundation.
76. Katherine Speirs. 2008. "Access to Flexible Work Schedules: Differences by Gender, Education Level, and Occupation." Conference Papers, American Sociological Association:1.
77. Jeremy R. Hayman. 2010. "Flexible Work Schedules and Employee Well-being." *New Zealand Journal of Employment Relations* 35(2):76–87.
78. Diane E. Schmidt and Gilbert Duenas. 2002. "Incentives to Encourage Worker-friendly Organizations." *Public Personnel Management* 31(3):293–308.
79. Speirs, "Access to Flexible Work Schedules."
80. Speirs, "Access to Flexible Work Schedules."
81. Lonnie Golden. 2008. "Limited Access: Disparities in Flexible Work Schedules and Work-at-home." *Journal of Family & Economic Issues* 29(1):86–109. (https://doi.org/10.1007/s10834-007-9090-7).
82. Ernest Gonzales, Nancy Morrow-Howell, and Huy Ho. 2017. "Expanding Paid Family & Medical Leave. A Policy Action to Advance Long and Productive Lives." CSD Perspective. St. Louis, MO: Washington University, Center for Social Development.
83. Nancy Morrow-Howell, Ernest Gonzales, and Christina Matz-Costa. 2016. "Policy Recommendations for Meeting the Grand Challenge to Advance Long and Productive Lives." CSD Perspective. St. Louis, MO: Washington University, Center for Social Development.
84. Edwina S. Uehara et al. 2013. "Grand Challenges for Social Work." *Journal of the Society for Social Work and Research* 4(3):165–70.
85. Ernest Gonzales and W. Benjamin Nowell. 2015. "Social Capital and Unretirement: Exploring the Bonding, Bridging, and Linking Aspects of Social Relationships." *Research on Aging* 39(10):1100–17. (https://doi.org/10.1177/0164027516664569).
86. Ernest Gonzales et al. 2015. "Formal Volunteering: A Solution to Bolster Health and Retirement Security in Later Life." Boston University, *Currents*.
87. Anthony Bonen and Teresa Ghilarducci. 2015. "The Surprising Equality of Retirement Time: Evidence from the Health and Retirement Study." *Connecticut Insurance Law Journal*.
88. Gonzales et al., "Theoretical Orientations to Intergenerational Home Sharing."

89. Cal J. Halvorsen and Olga Yulikova. 2020. "Job Training and So Much More for Low-income Older Adults: The Senior Community Service Employment Program." *Clinical Social Work Journal* 48:223–29. (https://doi.org/10.1007/s10615-019-00734-y).

90. Ofra Mayseless and Einat Keren. 2013. "Finding a Meaningful Life as a Developmental Task in Emerging Adulthood: The Domains of Love and Work across Cultures." *Emerging Adulthood* 2(1):63–73. (https://doi.org/10.1177216769681351544 6).

91. Smyer and Pitt-Catsouphes, "Meanings of Work for Older Workers."

92. Frances Reynolds, Alexandra Farrow, and Alison Blank. 2012. "Otherwise It Would Be Nothing but Cruises: Exploring the Subjective Benefits of Working past 65." *Intergenerational Journal of Ageing and Later Life* 7(1):79–106. (https://doi.org/10.3384/ijal.1652-8670.127179).

93. Erik Kojola and Phyllis Moen. 2016. "No More Lock Step Retirement: Boomers' Shifting Meaning of Work and Retirement." *Journal of Aging Studies* 36:59–70.

94. Kojola and Moen, "No More Lock Step Retirement."

95. Kate Shacklock and Yvonne Brunetto. 2011. "A Model of Older Workers' Intentions to Continue Working." *Personnel Review* 40(1):252–74.

96. C. Stamov-Roßnagel and G. Hertel. 2010. "Older Workers' Motivation: Against the Myth of General Decline." *Management Decision* 48(6):894–906.

97. Reynolds, Farrow, and Blank, "Otherwise It Would Be Nothing but Cruises."

98. Smyer and Pitt-Catsouphes, "Meanings of Work for Older Workers."

99. Maria Eismann, Kene Henkens, and Matthijs Kalmijn. 2019. "Why Singles Prefer to Retire Later." *Research on Aging*, 41(10):936–60. (https://doi.org/10.1177/0164027519873537).

## REFERENCES


AARP. 2015. "Caregiving in the U.S." *Research Report.* (https://www.aarp.org/content/dam/aarp/ppi/2015/caregiving-in-the-united-states-2015-report-revised.pdf).

AARP. 2020. "The Economic Impact of Age Discrimination." (https://www.aarp.org/content/dam/aarp/research/surveys_statistics/econ/2020/impact-of-age-discrimination.doi.10.26419-2Fint.00042.003.pdf).

Bass, Scott, Francis J. Caro, and Yung-Ping Chen. 1993. *Toward a Productive Aging Society.* Westport, CT: Auburn House.

Bonen, Anthony and Teresa Ghilarducci. 2015. "The Surprising Equality of Retirement Time: Evidence from the Health and Retirement Study." *Connecticut Insurance Law Journal*.

Brown, Melissa, et al. 2014. "Returning to the Workforce after Retiring: Perceptions of Job Demands, Job Control, and Social Support." *International Journal of Human Resource Management* 25(22):3113–33. (https://doi.org/10.1080/09585192.2014.919951).

Cahill, Kevin E., Michael D. Giandrea, and Joseph F. Quinn. 2015. "Evolving Patterns of Work and Retirement." Pp. 271–92 in *Handbook of Aging and the Social Sciences*, 8th ed., edited by Linda K. George and Kenneth F. Ferraro. London: Elsevier.

Calvo, Esteban, Ignacio Madero-Cabib, and Ursula M. Staudinger. 2018. "Retirement Sequences of Older Americans: Moderately Destandardized and Highly Stratified across Gender, Class, and Race." *The Gerontologist* 58(6):1166–76. (https://doi.org/10.1093/geront/gnx052).

Carolan, Kelsi, et al. 2018. "Institutional and Individual Factors Affecting Health and Employment among Low-income Women with Chronic Health Conditions." *Journals of Gerontology: Social Sciences*. (https://doi.org/10.1093/geronb/gby149).

Carr, Dawn, et al. Forthcoming. "Post-recession Retirement Transition Profiles in the United States: An Exploratory Analysis."

Chiu, Warren C. K., et al. 2001. "Age Stereotypes and Discriminatory Attitudes towards Older Workers: An East–West Comparison." *Human Relations* 54(5):629–61.

Congressional Research Service. 2017. H.R. 2942—115th Congress (2017–2018): Schedules That Work Act. 2017. Congress.gov. (www.congress.gov/bill/115th-congress/house-bill/2942).

Congressional Research Service. July 31, 2019. H.R. 4126—116th Congress (2019–2020). Social Security Caregiver Credit Act of 2019. Congress.gov. (www.congress.gov/bill/116th

-congress/house-bill/4126?q=%7B%22search%22%3A%5B%22social+security+caregiver+credit+act%22%5D%7D).

Dentinger, Emma and Marin Clarkberg. 2002. "Informal Caregiving and Retirement Timing among Men and Women: Gender and Caregiving Relationships in Late Midlife." *Journal of Family Issues* 23(7):857–79.

Donovan, Sarah A. 2019. "Paid Family Leave in the United States." Congressional Research Service. *Report*:1–16.

Eismann, Maria, Kene Henkens, and Matthijs Kalmijn. 2019. "Why Singles Prefer to Retire Later." *Research on Aging* 41(10):936–60. (https://doi.org/10.1177/0164027519873537).

Feinberg, Lynn F. 2019. "Paid Family Leave: An Emerging Benefit for Employed Family Caregivers of Older Adults." *Journal of the American Geriatrics Society* 67(7):1336–41. (https://doi.org.proxy.library.nyu.edu/10.1111/jgs.15869).

Finkelstein, Lisa M. and Michael J. Burke. 1998. "Age Stereotyping at Work: The Role of Rater and Contextual Factors on Evaluations of Job Applicants." *Journal of General Psychology* 125(4):317–45.

Flinn, Brendan. 2018. "Millennials: The Emerging Generation of Family Caregivers." Washington, DC: AARP Public Policy Institute. *Spotlight* 33:1–11.

Fritzsche, Barbara and Justin Marcus. 2013. "The Senior Discount: Biases against Older Career Changers." *Journal of Applied Social Psychology* 43(2):350–62.

Golden, Lonnie. 2008. "Limited Access: Disparities in Flexible Work Schedules and Work-at-home." *Journal of Family & Economic Issues* 29(1):86–109. (https://doi.org/10.1007/s10834-007-9090-7).

Gonzales, Ernest. 2013. "An Examination on Un-retirement: Retirees Returning to Work." PhD dissertation. Washington University, St. Louis, MO. (https://openscholarship.wustl.edu/etd/1132).

Gonzales, Ernest. 2015. "Workplace Policies and Practices: Opportunities for and Barriers to Accumulating Assets in Midlife and Later." In *Financial Capabilities across the Life Course*, edited by Nancy Morrow-Howell and Michael Sherraden. New York: Oxford University Press.

Gonzales, Ernest, et al. 2015. "Formal Volunteering: A Solution to Bolster Health and Retirement Security in Later Life." Boston University, *Currents*.

Gonzales, Ernest, et al. 2018. "Exploring the Consequences of Discrimination and Health for Retirement by Race and Ethnicity: Results from the Health and Retirement Study." Chestnut Hill, MA: Center for Retirement Research, Boston College. *Working Paper* 6.

Gonzales, Ernest, et al. 2019. "Theoretical Orientations to Intergenerational Home Sharing: Implications for Direct Social Work Practice on Addressing Student Debt and Aging-in-community." *Clinical Social Work Journal*:1–10.

Gonzales, Ernest, Kathy Lee, and Robert Harootyan. Forthcoming. "Voices from the Field: Ecological Factors That Promote Employment and Health among Low-income Older Adults with Implications for Direct Social Work Practice." *Clinical Social Work Journal*. (https://doi.org/10.1007/s10615-019-00719-x).

Gonzales, Ernest, Yeonjung Jane Lee, and Lisa A. Marchiondo. December 11, 2019. "Exploring the Consequences of Major Lifetime Discrimination, Neighborhood Conditions, Chronic Work, and Everyday Discrimination on Health and Retirement." *Journal of Applied Gerontology*. (https://doi.org/10.1177/0733464819892847).

Gonzales, Ernest, Christina Matz-Costa, and Nancy Morrow-Howell. 2015. "White House Conference on Aging 2015. Increasing Opportunities for the Productive Engagement of Older Adults: A Response to Population Aging." *The Gerontologist* 55(2):252–61. (https://doi.org/10.1093/geront/gnu176).

Gonzales, Ernest, Nancy Morrow-Howell, and Huy Ho. 2017. *Expanding Paid Family & Medical Leave. A Policy Action to Advance Long and Productive Lives*. CSD Perspective. St. Louis, MO: Washington University, Center for Social Development.

Gonzales, Ernest and W. Benjamin Nowell. 2015. "Social Capital and Unretirement: Exploring the Bonding, Bridging, and Linking Aspects of Social Relationships." *Research on Aging* 39(10):1100–17. (https://doi.org/10.1177/0164027516664569).

Greenfield, Jennifer Crane. 2013. "The Long-term Costs of Caring: How Caring for an Aging Parent Impacts Wealth Trajectories of Caregivers." PhD dissertation. Washington University, St. Louis, MO. (https://openscholarship.wustl.edu/etd/1108).

Halvorsen, Cal J. and Olga Yulikova. 2020. "Job Training and So Much More for Low-income Older Adults: The Senior Community Service Employment Program." *Clinical Social Work Journal* 48:223–29. (https://doi.org/10.1007/s10615-019-00734-y).

Hayman, Jeremy R. 2010. "Flexible Work Schedules and Employee Well-being." *New Zealand Journal of Employment Relations* 35(2):76–87.

James, Jacquelyn B. and Marcie Pitt-Catsouphes. 2016. "Introduction to the Special Issue: Change in the Meaning and Experience of Work in Later Life." *Work, Aging, and Retirement* 2(3):281–85. (https://doi.org/10.1093/workar/waw020).

Johnson, Richard W. November 12, 2018. "A Tale of Two Retirements: Working Longer Is Exacerbating Income Inequality among Older Adults." Washington, DC: Urban Institute blog. (https://www.urban.org/urban-wire/tale-two-retirements-working-longer-exacerbating-income-inequality-among-older-americans).

Kamakura, Wagner A. 2009. "American Time-styles: A Finite-mixture Allocation Model for Time-use Analysis." *Multivariate Behavioral Research* 44(3):332–61.

Kane, Robert L. 2015. "A New Long-term Care Manifesto." *The Gerontologist* 55:296–301.

Kojola, Erik and Phyllis Moen. 2016. "No More Lock Step Retirement: Boomers' Shifting Meaning of Work and Retirement." *Journal of Aging Studies* 36:59–70.

Kornfeld, Seth K. 2018. "A Need Not Being Met: Providing Paid Family and Medical Leave for All Americans." *Family Court Review* 56(1):165–79. (https://doi.org/10.1111/fcre.12329).

Krings, Franciska, Sabine Sczesny, and Annette Kluge. 2011. "Stereotypical Inferences as Mediators of Age Discrimination: The Role of Competence and Warmth." *British Journal of Management* 22(2):187–201.

Lee, Yeonjung, et al. 2015. "The Vicious Cycle of Parental Caregiving and Financial Well-being: A Longitudinal Study of Women." *Journals of Gerontology, Series B: Psychological Sciences and Social Sciences* 70(3):425–31.

Levy, Becca R., et al. 2020. "Ageism Amplifies Cost and Prevalence of Health Conditions." *The Gerontologist* 60(1):174–81. (https://doi.org/10.1093/geront/gny131).

Maestas, Nicole. 2010. "Back to Work: Expectations and Realizations of Work after Retirement." *Journal of Human Resources* 45(3):718–48.

Maestas, Nicole and Julie Zissimopoulos. 2010. "How Longer Work Lives Ease the Crunch of Population Aging." *Journal of Economic Perspectives* 24(1):139–60.

Marchiondo, Lisa A., Ernest Gonzales, and Shan Ran. 2015. "Development and Validation of the Workplace Age Discrimination Scale (WADS)." *Journal of Business and Psychology* 4. (https://doi.org/10.1007/s10869-015-9425-6).

Marchiondo, Lisa A., Ernest Gonzales, and Larry J. Williams. 2017. "Trajectories of Perceived Workplace Age Discrimination and Long-term Associations with Mental, Self-rated, and Occupational Health." *Journal of Gerontology: Social Sciences* 74(4):655–63. (https://doi.org/10.1093/geronb/gbx095).

Marin, Marie-France, et al. 2011. "Chronic Stress, Cognitive Functioning and Mental Health." *Neurobiology of Learning and Memory* 96(4):583–95.

Mayseless, Ofra and Einat Keren. 2013. "Finding a Meaningful Life as a Developmental Task in Emerging Adulthood: The Domains of Love and Work across Cultures." *Emerging Adulthood* 2(1):63–73. (https://doi.org/10.11772167696813515446).

Moen, Phyllis, Julie Robison, and Donna Dempster-McClain. 1995. "Caregiving and Women's Well-being: A Life-course Approach." *Journal of Health and Social Behavior* 36(3):259–73.

Morrow-Howell, Nancy, et al. 2017. "Approaches, Policies, and Practices to Support the Productive Engagement of Older Adults." *Journal of Gerontological Social Work* 60(3):193–200. (https://doi.org/10.1080.01634372.2016.1275912).

Morrow-Howell, Nancy, Ernest Gonzales, and Christina Matz-Costa. 2016. "Policy Recommendations for Meeting the Grand Challenge to Advance Long and Productive Lives." CSD Perspective. St. Louis, MO: Washington University, Center for Social Development.

Munnell, Alicia H. 2011. "What Is the Average Retirement Age?" Chestnut Hill, MA: Center for Retirement Research, Boston College. Brief 11:1–7.

Munnell, Alicia H. and Steven A. Sass. 2009. *Working Longer: The Solution to the Retirement Income Challenge*. Washington, DC: Brookings Institution.

National Organization for Women. 2014. "Background on Rep. Lowey's Social Security Caregiver Credit Act." (https://now.org/wp-content/uploads/2014/08/Background-on-Rep.-Nita-Loweys-Social-Security-Caregiver-Credit-Act.pdf).

National Partnership for Women & Families. 2017. "Schedules That Work" [Fact sheet]. (https://www.nationalpartnership.org/our-work/resources/economic-justice/equal-opportunity/schedules-that-work-act-fact-sheet.pdf).

Pavalko, Eliza K. and Julie E. Artis. 1997. "Women's Caregiving and Paid Work: Causal Relationships in Late Midlife." *Journals of Gerontology, Series B: Psychological Sciences and Social Sciences* 52(4):S170–79.

Pettigrew, Thomas F. and Linda R. Troop. 2006. "A Meta-analytic Test of Intergroup Contact Theory." *Journal of Personality and Social Psychology* 90(5):751–83. (https://doi.org/10.1037/0022-3514.90.5.751).

Posthuma, Richard A. and Michael A. Campion. 2009. "Age Stereotypes in the Workplace: Common Stereotypes, Moderators, and Future Research Directions." *Journal of Management* 35(1):158–88.

Reynolds, Frances, Alexandra Farrow, and Alison Blank. 2012. "Otherwise It Would Be Nothing but Cruises: Exploring the Subjective Benefits of Working past 65." *Intergenerational Journal of Ageing and Later Life* 7(1):79–106. (https://doi.org/10.3384/ijal.1652-8670.127179).

Rubin, Sadie E., et al. 2015. "Challenging Gerontophobia and Ageism through a Collaborative Intergenerational Art Program." *Journal of Intergenerational Relationships* 13(3):241–54. (https://doi.org/10.1080/15350770.2015.1058213).

Schmidt, Diane E. and Gilbert Duenas. 2002. "Incentives to Encourage Worker-friendly Organizations." *Public Personnel Management* 31(3):293–308.

Shacklock, Kate and Yvonne Brunetto. 2011. "A Model of Older Workers' Intentions to Continue Working." *Personnel Review* 40(1):252–74.

Smith, Peter M., et al. 2019. "Male/female Differences in the Impact of Caring for Elderly Relatives on Labor Market Attachment and Hours of Work: 1997–2015." *Journals of Gerontology: Social Sciences* 75(3):694–704. (https://doi.org/10.1093/geronb/gbz026).

Smyer, Michael A. and Marcie Pitt-Catsouphes. 2007. "The Meanings of Work for Older Workers." *Generations* 31(1):23–30.

Southerton, Dale and Mark Tomlinson. 2005. "'Pressed for Time'–The Differential Impacts of a 'Time Squeeze.'" *Sociological Review* 53(2):215–39.

Speirs, Katherine. 2008. "Access to Flexible Work Schedules: Differences by Gender, Education Level, and Occupation." Conference Papers, American Sociological Association:1.

Stamov-Roßnagel, C. and Hertel, G. 2010. "Older Workers' Motivation: against the Myth of General Decline." *Management Decision* 48(6):894–906.

Sullivan, Sherry E. and Akram Al Ariss. 2018. "Employment after Retirement: A Review and Framework for Future Research." *Journal of Management* 45(1):262–84.

Szinovacz, Maximiliane E. and Adam Davey. 2005. "Predictors of Perceptions of Involuntary Retirement." *The Gerontologist* 45(1):36–47.

Uehara, Edwina S., et al. 2013. "Grand Challenges for Social Work." *Journal of the Society for Social Work and Research* 4(3):165–70.

Wakabayashi, Chizuko and Katharine M. Donato. 2006. "Does Caregiving Increase Poverty among Women in Later Life? Evidence from the Health and Retirement Survey." *Journal of Health and Social Behavior* 47(3):258–74.

Wilson, Mark and Rebecca Lukens. 1997. "Flex-time for Families: What Works for the Government Can Work for the Private Sector." Washington, DC: Heritage Foundation.

CHAPTER 4

# The Choices of (Low-Income) Aging Workers on the Margins

## Expanding the Narrative

Christina Matz and Melissa Brown

### OVERVIEW

Today's health and demographic trends have given rise to concepts such as "active," "productive," "positive," and "successful" aging. These concepts and others have moved the field of gerontology away from the harmful deficits model of aging where aging is equated only with decline, skill loss, burden, and pathology, and toward a more strengths-based, positive aging framework that highlights the skills and talents that an aging population brings.[1] This important paradigm shift has fueled anti-ageist advocacy and represents important progress on behalf of gerontological theory building and conceptual development over the past several decades. When it comes to aging and work specifically, concepts such as working longer and "encore work" have received increasing attention, as have other approaches to reinventing retirement, especially among the more socioeconomically advantaged. However, some of these positive approaches have also been criticized for contributing to a public discourse that has not necessarily captured (or has sometimes even mischaracterized) the variety and complexity of lived experiences pertaining to later life—in particular, the issues faced by low-income workers, workers of Color,[2] and others marginalized due to their social positionality.[3] (See also chapters 3, 5, and 6.)

At the individual level, ageism is evident in feelings one has toward older adults (including oneself), beliefs about older people, and discrimination against older people. (See also chapter 12 and elsewhere in this volume.) These beliefs are rooted in culture-based age stereotypes and have a negative effect on the health of older persons.[4]

Older workers are often stereotyped as incompetent, incapable, or a burden to society and as a result end up sidelined. Ageism in the context of the labor market can manifest as being denied a job based on age, being treated as less capable, being passed over for a work role, receiving less social support, or being blamed for failures or problems due to age, among other examples.[5] Ageist messages are everywhere—in our everyday language (e.g., addressing an older woman as "young lady"), in greeting cards, in children's games and toys, and popular entertainment—all of which unconsciously reinforce that young is good and old is bad.[6] We even self-stereotype when it comes to age (e.g., "I am getting stubborn in my old age").

Ageism is deeply ingrained and operates at the institutional or structural level as well. Structural ageism occurs when societal institutions promote bias against older persons (e.g., denied access to health care based on age, mandated age-based retirement policies, lack of work opportunities, devaluing of lives). In a recent landmark systematic review of hundreds of research studies and millions of research participants conducted by Yale researchers, Chang and colleagues documented what they refer to as "the pernicious reach of ageism" at both the structural and individual levels.[7] Ageism led to worse outcomes in a number of mental health conditions, including depression, and a number of physical health conditions, including shorter life expectancy. Ageism affected older persons regardless of their age, sex, and racial/ethnic membership. Further, 85 percent of all relevant studies reviewed found evidence of denied access to health care treatments, and 92 percent found indications of ageism in medical decisions. When it came to studies that focused on lack of work opportunities, the study found evidence that employers were significantly less likely to hire older than younger job applicants; older workers had less access to training, and those who faced ageism in the workplace were more likely to retire early.

Ageism is, of course, intimately entangled with ableism—the privileging of the "normal" or able bodied. Indeed, "anything and everything can be cast under the light of normality, the light of ever-intertwined assumptions about how bodies are and should be."[8] Examples include older adults distancing themselves from and judging other older adults who are disabled or ill (e.g., believing that "those old people" do not include oneself). Positive aging discourse, while strengths based in its intentions, often leads to public discourse in which we define and uplift the healthy older adult as one who is not disabled and is active, productive, and "not looking his/her age."[9] Thus, the "preferred way of being old is to not be old at all, but rather to maintain some image of middle-age functionality and appearance."[10]

The main aim of this chapter is to question the assumptions that shape access to choice and opportunity in later life and drive some of these more dominant narratives around retirement planning and decision-making. To be clear, there is *no* age wherein engaging in paid or unpaid labor is merely a question of individual will or effort or choice. Such choice is always in intricate concert with a vast range of social, political, economic, legal, and other factors.[11] This does not change when one reaches "traditional" retirement age. Recent qualitative[12] and quantitative[13] research has pointed to a variety of issues that may affect low-income and marginalized workers during the retirement transition including financial vulnerability, limited work prospects, significant caregiving responsibilities, health complications, cultural and familial factors, and perceptions of control. Many adults approaching retirement age come to the realization that there often is no choice—no good choice, at least—when it comes to the alternative of work versus retirement.

## UNDERSTANDING CONSTRAINED CHOICES

By definition, choice is "an act of selecting or making a decision when faced with two or more possibilities."[14] It suggests the opportunity or privilege of choosing freely, the "power" to choose. However, a variety of terms exists to describe situations where one's choices may be limited or only poor options are available. There is a "Hobson's choice," which is a choice of taking what is available or nothing at all; a dilemma, which is a choice between two or more unattractive options; a "catch-22," which is a paradox that arises from a situation where an individual needs something that can only be acquired by not being in that very situation; and even a "Morton's fork," which is a double bind where choices yield equivalent, and often undesirable, results.[15] We make thousands of choices each day. In fact, Wansink and Sobal found that we make more than 221 choices per day just about food.[16] The ability to make choices and manage one's own life, a tenet of self-determination theory, plays an important role in psychological health and well-being.[17]

Constrained choice theory articulates how social position (such as gender, class, race/ethnicity, immigration status, or sexual orientation) determines the freedom individuals have in making everyday choices that cumulatively impact their lives and health.[18] Personal agency or choice is impeded (or enhanced) by interactions among social positions (e.g., being gay and Black, being working class and an immigrant). The constraints that affect an individual's agency and decision-making can occur at the levels of family, work, community, and broader public policy and operate to narrow or expand the range and relative costs—economic and noneconomic—associated with options. This, in turn, affects the promotion or restoration of health and the risk of early death.

Aging workers who have been marginalized for various reasons often lose out on both the ability to make choices for themselves and the opportunity to net psychological and other benefits as a result of those choices. For instance, older Black workers may not have the choice to speak up at work about a decision they don't agree with (and act on their self-determination) for fear that they will be perceived by white peers as "difficult" and that will be negatively attributed to their race. White or white-passing workers in a similar position may also choose not to speak up at work, but they have the privilege to choose to take the path of least resistance and not say anything or to say something and be confident that what they have said will not be attributed to their race. Thus, this is always less of a high-stakes decision for white workers than for Black workers. When multiple marginalized identities produce untold numbers of constrained choices that accumulate over a lifetime, it drives increasing distance between the privileged and the marginalized on a variety of life outcomes. All the while, these dynamics are invisible to many. This is what constrained choice is really about. We now consider three case examples that demonstrate how constrained choice functions for populations relegated to society's margins when approaching traditional retirement age.

## Case Example 1: Jane

As Jane stands on the hard concrete floor of the flower shop's back room, she feels the familiar ache in her legs from being on her feet for more than ten hours that day, after having already worked a full week. There are four weddings tomorrow, and they *have* to get these flower arrangements done before they can go home, but she has just about had it. She says, looking down at her raw and cracked hands, "I am too old for this! I can't be working sixty-hour weeks at this point in my life!" The owner looks at her with disdain and says, "What choice do you have? It's either work these hours or I will find someone else who will!" Shocked by this callous and hurtful comment after more than fifteen years of hard work and loyalty to this small business, Jane thinks about it for a second and then declares, "I quit, then!" As she furiously drives home, her mind is racing. "What have I done?"

Jane has worked as a florist her entire life. Her first job out of high school was working in her father's greenhouses. She enjoyed the work, and besides, college was an expense that her family could not afford. Now, at age fifty-nine, her body is tired from the grueling and physically demanding work, and while she would like nothing more than to be able to retire and live a life of her own choosing, how can she? She is a single mother with significant loan debt from helping her two adult children pay for college.[19] She doesn't regret working part-time during their younger years, but her Social Security earnings are diminished as a result; early retirement is not feasible.[20] In addition, she's already experienced several health issues that have required expensive surgery—she can't take the risk of going without health insurance, and purchasing private health insurance is out of her price range.[21] Even with a job, some months she finds herself struggling to make ends meet, never mind trying to live on the meager savings that she has accumulated over the years. And, the odds of finding another job at this point are minimal.

Jane thinks to herself, "Why would another florist hire me at what I am being paid now when they could easily hire a college student at a much lower rate?" As she cries in the car, she realizes that she will have to turn around, apologize, and beg for her job back—"I can hold out another eight years till sixty-seven," she convinces herself. "What choice do I have?"[22]

None of Jane's choices (early retirement, quitting and looking for a new job, or returning to the job) are self-determined; in fact, they will result in additional constrained choices. Jane's specific social position as a single mother with limited education, significant debt, and little safety net to fall back on leaves her at much greater risk for poor health and well-being outcomes. On the other hand, Jane enjoys the privileges of various other social positions that she holds as a heterosexual, cisgender white woman who is able bodied and born in the U.S.

## Case Example 2: Giang

Giang is in the same situation Jane faced, working for the same flower shop with the same boss, facing the same crossroads: to quit or not to quit? She is also fifty-nine years old and a single mother of two from a working-class background. However, Giang is Vietnamese, bilingual, and a 1.5 generation immigrant (meaning that she was born in another country but immigrated to the U.S. before her early teens). Like many immigrants, Giang is paid less than her native-born coworker who holds the same position.[23] Decades of lower wages meant taking out larger loans to pay for her children's education. Because her cultural traditions strongly emphasize adult children's responsibility for aging parents in later life, she is now also taking care of her eighty-three-year-old father, who speaks only a little English and suffers from dementia.[24]

Like Jane, Giang weighs whether she can walk out on her employer due to the extraordinary demands that her job puts on her physical and mental health. As she looks down at her raw and cracked hands, she thinks, "I am too old for this! I can't be working sixty-hour weeks at this point in my life!" But years of discrimination in this country have taught her that not only does she not have the luxury of either asking for her hours to be scaled back or of quitting her job, but also that if she shows signs of fatigue and her production rate diminishes, the owner will have no problem letting her go. She cannot let that happen. Further, it is likely that while Jane is holding out for age sixty-seven when she can claim full Social Security (SS) benefits, Giang is hoping that she can hold out much longer than that, as she expects her SS benefits will be inadequate to cover her bills.[25] As these two examples demonstrate, the options that an individual has, or can afford to choose from, are socially and economically patterned in ways that contribute to differential exposures and risks; these, in turn, are exacerbated by multiple intersectional identities, shaping life chances and lifespans across various health conditions and outcomes.

## Case Example 3: Jeanette

Again, let's take the same situation that Jane and Giang face, but instead it is Jeanette who works in the flower shop. Jeanette, too, is fifty-nine years old, single, and from a working-class background; however, she never had children. As a child, Jeanette always wanted to be an engineer. She studied hard, went to a prestigious engineering school, and received her bachelor's degree in civil engineering. Toward the end of college, in the early 1980s, Jeanette came out to her family and friends as transgender. Assigned male at birth and raised as a boy (then John), Jeanette began transitioning to female. And though she was eventually accepted by her family and closest friends, when she started to apply to civil engineering positions after she graduated, no one would hire her. Despite literally hundreds of interviews for jobs that she was highly qualified for, she had no job offers. After living with the support of her parents for two years, still holding out on a civil engineering job, she decided to take a job at a local bookstore to pay the bills. Fast-forward to age fifty-nine; Jeanette, like many transgender individuals, has struggled with employment discrimination her entire life.[26] More than half of states in the U.S. do not have full discrimination protections regarding sexual orientation or gender identity.[27] Jeanette has had to rely on low-wage and often part-time or temporary positions to get by.

Standing on the hard concrete floor of the flower shop, her most recent place of employment, Jeanette (like Jane and Giang) looks down at her raw and cracked hands and thinks to herself, "I am too old for this! I can't be working sixty-hour weeks at this point in my life!" But, after enduring harassment from many prior employers,[28] she appreciates having a workplace that at least accepts her for who she is, even if management makes it clear on a regular basis that she is easily replaceable. She knows that she had better not complain and that she needs to work while she still can. Due to the nature of the various jobs she has held over the years, she is facing extreme financial strain and has little to no retirement savings. She can't imagine ever being able to retire, yet her health may soon force her to. Having had horrific experiences seeking medical care and even being refused care, Jeanette continues to struggle with several untreated health issues.[29] Her current job, thankfully, provides private insurance that covers her monthly hormone treatments, and her gender-affirming primary care physician is in network. She knows from her friends' experience that Medicare and Medicaid programs frequently place arbitrary and discriminatory limits on coverage for transition-related and preventive care and often require transgender older adults to pay out of pocket for many expenses—she just wouldn't be able to afford those and keep a roof over her head.[30] She's really not sure what her future holds at this point.

## NEW DIRECTIONS FOR EXPANDING THE NARRATIVE IN AGING AND WORK

In 2020, the COVID-19 pandemic has put the spotlight on older adults globally. On one hand, it is increasing awareness of important issues older adults typically face that younger adults may never before have thought critically about (e.g., social isolation, comorbidities). The crisis has also enabled innovations that gerontologists have been recommending for quite some time to become available quickly (e.g., needed technology investments and acceptance of telehealth and tele–mental health options).[31] On the other hand, however, this crisis has highlighted and exacerbated the ageism in our society and the "otherizing" of older adults (e.g., rampant and open discussion of willingness to sacrifice the lives of older adults for the economy, a form of age-based rationing of care). We are also seeing a return to the deficits model of aging, with older adults being portrayed as a weak, vulnerable, and monolithic group.[32] Unfortunately, but not unexpectedly, older adults who occupy other targeted social identities are particularly at risk. Higher rates of disease prevalence and mortality from COVID-19 are found in communities made vulnerable through racism—the same communities facing longstanding structural inequities in access to health care. In other words, the pandemic has laid bare existing inequalities like never before.[33]

Older workers in their fifties and sixties, especially women, have been among the hardest hit by the economic downturn, with the unemployment rate for women fifty-five and older rising from 3.3 percent in March to 15.5 percent in April 2020 and for men from 3.4 percent to 12.1 percent.[34] Job losses and depleted retirement savings will have long-lasting, painful financial implications, even for those who are middle class. For lower-income and marginalized workers, it could be deadly.[35] Combine that with the loss of normal care structures and less backing from extended family and support networks, lack of sick leave, underemployment, and poor existing supports before the pandemic struck, already-marginalized older workers are being pushed to the brink.[36]

Thus, it is a critical time to expand the narrative on aging and work in ways that: (1) draw on our profession's progress in moving the field toward more strengths-based approaches, and (2) bring in new narratives focused on the variety and complexity of lived experiences pertaining to later life. Below, we highlight several possible directions for doing so that could further advance our understanding of constrained choice in the context of the retirement transition. Those potential avenues will also challenge us to consider the privilege from which the ideals we put forward are derived, and recognize the social contexts and environments that need to be present to support them.

## DO NOT IGNORE CARE WORK

Unpaid care work plays a very important role in constrained choices across the lifespan. (See also chapter 20.) Growing numbers of older adults are providing various forms of unpaid care, yet the wide spectrum of different types of caregiving and the intensity of some forms of caregiving for workers, even under the most privileged of circumstances, are often underestimated.[37] For instance, aging workers could be raising grandchildren or providing significant unpaid care for them or other children. In 2010, about one in fourteen children lived in a household headed by a grandparent—this percentage has increased steadily over recent decades.[38] More than half of children who were living with grandparents in 2012 were being raised primarily by (those) grandparent(s).[39] Aging workers could be caring for young or midlife adults who are ill or disabled. Approximately 16.6 percent of people nationwide provide care to an adult child, sibling, spouse, or other family member who may have been ill or disabled from birth or have become ill or disabled through accident or disease.[40] When we look at development disabilities (e.g., cerebral palsy, Down syndrome, epilepsy) alone, we see that about 76 percent of individuals with developmental disabilities reside at home, and in 25 percent of these homes, the family caregiver is over sixty years of age, while the average age of the care recipient is thirty-eight.[41]

Aging workers could be caring for elders who are ill or disabled. Eldercare is defined by the Bureau of Labor Statistics (BLS) as providing "unpaid care to someone age 65 or older who needs help because of a condition related to aging."[42] This can include care for loved ones who are living in the same household, a different household, or a nursing home or assisted living facility. BLS data from 2017 to 2018 show that 58 percent of all eldercare providers are women and 42 percent are aged fifty-five or older.[43] One study found that, among U.S. workers, more than 40 percent have provided care for an aging relative or friend in the past five years, and almost half anticipate doing so within the next five years.[44] And lastly, some aging workers are "sandwiched" between multiple forms of caregiving (e.g., care for children and parents simultaneously). Approximately 30 percent of the U.S. population is part of the "sandwich generation."[45] Eighty-two percent of eldercare providers who were parents were employed and 69 percent were employed full-time.[46]

Those providing unpaid family care often struggle to manage demands from work and other life roles while simultaneously confronting their own age-related changes—

often with inadequate support from health care and social service systems. As shown with the case of Giang, asking for accommodations or flexibility due to care responsibilities of a loved one is a constrained choice for some aging workers, especially those who work hourly, low-wage jobs that provide minimal benefits.[47] Lahaie, Earle, and Heymann found that for women and first-generation immigrants, providing eldercare may result in early retirement and involuntary reduction of work hours to meet the demands of caregiving. Moreover, Hispanics and first-generation immigrant elder caregivers had less access to paid leave, had less schedule flexibility, and faced an unsupportive work culture.[48] Those forced into reducing their hours or permanently exiting the workplace due to care responsibilities are at greater risk of poverty in later life, due to reduced earnings, lower Social Security benefits, and loss of employer-sponsored health insurance.[49]

Research and discourse on aging and work must acknowledge the plentitude of forms of caregiving and the ways in which they constrain or expand choice in later life, especially for lower-income workers (e.g., grandparents raising grandchildren may have to give up retirement completely). This can also include financial assistance to adult children who are not ill or disabled, including financial transfers to kin and taking on their children's student loan debt. There is also a need for narratives that uphold the value of the work that unpaid caregivers do, that highlight and celebrate the racial, ethnic, and cultural contexts that shape caregiving, and seek to understand the ways in which caregiving can be both excruciating and rich in meaning simultaneously.[50]

## CONSIDER CULTURALLY RESPONSIVE APPROACHES

Many of our models and theories of aging and work were based on Western (specifically American) and middle-class values, and thus may not readily apply to other cultures or social classes. Let's use retirement saving behaviors as an example. BLS data show that in 2018, 78 percent of workers in management and professional occupations participated in a defined contribution retirement plan if they had access to one, while only 52 percent of service workers did. Among the top 25 percent of earners, 80 percent participated, while among the bottom 25 percent of earners only 50 percent did.[51] In trying to understand these differences, we should examine the underlying economics as well as the influence of class position on people's behavior, which is just as important ("class as culture").[52]

An emerging body of research suggests that there are considerable ethno-racial disparities in retirement savings and preparedness that we do not yet fully understand.[53] Lytle and colleagues point out that ethno-racial and cultural variables are some of the most understudied variables in the retirement planning literature and call for an increased focus on this area moving forward.[54] Some recent qualitative[55] and quantitative research (see chapter 6 in this volume)[56] has shown that among Hispanics in particular, there may be cultural and familial factors at play. Díaz-Valdes's study proposes that the commonly identified predictors of delayed retirement ("working longer") in the general population do not necessarily extend to Hispanics, indicating that there are other factors at play that researchers and practitioners should explore and that cultural and familial factors appear to play an important role in the retirement decision-making process.[57]

Calvo and colleagues suggest that traditional indicators in the aging literature, like education, wealth, or health, may not be sufficient to understand the experiences of aging persons of Color. They found, for example, that older Hispanic adults are more satisfied with their lives than any other group of older adults in the U.S. Furthermore, there seemed to be some nontraditional factors behind this finding: co-residing with children actually increased the happiness of Hispanics, while educational attainment only had a positive effect on the happiness of non-Hispanic whites.[58]

Research and discourse on aging and work that use only culturally dominant indicators of "success" will fail to reflect the diversity of experience within the population of older workers. We must look deeply at specific sociocultural contexts and how they play a role in understanding observed disparities in choice, agency, and opportunity as well as antecedents and outcomes related to various aging and work phenomena. This will not be easy because it requires that we step out of our own cultural awareness to try to understand another's—but it is crucial that we challenge ourselves to do this critical work.

## CENTER MARGINALIZED VOICES WITH EMPHASIS ON INTERSECTIONALITY

Research and discourse on aging and work must take an explicitly intersectional approach in order for the field to gain a better understanding of how multiple sources of oppression intersect to shape choice and opportunity and, subsequently, divergent work and retirement trajectories. For example, while the unemployment rate in 2016–2018 ranged from 3.9 to 4.9 percent in the U.S., the unemployment rate for transgender adults averaged 12.8 percent,[59] and for transgender people of Color, it was 20 percent.[60] Documenting such intersectional disparities in the context of work will help the field move beyond approaches that focus solely on individual agency and choice (i.e., depicting "successful" agers as those who make good choices to secure their health and well-being, employment security, and pension and welfare provision in later life, etc.) and toward broader approaches that identify socioeconomic, structural, historical, and cultural factors contributing to unfair workplace practices, poor employee health, early retirement, and employment/retirement insecurity.[61]

When people think of working in retirement, they imagine choosing to work part-time at a job that is fulfilling for any number of reasons. Part-time work is often glorified as a great option for older adults who want or need to continue working but do not want to continue at the same pace, and it can be just that. However, the reality for a lot of people working part-time is that it is a form of *under*employment not always recognized as such. Lower-income workers and those with multiple marginalized identities may be "stuck" with part-time work when what they really need is full-time work.

A variety of factors can contribute to forced or involuntary reduction of hours as well, including family caregiving responsibilities, a health crisis/shock or disability, company closure or layoffs,[62] or no longer being able to tolerate the physical or emotional demands of the job (e.g., construction workers, hotel housekeepers, retail workers). Involuntary underemployment in later life potentially puts such workers on a very different, and more precarious, trajectory for retirement than they expected. For instance, it can present problems with regard to financial stability and maintaining overall health and well-being in both the short term and long term.[63] Certain groups of older workers are more "at risk" for this type of constrained choice. Almost two-thirds (62 percent) of transgender older adults have some form of disability, and these rates are even higher for Black and Latinx transgender older adults.[64]

The informal economy, meaning employment and production that operate outside the regulatory and tax systems, tends to be overlooked in discussions of aging and work.[65] While working "under the table" or "off the books" is illegal, millions of workers are involved in such arrangements. Common types of unreported jobs include domestic work, such as housekeeping, babysitting, or food service; construction work, landscaping, farmwork; taxicab service; various types of self-employment, such as plumbing, electrical repair, window cleaning, painting and decorating, street market trading, and gardening; and short-term work and day labor. It is very challenging to measure this type of work; thus, studies have produced estimates of total informal employment that range from 3 percent to 40 percent of the total U.S. labor force.[66] Informal workers are at much higher risk of income insecurity and poverty during their work lives and in retirement than standard, traditional workers who have formal full-time, permanent employment arrangements and are usually covered by labor and social protection policies. Further, those who are employed under the table, including undocumented immigrants, may be denied rights that legally employed workers have, such as minimum wage, various benefits (particularly unemployment benefits), and fair treatment.[67] Much more effort should be made to study informal work as a primary source of income and those who engage in it as a "side hustle," as well as the increasing number of older adults who work in the "gig economy" as a retirement job.

## CONCLUSION

Everyone should have the right to choice and opportunity when it comes to paid and unpaid work as they approach and pass retirement age. We know, however, that birthplace, social and economic class, and earnings impact not only our life expectancy but also quality of life. Rising levels of inequality mean wealthier people can retire whenever they see fit and enjoy at least a modicum of financial comfort while those with lower incomes and additional layers of being "othered" face impossible choices, like whether to continue working at a job that is killing them or risk impoverishment by retiring. That is, if they live long enough to have the opportunity to make "choices" about retirement. The number of Americans facing these types of choices was already on the rise before COVID-19, and early data show that downward mobility among older workers since the economic downturn is escalating at a staggering rate. The Retirement Equity Lab (ReLab) estimates that the COVID-19 recession will force 3.1 million older workers and their spouses into de facto poverty in retirement.[68]

Now is the time to take action on this front. Portraying the experiences of older workers holistically is important to advancing this area of scholarship. What is most critical, though, is ensuring that we approach this work with intentionality and purpose. We need to have representation on research teams of older workers across various identities. We need to be asking, before we do a study, which workers would benefit from the research, who is represented, and who is left out? We also need to be ensuring that older workers—particularly those who occupy marginalized social identities—are being centered in policy discussions and government responses to the COVID-19 recession.

## NOTES

1. For a review of theories and critical perspectives, see Hannes Zacher and Cort W. Rudolph. 2017. "Successful Aging at Work and Beyond: A Review and Critical Perspective." Pp. 35–64 in *Age Diversity in the Workplace: An Organizational Perspective*, edited by Silvia Profili, Alessia Sammarra, and Laura Innocenti. Bingley, UK: Emerald Publishing.

2. The authors prefer to capitalize the words "black" and "color" when referencing racial/ethnic/cultural identity. Please see Mike Laws. June 16, 2020. "Why We Capitalize 'Black' (and Not 'White')." *Columbia Journalism Review*. (https://www.cjr.org/analysis/capital-b-black-style guide.php).

3. Jiayin Liang and Baozhen Luo. August 2012. "Toward a Discourse Shift in Social Gerontology: From Successful Aging to Harmonious Aging." *Journal of Aging Studies* 26(3):327–34. (https://doi.org/10.1016/j.jaging.2012.03.001); Marty Martinson and Clara Berridge. 2015. "Successful Aging and Its Discontents: A Systematic Review of the Social Gerontology Literature" *The Gerontologist* 55(1):58–69; Alicia H. Munnell. Fall 2019. "Socioeconomic Barriers to Working Longer." *Generations* 43(3):42–50.

4. E-Shien Chang et al. 2020. "Global Reach of Ageism on Older Persons' Health: A Systematic Review." *PLoS ONE* 15(1):e0220857. (https://doi.org/10.1371/journal.pone.0220857).

5. Ernest Gonzales et al. April 2015. "Age Discrimination in the Workplace and Its Association with Health and Work: Implications for Social Policy." *Research Brief* 2015-02. Boston: Boston University.

6. Tracey L. Gendron et al. 2015. "The Language of Ageism: Why We Need to Use Words Carefully." *The Gerontologist* 56(6):997–1006. (https://doi.org/10.1093/geront/gnv066).

7. Chang et al., "Global Reach."

8. Joel Michael Reynolds. 2018. "The Extended Body: On Aging, Disability, and Well-being." *Report* No. 48:S33. Cambridge, MA: Hastings Center.

9. Clara W. Berridge and Marty Martinson. 2018. "Valuing Old Age without Leveraging Ableism." *Generations* 41(4):83.

10. Berridge and Martinson, "Valuing Old Age," 83.

11. Reynolds, "Extended Body."

12. Nicole Ruggiano et al. 2017. "'Work Is Like a Therapy That Prevents Aging': Perceptions of Retirement, Productivity, and Health among Minorities and Immigrants." *SAGE Open* 7(1):1–11. (https://doi.org/10.1177/2158244016687234); Luisa R. Blanco et al. 2016. "Retirement Planning among Hispanics: In God's Hands?" *Journal of Aging & Social Policy* 29(4):311–31. (https://doi.org/10.1080/08959420.2016.1272161); Mary Gatta. 2018. *Waiting on Retirement: Aging and Economic Insecurity in Low-Wage Work*. Stanford, CA: Stanford University Press.

13. Dawn C. Carr et al. 2020. "Postretirement Life Satisfaction and Financial Vulnerability: The Moderating Role of Control." *The Journals of Gerontology, Series B* 75(4):849–60. (https://doi.org/10.1093/geronb/gby105); Rocio Calvo, Dawn Carr, and Christina Matz-Costa. 2019. "Expanding the 'Happiness Paradox': Racial/Ethnic Disparities in Life Satisfaction among Older Immigrants in the United States." *Journal of Aging and Health* 31(2):231–55; Antonia Díaz-Valdes. 2019. "Retirement Intentions and Behaviors of Hispanics Compared to Non-Hispanics in the United States: A Three-paper Dissertation." PhD Dissertation. Boston College, Chestnut Hill, MA.

14. Lexico. N.d. "Choice." Retrieved May 19, 2020 (https://www.lexico.com/en/definition/choice).

15. Wikipedia. N.d. "Hobson's Choice." (https://en.wikipedia.org/wiki/Hobson%27s_choice).

16. Brian Wansink and Jeffery Sobal. January 2007. "Mindless Eating: The 200 Daily Food Decisions We Overlook." *Environment and Behavior* 39(1):106–23.

17. Richard M. Ryan and Edward L. Deci. 2000. "Self-determination Theory and the Facilitation of Intrinsic Motivation, Social Development, and Well-being." *American Psychologist* 55:68–78.

18. Chloe E. Bird and Patricia P. Rieker. 2008. *Gender and Health: The Effects of Constrained Choices and Social Policies*. New York: Cambridge University Press.

19. Samantha Brady et al. 2019. "Retiring and Caregiving in the Age of Student Loans: The Impact of Student Debt on Retirement and Longevity Planning." *Innovation in Aging* 3 (Suppl 1):S42. (https://doi.org/10.1093/geroni/igz038.163).

20. Matthew S. Rutledge, Alice Zulkarnain, and Sara Ellen King. 2017. "How Much Does Motherhood Cost Women in Social Security Benefits?" *CRR WP* 2017-14. Chestnut Hill, MA: Center for Retirement Research, Boston College.

21. Schwartz Center for Economic Policy Analysis. August 4, 2017. "1 in 4 Older Workers Lack On-the-job Health Insurance." Older Workers Report. New York: The New School for Social Research. (https://www.economicpolicyresearch.org/jobs-report/july-2017-unemployment-report-for-workers-over-55).

22. Social Security Administration. N.d. "Benefits Planner: Retirement." (https://www.ssa.gov/planners/retire/).

23. Bureau of Labor Statistics. May 24, 2017. "Foreign-born Workers Made 83.1 Percent of the Earnings of Their Native-born Counterparts in 2016." *Economics Daily*. Washington, DC: U.S. Department of Labor. (https://www.bls.gov/opub/ted/2017/foreign-born-workers-made-83-point-1-percent-of-the-earnings-of-their-native-born-counterparts-in-2016.htm).

24. Oanh L. Meyer et al. 2015. "The Sociocultural Context of Caregiving Experiences for Vietnamese Dementia Family Caregivers." *Asian American Journal of Psychology* 6(3):263–72.

25. Purvi Sevak and Lucie Schmidt. February 26, 2014. "Immigrants and Retirement Resources." *Social Security Bulletin* 74(1):27–45.

26. Sandy E. James et al. 2016. *The Report of the 2015 U.S. Transgender Survey*. Washington, DC: National Center for Transgender Equality.

27. Job discrimination based on sexual orientation or gender identity was legal in twenty-nine U.S. states just prior to the landmark June 2020 Supreme Court decision that formally prohibited such discrimination on the federal level. However, it remains legal in these twenty-nine states for stores, restaurants, and hotels to deny service; for adoption agencies to refuse help; and for many public institutions and services to turn people away based on LGBTQ identity. See: Megan Clayton. June 16, 2020. *A Historic Decision Just Came Down from the Supreme Court. Here's What It Means for LGBTQ Freedom*. Washington, DC: Freedom for All Americans. (https://www.freedomforallamericans.org/a-historic-decision-just-came-down-from-the-supreme-court-heres-what-it-means-for-lgbtq-freedom/).

28. James et al., *Report of the 2015 U.S. Transgender Survey*.

29. James et al., *Report of the 2015 U.S. Transgender Survey*.

30. Jaime M. Grant et al. 2011. *Injustice at Every Turn: A Report of the National Transgender Discrimination Survey*. Washington, DC: National Center for Transgender Equality and National Gay and Lesbian Task Force.

31. Rani Snyder. May 21, 2020. "Is Availability of Telehealth for Older Adults a COVID-19 Silver Lining?" John A. Hartford Foundation Blog.

32. Elizabeth Yuko. May 20, 2020. "Why Older People Might Suffer Most, Post-pandemic." *Rolling Stone*. (https://www.rollingstone.com/culture/culture-features/covid-19-pandemic-ageism-older-americans-1002935/).

33. Monica Webb Hooper, Anna María Nápoles, and Eliseo J. Pérez-Stable. May 11, 2020. "COVID-19 and Racial/Ethnic Disparities." *JAMA*. (https://doi.org/10.1001/jama.2020.8598).

34. Jennifer Schramm. May 8, 2020. "Employment Data Digest." Washington, DC: AARP Public Policy Institute. (https://www.aarp.org/ppi/info-2020/employment-data-digest.html).

35. Michael Papadopoulos et al. 2020. "Recession Increases Downward Mobility in Retirement: Middle Earners Hit from Both Sides." Status of Older Workers Report Series. Retirement Equity Lab. New York: Schwartz Center for Economic Policy Analysis, New School for Social Research.
36. Papadopoulos et al., "Recession."
37. Arthur Kleinman. 2019. *The Soul of Care*. New York: Viking Press.
38. Paola Scommegna. March 26, 2012. "More U.S. Children Raised by Grandparents." Washington, DC: Population Reference Bureau.
39. Scommegna, "More U.S. Children Raised by Grandparents."
40. Family Caregiver Alliance. April 17, 2019. "Caregiver Statistics: Demographics." San Francisco: National Center on Caregiving. (https://www.caregiver.org/caregiver-statistics-demographics).
41. Family Caregiver Alliance, "Caregiver Statistics."
42. Bureau of Labor Statistics. November 22, 2019. "Unpaid Eldercare in the United States." News Release. Washington, DC: United States Department of Labor. (https://www.bls.gov/news.release/pdf/elcare.pdf).
43. Bureau of Labor Statistics, "Unpaid Eldercare."
44. Kersin Aumann et al. October 2010. *The Elder Care Study: Everyday Realities and Wishes for Change*. New York: Families and Work Institute.
45. Gretchen Livingston. November 29, 2018. *More Than One-in-ten U.S. Parents Are Also Caring for an Adult*. Washington, DC: Pew Research Center. (https://www.pewresearch.org/fact-tank/2018/11/29/more-than-one-in-ten-u-s-parents-are-also-caring-for-an-adult/).
46. Bureau of Labor Statistics, "Unpaid Eldercare."
47. Anna Jacobs and Irene Padavic. 2015. "Hours, Scheduling, and Flexibility for Women in the U.S. Low-wage Labor Force." *Gender Work and Organization* 22.
48. Claudia Lahaie, Alison Earle, and Jody Heymann. 2013. "An Uneven Burden: Social Disparities in Adult Caregiving Responsibilities, Working Conditions, and Caregiver Outcomes." *Research on Aging* 35(3):243–74. (https://doi.org/10.1177/0164027512446028).
49. Lynn Friss Feinberg and Rita Choula. 2012. *Understanding the Impact of Family Caregiving on Work*. Washington, DC: AARP Public Policy Institute. (https://www.aarp.org/content/dam/aarp/research/public_policy_institute/ltc/2012/understanding-impact-family-caregiving-work-AARP-ppi-ltc.pdf).
50. Katrina A. Burch, Alicia G. Dugan, and Janet L. Barnes-Farrell. January 2019. "Understanding What Eldercare Means for Employees and Organizations: A Review and Recommendations for Future Research." *Work, Aging and Retirement* 5(1):44–72. (https://doi.org/10.1093/workar/way011).
51. Bureau of Labor Statistics. 2018. *Retirement Benefits: Access, Participation, and Take-Up Rates*. Washington, DC: United States Department of Labor. (https://www.bls.gov/ncs/ebs/benefits/2018/ownership/civilian/table02a.htm?mod=article_inline).
52. Andrea Dittmann. August 12, 2016. "Understanding Social Class as Culture." *Behavioral Scientist*.
53. Luisa R. Blanco et al. 2015. "A Qualitative Analysis of the Use of Financial Services and Saving Behavior among Older African Americans and Latinos in the Los Angeles Area." *SAGE Open* 5(1):1–14.
54. Megan C. Lytle et al. 2015. "Current Trends in Retirement: Implications for Career Counseling and Vocational Psychology." *Journal of Career Development* 42(3):170–84. (https://doi.org/10.1177/0894845314545785).
55. Blanco et al., "Retirement Planning."
56. Díaz-Valdes, "Retirement Intentions."
57. Díaz-Valdes, "Retirement Intentions."
58. Calvo et al., "Expanding the 'Happiness Paradox.'"
59. Jody L. Herman and Kathryn O'Neill. April 2020. "Vulnerabilities to COVID-19 among Transgender Adults in the U.S." *Brief*. Los Angeles: UCLA School of Law, Williams Institute.
60. James et al., *Report of the 2015 U.S. Transgender Survey*.
61. Zacher and Rudolph, "Successful Aging."

62. Ruth Helman, Craig Copeland, and Jack VanDerhei. March 2012. "The 2012 Retirement Confidence Survey: Job Insecurity, Debt Weigh on Retirement Confidence, Savings." *EBRI Issue Brief* No. 369. Washington, DC: Employee Benefit Research Institute.

63. Min-Kyoung Rhee, Michàlle E. Mor Barak, and William T. Gallo. 2016. "Mechanisms of the Effect of Involuntary Retirement on Older Adults' Self-rated Health and Mental Health." *Journal of Gerontological Social Work* 59(1):35–55. (https://doi.org/10.1080/01634372.2015.1128504).

64. Grant et al., *Injustice at Every Turn.*

65. Tamila Nutsubidze and Khatuna Nutsubidze. 2019. "Informal and Non-standard Employment: A Look at the Impact on Social Protection Policy." *CRR WP* 2019-11. Chestnut Hill, MA: Center for Retirement Research, Boston College.

66. Demetra Smith Nightingale and Stephen A. Wandner. 2011. *Informal and Nonstandard Employment in the United States: Implications for Low-income Working Families.* Washington, DC: Urban Institute.

67. Nutsubidze and Nutsubidze, "Informal and Non-standard Employment."

68. Papadopoulos et al., "Recession."

## REFERENCES


Aumann, Kersin, et al. October 2010. *The Elder Care Study: Everyday Realities and Wishes for Change.* New York: Families and Work Institute.

Berridge, Clara W. and Marty Martinson. 2018. "Valuing Old Age without Leveraging Ableism." *Generations* 41(4):83–91.

Bird, Chloe E. and Patricia P. Rieker. 2008. *Gender and Health: The Effects of Constrained Choices and Social Policies.* New York: Cambridge University Press.

Blanco, Luisa R., et al. 2015. "A Qualitative Analysis of the Use of Financial Services and Saving Behavior among Older African Americans and Latinos in the Los Angeles Area." *SAGE Open* 5(1):1–14.

Blanco, Luisa R., et al. 2016. "Retirement Planning among Hispanics: In God's Hands?" *Journal of Aging & Social Policy* 29(4):311–31. (https://doi.org/10.1080/08959420.2016.1272161).

Brady, Samantha, et al. 2019. "Retiring and Caregiving in the Age of Student Loans: The Impact of Student Debt on Retirement and Longevity Planning." *Innovation in Aging* 3 (Suppl 1):S42. (https://doi.org/10.1093/geroni/igz038.163).

Burch, Katrina A., Alicia G. Dugan, and Janet L. Barnes-Farrell. January 2019. "Understanding What Eldercare Means for Employees and Organizations: A Review and Recommendations for Future Research." *Work, Aging and Retirement* 5(1):44–72. (https://doi.org/10.1093/workar/way011).

Bureau of Labor Statistics. May 24, 2017. "Foreign-born Workers Made 83.1 Percent of the Earnings of Their Native-born Counterparts in 2016." *Economics Daily*. Washington, DC: United States Department of Labor. (https://www.bls.gov/opub/ted/2017/foreign-born-workers-made-83-point-1-percent-of-the-earnings-of-their-native-born-counterparts-in-2016.htm).

Bureau of Labor Statistics. 2018. "Retirement Benefits: Access, Participation, and Take-up Rates." Washington, DC: United States Department of Labor. (https://www.bls.gov/ncs/ebs/benefits/2018/ownership/civilian/table02a.htm?mod=article_inline).

Bureau of Labor Statistics. November 22, 2019. "Unpaid Eldercare in the United States." News Release. Washington DC: United States Department of Labor. (https://www.bls.gov/news.release/pdf/elcare.pdf).

Calvo, Rocio, Dawn Carr, and Christina Matz-Costa. 2019. "Expanding the 'Happiness Paradox': Racial/Ethnic Disparities in Life Satisfaction among Older Immigrants in the United States." *Journal of Aging and Health* 31(2):231–55.

Carr, Dawn C., et al. 2020. "Postretirement Life Satisfaction and Financial Vulnerability: The Moderating Role of Control." *Journals of Gerontology, Series B* 75(4):849–60. (https://doi.org/10.1093/geronb/gby105).

Chang, E-Shien, et al. 2020. "Global Reach of Ageism on Older Persons' Health: A Systematic Review." *PLoS ONE* 15(1):e0220857. (https://doi.org/10.1371/journal.pone.0220857).

Clayton, Megan. June 16, 2020. *A Historic Decision Just Came Down from the Supreme Court: Here's What It Means for LGBTQ Freedom*. Washington, DC: Freedom for All Americans. (https://www.freedomforallamericans.org/a-historic-decision-just-came-down-from-the-supreme-court-heres-what-it-means-for-lgbtq-freedom/).

Coughlin, Joseph. May 2010. "Estimating the Impact of Caregiving and Employment on Well-being." *Outcomes & Insights in Health Management* 2(1).

Díaz-Valdes, Antonia. 2019. "Retirement Intentions and Behaviors of Hispanics Compared to Non-Hispanics in the United States: A Three-paper Dissertation." PhD Dissertation. Boston College, Chestnut Hill, MA.

Dittmann, Andrea. August 12, 2016. "Understanding Social Class as Culture." *Behavioral Scientist*.

Family Caregiver Alliance. April 17, 2019. "Caregiver Statistics: Demographics." San Francisco: National Center on Caregiving. (https://www.caregiver.org/caregiver-statistics-demographics).

Feinberg, Lynn Friss and Rita Choula. 2012. *Understanding the Impact of Family Caregiving on Work*. Washington, DC: AARP Public Policy Institute. (https://www.aarp.org/content/dam/aarp/research/public_policy_institute/ltc/2012/understanding-impact-family-caregiving-work-AARP-ppi-ltc.pdf).

Gatta, Mary. 2018. *Waiting on Retirement: Aging and Economic Insecurity in Low-wage Work*. Stanford, CA: Stanford University Press.

Gendron, Tracey L., et al. 2015. "The Language of Ageism: Why We Need to Use Words Carefully." *The Gerontologist* 56(6):997–1006. (https://doi.org/10.1093/geront/gnv066).

Gonzales, Ernest, et al. April 2015. "Age Discrimination in the Workplace and Its Association with Health and Work: Implications for Social Policy." *Research Brief* 2015-02. Boston: Boston University,

Grant, Jaime M., et al. 2011. *Injustice at Every Turn: A Report of the National Transgender Discrimination Survey*. Washington, DC: National Center for Transgender Equality and National Gay and Lesbian Task Force.

Griggs, Tracy L., et al. 2020. "Eldercare and the Psychology of Work Behavior in the Twenty-first Century." *Journal of Business and Psychology* 35:1–8.

Helman, Ruth, Craig Copeland, and Jack VanDerhei. March 2012. "The 2012 Retirement Confidence Survey: Job Insecurity, Debt Weigh on Retirement Confidence, Savings." *EBRI Issue Brief* No. 369. Washington, DC: Employee Benefit Research Institute.

Herman, Jody L. and Kathryn O'Neill. April 2020. "Vulnerabilities to COVID-19 among Transgender Adults in the US." *Brief*. Los Angeles: UCLA School of Law, Williams Institute.

Hooper, Monica Webb, Anna María Nápoles, and Eliseo J. Pérez-Stable. May 11, 2020. "COVID-19 and Racial/Ethnic Disparities." *JAMA*. (https://doi.org/10.1001/jama.2020.8598).

Jacobs, Anna and Irene Padavic. 2015. "Hours, Scheduling, and Flexibility for Women in the U.S. Low-wage Labor Force." *Gender Work and Organization* 22.

James, Sandy E., et al. 2016. *The Report of the 2015 U.S. Transgender Survey*. Washington, DC: National Center for Transgender Equality.

Kijakazi, Kilolo. May 28, 2020. *Older Workers and COVID-19: The Harsh Economic Realities*. Washington, DC: Urban Institute. (https://www.economicpolicyresearch.org/images/Retirement_Project/Presentations/May28_OlderWorkersWebinar/5-28-_2020_Webinar_Kilolo_reformat.pdf).

Kleinman, Arthur. 2019. *The Soul of Care*. New York: Viking Press.

Lahaie, Claudia, Alison Earle, and Jody Heymann. 2013. "An Uneven Burden: Social Disparities in Adult Caregiving Responsibilities, Working Conditions, and Caregiver Outcomes." *Research on Aging* 35(3):243–74. (https://doi.org/10.1177/0164027512446028).

Laws, Mike. June 16, 2020. "Why We Capitalize 'Black' (and Not 'White')." *Columbia Journalism Review*. (https://www.cjr.org/analysis/capital-b-black-styleguide.php).

Lexico. N.d. "Choice." Retrieved May 19, 2020 (https://www.lexico.com/en/definition/choice).

Liang, Jiayin and Baozhen Luo. August 2012. "Toward a Discourse Shift in Social Gerontology: From Successful Aging to Harmonious Aging." *Journal of Aging Studies* 26(3):327–34. (https://doi.org/10.1016/j.jaging.2012.03.001).

Livingston, Gretchen. November 29, 2018. *More Than One-in-ten U.S. Parents Are Also Caring for an Adult*. Washington, DC: Pew Research Center. (https://www.pewresearch.org/fact-tank/2018/11/29/more-than-one-in-ten-u-s-parents-are-also-caring-for-an-adult/).

Lytle, Megan C., et al. 2015. "Current Trends in Retirement: Implications for Career Counseling and Vocational Psychology." *Journal of Career Development* 42(3):170–84. (https://doi.org/10.1177/0894845314545785).

Martinson, Marty and Clara Berridge. 2015. "Successful Aging and Its Discontents: A Systematic Review of the Social Gerontology Literature." *The Gerontologist* 55(1):58–69.

Meyer, Oanh L., et al. 2015. "The Sociocultural Context of Caregiving Experiences for Vietnamese Dementia Family Caregivers." *Asian American Journal of Psychology* 6(3):263–72.

Munnell, Alicia H. Fall 2019. "Socioeconomic Barriers to Working Longer." *Generations* 43(3):42–50.

Nightingale, Demetra Smith and Stephen A. Wandner. 2011. *Informal and Nonstandard Employment in the United States: Implications for Low-income Working Families.* Washington, DC: Urban Institute.

Nutsubidze, Tamila and Khatuna Nutsubidze. 2019. "Informal and Non-standard Employment: A Look at the Impact on Social Protection Policy." *CRR WP* 2019-11. Chestnut Hill, MA: Center for Retirement Research, Boston College.

Papadopoulos, Michael, et al. 2020. "Recession Increases Downward Mobility in Retirement: Middle Earners Hit from Both Sides." Status of Older Workers Report Series. Retirement Equity Lab. New York: Schwartz Center for Economic Policy Analysis, New School for Social Research.

Reynolds, Joel Michael. 2018. "The Extended Body: On Aging, Disability, and Well-being." *Report* No. 48:S33. Cambridge, MA: Hastings Center.

Rhee, Min-Kyoung, Michàlle E. Mor Barak, and William T. Gallo. 2016. "Mechanisms of the Effect of Involuntary Retirement on Older Adults' Self-rated Health and Mental Health." *Journal of Gerontological Social Work* 59(1):35–55. (https://doi.org/10.1080/01634372.2015.1128504).

Ruggiano, Nicole, et al. 2017. "'Work Is Like a Therapy That Prevents Aging': Perceptions of Retirement, Productivity, and Health among Minorities and Immigrants." *SAGE Open* 7(1):1–11. (https://doi.org/10.1177/2158244016687234).

Rutledge, Matthew S., Alice Zulkarnain, and Sara Ellen King. 2017. "How Much Does Motherhood Cost Women in Social Security Benefits?" *CRR WP* 2017-14. Chestnut Hill, MA: Center for Retirement Research, Boston College.

Ryan, Richard M. and Edward L. Deci. 2000. "Self-determination Theory and the Facilitation of Intrinsic Motivation, Social Development, and Well-being." *American Psychologist* 55:68–78.

Schramm, Jennifer. May 8, 2020. "Employment Data Digest." Washington, DC: AARP Public Policy Institute. (https://www.aarp.org/ppi/info-2020/employment-data-digest.html).

Schwartz Center for Economic Policy Analysis. August 4, 2017. "1 in 4 Older Workers Lack On-the-job Health Insurance." Older Workers Report. New York: New School for Social Research. (https://www.economicpolicyresearch.org/jobs-report/july-2017-unemployment-report-for-workers-over-55).

Scommegna, Paola. March 26, 2012. "More U.S. Children Raised by Grandparents." Washington, DC: Population Reference Bureau.

Sevak, Purvi and Lucie Schmidt. February 26, 2014. "Immigrants and Retirement Resources." *Social Security Bulletin* 74(1):27–45.

Snyder, Rani. May 21, 2020. "Is Availability of Telehealth for Older Adults a COVID-19 Silver Lining?" John A. Hartford Foundation Blog.

Social Security Administration. N.d. "Benefits Planner: Retirement." (https://www.ssa.gov/planners/retire/).

Wansink, Brian and Jeffery Sobal. January 2007. "Mindless Eating: The 200 Daily Food Decisions We Overlook." *Environment and Behavior* 39(1):106–23.

Wikipedia. N.d. "Hobson's Choice." (https://en.wikipedia.org/wiki/Hobson%27s_choice).

Yuko, Elizabeth. May 20, 2020. "Why Older People Might Suffer Most, Post-pandemic." *Rolling Stone.* (https://www.rollingstone.com/culture/culture-features/covid-19-pandemic-ageism-older-americans-1002935/).

Zacher, Hannes and Cort W. Rudolph. 2017. "Successful Aging at Work and Beyond: A Review and Critical Perspective." Pp. 35–64 in *Age Diversity in the Workplace: An Organizational Perspective,* edited by Silvia Profili, Alessia Sammarra, and Laura Innocenti. Bingley, UK: Emerald Publishing.

CHAPTER 5

# Precariously and Securely Employed Older Women and Prospects for Extended Working Lives

Debra Street and Áine Ní Léime

## OVERVIEW

This chapter provides an overview of issues associated with older women's employment in the first two decades of the twenty-first century, contextualized within a policy arena linked to the need to extend working life/delay retirement. We first define extended working life and contrast that with delaying retirement. The ability to extend work or delay retirement hinges, in part, on whether employment is secure or precarious. The long reach of gendered life course trajectories accumulates by later ages to shape older women's current employment circumstances and their potential to work longer. In fact, the gap between an imagined potential for many older women's extended employment and the reality of current and likely future labor markets is considerable. Emerging trends in the United States in the early months of the pandemic underscore the shifting sands of precarity and security for women workers in general, and older women in particular. The economic havoc wreaked by the global pandemic seems likely to persist. If it does, that will exacerbate unresolved problems that have shaped contemporary older women's employment experiences and the effort to extend employment to later ages in the future. Researchers and policy makers alike will need to rethink employment prospects if postpandemic policies are to yield outcomes that can minimize the challenges inherent in precarious employment, inadequate income, and family demands for many older women.

Following a general discussion of affluent countries' pursuit of extended working lives and the continuum between secure and precarious employment, we outline characteristics of older women's employment in the U.S. Some older women have rewarding careers and little interest in retiring at traditional ages. Others toil in very different kinds of jobs and are eager to retire. At best, many older women have steady, if not particularly rewarding, employment that pays the bills and permits saving—but are happy to retire given the opportunity. At worst, older women in precarious jobs work under adverse, uncertain conditions, negatively affecting their health and economic well-being. Is it reasonable to expect such disadvantaged older women to stay in paid work to older ages? We consider the prospects for extending women's employment, taking family and work experiences and early evidence from the pandemic-disrupted labor market into account.

## THE NEOLIBERAL TURN AND EXTENDED WORKING LIVES

Internationally, the ascendance of neoliberalism has stoked concerns about the sustainability of spending on pension expenditures for aging populations. The combination of population aging and more pensioners has triggered a transnational political movement to extend working lives.[1,2] In the United States, pro-market neoliberal ideology has fostered a sustained offensive against redistributive public policies via lower taxes, spending cuts, and deregulation. Neoliberalism's "radically free market" agenda yields "social policies favorable to business and indifferent toward poverty,"[3] providing a rationale both for cutting public spending on pensions and for "freeing" employers from the expectation that they should provide traditional occupational pensions for their retirees. Neoliberal politicians and scholars have targeted older people as an expensive and "unaffordable" component of public spending, given their (increasingly expensive) health care needs and entitlement to state pensions. They promote policy initiatives that reassign what previously were public responsibilities (like income security in old age) to the private sector, increasing the responsibility of individuals to provide (pensions) for themselves.[4]

Both in the United States and internationally, the refrain "live longer, work longer" has led to a revised social contract that leans more on individual responsibility than on collective guarantees.[5] In most countries, the age for full state pension entitlement is increasing, and eligibility requirements for receiving public pensions and benefit values are linked more tightly to paid employment. Simultaneously, employers have withdrawn from traditional defined benefit (DB) pensions, which used to provide retirees with predictable monthly pensions for life. Those DB plans (whose funding was largely the responsibility of employers) have been replaced by much riskier individual defined contribution (DC) retirement savings accounts.

Some recent U.S. policies encourage employers to retain older workers by creating more flexible arrangements for preretirement employment. Unfortunately, such policies are exhortatory rather than mandated. Employment-related legislation intended to mitigate the pervasive effects of ageism, sexism, and racism in labor markets has been enacted but is difficult to enforce. Disability accommodation rights have also been introduced, a welcome adjustment to the evolving needs of older workers when employers cooperate with "reasonable accommodations." However, it is unclear to what extent such de jure rights are enjoyed by older workers, enacted by employers, or enforced by the state.[6]

Efforts to persuade or compel people to work longer occur within specific national contexts, reflecting distinctive sociopolitical and economic circumstances, policy legacies and initiatives, and evolving labor markets. Internationally, finding the best combination of carrots and sticks to encourage most people to forgo retirement at a well-established normative retirement age and to work to later ages has been elusive so far.[7]

One approach to extending working lives in the United States has been to change the Social Security program. Until the 1983 Social Security Amendments changed eligibility for individuals, sixty-five was the normal (full) retirement age (NRA). It was not until 2003 that individuals born in 1938 and later saw their NRA increase. Yet the traditional retirement age of sixty-five is still used in research and policy circles as the marker to categorize "working aged" people (under sixty-five) from "retired" or "elderly people" (sixty-five-plus) and is also the age of entitlement for the second most important national policy affecting their well-being—Medicare.

The prospect of the large baby boom cohort claiming Social Security benefits has been one of the rationales provided by proponents of extending work/delaying retirement. Because the boomer cohort is, on average, healthier and wealthier than earlier generations, the assumption is that most of this generation in the U.S. as elsewhere, can—and *should*—work longer than previous cohorts before claiming public pensions.[8] Although early retirement from age sixty-two with reduced Social Security benefits is possible, the "should work longer" idea is embedded in the gradual increase to age sixty-seven for eligibility for unreduced Social Security retirement benefits. Compelling delayed retirement in order to receive full public pension benefits is one "stick" that can be used to extend working lives. While the average American still *prefers* to retire significantly earlier (often giving age sixty-one or sixty-two as their ideal age), table 5.1 shows that older workers in particular *expect* to retire around the soon-to-be Social Security normal retirement age of sixty-seven, although younger age groups seem less willing to work to later ages.

Who extends their working lives? As figure 5.1 shows, compared to 1988, by 2016 Americans were already more likely to be working at older ages. While nearly one in five sixty-five-plus individuals were still working in 2016, by February 2020 (the month before the pandemic), 26 percent of individuals sixty-five-plus were employed.[9] Pre-pandemic, the steady increase in older people remaining in work was expected to continue. However, whether projections for 2026 will materialize postpandemic is very uncertain. Only two months into the pandemic, sixty-five-plus employment had already declined by 3 percent to its lowest point in eight years.

**TABLE 5.1.** Retirement Age Expectations by Age Group

*When do you expect to retire (non-retirees)?*

| *Current Age* | *Average Age (Years) Expect to Retire* |
|---|---|
| 18–29 | 63 |
| 30–49 | 65 |
| 50–64 | 67 |

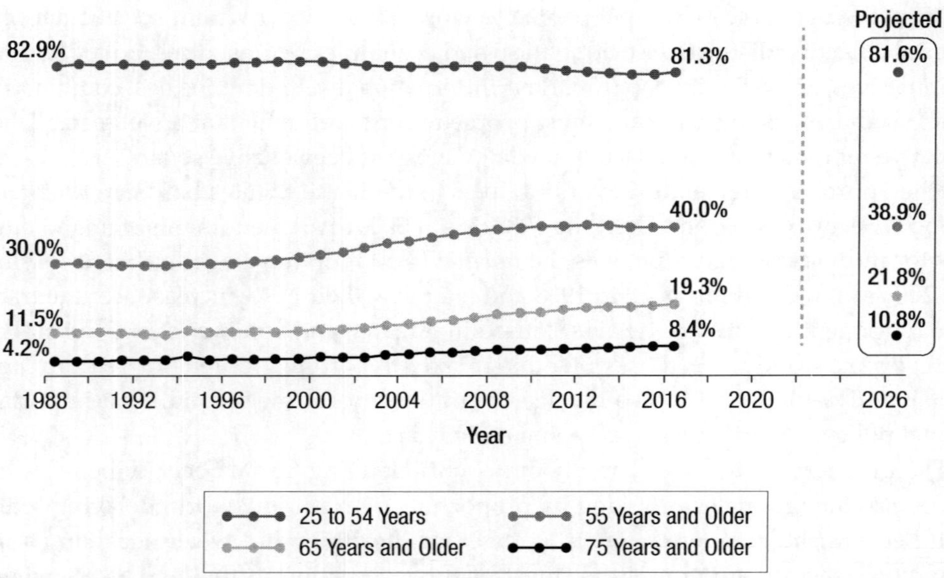


**FIGURE 5.1.** Labor Force Participation Rates by Age Group, 1988–2016, and Projections for 2026
*Source:* U.S. Senate Special Committee on Aging, 2017.

As we argue elsewhere,[10] extending work and delaying retirement are conceptually distinct. The "stick" compelling people to work longer lies in the capacity of governments to tighten eligibility rules for public pension entitlements and raise state retirement ages. Withholding retirement income beyond a person's preferred retirement date is a formidable incentive to remain employed, as are losses in individual retirement accounts when economic markets plunge as they did in the global recession of 2008.[11] "Carrots" encouraging people to work longer include state policies and employment practices that support employment to later ages and provide adequate income and appropriate working conditions, suited to older workers' skills.

## SECURE VERSUS PRECARIOUS EMPLOYMENT

Comparisons among women in varied family and occupational circumstances are not always crisp. Part of the debate about extended working lives centers on whether past, current, or future jobs are secure or precarious, what family responsibilities are in play, and how those circumstances feed into the potential for a particular individual to extend work. Kalleberg and Vallas define precarious work as work that "is *uncertain, unstable,* and *insecure* and in which employees *bear the risks of work* (as opposed to businesses or the government) and *receive limited social benefits and statutory protections.*"[12] Secure jobs typically feature full-time work, predictable hours, workplace protections, and employee benefits. For individuals in nonstandard employment, one worker's flexibility is another's precarity. The proportion of workers in such precarious positions—in seasonal, on-call, or short-term work, on "zero hours" contracts, or working in the "gig" economy, for example[13]—has been steadily growing.[14]

Transitions into retirement have become increasingly diverse and less sharply delineated than the traditional tripartite school/work/retirement model. The boundaries between later-life employment and retirement statuses are fluid, featuring bridge employment, second careers, flexible work, and unretirement.[15] (See chapters 21 and 22.) Which women can take advantage of desired flexible work choices, contrasted with women who have few choices, is central to the issue of extending older women's working lives. How transitions are experienced reflects a range of more and less favorable employment conditions among older women with differing employment-related choices, family circumstances, and health statuses.

The ability of older workers to extend employment depends on employer behavior, not just individual choices. (See also chapters 7, 8, 10, and 11.) Employers set the parameters for job-related choice and are often encouraged to permit nonstandard working arrangements for older workers to ease into retirement,[16] as policy makers advocate flexibility to permit workers to design their own particular exit from employment.[17] This assumes that: (1) flexibility permits employers to keep highly skilled workers they value and perhaps incentivize retirement for older workers who are valued less;[18] and (2) older workers may want to ease into their own exit arrangements—via phased retirement, part-time work, home-based working, or other flexible options. Yet it is employers who determine which occupations and jobs are secure and well paid, which are flexible in ways that appeal to older workers, and which are precarious and poorly paid. Employees typically have much less control over working conditions, in terms of pay, hours, stability, or physical demands.

Other considerations shape the categories of secure, flexible, and precarious jobs available for older women's employment. Historically, there was skepticism that employers would support sufficient job flexibility (particularly in the private sector) to appeal to both employers and older workers. The pandemic may reverse the skepticism about flexible work arrangements (particularly remote work), at least for some employers. Millions of Americans—especially workers in good jobs—have had the ability to work from home, potentially supplying the productivity evidence to reassure employers that future flexibility is possible. That in turn could present new opportunities for older full-time workers to ease into more flexible jobs. Flexible, at-home work could also be very beneficial for older women who want to remain employed, but to work less or work remotely in the run-up to retirement, whether in response to preference or family care needs.

Additional issues associated with extending work highlight the tension between high- and low-quality employment, and the contrast between choice and compulsion. In part, flexible or precarious definitions depend on job quality, whether it is well paid and rewarding, and accommodates competing family demands and physical capabilities. When chosen, flexibility is valued and can be a motivating factor for extending work. In contrast, imposed flexibility (fewer working hours, or lower pay) is typically unwelcome, rendering it a form of precarity and, often, underemployment. U.S. employment policies and practices to date do not adequately address the complexities of older women's income and retirement savings needs, a policy vacuum made even more obvious given labor market disruptions associated with the pandemic.

## GENDER AND EXTENDED WORK

Women's and men's typical life course patterns, occupational opportunities, employment histories, patterns of pay and pension eligibility, and expectations related to unpaid family caregiving mesh to create gendered experiences for work at later ages. The focus on older women workers highlights the role that gendered life courses play in the lives of older women workers and their prospects for extending their working lives.[19] Current scholarship contrasts precarious and secure work to reveal sources of systematic inequality and insecurity among older women workers. The gendered effects of employment and expectations to work longer are enacted across several life domains: from the gender composition of occupations; to the normative expectation that women do most unpaid family caregiving (childcare or eldercare); to the ways that women's lower lifetime incomes and pension entitlement combine with greater longevity to create financial vulnerabilities in old age. Many women's labor market disadvantages highlight the need for facilitative policies to support current women's employment and older women's future employment, especially if they are expected to continue working to older ages. The conundrum of how best to support older women's employment needs and ensure income security in old age has become even more perplexing, given the collapse of some components of labor markets arising from the COVID-19 pandemic fallout.

## OLDER WOMEN'S EMPLOYMENT

The rate of older American women in paid work has increased about 5 percent since 2000. Contemporary U.S. women are better educated, on average, than earlier cohorts, scaling career hierarchies into fulfilling professional and managerial positions and remaining in work longer.[20] Women workers with the highest levels of education and professional credentials are more likely to work to later ages than others with fewer credentials. Another contributor to employment trends for women of all ages is the U.S.'s notorious stinginess or absence of family-friendly policies, whether paid sick leave, paid maternity leave, paid care leave, or affordable high-quality childcare, which depresses younger women's labor force participation and makes it impossible for some older women to simultaneously maintain employment and caring responsibilities. (See also chapter 20.)

Many women must balance paid work and unpaid family care responsibilities throughout the life course. Family care needs might be childcare for grandchildren[21] or eldercare for parents, parents-in-law, and spouses.[22] One way some older women manage the expectation that women provide family care is to buy domestic assistance. That is easiest when women can afford to do so, using resources from secure employment, decent pay, full-time hours, and employer-provided benefits. However, many older women need to trade employment security for part-time work or precarity to accommodate unpaid caring responsibilities, despite needing more income or help with care. Sometimes a part-time job can be enough for such women to cope. However, the most vulnerable among older women workers confront both heavy family care demands and desperate income needs. When such older women toil in substandard jobs, with very low pay, physically demanding work, and insufficient wages, they cannot simultaneously earn a secure living, save for retirement,[23] or ever hope to purchase care assistance, domestic services or care respite they desperately need.

## Good and "Good Enough" Jobs

The job elite—professional women in stable, secure employment, with good wage and benefit packages, secure positions, and interesting work—have careers that may be appealing enough to entice women to remain in work longer.[24,25] Such *good* jobs were more prevalent in 2019 than ever before, as women's educational attainment and enterprise made inroads into the professions, to management, and sometimes to the upper echelon of occupations, previously the exclusive reserve of men. However, such appealing careers are still the exception for most older women. The best many can hope for is a *good enough* job, one that can be performed within their physical capacities and that can sustain income and savings until a later retirement date is reached. The third category is the *not good enough* job. While it is true that some women may have part-time, episodic, low-paid employment that they enjoy and that meets their employment needs, too many older women have to settle for low-quality work. Such work is typically done under adverse or stressful conditions and at relatively low levels of pay, is often physically demanding, and lacks certainty that hours or duration of work will generate income sufficient to meet current needs or to enable pension contributions.[26]

## Choice versus Compulsion

There is ample evidence of the importance of autonomy for psychological well-being, and having choices about whether to continue working or to stop at older ages is important.[27] Individuals with meaningful, interesting, and rewarding jobs often characterize the choice to work longer as a positive experience.[28,29] In contrast, being desperate to remain in work or become employed at older ages because of financial need is stressful and unpleasant for individuals who have to settle for a poorly paid, boring, or physically demanding job.[30,31,32]

## Variation in Older Women's Employment Experiences

Changes in pension policies (both public and private) force many women to work longer because they have earned too little to have a surplus to save for retirement. Increasing state pension ages lengthens the time that many older workers are compelled to work longer in low-paid, stressful jobs[33] because such jobs typically do not have occupational pensions and workers cannot afford private pension savings that might allow them to retire sooner. This has negative health implications for their later years.[34,35]

## The Intersection of Age, Sex, and Race

Age discrimination by employers is widespread in relation to recruitment, retention, and reemployment of older workers.[36,37] (See also chapter 12.) In the U.S. labor market, even with historically low levels of unemployment until March 2020, older workers often experience problems becoming employed or reemployed after a "certain" age.[38] When state pension ages are increased and older job seekers face age discrimination, they are apt to remain involuntarily unemployed. Further, evidence indicates that age discrimination in the workplace is gendered.[39] In many occupations, employers consider women "too old" at younger ages than men,[40] disadvantaging older female workers and job seekers. The intersection of age, sex, and race in the U.S. means that many older women of color are triply disadvantaged in terms of their capacity to extend work. In the current recession, pandemic unemployment has been dominated by women of color, many of them older workers in low-paid service jobs.[41]

## POLICIES TO EXTEND WORKING LIFE/DELAY RETIREMENT IN THE U.S.

Several U.S. measures have sought to extend working lives or to delay retirement. With few exceptions (e.g., public safety occupations), there is no mandatory retirement age in the U.S. This is a "carrot" for extending working life, since people who enjoy their work are not compelled to retire involuntarily at a particular age. The Social Security Amendments that gradually increase the NRA to age sixty-seven by 2025 are a "stick" as many must work longer than expected to obtain the highest Social Security retirement benefits.[42] While U.S. workers may still choose to retire early at age sixty-two, doing so permanently reduces Social Security benefits (another "stick"). A Social Security provision that permits older workers to earn wages from employment and still collect at least partial benefits is a "carrot" to remain employed. So too is the ability to continue working (increasing Social Security contributions and the ultimate value of benefits) until age seventy (three years past the NRA), for workers healthy enough to continue working and able to wait for higher Social Security benefits. In one sense, this actually makes seventy the de facto NRA since seventy thus becomes the age at which the highest Social Security benefits are earned.[43,44]

While extending work is partly shaped by statutory retirement ages, what people plan to do and actually do often differ. One way to capture that gap is to observe actual labor market withdrawal for recent cohorts of workers by considering the average effective age of retirement over a five-year period, based on actual labor market exits. Despite a Social Security NRA of 66 in 2018, the average effective date of retirement for U.S. women (the 2013–2018 older cohort's average age of actual withdrawal from employment) was 66.5, compared to 67.9 for men.[45] Higher effective retirement ages reflect myriad factors: needing to work longer to try to recoup pension plan losses due to the global recession of 2008–2009; the gradual increase in the Social Security NRA for recent cohorts; and, (until recently) a booming U.S. economy with ample employment opportunities.[46]

Yet, on average, older women in the U.S. have more interrupted careers, have fewer Social Security contributions, and are more likely to work part time and to have lower wages over their working lives than men.[47] From 2001 to 2016, those gendered differences in employment created a 51 percent gap in fifteen-year earnings between average female and male workers.[48] After forty years of full-time employment, a twenty-year-old woman who started to work in 2018 will average an estimated $407,760 less in earnings than white, non-Hispanic men. That translates into a lifetime pay gap of $527,000 for white women, $941,600 for black women, and $1,121,440 for Latinas.[49] This gendered lifetime earnings gap is but one reason that older women depend more on Social Security for their income in retirement than men.

## OLDER WOMEN'S EMPLOYMENT, UNEMPLOYMENT, AND RETIREMENT

The stay-at-home and social distancing required in response to the pandemic has changed many employment relations. The unprecedentedly high employment rates of 2019 have given way to unemployment rates (as of June 2020) at historic post-1930s Depression-era levels in the United States. What is the likely future of older women's employment, when most analysts expect many jobs to disappear forever?

The most recent period for which similar data are available is after the Great Recession of 2008–2009. That period featured high levels of unemployment yet simultaneously accelerated a trend: attempts to weather the financial turmoil undermining retirement income security by hanging on to one's job, secure or precarious. For displaced older workers laid off or terminated during the recession, finding new jobs was difficult; older women were particularly disadvantaged due to the intersection of ageism and sexism. There is little reason to be more hopeful now, given the sheer extent of global pandemic employment displacements.

"Long-term unemployed" are individuals out of work for six-plus months, while "discouraged" workers have given up looking because they believe no jobs are available for them or there were none for which they qualify. Unsurprisingly, long-term unemployment increases with age. Workers over age fifty-five are the most at risk of long-term unemployment once they lose a job (even when labor markets are thriving), and reemployment is difficult. For example, older women's unemployment rates more than tripled in the aftermath of the Great Recession.[50] Given the disproportionately high rates of women's unemployment early in the pandemic, it is logical to assume that older women suffering job loss will remain unemployed for long spells or may give up seeking employment altogether.[51] Even when older individuals want or need jobs, they often self-identify as retired to avoid the stigma of being labeled unemployed.[52,53]

Another age-related employment risk in the aftermath of the most recent recession was *under*employment, affecting part-timers who would prefer full-time work and workers who took jobs that did not fully use their skills and qualifications.[54] When older job seekers do find work, it is often with fewer hours of work or lower pay, or both.[55,56] Skills/job mismatches can make reemployment especially difficult. Older workers who are displaced due to businesses closing or downsizing may lack the technical skills needed to compete for available jobs, and workplace ageism reduces their access to training opportunities.[57]

Whether sufficient jobs, private or public, can be created, how they can be distributed throughout the U.S., what skills would be needed, and what pay could be offered are all missing pieces in the future older worker/labor market participation puzzle.

Demand-side issues receive scant attention in extended working life debates, yet asserting the prospect of looming labor shortages or having low levels of unemployment—as in the recent past—has not meant that employers were eager to retain or recruit older workers. Research based on the University of Michigan Health and Retirement Study shows that over half of retired older Americans said they wanted to work but were involuntarily pushed or encouraged out of employment.[58]

## Work-Family Balance, Health, and Discrimination

Paid family leave in the U.S. is rare and usually at the employer's discretion. The Family and Medical Leave Act (FMLA) provides for leave due to parenthood or providing care to immediate family members, covering employees who meet minimum standards of job tenure and hours worked annually and who are employed by the government or large private-sector organizations. Job-protected FMLA leave can be taken for up to six months, but there is no requirement that the leave be paid. Most workers have no entitlement to paid or unpaid leave at all. Caregivers face short- and long-term costs, including out-of-pocket expenses, shifting to part-time work, and lower incomes (and thus less surplus to save for retirement or contribute to Social Security). While the thirty-five highest years of pay used in Social Security calculations for retirement benefits may give working caregivers some leeway in maximizing benefits despite shorter periods of employment, there is no deliberate policy mechanism within Social Security to compensate them for essential, unpaid work.[59]

A unique component of the American political economy that encourages or compels older workers to remain employed is the linkage of health insurance to employment. Most Americans younger than sixty-five depend on employers for affordable group health insurance—a source of "job lock" that keeps many in full-time employment until they become eligible for state-provided Medicare at age sixty-five. While the Patient Protection and Affordable Care Act 2010 (a.k.a. Obamacare) might have minimized some of the perverse effects embedded in the structure of U.S. health insurance, rollbacks under the Trump administration coupled with the devastating toll the pandemic has taken on jobs, health, and especially employer-provided health insurance coverage have created a "triple whammy" for many older workers. Current U.S. health policies do not adequately support older workers with health problems who seek to remain employed.

Economic trends that decreased manufacturing and clerical jobs from the mid-to-late twentieth century due to globalization and automation, combined with many older workers' lower levels of education and age discrimination, left few good choices for former older job seekers who wanted or needed to work longer. Today as well, older workers are often forced into the only readily available jobs—low-paid precarious employment in the services sector.[60] The effects on workers relegated to service jobs have been particularly acute during the pandemic. Many older women were deemed essential workers, occupying frontline service positions and paid caring jobs—employment undertaken with grueling schedules and hard physical work—at risk to their own health.[61]

Even when jobs are abundant, employers prefer to hire younger rather than older workers. While the U.S. pioneered legislation for workers forty and older with the Age

Discrimination in Employment Act of 1967 (ADEA), its impact has been limited. There is a widespread perception that age discrimination is pervasive in the American workplace.[62,63] A barrier for older Americans in general, age discrimination can push willing older female workers out of employment altogether. (See also chapter 12 and elsewhere in this volume.)

A policy that could help older women remain in employment longer is the Americans with Disabilities Act (ADA) of 1990. Because older women report having more chronic conditions than men, a workplace accommodation could be the difference between working and becoming unemployed. Workplaces of a certain size must offer reasonable accommodation for employees who need adaptations to their conditions of work. Both anti–age discrimination and disability accommodation legislation (when effective and enforced) could potentially help older women seeking to remain employed. However, neither the ADEA nor the ADA have shown particular effectiveness in helping older workers extend their working lives.[64]

On the demand side of the extended working life equation, employers seem to have few jobs for which the skills of most older workers are in high demand. Even when age is not an overt part of the job recruitment strategy, the language of job ads and the practice of targeting younger adults on social media reflect entrenched ageist attitudes in the American workplace. Although unemployment rates in 2019 skirted record lows, even then the demand-side conditions favorable for extending work were uncertain. Older women workers whose jobs disappear during the pandemic are likely to remain unemployed or redefine themselves as retired.

## UNWANTED AND UNAFFORDABLE? GENDERED PERCEPTIONS OF THE OLDER POPULATION

Before the pandemic, growing demands for public spending on pensions, health, and social care systems were associated with population aging. A smaller proportion of "working-age" people were contributing to national tax bases that sustained health and pension systems for aging populations. The transition from industrial to postindustrial and from national/local to global labor markets introduced new complexities in employment patterns. Simultaneously, the large and still growing proportions of women in gendered labor markets rendered social policies devised around the assumptions of the male breadwinner/female homemaker model outdated. Systemic ageism, sexism, and racism plague employment relations.[65] The chronic lack of adequate social care options across the life course, given normative expectations that women should perform most unpaid care, contributes to insurmountable problems for many women trying to establish feasible work-family balance, regardless of age. The challenges that employed women with family responsibilities face have real consequences. The combination of time out of work or in part-time employment, the missed opportunities for advancement in jobs, and the persistent gender pay gap translates into nearly half a million dollars' shortfall in average earnings over a lifetime, for women compared to men.

## CURRENT EXTENDED WORKING LIFE DEBATES AND THEIR POTENTIAL POLICY FUTURES

Proponents of extended working life often use vague language that emphasizes the positive side of policies that governments enact, motivated more by pension cost-saving than enhancing employment opportunities for older workers. Positive but nonspecific rhetoric associated with the hegemonic "active aging" agenda naturalizes the idea of extending working lives. The sleight of hand invoked by "extending working life" language masks the more specific, less optimistic "delaying retirement" reality, obscuring both the intent and outcomes associated with current policies. Public audiences have been conditioned with messaging about "too many, too expensive" applied to aging populations.[66] The inevitable conclusion is that, with rare exceptions, everyone everywhere must work longer—not just the job elite, but women with bad jobs too. Sociologist John Myles characterizes routine expectations of retirement as a crowning twentieth-century social policy achievement, bestowing "the right to stop working before wearing out."[67] For the financially insecure, retirement may be an elusive twenty-first-century entitlement.

## CONCLUSION

Both the policies that have shaped older women's employment in recent pre-pandemic years and current policy proposals to extend working lives tend to encompass simplistic, one-size-fits-all approaches. Most policies designed to compel or encourage extended work, whether by choice or necessity, assume all (older) workers to be undifferentiated, unencumbered, unhealthed, and ungendered.[68]

The culmination of the neoliberal political agenda has been increased income inequality and insecurity for individuals in all affluent countries, and the U.S. is no exception. There is no surprise that, pre-pandemic, the idea that dominated policy circles was the "live longer, work longer" solution[69]—even for older employed women who routinely put in the "second shift" of unpaid work.[70]

The *New York Times* recently referred to the current pandemic-induced recession in the U.S. as a "shecession"—with furloughs and layoffs disproportionately experienced by women.[71] Women in low-paid service occupations who return to work after a furlough may put their health at risk. Older women workers may be permanently displaced by the pandemic, especially if history repeats itself and unemployed older women cannot find jobs when the economy slowly recovers. One glimmer of hope is that some kinds of jobs can be performed from home. Still, fewer than half of older workers have those kinds of jobs.[72] The challenges that plagued many older women's employment needs and opportunities pre-pandemic are a point of departure for what happens next in terms of their security or precarity. At best, the postpandemic crystal ball for women's later-life employment provides but an uncertain, and not entirely hopeful, glimpse at their prospects.

## NOTES

1. Áine Ní Léime et al., eds. 2017. *Gender, Ageing and Extended Working Life: Cross-national Perspectives*. Bristol, UK: Policy Press.

2. Áine Ní Léime et al., eds. 2020. *Extended Working Life Policies: International Gender and Health Perspectives*. Cham, Switzerland: SpringerOpen. (https://link.springer.com/content/pdf/10.1007%2F978-3-030-40985-2.pdf).

3. Wendy Brown. 2003. "Neo-liberalism and the End of Liberal Democracy." *Theory & Event* 7(1). (https://doi.org/10.1353/tae.2003.0020).

4. Larry Polivka and Luo Baozhen. 2015. "The Neo-liberal Political Economy and Erosion of Retirement Security." *The Gerontologist* 55(2):183–90. (https://doi.org/10.1093/geront/gnv006).

5. OECD. 2006. *Live Longer, Work Longer*. Paris: OECD Publishing.

6. Debra Street. 2020. "United States." Pp. 481–93 in *Extended Working Life Policies: International Gender and Health Perspectives*, edited by Áine Ní Léime et al. Cham, Switzerland: SpringerOpen. (https://link.springer.com/content/pdf/10.1007%2F978-3-030-40985-2.pdf).

7. Debra Street and Áine Ní Léime. 2020. "Problems and Prospects for Current Policies to Extend Working Lives." Pp. 85–113 in *Extended Working Life Policies: International Gender and Health Perspectives*, edited by Áine Ní Léime et al. Cham, Switzerland: SpringerOpen. (https://link.springer.com/content/pdf/10.1007%2F978-3-030-40985-2.pdf).

8. Sarah Vickerstaff. 2010. "Older Workers: The Unavoidable Obligation of Extending Our Working Lives." *Sociology Compass* 4(10):869–79.

9. Bureau of Labor Statistics, U.S. Department of Labor. 2020. "Labor Force Participation Rate—With No Disability, 65 Years and Over." [LNU01375379]. FRED, Federal Reserve Bank of St. Louis. Retrieved June 13, 2020 (https://fred.stlouisfed.org/series/LNU01375379).

10. Street and Ní Léime, "Problems and Prospects."

11. Nata Duvvury, Áine Ní Léime, and Aoife Callan. 2017. "Erosion of Pension Rights. Experiences of Women in Ireland." *European Journal of Cultural and Political Sociology* 5(3):266–94. (https://doi.org/10.1080/23254823.2017.1381034).

12. Arne L. Kalleberg and Steven P. Vallas. 2018. "Probing Precarious Work: Theory, Research, and Politics." *Precarious Work: Research in the Sociology of Work* 31(1):1–30. (https://doi.org/10.1108/S0277-283320170000031017). Emphasis in original.

13. Guy Standing. 2011. *The Precariat: The New Dangerous Class*. New York: Bloomsbury.

14. International Labor Organization. 2016. *Non-standard Employment around the World: Understanding Challenges, Shaping Prospects*. Geneva: ILO.

15. Mo Wang and Kenneth Shultz. 2010. "Employee Retirement: A Review and Recommendations for Future Investigation." *Journal of Management* 36(1):172–206.

16. Stephen Miller. 2019a. "Many Older Workers Would Prefer to Ease into Retirement." Society for Human Resource Management. (November 4, 2019):1–30. (https://www.shrm.org/resourcesandtools/hr-topics/benefits/pages/manyolder-workers-prefer-easing-into-retirement.aspx).

17. U.S. Senate, Special Committee on Aging. 2017. *America's Aging Workforce: Opportunities and Challenges*. Washington, DC: U. S. Government Printing Office.

18. Stephen Miller. November 4, 2019b. "Targeted Benefits Help Baby Boomers to Stay at Work, Ease into Retirement." Society for Human Resource Management. (November 4, 2019). (https://www.shrm.org/ResourcesAndTools/hr-topics/benefits/Pages/targeted-benefits-help-baby-boomers-stay-at-work-prepare-to-retire.aspx).

19. Jay Ginn, Debra Street, and Sara Arber, eds. 2001. *Women, Work, and Pensions: International Issues and Prospects*. Buckingham, UK: Open University Press.

20. Elizabeth Fideler. 2012. *Women Still at Work: Professionals over 60 and on the Job*. Lanham, MD: Rowman & Littlefield.

21. Madonna Harrington Meyer and Ynesse Abdul-Malak, eds. 2016. *Grandparenting in the United States*. Amityville, NY: Baywood Press.

22. Kim Parker and Eileen Patten. 2013. "The Sandwich Generation: Rising Financial Burdens for Middle-aged Americans." Washington, DC: Pew Research Center. Retrieved July 7, 2020 (http://www.pewsocialtrends.org/2013/01/30/the-sandwich-generation/).

23. Áine Ní Léime and Debra Street. 2019. "Working Later in the USA and Ireland: Implications for Precarious and Securely Employed Women." *Ageing & Society* 39(10):2194–218. (https://doi.org/10.1017/S0144686X18000508).

24. AARP. 2014. *Staying Ahead of the Curve 2013: The AARP Work and Career Study, Older Workers in an Uneasy Job Market.* Washington, DC: AARP.

25. Fideler, *Women Still at Work.*

26. Ní Léime and Street, "Working Later in the USA and Ireland."

27. Estaban Calvo, Kelly Haverstick, and Steven Sass. 2009. "Gradual Retirement, Sense of Control, and Retirees' Happiness." *Research on Aging* 31(1):112–35.

28. Fideler, *Women Still at Work.*

29. Ní Léime and Street, "Working Later in the USA and Ireland."

30. Nathalie Burnay. 2019. "Belgian Temporary Workers at End of Working Life: An Intersectional Life Course Analysis." *Ageing & Society* 39(10):2267–89.

31. Ní Léime and Street, "Working Later in the USA and Ireland."

32. Vickerstaff, "Older Workers."

33. Lena Hünefeld, Susanne Gerstenberg, and Joachim Hüffmeier. 2019. "Satisfaction and Mental Health of Temporary Agency Workers in Europe: A Systematic Review and Research Agenda." *Work and Stress*:1–29.

34. Ill-Yo Kim. 2011. "Welfare States, Flexible Employment and Health: A Critical Review." *Health Policy* 104(2):99–127. (https://doi.org/10.1016/j.healthpol.2011).

35. Ní Léime and Street, "Working Later in the USA and Ireland."

36. Kasia Karpinska, Kene Henkens, and Joop Schippers. 2011. "The Recruitment of Early Retirees: A Vignette Study of the Factors That Affect Managers' Decisions." *Ageing & Society* 31(4):570–89.

37. David Neumark, Ian Burn, and Patrick Button. 2015. "Is It Harder for Older Workers to Find Jobs? New and Improved Evidence from a Field Experiment." *NBER Working Paper* 21669. Cambridge, MA: National Bureau of Economic Research.

38. Joanna Lahey. 2008. "Age, Women, and Hiring: An Experimental Study." *Journal of Human Resources* 43:30–56. (https://doi.org/10.3368/jhr.43.1.30).

39. Lahey, "Age, Women, and Hiring."

40. Colin Duncan and Wendy Loretto. 2004. "Never the Right Age? Gender and Age-based Discrimination in Employment." *Gender, Work & Organization* 11:95–115.

41. Alisha Haridasani Gupta. May 9, 2020. "Why Some Women Call This Recession a 'Shecession.'" *New York Times*.

42. Debra Street and Joanne Tompkins. 2017. "Is 70 the New 60? Extending American Women's and Men's Working Lives." Pp. 193–215 in *Gender, Ageing and Extended Working Life: International Analysis from a Critical Perspective*, edited by Áine Ní Léime et al. Bristol, UK: Policy Press:193–215.

43. Alicia Munnell. 2013. "Social Security's Real Retirement Age Is 70." *Issue Brief* 13-5. Chestnut Hill, MA: Center for Retirement Research, Boston College.

44. Ní Léime and Street, "Working Later in the USA and Ireland."

45. OECD. 2019. *Pensions at a Glance 2019: OECD and G20 Indicators.* Paris: OECD Publishing. (https://doi.org/10.1787/b6d3dcfc-en).

46. OECD, *Pensions at a Glance 2019.*

47. Street, "United States."

48. Stephen J. Rose and Heidi Hartmann. 2018. *It's Still a Man's Labor Market: The Slowly Narrowing Gender Wage Gap.* Institute for Women's Policy Research. Retrieved July 7, 2020 (https://iwpr.org/publications/still-mans-labor-market/).

49. Amanda Fins. 2020. *Women and the Lifetime Wage Gap: How Many Woman Years Does It Take to Equal 40 Man Years?* Washington, DC: National Women's Law Center. (https://nwlc-ciw49tixgw5lbab.stackpathdns.com/wp-content/uploads/2019/03/Women-and-the-Lifetime-Wage-Gap-v2.pdf).

50. Federal Reserve Bank of St. Louis. 2015. "Age and Gender Differences in Long-term Unemployment: Before and after the Great Recession." *Economic Synopses* 26. Retrieved July 7, 2020 (https://research.stlouisfed.org/publications/economic-synopses/2015-11-10/age-andgender differences-in-long-term-unemployment-before-and-after-thegreat-recession.pdf).

51. Gupta, "Why Some Women Call This Recession a 'Shecession.'"

52. Peter Heslin, Myrtle Bell, and Pinar Fletcher. 2012. "The Devil Without and Within: A Conceptual Model of Social Cognitive Processes Whereby Discrimination Leads Stigmatized Minorities to Become Discouraged Workers." *Journal of Organizational Behavior* 33(6):840–62.

53. Ariane Froideveau, Andreas Hirschi, and Mo Wang. 2019. "Identity Incongruence and Negotiation in the Transition from Work to Retirement: A Theoretical Model." *Organizational Psychology Review* 8(4):228–55. (https://doi.org/10.1177/2041386619830754).

54. Bureau of Labor Statistics, U.S. Department of Labor. 2016. *Local Area Unemployment Statistics*. Retrieved June 13, 2020 (http://www.bls.gov/lau/stalt.htm).

55. General Accounting Office. 2012. *Unemployed Older Workers: Many Experience Challenges Regaining Employment and Face Reduced Retirement Security*. Washington, DC: GAO.

56. David Lain. 2012. "Working past 65 in the UK and the USA: Segregation into 'Lopaq' Occupations?" *Work, Employment & Society* 26(1):78–94. (https://doi.org/10.1177/0950017011426312).

57. Neil Charness. 2013. "Job Security in an Insecure World: Adaptations of Older Workers in the IT Industry." Pp. 109–14 in *Older Workers in an Ageing Society: Critical Topics in Research and Policy*, edited by Philip Taylor. Cheltenham, UK: Edward Elgar.

58. Richard Johnson and Peter Gosselin. 2018. *How Secure Is Employment at Older Ages?* Washington, DC: Urban Institute. Retrieved January 16, 2020 (Tinyurl.com/y43zwj8d).

59. Ní Léime and Street, "Working Later in the USA and Ireland."

60. Standing, *The Precariat.*

61. Teresa Ghilarducci and Aida Farmand. 2020. "Older Workers on the COVID-19-Frontlines without Paid Sick Leave." *Journal of Aging & Social Policy* 32(4–5):471–76, (https://doi.org/10.1080/08959420.2020.1765685).

62. AARP, *Staying Ahead of the Curve.*

63. Teresa Ghilarducci. 2015. "Senior Class: America's Unequal Retirement." *American Prospect.* (https://prospect.org/article/senior-class-americas-unequal-retirement).

64. David Wegman and James McGee, eds. 2004. "Programs and Policies Related to the Older Workforce and Safe Work." In *Health and Safety Needs of Older Workers.* U.S. National Research Council and Institute of Medicine Committee on the Health and Safety Needs of Older Workers. Washington, DC: National Academies Press. Retrieved August 10, 2020 (https://www.ncbi.nlm.nih.gov/books/NBK207714/).

65. David Neumark, Ian Burn, and Patrick Button. 2017. *Age Discrimination and Hiring of Older Workers,* Federal Reserve Bank of San Francisco. Retrieved July 7, 2020 (http://w.frbsf.org/economic-research/publications/economic-letter/2017/february/age-discrimination-and-hiring-older-workers/).

66. David Willetts. 2010. *The Pinch: How the Baby Boomers Took Their Children's Future—and Why They Should Give It Back*. London: Atlantic Books.

67. John Myles. 1989. *Old Age and the Welfare State: The Political Economy of Public Pensions.* Lawrence: University of Kansas Press.

68. Ní Léime and Street, "Working Later in the USA and Ireland."

69. OECD, *Live Longer, Work Longer*.

70. Arlie Hochschild. 2003. *The Second Shift.* New York: Penguin Books.

71. Gupta, "Why Some Women Call This Recession a 'Shecession."

72. Anqi Chen and Alicia Munnell. 2020. "Can Older Workers Work from Home?" *Issue Brief* 20-9. Chestnut Hill, MA: Center for Retirement Research, Boston College.

## REFERENCES

AARP. 2014. *Staying Ahead of the Curve 2013: The AARP Work and Career Study, Older Workers in an Uneasy Job Market.* Washington, DC: AARP.

Brown, Wendy. 2003. "Neo-liberalism and the End of Liberal Democracy." *Theory & Event* 7(1). (https://doi.org/10.1353/tae.2003.0020).

Bureau of Labor Statistics, U.S. Department of Labor. 2016. *Local Area Unemployment Statistics*. Retrieved June 13, 2020 (http://www.bls.gov/lau/stalt.htm).

Bureau of Labor Statistics, U.S. Department of Labor. 2020. "Labor Force Participation Rate—With No Disability, 65 Years and Over." [LNU01375379] FRED, Federal Reserve Bank of St. Louis. Retrieved June 13, 2020 (https://fred.stlouisfed.org/series/LNU01375379).

Burnay, Nathalie. 2019. "Belgian Temporary Workers at End of Working Life: An Intersectional Life Course Analysis." *Ageing & Society* 39(10):2267–89.

Calvo, Estaban, Kelly Haverstick, and Steven Sass. 2009. "Gradual Retirement, Sense of Control, and Retirees' Happiness." *Research on Aging* 31(1):112–35.

Charness, Neil. 2013. "Job Security in an Insecure World: Adaptations of Older Workers in the IT Industry." Pp. 109–14 in *Older Workers in an Ageing Society: Critical Topics in Research and Policy*, edited by Philip Taylor. Cheltenham, UK: Edward Elgar.

Chen, Anqi and Alicia Munnell. 2020. "Can Older Workers Work from Home?" *Issue Brief* 20-9. Chestnut Hill, MA: Center for Retirement Research, Boston College.

Duncan, Colin and Wendy Loretto. 2004. "Never the Right Age? Gender and Age-based Discrimination in Employment." *Gender, Work & Organization* 11:95–115.

Duvvury, Nata, Áine Ní Léime, and Aoife Callan. 2017. "Erosion of Pension Rights. Experiences of Women in Ireland." *European Journal of Cultural and Political Sociology* 5(3):266–94. (https://doi.org/10.1080/23254823.2017.1381034).

Federal Reserve Bank of St. Louis. 2015. "Age and Gender Differences in Long-term Unemployment: Before and after the Great Recession." *Economic Synopses* 26. Retrieved July 7, 2020 (https://research.stlouisfed.org/publications/economic-synopses/2015-11-10/age-andgenderdifferences-in-long-term-unemployment-before-and-after-thegreat-recession.pdf).

Fideler, Elizabeth. 2012. *Women Still at Work: Professionals over 60 and on the Job*. Lanham, MD: Rowman & Littlefield.

Fins, Amanda. 2020. *Women and the Lifetime Wage Gap: How Many Woman Years Does It Take to Equal 40 Man Years?* Washington, DC: National Women's Law Center. (https://nwlc-ciw49tixgw5lbab.stackpathdns.com/wp-content/uploads/2019/03/Women-and-the-Lifetime-Wage-Gap-v2.pdf).

Froideveau, Ariane, Andreas Hirschi, and Mo Wang. 2019. "Identity Incongruence and Negotiation in the Transition from Work to Retirement: A Theoretical Model." *Organizational Psychology Review* 8(4):228–55. (https://doi.org/10.1177/2041386619830754).

General Accounting Office. 2012. *Unemployed Older Workers: Many Experience Challenges Regaining Employment and Face Reduced Retirement Security*. Washington, DC: GAO.

Ghilarducci, Teresa. 2015. "Senior Class: America's Unequal Retirement." *American Prospect*. (https://prospect.org/article/senior-class-americas-unequal-retirement).

Ghilarducci, Teresa and Aida Farmand. 2020. "Older Workers on the COVID-19-Frontlines without Paid Sick Leave." *Journal of Aging & Social Policy* 32(4–5):471–76. (https://doi.org/10.1080/08959420.2020.1765685).

Ginn, Jay, Debra Street, and Sara Arber, eds. 2001. *Women, Work and Pensions: International Issues and Prospects*. Buckingham, UK: Open University Press.

Gupta, Alisha Haridasani. May 9, 2020. "Why Some Women Call This Recession a 'Shecession.'" *New York Times*.

Harrington Meyer, Madonna and Ynesse Abdul-Malak, eds. 2016. *Grandparenting in the United States*. Amityville, NY: Baywood Press.

Heslin, Peter, Myrtle Bell, and Pinar Fletcher. 2012. "The Devil Without and Within: A Conceptual Model of Social Cognitive Processes Whereby Discrimination Leads Stigmatized Minorities to Become Discouraged Workers." *Journal of Organizational Behavior* 33(6):840–62.

Hochschild, Arlie. 2003. *The Second Shift*. New York: Penguin Books.

Hünefeld, Lena, Susanne Gerstenberg, and Joachim Hüffmeier. 2019. "Satisfaction and Mental Health of Temporary Agency Workers in Europe: A Systematic Review and Research Agenda." *Work and Stress*:1–29.

International Labor Organization. 2016. *Non-standard Employment around the World: Understanding Challenges, Shaping Prospects*. Geneva: ILO.

Johnson, Richard and Peter Gosselin. 2018. *How Secure Is Employment at Older Ages?* Washington, DC: Urban Institute. Retrieved January 16, 2020 (Tinyurl.com/y43zwj8d).

Kalleberg, Arne L. and Steven P. Vallas. 2018. "Probing Precarious Work: Theory, Research, and Politics." *Precarious Work: Research in the Sociology of Work* 31(1):1–30. (https://doi.org/10.1108/S0277-283320170000031017).

Karpinska, Kasia, Kene Henkens, and Joop Schippers. 2011. "The Recruitment of Early Retirees: A Vignette Study of the Factors That Affect Managers' Decisions." *Ageing & Society* 31(4):570–89.

Kim, Ill-Yo. 2011. "Welfare States, Flexible Employment and Health: A Critical Review." *Health Policy* 104(2):99–127. (https://doi.org/10.1016/j.healthpol.2011).

Lahey, Joanna. 2008. "Age, Women, and Hiring: An Experimental Study." *Journal of Human Resources* 43:30–56. (https://doi.org/10.3368/jhr.43.1.30).

Lain, David. 2012. "Working past 65 in the UK and the USA: Segregation into 'Lopaq' Occupations?" *Work, Employment & Society* 26(1):78–94. (https://doi.org/10.1177/0950017011426312).

Miller, Stephen. 2019a. "Many Older Workers Would Prefer to Ease into Retirement." Society for Human Resource Management. (November 4, 2019):1–30. (https://www.shrm.org/resourcesandtools/hr-topics/benefits/pages/manyolder-workers-prefer-easing-into-retirement.aspx).

Miller, Stephen. 2019b. "Targeted Benefits Help Baby Boomers to Stay at Work, Ease into Retirement." Society for Human Resource Management. (November 4, 2019). (https://www.shrm.org/resourcesandtools/hr-topics/benefits/pages/targeted-benefits-help-baby-boomers-stay-at-work-prepare-to-retire.aspx).

Munnell, Alicia. 2013. "Social Security's Real Retirement Age Is 70." *Issue Brief* 13-5. Chestnut Hill, MA: Center for Retirement Research, Boston College.

Myles, John. 1989. *Old Age and the Welfare State: The Political Economy of Public Pensions.* Lawrence: University of Kansas Press.

Neumark, David, Ian Burn, and Patrick Button. 2015. "Is It Harder for Older Workers to Find Jobs? New and Improved Evidence from a Field Experiment." *NBER Working Paper* 21669. Cambridge, MA: National Bureau of Economic Research.

Neumark, David, Ian Burn, and Patrick Button. 2017. *Age Discrimination and Hiring of Older Workers.* Federal Reserve Bank of San Francisco. Retrieved July 7, 2020 (http://w.frbsf.org/economic-research/publications/economic-letter/2017/february/age-discrimination-and-hiring-older-workers/).

Ní Léime, Áine, et al., eds. 2017. *Gender, Ageing and Extended Working Life: Cross-national Perspectives*. Bristol, UK: Policy Press.

Ní Léime, Áine, et al., eds. 2020. *Extended Working Life Policies: International Gender and Health Perspectives*. Cham, Switzerland: SpringerOpen. (https://link.springer.com/content/pdf/10.1007%2F978-3-030-40985-2.pdf).

Ní Léime, Áine and Wendy Loretto. 2017. "Gender Perspectives on Extended Working Life Policies." Pp. 53–76 in *Gender, Ageing and Extended Working Life: Cross-national Perspectives*, edited by Áine Ní Léime, et al. Bristol, UK: Policy Press.

Ní Léime, Áine and Debra Street. 2019. "Working Later in the USA and Ireland: Implications for Precarious and Securely Employed Women." *Ageing & Society* 39(10):2194–218. (https://doi.org/10.1017/S0144686X18000508).

OECD. 2006. *Live Longer, Work Longer*. Paris: OECD Publishing.

OECD. 2019. *Pensions at a Glance 2019: OECD and G20 Indicators.* Paris: OECD Publishing. (https://doi.org/10.1787/b6d3dcfc-en).

Parker, Kim and Eileen Patten. 2013. "The Sandwich Generation: Rising Financial Burdens for Middle-aged Americans." Washington, DC: Pew Research Center. Retrieved July 7, 2020 (http://www.pewsocialtrends.org/2013/01/30/the-sandwich-generation/).

Polivka, Larry and Luo Baozhen. 2015. "The Neo-liberal Political Economy and Erosion of Retirement Security." *The Gerontologist* 55(2):183–90. (https://doi.org/10.1093/geront/gnv006).

Rose, Stephen J. and Heidi Hartmann. 2018. *It's Still a Man's Labor Market: The Slowly Narrowing Gender Wage Gap.* Institute for Women's Policy Research. Retrieved July 7, 2020 (https://iwpr.org/publications/still-mans-labor-market/).

Standing, Guy. 2011. *The Precariat: The New Dangerous Class.* New York: Bloomsbury.

Street, Debra. 2020. "United States." Pp. 481–93 in *Extended Working Life Policies: International Gender and Health Perspectives*, edited by Áine Ní Léime et al. Cham, Switzerland: SpringerOpen. (https://link.springer.com/content/pdf/10.1007%2F978-3-030-40985-2.pdf).

Street, Debra and Áine Ní Léime. 2020. "Problems and Prospects for Current Policies to Extend Working Lives." Pp. 85–113 in *Extended Working Life Policies: International Gender and Health Perspectives*, edited by Áine Ní Léime et al. Cham, Switzerland: SpringerOpen. (https://link.springer.com/content/pdf/10.1007%2F978-3-030-40985-2.pdf).

Street, Debra and Joanne Tompkins. 2017. "Is 70 the New 60? Extending American Women's and Men's Working Lives." Pp. 193–215 in *Gender, Ageing and Extended Working Life: International Analysis from a Critical Perspective*, edited by Áine Ní Léime et al. Bristol, UK: Policy Press.

U.S. Senate, Special Committee on Aging. 2017. *America's Aging Workforce: Opportunities and Challenges*. Washington, DC: U.S. Government Printing Office.

Vickerstaff, Sarah. 2010. "Older Workers: The Unavoidable Obligation of Extending Our Working Lives." *Sociology Compass* 4(10):869–79.

Wang, Mo and Kenneth Shultz. 2010. "Employee Retirement: A Review and Recommendations for Future Investigation." *Journal of Management* 36(1):172–206.

Wegman, David and James McGee, eds. 2004. "Programs and Policies Related to the Older Workforce and Safe Work." In *Health and Safety Needs of Older Workers*. U.S. National Research Council and Institute of Medicine Committee on the Health and Safety Needs of Older Workers. Washington, DC: National Academies Press. Retrieved August 10, 2020. (https://www.ncbi.nlm.nih.gov/books/NBK207714/).

Willetts, David. 2010. *The Pinch: How the Baby Boomers Took Their Children's Future—and Why They Should Give It Back*. London: Atlantic Books.

CHAPTER 6

# Retirement Security and Timing among Hispanics

## Is Working Longer a Fair Expectation for Everyone in the U.S.?

Antonia Díaz-Valdés I.

### OVERVIEW

The landscape of factors that affect retirement security and planning in this era of longevity are complex and continuously emerging. Unfortunately, many older adults in the United States are facing their later life having been hit hard by the Great Recession of 2008 and the unforgiving economy that followed. They are saddled with debt, have accumulated minimal pension or retirement savings, and see poor options for continued work.[1,2] Moreover, social security systems were designed to help people insure themselves against certain events, such as old age, unemployment, disability, and death of the head of household.[3] However, the aging of the population has imposed sustainability problems on the Social Security system[4,5] and has raised concerns about retirement security, not just in terms of finances, but also in terms of health and well-being.

Given these concerns, debate has intensified about what the full retirement age (FRA) should be and whether individuals should postpone retirement (i.e., work longer). These are extremely complex issues with multiple economic and social consequences—at the individual and societal levels. One of the main questions in this debate is whether postponing retirement or working longer is a fair expectation or goal for all individuals, or just for those who have a certain level of control over their retirement decision.[6,7]

Most literature about retirement in the U.S. has focused on middle-class whites, and little is known about ethno-racial groups, particularly about Hispanics. Current literature states that those who tend to work longer are wealthier males, who are healthier, have higher levels of education, and tend to have old-age benefits such as employer-sponsored pensions and health insurance.[8,9] When compared to non-Hispanics, Hispanics' particular migration experiences and accumulation of disadvantages over the life course might differentially influence their retirement behaviors and opportunities. Factors such as socioeconomic status, immigration status, educational attainment, degree of acculturation, and English proficiency have an enormous impact on a person's beliefs and behaviors. Hispanics are less likely to plan for retirement, and when they do retire, they are often financially unprepared.[10] Even if Hispanics are more likely to state they will "never" retire and that they want to work until they are not able to do so, they are more likely to retire earlier than non-Hispanics.[11] Although Hispanics' life expectancies are among the longest in the U.S., they enter old age with higher prevalence of chronic diseases and generally poorer health in comparison to other ethno-racial groups in the U.S.—as a result of lifelong deprivation of health care access and utilization.[12] Given that Hispanics face retirement with limited resources and complex health issues, they could benefit greatly from extended work lives.

For Hispanics, the decision to stay in the workforce longer may have less to do with projected finances and more with cultural values, such as religion and family.[13] Failure to put Hispanics' retirement planning and behaviors in the context of normative cultural values limits our ability to understand the dynamics and to create culturally sensitive supports and programs to improve their outcomes. However, a discussion of cultural values should be prefaced with an understanding that significant variation occurs between Hispanic cultural subgroups—just as individuals subscribe to group norms to varying degrees.

In this chapter, I will first discuss Hispanic migration histories and life course conditions. Second, I will describe Hispanics' retirement planning, followed by a description of the discrepancy between retirement expectation and reality. Finally, I will sightsee the potential effect of the discrepancy between planned and actual retirement timing on Hispanics, from the productive aging framework.

## HISPANICS' MIGRATION HISTORY AND LIFE COURSE

Life course theory recognizes the relationship between environmental factors and personal agency. From a life course perspective, earlier events have an impact on later-life outcomes. Individuals do not pass through fixed and irreversible stages during their lives, and there are biographical and historical components that shape the life outcomes of people.[14,15] Hispanics as a group have unique characteristics that influence their retirement experience.

This is important, as Hispanics are the largest minority group in the U.S. and their life trajectory will increasingly influence the overall well-being of the society.[16] Hispanics' share of the U.S. population has increased steadily since 1960, comprising about 18 percent of the population in 2015, and is expected to continue to increase over the next decades to about 24 percent by 2060.[17,18] Hispanic older adults' share of the population (those aged sixty-five and older) has been growing especially rapidly. Between 1980 and 2014, the older Hispanic population quintupled, and it is projected to increase from 8 percent in 2014 to 15 percent by 2040.[19]

The share of foreign-born Hispanics increased between the 1960s and the 2000s. Since 2000, the share of foreign born compared to native born has started to decrease—from about 40 percent in 2000 to 34 percent by 2015, and is expected to continue to decrease over the following decades as second- and third-generation Hispanics are increasing in number.[20] Since 2000, the increase of Hispanics in the U.S. has been due to births, while before 2000 the main cause was immigration.[21] Hispanics aged sixty-four and younger are mostly (67 percent) native born, while Hispanics aged sixty-five and older are mostly foreign born (54 percent)—about one in four are undocumented immigrants.[22] This represents several changes within the Hispanic population. Second-generation Hispanics tend to have higher levels of education and of English proficiency.

Hispanic migration has gained importance since the 1960s; there were some significant shifts in migration during this decade and after in the U.S. Until the 1960s, immigrants in the U.S. came mostly from European countries.[23] Since 1990, Hispanics have become the largest foreign-born population in the U.S. Hispanics' migration before the 1960s was marked by the need for manual labor brought on by World War II.[24]

Most Hispanics migrated to the U.S. seeking better employment and financial opportunities.[25,26] However, their migration was shaped by diminished labor market conditions. By the 1970s–1980s, high unemployment and inflation followed the economic proliferation of the post–World War II era.[27] This migration context combined with low levels of education and poor English proficiency burdened them with unique traits that have defined Hispanics in the U.S.[28] Level of education and English proficiency have been linked to social mobility.[29,30] Hispanic immigrants' limited education and lack of English skills concentrated them in low-wage jobs, which, along with labor market conditions, decreased their ability to join the U.S. mainstream.[31,32]

The English proficiency of Hispanics in the U.S. has been steadily increasing since 2000. Not surprisingly, native-born Hispanics have historically had higher English proficiency than foreign-born Hispanics. From 1980 to 2015, the share of native-born Hispanics who spoke English at least very well increased by 18 percentage points (from 72 percent to 90 percent), compared to only a 4 percentage point increase among foreign-born Hispanics (from 31 percent to 35 percent).[33] Thus, it is possible to observe that the increase in English proficiency is driven by younger, mostly second-generation Hispanics. About 33 percent of foreign-born working-age Hispanics are fluent in English, compared to about 88 percent of native-born Hispanics. There are significant differences given country of origin and length of stay. About 25 percent of Mexican-origin Hispanics state they are fluent in English, compared to 50 percent of Cubans and even larger shares of Puerto Ricans. Overall, 90 percent of native-born Hispanics are fluent in English, independent of their country of origin.[34]

Two of the most decisive factors in English proficiency are educational attainment and length of stay. Historically, Hispanics as a group have had the lowest educational attainment in the U.S.; they are less likely than non-Hispanic whites and blacks to earn a high school diploma or equivalent.[35] Even as educational attainment has been increasing for all ethnic groups, Hispanics have the lowest levels. The percentage of Hispanics with less than a high school degree has decreased from 45 percent to 33 percent, while for non-Hispanics the decrease was from 17 percent to 12 percent.[36] This decrease is due to younger Hispanics; second-generation Hispanics tend to have higher levels of education, which is aligned with differences in educational attainment between older Hispanics and older non-Hispanics. Based on 2017 census data,[37] about 14 percent of Hispanics aged sixty-five years and older had a bachelor's degree or higher, compared to 25 percent of non-Hispanics of the same age group. Similarly, about 42 percent of Hispanics aged sixty-five years and older had less than a high school education, compared to just 11 percent of non-Hispanics of the same age group. There are also significant differences by country of origin; of all Hispanics, Mexican-origin Hispanics are more likely to drop out of high school.[38] Younger Hispanics, as a group, are more likely to acquire higher education levels, thus, higher English proficiency.

As mentioned previously, Hispanics face several challenges when merging into the U.S. mainstream. Lower levels of education and English proficiency, especially on the part of foreign-born Hispanics, make it harder for them. Undocumented Hispanic immigrants face additional challenges. The large share of undocumented immigrants is a result of both the demand for cheap, hardworking employees and failed immigration laws; in fact, laws designed to decrease the proportion of undocumented immigrants have actually increased it.[39] For instance, the 1920s immigration laws designed to limit the number of immigrants from Asia, Africa and northwestern Europe, the Dominican Republic, and independent countries from South and Central America excluded Mexico. Additionally, the "bracero" program, a guest worker program that had started in 1942, was formally ended in 1964. However, the need for a manual labor force did not end, and Hispanics continued to enter legally and illegally.[40,41] The termination of this program corresponded with economic pressures in Mexico, which increased the share of undocumented immigrants. Similarly, the 1978 amendment to the Hart-Celler Act strengthened requirements for legal migration but ended up increasing the pressure to enter the U.S. illegally.[42]

Today, about 40 percent of Hispanics are undocumented immigrants, and most of them are long-standing immigrants—with stays of ten years or longer.[43,44] Unauthorized immigration has stabilized since 2009, due to a decrease in unauthorized migration from Mexico and South America. However, the number of unauthorized immigrants from Central America has increased since the 1990s. Mexican unauthorized immigrants still make up more than 50 percent of the unauthorized immigrants from Latin American countries, followed by 21 percent of immigrants from Central America, and 8 percent of unauthorized immigrants from South America.[45] Undocumented Hispanics are in limbo; their migration status leaves them unprotected and limits their immersion into the U.S. mainstream. They do not have access to social welfare, lack civil rights protections, and have limited employment opportunities because they are not legally entitled to work in the U.S.[46]

## THE ROLE OF *FAMILISMO* IN RETIREMENT PLANNING AMONG HISPANICS

Hispanics, as a group, tend to share a collectivist or group-oriented view of life, also known as *familismo*, which shapes their financial, social, and retirement decisions. A strong emphasis is placed on family—extended family, including grandparents, aunts, cousins, and even those not biologically related—as the major source of one's identity and protection against hardships in life.[47,48] This collectivist view of life derives from the belief that family takes care of the family: children take care of their parents when they get older, and older parents help with their grandchildren as they get older or their own children if they need them to, which might reduce the urgency of saving for retirement, even the possibility of saving for retirement.[49] The *familia* (family) is a key element among Mexican-origin Hispanics. Their family gives them a sense of collective ownership, connection, and cooperation; as a family, they share caregiving responsibilities, emotional support, and financial responsibilities.[50]

Attitudes toward material exchange and investments are complex, shaped during childhood and rooted in moral and reciprocal relationships. Material exchanges within families are shaped by complex interactions and emotional exchanges that at the same time influence the expectations regarding these exchanges.[51,52] Thus, Hispanics invest in people and expect returns from it. These investments can be monetary assistance (e.g., intergenerational transfer to/from children, to relatives, to friends) or nonmonetary assistance (e.g., co-residing, taking care of grandchildren, taking care of older parents, food preparation, cleaning).[53,54] Because Hispanics, as a group, tend to lack financial resources, they often support their family in nonmonetary ways, such as caregiving and co-residing to reduce expenses (e.g., renting).[55]

Paradoxically, a qualitative study of older Hispanics in the U.S. by Blanco and colleagues found that most participants did not expect to rely on family networks for support in old age. For example, some study participants stated that they help their parents, but they do not expect their children to help them. However, Richman and colleagues report strong evidence of a culture of familial interdependence, where Hispanic adults felt obliged to support elderly parents without complaining and there was a generalized reciprocity between Hispanic older adults and their children.[56] Both first and second generations have an affinity to help the family; however, second-generation Hispanics were more likely to indicate that they did not expect the same in return.[57]

Similarly, Blanco and colleagues found that first-generation Hispanics did not expect their native-born children to help them the way they had helped their parents, stating that their children have another culture: they are Americans.[58] For first-generation Hispanics, gifting and giving are rooted values that they embrace unconditionally. However, for second- and third- generation Hispanics who are more acculturated, these values might take a different shape or fade. Even when seniors do not have much to share, which limits their gifting, they do so unconditionally.[59] First-generation Hispanics were more likely to support relatives unconditionally (e.g., they borrow money to support their family), while second-generation help was more limited and less unconditional (e.g., they will not borrow money to support relatives and/or they will support them only if they ask them to).[60] This collectivist view of Hispanics shapes their retirement preparedness, especially, among first-generation Hispanics. However, the extent to which this view shapes retirement timing among Hispanics is not yet explored.

For workers who experienced more unemployment events and who worked in low-wage jobs, diminishing employment opportunities and growing family responsibilities would seem to be strong predictors of retirement timing.[61] This is aligned with the Hispanics' collectivist view of life and *familismo*.

Recent research has found that there are differences regarding common predictors of retirement planning and timing.[62] For Hispanics, nonfinancial transfers and employer-sponsored benefits were predictors of retirement timing, and the results reflect Hispanics' financial disadvantages over the life course and provide insights about their collectivist view of life. For instance, unlike non-Hispanics, having medical insurance was significantly associated with an increased probability of planning for delayed retirement among Hispanics. Hispanics are less likely to be offered health insurance, and having access to it is an incentive to delay retirement. Furthermore, unlike non-Hispanics, health status does not significantly influence the discrepancy between planned and actual retirement timing for Hispanics. For Hispanics, taking care of grandchildren decreased the probability of "never" retiring, and the number of dependents strongly affected the decision to retire earlier than planned. It appears that fulfilling caregiving roles and the needs of their families are stronger predictors for Hispanics than for non-Hispanics.

This is especially important when designing interventions and public policy seeking to increase Hispanics' retirement preparedness and to help them fulfill their retirement expectations. Failing to account for Hispanics' collectivist view of life and the role of extended families might lead to worse retirement outcomes. Even if they might financially benefit from extended work life, it could be that for them, taking care of family brings increased satisfaction and well-being.

## HISPANICS' RETIREMENT PLANNING

The lack of retirement planning is not unique to Hispanics; most Americans do not plan for retirement. However, evidence suggests that Hispanics tend to engage in little to no retirement planning—estimating a retirement age, calculating how much one will need to save for retirement, and identifying potential sources of retirement income. According to Sun and colleagues, only 35 percent of Hispanics stated they planned for retirement savings, compared to over 70 percent of non-Hispanics whites.[63] Moreover, Blanco and colleagues, in a qualitative study on retirement preparedness among middle-aged and older low-income Hispanics in Los Angeles, found that most of them did not have a set age planned for retirement because they wanted to work until they could no longer, and they were not sure when that would be.[64]

Furthermore, Blanco and colleagues found a lack of tradition regarding preparation for retirement: Hispanics stated their parents did not plan for retirement nor did they speak or teach them about it. Evidence suggested that religiosity and spirituality played a key role as a coping mechanism regarding retirement saving and preparedness among Hispanics in the U.S.: some felt that their retirement and future were in God's hands.[65]

Financial literacy (knowing strategies for managing one's income and assets) and financial capability (the ability to use that knowledge regarding effective management of one's income and assets) are key skills to ensure financial security at old age.[66] Hispanics lack knowledge about retirement investing and savings.[67] For instance, 43 percent of Latino workers had no knowledge about investing or saving for retirement compared to only 12 percent of all workers.[68] Moreover, Hispanics' low trust in financial institutions limits their participation in such institutions.[69] And according to the Social Security Administration, Hispanics are less likely than any other ethno-racial group to be knowledgeable at all about Social Security. Hispanics are less likely than non-Hispanic whites (13 percent versus 24 percent), to know what their full retirement age (FRA) is. Similarly, Hispanics are about 15 percent less likely than non-Hispanic whites to know whether Social Security benefits are adjusted for inflation or what delayed retirement credits are.[70]

Over 50 percent of Hispanics stated they do not feel financially prepared for retirement. They are more likely than any other ethno-racial group to state they are not prepared.[71] Most Hispanics live day to day and are not able to save for retirement or other life expenses, such as college education for their children.[72,73] As mentioned previously, Hispanics tend to think less often about retirement compared to non-Hispanics—about 60 percent have never calculated how much they need to save to maintain their lifestyle in retirement, and about 70 percent of Hispanics lack a retirement investment plan.[74] This reflects their precarious financial situation, unstable work histories, and lack of control over the retirement decision.

Hispanics' migration experience, marked by diminished labor market conditions, combined with their low level of education and lack of English proficiency, has shaped Hispanics' employment opportunities.[75] Hispanics tend to be concentrated in low-wage jobs, which are also associated with limited or nonexistent access to employer-sponsored retirement plans and limited access to health insurance coverage.[76,77] Additionally, Hispanics are less likely to participate in employer-sponsored plans, and even if they do participate in such plans, they tend to make smaller contributions and for shorter periods of time.[78,79] By 2014, about 38 percent of male Hispanics aged twenty-five to sixty-four were offered pension coverage, compared to 61 percent of non-Hispanic whites and 57 percent of non-Hispanic blacks. The rate is even lower for foreign-born Hispanics compared to native-born Hispanics—29 percent versus 53 percent.[80] Over time, the proportion of Hispanics covered by an employer-sponsored plan has decreased (from 32 percent in 1989 to 27 percent in 2010), while white non-Hispanic coverage increased (from 48 percent to 50 percent) over the same time period. Similarly, there has been a shift from defined benefit (DB) plans to defined contribution (DC) plans, mostly to 401(k) plans, and the enrollment in DB plans is automatic while the enrollment of DC plans is voluntary.[81]

Along with limited access to retirement plans Hispanics have lower wealth accumulation in such plans. They have on average $54,000 less in savings when compared to the average balance for all ethno-racial groups—about $69,000.[82] Furthermore, they tend to have the highest poverty rates in old age, which they also tend to carry over the life course.[83] This situation is even more disadvantageous for foreign-born Hispanics, especially for those who are undocumented. Undocumented Hispanics usually contribute to Social Security; however, they are not eligible to receive benefits because they do not meet the requirements. Moreover, twice as many native-born Hispanics than foreign-born Hispanics receive employer-sponsored pension benefits, yet native-born Hispanics are 14 percent less likely to receive Social Security than non-Hispanics.[84]

Finally, lifelong financial disadvantage, inadequate savings, and longer life expectancies put Hispanics at a higher risk of experiencing poverty and of relying on Social Security (SS) and Medicaid at old age.[85] Hispanics aged sixty-five and older are three times more likely than non-Hispanics to live in poverty—about 19 percent versus 7 percent.[86] Over 70 percent of Hispanics rely on SS for at least half of their income, and over 30 percent of Hispanics rely on it for at least 90 percent of their income, compared to 61 percent and 24 percent of non-Hispanics, respectively.[87] Even if they tend to rely more on Social Security compared to non-Hispanic whites, Hispanics are less likely to benefit from SS—about 75 percent of Hispanics receive SS compared to 90 percent of non-Hispanic whites, as many of them do not have the minimum requirements to make a claim.[88] Furthermore, Hispanics over sixty-five years of age are more likely than non-Hispanics to rely solely on Medicare or Medicare Advantage—47 percent versus 41 percent, and are less likely to complement it with other health insurance.[89] Hispanics are less likely than any other ethno-racial group to supplement their health coverage with employer-sponsored health coverage—14 percent of Hispanics, compared to 32 percent of whites. In addition, Hispanics (22 percent) are more likely than non-Hispanic whites to supplement Medicare with Medicaid.[90]

Retirement preparedness and well-being are influenced by one's financial behavior and circumstances earlier in life. Researchers have found that life trajectories influence later-life well-being, and later-life inequalities can be traced to preretirement years.[91,92] Similarly, evidence suggests that retirement experiences and outcomes are shaped to a very large extent by career trajectories.[93] For Hispanics, the possibility of and planning for extended work life might not be as straightforward as it is for other groups that tend to have better employment opportunities and more stable job histories.

## RETIREMENT TIMING: EXPECTATIONS VERSUS REALITY

In the U.S., most workers (over 70 percent) plan to work for pay at age sixty-five and older.[94] Evidence suggests that in order to make ends meet, workers intend to stay on the job longer.[95] According to U.S. Federal Reserve data, among people aged fifty-five to sixty-four who have not retired yet, 79 percent state that they plan to work for pay in retirement. Moreover, 38 percent reported that they planned to retire at seventy years or older, while 26 percent reported they planned to retire before age sixty-five years, 23 percent planned to retire at age sixty-five, and 14 percent planned to retire between sixty-five and sixty-nine years.[96] Even if people say they plan to continue to work at old age, a large percentage of people are not meeting those expectations. About 50 percent of retirees of all racial/ethnic groups retired earlier than they planned, and of those only

24 percent retired earlier because they realized they could afford it, while others retired earlier when facing health hardship or changes at their companies.[97]

For all the reasons already discussed, Hispanics are more likely than non-Hispanics to state they do not know when they will retire.[98] However, researchers have found that Hispanics are less likely to postpone or plan to postpone retirement when compared to their non-Hispanic counterparts.[99,100] Evidence suggests there are ethno-racial differences regarding retirement intentions and behavior.[101] Research about retirement timing, conducted mostly in the U.S. with middle-class whites, suggests that those who tend to work longer are wealthier, have higher levels of education, have good health, and are males (as indicated in the overview). However, with the lowest level of education than all other ethno-racial groups in the U.S., Hispanics are overrepresented in low-wage jobs, which are also associated with limited access to pension plans and health insurance and with less flexibility and labor stability.[102,103] Therefore, there might be extra hardships for Hispanics when planning to retire or delay retirement.

Despite their insistence that they do not know when they will retire and apparent determination not to retire before age sixty-five,[104] Hispanics are retiring earlier than other ethno-racial groups, as depicted in figure 6.1.

Based on Health and Retirement Study/RAND data (1992–2014)[105] and as depicted in table 6.1, it is possible to infer that the overall planned and actual retirement age has been increasing over the last two decades for Hispanics and non-Hispanics. However, foreign-born Hispanics are less likely to state they plan to retire at sixty-one or younger, compared to white non-Hispanics and native-born Hispanics. Moreover, all respondents were more likely to state they will "never" retire.

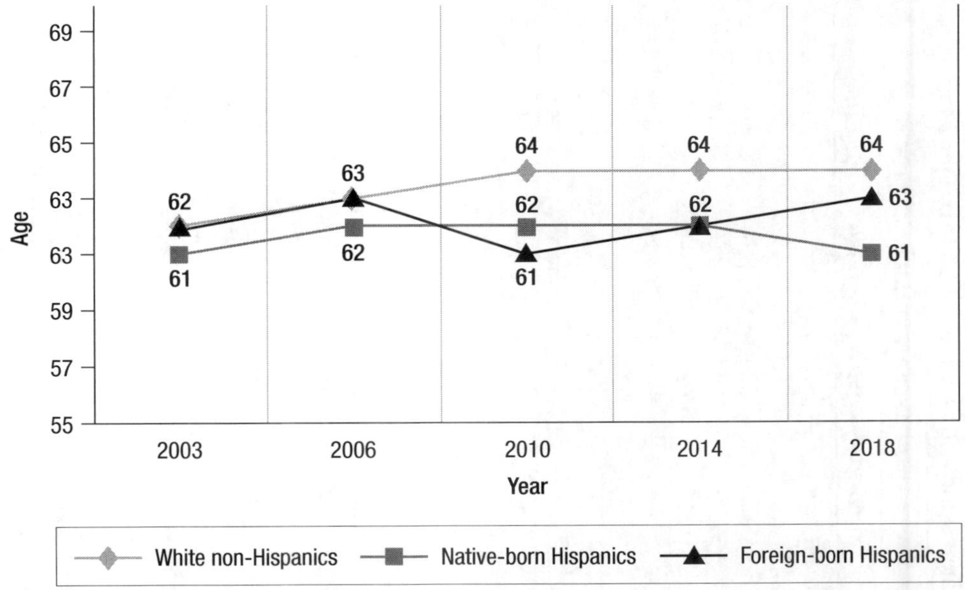


**FIGURE 6.1.** Average Retirement Age by Race and Ethnicity Using CPS Data. Note: Average retirement age is measured as the age at which the employment rate drops under 50 percent.

*Source:* Díaz-Valdes I., A., based on U.S. Census Bureau's Current Population Survey, 2017.

**TABLE 6.1.** Planned and Actual Retirement Age by Ethno-racial Group over Time

| | *White Non-Hispanics* | | | | *Native-Born Hispanics* | | | | *Foreign-Born Hispanics* | | | |
|---|---|---|---|---|---|---|---|---|---|---|---|---|
| | *1992* | *1998* | *2002* | *2014* | *1992* | *1998* | *2002* | *2014* | *1992* | *1998* | *2002* | *2014* |
| ***Planned Retirement Year*** | | | | | | | | | | | | |
| Younger than 62 years | 15% | 9% | 5% | 3% | 19% | 13% | 6% | 3% | 8% | 2% | 5% | 2% |
| | (1,024) | (529) | (214) | (107) | (63) | (31) | (13) | (11) | (33) | (7%) | (15) | (17) |
| 62–64 years | 25% | 11% | 8% | 7% | 26% | 11% | 14% | 8% | 29% | 15% | 11% | 9% |
| | (1,683) | (690) | (349) | (257) | (84) | (26) | (32) | (28) | (120) | (43) | (32) | (60) |
| 65 years | 17% | 12% | 10% | 10% | 17% | 18% | 10% | 13% | 20% | 17% | 9% | 16% |
| | (1,153) | (734) | (459) | (392) | (54) | (45) | (24) | (45) | (84) | (48) | (24) | (113) |
| 66–70 years | 11% | 8% | 14% | 19% | 11% | 5% | 11% | 22% | 10% | 7% | 10% | 14% |
| | (726) | (478) | (660) | (741) | (36) | (13) | (25) | (74) | (42) | (20) | (27) | (95) |
| Over 70 years | 2% | 9% | 9% | 14% | 2% | 2% | 7% | 11% | 3% | 2% | 2% | 4% |
| | (165) | (529) | (403) | (554) | (6) | (5) | (16) | (39) | (13) | (5) | (5) | (25) |
| Never | 30% | 51% | 55% | 47% | 26% | 51% | 52% | 42% | 31% | 57% | 63% | 56% |
| | (2,046) | (3,107) | (2,520) | (1,812) | (85) | (124) | (120) | (144) | (129) | (166) | (178) | (395) |
| ***Actual Retirement Year*** | | | | | | | | | | | | |
| Younger than 62 years | 51% | 41% | 39% | 19% | 62% | 47% | 27% | 18% | 39% | 43% | 20% | 15% |
| | (270) | (217) | (158) | (19) | (18) | (9) | (7) | (2) | (11) | (12) | (9) | (2) |
| 62–64 years | 24% | 26% | 26% | 21% | 28% | 26% | 39% | 46% | 32% | 32% | 49% | 46% |
| | (129) | (136) | (105) | (21) | (8) | (5) | (10) | (5) | (9) | (9) | (22) | (6) |
| 65 years | 5% | 6% | 7% | 13% | 3% | 0% | 12% | 0% | 4% | 7% | 18% | 23% |
| | (27) | (32) | (30) | (13) | (1) | (0) | (3) | (0) | (1) | (2) | (8) | (3) |
| 66–70 years | 13% | 15% | 16% | 29% | 3% | 26% | 19% | 18% | 14% | 11% | 9% | 15% |
| | (67) | (78) | (65) | (28) | (1) | (5) | (5) | (2) | (4) | (3) | (4) | (2) |
| Over 70 years | 8% | 12% | 12% | 17% | 3% | 0% | 4% | 18% | 11% | 7% | 4% | 0% |
| | (42) | (61) | (49) | (17) | (1) | (0) | (1) | (2) | (3) | (2) | (2) | (0) |

*Source:* Health and Retirement Study/RAND data, 1992–2014.

Even if Hispanics intend to work longer and delay retirement, they might not be able to fulfill those expectations, owing to limited employment opportunities in old age, poorer health resulting from lack of access to health care, and limited saving capacity throughout the life course.[106] Since Hispanics tend to have higher poverty rates in old age and rely mostly on Social Security, they could greatly benefit from extended work lives, not just in financial terms, but also because having the choice to postpone retirement, for those who are physically and mentally able to work and who want to work, can lead to better health and well-being.[107,108] (See also chapter 19.) Thus, it is important to understand Hispanics' uniqueness regarding retirement planning and timing, because this would help greatly to improve their lives as they age.

## HISPANICS' INTENTIONS TO WORK LONGER VIEWED THROUGH THE PRODUCTIVE AGING FRAMEWORK

The productive aging framework states that engaging in productive activities in old age can lead to better health outcomes and well-being of older adults. Productive aging theory has been based mostly on white Americans without considering that minorities often assign different meanings to different roles and, therefore, that engagement in different activities could lead to different effects.[109] Engagement refers to the individual's experience of meaningfully connecting to such role(s).[110] There are several definitions of productive activities. The broadest definition includes activities that are personally and financially productive, such as recreation, leisure, and paid work.[111] (See also chapter 14.)

Cultural and ethno-racial diversity within the U.S. population calls for a better understanding of productive engagement among older adults, whose numbers and ethno-racial diversity are projected to increase in the following decades.[112] For instance, Hispanics and non-Hispanics describe aging differently.[113] While Hispanics tend to have a positive view of aging focused on the present and social relationships, non-Hispanics tend to focus on the past and the future and coping. What's more, Hispanics recognize that retirement is different for them compared to what it was for their parents; they say they feel younger and more energized.[114] As discussed previously, there are substantial differences between Hispanics and non-Hispanics regarding health and well-being at old age. Hispanics enjoy better health while young and during the working years, despite their financial disadvantages—what some have called the *Hispanic health paradox*.[115] However, the prevalence of chronic diseases as a result of lifelong deprivation, and the disability rates at ages sixty-five and older, tend to match or even surpass non-Hispanic whites' prevalence and rates,[116,117] which suggests a higher detrimental effect of aging for Hispanics than for non-Hispanics. Hispanics and non-Hispanics also tend to report similar levels of mental health disorders during their lifetimes.[118,119,120] However, as a group, Hispanics tend to report greater happiness and life satisfaction than non-Hispanic whites—what is known as the *Hispanic happiness paradox*.[121]

The effect of retirement timing on health and well-being is mixed. Researchers have found that retirement has a reversible detrimental effect on cognition[122] and a positive effect on mental health and well-being,[123] but no effect on incidence of certain physical illnesses.[124] Evidence suggests that working conditions influence the association between retirement and health and/or well-being: for those who work in low-quality jobs with poor conditions, retirement has a positive effect on health and well-being.[125,126] There is also evidence that individuals' experiences during the preretirement years and the time at which they retired compared to normative cultural and institution-specified time are predictors of health and well-being in retirement.[127,128] Furthermore, retiring *involuntarily* is associated with poorer health and well-being in retirement.[129,130] Thus, Hispanics' unique circumstances often influence their retirement outcomes differently, when compared to non-Hispanics.

Even Hispanics who plan to continue to work in later life are apt to encounter complications that interfere with fulfilling their expectations. This is especially true of lower-educated Hispanics. Higher-income Hispanics report having flexibility to reduce working hours or switch careers, while lower-income respondents report limited opportunities and set working hours they could not reduce due to employer inflexibility or the risk of financial hardship. Lower-income Hispanics also report being forced to leave their jobs to fulfill caregiving responsibilities.[131] This is particularly important for one of the most disadvantaged groups in the U.S., given their lower educational levels and limited English proficiency.

When Hispanics retire later than planned because they cannot afford to stop, and they are exposed to poor working conditions, their health and well-being in later life can be negatively affected. Similarly, the inability to fulfill retirement expectations might negatively influence their health and well-being. Then, too, involuntary early retirement owing to lack of job opportunities and/or for personal reasons (e.g., layoff, lack of flexibility in the workplace, failing health, need to take care of the family) has been linked to worsening outcomes during retirement, as the productive aging hypothesis would suggest. However, and in line with the "role overload hypothesis," those who are stressed and experience poor working conditions might find relief in retirement, as they can leave behind some of those problems.[132] Still, financial need might outweigh the relief of leaving the job, and Hispanics might not be able to afford retirement. This vulnerable economic situation, especially for foreign-born Hispanics, prevents wealth accumulation, which in turn limits retirement preparedness and savings.

Further research should continue to explore ethno-racial differences as part of efforts to promote better retirement preparedness and outcomes among Hispanics. We need culturally relevant interventions and policies that move from an individualistic view to a collectivist view, to increase Hispanic engagement in such programs. Furthermore, identifying interventions and programs that reduce the educational gap are a must—for example, recognizing that Hispanics prefer to receive information about retirement planning and saving through email, through physical mail, and via the Social Security Administration website rather than in person.[133] Generating noncontact and culturally relevant tools would be a good strategy to increase financial literacy and financial capability among Hispanics.[134]

## NOTES

1. John M. Glionna. January 2016. "Too Poor to Retire and Too Young to Die." *Los Angeles Times*:1. (https://graphics.latimes.com/retirement-nomads/?track=lat-pick).

2. Alicia H. Munnell. April 2015. "Falling Short: The Coming Retirement Crisis and What to do About It." *Issue Brief* 15(7):1–8. Chestnut Hill, MA: Center for Retirement Research, Boston College. (https://crr.bc.edu/wp-content/uploads/2015/04/IB_15-7_508.pdf).

3. Diana M. DiNitto and David H. Johnson. 2012. *The Essentials of Social Welfare: Politics and Public Policy. Connecting Core Competencies Series*. Boston: Allyn & Bacon.

4. Catherine P. Montalto, Yoonkyung Yuh, and Sherman D. Hanna. May 2000. "Determinants of Planned Retirement Age." *Financial Services Review* 9(1):1–15. (10.1016/S1057-0810(00)00052-4).

5. DiNitto and Johnson, *Essentials of Social Welfare*.

6. Alicia H. Munnell and Steven S. Sass. 2008. *Working Longer: The Solution to the Retirement Income Challenges*. Washington, DC: Brookings Institution.

7. Tay K. McNamara and John Williamson. 2013. *Unequal Prospects: Is Working Longer the Answer?* New York: Taylor & Francis.

8. John B. Williamson and Tay K. McNamara. November 2001. "Why Some Workers Remain in the Labor Force beyond the Typical Age of Retirement." Chestnut Hill, MA: Center for Retirement Research, Boston College. *CRR Working Paper* 2001-09. (http://crr.bc.edu/working-papers/why-some-workers-remain-in-the-labor-force-beyond-the-typical-age-of-retirement/).

9. Alicia H. Munnell, Robert K. Triest, and Natalia Jivan. November 2004. "How Do Pensions Affect Expected and Actual Retirement Ages?" Chestnut Hill, MA: Center for Retirement Research, Boston College. *CRR Working Paper* 2004-27. (http://crr.bc.edu/working-papers/how-do-pensions-affect-expected-and-actual-retirement-ages/).

10. Luisa Blanco et al. March 2015. "Retirement Planning among Middle-aged and Older Hispanics." Malibu, CA: Pepperdine University, School of Public Policy, *Working Paper* 54. (http://digitalcommons.pepperdine.edu/sppworkingpapers/54).

11. Blanco et al., "Retirement Planning among Middle-aged and Older Hispanics."

12. U.S. Census Bureau. 2017. "Current Population Survey 2017." (https://www.census.gov/cps/data/cpstablecreator.html).

13. Rocio Calvo, Dawn Carr, and Christina Matz-Costa. August 2017. "Expanding the Happiness Paradox: Ethno-racial Disparities in Life Satisfaction among Older Immigrants in the United States." *Journal of Aging and Health* 3(2):231–55. (https://doi.org/10.1177/0898264317726608).

14. Megan C. Lytle et al. May 2015. "Current Trends in Retirement: Implications for Career Counseling and Vocational Psychology." *Journal of Career Development* 42(3):170–84. (10.1177/0894845314545785).

15. Angela O'Rand. 2009. "Cumulative Processes in the Life Course." In *The Craft of Life Course Research*, edited by Glen H. Elder Jr. and Janet Z. Giele. London: Guilford Press.

16. Glen H. Elder Jr., Monica Kirkpatrick Johnson, and Robert Crosnoe. 2006. "The Emergence and Development of Life Course Theory." In *Handbook of the Life Course*, edited by Jeylan T. Mortimer and Michael J. Shanahan. Berlin, Germany: Springer.

17. Luisa Blanco et al. July–September 2017. "Retirement Planning among Hispanics: In God's Hands?" *Journal of Aging & Social Policy* 24(9):311–31. (http://dx.doi.org/10.1080/08959420.2016.1272161).

18. Antonio Flores. September 2017a. "Facts on U.S. Latinos, 2015: Statistical Portrait of Hispanics in the United States." (http://www.pewhispanic.org/2017/09/18/facts-on-u-s-latinos/#share-mexican-origin).

19. U.S. Census Bureau, "Current Population Survey 2017."

20. Richard W. Johnson, Stipica Mudrazija, and Claire X. Wang. June 2017. "Hispanics' Retirement Transitions and Differences by Nativity." *Journal of Aging and Health* 19(6):1096–115. (https://doi.org/10.1177/0898264317711608).

21. Flores, "Facts on U.S. Latinos, 2015."

22. U.S. Census Bureau, "Current Population Survey 2017."

23. Antonio Flores. September 18, 2017b. "How the U.S. Hispanic Population Is Changing." Washington, DC: Pew Research Center, Fact Tank. (http://www.pewhispanic.org/2017/09/18/facts-on-u-s-latinos/).

24. Örn B. Bodvarsson and Hendrik F. Van den Berg. 2009. "Hispanic Immigration to the United States." Pp. 315–41 in *The Economics of Immigration: Theory and Policy*, edited by Örn B. Bodvarsson and Hendrik F. Van den Berg. New York: Springer-Verlag.

25. Marta Tienda and Faith Mitchell. 2006. *Multiple Origins, Uncertain Destinies: Hispanics and the American Future*. Washington, DC: National Academies Press.

26. Tienda and Mitchell, *Multiple Origins, Uncertain Destinies.*

27. Ronald J. Angel and Jacqueline Angel. 2015. *Latinos in an Aging World: Social, Psychological, and Economic Perspective*. New York: Routledge.

28. Angel and Angel, *Latinos in an Aging World.*

29. Angel and Angel, *Latinos in an Aging World.*

30. Johnson, Mudrazija and Wang, "Hispanics' Retirement Transitions."

31. Tienda and Mitchell, *Multiple Origins, Uncertain Destinies.*

32. Stipica Mudrazija and Jacqueline L. Angel. 2014. "Diversity and the Economic Security of Older Americans." Pp. 138–54 in *The New Politics*, edited by Robert B. Hudson. Baltimore: Johns Hopkins University Press.

33. Flores, "Facts on U.S. Latinos, 2015."

34. Tienda and Mitchell, *Multiple Origins, Uncertain Destinies.*

35. Tienda and Mitchell, *Multiple Origins, Uncertain Destinies.*

36. Tienda and Mitchell, *Multiple Origins, Uncertain Destinies.*

37. U.S. Census Bureau, "Current Population Survey 2017."

38. U.S. Census Bureau, "Current Population Survey 2017."

39. Centers for Disease Control and Prevention. 2018. "Summary Health Statistics (2013–2018)." National Center for Health Statistics: Summary Tables. (https://www.cdc.gov/nchs/nhis/shs/tables.htm).

40. Tienda and Mitchell, *Multiple Origins, Uncertain Destinies.*

41. Tienda and Mitchell, *Multiple Origins, Uncertain Destinies.*

42. Angel and Angel, *Latinos in an Aging World.*

43. Tienda and Mitchell, *Multiple Origins, Uncertain Destinies.*

44. Tienda and Mitchell, *Multiple Origins, Uncertain Destinies.*

45. Jeffrey S. Passel and D'vera Cohn. November 27, 2018. "U.S. Unauthorized Immigrant Total Dips to Lowest Level in a Decade." Washington, DC: Pew Research Center. (http://www.pewhispanic.org/2018/11/27/u-s-unauthorized-immigrant-total-dips-to-lowest-level-in-a-decade/).

46. Pew Research Center. November 27, 2016. "Unauthorized Immigrant Population Trends for States, Birth Countries and Regions." Washington, DC: Pew Research Center. (http://www.pewhispanic.org/interactives/unauthorized-trends/).

47. Tienda and Mitchell, *Multiple Origins, Uncertain Destinies.*

48. Jacqueline L. Angel. 2008. *Inheritance in Contemporary America: The Social Dimension of Giving across Generations.* Baltimore: Johns Hopkins University Press.

49. Karen Richman et al. February 2012. *Confianza, Savings, and Retirement: A Study of Mexican Immigrants.* Research Report 2012.1. Notre Dame, IN: University of Notre Dame Institute for Latino Studies. (https://latinostudies.nd.edu/assets/95267/original/confianza_savings_retirement.pdf).

50. Angel, *Inheritance in Contemporary America.*

51. Richman et al., *Confianza, Savings, and Retirement.*

52. Brent Berry. November 2006. "What Accounts for Race and Ethnic Differences in Parental Financial Transfers to Adult Children in the United States?" *Journal of Family Issues* 27(11):1583–1604. (https://doi.org/10.1177/0192513X06291498).

53. Angel, *Inheritance in Contemporary America.*

54. Angel, *Inheritance in Contemporary America.*

55. Richman et al., *Confianza, Savings, and Retirement.*

56. Berry, "What Accounts for Race."

57. Richman et al., *Confianza, Savings, and Retirement.*

58. Richman et al., *Confianza, Savings, and Retirement.*

59. Blanco et al., "Retirement Planning among Middle-aged and Older Hispanics."

60. Karen Richman et al. June 2008. *La Tercera Edad: Latinos' Pensions, Retirement, and Impact on Families.* Research Report 2008.1. Notre Dame, IN: University of Notre Dame Institute for Latino Studies. (https://www.researchgate.net/publication/237581893_La_Tercera_Edad_Latinos'_Pensions_Retirement_and_Impact_on_Families).

61. Richman et al., *Confianza, Savings, and Retirement.*

62. Cheboa Flippen and Marta Tienda. January 2000. "Pathways to Retirement: Patterns of Labor Force Participation and Labor Market Exit among the Pre-retirement by Race, Hispanic Origin, and Sex." *Journal of Gerontology* 51(1):14–27. (https://doiorg./10.1093/geronb/55.1.S14).

63. Antonia Díaz-Valdes. 2019. "Retirement Intentions and Behaviors of Hispanics Compared to Non-Hispanics in the United States: A Three-paper Dissertation." PhD dissertation. Boston College, Chestnut Hill, MA.

64. Wei Sun, Gia Barboza, and Karen Richman. December 2007. "Preparing for the Future: Latinos' Financial Literacy and Retirement Planning." *Business Journal of Hispanics Research* 1(2):54–68. (https://latinostudies.nd.edu/assets/95325/original/preparing_for_the_future.pdf).

65. Blanco et al., "Retirement Planning among Middle-aged and Older Hispanics."

66. Blanco et al., "Retirement Planning among Middle-aged and Older Hispanics."

67. Angel and Angel, *Latinos in an Aging World.*

68. National Council of La Raza. July 2005. "Retirement Security for Latinos." (http://publications.nclr.org/handle/123456789/888).

69. Richman et al., *Confianza, Savings, and Retirement.*

70. Social Security Administration. April 2016. "Income of the Population 55 or Older, 2014." (https://www.ssa.gov/policy/docs/statcomps/income_pop55/2014/index.html).

71. Angel and Angel, *Latinos in an Aging World.*

72. Angel and Angel, *Latinos in an Aging World.*

73. Richman et al., *Confianza, Savings, and Retirement.*

74. Angel and Angel, *Latinos in an Aging World.*

75. Tienda and Mitchell, *Multiple Origins, Uncertain Destinies.*

76. Richman et al., *Confianza, Savings, and Retirement.*

77. Angel and Angel, *Latinos in an Aging World.*

78. Johnson, Mudrazija, and Wang, "Hispanics' Retirement Transitions."

79. Jacqueline L. Angel, Kate Prickett, and Ronald J. Angel. 2014. "Retirement Security for Black, Non-Hispanic White, and Mexican-origin Women: The Changing Roles of Marriage and Work." *Journal of Women, Politics & Policy* 3(53):222–41. (https://doi.org/10.1080/1554477X.2014.921541).

80. Angel and Angel, *Latinos in an Aging World.*

81. Richard W. Johnson, Stipica Mudrazija, and Claire X. Wang. September 2016. *Hispanics' Retirement Security: Past Trends and Future Prospects.* Research Report. Washington, DC: Urban Institute. (https://www.dol.gov/sites/default/files/ebsa/researchers/analysis/retirement/hispanics-retirement-security-past-trends-and-future-prospects.pdf).

82. Monique Morrissey. September 11, 2013. "Blacks and Hispanics Are Falling behind Whites in Retirement Coverage." Washington, DC: Economic Policy Institute, *The Retirement Inequality Chartbook.* (https://www.epi.org/publication/snapshot-blacks-hispanics-whites-retirement/).

83. Angel and Angel, *Latinos in an Aging World.*

84. U.S. Census Bureau, "Current Population Survey 2017."

85. Johnson, Mudrazija, and Wang, "Hispanics' Retirement Transitions."

86. Angel and Angel, *Latinos in an Aging World.*

87. Johnson, Mudrazija, and Wang, "Hispanics' Retirement Transitions."

88. Johnson, Mudrazija, and Wang, "Hispanics' Retirement Transitions."

89. Holly Birkett, Fiona Carmichael, and Joanne Duberley. December 2017. "Activity in the Third Age: Examining the Relationship between Careers and Retirement Experiences." *Journal of Vocational Behavior* 103:55–65. (https://doi.org/10.1016/j.jvb.2017.08.002).

90. Henry J. Kaiser Family Foundation. 2016. "Profile of Medicare Beneficiaries by Race and Ethnicity: A Chartpack." (http://files.kff.org/attachment/chartpack-profile-of-medicare-beneficiaries-by-race-and-ethnicity-a-chartpack).

91. Centers for Disease Control and Prevention. "Summary Health Statistics (2013–2018)."

92. Melissa Hardy and Adriana M. Reyes. 2016. "Theories of Work and Retirement: Culture, Trust, and the Social Contract." In *Handbook of Theories of Aging*, edited by Vern L. Bengston and Richard A. Settersen Jr. New York: Springer.

93. Stephen Crystal, Dennis G. Shea, and Adriana M. Reyes. October 2017. "Cumulative Advantage, Cumulative Disadvantage, and Evolving Patterns of Late-life Inequality." *The Gerontologist* 57(5):910–20. (https://doi.org/10.1093/geront/gnw056).

94. Birkett, Carmichael, and Duberley, "Activity in the Third Age."

95. Employment Benefit Research Institute (EBRI). March 21, 2017. "Retirement Confidence Survey." Washington, DC. (https://www.ebri.org/surveys/rcs/2017/).

96. U.S. Federal Reserve Data. 2014. "Federal Reserve Board Issues Report on the Economic Well-being of U.S. Households in 2013." Washington, DC: Board of Governors of the Federal Reserve System. (https://www.federalreserve.gov/econresdata/2013-report-economic-well-being-us-households-201407.pdf).

97. EBRI, "Retirement Confidence Survey," 3.

98. U.S. Federal Reserve Data, "Federal Reserve Board Issues Report."

99. Employment Benefit Research Institute (EBRI). June 5, 2007. "2007 Minority Retirement Confidence Survey." Washington, DC. (https://www.ebri.org/surveys/mrcs/).

100. Geoffrey Sanzenbacher, Steven A. Sass, and Christopher Gillis. February 2017. "How Job Changes Affect Retirement Timing by Socioeconomic Status." *Issue Brief* 17(3):1–8. Chestnut Hill, MA: Center for Retirement Research, Boston College. (http://crr.bc.edu/briefs/how-job-changes-affect-retirement-timing-by-socioeconomic-status/).

101. Lytle et al. "Current Trends in Retirement Implications."

102. Montalto, Yuh, and Hanna, "Determinants of Planned Retirement Age."

103. U.S. Census Bureau, "Current Population Survey 2017."

104. U.S. Census Bureau, "Current Population Survey 2017."

105. RAND. 2018. "RAND HRS Longitudinal File, February, 2018." Funded by the National Institute of Aging and the Social Security Administration; distributed by RAND. (https://ssl.isr.umich.edu/hrs/files2.php).

106. EBRI, "2007 Minority Retirement Confidence Survey."

107. Scott A. Bass and Francis G. Caro. 2001. "Productive Aging: A Conceptual Framework." Pp. 37–80 in *Productive Aging: Concepts and Challenges*, edited by Nancy Morrow-Howell, James Hinterlong, and Michael Sherraden. Baltimore: Johns Hopkins University Press.

108. Stefanie König, Magnus Lindwall, and Boo Johansson. November 2018. "Involuntary and Delayed Retirement as a Possible Health Risk for Lower Educated Retirees." *Journal of Population Ageing*:1–15. (https://doi.org/10.1007/s12062-018-9234-6).

109. Jennifer Hale-Gallardo, Hisako Matsuo, and Lisa Willoughby. June 2013. "Exploring Successful Aging among Foreign-born Latinos and Other Immigrant Groups in Saint Louis, Missouri." (https://mospace.umsystem.edu/xmlui/handle/10355/48889).

110. Bass and Caro, "Productive Aging."

111. Christina Matz-Costa, et al. April 2014. "Differential Impact of Multiple Levels of Productive Activity Engagement on Psychological Well-being in Middle and Later Life." *The Gerontologist* 54(2):277–89. (https://doi.org/10.1093/geront/gns148).

112. Ernest Gonzales, Christina Matz-Costa, and Nancy Morrow-Howell. April 2015. "Increasing Opportunities for the Productive Engagement of Older Adults: A Response to Population Aging." *The Gerontologist* 55(2):252–61. (https://doi.org/10.1093/geront/gnu176).

113. U.S. Census Bureau, "Current Population Survey 2017."

114. Jeanne M. Hilton et al. July 2012. "Perceptions of Successful Aging among Older Latinos, in Cross-cultural Context." *Journal of Cross Cultural Gerontology* 27:183–99. (https://doi.org/10.1007/s10823-012-9171-4).

115. Nicole Ruggiano, Janice O'Driscoll, and Andreja Lukic. February 2017. "'Work Is Like a Therapy That Prevents Aging': Perceptions of Retirement, Productivity, and Health among Minorities and Immigrants." *Sage Open, Special Issue*:1–11. (https://doi.org/10.1177/2158244016687234).

116. Calvo, Carr, and Matz-Costa, "Expanding the Happiness Paradox."

117. Joseph J. Sudano and David W. Baker. 2006. "Explaining U.S. Racial/Ethnic Disparities in Health Declines and Mortality in Late Middle Age: The Roles of Socio-economic Status, Health Behaviors, and Health Insurance." *Social Science & Medicine* 62(4):909–22. (https://doi.org/10.1016/j.socscimed.2005.06.041).

118. Calvo, Carr, and Matz-Costa, "Expanding the Happiness Paradox."

119. U.S. Census Bureau, "Current Population Survey 2017."

120. Margarita Alegría et al. March 2008. "Prevalence of Mental Illness in Immigrant and Non-immigrant U.S. Latino Groups." *American Journal of Psychiatry* 165(3):359–69.

121. Hector M. González et al. 2010. "The Epidemiology of Major Depression and Ethnicity in the United States." *Journal of Psychiatric Research* 44:1043–51. (https://doi.org/10.1016/j.jpsychires.2010.03.017).

122. Calvo, Carr, and Matz-Costa, "Expanding the Happiness Paradox."

123. Sean A. P. Clouston and Nicole Denier. April 2017. "Mental Retirement and Health Selection: Analyses from the U.S. Health and Retirement Study." *Journal of Social Science & Medicine* 178:78–86. (http://dx.doi.org/10.1016/j.socscimed.2017.01.019).

124. Elizabeth Mokyr Horner and Mark Cullen. 2016. "The Impact of Retirement on Health: Quasi-experimental Methods Using Administrative Data." *BMC Service Research* 16:1–9. (10.1186/s12913-016-1318-5).

125. Ehsan Latif. 2011. "The Impact of Retirement on Psychological Well-being in Canada." *Journal of Socio-economics* 40:373-80. (https://doi.org/10.1016/j.socec.2010.12.011).

126. Peter Eibich. September 2015. "Understanding the Effect of Retirement on Health: Mechanisms and Heterogeneity." *Journal of Health Economics* 43:1–12. (https://doi.org/10.1016/j.jhealeco.2015.05.001).

127. Alan Marshall and James Nazroo. August 2015. "Trajectories in the Prevalence of Self-reported Illness around Retirement." *Journal of Population Ageing* 9:11–48. (https://doi.org/10.1007/s12062-015-9130-2).

128. Katey Matthews. 2014. "Is Working beyond State Pension Age Beneficial for Health? Evidence from the English Longitudinal Study of Ageing." Doctoral thesis. University of Manchester, Manchester, England.

129. Esteban Calvo, Natasha Sarkisian, and Christopher Tamborini. January 2013. "Causal Effects of Retirement Timing on Subjective Physical and Emotional Health." *Journals of Gerontology, Series B: Psychological Sciences and Social Sciences*, 68(1):73–84. (https://doi.org/10.1093/geronb/gbs097).

130. König, Lindwall, and Johansson, "Involuntary and Delayed Retirement."

131. William T. Gallo et al. May 2000. "Health Effect of Involuntary Job Loss among Older Workers: Findings from the Health and Retirement Study." *Journal of Gerontology* 55B(3):S131-40. (https://doi.org/10.1093/geronb/55.3.s131).

132. Ruggiano, O'Driscoll, and Lukic, "'Work Is Like a Therapy That Prevents Aging.'"

133. Stephanie Creary and Judith R. Gordon. 2016. "Role Conflict, Role Overload, and Role Strain." In *The Wiley Blackwell Encyclopedia of Family Studies*, edited by Stephanie Creary and Judith R. Gordon. Hoboken, NJ: Wiley Blackwell.

134. Lila Rabinovich et al. 2016. "Preparing for Retirement, Social Security Literacy and Information Preferences among Hispanics: A Qualitative Study." *CESR-Schaeffer Working Paper Series*, 2016-12. Los Angeles: Center for Economic and Social Research, University of Southern California. (https://cesr.usc.edu/documents/WP_2016_012.pdf).

## REFERENCES


Alegría, Margarita, et al. March 2008. "Prevalence of Mental Illness in Immigrant and Non-immigrant U.S. Latino Groups." *American Journal of Psychiatry* 165(3):359–69.

Angel, Jacqueline L. 2008. *Inheritance in Contemporary America: The Social Dimension of Giving across Generations*. Baltimore: Johns Hopkins University Press.

Angel, Jacqueline L., Kate Prickett, and Ronald J. Angel. July 2014. "Retirement Security for Black, Non-Hispanic White, and Mexican-origin Women: The Changing Roles of Marriage and Work." *Journal of Women, Politics & Policy* 3(53):222–41. (https://doi.org/10.1080/1554477X.2014.921541).

Angel, Ronald J. and Jacqueline Angel. 2015. *Latinos in an Aging World: Social, Psychological, and Economic Perspective*. New York: Routledge.

Bass, Scott A. and Francis G. Caro. 2001. "Productive Aging: A Conceptual Framework." Pp. 37–80 in *Productive Aging: Concepts and Challenges*, edited by Nancy Morrow-Howell, James Hinterlong, and Michael Sherraden. Baltimore: Johns Hopkins University Press.

Berry, Brent. November 2006. "What Accounts for Race and Ethnic Differences in Parental Financial Transfers to Adult Children in the United States?" *Journal of Family Issues* 27(11):1583–1604. (https://doi.org/10.1177/0192513X06291498).

Birkett, Holly, Fiona Carmichael, and Joanne Duberley. December 2017. "Activity in the Third Age: Examining the Relationship between Careers and Retirement Experiences." *Journal of Vocational Behavior* 103:55–65. (https://doi.org/10.1016/j.jvb.2017.08.002).

Blanco, Luisa, et al. March 2015. "Retirement Planning among Middle-aged and Older Hispanics." Malibu, CA: Pepperdine University, School of Public Policy. *Working Paper* 54. (http://digitalcommons.pepperdine.edu/sppworkingpapers/54).

Blanco, Luisa., et al. July–September 2017. "Retirement Planning among Hispanics: In God's Hands?" *Journal of Aging & Social Policy* 24(9):311–31. (http://dx.doi.org/10.1080/08959420.2016.1272161).

Bodvarsson, Örn B. and Hendrik F. Van den Berg. 2009. "Hispanic Immigration to the United States." Pp. 315–41 in *The Economics of Immigration: Theory and Policy*, edited by Örn B. Bodvarsson and Hendrik F. Van den Berg. New York: Springer-Verlag.

Calvo, Esteban, Natasha Sarkisian, and Christopher Tamborini. January 2013. "Causal Effects of Retirement Timing on Subjective Physical and Emotional Health." *Journals of Gerontology, Series B: Psychological Sciences and Social Sciences* 68(1):73–84. (https://doi.org/10.1093/geronb/gbs097).

Calvo, Rocío, Dawn Carr, and Christina Matz-Costa. August 2017. "Expanding the Happiness Paradox: Ethno-racial Disparities in Life Satisfaction among Older Immigrants in the United States." *Journal of Aging and Health* 3(2):231–55. (https://doi.org/10.1177/0898264317726608).

Centers for Disease Control and Prevention. 2018. "Summary Health Statistics (2013–2018)." National Center for Health Statistics: Summary Tables. (https://www.cdc.gov/nchs/nhis/shs/tables.htm).

Clouston, Sean A. P. and Nicole Denier. April 2017. "Mental Retirement and Health Selection: Analyses from the U.S. Health and Retirement Study." *Journal of Social Science & Medicine* 178:78–86. (http://dx.doi.org/10.1016/j.socscimed.2017.01.019).

Creary, Stephanie and Judith R. Gordon. 2016. "Role Conflict, Role Overload, and Role Strain." In *The Wiley Blackwell Encyclopedia of Family Studies*, edited by Stephanie Creary and Judith R. Gordon. Hoboken, NJ: Wiley Blackwell.

Crystal, Stephen, Dennis G. Shea, and Adriana M. Reyes. October 2017. "Cumulative Advantage, Cumulative Disadvantage, and Evolving Patterns of Late-life Inequality." *The Gerontologist* 57(5):910–20. (https://doi.org/10.1093/geront/gnw056).

Díaz-Valdes, Antonia. 2019. "Retirement Intentions and Behaviors of Hispanics Compared to Non-Hispanics in the United States: A Three-paper Dissertation." PhD dissertation. Boston College, Chestnut Hill, MA.

DiNitto, Diana M. and David H. Johnson. 2012. *The Essentials of Social Welfare: Politics and Public Policy: Connecting Core Competencies Series.* Boston: Allyn & Bacon.

Eibich, Peter. September 2015. "Understanding the Effect of Retirement on Health: Mechanisms and Heterogeneity." *Journal of Health Economics* 43:1–12. (https://doi.org/10.1016/j.jhealeco.2015.05.001).

Elder, Glen H., Jr., Monica Kirkpatrick Johnson, and Robert Crosnoe. 2006. "The Emergence and Development of Life Course Theory." In *Handbook of the Life Course*, edited by Jeylan T. Mortimer and Michael J. Shanahan. Berlin, Germany: Springer.

Employment Benefit Research Institute (EBRI). June 5, 2007. "2007 Minority Retirement Confidence Survey." Washington, DC. (https://www.ebri.org/surveys/mrcs/).

Employment Benefit Research Institute (EBRI). March 21, 2017. "Retirement Confidence Survey." Washington, DC. (https://www.ebri.org/surveys/rcs/2017/).

Flippen, Cheboa and Marta Tienda. January 2000. "Pathways to Retirement: Patterns of Labor Force Participation and Labor Market Exit among the Pre-retirement by Race, Hispanic Origin, and Sex." *Journal of Gerontology* 51(1):14–27. (https://doi.org/10.1093/geronb/55.1.s14).

Flores, Antonio. September 18, 2017a. "Facts on U.S. Latinos, 2015: Statistical Portrait of Hispanics in the United States." (http://www.pewhispanic.org/2017/09/18/facts-on-u-s-latinos/#share-mexican-origin).

Flores, Antonio. September 18, 2017b. "How the U.S. Hispanic Population Is Changing." Washington, DC: Pew Research Center, Fact Tank. (http://www.pewhispanic.org/2017/09/18/facts-on-u-s-latinos/).

Gallo, William T., et al. May 2000. "Health Effect of Involuntary Job Loss among Older Workers: Findings from the Health and Retirement Study." *Journal of Gerontology* 55B(3):S131–40. (https://doi.org/10.1093/geronb/55.3.s131).

Glionna, John M. January 2016. "Too Poor to Retire and Too Young to Die." *Los Angeles Times*:1. (https://graphics.latimes.com/retirement-nomads/?track=lat-pick).

Gonzales, Ernest, Christina Matz-Costa, and Nancy Morrow-Howell. April 2015. "Increasing Opportunities for the Productive Engagement of Older Adults: A Response to Population Aging." *The Gerontologist* 55(2):252–61. (https://doi.org/10.1093/geront/gnu176).

González, Hector M., et al. November 2010. "The Epidemiology of Major Depression and Ethnicity in the United States." *Journal of Psychiatric Research* 44:1043–51. (https://doi.org/10.1016/j.jpsychires.2010.03.017).

Hale-Gallardo, Jennifer, Hisako Matsuo, and Lisa Willoughby. June 2013. "Exploring Successful Aging among Foreign-born Latinos and Other Immigrant Groups in Saint Louis, Missouri." (https://mospace.umsystem.edu/xmlui/handle/10355/48889).

Hardy, Melissa and Adriana M. Reyes. 2016. "Theories of Work and Retirement: Culture, Trust, and the Social Contract." In *Handbook of Theories of Aging*, edited by Vern L. Bengston and Richard A. Settersen Jr. New York: Springer.

Henry J. Kaiser Family Foundation. 2016. "Profile of Medicare Beneficiaries by Race and Ethnicity: A Chartpack." (http://files.kff.org/attachment/chartpack-profile-of-medicare-beneficiaries-by-race-and-ethnicity-a-chartpack).

Hilton, Jeanne M., et al. July 2012. "Perceptions of Successful Aging among Older Latinos, in Cross-cultural Context." *Journal of Cross Cultural Gerontology* 27:183–99. (https://doi.org/10.1007/s10823-012-9171-4).

Johnson, Richard W., Stipica Mudrazija, and Claire X. Wang. September 2016. *Hispanics' Retirement Security: Past Trends and Future Prospects.* Research Report. Washington, DC: Urban Institute. (https://www.dol.gov/sites/default/files/ebsa/researchers/analysis/retirement/hispanics-retirement-security-past-trends-and-future-prospects.pdf).

Johnson, Richard W., Stipica Mudrazija, and Claire X. Wang. June 2017. "Hispanics' Retirement Transitions and Differences by Nativity." *Journal of Aging and Health* 19(6):1096–115. (https://doi.org/10.1177/0898264317711608).

König, Stefanie, Magnus Lindwall, and Boo Johansson. November 2018. "Involuntary and Delayed Retirement as a Possible Health Risk for Lower Educated Retirees." *Journal of Population Ageing*:1–15. (https://doi.org/10.1007/s12062-018-9234-6).

Latif, Ehsan. August 2011. "The Impact of Retirement on Psychological Well-being in Canada." *Journal of Socio-economics* 40:373–80. (https://doi.org/10.1016/j.socec.2010.12.011).

Lytle, Megan C., et al. May 2015. "Current Trends in Retirement: Implications for Career Counseling and Vocational Psychology." *Journal of Career Development* 42(3):170–84. (https://doi.org/10.1177/0894845314545785).

Marshall, Alan and James Nazroo. August 2015. "Trajectories in the Prevalence of Self-reported Illness around Retirement." *Journal of Population Ageing* 9:11–48. (https://doi.org/10.1007/s12062-015-9130-2).

Matthews, Katey. 2014. "Is Working beyond State Pension Age Beneficial for Health? Evidence from the English Longitudinal Study of Ageing." Doctoral thesis. University of Manchester, Manchester, England.

Matz-Costa, Christina, et al. April 2014. "Differential Impact of Multiple Levels of Productive Activity Engagement on Psychological Well-being in Middle and Later Life." *The Gerontologist* 54(2):277–89. (https://doi.org/10.1093/geront/gns148).

McNamara, Tay K. and John Williamson. 2013. *Unequal Prospects: Is Working Longer the Answer?* New York: Taylor & Francis.

Mokyr Horner, Elizabeth and Mark Cullen. February 2016. "The Impact of Retirement on Health: Quasi-experimental Methods Using Administrative Data." *BMC Service Research* 16:1–9. (https://doi.org/10.1186/s12913-016-1318-5).

Montalto, Catherine P., Yoonkyung Yuh, and Sherman D. Hanna. May 2000. "Determinants of Planned Retirement Age." *Financial Services Review* 9(1):1–15. (https://doi.org/10.1016/S1057-0810(00)00052-4).

Morrissey, Monique. September 11, 2013. "Blacks and Hispanics Are Falling behind Whites in Retirement Coverage." Washington, DC: Economic Policy Institute, *The Retirement Inequality Chartbook*. (https://www.epi.org/publication/snapshot-blacks-hispanics-whites-retirement/).

Mudrazija, Stipica and Jacqueline L. Angel. 2014. "Diversity and the Economic Security of Older Americans." Pp. 138–54 in *The New Politics*, edited by Robert B. Hudson. Baltimore: Johns Hopkins University Press.

Munnell, Alicia. April 2015. "Falling Short: The Coming Retirement Crisis and What to Do about It." *Issue Brief* 15(7):1–8. Chestnut Hull, MA: Center for Retirement Research, Boston College. (https://crr.bc.edu/wp-content/uploads/2015/04/IB_15-7_508.pdf).

Munnell, Alicia and Steven S. Sass. 2008. *Working Longer: The Solution to the Retirement Income Challenges*. Washington, DC: Brookings Institution.

Munnell, Alicia H., Robert K. Triest, and Natalia Jivan. November 2004. "How Do Pensions Affect Expected and Actual Retirement Ages?" Chestnut Hill, MA: Center for Retirement Research, Boston College. *CRR Working Paper* 2004-27. (http://crr.bc.edu/working-papers/how-do-pensions-affect-expected-and-actual-retirement-ages/).

National Council of La Raza. July 2005. "Retirement Security for Latinos." (http://publications.nclr.org/handle/123456789/888).

O'Rand, Angela. 2009. "Cumulative Processes in the Life Course." In *The Craft of Life Course Research*, edited by Glen H. Elder Jr. and Janet Z. Giele. London: Guilford Press.

Passel, Jeffrey S. and D'vera Cohn. November 27, 2018. "U.S. Unauthorized Immigrant Total Dips to Lowest Level in a Decade." Washington, DC: Pew Research Center. (http://www.pewhispanic.org/2018/11/27/u-s-unauthorized-immigrant-total-dips-to-lowest-level-in-a-decade/).

Pew Research Center. November 27, 2016. "Unauthorized Immigrant Population Trends for States, Birth Countries and Regions." Washington, DC: Pew Research Center. (http://www.pewhispanic.org/interactives/unauthorized-trends/).

Pew Research Center. September 18, 2017. "Key Findings about U.S. Immigrants." Washington, DC: Pew Research Center. (http://www.pewhispanic.org/2017/09/18/facts-on-u-s-latinos/).

Rabinovich, Lila, et al. 2016. "Preparing for Retirement, Social Security Literacy and Information Preferences among Hispanics: A Qualitative Study." *CESR-Schaeffer Working Paper Series*, 2016-12. Los Angeles: Center for Economic and Social Research, University of Southern California. (https://cesr.usc.edu/documents/WP_2016_012.pdf).

RAND. 2018. "RAND HRS Longitudinal File, February, 2018." Funded by the National Institute of Aging and the Social Security Administration; distributed by RAND. (https://ssl.isr.umich.edu/hrs/files2.php).

Richman, Karen, et al. June 2008. *La Tercera Edad: Latinos' Pensions, Retirement, and Impact on Families.* Research Report 2008.1. Notre Dame, IN: University of Notre Dame, Institute for Latino Studies. (https://www.researchgate.net/publication/237581893_La_Tercera_Edad_Latinos'_Pensions_Retirement_and_Impact_on_Families).

Richman, Karen, et al. February 2012. "Confianza, Savings, and Retirement: A Study of Mexican Immigrants." Research Report 2012.1. Notre Dame, IN: University of Notre Dame, Institute for Latino Studies. (https://latinostudies.nd.edu/assets/95267/original/confianza_savings_retirement.pdf).

Ruggiano, Nicole, Janice O'Driscoll, and Andreja Lukic. February 2017. "'Work Is Like a Therapy That Prevents Aging': Perceptions of Retirement, Productivity, and Health among Minorities and Immigrants." *Sage Open, Special Issue*:1–11. (https://doi.org/10.1177/2158244016687234).

Sanzenbacher, Geoffrey, Steven A. Sass, and Christopher Gillis. February 2017. "How Job Changes Affect Retirement Timing by Socioeconomic Status." *Issue Brief* 17(3):1–8. Chestnut Hill, MA: Center for Retirement Research, Boston College. (http://crr.bc.edu/briefs/how-job-changes-affect-retirement-timing-by-socioeconomic-status/).

Social Security Administration. April 2016. "Income of the Population 55 or Older, 2014." (https://www.ssa.gov/policy/docs/statcomps/income_pop55/2014/index.html).

Sudano, Joseph J. and David W. Baker. February 2006. "Explaining U.S. Racial/Ethnic Disparities in Health Declines and Mortality in Late Middle Age: The Roles of Socio-economic Status, Health Behaviors, and Health Insurance." *Social Science & Medicine* 62(4):909–22. (https://doi.org/10.1016/j.socscimed.2005.06.041).

Sun, Wei, Gia Barboza, and Karen Richman. December 2007. "Preparing for the Future: Latinos' Financial Literacy and Retirement Planning." *Business Journal of Hispanics Research* 1(2):54–68. (https://latinostudies.nd.edu/assets/95325/original/preparing_for_the_future.pdf).

Tienda, Marta and Faith Mitchell. 2006. *Multiple Origins, Uncertain Destinies: Hispanics and the American Future.* Washington, DC: The National Academies Press.

U.S. Census Bureau. 2017. "Current Population Survey 2017." (https://www.census.gov/cps/data/cpstablecreator.html).

U.S. Federal Reserve Data. 2014. "Federal Reserve Board Issues Report on the Economic Well-being of U.S. Households in 2013." Washington, DC: Board of Governors of the Federal Reserve System. (https://www.federalreserve.gov/econresdata/2013-report-economic-well-being-us-households-201407.pdf).

Williamson, John B. and Tay K. McNamara. November 2001. "Why Some Workers Remain in the Labor Force beyond the Typical Age of Retirement." Chestnut Hill, MA: Center for Retirement Research, Boston College. *CRR Working Paper* 2001-09. (http://crr.bc.edu/working-papers/why-some-workers-remain-in-the-labor-force-beyond-the-typical-age-of-retirement/).

# PART II

# DEMOGRAPHIC SHIFTS AND WORKFORCE MANAGEMENT

CHAPTER 7

# Adapting to an Aging Workforce

## Evolving Talent Strategies and HR Practices

Jennifer Schramm

### A CHANGING WORKFORCE

Economists, demographers, HR managers, and business leaders have long known that the workforce is aging. Forecasts for the future show that older workers will continue to represent the fastest-growing segment of U.S. workers over the coming decade. While employers' responses to these trends have varied, many have failed to adapt to current shifts or create a talent strategy for the future based on a multigenerational workforce. This is to their detriment. Age discrimination continues to be widespread. Workforce planning for many organizations looks only to the short term with phased retirement options rarely offered. Even now, after years of attention to diversity issues, few organizations include age in their diversity and inclusion (D&I) programs, or recognize the intersection of age bias with gender and racial discrimination.

Economic conditions, new technologies, and other factors will all influence the workplace in the years ahead, but through it all, the aging population will remain an underlying and forceful driver of change—one requiring a strategic response. Forward-thinking leaders will not ignore these demographic shifts, either in the greater population or in their workforce. Instead, they will recognize both the value of older workers as a source of talent and the competitive advantage that building an age-diverse workforce will give them.

## LABOR FORCE PARTICIPATION RATES ARE RISING FOR OLDER WORKERS

Over the past thirty years, labor force participation rates (LFPRs) among age groups traditionally considered at or beyond retirement age have increased. Compared with previous decades, a higher proportion of today's U.S. older population is either working or actively seeking work. Even the Great Recession did not reverse this trend; since the start of the downturn in 2007, the LFPR of older age groups continued to rise.[1]

In 2019, the majority of baby boomers (born between 1946 and 1964) were still in the labor force, and the oldest boomers have stayed in the labor force at the highest annual rate for people their age in more than half a century.[2] The U.S. Bureau of Labor Statistics (BLS) forecasts that by 2026, of the almost 170 million people in the U.S. labor force, 42 million will be ages fifty-five and older. The fastest rates of growth in the years ahead will be among the oldest demographic of workers, the sixty-five and older age groups.[3]

While both men and women are working longer, the growing share of older women in the workforce is an important contributing factor. Labor force participation rates among women ages sixty-five and older were below 10 percent as recently as 2002. By 2018, they had reached 15.9 percent. Among those aged seventy-five and above, women's increases in labor force participation are forecast to significantly outpace those of men in the same age category, a 106.8 percent change in the labor force compared with 80.4 percent for men.[4]

## A DECLINE IN YOUNGER WORKERS

The increase in the number of older workers contrasts most sharply against the participation rates of the youngest cohorts of workers, which declined during the past three decades. The annual average LFPR for the sixteen-to-twenty-four age group declined from 68.4 percent in 1988 to 55.2 percent in 2018 but rose from 11.5 percent to 19.6 percent for workers ages sixty-five and older, according to the BLS.

The LFPR of the "prime-age" male workforce (i.e., those ages twenty-five to fifty-four) increased slightly during 2018 as the economy continued to grow, but for more than sixty years prior, this rate had also been in decline. In the 1950s, the LFPR of the male prime-age workforce was as high as 98 percent; it has since decreased and remained at around 88 percent in the past few years. Employment rates for this group have dropped at a higher rate in the United States than in other comparable countries[5] and for men at all education levels.[6] In comparison, the sixty-five-plus male LFPR fell as low as 14.8 percent in 1991, but by 2018, it had reached 24 percent.

The participation rates of young women have also declined. The LFPR of sixteen-to-twenty-four-year-old women reached its highest level in 1987 (64.6 percent) but has significantly declined since 2000. In 2019, the annual average LFPR for women in this age group was 54.5 percent. Since that time, the median age of the women in the labor force has surpassed that of men, and in the years ahead, forecasts for the fastest increases in participation are for older women.[7]

The rise in the number of prime-age workers staying outside of the workforce during their main earning years will have implications for individual lifetime earnings, savings, and living standards and will influence labor supply. The increased participation of both men and women at ages sixty-five-plus may offset at least some, though not all, of the loss of younger workers from the labor force. Employers will increasingly need to focus efforts on recruiting and retaining older workers while maximizing the productivity of a multigenerational workforce.

## DRIVERS OF OLDER WORKERS' LABOR FORCE PARTICIPATION

Along with population projections, government employment forecasts also take into account how industries will distribute jobs across occupations, and how trends in technology, changing skill requirements, and other factors will change labor supply and demand in the future. Economic conditions, and individual finances and savings, skills and education, occupational shifts, and working conditions all influence the rise in the number of older workers.

### Demographics and Longevity

Labor market forecasters have long predicted that the large size of the baby boom generation would lead to increases in the number of older workers in the labor force. Meanwhile, life expectancy in the U.S. has increased. For the total U.S. population, life expectancy at birth increased between 2006 and 2016, from 77.8 years to 78.6 years, according to the U.S. Centers for Disease Control and Prevention's (CDC) U.S. population data. Although in recent years, life expectancy at birth decreased slightly, the previous years' gains remain a factor in longer working lives.[8]

### Finances

Among the reasons why labor force participation rates for older workers reached their lowest point in the mid-1980s were greater access to employer-based retirement benefits, such as pensions, and favorable wage growth that enabled people to save for retirement. Today, increasing longevity means that people need to finance a longer period of retirement. With fewer workers having access to traditional defined benefit pension plans, more must finance their retirement through their savings. A large number of workers also do not have access to defined contribution savings plans, making it even harder to save enough money for retirement. Increased costs of living are another obstacle to financial security in retirement. High housing costs and medical expenses have become particularly burdensome. (See chapter 2 for further discussion of fiscal matters.)

Financial reasons are the main factor most frequently cited by older workers for remaining in the workforce. AARP research found that older workers' most common "very important" reasons for staying on the job are the need for money, to save more for retirement, and to maintain or get health insurance through an employer.[9]

## Education

While the decline in defined benefit retirement plans and a need for more savings has led many older workers to remain on the job longer for financial reasons, other factors have also played a role. Education appears to be among the most important factors behind the rise in the number of older workers. Due to educational improvements, achieved across decades, today's older workforce is more educated than were previous generations. Women, especially, have made steady gains in educational achievement, and this may play a role in the more rapid increases in LFPR among older women. A study examining the labor supply of older workers in advanced economies attributes more than two-thirds of the median increase in the participation rates of fifty-five- to seventy-four-year-olds between 2002 and 2017 to rising life expectancy and educational attainment changes.[10]

Workers with higher levels of education often have more opportunities to remain in the workforce longer. Between 2007 and 2017, labor force participation rates of people ages sixty-five and older increased across the education spectrum. However, those least likely to be working had less than a high school education while the LFPR for those ages sixty-five-plus with a master's degree or higher was over 30 percent in 2017.[11] Other research has found that opportunities for older workers improved significantly between the late 1990s and the early part of this decade, but gains mainly went to better-educated older workers.[12]

## Occupation

Workers in occupations and with skills that are in high demand have better prospects for working longer, and employers are more likely to provide incentives to encourage them to remain on the job. Education requirements are rising for many of the fastest-growing occupations and occupations projected to grow fastest are high-earning jobs requiring a doctoral, professional, or master's degree for entry.[13] In addition, more jobs are requiring professional certifications and occupational licenses.[14]

Meanwhile, workers in lower-skilled occupations earning low wages may be more likely to have to continue to work beyond traditional retirement age out of financial necessity. (See chapters 2–6 for further discussion.) An analysis of U.S. occupational distribution data by age found that the share of workers ages sixty-five-plus decreased in occupations with middle-range wages and salaries to a greater extent than did the share of workers ages forty-five to sixty-five. At the same time, the share of sixty-five-plus workers increased in occupations with both relatively high or relatively low wages and salaries.[15] High-wage workers may be working longer because they enjoy their jobs, have good working conditions, and are well compensated. Low-wage workers may work longer because they must in order to make ends meet.

The aging population is also influencing both the types of occupations that will grow and the number of older workers filling those fast-growing occupations. For example, the BLS projects that health care industries and their associated occupations will account for a substantial share of new jobs projected through 2026, largely driven by the aging population's demand for health care services. Many of these occupations require high levels of education, skills, and experience; in the years ahead, older workers with these qualifications may be able to work longer because of the high demand for their skills and credentials.

While many people intend to work longer, some face health conditions or other situations, such as family caregiving responsibilities, that ultimately lead to an earlier exit from the workforce than they had planned. For many older workers, however, the challenges they face in the labor market, not life circumstances, are the deciding factor that leads to them dropping out of the workforce sooner than they would like.[16]

### Age Discrimination

Research shows that age discrimination is common in the workplace. (See additional discussions of ageism, e.g., chapter 12 and elsewhere in this volume.) Among American workers ages forty-five and older, 61 percent reported either seeing or experiencing age discrimination in the workplace. Older job seekers are very aware of how age discrimination acts as a barrier to working; unemployed people were more likely than their working counterparts to say they had seen or experienced age discrimination, and 38 percent believed they had not been hired for a job because of their age.[17]

There is evidence that age discrimination is an even bigger problem for older women. Field studies have demonstrated a higher prevalence of age discrimination in hiring against older female job applicants compared with their male counterparts.[18] Women are more likely to say that they have seen or experienced age discrimination (64 percent versus 59 percent of men). An individual's race may also intensify the effects of age discrimination; black/African American workers were most likely to say they had experienced age discrimination.[19]

Age discrimination may lead older workers to drop out of the labor market entirely. The BLS's broadest measure of unemployment includes people not counted in the standard rate, that is, the "marginally attached." These are individuals who, though they would like to work, are not actively job seeking. The number of marginally attached workers can reach high levels in a weak economy; it reached over two million during the Great Recession.[20] A subset of the marginally attached includes a category considered "discouraged workers." Though they would like to work, discouraged workers are not currently looking because they believe no job is available in their line of work or area, they could not find any work, or they lack the necessary schooling, training, skills, or experience. Marginally attached workers are also considered discouraged if they say they gave up looking for work because they encountered discrimination or believe employers think they are too young or too old. Compared with people in other age groups, discouraged workers ages sixty-five and older are more likely to say that they have given up looking for work because employers do not want to hire someone their age.[21]

## LONG-TERM UNEMPLOYMENT AND ITS LASTING EFFECTS

One of the most well-known challenges older job seekers face is long-term unemployment. This was especially apparent during the Great Recession of 2007–2009 and its aftermath. The long-term unemployed are individuals who have been looking for work for about seven months or more (twenty-seven weeks and above). The effects of these longer bouts of joblessness can have a lifetime impact on wages and savings. Those ages fifty-five-plus are more likely to experience long-term unemployment (LTU) than younger job seekers. During the recession, LTU levels reached a record high of 45.1 percent; older workers were among those the hardest hit. In 2014, 44.6 percent of the unemployed ages fifty-five years and older had looked for work for twenty-seven weeks or longer, compared to 22.1 percent of those under age twenty-five.[22]

LTU has many negative outcomes. It increases the risk that a job seeker will drop out of the labor market altogether. Individuals in their late fifties to early sixties who experience unemployment during a recession are less likely to have health insurance coverage and use health care services, and show an increase in mortality rates over the longer term.[23] LTU also frequently has a significant and lasting financial impact, even for those who eventually find reemployment. About 59 percent of forty-five- to seventy-year-olds who had previously been jobless six months or more were earning less in their current jobs than they had in their previous jobs, compared with 41 percent of those who had been unemployed for a shorter period. This difference in earnings results in lower savings, decreased retirement investments, and delayed or abandoned investments in education or homeownership.[24]

A study of baby boomers found that those most likely to experience lasting employment effects in the aftermath of the Great Recession were individuals with less than a high school education and those with health limitations. The workers who left their jobs between the early months of the Great Recession through a full year after the recession ended faced a harsh labor market. Both men and women with less than a high school diploma were more likely to leave their jobs than those with a bachelor's degree or more, but the difference in the likelihood of job leaving based on educational attainment was much greater among women. Older women with low levels of education may be especially susceptible to longer stretches of unemployment during tough economic times.[25]

## Job Displacement

Job displacement refers to the process of losing or leaving a job due to plant or company closures, insufficient work, or the abolishment of a position or shift. When older workers' jobs are displaced, they are less likely than their younger counterparts to find reemployment. BLS job displacement data find that while 76 percent of workers ages twenty-five to fifty-four who had lost their jobs during the 2015 to 2017 survey period were back at work, only 60 percent of workers ages fifty-five to sixty-four and 31 percent of those ages sixty-five-plus were reemployed by January 2018. Over half (57 percent) of workers ages sixty-five and older who had been displaced had dropped out of the labor force entirely.[26] In the coming years, policy makers looking for ways to encourage longer working lives will have to consider policies to help displaced workers regain their footing in the job market. This will be especially important if, as many business and technology forecasters anticipate, large numbers of workers are displaced due to automation.

Even among older workers who do not experience job displacement, there is evidence that a large number are effectively pushed out of their jobs. Analysis of data from the Health and Retirement Study found that over half of U.S. older workers were laid off at least once or left jobs "under such financially damaging circumstances" that it is unlikely that they chose to leave voluntarily. Only one in ten ever again earn as much as they did before, and even years afterward, the household incomes of over half remain well below those of workers who did not experience these types of employment setbacks.[27]

### Labor Market Reentry

Reentering the workforce after an absence is the most common reason older job seekers give for being unemployed, and overall, they are more likely to be reentering the labor market than younger job seekers. Women are more likely than men are to cite reentry as their reason for unemployment at all ages.[28] Finding a job after time out of the workforce may be especially challenging, presenting a range of disadvantages for the job seeker—a career network that has weakened over time, a skill set that may no longer be up to date, and gaps in a resume they must explain to potential employers. Because the sixty-five and older demographic is expected to grow the fastest in the labor market, the number of labor market reentrants is likely to rise in the coming years. Policy makers will need to consider how they can help individuals reenter the workforce successfully. Employers, for their part, will have to adjust their recruiting practices to be more open to job seekers who have taken time out of work.

### Gig Work and Self-Employment

Workers ages fifty and older are more likely to report that they are self-employed compared with workers age twenty-five to forty-nine, and workers ages seventy-five and older are the most likely to report that they are self-employed.[29] There are different reasons for choosing contract, gig work, or self-employment. Some older job seekers decide to work for themselves because it is something they have always wanted to try. Others, because factors like age discrimination have made finding employment difficult. Likewise, many older workers only reluctantly engage in the gig economy as a way to make ends meet, while others find it is a good option for their current needs.

Research has found that the majority of individuals who work solely as temporary or contract workers make on average only 58 percent as much as those who hold traditional full-time jobs, and also do not have access to employer-sponsored retirement or insurance plans.[30] However, some older workers do find a way to make gig work a reasonable option for them. A study that examined outcomes of gig workers by generation found that gig work seemed to function best for baby boomers compared with other generations, probably because they were using it as a bridge to retirement rather than their full-time career. Seventy-five percent of the boomer gig workers surveyed said they liked their current situation and would not want to change it, the highest of any generation. They also earned more from their gig work compared with younger generations despite not working as many hours. They were less likely to use online gig platforms, suggesting that the type of gig work older workers are doing may often be more skilled or higher-earning consulting work. Subsequent generations of gig workers, especially Gen Xers, were less financially secure and less satisfied with their employment situation.[31]

Other research also indicates that older workers are using self-employment as a type of bridge employment to retirement. It found that increases in self-employment at popular retirement ages were associated with Social Security eligibility, especially for individuals with more retirement savings, and that individuals worked fewer hours after they switched to self-employment.[32] Few employers offer formal or informal phased retirement programs.[33] As a result, some older workers may view self-employment or contract and gig work as the best ways to phase down their working hours and control their schedules as they head toward retirement.

## Re-careering

As automation threatens a growing number of jobs, career counselors and policy makers may increasingly promote occupational change or "re-careering" as the answer to the problem of older workers' job displacement or long stretches of unemployment. The current reality, however, is that the likelihood of changing from one occupation to a different one peaks at ages eighteen to nineteen and after that declines with age. Individuals with higher levels of educational attainment may have more options when it comes to re-careering, but this varies by occupation.[34]

The choice to re-career is often not a choice at all, but a response to involuntary job loss. Older workers who change occupations usually experience a drop in pay. Making an occupational transition, however, is not always negative. Older career changers often report enjoying their new careers even more than their previous one, citing the benefits of more flexibility and less stress.[35] Overall, however, we have a long way to go before re-careering will be the solution for reemploying most displaced older workers.

## Working Hours and Flexibility

As they phase toward retirement or face more caregiving responsibilities, many older workers seek more control over their working hours. Though some would like to work more hours but only manage to find part-time work, many actually want to phase down the number of hours they work per week but find it impossible to do so within the parameters of their current occupation, industry, or employer.

A part-time worker usually works one to thirty-four hours per week,[36] and workers ages sixty-five and older are more likely to be working part-time compared with workers ages twenty-five to sixty-four. By the time they reach age seventy-five and older, about half of workers are working part-time.[37] Reasons for working part-time vary by age. For older workers, common reasons include retirement from full-time employment and the Social Security[38] earnings limit.[39] Other reasons for working part-time include caregiving responsibilities and economic reasons, such as unfavorable labor market conditions or the inability to find full-time work, but these reasons are more common for workers under fifty. Even among older workers, few say that health or medical conditions are the reason they are working part-time. Workers over fifty who are working part-time are more likely than their full-time counterparts are to be working in the service sector, suggesting that it may be easier for some older workers to find part-time work in services. Some may even transition out of industries in which part-time work is less available into industries, like services, where they have the option to work fewer hours per week.[40]

Lifestyle factors such as commuting time, flexible work schedules, the ability to phase into retirement, and the option to work from home are important to older job seekers,[41] and though only 6 percent of organizations offer formal phased retirement programs, informal work flex arrangements are increasingly common. These are job factors that workers of all ages value. The majority of companies already offer some form of telecommuting,[42] but as technology develops, more employers may expand their flexible work offerings. (See also chapters 10 and 11.)

## THE AGING POPULATION IS A STRATEGIC BUSINESS ISSUE

The aging population is a global business issue. It influences markets and consumer demand. It drives outcomes and determines necessary and available resources. Because of its wide-ranging effects, organizations will increasingly address the aging population and longevity economy in their strategic planning processes. The most forward-thinking business leaders are already beginning to develop a set of guiding principles around aging that drive their decision-making in a range of areas, including product development, talent management, and workforce planning. A key underlying principle is that an aging population represents a business *opportunity* to those who are willing to act on it, as well as a chance to help realize human potential. Insightful business leaders recognize the value of their older workers and know that there are many strategic reasons for maintaining age diversity in their workforce.

### Leveraging Knowledge and Skills

Workers who remain in the workforce the longest are often in occupations requiring the deepest levels of skills and experience.[43] The expansion of career lifespans will give organizations unprecedented access to deep reserves of experience and institutional knowledge, a valuable resource in a tight labor market when employers are concerned about skills shortages. An age-diverse workforce helps to maintain the skills base of the organization through facilitating intergenerational knowledge transfer.[44] It offers the benefits of mentoring, helping to improve employee soft skills, career-related knowledge, and other job skills. Moreover, employees who have had a mentor are more likely to become mentors themselves. This mentorship paid forward can benefit industries and organizations over decades and even generations.[45]

### Maintaining Stability and Managing Turnover

Research has found higher levels of stability, consistency, and reliability among older workers compared with younger employees, helping to support a stable organization and culture.[46] Maintaining a balance of age groups within the workforce can also help employers manage their turnover rates. Older workers stay with their employers longer compared with their younger counterparts, with the median tenure of workers ages fifty-five to sixty-four more than three times that of workers ages twenty-five to thirty-four.[47] This added stability reduces the cost of turnover. Grit, defined as passion and sustained persistence applied toward long-term achievement, with no particular concern for rewards or recognition along the way, has been observed to reach its highest average levels in individuals in their late sixties and older.[48]

## Building Employee Engagement and an Inclusive Culture

There is a direct line between an organization's diversity practices and employee engagement. Employers with well-developed diversity and inclusion (D&I) practices promote trust, an important factor in employee job satisfaction,[49] and employee engagement.[50] Age diversity may promote engagement in other ways. Research has found that those ages forty and older are the most engaged employees and also demonstrate the highest level of organizational commitment.[51] High employee engagement has a measurable, bottom-line result; business units in the top quartile of engagement realize 21 percent higher profitability than those in the bottom quartile.[52]

We are all aging, and even younger workers who witness age discrimination are affected by it, as they see how they too, could one day be treated. Age-diverse teams, therefore, promote feelings of inclusivity and belonging for employees of all ages. Furthermore, employees themselves prefer working in a multigenerational workplace. Younger workers value their older colleagues for their skill as teachers and for making the workplace more productive, while older workers value the creativity of their younger colleagues.[53]

## Optimizing Team Performance

Modern talent management not only focuses on individual performance but takes on the challenge of understanding and managing the complexities of team performance. In a networked age, there are many new ways employees can interact to complete tasks and improve performance. In this environment, however, the drivers of team performance can be much more difficult to measure, especially because identifying teams themselves is not always straightforward. There is evidence to suggest that the most engaged employees work together in ways their organizations do not even realize and do not measure.[54] This may be especially true of older workers, who we know are among the most engaged employees and whom younger workers value for their role as teachers. There is still a lot to learn about these "hidden teams" and the factors that bring such teams together and make them effective. However, evidence suggests that productivity of both older and younger workers is significantly higher in companies that used mixed-age teams than in companies that do not.[55] (See also chapters 8, 9, 13, and 14.)

Moreover, greater diversity appears to support innovation. Companies with above-average diversity, including age, on their management teams, report higher innovation revenue and profit margins.[56] Research has found that age-diverse design teams create innovative products and services for consumers of all ages and can more effectively target the fast-growing longevity economy.[57]

## HR PRACTICES TO ADAPT TO AN AGING WORKFORCE

Leading organizations are taking a range of steps to adapt to an aging population and use it to gain competitive advantage. These steps include recognizing age diversity in broader diversity efforts, improving strategic planning to include aspects related to an aging workforce, rethinking talent management and hiring practices, and offering flexible work schedules and educational training opportunities.

### Recognizing Age as a Fundamental Aspect of Diversity Strategy

A key first step most employers, HR, and diversity leaders can take to adapt to an aging workforce is to include age in their organization's diversity strategy. Only 8 percent of CEOs say they are including age in their D&I programs.[58] Organizations that recognize the value of older workers and of including age diversity in their D&I programs understand that this is about more than adding an overlooked demographic to existing initiatives; it is essential to building a cohesive and effective talent management strategy.[59] And because there is evidence that women and some racial minorities may be more likely to experience age discrimination, D&I programs that do not include age also do not fully address the challenges faced by individuals in these other worker demographics.

Although D&I strategies should include age, leaders and managers should avoid emphasizing age and generational differences. Studies show that, overall, generational differences are small. Cultivating beliefs in such differences, however, can impair collaboration and team building and create management and training inequities.[60]

### Understanding the Risks and Costs of Inaction

A failure to plan for and respond to an aging population and workforce puts organizations at risk. From a human capital standpoint, organizations can face unexpectedly high retirement rates leading to high replacement and turnover costs. They can experience skills shortages and a loss of institutional and tacit knowledge. Organizations that exclude age from their diversity programs and practices risk leaving themselves open to age discrimination litigation.

### Improving Workforce Planning Capabilities

Many organizations have not conducted a strategic workforce planning assessment to determine the impact of an aging workforce on their business. Most that have done so concentrate their analysis on only one to five years into the future.[61] The scale of demographic shifts merits a more long-term approach to workforce planning. At a minimum, organizations should have a good understanding of the essential types of expertise needed to carry out their mission and a sense of how their talent base will evolve to meet these requirements. Workforce planners should not only consider the influence of planned retirements among older workers, but also understand the role of other employment trends. These include the declining number of prime-age workers, as well as changes in worker competencies and educational attainment levels.

### Taking a Holistic View of Talent Management

Effective talent management is not only about locating, recruiting, and retaining star performers, but also the understanding and management of how individuals work *together.* By cultivating strong teamwork, managers can increase the overall productivity, engagement, and performance of the total organization. Researchers are learning more about how both formal and informal teams benefit from diversity, including age diversity. In the future, business and HR leaders will have an even better understanding of these complex interactions.

### Managing Recruiting Processes to Reduce Age Bias

HR and staffing professionals are under pressure to build faster and more effective recruiting processes, but organizations must use caution when leveraging new recruiting technologies. Online networking platforms have given hiring managers direct access to potential candidates, making them much more involved in the hiring process and raising expectations of the "perfect hire"—often someone who looks a lot like them. Even new technologies that use artificial intelligence (AI) to sort through data about potential and current job applicants, target passive job seekers, and manage administrative tasks can embed bias that harms older job seekers. As these predictive technologies look for patterns in data to forecast outcomes, they may not only reproduce existing bias but also exponentially intensify it. Developers will need to continually audit such systems for bias, including unconscious bias, which may be the hardest to eradicate.

### Offering Flexible Work Arrangements to Employees of All Ages

Individuals across all life stages already face time pressures, but the reality of an aging population means that flexible work situations for employees of all ages could help mitigate some of the stress. For example, many millennials have caregiving responsibilities for an adult relative with a serious illness or disability.[62] Job characteristics, not the demographic characteristics of the worker, determine the effectiveness of flexible work options, but as technology advances, there will be more opportunities for employers to offer flexible work options. Along with competitive pay and benefits, older workers and job seekers say they are looking for a good commute, flexible hours, telecommuting, and the ability to phase toward retirement.[63] Sometimes only minor changes in work hours or location can be enough to retain employees facing challenges such as caregiving responsibilities or those who want to devote more of their time to travel and family. (See also chapters 11 and 20.)

### Creating Inclusive Learning and Development Strategies

Especially for those with low levels of skills and education, transitioning out of shrinking job sectors and into new and growing fields will require much greater investments in training than are currently being made. The costs of recruiting, hiring, and onboarding employees with the needed new and emerging skills are a strong incentive for employers to retrain existing employees. Evolving technologies drive the need for constant upskilling and retraining. (See also chapters 15, 17, and 18.) On-the-job learning opportunities that are inclusive and allow for individual learning styles and cognitive approaches will be most effective. Benefits that assist employees in obtaining further education will be important to employees of all ages. As career lifespans grow, age should not be a barrier to accessing learning and career growth opportunities.

*Disclaimer: This chapter, including its views and interpretation of data, are those of the author and do not necessarily represent the views or official policies of AARP.*

## NOTES

1. U.S. Bureau of Labor Statistics. Historical data derived from the Current Population Survey public use dataset.
2. Richard Fry. July 24, 2019. "Baby Boomers Are Staying in the Labor Force at Rates Not Seen in Generations for People Their Age." Washington, DC: Pew Research Center. (https://www.pewresearch.org/fact-tank/2019/07/24/baby-boomers-us-labor-force/).
3. Mitra Toossi and Elka Torpey. May 2017. "Older Workers: Labor Force Trends and Career Options." *Career Outlook.* Washington, DC: U.S. Bureau of Labor Statistics. (https://www.bls.gov/careeroutlook/2017/article/older-workers.htm).
4. U.S. Bureau of Labor Statistics. November 2017. "Projections of the Labor Force, 2016–26." *Career Outlook.* Washington, DC: U.S. Bureau of Labor Statistics. (https://www.bls.gov/careeroutlook/2017/article/projections-laborforce.htm).
5. OECD. "Employment Rate by Age Group: Indicator." Retrieved on July 18, 2019 (https://doi.org/10.1787/084f32c7-en).
6. Alexander W. Richter, Daniel Chapman, and Emil Mihaylov. April 2018. "Declining U.S. Labor Force Participation Rates Stand Out." *Economic Letter* 13(6). Dallas: Federal Reserve Bank of Dallas. (https://www.dallasfed.org/research/~/media/documents/research/eclett/2018/el1806.pdf).
7. Mitra Toossi and Teresa L. Morisi. July 2017. "Women in the Workforce before, during, and after the Great Recession." *Spotlight on Statistics.* Washington, DC: U.S. Bureau of Labor Statistics. (https://www.bls.gov/spotlight/2017/women-in-the-workforce-before-during-and-after-the-great-recession/pdf/women-in-the-workforce-before-during-and-after-the-great-recession.pdf).
8. National Center for Health Statistics. 2018. *Health, United States, 2017.* Hyattsville, Maryland: U.S. Centers for Disease Control and Prevention. (https://www.cdc.gov/nchs/hus/description.htm).
9. AARP. 2018. *The Value of Experience: The AARP Work and Career Study.* Washington, DC: AARP Research. (http://www.aarp.org/ValueofExperience).
10. Christian Geppert et al. June 11, 2019. "Labour Supply of Older People in Advanced Economies: The Impact of Changes to Statutory Retirement Ages." *OECD Economics Department Working Paper* 1554. Paris: OECD Publishing. (https://doi.org/10.1787/b9f8d292-en).
11. Jennifer Schramm. September 2018. *An Aging Labor Force and the Challenges of 65+ Jobseekers.* Washington, DC: AARP Public Policy Institute. (https://www.aarp.org/ppi/info-2018/an-aging-labor-force.html).
12. Matthew S. Rutledge, Steven A. Sass, and Jorge D. Ramos-Mercado. August 2015. "How Does Occupational Access for Older Workers Differ by Education?" *CRR Working Paper* 2015-20.

Chestnut Hill, MA: Center for Retirement Research, Boston College. (http://crr.bc.edu/wp-content/uploads/2015/08/wp_2015-20.pdf).

13. Emily Rolen. January 2019. "Occupational Employment Projections through the Perspective of Education and Training." *Spotlight on Statistics*. Washington, DC: U.S. Bureau of Labor Statistics. (https://www.bls.gov/spotlight/2019/education-projections/home.htm).

14. Evan Cunningham. June 2019. "Professional Certifications and Occupational Licenses: Evidence from the Current Population Survey." *Monthly Labor Review.* Washington, DC: U.S. Bureau of Labor Statistics. (https://doi.org/10.21916/mlr.2019.15).

15. Frederic Pryor. February 2017. "Occupational Choices of the Elderly." *Monthly Labor Review.* Washington, DC: U.S. Bureau of Labor Statistics. (https://doi.org/10.21916/mlr.2017.4).

16. Employee Benefit Research Institute and Greenwald & Associates. April 23, 2019. *2019 Retirement Confidence Survey*. Washington, DC. (https://www.ebri.org/retirement/retirement-confidence-survey).

17. AARP, *Value of Experience.*

18. David Neumark, Ian Burn, and Patrick Button. February 27, 2017. "Age Discrimination and Hiring of Older Workers." *FRBSF Economic Letter* 2017-06. San Francisco: Federal Reserve Bank of San Francisco. (https://unbound.upcea.edu/innovation/alternative-credentialing/microdegrees/national-survey-suggests-that-employers-will-lead-way-on-digital-badging/).

19. AARP, *Value of Experience.*

20. U.S. Bureau of Labor Statistics. April 2009. "Ranks of Discouraged Workers and Others Marginally Attached to the Labor Force Rise during Recession." *Issues in Labor Statistics*. Washington, DC: U.S. Bureau of Labor Statistics. (https://www.bls.gov/opub/btn/archive/ranks-of-discouraged-workers-and-others-marginally-attached-to-the-labor-force-rise-during-recession.pdf).

21. Schramm, *An Aging Labor Force.*

22. Karen Kosanovich and Eleni T. Sherman. March 2015. "Trends in Long-term Unemployment." *Spotlight on Statistics.* Washington, DC: U.S. Bureau of Labor Statistics. (https://www.bls.gov/spotlight/2015/long-term-unemployment/pdf/long-term-unemployment.pdf).

23. Courtney Coile, Phillip Levine, and Robin McKnight. September 2012. "Recessions, Older Workers, and Longevity: How Long Are Recessions Good for Your Health?" *American Economic Journal: Economic Policy* 6(3):92–119. (https://www.nber.org/papers/w18361).

24. Gary Koenig, Lori Trawinski, and Sara Rix. March 2015. *The Long Road Back: Struggling to Find Work after Unemployment.* Washington, DC: AARP Public Policy Institute. (https://www.aarp.org/content/dam/aarp/ppi/2015-3/The%20Long%20Road%20Back_INSIGHT-new.pdf).

25. Donna Rothstein. December 2018. "Leaving a Job during the Great Recession: Evidence from the National Longitudinal Survey of Youth 1979." *Monthly Labor Review.* Washington, DC: U.S. Bureau of Labor Statistics. (https://doi.org/10.21916/mlr.2018.28).

26. U.S. Bureau of Labor Statistics. August 28, 2018. *Worker Displacement: 2015–17.* Washington, DC: U.S. Bureau of Labor Statistics. (https://www.bls.gov/news.release/disp.nr0.htm).

27. Peter Gosselin. December 28, 2018. "If You're over 50, Chances Are the Decision to Leave a Job Won't Be Yours." ProPublica and the Urban Institute. (https://www.propublica.org/article/older-workers-united-states-pushed-out-of-work-forced-retirement).

28. Schramm, *An Aging Labor Force.*

29. Toossi and Torpey, "Older Workers."

30. Prudential Financial. August 1, 2017. *Gig Workers in America: Profiles, Mindsets, and Financial Wellness.* (https://www.prudential.com/corporate-insights/gig-workers-in-america-profiles-mindsets-and-financial-wellness?utm_medium=distribution&utm_source=newsroom&utm_content=gc&utm_campaign=gig_workers_lp).

31. Prudential Financial. July 12, 2019. *Gig Economy Impact by Generation.* (https://www.prudential.com/corporate-insights/gig-economy-impact-by-generation).

32. Shanthi Ramnath, John B. Shoven, and Sita N. Slavov. June 2017. "Pathways to Retirement through Self-Employment." *NBER Working Paper* 23551. (https://www.nber.org/papers/w23551?utm_campaign=ntw&utm_medium=email&utm_source=ntw).

33. Society for Human Resource Management. June 2019. *2019 Employee Benefits.* Alexandria, VA: SHRM Research. (https://shrm.org/hr-today/trends-and-forecasting/research-and-surveys/Pages/Benefits19.aspx).

34. Andrew O'Bar. June 2019. "What's behind Occupational Separations?" *Monthly Labor Review*. Washington, DC: U.S. Bureau of Labor Statistics. (https://doi.org/10.21916/mlr.2019.13).

35. Richard Johnson, Janette Kawachi, and Eric Lewis. 2009. *Older Workers on the Move: Recareering in Later Life*. Washington, DC: AARP Public Policy Institute and the Urban Institute. (https://assets.aarp.org/rgcenter/econ/2009_08_recareering.pdf).

36. While hours are based on the usual number of hours worked from all jobs, some exceptions are made for certain types of workers, who, though they work fewer than thirty-five hours per week, are considered full-time workers.

37. The only age group more likely than those ages sixty-five and older to work part-time is ages sixteen to twenty-four, mainly because of school and training.

38. Social Security is the term generally used to describe the Old Age, Survivors Insurance program, or OASI, created by Title II of the Social Security Act of 1935. The Current Population Survey combines "retirement" and "the Social Security earnings limit" into one survey response option. Therefore, it is not possible to distinguish between these two factors as the main reason for working part-time. The Social Security Administration reduces the benefits of workers who have not reached their full retirement age if their earnings exceed a certain threshold. Generally, this reduction in retirement benefits is temporary, and amounts withheld because of the earnings limit are repaid over the worker's life beginning at full retirement age.

39. Research suggests that the Social Security Retirement Earnings Test (RET) may influence some OASI claimants to retire sooner than they would have otherwise. Looking solely at those ages sixty-two to sixty-five, whose decision to work part-time is most likely to be influenced by the earnings limit, 40 percent are working part-time due to retirement and/or the Social Security earnings limit compared with 57 percent of those ages sixty-five to seventy-four, who are unlikely to be affected by the RET. See Alexander Gelber, Damon Jones, and Daniel Sacks. November 2015. *Earnings Adjustment Frictions: Evidence from the Social Security Earnings Test*. Cambridge, MA: National Bureau of Economic Research. (http://users.nber.org/~agelber/papers/adjustment111915.pdf).

40. Jennifer Schramm. 2018. *Older Workers and Part-Time Employment*. Washington, DC: AARP Public Policy Institute. (https://www.aarp.org/ppi/info-2018/older-workers-and-part-time-employment.html).

41. AARP, *Value of Experience*.

42. Society for Human Resource Management, *2019 Employee Benefits*.

43. AARP and Oxford Economics. September 2016. *The Longevity Economy*. (https://www.aarp.org/content/dam/aarp/research/surveys_statistics/econ/2017/2016-natl-longevity-economy.doi.10.26419%252Fres.00172.001.pdf).

44. Uschi Backes-Gellner and Stephan Veen. January 2, 2009. "The Impact of Aging and Age Diversity on Company Performance." (http://dx.doi.org/10.2139/ssrn.1346895).

45. G. Oscar Anderson. January 2019. *Mentorship and the Value of a Multigenerational Workforce*. Washington, DC: AARP Research. (https://www.aarp.org/research/topics/economics/info-2019/multigenerational-work-mentorship.html).

46. Florian Schmiedek, Martin Lövdén, and Ulman Lindenberger. September 2013. "Keeping It Steady: Older Adults Perform More Consistently on Cognitive Tasks Than Younger Adults." *Psychological Science* 24(9):1747–54. (https://doi.org/10.1177/0956797613479611).

47. U.S. Bureau of Labor Statistics. September 20, 2018. *Employee Tenure in 2018*. Washington, DC: U.S. Bureau of Labor Statistics. (https://www.bls.gov/news.release/pdf/tenure.pdf).

48. Angela Duckworth et al. 2007. "Grit: Perseverance and Passion for Long-term Goals." *Journal of Personality and Social Psychology* 92(6):1087–101. (https://doi.org/10.1037/0022-3514.92.6.1087).

49. Society for Human Resource Management. April 24, 2017. *2017 Employee Job Satisfaction and Engagement: The Doors of Opportunity Are Open*. Alexandria, VA: SHRM Research. (https://www.shrm.org/hr-today/trends-and-forecasting/research-and-surveys/Pages/2017-Job-Satisfaction-and-Engagement-Doors-of-Opportunity-Are-Open.aspx).

50. Stephanie Downey et al. January 2015. "The Role of Diversity Practices and Inclusion in Promoting Trust and Employee Engagement." *Journal of Applied Social Psychology* 45(1):35–44. (https://doi.org/10.1111/jasp.12273).

51. Natalia Sarkisian et al. December 2011. "Effects of Country & Age on Work Engagement, Job Satisfaction & Organizational Commitment among Employees in the United States." Chestnut

Hill, MA: Sloan Center on Aging and Work, Boston College. (https://www.bc.edu/content/dam/files/research_sites/agingandwork/pdf/publications/GOT_USEmployee.pdf).

52. Jim Harter. August 26, 2018. "Employee Engagement on the Rise in the U.S." *Gallup News*. (https://news.gallup.com/poll/241649/employee-engagement-rise.aspx).

53. Anderson, *Mentorship*.

54. Marcus Buckingham and Ashley Goodall. May 2019. "The Power of Hidden Teams." *Harvard Business Review*. (https://hbr.org/cover-story/2019/05/the-power-of-hidden-teams).

55. Backes-Gellner and Veen, "Impact of Aging."

56. Rocío Lorenzo et al. 2018. *How Diverse Leadership Teams Boost Innovation*. Boston Consulting Group.

57. Susan Wilner Golden and Laura Carstensen. March 4, 2019. "How Merrill Lynch Is Planning for Its Customers to Live to 100." *Harvard Business Review*. (https://hbr.org/2019/03/how-merrill-lynch-is-planning-for-its-customers-to-live-to-100).

58. PWC. 2018. *18th Annual Global CEO Survey*. (https://www.pwc.com/gx/en/ceo-survey/2015/assets/pwc-18th-annual-global-ceo-survey-jan-2015.pdf).

59. Lori A. Trawinski. October 2016. *Disrupting Aging in the Workplace: Profiles in Intergenerational Diversity Leadership*. Washington, DC: AARP Public Policy Institute. (https://www.aarp.org/content/dam/aarp/ppi/2017/08/disrupt-aging-in-the-workforce.pdf).

60. Eden King et al. August 1, 2019. "Generational Differences at Work Are Small. Thinking They're Big Affects Our Behavior." *Harvard Business Review*. (https://hbr.org/2019/08/generational-differences-at-work-are-small-thinking-theyre-big-affects-our-behavior).

61. Society for Human Resource Management. 2014. *SHRM Survey Findings: The Aging Workforce—The State of Older Workers in U.S. Organizations*. Alexandria, VA: SHRM Research. (https://www.shrm.org/hr-today/trends-and-forecasting/research-and-surveys/Documents/2014-Older-Workers-Survey-Overall-Results-Part1-State-of-Older-Workers.pdf).

62. National Alliance for Caregiving (NAC) and AARP Public Policy Institute. June 2015. *Caregiving in the U.S. 2015*. Bethesda, MD, and Washington, DC: NAC and AARP.

63. AARP, *Value of Experience*.

## REFERENCES


AARP. 2018. *The Value of Experience: The AARP Work and Career Study*. Washington, DC: AARP Research. (http://www.aarp.org/ValueofExperience).

AARP and Oxford Economics. September 2016. *The Longevity Economy*. (https://www.aarp.org/content/dam/aarp/research/surveys_statistics/econ/2017/2016-natl-longevity-economy.doi.10.26419%252Fres.00172.001.pdf).

Anderson, G. Oscar. January 2019. *Mentorship and the Value of a Multigenerational Workforce*. Washington, DC: AARP Research. (https://www.aarp.org/research/topics/economics/info-2019/multigenerational-work-mentorship.html).

Backes-Gellner, Uschi and Stephan Veen. January 2, 2009. "The Impact of Aging and Age Diversity on Company Performance." (http://dx.doi.org/10.2139/ssrn.1346895).

Buckingham, Marcus and Ashley Goodall. May 2019. "The Power of Hidden Teams." *Harvard Business Review*. (https://hbr.org/cover-story/2019/05/the-power-of-hidden-teams).

Coile, Courtney, Phillip Levine, and Robin McKnight. September 2012. "Recessions, Older Workers, and Longevity: How Long Are Recessions Good for Your Health?" *American Economic Journal: Economic Policy* 6(3):92–119. (https://www.nber.org/papers/w18361).

Cunningham, Evan. June 2019. "Professional Certifications and Occupational Licenses: Evidence from the Current Population Survey." *Monthly Labor Review*. Washington, DC: U.S. Bureau of Labor Statistics. (https://doi.org/10.21916/mlr.2019.15).

Downey, Stephanie, et al. January 2015. "The Role of Diversity Practices and Inclusion in Promoting Trust and Employee Engagement." *Journal of Applied Social Psychology* 45(1):35–44. (https://doi.org/10.1111/jasp.12273).

Duckworth, Angela, et al. 2007. "Grit: Perseverance and Passion for Long-term Goals." *Journal of Personality and Social Psychology* 92(6):1087–101. (https://doi.org/10.1037/0022-3514.92.6.1087).

Employee Benefit Research Institute and Greenwald & Associates. April 23, 2019. *2019 Retirement Confidence Survey*. Washington, DC. (https://www.ebri.org/retirement/retirement-confidence-survey).

Fry, Richard. July 24, 2019. "Baby Boomers Are Staying in the Labor Force at Rates Not Seen in Generations for People Their Age." Washington, DC: Pew Research Center. (https://www.pewresearch.org/fact-tank/2019/07/24/baby-boomers-us-labor-force/).

Gelber, Alexander, Damon Jones, and Daniel Sacks. November 2015. *Earnings Adjustment Frictions: Evidence from the Social Security Earnings Test*. Cambridge, MA: National Bureau of Economic Research. (http://users.nber.org/~agelber/papers/adjustment111915.pdf).

Geppert, Christian, et al. June 11, 2019. "Labor Supply of Older People in Advanced Economies: The Impact of Changes to Statutory Retirement Ages." *OECD Economics Department Working Paper* 1554. Paris: OECD Publishing. (https://doi.org/10.1787/b9f8d292-en).

Gosselin, Peter. December 28, 2018. "If You're over 50, Chances Are the Decision to Leave a Job Won't Be Yours." ProPublica and the Urban Institute. (https://www.propublica.org/article/older-workers-united-states-pushed-out-of-work-forced-retirement).

Harter, Jim. August 26, 2018. "Employee Engagement on the Rise in the U.S." *Gallup News*. (https://news.gallup.com/poll/241649/employee-engagement-rise.aspx).

Johnson, Richard, Janette Kawachi, and Eric Lewis. 2009. *Older Workers on the Move: Recareering in Later Life*. Washington, DC: AARP Public Policy Institute and the Urban Institute. (https://assets.aarp.org/rgcenter/econ/2009_08_recareering.pdf).

King, Eden, et al. August 1, 2019. "Generational Differences at Work Are Small. Thinking They're Big Affects Our Behavior." *Harvard Business Review*. (https://hbr.org/2019/08/generational-differences-at-work-are-small-thinking-theyre-big-affects-our-behavior).

Koenig, Gary, Lori Trawinski, and Sara Rix. March 2015. *The Long Road Back: Struggling to Find Work after Unemployment*. Washington, DC: AARP Public Policy Institute. (https://www.aarp.org/content/dam/aarp/ppi/2015-3/The%20Long%20Road%20Back_INSIGHT-new.pdf).

Kosanovich, Karen and Eleni T. Sherman. March 2015. "Trends in Long-term Unemployment." *Spotlight on Statistics*. Washington, DC: U.S. Bureau of Labor Statistics. (https://www.bls.gov/spotlight/2015/long-term-unemployment/pdf/long-term-unemployment.pdf).

Lorenzo, Rocío, et al. 2018. *How Diverse Leadership Teams Boost Innovation*. Boston Consulting Group.

National Alliance for Caregiving (NAC) and AARP Public Policy Institute. June 2015. *Caregiving in the U.S. 2015*. Bethesda, MD, and Washington, DC: NAC and AARP.

National Center for Health Statistics. 2018. *Health, United States, 2017*. Hyattsville, MD: U.S. Centers for Disease Control and Prevention. (https://www.cdc.gov/nchs/hus/description.htm).

Neumark, David, Ian Burn, and Patrick Button. February 27, 2017. "Age Discrimination and Hiring of Older Workers." *FRBSF Economic Letter* 2017-06. San Francisco: Federal Reserve Bank of San Francisco. (https://unbound.upcea.edu/innovation/alternative-credentialing/microdegrees/national-survey-suggests-that-employers-will-lead-way-on-digital-badging/).

O'Bar, Andrew. June 2019. "What's behind Occupational Separations?" *Monthly Labor Review*. Washington, DC: U.S. Bureau of Labor Statistics. (https://doi.org/10.21916/mlr.2019.13).

OECD. "Employment Rate by Age Group: Indicator." Retrieved July 18, 2019 (https://doi.org/10.1787/084f32c7-en).

Prudential Financial. August 1, 2017. *Gig Workers in America: Profiles, Mindsets, and Financial Wellness*. (https://www.prudential.com/corporate-insights/gig-workers-in-america-profiles-mindsets-and-financial-wellness?utm_medium=distribution&utm_source=newsroom&utm_content=gc&utm_campaign=gig_workers_lp).

Prudential Financial. July 12, 2019. *Gig Economy Impact by Generation*. (https://www.prudential.com/corporate-insights/gig-economy-impact-by-generation).

Pryor, Frederic. February 2017. "Occupational Choices of the Elderly." *Monthly Labor Review*. Washington, DC: U.S. Bureau of Labor Statistics. (https://doi.org/10.21916/mlr.2017.4).

PWC. 2018. *18th Annual Global CEO Survey*. (https://www.pwc.com/gx/en/ceo-survey/2015/assets/pwc-18th-annual-global-ceo-survey-jan-2015.pdf).

Ramnath, Shanthi, John B. Shoven, and Sita N. Slavov. June 2017. "Pathways to Retirement through Self-Employment." *NBER Working Paper* 23551. (https://www.nber.org/papers/w23551?utm_campaign=ntw&utm_medium=email&utm_source=ntw).

Richter, Alexander, Daniel Chapman, and Emil Mihaylov. April 2018. "Declining U.S. Labor Force Participation Rates Stand Out." *Economic Letter* 13(6). Dallas: Federal Reserve Bank of Dallas. https://www.dallasfed.org/research/~/media/documents/research/eclett/2018/el1806.pdf.

Rolen, Emily. January 2019. "Occupational Employment Projections through the Perspective of Education and Training." *Spotlight on Statistics*. Washington, DC: U.S. Bureau of Labor Statistics. (https://www.bls.gov/spotlight/2019/education-projections/home.htm).

Rothstein, Donna. December 2018. "Leaving a Job during the Great Recession: Evidence from the National Longitudinal Survey of Youth 1979." *Monthly Labor Review.* Washington, DC: U.S. Bureau of Labor Statistics. (https://doi.org/10.21916/mlr.2018.28).

Rutledge, Matthew, Steven Sass, and Jorge Ramos-Mercado. August 2015. "How Does Occupational Access for Older Workers Differ by Education?" *CRR Working Paper* 2015-20. Chestnut Hill, MA: Center for Retirement Research, Boston College. (http://crr.bc.edu/wp-content/uploads/2015/08/wp_2015-20.pdf).

Sarkisian, Natalia, et al. December 2011. "Effects of Country & Age on Work Engagement, Job Satisfaction & Organizational Commitment among Employees in the United States." Chestnut Hill, MA: Sloan Center on Aging and Work, Boston College. (https://www.bc.edu/content/dam/files/research_sites/agingandwork/pdf/publications/GOT_USEmployee.pdf).

Schmiedek, Florian, Martin Lövdén, and Ulman Lindenberger. September 2013. "Keeping It Steady: Older Adults Perform More Consistently on Cognitive Tasks Than Younger Adults." *Psychological Science* 24(9):1747–54. (https://doi.org/10.1177/0956797613479611).

Schramm, Jennifer. September 2018. *An Aging Labor Force and the Challenges of 65+ Jobseekers.* Washington, DC: AARP Public Policy Institute. (https://www.aarp.org/ppi/info-2018/an-aging-labor-force.html).

Schramm, Jennifer. 2018. *Older Workers and Part-time Employment.* Washington, DC: AARP Public Policy Institute. (https://www.aarp.org/ppi/info-2018/older-workers-and-part-time-employment.html).

Society for Human Resource Management. 2014. *SHRM Survey Findings: The Aging Workforce—The State of Older Workers in U.S. Organizations.* Alexandria, VA: SHRM Research. (https://www.shrm.org/hr-today/trends-and-forecasting/research-and-surveys/Documents/2014-Older-Workers-Survey-Overall-Results-Part1-State-of-Older-Workers.pdf).

Society for Human Resource Management. April 24, 2017. *2017 Employee Job Satisfaction and Engagement: The Doors of Opportunity Are Open.* Alexandria, VA: SHRM Research. (https://www.shrm.org/hr-today/trends-and-forecasting/research-and-surveys/Pages/2017-Job-Satisfaction-and-Engagement-Doors-of-Opportunity-Are-Open.aspx).

Society for Human Resource Management. June 2019. *2019 Employee Benefits.* Alexandria, VA: SHRM Research. (https://shrm.org/hr-today/trends-and-forecasting/research-and-surveys/Pages/Benefits19.aspx).

Toossi, Mitra and Teresa L. Morisi. July 2017. "Women in the Workforce before, during, and after the Great Recession." *Spotlight on Statistics.* Washington, DC: U.S. Bureau of Labor Statistics. (https://www.bls.gov/spotlight/2017/women-in-the-workforce-before-during-and-after-the-great-recession/pdf/women-in-the-workforce-before-during-and-after-the-great-recession.pdf).

Toossi, Mitra and Elka Torpey. May 2017. "Older Workers: Labor Force Trends and Career Options." *Career Outlook.* Washington, DC: U.S. Bureau of Labor Statistics. (https://www.bls.gov/careeroutlook/2017/article/older-workers.htm).

Trawinski, Lori. October 2016. *Disrupting Aging in the Workplace: Profiles in Intergenerational Diversity Leadership.* Washington, DC: AARP Public Policy Institute. (https://www.aarp.org/content/dam/aarp/ppi/2017/08/disrupt-aging-in-the-workforce.pdf).

U.S. Bureau of Labor Statistics. April 2009. "Ranks of Discouraged Workers and Others Marginally Attached to the Labor Force Rise during Recession." *Issues in Labor Statistics.* Washington, DC: U.S. Bureau of Labor Statistics. (https://www.bls.gov/opub/btn/archive/ranks-of-discouraged-workers-and-others-marginally-attached-to-the-labor-force-rise-during-recession.pdf).

U.S. Bureau of Labor Statistics. November 2017. "Projections of the Labor Force, 2016–26." *Career Outlook*. Washington, DC: U.S. Bureau of Labor Statistics. (https://www.bls.gov/careeroutlook/2017/article/projections-laborforce.htm).

U.S. Bureau of Labor Statistics. August 28, 2018. *Worker Displacement: 2015–17*. Washington, DC: U.S. Bureau of Labor Statistics. (https://www.bls.gov/news.release/disp.nr0.htm).

U.S. Bureau of Labor Statistics. September 20, 2018. *Employee Tenure in 2018*. Washington, DC: U.S. Bureau of Labor Statistics. (https://www.bls.gov/news.release/pdf/tenure.pdf).

Wilner Golden, Susan and Laura Carstensen. March 4, 2019. "How Merrill Lynch Is Planning for Its Customers to Live to 100." *Harvard Business Review*. (https://hbr.org/2019/03/how-merrill-lynch-is-planning-for-its-customers-to-live-to-100).

CHAPTER 8

# Managing Aging and Age-Diverse Workforces

Hannes Zacher and Cort W. Rudolph

Due to demographic changes (e.g., low or decreasing birth rates, higher life expectancy) and changing employment participation patterns (e.g., delayed retirement), the workforces in developed countries and also many developing countries (e.g., China, India) are aging and becoming increasingly age diverse.[1] These trends pose a number of labor supply challenges and opportunities. Small- and medium-sized businesses as well as large organizations increasingly compete for a shrinking number of highly qualified young workers, while trying to motivate and retain their middle-aged and older incumbents.[2] Moreover, bridge employment arrangements with senior experts, who have left their career jobs but are not yet fully retired, are becoming more and more common.[3] Today's employees are also more likely to work in age-diverse teams and to have supervisors who are much younger or older than they are, which can have both positive (e.g., knowledge exchange) and negative consequences (e.g., discrimination).[4]

In this context, organizational leaders and human resources managers have to identify ways to successfully manage—that is, to attract, hire, motivate, retain, and potentially reemploy—workers of different ages.[5] Fortunately, theory and empirical studies on the role of age at work have accumulated over the last few decades. This research allows deriving evidence-based recommendations on topics relevant to aging and age diversity at work, including personnel recruitment, selection, and development; work design and performance and health management; as well as leadership and teamwork.[6] Before we discuss this research and associated recommendations for employers and managers, we set the stage by describing various important individual age-related changes that influence work outcomes, and by reviewing the literature on common negative age stereotypes toward older and younger employees. We suggest that the combination of individual age-related changes across the lifespan, active behaviors of employees, and supportive job, team, and organizational contexts allows employees to age successfully at work.[7] We conclude this chapter by outlining implications for future research that rigorously addresses important theoretical and practical questions.

## AGE-RELATED CHANGES THAT INFLUENCE WORK OUTCOMES

Most research on individual age-related changes that have implications for the work context is based on the lifespan developmental perspective.[8] This metatheory suggests that age-related changes are multidimensional and multidirectional, including growth, decline, and maintenance in various psychological characteristics across the lifespan. In the work context, five categories of age-related characteristics have received the most attention: cognitive abilities, personality, goal orientation, socioemotional experience, and health.[9] Cognitive abilities are important predictors of job performance, particularly the efficiency with which employees carry out their tasks.[10] Lifespan research has shown that fluid cognitive abilities, such as fast information processing, logical reasoning, and memory, are negatively related to age, whereas crystallized cognitive abilities, such as verbal knowledge and wise judgment, are positively related to age.[11]

With regard to personality characteristics relevant to the work context, both cross-sectional and longitudinal studies have demonstrated that people, on average, become more mature and well adjusted with age (i.e., conscientious, agreeable, emotionally stable), whereas the sociability dimension of extraversion and openness to experience show some declines at higher ages.[12] Researchers have proposed that these favorable personality changes could be one of the reasons for positive associations documented between age and organizational citizenship behaviors (e.g., helping others, promoting the organization) and for negative links between age and counterproductive work behaviors (e.g., aggression, voluntary absenteeism).[13]

Lifespan research further shows that people's goal orientation changes across the adult lifespan from striving for gains (e.g., knowledge, social contacts) at younger ages to maintenance and prevention of losses (e.g., use of technical aids, compensation strategies) at higher ages.[14] In particular, the lifespan model of selection, optimization, and compensation outlines the processes of setting, pursuing, and maintaining personal goals.[15] Older adults can use action regulation strategies related to these three processes to better invest their increasingly limited personal resources (e.g., physical strength), with positive effects on their well-being and performance.[16] Relatedly, research on socioemotional selectivity theory suggests that, with increasing age, people perceive that they have less time left in life and, therefore, their socioemotional priorities shift from rather instrumental pursuits at younger ages to more pleasant and meaningful experiences and activities at higher ages.[17] For instance, research has shown that, on average, learning and development motives are stronger among young employees, whereas generativity (i.e., supporting the next generation) is a more important concern of older employees.[18] Overall, these motivational lifespan theories assume that people more or less successfully adapt to age-related changes and challenges.[19]

Finally, research shows that some physical abilities (e.g., strength, flexibility) decline with age,[20] whereas specific indicators of physical ill health (e.g., blood pressure, cholesterol level, body mass index) are weakly positively associated with age.[21] In contrast, meta-analytic research neither finds age-related declines in self-reported physical health nor mental health.[22] Consistently, associations between employee age and favorable work-related attitudes (e.g., job satisfaction, involvement) appear to be generally positive.[23] When interpreting these findings, however, it is important to consider that, due to technological advancements and the changing nature of industries, most of today's employees do not work any longer in jobs that are physically very demanding. In addition, research reporting associations with age could be biased by the "healthy worker effect," which suggests that workers with relatively poor health and well-being have left the workforce early and, thus, may be not represented in samples of older employees.

## AGE-RELATED STEREOTYPES IN ORGANIZATIONS

Negative age stereotypes, which typically portray older as compared to younger workers as low in competence and adaptability (but higher in the interpersonal dimension of warmth), are a key hindrance to successful aging at work.[24] Negative age-related attitudes and stereotypes are still widespread in modern organizations, despite overwhelming empirical evidence that refutes most of them.[25] For instance, a meta-analysis on six common age stereotypes did not find support for the assumptions that older workers are generally less motivated, less willing to change, less trusting, less healthy, and more vulnerable to work-family imbalance than younger workers.[26] The only age stereotype for which some empirical support was found was that older workers are less willing to participate in training and career development activities. However, research has shown that lower training-related motivation (e.g., lower self-efficacy due to a lack of prior mastery experiences in the training context), and not generally lower learning ability, is largely responsible for this difference between older and younger workers.[27] Whereas learning ability is an individual difference characteristic that is difficult to change, training motivation is a more malleable state that can be enhanced through, for instance, positive feedback. (See also chapter 15.) The lack of evidence for common age stereotypes suggests that it is important to eliminate these generalized negative beliefs in organizations, because they can lead to age-based discrimination, reduce worker well-being, and may increase their withdrawal behavior.[28] Moreover, a climate for successful aging, including appreciation of age-related strengths and challenges as well as nondiscriminatory treatment, can help older employees maintain a positive view of their occupational future.[29]

Importantly, not only older employees but also younger employees may face negative age-based stereotypes and discrimination. For example, younger employees are often stereotyped as inexperienced, immature, and unreliable.[30] Some research suggests that younger employees are less vulnerable than older employees to the detrimental consequences of negative age stereotypes for well-being and work behavior.[31] However, negative age stereotypes toward young employees today can be hidden in generalized assumptions about "the younger generation" and "generational differences," and these assumptions might be internalized and negatively affect younger employees' well-being and work behavior.[32] Thus, it is important to reduce both ageism and "generationalism" in the workplace.

Research at the company level has shown that greater age diversity is associated with a stronger age discrimination climate (i.e., employees' shared perception that their organization discriminates against employees based on their age), which, subsequently, negatively impacts firm performance.[33] This detrimental chain of effects can be prevented by reducing top managers' negative age stereotypes, by implementing diversity-friendly human resource policies, and by facilitating a positive age-diversity climate.[34] Moreover, a study with chief executive officers of small- and medium-sized businesses showed that the combination of leaders' own age and their age-related attitudes can shape the extent to which the culture in their organizations was supportive of employees from different age groups.[35] Overall, these studies show that negative age stereotypes are not only harmful for employees, but can also have negative consequences for the culture, climate, and outcomes of organizations. Fortunately, this line of research also suggests that organizations can reduce these negative effects by implementing age-inclusive human resource practices.

## AGE-INCLUSIVE HUMAN RESOURCE PRACTICES

Having reviewed the literature on important individual age-related changes and common negative stereotypes about different age groups, we now turn to an overview of more specific human resource practices that could be implemented to attract, hire, motivate, and retain employees from different age groups.[36] (See also chapters 7 and 9–12.)

### Personnel Recruitment, Selection, and Development

Scholars have suggested that organizations aiming to recruit employees from specific age groups (e.g., older adults) should consider five key aspects.[37] First, for targeted recruitment to be successful, they have to gain an understanding of the strengths and motives of the age group (see our review on individual age-related changes above). Second, in their recruitment messages, they should particularly communicate those job and organizational attributes that members of this age group consider attractive (e.g., task variety).[38] Third, the recruitment source should match the job search behaviors of the targeted age group (e.g., specialized media outlets and employment agencies). Fourth, recruiters should be sensitive to the strengths and needs of the targeted age group and avoid age discriminatory behaviors (e.g., ignoring older employees' knowledge and ability). Finally, organizations should make clear that they value members of this age group and age diversity more generally.[39] Recruitment and selection researchers have suggested that human resource practitioners, in the context of an aging and age-diverse workforce, should particularly focus on enhancing (perceived) applicant-organization fit.[40]

With regard to selection practices, it is important (and legally mandated in most Western countries) that organizations do not explicitly, or implicitly, discriminate against older or younger employees. Specific restrictions with regard to applicant and retirement age have to be clearly justified and based on rigorous empirical evidence (e.g., due to well-documented declines in fluid cognitive abilities, older adults cannot apply to work as air traffic controllers, and there is often a mandated earlier retirement in this occupation). Organizations also need to prevent age-based adverse impact of their selection practices. Specifically, research shows that tests emphasizing fluid cognitive abilities may discriminate against older job applicants, whereas tests focused on assessing crystallized cognitive abilities may discriminate against younger applicants.[41]

Age-based discrimination should also be avoided when assigning employees to training and development activities intended to improve their knowledge, skills, and other characteristics. Research suggests that employees are able to learn new knowledge and skills independent of age, but that the learning process of older adults may be optimized by designing training according to their altered abilities and needs.[42] For instance, recommendations to optimize training for older adults include enhancing learning self-efficacy by allowing mastery experiences, linking training to past work experience, emphasizing transferability of existing knowledge and skills during training, and allowing for active practice of training content.[43]

## Work Design

Research on age-differentiated work design is concerned with the question of how younger and older employees react to and perform in jobs that differ in their task, knowledge, social, and contextual characteristics.[44] With regard to task characteristics, research on age as a moderator of effects of employees' experiences of job autonomy and feedback from the job on important work outcomes, such as employees' sense of job satisfaction and supervisor ratings of employees' performance, is inconclusive and complex.[45] In contrast, studies have shown that younger employees benefit more from high task variety than older employees,[46] whereas older employees benefit more from high levels of task significance and task identity (i.e., the degree to which employees are involved in the entire work process) than younger employees.[47]

Among the knowledge characteristics of jobs, high levels of job complexity, information processing demands, and problem-solving demands may, depending on individual development and cognitive resources, pose greater challenges for older than for younger employees, whereas high skill variety and specialization of job seem to have a greater fit with older employees' accumulated knowledge and experience.[48] In terms of social job characteristics, social support appears to benefit workers independent of their age. In line with propositions of socioemotional selectivity theory,[49] interdependence (i.e., links between one's own and others' jobs) may be more beneficial for older employees, and interaction outside the organization (i.e., the requirement to interact with people who are not employed by one's organization) may be perceived as more rewarding by younger employees.[50] Finally, the extent to which various work context factors, such as ergonomics, physical demands, working conditions, and equipment use, are favorable or unfavorable may play a greater role for older compared to younger employees due to declines in some physical abilities, as well as age-related increases in the need for positive and meaningful experiences at work.[51]

## Performance and Health Management

Meta-analyses have shown that most bivariate relationships between age and different indicators of job performance and health are rather weak,[52] suggesting that stereotypes of age-related declines in performance and health are unfounded. (See also chapters 13 and 14.) Nevertheless, to enable successful aging at work, research shows that effective human resource practices to manage employee performance and health are important.[53] For example, supervisors should provide employees from all age groups with regular performance feedback; however, they should be aware that, consistent with socioemotional selectivity theory,[54] younger employees focus more on the utility of feedback information provided, whereas older employees focus more on the social implications of feedback information.[55] Importantly, supervisors should receive performance appraisal training to minimize bias due to negative age stereotypes.[56] When developing and setting performance goals, supervisors should take age-related differences in employees' occupational future time perspective, including their perceived remaining time and opportunities, into account.[57]

With regard to health management, research has identified a number of factors that could help buffer potential age-related declines in occupational health and well-being indicators. (See also chapter 19.) For instance, research showed that high levels of job autonomy and the use of selection, optimization, and compensation strategies can buffer the negative association between age and work ability,[58] that is, foster older employees' perception that they can fulfill the physical, mental, and emotional demands of their work.[59] Similarly, a study has demonstrated that high levels of job autonomy facilitate the use of selection, optimization, and compensation strategies, which in turn reduce depressive symptoms in older workers.[60] Moreover, a favorable team health climate (e.g., regular communication among team members about health-related topics) positively influences the link between age and work ability.[61]

## Leadership and Teamwork

Effective leadership plays a key role in supporting employees across the lifespan and in successfully leading age-diverse teams.[62] Research has suggested that contingent reward (e.g., rewarding employees when they have achieved their identified goals), a transactional form of leadership, is more effective when used by younger leaders (who, compared to older leaders, are less prototypical of effective leaders and lack social status) in terms of reducing voluntary turnover.[63] In contrast, the study's findings suggest that younger leaders, as compared to older leaders, should not make use of participative leadership behaviors (e.g., asking employees for their opinion before making an important decision). Other researchers have shown that the greater the extent to which younger supervisors and older subordinates differ in age is associated with increased prevalence of negative emotions among older subordinates and their coworkers, which, in turn, negatively predicts company performance if subordinates express their feelings toward their supervisor.[64]

A meta-analysis found no significant associations between age diversity in teams and several important team outcomes, including performance quality, financial performance, innovation and creativity, effectiveness, and satisfaction.[65] However, team age diversity was weakly and positively related to turnover. Age diversity is often considered to be a double-edged sword with regard to team performance and innovation, as it has positive effects on the exchange of task-related information, but negative effect on social cohesion and social identity.[66] Research suggests that transformational leaders, who encourage creativity and emphasize common goals, can maximize the positive effects of age diversity and minimize the negative effects of age diversity.[67] Thus, organizations should train their leaders in dealing with age diversity.

## DISCUSSION

In this chapter, we have offered an overview of various issues that have implications for the management of aging and age-diverse workforces. We began by describing the general nature of the aging process in terms of individual age-related changes, and likewise discussed the influence that such changes bring to bear on work outcomes. We additionally reviewed research evidence concerning negative age stereotypes toward older and younger workers. Against this backdrop, we then summarized evidence-based practices for attracting, hiring, retaining, and reemploying workers of different ages. In this regard, we particularly focused on personnel recruitment, selection, and development; work design and performance and health management; and leadership and teamwork in the context of aging and age-diverse workforces. We now conclude this chapter by offering suggestions for rigorous future work to address challenges to our understanding of these phenomena, and in particular those that have implications for theory, research, and practice. We also offer methodological guidance to help researchers address these challenges through enhanced programs of research.

One challenge to managing aging and age-diverse workforces concerns how to optimally harness older workers' potential cognitive and emotional strengths and contributions. Indeed, economists have long lamented the "underutilization" of older workers.[68] Concerning cognitive contributions, various challenges associated with how to both retain and maximize the accumulated job knowledge and experience of older workers have long been noted in the literature.[69] Similarly, concerning emotional contributions, research has suggested that older individuals are generally better than younger individuals at emotion regulation, and that this advantage carries over to interpersonal behavior in the workplace.[70] For example, older workers are generally better at engaging in more adaptive forms of emotional labor (i.e., the regulation of felt and expressed emotions as required by one's job).[71] Although recent experience-sampling studies have demonstrated the short-term advantages that older workers have in the expression of emotional labor,[72] there has thus far been little long-term longitudinal research on this topic. This is important to note, as emotion regulation skills, like emotional labor, are particularly relevant for success in customer service roles and beyond.

Another challenge to managing aging and age-diverse workforces concerns how best to integrate the accumulated research evidence into actionable policies, procedures, and practices. For example, although quite a bit of research concerning work and aging has focused on lifespan development theories, there has been little attempt to develop interventions to enhance the developmental mechanisms that are purported to exert an influence on work outcomes. There are exceptions to this, however. For example, recent work supports the efficacy of training interventions to enhance the use of selection, optimization, and compensation adaptive coping strategies.[73] Still, there remain numerous opportunities for research to develop interventions, for example, interventions aimed at enhancing the employee's occupational future time perspective.[74] Given strong links between future time perspective and well-being, both inside and outside of work,[75] such efforts would be especially beneficial.

Finally, addressing challenges such as these will require the advancement of more rigorous research programs. Thus, we offer some methodological advice for future research on work and aging that attempts to address these and related issues. Indeed, recent work outlines an enhanced agenda and set of "best practices" for research concerning work and aging.[76] Specifically, eight methodological recommendations are outlined that, if adopted, would serve to enhance our understanding of the complexities of aging and work through better-conducted research. These recommendations include: (1) testing age-related mediators that link age as a predictor to various work outcomes; (2) testing moderators to examine the variability in work outcomes among older and younger workers; (3) moving away from cross-sectional, and toward longitudinal, experience-sampling, and experimental research designs; (4) sampling workers across the entire work lifespan; (5) operationalizing age as a continuous variable; (6) studying nonlinear effects of age on work outcomes; (7) controlling for alternative time-related constructs, such as tenure; and finally (8) studying age (in)congruence via polynomial regression and related methodologies. A complete description of each of these recommendations, as well as practical advice for their implementation, can be found in the article.[77] Given the implications of an aging workforce discussed here, the imperative for "better" research to be conducted in this area should be apparent. Accordingly, we strongly suggest that researchers consider these recommendations and how they can be integrated into their own programs of research. We also suggest that researchers and practitioners critically evaluate the quality of existing evidence against these recommendations before embarking on work for which the quality of available support is weak or equivocal.

## CONCLUSION

From the preceding, it should be clear that there are a number of challenges and opportunities associated with the aging and increased age diversity of the workforce that have implications for organizational leaders, human resource management, and work organizations, more broadly. Although there is still much to be learned about our aging and age-diverse workforce, we have so far developed a solid base of evidence upon which management practices can be shaped. At the same time, our hope is that the present work inspires researchers and practitioners to consider ways of optimizing opportunities to further our understanding of the aging and age-diverse workforce, and to work toward evidence-based ways to rigorously address the given barriers to our broader understanding of these issues.

## NOTES

Acknowledgment: We thank Kahea Chang for his help in preparing this chapter.

1. Guido Hertel and Hannes Zacher. 2018. "Managing the Aging Workforce." Pp. 396–428 in *The SAGE Handbook of Industrial, Work and Organizational Psychology*, edited by Deniz Ones et al. Thousand Oaks, CA: SAGE; Carol Kulik et al. 2014. "From the Editors: Aging Populations and Management." *Academy of Management Journal* 57(4):929–35. (https://doi.org/10.5465/amj.2014.4004).
2. Cort Rudolph and Hannes Zacher. 2019. "Managing Employees across the Lifespan." Pp. 425–45 in *The Cambridge Handbook of the Changing Nature of Work*, edited by Brian Hoffman, Mindy Shoss, and Lauren Wegman. Cambridge: Cambridge University Press.
3. Terry Beehr and Misty Bennett. 2015. "Working after Retirement: Features of Bridge Employment and Research Directions." *Work, Aging and Retirement* 1(1):112–28. (https://doi.org/10.1093/workar/wau007); Yujie Zhan and Mo Wang. 2015. "Bridge Employment: Conceptualizations and New Directions for Future Research." Pp. 203–20 in *Aging Workers and the Employee-employer Relationship*, edited by Matthis Bal, Dorien Kooij, and Denise Rousseau. Cham, Switzerland: Springer.
4. Claudia Buengeler, Astrid Homan, and Sven Voelpel. 2016. "The Challenge of Being a Young Manager: The Effects of Contingent Reward and Participative Leadership on Team-level Turnover Depend on Leader Age." *Journal of Organizational Behavior* 37(8):1224–45. (https://doi.org/10.1002/job.2101); Matthias Schneid et al. 2016. "Age Diversity and Team Outcomes: A Quantitative Review." *Journal of Managerial Psychology* 31(1):2–17. (https://doi.org/10.1108/JMP-07-2012-0228).
5. Stephan Böhm, Heike Schröder, and Florian Kunze. 2013. "Comparative Age Management: Theoretical Perspective and Practical Implications." Pp. 211–37 in *The SAGE Handbook on Work, Aging, and Society*, edited by John Field, Ronald Burke, and Cary Cooper. Thousand Oaks, CA: SAGE; Gerhard Naegele and Alan Walker. 2011. "Age Management in Organisations in the European Union." Pp. 251–67 in *The SAGE Handbook of Workplace Learning*, edited by Margaret Malloch et al. London: SAGE; Cort Rudolph, Eileen Toomey, and Boris Baltes. 2017. "Considering Age Diversity in Recruitment and Selection: An Expanded Work Lifespan View of Age Management." Pp. 607–38 in *Handbook of Age Diversity and Work*, edited by Jean McCarthy and Emma Parry. London: Palgrave-Macmillan.
6. See also Hannes Zacher, Dorien Kooij, and Margaret Beier. 2018. "Active Aging at Work: Contributing Factors and Implications for Organizations." *Organizational Dynamics* 47(1):37–45. (https://doi.org/10.1016/j.orgdyn.2017.08.001).
7. Dorien Kooij et al. 2019. "Successful Aging at Work: A Process Model to Guide Future Research and Practice." *Industrial and Organizational Psychology*. (https://doi.org/10.1017/iop.2020.1); Donald Truxillo, David Cadiz, and Leslie Hammer. 2015. "Supporting the Aging Workforce: A Research Review and Recommendations for Workplace Intervention Research." *Annual Review of Organizational Psychology and Organizational Behavior* 2:351–81. (https://doi.org/10.1146/annurev-orgpsych-032414-111435); Hannes Zacher and Cort Rudolph. 2017. "Successful Aging at Work and Beyond: A Review and Critical Perspective." Pp. 35–64 in *Age Diversity in the Workplace: An Organizational Perspective*, edited by Silvia Profili, Alessia Sammarra, and Laura Innocenti. Bingley, UK: Emerald.
8. Paul Baltes. 1987. "Theoretical Propositions of Life-span Developmental Psychology: On the Dynamics between Growth and Decline." *Developmental Psychology* 23(5):611–26. (https://doi.org/10.1037/0012-1649.23.5.611); See also Hannes Zacher, Cort Rudolph, and Boris Baltes. 2019. "An Invitation to Lifespan Thinking." Pp. 1–14 in *Work across the Lifespan*, edited by Boris Baltes, Cort Rudolph, and Hannes Zacher. London: Academic Press.

9. Thomas Ng and Daniel Feldman. 2013b. "How Do Within-person Changes Due to Aging Affect Job Performance?" *Journal of Vocational Behavior* 83(3):500–13. (https://doi.org/10.1016/j.jvb.2013.07.007).

10. Gwenith Fisher, Marisol Chacon, and Dorey Chaffee. 2019. "Theories of Cognitive Aging and Work." Pp. 17–45 in *Work across the Lifespan*, edited by Boris Baltes, Cort Rudolph, and Hannes Zacher. London: Academic Press.

11. Rachael Klein et al. 2015. "Cognitive Predictors and Age-based Adverse Impact among Business Executives." *Journal of Applied Psychology* 100(5):1497–510. (https://doi.org/10.1037/a0038991); Timothy Salthouse. 2012. "Consequences of Age-related Cognitive Declines." *Annual Review of Psychology* 63:201–26. (https://doi.org/10.1146/annurev-psych-120710-100328).

12. Christopher Nye and Brent Roberts. 2019. "A Neo-socioanalytic Model of Personality Development." Pp. 47–79 in *Work across the Lifespan*, edited by Boris Baltes, Cort Rudolph, and Hannes Zacher. London: Academic Press; Brent Roberts, Kate Walton, and Wolfgang Viechtbauer. 2006. "Patterns of Mean-level Change in Personality Traits across the Life Course: A Meta-analysis of Longitudinal Studies." *Psychological Bulletin* 132(1):1–25. (https://doi.org/10.1037/0033-2909.132.1.1).

13. Thomas Ng and Daniel Feldman. 2008. "The Relationship of Age to Ten Dimensions of Job Performance." *Journal of Applied Psychology* 93(2):392–423. (https://doi.org/10.1037/0021-9010.93.2.392).

14. Natalie Ebner, Alexandra Freund, and Paul Baltes. 2006. "Developmental Changes in Personal Goal Orientation from Young to Late Adulthood: From Striving for Gains to Maintenance and Prevention of Losses." *Psychology and Aging* 21(4):664–78. (https://doi.org/10.1037/0882-7974.21.4.664).

15. Paul Baltes and Margret Baltes. 1990. "Psychological Perspectives on Successful Aging: The Model of Selective Optimization with Compensation." Pp. 1–34 in *Successful Aging: Perspectives from the Behavioral Sciences*, edited by Paul Baltes and Margret Baltes. New York: Cambridge University Press.

16. Baltes and Baltes, "Psychological Perspectives"; Darya Moghimi et al. 2017. "The Selection, Optimization, and Compensation Model in the Work Context: A Systematic Review and Meta-analysis of Two Decades of Research." *Journal of Organizational Behavior* 38(2):247–75. (https://doi.org/10.1002/job.2108).

17. Laura Carstensen, Derek Isaacowitz, and Susan Charles. 1999. "Taking Time Seriously: A Theory of Socioemotional Selectivity." *American Psychologist* 54(3):165–81. (https://doi.org/10.1037/0003-066X.54.3.165).

18. Dorien Kooij and Karina Van de Voorde. 2011. "How Changes in Subjective General Health Predict Future Time Perspective and Development and Generativity Motives over the Lifespan." *Journal of Occupational and Organizational Psychology* 84(2):228–47. (https://doi.org/10.1111/j.2044-8325.2010.02012.x).

19. Cort Rudolph. 2016. "Lifespan Developmental Perspectives on Working: A Literature Review of Motivational Theories." *Work, Aging and Retirement* 2:130–58. (https://doi.org/10.1093/workar/waw012).

20. Julie Maertens et al. 2012. "Physical Capabilities and Occupational Health of Older Workers." Pp. 215–35 in *The Oxford Handbook of Work and Aging*, edited by Jerry W. Hedge and Walter C. Borman. New York: Oxford University Press.

21. Thomas Ng and Daniel Feldman. 2013a. "Employee Age and Health." *Journal of Vocational Behavior* 83(3):336–45. (https://doi.org/10.1016/j.jvb.2013.06.004).

22. Ng and Feldman, "Employee Age and Health."

23. Thomas Ng and Daniel Feldman. 2010. "The Relationship of Age with Job Attitudes: A Meta-analysis." *Personnel Psychology* 63(3):667–718. (https://doi.org/10.1111/j.1744-6570.2010.01184.x).

24. Kooij et al., "Successful Aging at Work."

25. Jean McCarthy, Noreen Heraty, and Ashley Bamberg. 2019. "Lifespan Perspectives on Age-related Stereotypes, Prejudice, and Discrimination at Work (and Beyond)." Pp. 417–35 in *Work across the Lifespan*, edited by Boris Baltes, Cort Rudolph, and Hannes Zacher. London: Academic Press; Richard Posthuma and Laura Guerrero. 2013. "Age Stereotypes in the Workplace:

Multidimensionality, Cross-cultural Applications, and Directions for Future Research." Pp. 250–65 in *The SAGE Handbook of Aging, Work and Society*, edited by John Field, Ronald Burke, and Cary Cooper. Thousand Oaks, CA: SAGE.

26. Thomas Ng and Daniel Feldman. 2012. "Evaluating Six Common Stereotypes about Older Workers with Meta-analytical Data." *Personnel Psychology* 65(4):821–58. (https://doi.org/10.1111/peps.12003).

27. Todd Maurer. 2001. "Career-relevant Learning and Development, Worker Age, and Beliefs about Self-efficacy for Development." *Journal of Management* 27:123–40. (https://doi.org/10.1177/014920630102700201).

28. Barbara Griffin, Piers Bayl-Smith, and Beryl Hesketh. 2016. "The Longitudinal Effects of Perceived Age Discrimination on the Job Satisfaction and Work Withdrawal of Older Employees." *Work, Aging and Retirement* 2(4):415–27. (https://doi.org/10.1093/workar/waw014); Courtney von Hippel et al. 2018. "Age-based Stereotype Threat and Work Outcomes: Stress Appraisals and Rumination as Mediators." *Psychology and Aging* 34(1):68–84. (https://doi.org/10.1037/pag0000308); Sara Zaniboni. 2015. "The Interaction between Older Workers' Personal Resources and Perceived Age Discrimination Affects the Desired Retirement Age and the Expected Adjustment." *Work, Aging and Retirement* 1(3):266–73. (https://doi.org/10.1093/workar/wav010).

29. Hannes Zacher and Jie Yang. 2016. "Organizational Climate for Successful Aging." *Frontiers in Psychology* 7(1):1007. (https://doi.org/10.3389/fpsyg.2016.01007).

30. Lisa Finkelstein, Katherine Ryan, and Eden King. 2013. "What Do the Young (Old) People Think of Me? Content and Accuracy of Age-based Metastereotypes." *European Journal of Work and Organizational Psychology* 22(6):633–57. (https://doi.org/10.1080/1359432X.2012.673279).

31. Courtney von Hippel, Elise Kalokerinos, and Julie Henry. 2012. "Stereotype Threat among Older Employees: Relationships with Job Attitudes and Turnover Intentions." *Psychology and Aging* 28(1):17–27. (https://doi.org/10.1037/a0029825).

32. Rachel Rauvola, Cort Rudolph, and Hannes Zacher. May 2018. "Generationalism: Problems and Implications." *Organizational Dynamics* 48(4). (https://doi.org/10.1016/j.orgdyn.2018.05.006).

33. Florian Kunze, Stephan Böhm and Heike Bruch. 2011. "Age Diversity, Age Discrimination Climate and Performance Consequences: A Cross Organizational Study." *Journal of Organizational Behavior* 32(2):264–90. (https://doi.org/10.1002/job.698).

34. Stephan Böhm, Florian Kunze, and Heike Bruch. 2014. "Spotlight on Age-diversity Climate: The Impact of Age-inclusive HR Practices on Firm-level Outcomes." *Personnel Psychology* 67(3):667–704. (https://doi.org/10.1111/peps.12047); Florian Kunze, Stephan Böhm, and Heike Bruch. 2013. "Organizational Performance Consequences of Age Diversity: Inspecting the Role of Diversity-friendly HR Policies and Top Managers' Negative Age Stereotypes." *Journal of Management Studies* 50(3):413–42. (https://doi.org/10.1111/joms.12016).

35. Hannes Zacher and Michael Gielnik. 2012. "Organizational Age Cultures: The Interplay of Chief Executive Officers' Age and Attitudes toward Younger and Older Employees." *International Small Business Journal* 32(3):327–49. (https://doi.org/10.1177/0266242612463025).

36. See also Stephan Böhm and David Dwertmann. 2015. "Forging a Single-edged Sword: Facilitating Positive Age and Disability Diversity Effects in the Workplace through Leadership, Positive Climates, and HR Practices." *Work, Aging and Retirement* 1(1):41–63. (https://doi.org/10.1093/workar/wau008); Dorien Kooij et al. 2013. "How the Impact of HR Practices on Employee Well-being and Performance Changes with Age." *Human Resource Management Journal* 23(1):18–35. (https://doi.org/10.1111/1748-8583.12000); Jorg Korff et al. 2009. "HR Management for an Aging Workforce: A Life-span Psychology Perspective." *Journal of Personnel Psychology* 8(4):201–13; Rudolph, Toomey, and Baltes, "Considering Age Diversity."

37. Filip Lievens, Greet Van Hoye, and Hannes Zacher. 2012. "Recruiting/Hiring of Older Workers." Pp. 380–91 in *The Oxford Handbook of Work and Aging*, edited by Jerry W. Hedge and Walter C. Borman. New York: Oxford University Press.

38. Hannes Zacher et al. 2017. "Age-differential Effects of Job Characteristics on Job Attraction: A Policy-capturing Study." *Frontiers in Psychology* 8:1124. (https://doi.org/10.3389/fpsyg.2017.01124).

39. Florian Kunze and Andra Toader. 2019. "Lifespan Perspectives on Organizational Climate." Pp. 561–80 in *Work across the Lifespan*, edited by Boris Baltes, Cort Rudolph, and Hannes Zacher. London: Academic Press.

40. Dennis Doverspike, Catalina Flores, and Josh VanderLeest. 2019. "Lifespan Perspectives on Personnel Selection and Recruitment." Pp. 343–68 in *Work across the Lifespan*, edited by Boris Baltes, Cort Rudolph, and Hannes Zacher. London: Academic Press.

41. Klein et al., "Cognitive Predictors."

42. Margaret Beier, Mark Teachout, and Cody Cox. 2012. "The Training and Development of an Aging Workforce." Pp. 436–53 in *The Oxford Handbook of Work and Aging*, edited by Jerry W. Hedge and Walter C. Borman. New York: Oxford University Press.

43. Harvey Sterns and Katherine Harrington. 2019. "Lifespan Perspectives on Learning and Training." Pp. 323–41 in *Work across the Lifespan*, edited by Boris Baltes, Cort Rudolph, and Hannes Zacher. London: Academic Press.

44. David Cadiz, Jennifer Rineer, and Donald Truxillo. 2019. "Lifespan Perspectives on Job and Work Design." Pp. 263–90 in *Work across the Lifespan*, edited by Boris Baltes, Cort Rudolph, and Hannes Zacher. London: Academic Press; Donald Truxillo et al. 2012. "A Lifespan Perspective on Job Design: Fitting the Job and the Worker to Promote Job Satisfaction, Engagement, and Performance." *Organizational Psychology Review* 2(4):340–60. (https://doi.org/10.1177/2041386612454043).

45. Thomas Ng and Daniel Feldman. 2015. "The Moderating Effects of Age in the Relationships of Job Autonomy to Work Outcomes." *Work, Aging and Retirement* 1(1):64–78. (https://doi.org/10.1093/workar/wau003); Mo Wang et al. 2015. "Age Differences in Feedback Reactions: The Roles of Employee Feedback Orientation on Social Awareness and Utility." *Journal of Applied Psychology* 100:1296–1308. (https://doi.org/10.1037/a0038334).

46. Sara Zaniboni, Donald Truxillo, and Franco Fraccaroli. 2013. "Differential Effects of Task Variety and Skill Variety on Burnout and Turnover Intentions for Older and Younger Workers." *European Journal of Work and Organizational Psychology* 22(3):306–17. (https://doi.org/10.1080/1359432X.2013.782288).

47. Hannes Zacher, Winfried Hacker, and Michael Frese. 2016. "Action Regulation across the Adult Lifespan (ARAL): A Meta-theory of Work and Aging." *Work, Aging and Retirement* 2(3):286–306. (https://doi.org/10.1093/workar/waw015).

48. Cadiz, Rineer, and Truxillo, "Lifespan Perspectives."

49. Carstensen, Isaacowitz, and Charles, "Taking Time Seriously."

50. Donald Truxillo et al., "A Lifespan Perspective on Job Design."

51. Cadiz, Rineer, and Truxillo, "Lifespan Perspectives"; Susan Charles, "Strength and Vulnerability Integration: A Model of Emotional Well-being across Adulthood." *Psychological Bulletin* 136(6):1068–91. (https://doi.org/10.1037/a0021232).

52. Ng and Feldman, "Relationship of Age."

53. Jeanette Cleveland et al. 2019. "Lifespan Perspectives on Job Performance, Performance Appraisal/Management and Creative Performance." Pp. 291–321 in *Work across the Lifespan*, edited by Boris Baltes, Cort Rudolph, and Hannes Zacher. London: Academic Press; Antje Schmitt and Dana Unger. 2019. "Lifespan Perspectives on Occupational Health." Pp. 369–93 in *Work across the Lifespan*, edited by Boris Baltes, Cort Rudolph, and Hannes Zacher. London: Academic Press.

54. Carstensen, Isaacowitz, and Charles, "Taking Time Seriously."

55. Wang et al., "Age Differences in Feedback Reactions."

56. Cleveland et al., "Lifespan Perspectives on Job Performance."

57. Cort Rudolph et al. 2018. "Occupational Future Time Perspective: A Meta-analysis of Antecedents and Outcomes." *Journal of Organizational Behavior* 39(2):229–48. (https://doi.org/10.1002/job.2264).

58. Matthias Weigl et al. 2013. "The Moderating Effects of Job Control and Selection, Optimization, and Compensation Strategies on the Age–Work Ability Relationship." *Journal of Organizational Behavior* 34:607–28. (https://doi.org/10.1002/job.1810).

59. Alyssa McGonagle et al. 2015. "Individual and Work Factors Related to Perceived Work Ability and Labor Force Outcomes." *Journal of Applied Psychology* 100(2):376–98. (https://doi.org/10.1037/a0037974).

60. Andreas Müller et al. 2017. "The Age-related Effect of Job Autonomy on Depressive Symptoms through Selective Optimization with Compensation: A Two-wave Panel Study." *Work, Aging and Retirement* 3(4):379–92. (https://doi.org/10.1093/workar/wax004).

61. Heiko Schulz, Hannes Zacher, and Sonia Lippke. 2017. "The Importance of Team Health Climate for Health-related Outcomes of White-collar Workers." *Frontiers in Psychology* 8:74. (https://doi.org/10.3389/fpsyg.2017.00074).

62. Kathrin Rosing and Franziska Jungmann. 2019. *Lifespan Perspectives on Leadership*. London: Academic Press; Hannes Zacher et al. 2015. "A Lifespan Perspective on Leadership." Pp. 87–104 in *Aging Workers and the Employee-Employer Relationship*, edited by Mattiijs Bal, Dorien Kooij, and Denise Rousseau. Cham, Switzerland: Springer.

63. Buengeler, Homan, and Voelpel, "Challenge of Being a Young Manager."

64. Florian Kunze and Jochen Menges. 2017. "Younger Supervisors, Older Subordinates: An Organizational-level Study of Age Differences, Emotions, and Performance." *Journal of Organizational Behavior* 38(4):461–86. (https://doi.org/10.1002/job.2129).

65. Schneid et al., "Age Diversity and Team Outcomes."

66. Böhm and Dwertmann, "Forging a Single-Edged Sword."; Jurgen Wegge et al. 2008. "Age and Gender Diversity as Determinants of Performance and Health in a Public Organization: The Role of Task Complexity and Group Size." *Journal of Applied Psychology* 93(6):1301–13. (https://doi.org/10.1037/a0012680).

67. Eric Kearney and Diether Gebert. 2009. "Managing Diversity and Enhancing Team Outcomes: The Promise of Transformational Leadership." *Journal of Applied Psychology* 94(1):77–89. (https://doi.org/10.1037/a0013077).

68. Michael Barth, William McNaught, and Philip Rizzi. 1995. "Older Americans as Workers." Pp. 35–70 in *Older and Active: How Americans over 55 Are Contributing to Society*, edited by Scott Bass. New Haven, CT: Yale University Press.

69. David DeLong and John Storey. 2004. *Lost Knowledge: Confronting the Threat of an Aging Workforce*. New York: Oxford University Press.

70. Friederike Doerwald et al. 2016. "Emotional Competencies across Adulthood: State of Knowledge and Implications for the Work Context." *Work, Aging and Retirement* 2(2):159–216. (https://doi.org/10.1093/workar/waw013); Susanne Scheibe and Hannes Zacher. 2013. "A Lifespan Perspective on Emotion Regulation, Stress, and Well-being in the Workplace." Pp. 167–97 in *Research in Occupational Stress and Well-being*, edited by Pamela Perrewé, Jonathon Halbesleben, and Christopher Rosen. Bingley, UK: Emerald.

71. Alicia Grandey. 2000. "Emotion Regulation in the Workplace: A New Way to Conceptualize Emotional Labor." *Journal of Occupational Health Psychology* 5(1):95–110.

72. Cort Rudolph and Alyssa McGonagle. 2018. "Exploring Age-conditional Effects in the Emotional Labor–perceived Work Ability Linkage: A Daily Diary Study." *Work, Aging and Retirement* 5(2):163–74. (https://doi.org/10.1093/workar/way014); Eileen Toomey and Cort Rudolph. 2018. "Age-conditional Effects in the Affective Arousal, Empathy, and Emotional Labor Linkage: Within-person Evidence from an Experience Sampling Study." *Work, Aging and Retirement* 4(2):145–60. (https://doi.org/10.1093/workar/wax018).

73. Imad Maatouk et al. 2018. "Healthy Ageing at Work—Efficacy of Group Interventions on the Mental Health of Nurses Aged 45 and Older: Results of a Randomised, Controlled Trial." *PLoS ONE* 13(1). (https://doi.org/10.1371/journal.pone.0191000).

74. Hannes Zacher and Michael Frese. 2009. "Remaining Time and Opportunities at Work: Relationships between Age, Work Characteristics, and Occupational Future Time Perspective." *Psychology and Aging* 24(2):487–93. (https://doi.org/10.1037/a0015425).

75. Dorien Kooij et al. 2018. "Future Time Perspective: A Systematic Review and Meta-analysis." *Journal of Applied Psychology* 103(8):867–93 (https://doi.org/10.1037/apl0000306).

76. Clarissa Bohlmann, Cort Rudolph, and Hannes Zacher. 2018. "Methodological Recommendations to Move Research on Work and Aging Forward." *Work, Aging and Retirement* 4(3):225–37. (https://doi.org/10.1093/workar/wax023).

77. Bohlmann, Rudolph, and Zacher, "Methodological Recommendations."

## REFERENCES


Baltes, Paul. 1987. "Theoretical Propositions of Life-span Developmental Psychology: On the Dynamics between Growth and Decline." *Developmental Psychology* 23(5):611–26. (https://doi.org/10.1037/0012-1649.23.5.611).

Baltes, Paul and Margret Baltes. 1990. "Psychological Perspectives on Successful Aging: The Model of Selective Optimization with Compensation." Pp. 1–34 in *Successful Aging: Perspectives from the Behavioral Sciences*, edited by Paul Baltes and Margret Baltes. New York: Cambridge University Press.

Barth, Michael, William McNaught, and Philip Rizzi. 1995. "Older Americans as Workers." Pp. 35–70 in *Older and Active: How Americans over 55 Are Contributing to Society*, edited by Scott Bass. New Haven, CT: Yale University Press.

Beehr, Terry and Misty Bennett. 2015. "Working after Retirement: Features of Bridge Employment and Research Directions." *Work, Aging and Retirement* 1(1):112–28. (https://doi.org/10.1093/workar/wau007).

Beier, Margaret, Mark Teachout, and Cody Cox. 2012. "The Training and Development of an Aging Workforce." Pp. 436–53 in *The Oxford Handbook of Work and Aging*, edited by Jerry W. Hedge and Walter C. Borman. New York: Oxford University Press.

Bohlmann, Clarissa, Cort Rudolph, and Hannes Zacher. 2018. "Methodological Recommendations to Move Research on Work and Aging Forward." *Work, Aging and Retirement* 4(3):225–37. (https://doi.org/10.1093/workar/wax023).

Böhm, Stephan and David Dwertmann. 2015. "Forging a Single-edged Sword: Facilitating Positive Age and Disability Diversity Effects in the Workplace through Leadership, Positive Climates, and HR Practices." *Work, Aging and Retirement* 1(1):41–63. (https://doi.org/10.1093/workar/wau008).

Böhm, Stephan, Florian Kunze, and Heike Bruch. 2014. "Spotlight on Age-diversity Climate: The Impact of Age-inclusive HR Practices on Firm-level Outcomes." *Personnel Psychology* 67(3):667–704. (https://doi.org/10.1111/peps.12047).

Böhm, Stephan, Heike Schröder, and Florian Kunze. 2013. "Comparative Age Management: Theoretical Perspective and Practical Implications." Pp. 211–37 in *The SAGE Handbook on Work, Aging, and Society*, edited by John Field, Ronald Burke, and Cary Cooper. Thousand Oakes, CA: SAGE.

Buengeler, Claudia, Astrid Homan, and Sven Voelpel. 2016. "The Challenge of Being a Young Manager: The Effects of Contingent Reward and Participative Leadership on Team-level Turnover Depend on Leader Age." *Journal of Organizational Behavior* 37(8):1224–45. (https://doi.org/10.1002/job.2101).

Cadiz, David, Jennifer Rineer, and Donald Truxillo. 2019. "Lifespan Perspectives on Job and Work Design." Pp. 263–90 in *Work across the Lifespan*, edited by Boris Baltes, Cort Rudolph, and Hannes Zacher. London: Academic Press.

Carstensen, Laura, Derek Isaacowitz, and Susan Charles. 1999. "Taking Time Seriously: A Theory of Socioemotional Selectivity." *American Psychologist* 54(3):165–81. (https://doi.org/10.1037/0003-066X.54.3.165).

Charles, Susan. 2010. "Strength and Vulnerability Integration: A Model of Emotional Well-being across Adulthood." *Psychological Bulletin* 136(6):1068–91. (https://doi.org/10.1037/a0021232).

Cleveland, Jeanette, et al. 2019."Lifespan Perspectives on Job Performance, Performance Appraisal/Management and Creative Performance." Pp. 291–321 in *Work across the Lifespan*, edited by Boris Baltes, Cort Rudolph, and Hannes Zacher. London: Academic Press.

DeLong, David and John Storey. 2004. *Lost Knowledge: Confronting the Threat of an Aging Workforce*. New York: Oxford University Press.

Doerwald, Friederike, et al. 2016. "Emotional Competencies across Adulthood: State of Knowledge and Implications for the Work Context." *Work, Aging and Retirement* 2(2):159–216. (https://doi.org/10.1093/workar/waw013).

Doverspike, Dennis, Catalina Flores, and Josh VanderLeest. 2019. "Lifespan Perspectives on Personnel Selection and Recruitment." Pp. 343–68 in *Work across the Lifespan*, edited by Boris Baltes, Cort Rudolph, and Hannes Zacher. London: Academic Press.

Ebner, Natalie, Alexandra Freund, and Paul Baltes. 2006. "Developmental Changes in Personal Goal Orientation from Young to Late Adulthood: From Striving for Gains to Maintenance and Prevention of Losses." *Psychology and Aging* 21(4):664–78. (https://doi.org/10.1037/0882-7974.21.4.664).

Finkelstein, Lisa, Katherine Ryan, and Eden King. 2013. "What Do the Young (Old) People Think of Me? Content and Accuracy of Age-based Metastereotypes." *European Journal of Work and Organizational Psychology* 22(6):633–57. (https://doi.org/10.1080/1359432X.2012.673279).

Fisher, Gwenith, Marisol Chacon, and Dorey Chaffee. 2019. "Theories of Cognitive Aging and Work." Pp. 17–45 in *Work across the Lifespan*, edited by Boris Baltes, Cort Rudolph, and Hannes Zacher. London: Academic Press.

Grandey, Alicia. 2000. "Emotion Regulation in the Workplace: A New Way to Conceptualize Emotional Labor." *Journal of Occupational Health Psychology* 5(1):95–110.

Griffin, Barbara, Piers Bayl-Smith, and Beryl Hesketh. 2016. "The Longitudinal Effects of Perceived Age Discrimination on the Job Satisfaction and Work Withdrawal of Older Employees." *Work, Aging and Retirement* 2(4):415–27. (https://doi.org/10.1093/workar/waw014).

Hertel, Guido and Hannes Zacher. 2018. "Managing the Aging Workforce." Pp. 396–428 in *The SAGE Handbook of Industrial, Work and Organizational Psychology*, edited by Deniz Ones et al. Thousand Oaks, CA: SAGE.

Kearney, Eric and Diether Gebert. 2009. "Managing Diversity and Enhancing Team Outcomes: The Promise of Transformational Leadership." *Journal of Applied Psychology* 94(1):77–89. (https://doi.org/10.1037/a0013077).

Klein, Rachael, et al. 2015. "Cognitive Predictors and Age-based Adverse Impact among Business Executives." *Journal of Applied Psychology* 100(5):1497–510. (https://doi.org/10.1037/a0038991).

Kooij, Dorien, et al. 2013. "How the Impact of HR Practices on Employee Well-being and Performance Changes with Age." *Human Resource Management Journal* 23(1):18–35. (https://doi.org/10.1111/1748-8583.12000).

Kooij, Dorien, et al. 2018. "Future Time Perspective: A Systematic Review and Meta-analysis." *Journal of Applied Psychology* 103(8):867–93. (https://doi.org/10.1037/apl0000306).

Kooij, Dorien, et al. 2019. "Successful Aging at Work: A Process Model to Guide Future Research and Practice." *Industrial and Organizational Psychology*. (https://doi.org/10.1017/iop.2020.1).

Kooij, Dorien and Karina Van de Voorde. 2011. "How Changes in Subjective General Health Predict Future Time Perspective, and Development and Generativity Motives over the Lifespan." *Journal of Occupational and Organizational Psychology* 84(2):228–47. (https://doi.org/10.1111/j.2044-8325.2010.02012.x).

Korff, Jorg, et al. 2009. "HR Management for an Aging Workforce: A Life-span Psychology Perspective." *Journal of Personnel Psychology* 8(4):201–13.

Kulik, Carol, et al. 2014. "From the Editors: Aging Populations and Management." *Academy of Management Journal* 57(4):929–35. (https://doi.org/10.5465/amj.2014.4004).

Kunze, Florian, Stephan Böhm, and Heike Bruch. 2011. "Age Diversity, Age Discrimination Climate and Performance Consequences: A Cross Organizational Study." *Journal of Organizational Behavior* 32(2):264–90. (https://doi.org/10.1002/job.698).

Kunze, Florian, Stephan Böhm, and Heike Bruch. 2013. "Organizational Performance Consequences of Age Diversity: Inspecting the Role of Diversity-friendly HR Policies and Top Managers' Negative Age Stereotypes." *Journal of Management Studies* 50(3):413–42. (https://doi.org/10.1111/joms.12016).

Kunze, Florian and Jochen Menges. 2017. "Younger Supervisors, Older Subordinates: An Organizational-level Study of Age Differences, Emotions, and Performance." *Journal of Organizational Behavior* 38(4):461–86. (https://doi.org/10.1002/job.2129).

Kunze, Florian and Andra Toader. 2019. "Lifespan Perspectives on Organizational Climate." Pp. 561–80 in *Work across the Lifespan*, edited by Boris Baltes, Cort Rudolph, and Hannes Zacher. London: Academic Press.

Lievens, Filip, Greet Van Hoye, and Hannes Zacher. 2012. "Recruiting/Hiring of Older Workers." Pp. 380–91 in *The Oxford Handbook of Work and Aging*, edited by Jerry W. Hedge and Walter C. Borman. New York: Oxford University Press.

Maatouk, Imad, et al. 2018. "Healthy Ageing at Work—Efficacy of Group Interventions on the Mental Health of Nurses Aged 45 and Older: Results of a Randomised, Controlled Trial." *PLoS ONE* 13(1). (https://doi.org/10.1371/journal.pone.0191000).

Maertens, Julie, et al. 2012. "Physical Capabilities and Occupational Health of Older Workers." Pp. 215–35 in *The Oxford Handbook of Work and Aging*, edited by Jerry W. Hedge and Walter C. Borman. New York: Oxford University Press.

Maurer, Todd. 2001. "Career-relevant Learning and Development, Worker Age, and Beliefs about Self-efficacy for Development." *Journal of Management* 27:123–40. (https://doi.org/10.1177/014920630102700201).

McCarthy, Jean, Noreen Heraty, and Ashley Bamberg. 2019. "Lifespan Perspectives on Age-related Stereotypes, Prejudice, and Discrimination at Work (and Beyond)." Pp. 417–35 in *Work across the Lifespan*, edited by Boris Baltes, Cort Rudolph, and Hannes Zacher. London: Academic Press.

McGonagle, Alyssa, et al. 2015. "Individual and Work Factors Related to Perceived Work Ability and Labor Force Outcomes." *Journal of Applied Psychology* 100(2):376–98. (https://doi.org/10.1037/a0037974).

Moghimi, Darya, et al. 2017. "The Selection, Optimization, and Compensation Model in the Work Context: A Systematic Review and Meta-analysis of Two Decades of Research." *Journal of Organizational Behavior* 38(2):247–75. (https://doi.org/10.1002/job.2108).

Müller, Andreas, et al. 2016. "Improving Well-being at Work: A Randomized Controlled Intervention Based on Selection, Optimization, and Compensation." *Journal of Occupational Health Psychology* 21(2):169–81. (https://doi.org/10.1037/a0039676).

Müller, Andreas, et al. 2017. "The Age-related Effect of Job Autonomy on Depressive Symptoms through Selective Optimization with Compensation: A Two-wave Panel Study." *Work, Aging and Retirement* 3(4):379–92. (https://doi.org/10.1093/workar/wax004).

Naegele, Gerhard and Alan Walker. 2011. "Age Management in Organisations in the European Union." Pp. 251–67 in *The SAGE Handbook of Workplace Learning*, edited by Margaret Malloch et al. London: SAGE.

Ng, Thomas and Daniel Feldman. 2008. "The Relationship of Age to Ten Dimensions of Job Performance." *Journal of Applied Psychology* 93(2):392–423. (https://doi.org/10.1037/0021-9010.93.2.392).

Ng, Thomas and Daniel Feldman. 2010. "The Relationship of Age with Job Attitudes: A Meta-analysis." *Personnel Psychology* 63(3):667–718. (https://doi.org/10.1111/j.1744-6570.2010.01184.x).

Ng, Thomas and Daniel Feldman. 2012. "Evaluating Six Common Stereotypes about Older Workers with Meta-analytical Data." *Personnel Psychology* 65(4):821–58. (https://doi.org/10.1111/peps.12003).

Ng, Thomas and Daniel Feldman. 2013a. "Employee Age and Health." *Journal of Vocational Behavior* 83(3):336–45. (https://doi.org/10.1016/j.jvb.2013.06.004).

Ng, Thomas and Daniel Feldman. 2013b. "How Do Within-person Changes Due to Aging Affect Job Performance?" *Journal of Vocational Behavior* 83(3):500–13. (https://doi.org/10.1016/j.jvb.2013.07.007).

Ng, Thomas and Daniel Feldman. 2015. "The Moderating Effects of Age in the Relationships of Job Autonomy to Work Outcomes." *Work, Aging and Retirement* 1(1):64–78. (https://doi.org/10.1093/workar/wau003).

Nye, Christopher and Brent Roberts. 2019. "A Neo-socioanalytic Model of Personality Development." Pp. 47–79 in *Work across the Lifespan*, edited by Boris Baltes, Cort Rudolph, and Hannes Zacher. London: Academic Press.

Posthuma, Richard and Laura Guerrero. 2013. "Age Stereotypes in the Workplace: Multidimensionality, Cross-cultural Applications, and Directions for Future Research." Pp. 250–65 in *The SAGE Handbook of Aging, Work and Society*, edited by John Field, Ronald Burke, and Cary Cooper. Thousand Oaks, CA: SAGE.

Rauvola, Rachel, Cort Rudolph, and Hannes Zacher. May 2018. "Generationalism: Problems and Implications." *Organizational Dynamics* 48(4). (https://doi.org/10.1016/j.orgdyn.2018.05.006).

Roberts, Brent, Kate Walton, and Wolfgang Viechtbauer. 2006. "Patterns of Mean-level Change in Personality Traits across the Life Course: A Meta-analysis of Longitudinal Studies." *Psychological Bulletin* 132(1):1–25. (https://doi.org/10.1037/0033-2909.132.1.1).

Rosing, Kathrin and Franziska Jungmann. 2019. *Lifespan Perspectives on Leadership*. London: Academic Press.

Rudolph, Cort. 2016. "Lifespan Developmental Perspectives on Working: A Literature Review of Motivational Theories." *Work, Aging and Retirement* 2:130–58. (https://doi.org/10.1093/workar/waw012).

Rudolph, Cort, et al. 2018. "Occupational Future Time Perspective: A Meta-analysis of Antecedents and Outcomes." *Journal of Organizational Behavior* 39(2):229–48. (https://doi.org/10.1002/job.2264).

Rudolph, Cort and Alyssa McGonagle. 2018. "Exploring Age-conditional Effects in the Emotional Labor–perceived Work Ability Linkage: A Daily Diary Study." *Work, Aging and Retirement* 5(2):163–74. (https://doi.org/10.1093/workar/way014).

Rudolph, Cort, Eileen Toomey, and Boris Baltes. 2017. "Considering Age Diversity in Recruitment and Selection: An Expanded Work Lifespan View of Age Management." Pp. 607–38 in *Handbook of Age Diversity and Work*, edited by Jean McCarthy and Emma Parry. London: Palgrave-Macmillan.

Rudolph, Cort and Hannes Zacher. 2019. "Managing Employees across the Lifespan." Pp. 425–45 in *The Cambridge Handbook of the Changing Nature of Work*, edited by Brian Hoffman, Mindy Shoss, and Lauren Wegman. Cambridge: Cambridge University Press.

Salthouse, Timothy. 2012. "Consequences of Age-related Cognitive Declines." *Annual Review of Psychology* 63:201–26. (https://doi.org/10.1146/annurev-psych-120710-100328).

Scheibe, Susanne and Hannes Zacher. 2013. "A Lifespan Perspective on Emotion Regulation, Stress, and Well-being in the Workplace." Pp. 167–97 in *Research in Occupational Stress and Well-being*, edited by Pamela Perrewé, Jonathon Halbesleben, and Christopher Rosen. Bingley, UK: Emerald.

Schmitt, Antje and Dana Unger. 2019. "Lifespan Perspectives on Occupational Health." Pp. 369–93 in *Work across the Lifespan*, edited by Boris Baltes, Cort Rudolph, and Hannes Zacher. London: Academic Press.

Schneid, Matthias, et al. 2016. "Age Diversity and Team Outcomes: A Quantitative Review." *Journal of Managerial Psychology* 31(1):2–17. (https://doi.org/10.1108/JMP-07-2012-0228).

Schulz, Heiko, Hannes Zacher, and Sonia Lippke. 2017. "The Importance of Team Health Climate for Health-related Outcomes of White-collar Workers." *Frontiers in Psychology* 8:74. (https://doi.org/10.3389/fpsyg.2017.00074).

Sterns, Harvey and Katherine Harrington. 2019. "Lifespan Perspectives on Learning and Training." Pp. 323–41 in *Work across the Lifespan*, edited by Boris Baltes, Cort Rudolph, and Hannes Zacher. London: Academic Press.

Toomey, Eileen and Cort Rudolph. 2018. "Age-conditional Effects in the Affective Arousal, Empathy, and Emotional Labor Linkage: Within-person Evidence from an Experience Sampling Study." *Work, Aging and Retirement* 4(2):145–60. (https://doi.org/10.1093/workar/wax018).

Truxillo, Donald, et al. 2012. "A Lifespan Perspective on Job Design: Fitting the Job and the Worker to Promote Job Satisfaction, Engagement, and Performance." *Organizational Psychology Review* 2(4):340–60. (https://doi.org/10.1177/2041386612454043).

Truxillo, Donald, David Cadiz, and Leslie Hammer. 2015. "Supporting the Aging Workforce: A Research Review and Recommendations for Workplace Intervention Research." *Annual Review of Organizational Psychology and Organizational Behavior* 2:351–81. (https://doi.org/10.1146/annurev-orgpsych-032414-111435).

von Hippel, Courtney, et al. 2018. "Age-based Stereotype Threat and Work Outcomes: Stress Appraisals and Rumination as Mediators." *Psychology and Aging* 34(1):68–84. (https://doi.org/10.1037/pag0000308).

von Hippel, Courtney, Elise Kalokerinos, and Julie Henry. 2012. "Stereotype Threat among Older Employees: Relationships with Job Attitudes and Turnover Intentions." *Psychology and Aging* 28(1):17–27. (https://doi.org/10.1037/a0029825).

Wang, Mo, et al. 2015. "Age Differences in Feedback Reactions: The Roles of Employee Feedback Orientation on Social Awareness and Utility." *Journal of Applied Psychology* 100:1296–308. (https://doi.org/10.1037/a0038334).

Wegge, Jurgen, et al. 2008. "Age and Gender Diversity as Determinants of Performance and Health in a Public Organization: The Role of Task Complexity and Group Size." *Journal of Applied Psychology* 93(6):1301–13. (https://doi.org/10.1037/a0012680).

Weigl, Matthias, et al. 2013. "The Moderating Effects of Job Control and Selection, Optimization, and Compensation Strategies on the Age–Work Ability Relationship." *Journal of Organizational Behavior* 34:607–28. (https://doi.org/10.1002/job.1810).

Zacher, Hannes, et al. 2015. "A Lifespan Perspective on Leadership." Pp. 87–104 in *Aging Workers and the Employee-Employer Relationship*, edited by Mattiijs Bal, Dorien Kooij, and Denise Rousseau. Cham, Switzerland: Springer.

Zacher, Hannes, et al. 2017. "Age-differential Effects of Job Characteristics on Job Attraction: A Policy-capturing Study." *Frontiers in Psychology* 8:1124. (https://doi.org/10.3389/fpsyg.2017.01124).

Zacher, Hannes and Michael Frese. 2009. "Remaining Time and Opportunities at Work: Relationships between Age, Work Characteristics, and Occupational Future Time Perspective." *Psychology and Aging* 24(2):487–93. (https://doi.org/10.1037/a0015425).

Zacher, Hannes and Michael Gielnik. 2012. "Organizational Age Cultures: The Interplay of Chief Executive Officers' Age and Attitudes toward Younger and Older Employees." *International Small Business Journal* 32(3):327–49. (https://doi.org/10.1177/0266242612463025).

Zacher, Hannes, Winfried Hacker, and Michael Frese. 2016. "Action Regulation across the Adult Lifespan (ARAL): A Meta-theory of Work and Aging." *Work, Aging and Retirement* 2(3):286–306. (https://doi.org/10.1093/workar/waw015).

Zacher, Hannes, Dorien Kooij, and Margaret Beier. 2018. "Active Aging at Work: Contributing Factors and Implications for Organizations." *Organizational Dynamics* 47(1):37–45. (https://doi.org/10.1016/j.orgdyn.2017.08.001).

Zacher, Hannes and Cort Rudolph. 2017. "Successful Aging at Work and Beyond: A Review and Critical Perspective." Pp. 35–64 in *Age Diversity in the Workplace: An Organizational Perspective*, edited by Silvia Profili, Alessia Sammarra, and Laura Innocenti. Bingley, UK: Emerald.

Zacher, Hannes, Cort Rudolph, and Boris Baltes. 2019. "An Invitation to Lifespan Thinking." Pp. 1–14 in *Work across the Lifespan*, edited by Boris Baltes, Cort Rudolph, and Hannes Zacher. London: Academic Press.

Zacher, Hannes and Jie Yang. 2016. "Organizational Climate for Successful Aging." *Frontiers in Psychology* 7(1):1007. (https://doi.org/10.3389/fpsyg.2016.01007).

Zaniboni, Sara. 2015. "The Interaction between Older Workers' Personal Resources and Perceived Age Discrimination Affects the Desired Retirement Age and the Expected Adjustment." *Work, Aging and Retirement* 1(3):266–73. (https://doi.org/10.1093/workar/wav010).

Zaniboni, Sara, Donald Truxillo, and Franco Fraccaroli. 2013. "Differential Effects of Task Variety and Skill Variety on Burnout and Turnover Intentions for Older and Younger Workers." *European Journal of Work and Organizational Psychology* 22(3):306–17. (https://doi.org/10.1080/1359432X.2013.782288).

Zhan, Yujie and Mo Wang. 2015. "Bridge Employment: Conceptualizations and New Directions for Future Research." Pp. 203–20 in *Aging Workers and the Employee-employer Relationship*, edited by Matthis Bal, Dorien Kooij, and Denise Rousseau. Cham, Switzerland: Springer.

CHAPTER 9

# Collaborative Work in the Twenty-First Century

## An Intergenerational, Age-Diverse Perspective

Jensine Paoletti, Ruilin Wu, and Eduardo Salas

We are entering a new age of work. In the past decades, there have been several major workforce trends, but two have been especially transformative for employee experiences in their everyday work life. First, people have been living longer; correspondingly, employees have been delaying retirement. Second, organizations have transformed their structure to rely on collaboration and teams as the primary mechanism of goal and strategy achievement. These two phenomena set the stage for the contemporary employee experience, motivation, and affect. These are the building blocks of intergenerational collaborative work in the modern era.

The so-called silver tsunami refers to the high rate of aging across the country due to demographic changes leading to a more age-diverse population. As people are living longer, they are often choosing to remain in the workforce for longer periods of time. In fact, workers fifty-five and older have consistently increased their participation in the labor force from 1994 to 2014, a trend that is projected to continue until 2024, primarily because of the baby boomers.[1] These older workers are also more likely to try a historically nontraditional approach to retirement, including choosing to leave and subsequently return to the workforce, working part-time, or choosing self-employment, leading to more older adults at work.

## PURPOSE

Despite these changes, the largest portion of the labor market continues to be composed of young to middle-aged adults. Millennials currently make up the largest portion of the workforce compared to other generations in America. Millennial presence plus the higher proportion of older workers means there is more age diversity within organizations today, and therefore more age-diverse collaborative work. In fact, organizations are increasingly relying on teams and other forms of collaborative work to solve problems originating in the complexities of the modern economic and technological environment.[2] Relatedly, age-diverse teams have been shown to be no less effective than homogenous counterparts.[3] Additionally, there are argued benefits to age-diverse collaborations, such as older team members adopting a more cautioned and experienced role.[4] Certainly, there are potential challenges to collaborative work in this new era, which we will address throughout this chapter. (See also chapters 7, 8, and 10–12.)

## A NOTE ON GENERATIONS

A point of interest lies in intergenerational dynamics at work, as many popular press articles comment on benefits and challenges to employees and organizations stemming from intergenerational interactions. Generations are groups of people, often from a similar birth cohort, who have been collectively affected by historical or cultural changes or events during developmentally significant parts of their lives, often late childhood through early adulthood.[5] This definition relies on the assumption that shared experiences create a shared identity between generational members.[6]

In academic spheres, there is some contention to the value of studying generations.[7] Specifically, generational differences are seen as theoretically valid, but researchers argue that cross-sectional data collection is not rich enough to decipher any latent generational differences.[8] Unfortunately, most studies to date have used cross-sectional data collection techniques,[9] and objective measures of age that do not capture variables like employee perceptions or age salience, which may be why a meta-analysis of motivational and affective variables across generations found small or nonexistent generational differences.[10] To properly study generational effects, data must be longitudinal in nature and establish statistical differences between the specified generations; in fact the very notion of generational cutoffs, particularly for younger generations (Generation X, millennials, Generation Z), has been challenged as theoretically and empirically weak.[11]

This is not to imply that there are no age-related differences in work-related motivation and affect, as another meta-analysis found some differences;[12] however, these differences are continuous across the lifespan, differ by individual, and are not attributable to one generation. Therefore, we will simultaneously provide information on age diversity and generational effects on collaborative work. This chapter aims to highlight effects at several different organizational levels, from individuals to collaborative dyads and partnerships, to team dynamics, and organizations at large. We focus on how motivation and attitudes change over the lifespan, and how these changes may benefit and challenge employees, collaborative work, teams, and organizations.

## DIFFERENCES IN MOTIVATION AND ATTITUDES ACROSS THE LIFESPAN

### What the Science Says

Research and theory have investigated motivational and attitudinal changes as they occur throughout the lifespan, resulting in a scientific understanding of adult development as it relates to work and aging. Specifically, we focus on the role of socioemotional selectivity theory[13] and a theory of aging and work motivation.[14] There is decidedly much less robust theory and empirical research on the role of generational differences in motivation and attitudes. While meta-analytic evidence speaks to little to no effects of large generational differences,[15] some studies have found motivational differences at work by generational membership. Specifically, a study of boomers and Generation X found that Generation X members were more likely to focus on their own individual goals plus the organization's goals.[16] They were also more likely, relative to boomers, to say that working hard (even without supervisor attention) is an indication of personal worth.

Socioemotional selectivity theory details the effects of three social motives—emotion regulation, self-concept, and information seeking—throughout the course of a typical lifespan. This theory states that as people age and grow, they seek to increase social and emotional benefits while reducing related losses.[17] Practically, this means that younger, middle-aged, and older people are motivated differently. The driver of this effect is the quality and quantity of social interactions; younger people are motivated to seek information about the world via a larger quantity of social interactions; yet, as they age these social interactions provide less new information, and accordingly, older adults become less information oriented. However, the pattern is different for affective rewards, as aging increases the affective rewards experienced from social interactions with more selectively chosen relational partners. This theory indicates that younger workers are more likely to desire learning and growth and performance opportunities, while older workers are more likely to desire high-quality relationships from their work lives. Additionally, younger workers may be more motivated by external rewards, while older workers are more motivated by intrinsic rewards.

Theory on aging and work motivation takes a different approach, as it proposes ideas about a broader span of adulthood, including motivation, cognition, emotion, and personality.[18] This theory hinges on the findings of fluid and crystalized intelligence, two abilities that take opposing paths in adult development—fluid intelligence, the ability to reason through new problems, tends to decline with age, but crystalized intelligence, knowledge and experience, tends to increase with age. This theory states that as fluid intelligence decreases with age, motivation increases as a way to make up for the loss, which has been supported by empirical findings.[19] Likewise, older adults are thought to increase motivation for jobs that require high levels of crystalized intelligence.[20] However, with all else the same, this theory also predicts that older adults will be less motivated in information-oriented jobs relative to younger adults, echoing the findings of socioemotional selectivity theory. However, according to both theories, older adults may find relationally oriented jobs more motivating than younger adults.

## What Stereotypes Say

Stereotypes, or cross-group perceptions, are a cognitive form of bias that indicates what others think about a target group. (See also chapter 13.) We focus on *descriptive* age stereotypes, or stereotypes about what is common behavior for an age group.[21] Some stereotypes exist for younger (ages eighteen to thirty) and older (age fifty-one-plus) workers, with much less data to suggest there are common stereotypes for middle-aged (ages thirty-one to fifty) workers, who may represent an ideal worker. Importantly, not all age-related stereotypes are negative, as there are some positive associations for all three age groups.[22]

However, age-related stereotypes have potentially harmful effects, as older workers receive lower ratings in interviews and performance appraisals, with meta-analytic evidence demonstrating a preference for younger workers[23] despite the protections of the Age Discrimination in Employment Act of 1967, which protect workers over the age of forty from discrimination. Age-related stereotypes, particularly those leveraged against older workers, may be more common in industries like retail, hospitality, finance, and insurance, as these industries are considered to be "younger."[24] Stereotypes also promote internalization into metastereotypes, or what one assumes others think of them (e.g., "they must see me as incompetent because I'm young"). Metastereotypes create intraemployee reactions, which have been demonstrated to result in avoidance, conflict, and engagement at work.[25] Both stereotypes and metastereotypes provide important information about perceptions of age-related attitudes and motivation.

## Where the Science and Stereotypes Meet

### OLDER WORKERS

Research on age-related stereotypes has been studied in older workers for longer than other age groups. In one study, common stereotypes of older workers also include such positive attitudinal labels as "experienced," "mature," and "hardworking," with the majority of stereotypes mentioned as positive.[26] Negative stereotypes have claimed that older workers are less motivated, more resistant to change, and less trusting, all of which have been shown to be false from meta-analytic data.[27] In fact, theory suggests that motivation increases with age as a compensatory strategy for ability changes.[28] However, the stereotype that older workers are less motivated to participate in training and career development has been supported, although weakly, by research.[29] (See also chapters 15, 17, and 18.)

### YOUNGER AND MIDDLE-AGED WORKERS

Researchers have studied stereotypes of younger workers and middle-aged workers less than older workers. A study found a split between positive (i.e., enthusiastic) and negative (i.e., lazy and unmotivated) attitudinal stereotypes of younger workers.[30] However, younger workers had severely negative metastereotypes, which have been associated with negative mood and feelings of anxiety and threat.[31] In contrast, middle-aged workers are overwhelmingly associated with positive stereotypes like "knowledgeable" and "enthusiastic." Middle-aged workers were also likely to have positive metastereotypes, which have been shown to result in work engagement.[32] Overall, managers and employees should be cautious and avoid negatively stereotyping their colleagues (or stereotyping themselves via metastereotypes). Rather, age-related differences in attitudes and motivations should be viewed through a scientific lens with sensitivity to all members of the workforce.

## BENEFITS AND CHALLENGES OF PEOPLE-ORIENTED ATTITUDES

At work, attitudes are argued to be a summary of the ongoing cognitive evaluations of other coworkers, clients, supervisors, and teams.[33] This assertion is grounded in the "emotions as social information" theory, which says that emotional expressions have reactionary affective and influential processes in the relational partner.[34] Therefore, attitudes and motivational influences have their roots in discreet (1) intrapersonal emotional experiences and (2) interpersonal emotional reactions and influences.

A handful of said attitudes are considered "people oriented"; that is, these attitudes are a synthesis of information about the other people in the organization. (See table 9.1.) A meta-analysis that examined the effects of age and attitudes referred to the following as "people-oriented attitudes": (1) satisfaction with coworkers, (2) satisfaction with supervisors, (3) relationship conflict, (4) interpersonal trust, (5) perception of politics, (6) leader-member exchange (LMX), (7) interaction fairness, (8) coworker support, and (9) supervisor support.[35] This study found that satisfaction with coworkers, satisfaction with supervisors, interpersonal trust, and LMX were all positively correlated with age, and relationship conflict was negatively correlated with age. Older adults are more likely to have longer organizational tenure, because of their age and lower likelihood of leaving their organization.[36] When the meta-analysis controlled for the variance of organizational tenure, then supervisor support, in addition, was positively correlated with age.

### Benefits and Challenges to Individuals

For the purpose of this review, we consider satisfaction to be our primary individual-focused variable. As noted by Ng and Feldman, two satisfaction-related variables are positively related to age.[37] Specifically, satisfaction with coworkers and satisfaction with supervisors have small, positive correlations with age. For satisfaction with coworkers, the effect was moderate with employees who had high organizational tenure, defined as six or more years of tenure, but there was no correlation for those with less than six years of tenure. Research shows that coworker satisfaction (1) varies at the daily level and (2) is positively related to job satisfaction and life satisfaction.[38] This effect is intensified for individuals who are highly agreeable. Satisfaction with coworkers changes over the employee's lifespan and career, which may pose challenges to those with lower organizational tenure. Those who are new to an organization should understand that it is normal to have a varying sense of satisfaction with coworkers.

**TABLE 9.1.** Summary of Benefits and Challenges of Attitudes for Age-Diverse Teams

| | *Benefits* | | | *Challenges* | | |
|---|---|---|---|---|---|---|
| *Attitudes* | *Individuals* | *Dyads* | *Teams* | *Individuals* | *Dyads* | *Teams* |
| People-oriented attitudes | Satisfaction with coworkers and supervisors has positive correlations with age.<br>Older women have high levels of satisfaction with supervisors. | Higher trust, less relationship conflict experienced by older employees.<br>Quality of a leader-follower relationship found to be positively related to age. | Transformational leadership's effectiveness positively related to age gap between leaders and followers. | Satisfaction with coworkers changes over employee's career, which challenges those with lower organizational tenure. | Older employees may show more caution with new collaborative partners.<br>Men may be more prone to decreases in benevolence perceptions as they age. | Young leaders stereotyped as incompatible with leadership roles. |
| Task-oriented attitudes | As employees age, they will value different aspects of work. Intrinsic rewards become more important. | Employees' crafting of challenging job tasks led to a higher probability for their partner to also seek challenges. | Job crafting can be good for age-diverse teams by increasing job resources and decreasing hindering job demands. | Older and younger employees motivated by different incentives, which may be challenging for managers. | Asking for feedback and advice from coworkers is an information-seeking behavior that likely fades away as one ages. | Job crafting consumes resources and may create extra challenges. |
| Organization-oriented attitudes | Positive correlation between employee age and affective commitment. | Varying demands of older and younger employees may present complementary fit (one provides what other needs). | Outcomes optimized when both manager and team members consider organizational support to be high. | Older and younger workers have different reward preferences, so managers must be flexible while rewarding fairly. | Two individuals of different ages may clash in values. | Different generational definitions of fairness. |

In comparison, satisfaction with supervisors may incur a gendered, generational effect such that older women have the highest levels of satisfaction with supervisors.[39] More research is needed at a longitudinal level to understand whether there are generational effects related to satisfaction with supervisors. Perhaps generational effects also help explain why older women are more satisfied with their supervisors, as these employees are likely to have faced pervasive gender discrimination earlier in their careers, while modern supervisors may be less explicitly discriminatory, following patterns found by discrimination research.[40] Satisfaction with supervisors changes over the employee's lifespan, which may pose challenges to younger generations and men. Employees should take comfort in the relatively small effects of age, generational membership, and gender.

## Benefits and Challenges to Collaborative Dyads

Differences in affect and motivation may benefit and challenge the work of collaborative dyads, or any two people who work together. In particular, there is meta-analytic evidence for differences in interpersonal trust, relationship conflict, and leader-member exchange (LMX) by age.[41] The socioemotional selectivity theory provides some explanation for the higher levels of trust and lower levels of relationship conflict experienced by older employees, as the theory states that older adults are more motivated by emotional regulation than knowledge acquisition, while the opposite is thought to be true for younger adults.[42] If emotion regulation is more important for older employees, it would explain why there is more trust and less conflict among this sample. These two effects also serve to benefit work collaborations among older adults. However, there is also evidence that suggests older employees demonstrate more caution with new collaborative partners, as older adults perceive these new partners as less benevolent.[43] Some evidence suggests that men may be more prone to decreases in benevolence perceptions as they age. More research is needed, but those in new collaborations should understand that trust may take time to build.

Leader-member exchange (LMX), a variable describing the quality of a leader's relationship with a follower, was found to be positively related to employee age; thus older employees had a higher-quality LMX.[44] Perhaps this is due to older employees fitting the prototype of a leader;[45] older adults may have more in common with their older leaders based on their shared age. This notion is based on the social identity theory, which states that people prefer those whom they consider to be part of their in-group because it provides them with a feeling of belongingness and security.[46] This idea is expanded by the optimal distinctiveness theory, which states that there should be a certain amount of difference of self-to-group but not enough to reduce feelings of belongingness.[47] Therefore, followers who are the same age as their leaders may benefit from the optimal distinctiveness theory, as they can retain their sense of independence because of their rank and feel a sense of belongingness because of shared age with their leader. Indeed, a meta-analysis notes that perceptions of supervisor support are higher for older employees when controlling for organizational tenure.[48] Leaders should make efforts to treat all their followers with a sense of fairness so as to not exacerbate any age-related inequalities among the leader-follower relationships.

### Benefits and Challenges to Teams

Changes in attitudes and motivation across employees' careers have implications for teams. Teams are characterized by their shared goals and interdependent work. They are some of the most common modern units of work completion.[49] Research on intergenerational interactions in teams has uncovered patterns of team leadership expectations and behaviors. For instance, younger teammates are stereotyped as incompatible with a leadership role,[50] and there is evidence to suggest that younger leaders must behave differently than older leaders to be seen as effective in their job. One study noted that younger leaders relying on contingent rewards, an exchange process that rewards high levels of performance, had teams characterized by lower rates of voluntary turnover, while the older leaders who used this tactic had higher team voluntary turnover.[51] Instead, older leaders were seen as more effective when they used participative leadership styles (in which followers are included in decision-making processes), but younger leaders were not effective using this style. This finding is supported by other research indicating that transformational leadership's effectiveness, a style similar to participative leadership, was positively related to the age gap between the leader and followers.[52] These findings may be explained by another study that found that leaders who were highly generative (who focused on guiding the younger generation) were able to avoid the deprecation of leader effectiveness ratings that often come with age.[53] Leaders of intergenerational teams should understand that followers' perceptions of their leadership are related to their personal characteristics. These team leaders should carefully consider their teams when choosing a leadership style.

## BENEFITS AND CHALLENGES OF TASK-ORIENTED ATTITUDES

Task-based attitudes refer to employees' summary evaluations of the job tasks and role duties they perform, such as job satisfaction.[54] In this section, we discuss the variation trends in job satisfaction that accompany the aging process, as well as how individuals, dyads, and teams may utilize job crafting to experience more positive job attitudes. (See table 9.1.)

### Benefits and Challenges to Individuals

It is normal for managers of an age-diverse workforce to observe discrepancies between older and younger workers in their job satisfaction. Job satisfaction is understood as the pleasurable emotional state resulting from the appraisal of one's job. In general, research indicates that older workers are slightly more satisfied with their jobs than younger workers are. For example, a small positive association between overall job satisfaction and age is found by meta-analysis, which is mostly composed of cross-sectional primary studies and longitudinal research.[55] It is also anticipated that as employees age, they will value different aspects of work compared with what they previously used to value. Theories of lifespan development posit that as workers age, (1) they are more strongly motivated by intrinsic than extrinsic rewards,[56] and (2) they shift the goal of their social interactions from gaining information to gaining positive affect.[57] Both patterns receive some empirical support. Employees' evaluations of the intrinsic appeal of their work tasks correlated with older, but not younger (below forty-four years old) employees' motivations; the pattern was flipped with employees' motivation for career opportunities, as workers younger than forty-four but not older were motivated to enhance their careers.[58] Another study found that younger workers gained job satisfaction from interaction with people outside the organization.[59] As interacting with external people helps to broaden one's network, it reasonably appeals to younger people who perceive an extended future time perspective.

We are relatively less certain of how two important aspects of work—pay and promotion opportunity—relate to the job satisfaction of an age-diverse workforce. Because pay and promotion bring mostly extrinsic rewards (money and power), lifespan theories suggest that aging likely leads to less concern with pay and promotion. The empirical evidence is nevertheless inconclusive. In line with theoretical predictions, research found that older workers assessed pay and promotion prospects as less important than younger workers did.[60] Counterevidence found the association between promotion and job satisfaction strengthened with age;[61] additionally, research found income to be a significant antecedent of job satisfaction for American workers over fifty years old.[62] Future research is welcomed to shed light on younger and older workers' perceptions of pay and advancement opportunity and possible moderators.

## Benefits and Challenges to Collaborative Dyads and Teams

To facilitate positive job attitudes, work tasks and roles may be modified to better fit workers' needs. One form of work task modification, job crafting, can potentially benefit age-diverse work dyads and teams. Job crafting is the self-initiated changes that individuals (or teams) make in the task or relational boundaries of their work that are aimed at improving person-job fit.[63] A popular model proposes four forms of job-crafting behaviors: increasing structural job resources, increasing social resources, increasing challenging job demands, and decreasing hindering job demands.[64]

Job crafting has interesting applications in an intergenerational workforce. Truxillo and colleagues suggest a series of job redesigns based on lifespan development models.[65] For example, older workers may benefit from greater autonomy, more specialized job responsibilities, and greater interdependence with colleagues. Job-crafting activities can also be considered in three components—accommodative, developmental, and utilization. Older employees can reduce hindering job demands (e.g., by delegating work to assistants), expand work into new areas (e.g., by practicing tasks that use the full spectrum of their skills), and focus more on work that interests them (e.g., by mentoring coworkers). Still, job crafting may not readily appeal to older workers, as it consumes resources and potentially involves taking up extra challenges. One study finds that a limited future time perspective on work (which is presumably held by many older employees) is not related to any form of job crafting.[66] Further, a meta-analysis concluded a small negative correlation between age and job crafting,[67] explainable by the negative relationship between age and information-seeking behavior, such as asking for feedback and advice from coworkers. As these behaviors decline with age, employees may have less access to social job resources.

Fortunately, there is encouraging evidence on the efficacy of job crafting at dyadic and team levels to involve older workers. Analogous to individual job crafting, members of work pairs and teams can decide jointly what resources and demands they want to craft for their work.[68] Research has uncovered three useful outcomes of team and dyadic job crafting. First, team job crafting is positively related to teamwork engagement and performance. Second, team job crafting can promote the individual job crafting of its members. Third, daily job crafting behaviors can be transferred between two colleagues who work closely together; for example, an employee's crafting of challenging job tasks led to a higher probability for the partner to seek challenges also.[69] In this way, collective job crafting can create an atmosphere that encourages individual job crafting, and older workers who do not initially warm to the idea can be encouraged to craft their jobs and reap the benefits.

## BENEFITS AND CHALLENGES OF ORGANIZATION-ORIENTED ATTITUDES

Organization-oriented attitudes refer to employees' summary evaluations of the employer or the employment relationship. Examples of organization-oriented attitudes include perceived organizational support, procedural justice, and affective commitment. These attitudes pertain not only to organizational well-being at the moment but also long-term human resource strategies. In the light of the reported shift from the organizational career to the protean career, firms should be particularly interested in ways to engage and retain their talent. This section presents findings that are relevant to fostering positive organization-based attitudes in intergenerational teams. (See table 9.1.)

### Benefits and Challenges to Individuals

Employees' affective commitment to their organization is the primary organization-oriented attitude relevant for individuals. In general, older workers have greater affective commitment than younger workers.[70] Meta-analytic evidence indicates a moderate, positive correlation between employee age and affective commitment.[71] The same pattern has been replicated across industries and job levels,[72] suggesting that the relationship is robust. The positive correlation between age and affective commitment refutes the stereotype that older employees are marking time until retirement.[73] In reality, older adults remain engaged. Accordingly, we recommend that organizations recognize the positive role of older workers and work to mitigate any negative perceptions of them.

Allen and Meyer propose three causes of the positive link between age and commitment: (1) maturity, (2) better experiences, and (3) cohort effects. First, the maturity explanation posits that aging directly predisposes older employees to be more committed to organizations.[74] Second, the better experiences explanation argues that older workers have more positive work experiences, hence higher commitment; those positive experiences may stem from older workers' superior ability to perform their roles and cope with stress, or simply the fact that they occupy higher-status positions. Lastly, according to the cohort explanation, older generations prefer the traditional norm of lifelong employment, while younger workers, faced with a turbulent and intense work environment, shift careers more readily.[75] After testing the three hypotheses, researchers found that older workers tend to rate their job experiences better, lending support to the better experiences theory. However, age was a predictor of affective commitment above and beyond the experiences, implying the potential role of aging and generational values differences.[76] Thus, all three explanations are tenable and make a contribution to the overall effect.

Important questions remain as to how the commitment of intergenerational workers may be promoted. Three theoretical perspectives are particularly useful when discussing factors that promote positive work attitudes across a person's lifespan, (1) Super's career development theory,[77] (2) Carstensen's socioemotional selectivity theory,[78] and (3) Kanfer and Ackerman's framework of work motivation.[79] Put together, the theories predict that younger workers are more interested in organizations that offer them financial security and growth opportunities, while older workers stay longer in relationally comfortable workplaces.

There is much empirical evidence in support of younger and older workers' preferences when considering whether to keep working in an organization. Career development opportunity was the biggest predictor of work engagement for employees under thirty-nine years old, while supervisor support was most crucial for participants fifty-five and over.[80] Older workers felt low levels of organizational support when they experienced (1) lack of vertical movement in an organization *and* (2) lack of challenges from work, but this effect was stronger for lack of challenges.[81] Overall, it is arguable that career advancement, financial rewards, and learning opportunities are more effective in retaining younger talent, while providing meaningful relationships and intrinsic motivation fit older workers better. Organizational leaders interested in motivating an intergenerational workforce should take steps to address disparate desires by approaching rewards in a flexible manner, while maintaining fairness in rewarding different team members.

## Benefits and Challenges to Collaborative Dyads

What happens when two individuals from different generations are put to work together? The members of the dyad may develop tension due to differences in work values, yet the tension is manageable through positive contact. The varying demands of older and younger employees may present complementary fit, that is, the characteristics of one providing what the other needs, so that they can both benefit from a mentoring relationship. Elaboration on both propositions is presented below.

Discernible differences exist between older and younger workers' attitudes toward the organization. These differences are likely to surface quickly and frequently in a closely collaborative dyadic relationship. For example, a young worker's quest for pay increase and external opportunities may be interpreted as instrumental by the older partner, while a young worker may belittle an older colleague's willingness to remain in the same place. Fortunately, those clashes can be reasonably controlled and attenuated via frequent and positive interactions, per Allport's contact hypothesis of reducing stereotypes and conflicts.[82] In this way, members of an intergenerational dyad can be brought closer through cordial conversations and understand why they hold different attitudes toward work and the organization. Diversity training provided by the organization may also help to weaken age-based stereotypes and foster healthy dyadic relationships.

Intergenerational dyads may benefit from the complementary fit of their needs and resources. Young workers, early in their career, desire learning, and older workers, guided by generative values, are willing to share their knowledge. The mutual fit prompts the formation of mentorship pairs, which can be both emotionally rewarding and productive. Older workers may have advanced as far as they desire or can within the organizational hierarchy, but they are happy to see their protégés succeed. The transfer of knowledge from older to younger workers develops the young talent of the organization and preserves the wisdom and experience accumulated by older employees, partially offsetting the human capital loss that accompanies retirement waves. In this way, the formation of intergenerational dyads is not only essential given changing demographics, but also tangibly beneficial to employees and employers alike.

## Benefits and Challenges to Teams

Teams offer rich soil for studying organization-oriented attitudes. Due to frequent and sustained interactions in the team context, members know about one another's attitudes toward the organization and may compare and contrast their attitudes. Meaningful outcomes can emerge when team members concur or disagree among themselves. This section presents research on two important organization-oriented attitudes—procedural justice (employee perceptions of the procedures used to determine outcomes received)[83] and perceived organizational support (the extent to which employees feel their organizations care about their well-being and value their contributions)[84]—and relates these findings to intergenerational teams.

Two factors potentially make intergenerational teams more prone to internal disagreement about perceptions of organizational justice and support. For one thing, team members who belong to different generations are likely to have conflicting views on the nature of support and rewards an organization should offer, which allows room for inconsistency in what constitutes a perceived slight. Colquitt found that a team member's role performance was highest when treatment of all teammates was perceived to be fair, which different generational definitions of fairness may preclude.[85] Secondly, employee age tends to covary with hierarchical seniority, such that older employees typically occupy more influential positions for shaping the organization's values. Indeed, research shows that baby boomers perceived better fit between their values and the organization's than people from Generations X and Y.[86] In one study, team outcomes were optimized when both the manager and team members considered organizational support to be high. The worst team performance occurred when the manager perceived high support and team members perceived low support.[87] Thus, managers are advised to stay in tune with the rest of the team on organization-oriented attitudes. Researchers have recommended training on fostering consistency in justice treatment and two-way dialogue on organizational values as possible solutions.

## FUTURE DIRECTIONS

There is a wealth of opportunities for additional research on age-diverse, intergenerational collaborative work. We choose to organize our agenda according to the input-mediator-outcome-input (IMOI) model, a common model in teams research that denotes the different stages in team processes, while implying the recursive nature of these processes.[88] This is not to indicate that our suggestions all fall under one particular team process, as our future research directions fit under many team processes.

### Research Needs for Process Inputs

When studying teams and aging, there should be increased attention to team compositional changes at retirement and related end-of-career processes. Research from the U.S. Bureau of Labor Statistics suggests that more older workers may choose nontraditional paths such as retiring and reentering the workforce or moving to part-time work.[89] (See chapters 21–23.) When employees retire, reenter the workforce after leaving, or shift to part-time work, their workplace collaborations will change as well. Research is needed to determine how these processes adapt to the organization's microcomposition changes. This mirrors calls for team compositional change to be studied.[90] We are also arguing that compositional change research must include individual, dyadic, and organizational effects of a team's compositional change. Does the remaining collaborative partner aim to find a new collaborator similar in age, experience, or tenure to the retiree lost? Some researchers have argued that older teammates are more likely to be a more cautious voice in their teams due to their greater experience.[91] However, the literature would benefit from more direct research into how age, experience, and tenure are related to the roles enacted by members of a team. For example, does a person newer to the organization bring lots of new ideas? Are there generational or age-related effects to observed role behaviors?

### Mediating Processes That Deserve Attention

Research in the diversity literature sometimes uses the informational/decision-making perspective, which assumes that there is value inherent in diversity due to difference in perspective that can be exchanged within diverse groups to result in better decision outcomes for the group.[92] Building off this perspective, it has been suggested that age-diverse organizations should use mentoring programs to increase intergenerational contact and communication between employees.[93] Research has demonstrated that more communication is not always helpful for team performance,[94] but intergenerational mentoring programs may have positive affective and cognitive outcomes for dyads and teams, as we know mentoring is positively related to affective organizational commitment variables.[95]

### Agenda for Cyclical Effects of Outcome Variables

Age diversity and collaborative work are often studied with concerns about performance implications. There are weak to no interactions of age diversity on team performance,[96] but there is more room for research examining affect-specific team variables. While variables like intention to leave, organizational commitment, and employee engagement are common and use an affective lens, collaborative affect variables are less studied. In particular, there is room to include team viability, a construct that indicates the team's shared perception that they can continue to work together. This construct was recently adapted to the dyadic level[97] and has potential to illuminate direct effects of affect in intergenerational collaborations.

## CONCLUSION

As noted in the popular press, there are common perceptions of age- and generation-related differences that may cause conflict in the workplace. Is this true? Are there unseen benefits? Due to economic and social forces, contemporary work is increasingly completed in age-diverse collaborations. In this chapter, we review age-related differences in attitudes and motivation that employees commonly experience. Specifically, we highlight socioemotional selectivity theory[98] and the theory of aging and work motivation.[99] These theories indicate benefits and challenges associated with collaborative work in age-diverse, intergenerational environments. We discuss relevant science-supported strategies that organizational leaders may implement at multiple levels of interest (individual team members, collaborative dyads, and teams). Research on this topic is still nascent; therefore, we recommend three areas for future study: (1) team compositional change effects, (2) intergenerational mentoring processes, and (3) using viability as an affective outcome variable. Through an age-diverse perspective on collaborative work, we believe we can make organizations more productive and welcoming for all employees.

## NOTES

This work was partially supported by the Center for Clinical and Translational Sciences (UT Health Science Center, Houston, TX), which is funded by National Institutes of Health Clinical and Translational Award UL1 TR003167 from the National Center for Advancing Translational Sciences. The content is solely the responsibility of the authors and does not necessarily represent the official views of the National Center for Advancing Translational Sciences or the National Institutes of Health. Rice University is a partner in the award.

1. Mitra Toossi and Elka Torpey. May 2017. "Older Workers: Labor Force Trends and Career Options." *Career Outlook*. U.S. Bureau of Labor Statistics. (https://www.bls.gov/careeroutlook/2017/article/older-workers.htm).

2. David L. Blustein. 2006. *The Psychology of Working: A New Perspective for Career Development, Counseling, and Public Policy*. New York: Routledge.

3. Aparna Joshi and Hyuntak Roh. June 1, 2009. "The Role of Context in Work Team Diversity Research: A Meta-analytic Review." *Academy of Management Journal* 52(3):599–627. (https://doi.org/10.5465/amj.2009.41331491).

4. Franz J. Gellert and Ben S. Kuipers. 2008. "Short- and Long-term Consequences of Age in Work Teams." *Career Development International* 13(2):132–49. (https://doi.org/10.1108/13620430810860549).

5. David P. Costanza et al. December 2012. "Generational Differences in Work-related Attitudes: A Meta-analysis." *Journal of Business and Psychology* 27(4):375–94. (https://doi.org/10.1007/s10869-012-9259-4).

6. Cort W. Rudolph and Hannes Zacher. 2015. "Intergenerational Perceptions and Conflicts in Multi-age and Multigenerational Work Environments." Pp. 253–82 in *Facing the Challenges of a Multi-age Workforce: A Use-inspired Approach*, edited by Lisa M. Finkelstein et al. New York: Routledge.

7. Eden King et al. August 1, 2019. "Generational Differences at Work Are Small. Thinking They're Big Affects Our Behavior." *Harvard Business Review*. (https://hbr.org/2019/08/generational-differences-at-work-are-small-thinking-theyre-big-affects-our-behavior).

8. Emma Parry and Peter Urwin. April 1, 2017. "The Evidence Base for Generational Differences: Where Do We Go from Here?" *Work, Aging and Retirement* 3(2):140–48. (https://doi.org/10.1093/workar/waw037).

9. Jürgen Wegge and Bertolt Meyer. 2020. "Age Diversity and Age-based Faultlines in Teams: Understanding a Brezel Phenomenon Requires a Brezel Theory." *Work, Aging and Retirement* 6(1):8–14. (https://doi.org/10.1093/workar/waz017).

10. Costanza et al., "Generational Differences in Work-related Attitudes."

11. Karen Wey Smola and Charlotte D. Sutton. 2002. "Generational Differences: Revisiting Generational Work Values for the New Millennium." *Journal of Organizational Behavior* 23(4):363–82. (https://doi.org/10.1002/job.147).

12. Thomas W. H. Ng and Daniel C. Feldman. August 5, 2010. "The Relationships of Age with Job Attitudes: A Meta-analysis." *Personnel Psychology* 63(3):677–718. (https://doi.org/10.1111/j.1744-6570.2010.01184.x).

13. Laura L. Carstensen. 1998. "A Life-span Approach to Social Motivation." Pp. 341–64 in *Motivation and Self-Regulation across the Life Span*. New York: Cambridge University Press. (https://doi.org/10.1017/CBO9780511527869.015).

14. Ruth Kanfer and Phillip L. Ackerman. July 1, 2004. "Aging, Adult Development, and Work Motivation." *Academy of Management Review* 29(3):440–58. (https://doi.org/10.5465/amr.2004.13670969).

15. Costanza et al., "Generational Differences in Work-related Attitudes."

16. Smola and Sutton, "Generational Differences."

17. Carstensen, "A Life-Span Approach to Social Motivation."

18. Kanfer and Ackerman, "Aging, Adult Development, and Work Motivation."

19. Richard A. Posthuma and Michael A. Campion. February 1, 2009. "Age Stereotypes in the Workplace: Common Stereotypes, Moderators, and Future Research Directions." *Journal of Management* 35:158–88. (https://doi.org/10.1177/0149206308318617).

20. Kanfer and Ackerman, "Aging, Adult Development, and Work Motivation."

21. Rudolph and Zacher, "Intergenerational Perceptions."

22. Lisa M. Finkelstein, Katherine M. Ryan, and Eden B. King. December 1, 2013. "What Do the Young (Old) People Think of Me? Content and Accuracy of Age-based Meta-stereotypes." *European Journal of Work and Organizational Psychology* 22(6):633–57. (https://doi.org/10.1080/1359432X.2012.673279).

23. Randall A. Gordon and Richard D. Arvey. 2004. "Age Bias in Laboratory and Field Settings: A Meta-analytic Investigation." *Journal of Applied Social Psychology* 34(3):468–92. (https://doi.org/10.1111/j.1559-1816.2004.tb02557.x).

24. Posthuma and Campion, "Age Stereotypes in the Workplace."

25. Lisa M. Finkelstein et al. 2019. "A Daily Diary Study of Responses to Age Meta-stereotypes." *Work, Aging and Retirement*:1–18. (https://doi.org/10.1093/workar/waz005).

26. Finkelstein, Ryan, and King, "What Do the Young (Old) People Think of Me?"

27. Ng and Feldman, "Relationships of Age."

28. Kanfer and Ackerman, "Aging, Adult Development, and Work Motivation."

29. Ng and Feldman, "Relationships of Age."

30. Finkelstein, Ryan, and King, "What Do the Young (Old) People Think of Me?"

31. Finkelstein et al., "Daily Diary Study."

32. Finkelstein et al., "Daily Diary Study."

33. Ng and Feldman, "Relationships of Age."
34. Gerben A. Van Kleef, Astrid C. Homan, and Arik Cheshin. November 1, 2012. "Emotional Influence at Work: Take It EASI." *Organizational Psychology Review* 2(4):311–39. (https://doi.org/10.1177/2041386612454911).
35. Ng and Feldman, "Relationships of Age."
36. Posthuma and Campion, "Age Stereotypes in the Workplace."
37. Ng and Feldman, "Relationships of Age."
38. Lauren S. Simon, Timothy A. Judge, and Marie D. K. Halvorsen-Ganepola. June 1, 2010. "In Good Company? A Multi-study, Multi-level Investigation of the Effects of Co-worker Relationships on Employee Well-being." *Journal of Vocational Behavior* 76(3):534–46. (https://doi.org/10.1016/j.jvb.2010.01.006).
39. Ng and Feldman, "Relationships of Age."
40. Kristen P. Jones et al. September 1, 2016. "Not So Subtle: A Meta-analytic Investigation of the Correlates of Subtle and Overt Discrimination." *Journal of Management* 42(6):1588–1613. (https://doi.org/10.1177/0149206313506466).
41. Ng and Feldman, "Relationships of Age."
42. Carstensen, "A Life-Span Approach to Social Motivation."
43. Christopher Jay Roussin. February 9, 2015. "Age Differences in the Perception of New Co-worker Benevolence." *Journal of Managerial Psychology* 30(1):71–86. (https://doi.org/10.1108/JMP-07-2014-0214).
44. Ng and Feldman, "Relationships of Age."
45. Nina M. Junker and Rolf van Dick. December 1, 2014. "Implicit Theories in Organizational Settings: A Systematic Review and Research Agenda of Implicit Leadership and Followership Theories." *Leadership Quarterly* 25(6):1154–73. (https://doi.org/10.1016/j.leaqua.2014.09.002).
46. Matthew J. Hornsey. 2008. "Social Identity Theory and Self-categorization Theory: A Historical Review." *Social and Personality Psychology Compass* 2(1):204–22.
47. Geoffrey J. Leonardelli, Cynthia L. Pickett, and Marilynn B. Brewer. 2010. "Optimal Distinctiveness Theory: A Framework for Social Identity, Social Cognition, and Intergroup Relations." *Advances in Experimental Social Psychology* 43:63–113.
48. Ng and Feldman, "Relationships of Age."
49. Blustein, *Psychology of Working*.
50. Junker and van Dick, "Implicit Theories."
51. Claudia Buengeler, Astrid C. Homan, and Sven C. Voelpel. 2016. "The Challenge of Being a Young Manager: The Effects of Contingent Reward and Participative Leadership on Team-level Turnover Depend on Leader Age." *Journal of Organizational Behavior* 37(8):1224–45.
52. Eric Kearney. 2008. "Age Differences between Leader and Followers as a Moderator of the Relationship between Transformational Leadership and Team Performance." *Journal of Occupational and Organizational Psychology* 81(4):803–11. (https://doi.org/10.1348/096317907X256717).
53. Hannes Zacher et al. 2011. "Establishing the Next Generation at Work: Leader Generativity as a Moderator of the Relationships between Leader Age, Leader-member Exchange, and Leadership Success." *Psychology and Aging* 26(1):241.
54. Ng and Feldman, "Relationships of Age."
55. Shoshana D. Riza, Yoav Ganzach, and Yihao Liu. 2018. "Time and Job Satisfaction: A Longitudinal Study of the Differential Roles of Age and Tenure." *Journal of Management* 44(7):2558–79. (https://doi.org/10.1177/0149206315624962).
56. Kanfer and Ackerman, "Aging, Adult Development, and Work Motivation."
57. Carstensen, "A Life-Span Approach to Social Motivation."
58. Nicolle P. G. Boumans, Ad H. J. de Jong, and Sara M. Janssen. December 1, 2011. "Age-differences in Work Motivation and Job Satisfaction. The Influence of Age on the Relationships between Work Characteristics and Workers' Outcomes." *International Journal of Aging and Human Development* 73(4):331–50. (https://doi.org/10.2190/AG.73.4.d).
59. Sara Zaniboni et al. 2011. "Age Moderates the Effects of WDQ Factors on Job Attitudes." Paper presented at Society for Industrial and Organizational Psychology (SIOP) Conference, Chicago. K. James and G. Burlacu, chairs.

60. Peter Warr. 2008. "Work Values: Some Demographic and Cultural Correlates." *Journal of Occupational and Organizational Psychology* 81(4):751–75. (https://doi.org/10.1348/096317907X263638).

61. Dorien T. A. M. Kooij et al. 2010. "The Influence of Age on the Associations between HR Practices and Both Affective Commitment and Job Satisfaction: A Meta-analysis." *Journal of Organizational Behavior* 31(8):1111–36. (https://doi.org/10.1002/job.666).

62. David Drabe, Sven Hauff, and Nicole Franziska Richter. March 26, 2015. "Job Satisfaction in Aging Workforces: An Analysis of the USA, Japan and Germany." *International Journal of Human Resource Management* 26(6):783–805. (https://doi.org/10.1080/09585192.2014.939101).

63. Kooij et al., "Influence of Age."

64. Maria Tims, Arnold B. Bakker, and Daantje Derks. February 1, 2012. "Development and Validation of the Job Crafting Scale." *Journal of Vocational Behavior* 80(1):173–86. (https://doi.org/10.1016/j.jvb.2011.05.009).

65. Donald M. Truxillo et al. November 1, 2012. "A Lifespan Perspective on Job Design: Fitting the Job and the Worker to Promote Job Satisfaction, Engagement, and Performance." *Organizational Psychology Review* 2(4):340–60. (https://doi.org/10.1177/2041386612454043).

66. Dorien T. A. M. Kooij, Maria Tims, and Jos Akkermans. January 2, 2017. "The Influence of Future Time Perspective on Work Engagement and Job Performance: The Role of Job Crafting." *European Journal of Work and Organizational Psychology* 26(1):4–15. (https://doi.org/10.1080/1359432X.2016.1209489).

67. Rudolph and Zacher, "Intergenerational Perceptions."

68. Maria Tims et al. August 1, 2013. "Job Crafting at the Team and Individual Level: Implications for Work Engagement and Performance." *Group & Organization Management* 38(4):427–54. (https://doi.org/10.1177/1059601113492421).

69. Maria C. W. Peeters, Richard Arts and Evangelia Demerouti. November 1, 2016. "The Crossover of Job Crafting between Co-workers and Its Relationship with Adaptivity." *European Journal of Work and Organizational Psychology* 25(6):819–32. (https://doi.org/10.1080/1359432X.2016.1160891).

70. Costanza et al., "Generational Differences in Work-related Attitudes."

71. Ng and Feldman, "Relationships of Age."

72. Natalie J. Allen and John P. Meyer. January 1, 1993. "Organizational Commitment: Evidence of Career Stage Effects?" *Journal of Business Research*, Special Issue Loyalty in a Multi-commitment World 26(1):49–61. (https://doi.org/10.1016/0148-2963(93)90042-N).

73. Jacquelyn B. James, Sharon McKechnie, and Jennifer Swanberg. February 2011. "Predicting Employee Engagement in an Age-diverse Retail Workforce." *Journal of Organizational Behavior* 32(2):173–96. (https://doi.org/10.1002/job.681).

74. Allen and Meyer, "Organizational Commitment."

75. Charles J. Brody and Beth A. Rubin. February 7, 2011. "Generational Differences in the Effects of Insecurity, Restructured Workplace Temporalities, and Technology on Organizational Loyalty." *Sociological Spectrum* 31(2):163–92. (https://doi.org/10.1080/02732173.2011.541341).

76. Allen and Meyer, "Organizational Commitment."

77. Donald E. Super. 1980. "A Life-span, Life-space Approach to Career Development." *Journal of Vocational Behavior* 16(3):282–98.

78. Carstensen, "A Life-Span Approach to Social Motivation."

79. Kanfer and Ackerman, "Aging, Adult Development, and Work Motivation."

80. James, McKechnie, and Swanberg, "Predicting Employee Engagement."

81. Marjorie Armstrong-Stassen and Nancy D. Ursel. 2009. "Perceived Organizational Support, Career Satisfaction, and the Retention of Older Workers." *Journal of Occupational and Organizational Psychology* 82(1):201–20. (https://doi.org/10.1348/096317908X288838).

82. Gordon W. Allport. 1954. *The Nature of Prejudice*. Reading, MA: Addison-Wesley.

83. Robert H. Moorman. 1991. "Relationship between Organizational Justice and Organizational Citizenship Behaviors: Do Fairness Perceptions Influence Employee Citizenship?" *Journal of Applied Psychology* 76(6):845–55. (https://doi.org/10.1037/0021-9010.76.6.845).

84. Robert Eisenberger et al. 1986. "Perceived Organizational Support." *Journal of Applied Psychology* 71(3):500.

85. Jason A. Colquitt. 2004. "Does the Justice of the One Interact with the Justice of the Many? Reactions to Procedural Justice in Teams." *Journal of Applied Psychology* 89(4):633–46. (https://doi.org/10.1037/0021-9010.89.4.633).

86. Lucy Cennamo and Dianne Gardner. January 1, 2008. "Generational Differences in Work Values, Outcomes and Person-organisation Values Fit." *Journal of Managerial Psychology* 23(8):891–906. (https://doi.org/10.1108/02683940810904385).

87. Michael R. Bashshur, Ana Hernández, and Vicente González-Romá. 2011. "When Managers and Their Teams Disagree: A Longitudinal Look at the Consequences of Differences in Perceptions of Organizational Support." *Journal of Applied Psychology* 96(3):558.

88. Daniel R. Ilgen et al. 2005. "Teams in Organizations: From Input-process-output Models to IMOI Models." *Annual Review of Psychology* 56(1):517–43. (https://doi.org/10.1146/annurev.psych.56.091103.070250).

89. Toossi and Torpey, "Older Workers."

90. John E. Mathieu et al. January 1, 2014. "A Review and Integration of Team Composition Models: Moving toward a Dynamic and Temporal Framework." *Journal of Management* 40:130–60. (https://doi.org/10.1177/0149206313503014).

91. Gellert and Kuipers, "Short- and Long-term Consequences."

92. Katherine Y. Williams and C. A. O'Reilly III. 1998. "Demography and Diversity in Organizations: A Review of 40 Years of Research." *Research in Organizational Behavior* 20:77–140.

93. Eduardo Salas and Jensine Paoletti. July 19, 2019. "A Teams Perspective on Workplace Aging and Retirement." *Work, Aging and Retirement* 5(3):212–14. (https://doi.org/10.1093/workar/waz008).

94. Shannon L. Marlow et al. January 1, 2018. "Does Team Communication Represent a One-size-fits-all Approach? A Meta-analysis of Team Communication and Performance." *Organizational Behavior and Human Decision Processes* 144:145–70. (https://doi.org/10.1016/j.obhdp.2017.08.001).

95. Stephanie C. Payne and Ann H. Huffman. February 1, 2005. "A Longitudinal Examination of the Influence of Mentoring on Organizational Commitment and Turnover." *Academy of Management Journal* 48(1):158–68. (https://doi.org/10.5465/amj.2005.15993166).

96. Joshi and Roh, "Role of Context in Work Team Diversity Research."

97. Jane S. Thomas et al. August 14, 2019. "Dyadic Viability in Project Teams: The Impact of Liking, Competence, and Task Interdependence." *Journal of Business and Psychology*. (https://doi.org/10.1007/s10869-019-09647-6).

98. Carstensen, "A Life-Span Approach to Social Motivation."

99. Kanfer and Ackerman, "Aging, Adult Development, and Work Motivation."

## REFERENCES

Allen, Natalie J. and John P. Meyer. January 1, 1993. "Organizational Commitment: Evidence of Career Stage Effects?" *Journal of Business Research*, Special Issue Loyalty in a Multi-commitment World 26(1):49–61. (https://doi.org/10.1016/0148-2963(93)90042-N).

Allport, Gordon W. 1954. *The Nature of Prejudice*. Reading, MA: Addison-Wesley.

Armstrong-Stassen, Marjorie and Nancy D. Ursel. 2009. "Perceived Organizational Support, Career Satisfaction, and the Retention of Older Workers." *Journal of Occupational and Organizational Psychology* 82(1):201–20. (https://doi.org/10.1348/096317908X288838).

Bashshur, Michael R., Ana Hernández, and Vicente González-Romá. 2011. "When Managers and Their Teams Disagree: A Longitudinal Look at the Consequences of Differences in Perceptions of Organizational Support." *Journal of Applied Psychology* 96(3):558.

Blustein, David L. 2006. *The Psychology of Working: A New Perspective for Career Development, Counseling, and Public Policy*. New York: Routledge.

Boumans, Nicolle P. G., Ad H. J. de Jong, and Sara M. Janssen. December 1, 2011. "Age-differences in Work Motivation and Job Satisfaction. The Influence of Age on the Relationships between Work Characteristics and Workers' Outcomes." *International Journal of Aging and Human Development* 73(4):331–50. (https://doi.org/10.2190/AG.73.4.d).

Brimeyer, Ted M., Robert Perrucci, and Shelley M. Wadsworth. 2010. "Age, Tenure, Resources for Control, and Organizational Commitment." *Social Science Quarterly* 91(2):511–30. (https://doi.org/10.1111/j.1540-6237.2010.00705.x).

Brody, Charles J. and Beth A. Rubin. February 7, 2011. "Generational Differences in the Effects of Insecurity, Restructured Workplace Temporalities, and Technology on Organizational Loyalty." *Sociological Spectrum* 31(2):163–92. (https://doi.org/10.1080/02732173.2011.541341).

Buengeler, Claudia, Astrid C. Homan, and Sven C. Voelpel. 2016. "The Challenge of Being a Young Manager: The Effects of Contingent Reward and Participative Leadership on Team-level Turnover Depend on Leader Age." *Journal of Organizational Behavior* 37(8):1224–45.

Carstensen, Laura L. 1998. "A Life-span Approach to Social Motivation." Pp. 341–64 in *Motivation and Self-Regulation across the Life Span*. New York: Cambridge University Press. (https://doi.org/10.1017/CBO9780511527869.015).

Cennamo, Lucy and Dianne Gardner. January 1, 2008. "Generational Differences in Work Values, Outcomes and Person-organisation Values Fit." *Journal of Managerial Psychology* 23(8):891–906. (https://doi.org/10.1108/02683940810904385).

Colquitt, Jason A. 2004. "Does the Justice of the One Interact with the Justice of the Many? Reactions to Procedural Justice in Teams." *Journal of Applied Psychology* 89(4):633–46. (https://doi.org/10.1037/0021-9010.89.4.633).

Costanza, David P., et al. December 2012. "Generational Differences in Work-related Attitudes: A Meta-analysis." *Journal of Business and Psychology* 27(4):375–94. (https://doi.org/10.1007/s10869-012-9259-4).

Drabe, David, Sven Hauff, and Nicole Franziska Richter. March 26, 2015. "Job Satisfaction in Aging Workforces: An Analysis of the USA, Japan and Germany." *International Journal of Human Resource Management* 26(6):783–805. (https://doi.org/10.1080/09585192.2014.939101).

Eisenberger, Robert, et al. 1986. "Perceived Organizational Support." *Journal of Applied Psychology* 71(3):500.

Finkelstein, Lisa M., et al. 2019. "A Daily Diary Study of Responses to Age Meta-stereotypes." *Work, Aging and Retirement*:1–18. (https://doi.org/10.1093/workar/waz005).

Finkelstein, Lisa M., Katherine M. Ryan, and Eden B. King. December 1, 2013. "What Do the Young (Old) People Think of Me? Content and Accuracy of Age-based Meta-stereotypes." *European Journal of Work and Organizational Psychology* 22(6):633–57. (https://doi.org/10.1080/1359432X.2012.673279).

Gellert, Franz J. and Ben S. Kuipers. 2008. "Short- and Long-term Consequences of Age in Work Teams." *Career Development International* 13(2):132–49. (https://doi.org/10.1108/13620430810860549).

Gordon, Randall A. and Richard D. Arvey. 2004. "Age Bias in Laboratory and Field Settings: A Meta-analytic Investigation." *Journal of Applied Social Psychology* 34(3):468–92. (https://doi.org/10.1111/j.1559-1816.2004.tb02557.x).

Hornsey, Matthew J. 2008. "Social Identity Theory and Self-categorization Theory: A Historical Review." *Social and Personality Psychology Compass* 2(1):204–22.

Ilgen, Daniel R., et al. 2005. "Teams in Organizations: From Input-process-output Models to IMOI Models." *Annual Review of Psychology* 56(1):517–43. (https://doi.org/10.1146/annurev.psych.56.091103.070250).

James, Jacquelyn B., Sharon McKechnie, and Jennifer Swanberg. February 2011. "Predicting Employee Engagement in an Age-diverse Retail Workforce." *Journal of Organizational Behavior* 32(2):173–96. (https://doi.org/10.1002/job.681).

Jones, Kristen P., et al. September 1, 2016. "Not So Subtle: A Meta-analytic Investigation of the Correlates of Subtle and Overt Discrimination." *Journal of Management* 42(6):1588–1613. (https://doi.org/10.1177/0149206313506466).

Joshi, Aparna and Hyuntak Roh. June 1, 2009. "The Role of Context in Work Team Diversity Research: A Meta-analytic Review." *Academy of Management Journal* 52(3):599–627. (https://doi.org/10.5465/amj.2009.41331491).

Junker, Nina M. and Rolf van Dick. December 1, 2014. "Implicit Theories in Organizational Settings: A Systematic Review and Research Agenda of Implicit Leadership and Followership Theories." *Leadership Quarterly* 25(6):1154–73. (https://doi.org/10.1016/j.leaqua.2014.09.002).

Kanfer, Ruth and Phillip L. Ackerman. July 1, 2004. "Aging, Adult Development, and Work Motivation." *Academy of Management Review* 29(3):440–58. (https://doi.org/10.5465/amr.2004.13670969).

Kearney, Eric. 2008. "Age Differences between Leader and Followers as a Moderator of the Relationship between Transformational Leadership and Team Performance." *Journal of Occupational and Organizational Psychology* 81(4):803–11. (https://doi.org/10.1348/096317907X256717).

King, Eden, et al. August 1, 2019. "Generational Differences at Work Are Small. Thinking They're Big Affects Our Behavior." *Harvard Business Review*. (https://hbr.org/2019/08/generational-differences-at-work-are-small-thinking-theyre-big-affects-our-behavior).

Kooij, Dorien T. A. M., et al. 2010. "The Influence of Age on the Associations between HR Practices and Both Affective Commitment and Job Satisfaction: A Meta-analysis." *Journal of Organizational Behavior* 31(8):1111–36. (https://doi.org/10.1002/job.666).

Kooij, Dorien T. A. M., Maria Tims, and Jos Akkermans. January 2, 2017. "The Influence of Future Time Perspective on Work Engagement and Job Performance: The Role of Job Crafting." *European Journal of Work and Organizational Psychology* 26(1):4–15. (https://doi.org/10.1080/1359432X.2016.1209489).

Leonardelli, Geoffrey J., Cynthia L. Pickett, and Marilynn B. Brewer. 2010. "Optimal Distinctiveness Theory: A Framework for Social Identity, Social Cognition, and Intergroup Relations." *Advances in Experimental Social Psychology* 43:63–113.

Marlow, Shannon L., et al. January 1, 2018. "Does Team Communication Represent a One-size-fits-all Approach? A Meta-analysis of Team Communication and Performance." *Organizational Behavior and Human Decision Processes* 144:145–70. (https://doi.org/10.1016/j.obhdp.2017.08.001).

Mathieu, John E., et al. January 1, 2014. "A Review and Integration of Team Composition Models: Moving toward a Dynamic and Temporal Framework." *Journal of Management* 40:130–60. (https://doi.org/10.1177/0149206313503014).

Moorman, Robert H. 1991. "Relationship between Organizational Justice and Organizational Citizenship Behaviors: Do Fairness Perceptions Influence Employee Citizenship?" *Journal of Applied Psychology* 76(6):845–55. (https://doi.org/10.1037/0021-9010.76.6.845).

Ng, Thomas W. H. and Daniel C. Feldman. August 5, 2010. "The Relationships of Age with Job Attitudes: A Meta-analysis." *Personnel Psychology* 63(3):677–718. (https://doi.org/10.1111/j.1744-6570.2010.01184.x).

Noble, Stephanie M. and Charles D. Schewe. December 1, 2003. "Cohort Segmentation: An Exploration of Its Validity." *Journal of Business Research* 56(12):979–87. (https://doi.org/10.1016/S0148-2963(02)00268-0).

Parry, Emma and Peter Urwin. April 1, 2017. "The Evidence Base for Generational Differences: Where Do We Go from Here?" *Work, Aging and Retirement* 3(2):140–48. (https://doi.org/10.1093/workar/waw037).

Payne, Stephanie C. and Ann H. Huffman. February 1, 2005. "A Longitudinal Examination of the Influence of Mentoring on Organizational Commitment and Turnover." *Academy of Management Journal* 48(1):158–68. (https://doi.org/10.5465/amj.2005.15993166).

Peeters, Maria C. W., Richard Arts, and Evangelia Demerouti. November 1, 2016. "The Crossover of Job Crafting between Co-workers and Its Relationship with Adaptivity." *European Journal of Work and Organizational Psychology* 25(6):819–32. (https://doi.org/10.1080/1359432X.2016.1160891).

Posthuma, Richard A. and Michael A. Campion. February 1, 2009. "Age Stereotypes in the Workplace: Common Stereotypes, Moderators, and Future Research Directions." *Journal of Management* 35:158–88. (https://doi.org/10.1177/0149206308318617).

Riza, Shoshana D., Yoav Ganzach, and Yihao Liu. 2018. "Time and Job Satisfaction: A Longitudinal Study of the Differential Roles of Age and Tenure." *Journal of Management* 44(7):2558–79. (https://doi.org/10.1177/0149206315624962).

Roussin, Christopher Jay. February 9, 2015. "Age Differences in the Perception of New Co-worker Benevolence." *Journal of Managerial Psychology* 30(1):71–86. (https://doi.org/10.1108/JMP-07-2014-0214).

Rudolph, Cort W. and Hannes Zacher. 2015. "Intergenerational Perceptions and Conflicts in Multi-age and Multigenerational Work Environments." Pp. 253–82 in *Facing the Challenges of a Multi-age Workforce: A Use-inspired Approach*, edited by Lisa M. Finkelstein et al. New York: Routledge.

Ryan, Katherine M., Eden B. King, and Lisa M. Finkelstein. January 1, 2015. "Younger Workers' Metastereotypes, Workplace Mood, Attitudes, and Behaviors." *Journal of Managerial Psychology* 30(1):54–70. (https://doi.org/10.1108/JMP-07-2014-0215).

Salas, Eduardo and Jensine Paoletti. July 19, 2019. "A Teams Perspective on Workplace Aging and Retirement." *Work, Aging and Retirement* 5(3):212–14. (https://doi.org/10.1093/workar/waz008).

Simon, Lauren S., Timothy A. Judge, and Marie D. K. Halvorsen-Ganepola. June 1, 2010. "In Good Company? A Multi-study, Multi-level Investigation of the Effects of Co-worker Relationships on Employee Well-being." *Journal of Vocational Behavior* 76(3):534–46. (https://doi.org/10.1016/j.jvb.2010.01.006).

Smola, Karen Wey, and Charlotte D. Sutton. 2002. "Generational Differences: Revisiting Generational Work Values for the New Millennium." *Journal of Organizational Behavior* 23(4):363–82. (https://doi.org/10.1002/job.147).

Super, Donald E. 1980. "A Life-span, Life-space Approach to Career Development." *Journal of Vocational Behavior* 16(3):282–98.

Thomas, Jane S., et al. August 14, 2019. "Dyadic Viability in Project Teams: The Impact of Liking, Competence, and Task Interdependence." *Journal of Business and Psychology*. (https://doi.org/10.1007/s10869-019-09647-6).

Tims, Maria, et al. August 1, 2013. "Job Crafting at the Team and Individual Level: Implications for Work Engagement and Performance." *Group & Organization Management* 38(4):427–54. (https://doi.org/10.1177/1059601113492421).

Tims, Maria, Arnold B. Bakker, and Daantje Derks. February 1, 2012. "Development and Validation of the Job Crafting Scale." *Journal of Vocational Behavior* 80(1):173–86. (https://doi.org/10.1016/j.jvb.2011.05.009).

Toossi, Mitra and Elka Torpey. May 2017. "Older Workers: Labor Force Trends and Career Options." *Career Outlook*. U.S. Bureau of Labor Statistics. (https://www.bls.gov/careeroutlook/2017/article/older-workers.htm).

Truxillo, Donald M., et al. November 1, 2012. "A Lifespan Perspective on Job Design: Fitting the Job and the Worker to Promote Job Satisfaction, Engagement, and Performance." *Organizational Psychology Review* 2(4):340–60. (https://doi.org/10.1177/2041386612454043).

Van Kleef, Gerben A., Marc W. Heerdink, and Astrid C. Homan. October 1, 2017. "Emotional Influence in Groups: The Dynamic Nexus of Affect, Cognition, and Behavior." *Current Opinion in Psychology, Emotion* 17:156–61. (https://doi.org/10.1016/j.copsyc.2017.07.017).

Van Kleef, Gerben A., Astrid C. Homan, and Arik Cheshin. November 1, 2012. "Emotional Influence at Work: Take It EASI." *Organizational Psychology Review* 2(4):311–39. (https://doi.org/10.1177/2041386612454911).

Warr, Peter. 2008. "Work Values: Some Demographic and Cultural Correlates." *Journal of Occupational and Organizational Psychology* 81(4):751–75. (https://doi.org/10.1348/096317907X263638).

Wegge, Jürgen and Bertolt Meyer. 2020. "Age Diversity and Age-based Faultlines in Teams: Understanding a Brezel Phenomenon Requires a Brezel Theory." *Work, Aging and Retirement* 6(1):8–14. (https://doi.org/10.1093/workar/waz017).

Williams, Katherine Y. and C. A. O'Reilly III. 1998. "Demography and Diversity in Organizations: A Review of 40 Years of Research." *Research in Organizational Behavior* 20:77–140.

Zacher, Hannes, et al. 2011. "Establishing the Next Generation at Work: Leader Generativity as a Moderator of the Relationships between Leader Age, Leader-member Exchange, and Leadership Success." *Psychology and Aging* 26(1):241.

Zaniboni, Sara, et al. 2011. "Age Moderates the Effects of WDQ Factors on Job Attitudes." Paper presented at Society for Industrial and Organizational Psychology (SIOP) Conference, Chicago. K. James and G. Burlacu, chairs.

CHAPTER 10

# The Role of Employers in Shaping the Lives of Experienced Employees

## Moving from Awareness to Activity

Brian Kaskie and Hannah Rochford

### UNDERSTANDING EXPERIENCED EMPLOYEES AND THE WORKFORCE

Most employers are aware of the changing age composition of the labor force. In one study, 80 percent of employers agreed that experienced employees (persons over the age of fifty) are crucial to the firm and acknowledged they are challenged to replace skills and organizational knowledge held by older workers.[1] According to another study, four of five employers said they support employees who plan to work past the age of sixty-five and are aware of preferences to gradually transition from full-time positions into part-time, seasonal, or consultant roles.[2] In a study of human resource (HR) professionals across the United States, 71 percent described their workplaces as "age-friendly."[3] (See also chapter 11.) And, in our recent survey of employers across the state of Colorado (n = 146), 70 percent reported thinking it is important to develop programs for experienced employees, and 90 percent reported that their organization is supportive of employees working for as long as they wish.

Despite such generally positive attitudes, there is a large and growing gap between awareness of and action to implement age-inclusive workplace accommodations, policies, and programs.[4] In one study sampling HR professionals, researchers found only 12 percent implemented three or more efforts focused on aging employees and 25 percent had developed only one or two programs.[5] Another study revealed that under

10 percent of employers included age as a factor in developing workforce recruitment and retention strategies.[6]

It should be noted that the aging workforce impacts industries variably.[7] As shown in table 10.1, over one-third of all agriculture, forestry, fishing, and hunting workers already are age fifty-five or older while service and retail trades employ a substantially smaller number of experienced employees.[8]

As far as supporting experienced employees, HR professionals representing government agencies were statistically more likely to have begun planning for an aging workforce, and were more likely to initiate training efforts as well as adjust their retention and recruitment efforts targeting experienced employees.[9] While 29 percent of persons working in finance, insurance, and real estate companies are over the age of

**TABLE 10.1.** Age Cohort Proportions and Median Age of Each Industry (for 2019, Numbers in Thousands)

| *Industry* | *Total Workers* | *16 to 34 Years* | *35 to 54 Years* | *55 and Over* | *Median Age* |
|---|---|---|---|---|---|
| Total employed | 157,538 | 55,129 | 65,169 | 37,240 | 42.3 |
| | % of workers in each industry (number of workers) | % of industry workers in each age cohort (number of industry workers) | | | |
| Agriculture, forestry, fishing, and hunting | 1.5% (2,425) | 27.3% (661) | 34.8% (844) | 37.9% (920) | 47.8 |
| Mining, quarrying, and oil and gas extraction | 0.5% (750) | 32.1% (241) | 47.7% (358) | 20.3% (152) | 41.8 |
| Construction | 7.2% (11,373) | 31.4% (3,570) | 46.5% (5,285) | 22.1% (2,518) | 42.6 |
| Manufacturing | 10.0% (15,741) | 30.2% (4,753) | 44.7% (7,029) | 25.1% (3,958) | 44.1 |
| Wholesale and retail trade | 12.5% (19,742) | 42.0% (8,299) | 34.9% (6,896) | 23.0% (4,547) | 39.9 |
| Transportation and utilities | 5.7% (8,991) | 30.6% (2,755) | 43.2% (3,886) | 26.1% (2,349) | 44.4 |
| Information | 1.8% (2,766) | 38.0% (1,051) | 42.5% (1,176) | 19.5% (539) | 40.7 |
| Financial activities | 6.8% (10,765) | 29.4% (3,168) | 45.0% (4,847) | 25.5% (2,749) | 44.0 |
| Professional and business services | 12.4% (19,606) | 33.4% (6,544) | 42.8% (8,398) | 23.8% (4,664) | 42.8 |
| Education and health services | 22.8% (35,894) | 32.3% (11,603) | 43.4% (15,591) | 24.2% (8,699) | 43.1 |
| Leisure and hospitality | 9.3% (14,643) | 56.0% (8,202) | 29.4% (4,310) | 14.6% (2,132) | 31.9 |
| Other services | 4.8% (7,617) | 32.7% (2,488) | 40.1% (3,055) | 27.2% (2,073) | 43.6 |
| Public administration | 4.6% (7,225) | 24.8% (1,791) | 48.4% (3,494) | 26.9% (1,940) | 45.8 |

*Source:* Employed Persons by Detailed Industry and Age, January 22, 2020. Retrieved from https://www.bls.gov/cps/cpsaat18b.htm.

fifty-five, HR professionals representing these firms were significantly less likely to be doing anything for their aging workforce.[10] Similarly, HR professionals representing professional, scientific, and technical services were significantly less likely to examine policies and practices pertaining to aging employees. They also were less likely to conduct a formal analysis of workplace retirement patterns and more likely to believe their firm needed to make no changes for the aging workforce.[11] Moreover, even though health and social service occupations (e.g., registered nurses, personal care aides) are projected to be among the fastest growing in the next decade, HR professionals from these industries were unlikely to consider the challenges and opportunities associated with an aging workforce.[12]

Some would suggest that such a "voltage drop" between employers' awareness and actions addressing the aging workforce can be attributed to particular characteristics of the organization.[13,14] For example, HR personnel may not have the capacity to conduct an internal evaluation focusing on the aging workforce relative to other priorities. The employer may not have sufficient resources to support the development and implementation of age-appropriate policies or programs, or organizational leadership may not value targeted accommodations out of concern they are incompatible with core values, threaten profitability, or constitute a form of discrimination.

Others suggest the lack of progression from awareness to action is a reflection of ageism among employers.[15,16] (See also chapter 12.) A survey of workplace manager opinions of employees over fifty years old revealed several negative stereotypes (experienced employees are inflexible and neither willing or able to adapt to new technology). Dennis and Thomas found that traits most admired about older workers, such as job commitment and respect for authority, were not highly valued by employers.[17] The retail and hospitality industry, with a lower proportion of workers over age fifty-five, is less likely to assign a value to the experience, knowledge, and skills of aging workers.[18] Employers and managers also believe that experienced employees are not as well suited for the contemporary workplace and are more costly to train.[19] Some employers simply believe that older workers cost more in terms of salary and benefit payouts.[20]

Regardless of cause, the lack of a concerted effort to respond to the unique needs and preferences of experienced employees will become more problematic in the decade ahead. As the population of experienced employees is expected to double, an increasing number will engage in longer work lives and pursue varied pathways out of (and back into) the labor force. (See also chapters 21 and 26.) Moreover, recognizing age-related health challenges, employers seeking to retain their trained, talented workers will need to alter workplace environments and invest in employee health and wellness. If employers do not respond with appropriate policies and programs, they contribute to the expanding "structural lag."[21]

If lags between employee demands and employer responses persist, employers will miss opportunities to engage and retain productive employees.[22] In fact, employers who do not prepare for the aging workforce may find themselves at a competitive disadvantage when it comes to attracting and retaining talented workers and filling vacant positions. Arguably, as the average worker becomes older, employers who anticipate and address the needs of older workers will be better positioned to fill their own labor force demands.

At worst, the failure to bridge these gaps can create negative and hostile workplace climates that may contribute to complaints of age-related discrimination.[23,24] Such discrimination can take many forms, from older workers being treated differently in hiring, firing, promotion, and layoff decisions to being systematically offered inferior benefits, job assignments, and training opportunities. Age discrimination in the hiring process is a particularly significant challenge for older workers and may be undermining their ability to transition between jobs or reenter the workforce.[25] According to one 2013 AARP survey, nearly two-thirds of workers ages forty-five to seventy-four believed other workers face age discrimination.[26]

In the remainder of this chapter, we set out to change the narrative around employers' response to experienced employees. We first reflect upon an emerging perspective that experienced employees offer considerable value relative to perceived costs. Next, we review a set of nine strategies employers can implement to support experienced employees. We then consider driving forces for policy and program adoption that bridge current gaps.

## CHANGING THE NARRATIVE AROUND EXPERIENCED EMPLOYEES

Experienced employees can be an asset to their respective firms. Experienced employees tend to display personal involvement with their job, are more productive, and have lower turnover relative to younger employees.[27] Experienced workers are noteworthy sources of formal and informal mentorship, maturity, and work ethic,[28] and have a positive effect on the productivity of other workers.[29] Experienced employees can serve as a source of revenue as they uphold the reputation of the firm, maintain clients and contracts, and secure new opportunities for organizational growth.[30,31] For more than a decade, this "business case" for experienced employees has been developed. As employers uphold and maintain workforces that include individuals of all ages, they are more likely to engage a range of clients and customers and present a more positive public image.[32]

## EMPLOYER POLICIES AND PROGRAMS PERTAINING TO EXPERIENCED EMPLOYEES

Based on previous research[33] and our own work, we identified a total of nine distinct approaches to address the aging workforce (summarized in table 10.2).

### Organizational Culture

A diversified, multigenerational workforce expands a business's ability to cater to a greater pool of potential customers and clients.[34] (See also chapter 9.) Intergenerational workforces can also diminish stereotypes held by employees of all ages and promote an understanding that supporting the well-being of experienced employees offers organizational benefits.[35] For example, intergenerational apprenticeship programs can

**TABLE 10.2.** Types of Employer Policies and Programs Pertaining to Experienced Employees

| *Policy or Program Type* | *Description* |
|---|---|
| Organizational culture | Related to workplace attitudes, language, and visual content inclusive of persons of all ages. |
| Health insurance and retirement savings | Related to employer-sponsored health insurance and retirement savings benefits. |
| Health and wellness promotion | Related to wellness promotion and disease prevention. |
| Disability and injury prevention | Related to safety promotion as well as acute and accumulated injury prevention. |
| Caregiving support | Related to schedule and professional responsibility accommodations for those acting as caregivers. |
| Continuing education and training | Related to equitable creation and utilization of opportunities for continued education and professional development. |
| Flexible workplace options | Related to physical and temporal working environment adjustments. |
| Financial literacy and retirement counseling | Related to financial security and preparedness for financial and nonfinancial aspects of retirement. |
| Retirement pathways | Related to transitions from full-time work to full-time retirement that allow for continued engagement with and/or gradual transition from the workforce at the discretion of the employee. |

*Source:* Kaskie, B., and Rochford, H., 2020.

foster professional growth of employees of all ages and promote cross-generational knowledge transfer.[36] Maintaining an age-diverse workforce also positions employers to respond more effectively to labor shortages. As participation rates among younger workers remain flat, employers increasingly recognize the need to recruit and retain nontraditional sources of employees. Innovative employers have responded to this need with targeted strategies to attract experienced workers.

## Health Insurance and Retirement Savings

Benefits are a powerful driver for getting employees to remain in (or return to) the workforce. In fact, the need for health insurance is one of the factors workers between the ages of fifty and sixty-five cite most frequently when asked to identify their reasons for continuing to work. This finding suggests continued access to employer-sponsored health insurance may be used by organizations to retain their skilled and experienced workers. A 2017 study reported that 79 percent of employers offer health insurance to their employees,[37] a benefit shown to correlate with increased work output and reduced disability leaves.[38]

Access to employer-sponsored retirement savings is important to experienced employees as well. Nearly half of private industry workers lack access to an employer-sponsored retirement plan, a proportion, however, varying considerably across industries and worker demographics.[39] Even when adults have access to retirement plans, the savings secured through defined benefit plans may be withdrawn to address emergencies and other unexpected financial challenges, thereby offering less long-term security.[40]

## Health and Wellness Promotion

Another important dimension of fostering an intergenerational workforce is creating conditions that support experienced employees' health and well-being. (See also chapter 19.) While employers can positively impact the health and well-being of employees indirectly through the conferral of salary and providing health insurance and retirement benefits, workplace health promotions are especially important for experienced employees who are at increased risk of acute illness/injury, chronic disease/disability, and higher associated costs.

While such programs must be carefully structured to ensure they do not discriminate against any employee, studies suggest that effectively targeted wellness programs can provide benefits to workers and correspond with cost savings for employers. In one large study, implementation of comprehensive workplace cardiovascular health initiatives was found to correspond with reductions in health risks and incidence of cardiovascular disease, as well as decreased medical expenditures.[41] In another study, Medicare-eligible beneficiaries who participated in a comprehensive workplace wellness program were shown to have lower out-of-pocket health care costs.[42]

Nonetheless, employers have been slow to develop health and wellness programs for experienced employees. As of 2017, it was estimated that less than half of employers acknowledged the importance of wellness programs, and less than a quarter offered such programs.[43] Differences in capacity between small and large organizations provide a partial explanation for this lag. However, tax incentives encouraging the establishment of these programs may improve implementation feasibility for small-business owners.[44,45]

Given that the health status of all employees changes with age, individuals and employers should consider how: (a) employer-based health insurance becomes more critical for persons over fifty-five; (b) health insurance benefits and wellness programs can result in improved individual and organizational outcomes; and (c) access to Medicare supplemental and long-term health insurance options are desired among aging workers as they decide to transition into retirement.

## Disability and Injury Prevention

While many workers with a health condition or disability already occupy and can perform jobs without accommodation, others are unable to apply for, accept, or maintain jobs due to a health condition or disability barriers. Barriers can be physical in nature (e.g., inaccessible work locations) or by-products of workplace procedures or practices (e.g., rules pertaining to when work breaks can be taken).[46] Moreover, individuals who perform repetitive physical tasks for a sustained period of time are more likely to experience an injury, and such injuries may lead to compensation claims and long-term disability.[47] As such, workplace disability and injury prevention is a complementary dimension to worker health and wellness. Prevention mitigates both the direct and indirect costs of injury for employers and employees.[48]

Prevention strategies often include environment adjustments and ergonomic support. Adjustments can be integrated through job hazard analysis (breaking each job up into smaller tasks, determining the risk factors, and identifying modifications for each task).[49] This information can be used to develop job rotations, where workers are cross-trained to rotate jobs throughout the day and change tasks often within their own job to manage the associated risks. This information may also prove valuable when selecting workplace tools to minimize repetitive strain or unnatural positions.[50]

## Caregiving Support

As the population grows older, experienced employees are called upon to act as informal caregivers for their relatives and others who are experiencing chronic health-related challenges or who need assistance for a short period of time after an acute health event. (See also chapter 20.) Informal caregiving can lead to "phantom absences" as individuals may need to alter their schedules and/or use sick and personal days. Yet almost half of employed caregivers are not able to adjust their schedule or restructure their position; those in positions earning lower wages tend to have fewer options. A substantial number of employed elder caregivers end up reluctantly leaving the workforce because they cannot alter their current roles or find a suitable alternative.[51]

While many employers offer unpaid leave pursuant to the federally mandated Family and Medical Leave Act (FMLA), only 13 percent of private-sector workers have access to paid family leave at work.[52] According to one survey looking specifically at employers' approaches to individuals with elder caregiving responsibilities, less than 10 percent of HR professionals surveyed had a formal policy concerning elder caregiving, and less than half offered any sort of program (e.g., caregiver referral) or support (e.g., flextime) for employed informal elder caregivers.[53] Employers may also consider incorporating educational resources about caregiving within existing employee assistance programs (EAPs). EAPs can establish linkages with local caregiver support programs and encourage employees to use resources such as respite service and support groups.

## Continuing Education and Training

Many experienced employees find themselves needing to improve their professional skills or learn new ones in order to keep up to date with the requirements of their current job, receive a promotion, or find a new job. (See also chapters 15, 17, and 18.) The nature and magnitude of challenges experienced workers face when seeking to acquire new skills and training vary substantially across industries. Older workers encountering significant challenges may have their ability to succeed in a workplace or to secure employment compromised. Accordingly, these workers are at risk for prolonged periods of unemployment and some may leave the labor force altogether.

The more employers invest in education and training, the greater their organizational capacity for efficiency and productivity. Some employers, however, may be reluctant to invest in older worker training out of a concern employees are likely to leave or retire before seeing a return on investment. A recent survey of 1,731 employers revealed 42 percent had increased training and cross-training efforts in response to the aging workforce.[54] These stereotypes can have self-fulfilling effects should mature workers themselves share these assumptions and opt out of training even when it is available.[55]

## Flexible Workplace Options

As people age, their vision of an ideal work-life balance may change. (See also chapters 11 and 20.) While caregiving duties may create a need for restructured job roles, there are many other reasons experienced employees may want to rebalance their responsibilities. Some may wish to work part-time to open up leisure opportunities or spend more time with family and friends; others may want to work full-time on a seasonal basis so they can relocate to a more attractive climate for part of the year; some others may be tired of work-related travel or daily commuting and prefer to contribute from home or through "telework" arrangements.

Employers responding to these varied demands might provide flexible alternatives especially to long-serving and trusted employees. This makes a workplace more attractive and helps businesses capitalize on the skill sets of experienced workers, maintain operational continuity, and reduce costs associated with hiring and training new employees.[56] Increased availability of flexible work schedules or telework options promotes greater employee engagement, better physical and mental health, greater satisfaction with work-family balance, and lower perceptions of work as a hindrance to other interests.

Flexible roles can be defined formally or informally. A formal arrangement involves a management structure in which employees must request formal approval and meet eligibility criteria such as length of employment.[57] Informal arrangements are developed on an individual basis between a supervisor and an employee.

## Financial Literacy and Retirement Counseling

Many experienced employees remain unprepared for retirement as they are unaware of how best to convert salary into retirement savings and unfamiliar with different Social Security payout options. As such, many experienced employees continue working because they have not amassed sufficient savings to meet retirement income goals. (See also chapters 2 and 6.) Employees facing financial stressors are over three times more likely to be distracted and/or to be managing financial matters while at work, twice as likely to miss work due to personal financial issues, and more inclined to cite health issues caused by financial stress than workers without such stress.[58] A growing number of employers are choosing to invest in employee financial literacy and promoting access to retirement savings. By doing so, employers can increase employee job satisfaction, elevate productivity, and lower their administrative costs.[59]

It is less common, however, for employers to offer counseling services about the *non*financial aspects of transitioning into retirement. Prior research suggests that nonfinancial aspects of retirement, including fear of being "cut off" from meaningful roles, contribute significantly to retirement hesitancy and delay.[60] Some researchers have suggested that comprehensive retirement counseling is among the most effective ways to positively alter savings behavior and retirement preparation.[61]

### Retirement Pathways

A large and growing number of experienced employees prefer to transition from full-time work gradually and with control over when they begin the process. Individuals can continue their professional engagement by adopting a bridge role, engaging in a retire-rehire program, or transitioning through a period of phased retirement. Of these, bridge employment is by far the most common—approximately one half of older workers with full-time careers (FTCs) move to a bridge job before exiting the labor force. (See also chapters 21 and 22.) This trend has been remarkably stable since the early 1990s.[62,63] The next most common form of gradual retirement is reentry or "unretirement." Approximately 15 percent of retired career workers eventually return to the labor force within two years.[64] About 10 percent of older workers with career jobs "phase out" of their professional roles by reducing their hours by 20 percent or more.[65]

As with flexible professional pathways, establishing eligibility criteria for phased retirement can help to ensure understanding between employers and employees[66] and reconcile any legal or compensation implications.

## DRIVERS OF AGE-INCLUSIVE POLICY OR PROGRAM ADOPTION

Prior work suggests that taking action to implement the strategies discussed in the prior section corresponds with the size and type of firm. For example, firms with more than one hundred employees are more likely to conduct internal evaluations and implement program initiatives because they possess the necessary administrative and financial resources to mobilize workplace change initiatives.[67] Indeed, our analysis of survey responses from Colorado revealed those with more than one hundred employees, particularly public or government agencies, were more likely than smaller employers to offer health insurance and disability insurance and to make contributions to employee retirement savings. They also were more likely to offer leave programs, early retirement, and retire-rehire opportunities. Most employers, however, appear to take a piecemeal approach to supporting experienced employees, developing only a few policies and programs and doing so in response to acute changes in circumstance (e.g., to alleviate an immediate budget challenge) rather than developing and implementing a comprehensive strategic plan.

The three-stage model of institutional change[68] suggests discrete steps employers can take when making gradual and progressive advances in policies, practices, and organizational culture. Based on studies concerning employers' response to the increasing number of women who entered the workforce during the 1980s:[69,70] step one involves organizational leadership recognizing how an aging workforce presents unique challenges and opportunities that warrant formal consideration. In step two, after conducting an internal assessment and identifying the specific needs and preferences of aging workers, employers develop and implement appropriate personnel policies and supportive workplace programs. When such policies and programs become standard offerings, the employer has entered the third and final stage of the change process: institutionalization. At this point, organizations evaluate policy and program impact and support their continued growth and improvement.

Regardless of the size, industry type, or profit status of a firm, chief executives and HR specialists are necessary to lead and sustain the activation process.[71,72] Arguably, institutional leadership must recognize that an aging workforce, like any increasingly diverse workforce, presents unique benefits and concerns,[73,74] and call for formal review and subsequent action.[75,76] Ideally, HR directors would have some training in gerontology and would be at least partially dedicated to managing age-inclusive policies and programs.[77] This constitutes one of this chapter's most actionable notions. HR professionals with some training in aging can dispel stereotypes, highlight the immense organizational benefits provided by senior employees, conduct internal assessments, and create a workplace culture that supports employees at all life stages.[78,79] Unfortunately, three out of four HR specialists have little training in aging and are insufficiently informed about how to meet the challenges presented by experienced employees.[80,81]

## PUBLIC POLICY

Public policies play a pivotal role in encouraging employers to address the needs and preferences of experienced employees (See also chapter 25.) Most notably, the Age Discrimination in Employment Act (ADEA) of 1967 made employment discrimination against individuals forty years of age and older illegal, and specifically outlawed blatantly discriminatory hiring practices such as posting job openings that explicitly bar older workers from applying or forcing older workers to retire at specific ages.[82] Despite this important progress, combating age discrimination in the workplace has proven increasingly difficult, as discussed in other chapters.

In 2005, the U.S. Senate Special Committee on Aging recognized the lack of an overall federal policy agenda concerning the aging workforce and called for the creation of a federal "Taskforce on the Aging of the American Workforce." The task force represented nine federal agencies and considered how employers were responding to the aging workforce, identified opportunities for experienced employees, and illuminated the most salient legal and regulatory issues concerning work and retirement.[83]

The task force also identified financial disincentives and other barriers that impact an individual's decision to continue working. For example, the task force highlighted how laws and regulations concerning pensions and other retirement savings vehicles significantly altered an individual's decision to remain in or retire from the workforce, often in a way that was not consistent with the individual's preferences. The task force recognized the need to consider how ERISA (the Employee Retirement Income Security Act of 1974), the tax code, and other federal laws might be amended to facilitate transitions from full-time work into retirement and called for an interagency group to create an inventory of the legal and regulatory barriers and disincentives to employment of aging workers. In 2006, the U.S. Congress passed the Pension Protection Act, which allows employees to receive in-service distributions from a defined benefit pension plan as early as age sixty-two.[84] Now, some older employees who otherwise would have chosen to continue working full-time until reaching the plan's normal retirement age might instead reduce their work schedule and supplement their earnings with pension income.

In addition, federal efforts have been developed to help unemployed and dislocated workers acquire new skills and train for new careers. The Senior Community Service Employment Program explicitly targets low-income older adults and offers adults ages fifty-five and above job skills training, opportunities for placement, and wage subsidies until they exit the program.[85] The Department of Labor also supported the Aging Workforce Research Initiative and provided grants to ten organizations that developed education and training programs as well as job referral services for aging workers.[86]

In addition, the federal government has addressed policies and practices that already are "on the books" and serve as impediments to much-needed flexibilities for experienced employees. As an example, some corporations are prohibited by existing federal retirement policies from hiring their own recent retirees, predicated on outdated expectations of clear divides between work and retirement. Regulations in the Fair Labor Standards Act limit possible flexibility policies around the time and timing of work, and policy makers continually look to address such constraints to continued engagement.[87] Also, while mandatory retirement is no longer an issue in most occupations, mandatory retirement rules still prevail in some private- and public-sector occupations.[88]

The federal government not only develops policies and programs for experienced employees, but also employs a large number of experienced employees (27 percent of federal workers are age fifty-five or older).[89] In response to the continued aging of the public sector workforce, Congress approved offering full-time employees covered by the Civil Service Retirement System or the Federal Employees' Retirement System the option of moving to a part-time work schedule while simultaneously receiving partial retirement benefits.[90] This plan allows for the retention of qualified federal workers while reducing costs associated with training new employees. In addition, specific federal agencies offer supportive policies and programs. The U.S. Fish and Wildlife Service offers employees of all ages access to online, self-paced training courses to enable experienced employees to maintain skills.[91] The Department of Veterans Affairs administers the Program of Comprehensive Assistance for Family Caregivers to provide financial and other critical supports to family caregivers.[92]

State governments are similarly examining opportunities and challenges presented by an aging workforce. In 2017, the Tri-State Learning Collaborative on Aging convened a workshop called "Grey Is the New Green," calling together more than 170 employers from New Hampshire, Maine, and Vermont to identify and promote strategies for recruiting and retaining older workers.[93] Some states have expanded paid family leave options for employers unable to offer one internally[94] and/or have created retirement savings mechanisms that entail employee-only contributions and employer-only contributions, as well as hybrid approaches.[95] California expanded its paid family leave program so that the costs are fully covered by workers through a single payroll deduction.[96] Oregon took action to support retirement savings via OregonSaves: a voluntary retirement program that helped more than ninety-five thousand workers set aside $22.8 million within its first two years.[97]

## THE CRITICAL ROLE OF ACADEMIC RESEARCH

For more than three decades, the federal government has led the way in supporting research that improves our understanding of the aging workforce. The National Institute on Aging has supported research examining labor force participation and retirement patterns among aging Americans.[98] The Center for Retirement Research at Boston College, supported by the Social Security Administration, continues to advance research on retirement income and savings.[99] The National Institute on Occupational Safety and Health, under the Centers for Disease Control and Prevention, established the National Center for Productive Aging and Work, advancing efforts to identify best practices, such as ergonomic office designs, to meet the needs of aging employees.[100] In addition, the Bureau of Labor Statistics, the Congressional Research Service, and the Government Accountability Office have conducted several analyses and investigations concerning the aging labor force. These range from charting prolonged spells of unemployment among aging workers,[101] forecasting desired career pathways for aging workers,[102] and investigating age discrimination. Looking forward, we need to learn how various policies and programs differentially impact experienced employees and better understand organizational change processes across different types of firms. Why do some employers attend to experienced employees while others do not? There certainly are substantive reasons for concern given the large number of employers who have yet to mobilize a concerted effort to be age inclusive amid the changing workforce composition. By continuing to support such research, we increase the capacity to determine how public policies and employer actions can positively impact the lives of experienced employees.

## NOTES

Acknowledgments: The authors would like to thank the Colorado-based Next50 Initiative, the TransAmerica Center for Retirement Studies, and the University of Iowa College of Public Health for supporting our efforts.

1. Robert Steyer. December 13, 2018. "Employers Try to Balance Value of Older Workers' Experience with Costs of Retaining Them—Survey." *Pensions & Investments*. (https://www.pionline.com/article/20181213/ONLINE/181219824/employers-try-to-balance-value-of-older-workers-experience-with-costs-of-retaining-them-survey).
2. U.S. Senate, Special Committee on Aging. December 2017. "America's Aging Workforce." (https://www.aging.senate.gov/imo/media/doc/Aging percent 20Workforce percent 20Report percent 20FINAL.pdf).
3. U.S. Senate, Special Committee on Aging, "America's Aging Workforce."
4. U.S. Senate, Special Committee on Aging, "America's Aging Workforce."
5. Brian Kaskie, Mark Walker, and Matthew Andersson. October 2016. "Efforts to Address the Aging Academic Workforce: Assessing Progress through the Three Stage Model of Institutional Change." *Innovations in Higher Education* 42(3):225–37.
6. U.S. Senate, Special Committee on Aging, "America's Aging Workforce."
7. Aldo Svaldi. 2019. "Colorado's Economy Accelerated in 2018 at Fastest Pace in Three Years." *Denver Post*. (https://www.denverpost.com/2019/05/03/colorados-economic-gdp-in-2018).
8. U.S. Bureau of Labor Statistics. January 22, 2020. "Employed Persons by Detailed Industry and Age." Labor Force Statistics from the Current Population Survey. (https://www.bls.gov/cps/cpsaat18b.htm).

9. Society for Human Resource Management (SHRM) Foundation. 2015b. "Preparing for an Aging Workforce: Government Industry Report." (https://www.shrm.org/hr-today/trends-and-forecasting/research-and-surveys/Documents/Preparing_for_an_Aging_Workforce).

10. Society for Human Resource Management (SHRM) Foundation. 2015a. "Preparing for an Aging Workforce: Finance, Insurance and Real Estate Industry Report." (https://www.shrm.org/hr-today/trends-and-forecasting/research-and surveys/Documents/Preparing_for_an_Aging_Workforce).

11. Society for Human Resource Management (SHRM) Foundation. 2015d. "Preparing for an Aging Workforce: Professional and Technical Services Industry Report." (https://www.shrm.org/hr-today/trends-and-forecasting/research-and-surveys/Documents/Preparing_for_an_Aging_Workforce).

12. Society for Human Resource Management (SHRM) Foundation. 2015c. "Preparing for an Aging Workforce: Health Care and Social Insurance Industry Report." (https://www.shrm.org/hr-today/trends-and-forecasting/research-and-surveys/Documents/Preparing_for_an_Aging_Workforce).

13. Gregory A. Aarons et al. 2016. "The Roles of System and Organizational Leadership in System-wide Evidence-based Intervention Sustainment: A Mixed-method Study." *Administration and Policy in Mental Health* 43(6):991–1008. (https://doi.org/10.1007/s10488-016-0751-4).

14. Borsika A. Rabin and Ross C. Brownson. 2012. "Developing the Terminology for Dissemination and Implementation Research in Health." In *Dissemination and Implementation Research in Health: Translating Science to Practice*, edited by Ross C. Brownson, Graham A. Colditz, and Enola K. Proctor. New York: Oxford University Press.

15. Matilda W. Riley, Robert L. Kahn, Anne Foner, et al. 1994. *Age and Structural Lag: Society's Failure to Provide Meaningful Opportunities in Work, Family, and Leisure*. Hoboken, NJ: John Wiley & Sons.

16. Jacquelyn B. James, Jennifer E. Swanberg, and Sharon P. McKechnie. November 2007. "Generational Differences in Perceptions of Older Workers' Capabilities." *Issue Brief* 12. Chestnut Hill, MA: Center on Aging & Work/Workplace Flexibility, Boston College.

17. Helen Dennis and Kathryn Thomas. 2007. "Ageism in the Workplace." *Generations* 31(1):84.

18. Society for Human Resource Management (SHRM) Foundation. 2015e. "Preparing for an Aging Workforce: Retail and Hospitality Industry Report." (https://www.shrm.org/hr-today/trends-and-forecasting/research-and-surveys/Documents/Preparing_for_an_Aging_Workforce).

19. Steyer, "Employers Try to Balance Value."

20. Emily S. DeRocco et al. February 2008. *Report of the Taskforce on the Aging of the American Workforce.* U.S. Department of Labor, Employment and Training Administration. (https://www.doleta.gov/reports/FINAL_Taskforce_Report_2_27_08.pdf).

21. Riley et al., *Age and Structural Lag.*

22. Melissa J. Bjelland et al. December 2010. "Age and Disability Employment Discrimination: Occupational Rehabilitation Implications." *Journal of Occupational Rehabilitation* 20(4):456–71. (https://www.ncbi.nlm.nih.gov/pmc/articles/PMC2980632/).

23. U.S. Senate, Special Committee on Aging, "America's Aging Workforce."

24. Bjelland et al., "Age and Disability Employment Discrimination."

25. David Neumark, Ian Burn, and Patrick Button. 2017. "Age Discrimination and Hiring of Older Workers." Federal Reserve Bank of San Francisco. (http://www.frbsf.org/economic-research/publications/economic-letter/2017/february/age).

26. AARP. 2014. "Staying Ahead of the Curve 2013: The AARP Work and Career Study." (https://www.aarp.org/content/dam/aarp/research/surveys_statistics/general/2014/Staying-Ahead-of-the-Curve-2013-The-Work-and-Career-Study. AARP-res-gen.pdf).

27. U.S. Senate, Special Committee on Aging, "America's Aging Workforce."

28. U.S. Senate, Special Committee on Aging, "America's Aging Workforce."

29. Stanford Center on Longevity. April 18–19, 2013. "Adapting to an Aging Workforce." Conference Proceedings. Stanford, CA. (http://longevity.stanford.edu/adapting-to-an-aging-workforce).

30. Kaskie, Walker, and Andersson, "Efforts to Address the Aging Academic Workforce."

31. John Pencavel. 2004. *Faculty Retirement Incentives by Colleges and Universities.* Working Paper 03-28. Stanford Institute for Economic Research. Stanford, CA. (ftp://ftp.repec.org/opt/ReDIF/RePEc/sip/03-028.pdf).

32. Susan A. Murphy. 2007. "Leading a Multigenerational Workforce." AARP. (https://assets.aarp.org/www.aarp.org_/articles/money/employers/leading_multigenerational_workforce.pdf).

33. Employee Benefit Research Institute (EBRI). May 28, 2020. "Retirement Confidence Survey." (https://www.ebri.org/retirement/retirement-confidence-survey.mployee).

34. Academy to Innovate HR (AIHR). September 5, 2018. "Age Diversity in the Workplace: 5 Lessons from The Intern" AIHR Digital. (https://www.digitalhrtech.com/age-diversity-in-the-workplace).

35. Julie Sweetland, Andrew Volmert, and Moira O'Neil. February 2017. "Finding the Frame: An Empirical Approach to Reframing Aging and Ageism." Frameworks Institute. (http://frameworksinstitute.org/assets/files/aging_elder_abuse/aging_research_report_final_2017.pdf).

36. Lori A. Trawinski. 2015. "Disrupting Aging in the Workplace: Profiles in Intergenerational Diversity Leadership." AARP Public Policy Institute. (https://www.aarp.org/content/dam/aarp/ppi/2016-08/Disrupt percent 20Aging percent 20in percent 20the percent 20Workforce per cent 20Report_FINAL_WEB.pdf).

37. Kaiser Family Foundation (KFF). September 19, 2017. "2017 Employer Health Benefits Survey." (https://www.kff.org/health-costs/report/2017-employer-health-benefits-survey/view/print).

38. Kenneth Pelletier. October 2005. "A Review and Analysis of the Clinical and Cost-effectiveness Studies of Comprehensive Health Promotion and Disease Management Programs at the Worksite: Update VI 2000–2004." American College of Occupational and Environmental Medicine. *Journal of Occupational and Environmental Medicine* 47(10).

39. U.S. Bureau of Labor Statistics. October 2, 2018. "51 Percent of Private Industry Workers Had Access to Only Defined Contribution Retirement Plans." *Economics Daily*. (https://www.bls.gov/opub/ted/2018/51-percent-of-private-industry-workers-had-access-to-only-defined-contribution-retirement-plans-march-2018.htm?view_full).

40. Stephen C. Miller. 2019. "Financial Wellness Perks Expand to Address Employee Needs." Society for Human Resource Management. (https://www.shrm.org/resourcesandtools/hr-topics/benefits/pages/financial-wellness-perks-expand.aspx).

41. Ron Goetzel et al. 2017. "Workplace Programs, Policies, and Environmental Supports to Prevent Cardiovascular Disease." Project Hope. *Health Affairs* 36(2):229–36. (https://healthmetrics.heart.org/wp-content/uploads/2017/10/Workplace-Programs-Policies-and-Environmental-Supports.pdf).

42. Ronald Loeppke et al. May 2013. "Advancing Workplace Health Protection and Promotion for an Aging Workforce." American College of Occupational and Environmental Medicine. *Journal of Occupational and Environmental Medicine* 55(5).

43. U.S. Senate, Special Committee on Aging, "America's Aging Workforce."

44. Kevin Johnston. April 8, 2020. "Tax Write-offs for Businesses Implementing a Wellness Program Such as Chair Massage." (https://smallbusiness.chron.com/tax-writeoffs-businesses-implementing-wellness-program-such-chair-massage-30806.html).

45. Alexandra Black. May 17, 2017. "Five Reasons Employee Wellness Is Worth the Investment." News & Events. Rockville, MD: Office of Disease Prevention and Health Promotion. (https://health.gov/news-archive/blog/2017/05/five-reasons-employee-wellness-is-worth-the-investment/index.html).

46. U.S. Equal Employment Opportunity Commission (EEOC). 2002. "Enforcement Guidance: Reasonable Accommodation and Undue Hardship under the Americans with Disabilities Act." (https://www.eeoc.gov/policy/docs/accommodation.html#general).

47. Oregon Occupational Safety and Health (OSHA). 2008. "The Advantages of Ergonomics." (https://osha.oregon.gov/OSHAPubs/ergo/ergoadvantages.pdf).

48. OSHA, "Advantages of Ergonomics."

49. OSHA, "Advantages of Ergonomics."

50. OSHA, "Advantages of Ergonomics."

51. Bell Policy Center. December 6, 2019. "Colorado's Changing Economy & Future of Work." Denver, CO:65. (https://www.bellpolicy.org/wp-content/uploads/2018/01/Work-Policies-Guide-to-Economic-Mobility.pdf).

52. U.S. Bureau of Labor Statistics. September 2019. "Employee Benefits Survey, National Compensation Survey: Glossary of Employee Benefit Terms." (https://www.bls.gov/ncs/ebs/glossary20162017.htm).

53. Catherine Collinson. August 2017. "All about Retirement: An Employer Survey." TransAmerica Center for Retirement Studies. (https://www.transamericacenter.org/docs/default-source/employer-research/tcrs2017_sr_employer_research.pdf).

54. U.S. Senate, Special Committee on Aging, "America's Aging Workforce."

55. Society for Human Resource Management (SHRM) Foundation. 2014. "The Aging Workforce: Leveraging the Talents of Mature Employees." Effective Practice Guidelines Series. (https://www.shrm.org/foundation/ourwork/initiatives/the-aging-workforce/Documents/The%20Aging%20Workforce%20Leveraging%20the%20Talents%20of%20Mature%20Employees.pdf).

56. Society for Human Resource Management (SHRM) Foundation. 2006. "Phased Retirement and Flexible Retirement Arrangements: Strategies for Retaining Skilled Workers." (https://assets.aarp.org/www.aarp.org_/articles/money/employers/phased_retirement.pdf).

57. SHRM Foundation, "Phased Retirement and Flexible Retirement Arrangements."

58. Neighborhood Trust Financial Partners. May 2018. "Re-imagining the Workplace as a Hub for Financial Wellness." IssueLab. (http://www.neighborhoodtrust.org/wp-content/uploads/2018/04/EAC-NTFP-White-Paper_Citi-FINAL_4.17.18.pdf).

59. Neighborhood Trust Financial Partners, "Re-imagining the Workplace."

60. Adrianna Kezar. 2013. "Changing Faculty Workforce Models." TIAA-CREF Institute.

61. Patricia A. Krajnak, Sharon A. Burns, and Sally M. Natchek. 2008. "Retirement Education in the Workplace." *Financial Services Review* 17(2).

62. Kevin E. Cahill, Michael D. Giandrea, and Joseph F. Quinn. 2018. "Is Bridge Job Activity Overstated?" *Work, Aging and Retirement* 4(4):330–51.

63. Michael D. Giandrea, Kevin E. Cahill, and Joseph F. Quinn. 2009. "Bridge Jobs: A Comparison across Cohorts." *Research on Aging* 31(5):549–76.

64. Kevin E. Cahill, Michael D. Giandrea, and Joseph F. Quinn. 2011. "Reentering the Labor Force after Retirement." *Monthly Labor Review* 134(6):34–42.

65. Kevin E. Cahill, Michael D. Giandrea, and Joseph F. Quinn. 2015. "Retirement Patterns and the Macroeconomy, 1992–2010: The Prevalence and Determinants of Bridge Jobs, Phased Retirement, and Reentry among Three Recent Cohorts of Older Americans." *The Gerontologist* 55(3):384–403.

66. SHRM Foundation, "Phased Retirement and Flexible Retirement Arrangements."

67. Brian Kaskie et al. 2020. *Age-Friendly Workplace Programs: Recruiting and Retaining Experienced Employees Research Report*. Transamerica Institute. (https://www.transamericainstitute.org/docs/default-source/age-friendly-workplaces/ti2020_sr_age-friendly-workplaces-colorado-research-report.pdf?sfvrsn=336f5f9b_4).

68. Barbara K. Curry. 1992. "Instituting Enduring Innovations: Achieving Continuity of Change in Higher Education." ASHE-ERIC Publication No. ED 358809. Washington, DC: Office of Educational Research and Improvement.

69. Adrianna Kezar and Cecile Sam. 2013. "Institutionalizing Equitable Policies and Practices for Contingent Faculty." *Journal of Higher Education* 84(1):56–87.

70. Robyn Marschke et al. 2007. "Demographic Inertia Revisited: An Immodest Proposal to Achieve Equitable Gender Representation among Faculty in Higher Education." *Journal of Higher Education* 78(1):1–26.

71. Libby Brooke and Philip Taylor. 2005. "Older Workers and Employment: Managing Age Relations." *Ageing & Society* 25(3):415–29.

72. Florian Kunze, Stephan Boehm, and Heike Bruch. 2013. "Age, Resistance to Change, and Job Performance." *Journal of Managerial Psychology* 28(7-8):741–60.

73. Adrianna Kezar. 2007. "Tools for a Time and Place: Phased Leadership Strategies to Institutionalize a Diversity Agenda." *Review of Higher Education* 30(4):413–39.

74. Kezar and Sam, "Institutionalizing Equitable Policies and Practices."

75. Marschke et al., "Demographic Inertia Revisited."

76. Kelly Ward and Lisa Wolf-Wendel. 2012. *Academic Motherhood: How Faculty Manage Work and Family.* New Brunswick, NJ: Rutgers University Press.

77. William Little. 2014. "Aging and the Elderly." *Introduction to Sociology—1st Canadian Edition.* BCcampus. Open Textbook Project. (https://opentextbc.ca/introductiontosociology/chapter/chapter13-aging-and-the-elderly).

78. Brooke and Taylor, "Older Workers and Employment."

79. Peggy G. Koopman-Boyden and Lesley Macdonald. 2003. "Ageing, Work Performance and Managing Ageing Academics." *Journal of Higher Education Policy and Management* 25(1):29–40.

80. Brian Kaskie. February 2016. "The Academy Is Aging in Place: Assessing Alternatives for Modifying Institutions of Higher Education." *The Gerontologist* 57(5):1–8.

81. Deborah E. Rupp, Stephen J. Vodanovich, and Marcus Credé. 2005. "The Multidimensional Nature of Ageism: Construct Validity and Group Differences." *Journal of Social Psychology* 145(3):335–62.

82. Age Discrimination in Employment Act of 1967. December 15, 1967. Pub. L. 90–202, 81 Stat. 602 (29 U.S.C. 621 et seq.).

83. DeRocco et al., *Report of the Taskforce.*

84. Pension Protection Act of 2006. 2006. 29 USC §§ 1001. (https://www.congress.gov/109/plaws/publ280/PLAW-109publ280.pdf).

85. Senior Community Service Employment Program. May 28, 2020. U.S. Department of Labor. (https://www.dol.gov/agencies/eta/seniors).

86. Society for Human Resource Management (SHRM) Foundation. 2017. "The Aging Workforce Research Initiative." (https://www.shrm.org/hr-today/trends-and-forecasting/research-and-surveys/pages/aging-workforce-research-initiative.aspx).

87. Wages and the Fair Labor Standards Act. 2020. U.S. Department of Labor. (https://www.dol.gov/agencies/whd/flsa).

88. Richard V. Burkhauser and Joseph F. Quinn. 1983. "Is Mandatory Retirement Overrated? Evidence from the 1970s." *Journal of Human Resources* 18(3):337–58.

89. FedScope. September 2013. "From the Office of Personnel Management, for All Full-Time, Non-seasonal, Permanent Employees." (fedscope.opm.gov).

90. Civil Service Retirement System (CSRS). June 27, 2016. Information. (https://www.opm.gov/retirement-services/csrs-information).

91. SHRM Foundation, "Phased Retirement and Flexible Retirement Arrangements."

92. Program of Comprehensive Assistance for Family Caregivers Improvements and Amendments under the VA MISSION Act of 2018. March 6, 2020. (https://www.federalregister.gov/documents/2020/03/06/2020-04464/program-of-comprehensive-assistance-for-family-caregivers-improvements-and-amendments-under-the-va).

93. U.S. Senate, Special Committee on Aging, "America's Aging Workforce."

94. SHRM Foundation, "Phased Retirement and Flexible Retirement Arrangements."

95. SHRM Foundation, "Phased Retirement and Flexible Retirement Arrangements."

96. Bell Policy Center, "Colorado's Changing Economy & Future of Work," 57.

97. George Bridges. 2019. "State Mulls Retirement Savings Options." AARP Colorado. (https://states.aarp.org/colorado/state-mulls-retirement-savings-options).

98. U.S. Department of Health and Human Resources, National Institute on Aging. March 2007. "Growing Older in America: The Health & Retirement Study." (https://www.nia.nih.gov/sites/default/files/2017-06/health_and_retirement_study_0.pdf).

99. Steven A. Sass. 2009. "The Research Contributions of the Center for Retirement Research at Boston College." Social Security Administration, Office of Retirement and Disability Policy, *Social Security Bulletin* 69(4). (https://www.ssa.gov/policy/docs/ssb/v69n4/v69n4p35.html).

100. Centers for Disease Control and Prevention. The National Institute for Occupational Safety and Health. N.d. "Productive Aging and Work." (https://www.cdc.gov/niosh/topics/productiveaging/default.html).

101. Gerald Mayer. 2014. "The Trend in Long-term Unemployment and Characteristics of Workers Unemployed for Two Years or More." CRS Report R41559. (https://fas.org/sgp/crs/misc/R41559.pdf).

102. Mitra Toossi and Elka Torpe. May 2017. "Older Workers: Labor Force Trends and Career Options." Bureau of Labor Statistics, *Career Outlook*. (https://www.bls.gov/careeroutlook/2017/article/pdf/older-workers.pdf).

## REFERENCES


Aarons, Gregory A., et al. 2016. "The Roles of System and Organizational Leadership in System-wide Evidence-based Intervention Sustainment: A Mixed-method Study." *Administration and Policy in Mental Health* 43(6):991–1008. (https://doi.org/10.1007/s10488-016-0751-4).

AARP. 2014. "Staying Ahead of the Curve 2013: The AARP Work and Career Study." (https://www.aarp.org/content/dam/aarp/research/surveys_statistics/general/2014/Staying-Ahead-of-the-Curve-2013-The-Work-and-Career-Study-AARP-res-gen.pdf).

Academy to Innovate HR (AIHR). September 5, 2018. "Age Diversity in the Workplace: 5 Lessons from the Intern." AIHR Digital. (https://www.digitalhrtech.com/age-diversity-in-the-workplace).

Age Discrimination in Employment Act of 1967. December 15, 1967. Pub. L. 90–202, 81 Stat. 602 (29 U.S.C. 621 et seq.).

Bell Policy Center. December 6, 2019. "Colorado's Changing Economy & Future of Work." Denver, CO. (https://www.bellpolicy.org/wp-content/uploads/2018/01/Work-Policies-Guide-to-Economic-Mobility.pdf).

Bjelland, Melissa J., et al. December 2010. "Age and Disability Employment Discrimination: Occupational Rehabilitation Implications." *Journal of Occupational Rehabilitation* 20(4):456–71. (https://www.ncbi.nlm.nih.gov/pmc/articles/PMC2980632/).

Black, Alexandra. May 17, 2017. "Five Reasons Employee Wellness Is Worth the Investment." News & Events. Rockville, MD: Office of Disease Prevention and Health Promotion. (https://health.gov/news-archive/blog/2017/05/five-reasons-employee-wellness-is-worth-the-investment/index.html).

Bridges, George. 2019. "State Mulls Retirement Savings Options." AARP Colorado. (https://states.aarp.org/colorado/state-mulls-retirement-savings-options).

Brooke, Libby and Taylor, Philip. 2005. "Older Workers and Employment: Managing Age Relations." *Ageing & Society* 25(3):415–29.

Burkhauser, Richard V. and Joseph F. Quinn. 1983. "Is Mandatory Retirement Overrated? Evidence from the 1970s." *Journal of Human Resources* 18(3):337–58.

Cahill, Kevin E., Michael D. Giandrea, and Joseph F. Quinn. 2011. "Reentering the Labor Force after Retirement." *Monthly Labor Review* 134(6):34–42.

Cahill, Kevin E., Michael D. Giandrea, and Joseph F. Quinn. 2015. "Retirement Patterns and the Macroeconomy, 1992–2010: The Prevalence and Determinants of Bridge Jobs, Phased Retirement, and Reentry among Three Recent Cohorts of Older Americans." *The Gerontologist* 55(3):384–403.

Cahill, Kevin E., Michael D. Giandrea, and Joseph F. Quinn. 2018. "Is Bridge Job Activity Overstated?" *Work, Aging and Retirement* 4(4):330–51.

Centers for Disease Control and Prevention. The National Institute for Occupational Safety and Health. N.d. "Productive Aging and Work." (https://www.cdc.gov/niosh/topics/productiveaging/default.html).

Civil Service Retirement System (CSRS). June 27, 2016. Information. (https://www.opm.gov/retirement-services/csrs-information).

Collinson, Catherine. August 2017. "All about Retirement: An Employer Survey." Los Angeles: TransAmerica Center for Retirement Studies. (https://www.transamericacenter.org/docs/default-source/employer-research/tcrs2017_sr_employer_research.pdf).

Curry, Barbara K. 1992. "Instituting Enduring Innovations: Achieving Continuity of Change in Higher Education." ASHE-ERIC Publication No. ED 358809. Washington, DC: Office of Educational Research and Improvement.

Dennis, Helen and Kathryn Thomas. 2007. "Ageism in the Workplace." *Generations* 3(1):84.

DeRocco, Emily S., et al. February 2008. *Report of the Taskforce on the Aging of the American Workforce.* U.S. Department of Labor, Employment and Training Administration. (https://www.doleta.gov/reports/FINAL_Taskforce_Report_2_27_08.pdf).

Employee Benefit Research Institute (EBRI). May 28, 2020. "Retirement Confidence Survey." (https://www.ebri.org/retirement/retirement-confidence-survey.mployee).

FedScope. September 2013. "From the Office of Personnel Management, for All Full-Time, Non-seasonal, Permanent Employees." (fedscope.opm.gov).

Giandrea, Michael D., Kevin E. Cahill, and Joseph F. Quinn. 2009. "Bridge Jobs: A Comparison across Cohorts." *Research on Aging* 31(5):549–76.

Goetzel, Ron et al. 2017. "Workplace Programs, Policies, and Environmental Supports to Prevent Cardiovascular Disease." Project Hope. *Health Affairs* 36(2):229–36. (https://healthmetrics.heart.org/wp-content/uploads/2017/10/Workplace-Programs-Policies-and-Environmental-Supports.pdf).

James, Jacquelyn B., Jennifer E. Swanberg, and Sharon P. McKechnie. November 2007. "Generational Differences in Perceptions of Older Workers' Capabilities." *Issue Brief* 12. Chestnut Hill, MA: Center on Aging & Work/Workplace Flexibility, Boston College.

Johnston, Kevin. April 8, 2020. "Tax Write-offs for Businesses Implementing a Wellness Program Such as Chair Massage." (https://smallbusiness.chron.com/tax-writeoffs-businesses-implementing-wellness-program-such-chair-massage-30806.html).

Kaiser Family Foundation (KFF). September 19, 2017. "2017 Employer Health Benefits Survey." (https://www.kff.org/health-costs/report/2017-employer-health-benefits-survey/view/print).

Kaskie, Brian. February 2016. "The Academy Is Aging in Place: Assessing Alternatives for Modifying Institutions of Higher Education." *The Gerontologist* 57(5):1–8.

Kaskie, Brian, Mark Walker, and Matthew Andersson. October 2016. "Efforts to Address the Aging Academic Workforce: Assessing Progress through the Three Stage Model of Institutional Change." *Innovations in Higher Education* 42(3):225–37.

Kaskie, Brian, et al. 2020. *Age-Friendly Workplace Programs: Recruiting and Retaining Experienced Employees Research Report*. Transamerica Institute. (https://www.transamericainstitute.org/docs/default-source/age-friendly-workplaces/ti2020_sr_age-friendly-workplaces-colorado-research-report.pdf?sfvrsn=336f5f9b_4).

Kezar, Adrianna. 2007. "Tools for a Time and Place: Phased Leadership Strategies to Institutionalize a Diversity Agenda." *Review of Higher Education* 30(4):413–39.

Kezar, Adrianna. 2013. "Changing Faculty Workforce Models." TIAA-CREF Institute.

Kezar, Adrianna and Cecile Sam. 2013. "Institutionalizing Equitable Policies and Practices for Contingent Faculty." *Journal of Higher Education* 84(1):56–87.

Koopman-Boyden, Peggy G. and Lesley Macdonald. 2003. "Ageing, Work Performance and Managing Ageing Academics." *Journal of Higher Education Policy and Management* 25(1):29–40.

Krajnak, Patricia A., Sharon A. Burns, and Sally M. Natchek. 2008. "Retirement Education in the Workplace." *Financial Services Review* 17(2).

Kunze, Florian, Stephan Boehm, and Heike Bruch. 2013. "Age, Resistance to Change, and Job Performance." *Journal of Managerial Psychology* 28(7–8):741–60.

Little, William. 2014. "Aging and the Elderly." *Introduction to Sociology—1st Canadian Edition.* BCcampus. Open Textbook Project. (https://opentextbc.ca/introductiontosociology/chapter/chapter13-aging-and-the-elderly).

Loeppke, Ronald, et al. May 2013. "Advancing Workplace Health Protection and Promotion for an Aging Workforce." American College of Occupational and Environmental Medicine. *Journal of Occupational and Environmental Medicine* 55(5).

Marschke, Robyn, et al. 2007. "Demographic Inertia Revisited: An Immodest Proposal to Achieve Equitable Gender Representation among Faculty in Higher Education." *Journal of Higher Education* 78(1):1–26.

Mayer, Gerald. 2014. "The Trend in Long-term Unemployment and Characteristics of Workers Unemployed for Two Years or More." CRS Report R41559. (https://fas.org/sgp/crs/misc/R41559.pdf).

Miller, Stephen C. 2019. "Financial Wellness Perks Expand to Address Employee Needs." Society for Human Resource Management. (https://www.shrm.org/resourcesandtools/hr-topics/benefits/pages/financial-wellness-perks-expand.aspx).

Murphy, Susan A. 2007. "Leading a Multigenerational Workforce." AARP. (https://assets.aarp.org/www.aarp.org_/articles/money/employers/leading_multigenerational_workforce.pdf).

Neighborhood Trust Financial Partners. May 2018. "Re-imagining the Workplace as a Hub for Financial Wellness." IssueLab. (http://www.neighborhoodtrust.org/wp-content/uploads/2018/04/EAC-NTFP-White-Paper_Citi-FINAL_4.17.18.pdf).

Neumark, David, Ian Burn, and Patrick Button. 2017. "Age Discrimination and Hiring of Older Workers." Federal Reserve Bank of San Francisco. (http://www.frbsf.org/economic-research/publications/economic-letter/2017/february/age).

Oregon Occupational Safety and Health (OSHA). 2008. "The Advantages of Ergonomics." (https://osha.oregon.gov/OSHAPubs/ergo/ergoadvantages.pdf).

Pelletier, Kenneth. October 2005. "A Review and Analysis of the Clinical and Cost-effectiveness Studies of Comprehensive Health Promotion and Disease Management Programs at the Worksite: Update VI 2000–2004." American College of Occupational and Environmental Medicine. *Journal of Occupational and Environmental Medicine* 47(10).

Pencavel, John. 2004. "Faculty Retirement Incentives by Colleges and Universities." Working Paper 03-28. Stanford Institute for Economic Research. Stanford, CA. (ftp://ftp.repec.org/opt/ReDIF/RePEc/sip/03-028.pdf).

Pension Protection Act of 2006. 2006. 29 USC §§ 1001. (https://www.congress.gov/109/plaws/publ280/PLAW-109publ280.pdf).

Program of Comprehensive Assistance for Family Caregivers Improvements and Amendments under the VA MISSION Act of 2018. March 6, 2020. (https://www.federalregister.gov/documents/2020/03/06/2020-04464/program-of-comprehensive-assistance-for-family-caregivers-improvements-and-amendments-under-the-va).

Rabin, Borsika A. and Ross C. Brownson. 2012. "Developing the Terminology for Dissemination and Implementation Research in Health." In *Dissemination and Implementation Research in Health: Translating Science to Practice*, edited by Ross C. Brownson, Graham A. Colditz, and Enola K. Proctor. New York: Oxford University Press.

Riley, Matilda W., Robert L. Kahn, and Anne Foner, et al. 1994. *Age and Structural Lag: Society's Failure to Provide Meaningful Opportunities in Work, Family, and Leisure*. Hoboken, NJ: John Wiley & Sons.

Rupp, Deborah E., Stephen J. Vodanovich, and Marcus Credé. 2005. "The Multidimensional Nature of Ageism: Construct Validity and Group Differences." *Journal of Social Psychology* 145(3):335–62.

Sass, Steven A. 2009. "The Research Contributions of the Center for Retirement Research at Boston College." Social Security Administration, Office of Retirement and Disability Policy. *Social Security Bulletin* 69(4). (https://www.ssa.gov/policy/docs/ssb/v69n4/v69n4p35.html).

Senior Community Service Employment Program. May 28, 2020. U.S. Department of Labor. (https://www.dol.gov/agencies/eta/seniors).

Society for Human Resource Management (SHRM) Foundation. 2006. "Phased Retirement and Flexible Retirement Arrangements: Strategies for Retaining Skilled Workers." (https://assets.aarp.org/www.aarp.org_/articles/money/employers/phased_retirement.pdf).

Society for Human Resource Management (SHRM) Foundation. 2014. "The Aging Workforce: Leveraging the Talents of Mature Employees." Effective Practice Guidelines Series. (https://www.shrm.org/foundation/ourwork/initiatives/the-aging-workforce/Documents/The%20Aging%20Workforce%20Leveraging%20the%20Talents%20of%20Mature%20Employees.pdf).

Society for Human Resource Management (SHRM) Foundation. 2015a. "Preparing for an Aging Workforce: Finance, Insurance and Real Estate Industry Report." (https://www.shrm.org/hr-today/trends-and-forecasting/research-and-surveys/Documents/Preparing_for_an_Aging_Workforce).

Society for Human Resource Management (SHRM) Foundation. 2015b. "Preparing for an Aging Workforce: Government Industry Report." (https://www.shrm.org/hr-today/trends-and-forecasting/research-and-surveys/Documents/Preparing_for_an_Aging_Workforce).

Society for Human Resource Management (SHRM) Foundation. 2015c. "Preparing for an Aging Workforce: Health Care and Social Insurance Industry Report." (https://www.shrm.org/hr-today/trends-and-forecasting/research-and-surveys/Documents/Preparing_for_an_Aging_Workforce).

Society for Human Resource Management (SHRM) Foundation. 2015d. "Preparing for an Aging Workforce: Professional and Technical Services Industry Report." (https://www.shrm.org/hr-today/trends-and-forecasting/research-and-surveys/Documents/Preparing_for_an_Aging_Workforce).

Society for Human Resource Management (SHRM) Foundation. 2015e. "Preparing for an Aging Workforce: Retail and Hospitality Industry Report." (https://www.shrm.org/hr-today/trends-and-forecasting/research-and-surveys/Documents/Preparing_for_an_Aging_Workforce).

Society for Human Resource Management (SHRM) Foundation. 2017. "The Aging Workforce Research Initiative." (https://www.shrm.org/hr-today/trends-and-forecasting/research-and-surveys/pages/aging-workforce-research-initiative.aspx).

Stanford Center on Longevity. April 18–19, 2013. "Adapting to an Aging Workforce." Conference Proceedings. Stanford, CA. (http://longevity.stanford.edu/adapting-to-an-aging-workforce).

Steyer, Robert. December 13, 2018. "Employers Try to Balance Value of Older Workers' Experience with Costs of Retaining Them—Survey." *Pensions & Investments*. (https://www.pionline.com/article/20181213/ONLINE/181219824/employers-try-to-balance-value-of-older-workers-experience-with-costs-of-retaining-them-survey).

Svaldi, Aldo. 2019. "Colorado's Economy Accelerated in 2018 at Fastest Pace in Three Years." *Denver Post*. (https://www.denverpost.com/2019/05/03/colorados-economic-gdp-in-2018).

Sweetland, Julie, Andrew Volmert, and Moira O'Neil. February 2017. "Finding the Frame: An Empirical Approach to Reframing Aging and Ageism." Frameworks Institute. (http://frameworksinstitute.org/assets/files/aging_elder_abuse/aging_research_report_final_2017.pdf).

Toossi, Mitra and Elka Torpe. May 2017. "Older Workers: Labor Force Trends and Career Options." Bureau of Labor Statistics. *Career Outlook*. (https://www.bls.gov/careeroutlook/2017/article/pdf/older-workers.pdf).

Trawinski, Lori A. 2015. "Disrupting Aging in the Workplace: Profiles in Intergenerational Diversity Leadership." AARP Public Policy Institute. (https://www.aarp.org/content/dam/aarp/ppi/2016-08/Disrupt percent 20Aging percent 20in percent 20the percent 20Workforce percent 20Report_FINAL_WEB.pdf).

U.S. Bureau of Labor Statistics. October 2, 2018. "51 Percent of Private Industry Workers Had Access to Only Defined Contribution Retirement Plans." *Economics Daily*. (https://www.bls.gov/opub/ted/2018/51-percent-of-private-industry-workers-had-access-to-only-defined-contribution-retirement-plans-march-2018.htm?view_full).

U.S. Bureau of Labor Statistics. September 2019. "Employee Benefits Survey, National Compensation Survey: Glossary of Employee Benefit Terms." (https://www.bls.gov/ncs/ebs/glossary20162017.htm).

U.S. Bureau of Labor Statistics. January 22, 2020. "Employed Persons by Detailed Industry and Age." Labor Force Statistics from the Current Population Survey. (https://www.bls.gov/cps/cpsaat18b.htm).

U.S. Department of Health and Human Resources, National Institute on Aging. March 2007. "Growing Older in America: The Health & Retirement Study." (https://www.nia.nih.gov/sites/default/files/2017-06/health_and_retirement_study_0.pdf).

U.S. Equal Employment Opportunity Commission (EEOC). 2002. "Enforcement Guidance: Reasonable Accommodation and Undue Hardship under the Americans with Disabilities Act." (https://www.eeoc.gov/policy/docs/accommodation.html#general).

U.S. Senate, Special Committee on Aging. December 2017. "America's Aging Workforce." (https://www.aging.senate.gov/imo/media/doc/Agingpercent20Workforcepercent20Reportpercent20FINAL.pdf).

Wages and the Fair Labor Standards Act. 2020. U.S. Department of Labor. (https://www.dol.gov/agencies/whd/flsa).

Ward, Kelly and Lisa Wolf-Wendel. 2012. *Academic Motherhood: How Faculty Manage Work and Family*. New Brunswick, NJ: Rutgers University Press.

CHAPTER 11

# Creating Age-Friendly Workplaces for Older Workers

## Challenges and Opportunities

Amanda Sonnega

### OVERVIEW

Whether because they want to or because they have to, a growing number of workers in the U.S. and worldwide are working past traditional retirement ages.[1] For years, policy analysts have anticipated the retirement of the baby boom generation and the aging of the population overall and have sought policy options—including encouraging longer working lives—to relieve the attendant pressure on public budgets. Likewise, the private sector increasingly recognizes the desirability of keeping older workers on the job. Although in previous generations employers provided incentives to urge early retirement, the question in both the private and the public sectors has now largely become: What can we do to retain older people in the workforce in ways that balance the needs of workers and employers?

Increasingly, firms are recognizing the need to implement policies aimed at supporting older workers. The term "age-friendly workplace" (AFW) has emerged to describe this scenario. Yet large gaps remain in the implementation of AFW policies. Across the literature reviewed for this chapter, a common thread was that, although there is common acknowledgment of the desirability of creating AFWs to extend working lives, widespread implementation is relatively low. For example, the Society for Human Resource Management's 2014 Older Workers Survey (an SHRM survey of human resource professionals) indicated that only around one-third of organizations had introduced some kind of age-friendly policy in response to an aging workforce.[2]

## LIVING LONGER AND WORKING LONGER

Average life expectancy is rising, not just in industrialized countries but throughout the world. Globally, 962 million people were aged sixty years in 2017, which is double what it was in 1980. This figure is projected to double again by 2050 when the number will stand at almost 2.1 billion.[3] In addition, reversing the decades-long trend toward earlier retirement, workers in many countries are beginning to work longer.[4] In addition to working longer, individuals are taking a variety of paths—including phased retirement, bridge employment, unretirement, and self-employment—toward retirement.[5,6] (See also chapters 21–23.) In 2000, 12.5 percent of Americans aged sixty-five and older were working; by 2016 that figure was 18.6 percent.[7] The number of workers ages sixty-five to seventy-four is projected to grow by 4.2 percent annually between 2016 and 2026, and the percentage of seventy-five and older will grow by 6.7 percent annually in that time. Similar trends are seen in other countries as well.[8]

Part of the reversal in the U.S. stems from elimination of and changes to both public and private policies—especially through the 1980s—that had encouraged workers to retire at relatively young ages. In the U.S., changes, such as the ban on mandatory retirement ages and both state and federal age discrimination laws, reduced institutionalized discrimination against older workers.[9] Other changes in law removed barriers to working longer, such as the Social Security earnings test[10] and built in incentives to work longer, for example, by increasing the age of eligibility for full Social Security retirement benefits.[11] In the Organisation for Economic Co-operation and Development (OECD), governments have taken similar steps and enacted other policies that have resulted in an 8 percentage point increase in the fraction of fifty-five- to sixty-year-olds in the labor force and a two-and-a-half-year increase in the average retirement age in the decade leading up to 2018.[12] (See also chapter 25.)

Yet factors that may encourage earlier workforce departure are clearly still in effect. In the U.S., defined benefit pensions, which offer workers an income stream in retirement after a certain number of years of service, provide incentive to leave work and claim these benefits as soon as they are available.[13] In other countries, some features of pension and welfare systems continue to encourage earlier workforce departure. In short, policies encouraging longer work have simultaneously helped to increase choices for those who wish to work longer and have limited options for those who need or desire an earlier retirement. At the same time, various incentives continue to encourage earlier retirement for a significant proportion of the population.

In this context, it is important to note that it is not clear when and how to urge people to stay in the labor force in ways that are salutary; ideally, those who are near or at retirement age but want to keep working and are able to do so will have those opportunities. And those in poor health or with stressful or physically demanding jobs would be able to retire or have the option to transition gradually to retirement through part-time or bridge work. That is, even as we pursue the goal of extending work lives and supporting older workers, it is important to realize that longer work is not the optimal solution for everyone.[14]

## CHALLENGES FACING OLDER WORKERS

Considerable challenges face some older workers in maximizing the benefits and opportunities of work, including, but not limited to, age discrimination, elevated rates of health and physical functioning problems, increased risk of severe and fatal workplace injury, and caregiving responsibilities.[15,16] (See also chapters 12, 19, and 20.) Age discrimination laws may counter the most egregious forms of unfair treatment facing older workers, but they have not succeeded in eliminating negative stereotypes that may affect older workers.[17] Research shows that older workers continue to face discrimination in hiring and promotion decisions.[18] On the job, employers may overlook older employees in offering skills development and training opportunities. One survey found that 9 percent of older workers felt they had been denied a training opportunity because of their age.[19]

Older workers are more likely, on average, to be coping with health and physical functioning problems (see Truxillo, Cadiz, and Hammer for a review).[20] For example, over two-thirds of Medicare beneficiaries report two or more functional limitations.[21] Other capacities that can diminish with age include hearing, vision, and memory.[22] An important point is that age-related physical and cognitive decline is likely to matter more in occupations that require those capacities;[23] thus, "fit" between the workers' capacity and job demands is relevant.[24] Interestingly, older workers have an overall lower rate of workplace injuries, but the injuries they do experience are more severe. For example, workers over age sixty-six experience fatal injuries at four times the rate of eighteen- to nineteen- or twenty- to twenty-four-year-olds.[25] Moreover, older workers have slower recovery from nonfatal injuries.

Balancing work with the care of family is a concern at all stages of work life but may be especially relevant to older workers. Population aging will increase caregiving demands for older workers who may be called on to care for their aging parents and spouses. A 2015 report from AARP (formerly the American Association of Retired Persons) indicates that more than 43.5 million Americans are unpaid family caregivers and that 53 percent of them are age fifty and older. Moreover, 21 percent of caregivers over age sixty-five report being employed.[26]

Lastly, in the context of encouraging workers to remain at work to older ages, it is also important to call attention to the intersection of age with gender, race, and immigration status as research suggests that older women, older minorities, and older immigrants may face even greater challenges in the workplace.[27]

## WHAT IS AN AGE-FRIENDLY WORKPLACE?

A general issue arising from the decidedly good news that we are living longer is the concern that those extra years should be productive and lived well. Terms like "productive aging," "successful aging," and "active aging" have been coined to express this view. Indeed, a burgeoning research literature explores what it means and its implications for a range of outcomes including the emergence of the concept of the AFW (see Scholl et al. for a complete discussion).[28] An important point made by numerous authors in this arena is that productive aging is relevant *across the life course*. Therefore, although age-friendly refers most directly to policies and practices that affect older workers, investing in the health and safety of workers of all ages can reduce problems later in life.[29] Loeppke et al. list the following set of specific age-friendly practices that would characterize an age-friendly workplace: workplace flexibility at all ages, adaptive technology and work design for older workers, management of hazards, ergo-friendly work environments, healthy lifestyle interventions, accommodation of medical self-care and time away for medical appointments, training and skills building at all ages, management of return-to-work after illness or injury, and training of management around these issues.[30]

Few studies proffer a specific definition of the AFW beyond a workplace that fosters active or productive aging. In a recent review, however, Eppler-Hattab, Meshoulam, and Doron have proposed the following working definition of the AFW concept:

> A workplace that is considered "age-friendly" is a place that adopts and maintains an organizational culture and climate in which older employees are able to know and feel that they are accepted and treated according to their competencies and needs. The creation of such a culture and climate should be reflected in embedded policies, practices, and supportive culture traits that can leverage the talent and accumulated knowhow of older employees, in favor of the overall benefit of the organization and its members.[31]

## FRAMEWORKS FOR STUDYING AND CREATING AGE-FRIENDLY WORKPLACES

The past ten years have seen a rapid growth in the number of scholarly reports on the topic of workplace aging. For example, a review focused on organizational factors in workplace aging found that between 1990 and 2009 there were twenty-four papers on the topic of the aging workforce, but between 2010 and 2018 a total of ninety-eight articles were published on this topic.[32] This burgeoning scholarship is evidence of growing interest among employers, scholars, and practitioners in the U.S. and around the world in taking stock of where we are and where we need to go. In doing so, they have proposed conceptual and practical frameworks for advancing the field. This chapter draws on the recent reports to provide a foundation for readers in some of the key concerns.

In the U.S., the National Institute of Occupational Safety and Health (NIOSH) has played a major role in advancing health promotion and protection for older workers. In 2012, in collaboration with the American College of Occupational and Environmental Medicine, NIOSH convened a two-day national invitational summit titled "Advancing Workplace Health Protection and Promotion in the Context of an Aging Workforce."[33] The summit formed workgroups focused on why employers should care about the aging workforce and establish best practices, align relevant organizational structures to improve approaches to aging workers, and identify barriers and resources to overcome barriers. The summit issued a set of consensus statements related to these charges.

In terms of establishing best practices, the statements related to building a "culture of health" in the workplace, creating age-friendly practice, and broadening the dialogue and raising awareness about workplace aging. To align relevant organizations, they recommend increasing the use of incentives such as benefit programs (including flexible work), integrating workplace health standards as a business metric, and developing models that help workers "age out" of physically demanding jobs into other meaningful work. In addressing barriers, the summit noted the desirability of developing better collection of worker health data, demonstrating the investment value of health promotion efforts, and creating a culture of "shared accountability."

In 2015, NIOSH launched its National Center for Productive Aging and Work (NCPAW). In 2018, Scholl and colleagues proposed a model of productive aging and work based on the work of the NCPAW that has four main attributes.[34] According to their framework, age-friendly workplaces represent a "life-span perspective." A general implication of this perspective for aging workers is that aging throughout the life course in relation to work represents an adaptive process whereby aspects of a worker's health and functioning change over time. That is, the fit of job demands and the worker's ability to meet demands requires updating over time. A second feature of the framework is that it is necessarily comprehensive and integrated. This means that strategies to create AFWs should be multilevel and wide ranging in the aspects of work life that are considered relevant to productive aging in the workplace. A third aspect of the framework is that it appreciates the needs of not only workers but also of employers. An important point here is that strategies can and should be mutually beneficial. For example, a worker-centered outcome might be "fair treatment and respect," and the corollary organization-centered outcome might be a "transfer of expertise between generations." Relatedly, the fourth feature of the framework is an emphasis on a supportive multigenerational work culture. As we appreciate generational differences, however, it is important not to overgeneralize. Rather, this perspective aims to use the "diverse skills, knowledge, and perspectives of all workers to create a more . . . productive organization." An implication of a well-functioning multigenerational workplace is that there can be stronger collaboration and knowledge transfer across all ages.

Nagarajan and colleagues conducted a broad-based multinational review of literature published between 1990 and 2018 with the main goal of identifying organizational factors that contribute to successful implementation of AFWs.[35] Based on their review of 122 publications on this topic, they propose five categories of organizational factors that can influence the productivity of older workers: human resource management, human capital, institutional policies, health, and technology tools. Human resource management includes checking attitudes of managers and processes related to hiring and retaining workers, combating stereotype threat, creating an age-blind meritocracy and equality of opportunity, and conducting fair and efficient performance appraisals. Human capital factors include building information and communications technology, promoting digital skills technology, and investing overall in knowledge development. Institutional factors include workplace policies such as flexible schedules, job rotation, and work environment that matches the health and capability of the worker. Relatedly, health factors include potential assignment to less physically demanding jobs (especially for workers in occupations like construction) and less stressful work environments.

Technology can include things like workstation design for more ergonomic fitness and use of artificial intelligence, for example, in manufacturing processes that can make jobs easier to perform. (See also chapter 17.)

As with any model of this sort, these categorizations overlap in practice. The review reveals that human capital, human resource management, and institutional factors receive the most research and employer attention. An important point made by these researchers is that their review only included English-language publications, which necessarily limited its comprehensiveness.

Most recently, Eppler-Hattab, Meshoulam, and Doron have proposed a new multidimensional model of the AFW.[36] These authors note the wide range of dimensions of the AFW articulated in the literature that are variously organized and categorized. Their multidimensional model attempts to pull all the threads together. As in Scholl et al.,[37] they propose that success of the AFW depends on taking account of the needs of both workers and employers. A major contribution of the model is to consider them jointly along dimensions of growth and decline for workers and utility and maintenance for organizations. Programs and policies can be placed at the intersection of these dimensions. Overall, they note that AFW culture involves recognition and respect for the contributions of older workers as well as fairness and equality across generations. AFW culture involves raising awareness and changing attitudes about these issues and promotes supportive workplace relationships.

This person-organization typology of the AFW suggests worker-related and organization-related dimensions. Along the *worker orientation axis* are the age-related dimensions of growth and decline, which indicate the changes that can come with age. Grosch and Scholl propose a similar heuristic model that emphasizes "gains" and "losses" that can come with age.[38] The goal of the AFW is to minimize losses and maximize gains in the workplace as workers age. Growth reflects the fact that many older workers continue to be interested in building their knowledge, skills, and abilities as they age. Other changes are indicative of physical and cognitive decline that can come with age, and the dimension of decline reflects that the AFW would continue to support workers through workplace policies.

The *organizational axis* includes utilitarian and maintenance dimensions, which brings to the fore resource-based human resource practices and organizational substructures and supportive programs as practical solutions to worker growth and decline. At the intersection of worker growth and organizational utilitarianism is the career development cluster that includes policies supportive of lifelong learning, job enrichment and mentoring, for example. In the growth and maintenance quadrant are policies aimed at sustaining older workers such as health promotion, workplace design, and keeping skills up to date. As some workers experience decline, a utilitarian organizational focus would suggest modifications to help the workers adapt and remain productive. Policies in this area could include things like job design or redesign or redeployment to another work area. Job crafting is an interesting strategy that can come into play in this cluster. Job crafting is a process that workers initiate to try to create a job that is more meaningful and satisfying for them.[39] (See also chapters 13, 14, and 16.)

Finally, at the intersection of the decline and maintenance axes is flexibility. As will be explored in greater detail in the next section, flexible work policies have many advantages but may be especially useful for workers needing to reduce their workload overall and/or continue to work but in ways that allow them to meet caregiving obligations, for example. The culture that recognizes the value of these policies will be more likely to foster a positive workplace climate for workers of all ages. This model holds promise for serving as a guide for organizations looking to build or improve their age-friendliness. However, as others have suggested, these efforts will need to be validated with measurement and data collection to track outcomes.

This section has focused on conceptual models of productive aging in the workplace. Several other publications are especially useful in articulating a wide range of specific issues related to active aging at work. See Zacher, Kooij, and Beier,[40] for example, for an excellent review and selected bibliography for more in-depth reading on these topics and Smeaton and Perry[41] for an evidence report aimed at providing very practical advice to employers looking to become more age friendly. A report of the OECD summarizes experiences in Denmark, France, the Netherlands, Norway, Japan, Korea, Poland, Switzerland, and the U.S. and proposes a three-pronged policy agenda for promoting employment at older ages.[42] Although it is a higher level of analysis, it too offers concrete suggestions for governments and employers. The report emphasizes the importance of the lifespan as in Scholl et al.,[43] suggesting that investing in the health and skills of workers at *all* ages will be critical to foster AFWs in the context of rapid population aging. The agenda includes policy recommendations for rewarding work and later retirement, encouraging employers to retain and hire older workers, and promoting employability over the lifespan, suggesting many of the policies articulated in Eppler-Hattab et al.[44]

As this brief review illustrates, there is a wide range of important considerations in creating AFWs. In the next section, we focus on one that has received considerable research and practical attention: workplace flexibility.

## OPPORTUNITIES AND CHALLENGES TO IMPLEMENTING FLEXIBLE WORK ARRANGEMENTS

Workplace flexibility is a leading accommodation in which employees and supervisors have some degree of control over "when, where, and how work gets done."[45] Exploration of the potential interest in and benefits of flexible work arrangements (FWAs) has been in the research literature for decades.[46,47] More recent research indicates that FWAs continue to be highly valued by workers. For example, Rau and Adams show that older workers were more likely to apply to a job if the advertisement indicated flexible work.[48] Another study found that willingness to work among recent retirees was high at 30 percent but increases to 50 percent if the potential job offers FWA. About 60 percent of nonworking respondents would be willing to return to work with a flexible schedule. Furthermore, 20 percent of them would be willing to take more than a 20 percent hourly wage reduction to do so.[49] Johnson studied later-career job changes, finding significant increase in flexible work schedules in new versus old jobs.[50] A related literature addresses the question of whether workplace flexibility keeps people working longer. Overall, the finding is yes. For example, results of a randomized field experiment testing the effect of a workplace flexibility initiative found that those in the treatment group were more likely to remain at work.[51] In addition to better worker retention, FWAs have been associated with other positive outcomes such as increased productivity and reduced absenteeism.[52]

Given that human resource professionals are often on the front lines of the implementation of flexible work policy, the Society for Human Resource Management (SHRM) in the U.S. has created a range of useful publications summarizing key issues concerning flexible work policy.[53] Importantly, their guidance in this and other publications takes account of federal, state, and local laws that may bear on the implementation of FWA.[54] Similar recent reports in the UK provide thoughtful discussion of key issues along with practical guidance.[55,56] Drawing on these sources, we provide a brief overview of the major policies and practices involved in FWA.

## Types of Workplace Flexibility

The following summary of common FWAs is not exhaustive but illustrative of some of the more common current practices involving time, location, and format flexibility. An important dimension of FWAs that cuts across all forms is the extent to which the arrangement is formal or informal.

### TIME FLEXIBILITY

One common form of workplace flexibility is known as "flextime," which is the ability to have a flexible start and end time around certain core working hours. The overall number of hours worked is likely the same as with a traditional schedule. An alternative time flexibility option is compressed schedules, which allow employees to work full-time but in fewer than five workdays, for example, four 10-hour days instead of five 8-hour days. One interesting variant of this option is the so-called 9/80 schedule in which an additional hour is worked for nine consecutive workdays in order to be off every other Friday.

### LOCATION FLEXIBILITY

In the age of advancing technology, a flexible work arrangement that is growing in popularity is flexibility in work location, which allows employees to work off-site and communicate with their employer and others electronically and by phone. This is variously called flexplace, teleworking, or telecommuting. The off-site location is often home or some other relatively close worksite. In this case, the employee's schedule often involves a combination of one or two days per week telecommuting with the other days spent working on-site at the organization. Another variant of flexplace is working remotely, which often means working a far distance from the main organization, for example, in the U.S. living in one state and working remotely for an organization headquartered in another state. A relevant concept here is the results-only work environment (ROWE), the heart of which proposes that both the time spent on a job and the place where the job is done are less relevant metrics of work success than whether a job gets done.[57]

There may be hidden costs to FWAs, especially location flexibility that involves working at home. For example, Putnam, Myers, and Gailliard conducted a literature review of workplace flexibility and identified what they term the "autonomy-control paradox" to help understand tensions in the implementation of FWA.[58] This paradox emerges in situations where workers in FWAs maintain a high level of autonomy at the cost of greater organizational control in the sense that their time is less their own than for workers with set schedules and work that does not flow over to home, as is often the case with remote work. Moreover, it is important to note that not all employees using telecommuting are higher-status workers within the organization. It is important to be mindful of the potential for such policies to take advantage, especially of contingent workers.[59]

### FORMAT FLEXIBILITY

A range of options falls under this category involving how work is structured. Part-time schedules are considered flexible work arrangements when they are desired by employees. Another option that may be especially helpful to older workers who may be interested in moving toward less demanding work is reduced workload. Such an arrangement may come with a reduction in pay, but this may be deemed worthwhile for the benefit of less stress. Yet another alternative work format option is job sharing. In this scenario, one full-time position is shared by two employees, often dividing the time fifty-fifty or sixty-forty with some time overlapping during the week.

### FORMAL VERSUS INFORMAL ARRANGEMENTS AND ORGANIZATIONAL SIZE

An important aspect of FWAs that has received less research attention is the extent to which they reflect formal deals worked out through structured organizational channels, which may, in some countries, be legally binding, or whether they are implemented on an ad hoc basis in informal arrangements agreed upon by a particular employer and supervisor. Vickerstaff and Alden make the point that although less formal arrangements may seem less daunting to implement, they are susceptible to personnel changes and may evaporate when a supervisor leaves.[60] On the other hand, more formal arrangements may have to be offered equitably across organizations, making especially smaller firms reluctant to adopt them. Thus the size of the firm is a related relevant consideration in that smaller firms may be more likely to need the flexibility of less formal arrangements whereas larger firms may have the wherewithal to broadly implement organization-level formalized flexible work policy. Atkinson and Sandiford conducted qualitative interviews with owner managers and workers in smaller firms in the UK exploring the relative formality of FWA, finding that both types of arrangements are valuable in meeting the needs of older workers.[61]

## UNDERSTANDING BARRIERS TO IMPLEMENTATION

In the U.S., the Alfred P. Sloan Foundation's Program on Working Longer has provided leadership and support for several important research initiatives that have added importantly to understanding barriers to implementing FWA. In the American Working Conditions Survey, Maestas et al. found that the job attribute least likely to match workers' preferences was having the right number of hours. Around 55 percent of older workers considered having the right number of work hours to be an essential or very important work attribute, but only 33 percent felt they had it.[62]

The Sloan Center on Aging and Work fielded the Age and Generations Study, a large-scale study of over 2,200 employees across nine organizations that provided key information on attitudes about workplace flexibility.[63] A key conclusion was that fit between the flexibility strategies firms offered and those that are most helpful to employees made a difference for outcomes such as increased engagement and retention. Fit depends to some extent on an employer's willingness to offer a range of flexibility options and employees' willingness to customize those options to best meet their own needs. Another initiative, the National Study of Business Strategy and Workforce Development, uncovered barriers to workplace flexibility.[64] Findings from the survey indicated that even in organizations with favorable conditions for flexible work, only about 16 percent of workers use these options. Moreover, employers in the study cited a range of barriers to implementing flexible work. Their top concerns (to a "moderate" or "great extent") included abuse of policies, the reactions of customers and clients, difficulties with supervising employees in a flexible manner, loss of productivity, and treating all employees equally.

A smaller but growing literature focuses on attitudes and actual practices of *line managers* in implementing FWAs, as distinct from a focus at the organizational or employee level.[65] For example, Sweet, Pitt-Catsouphes, and James reported on the results of a workplace flexibility initiative offering training that encouraged supervisors to explore FWA options for those they supervise with the goal of increasing use of FWAs among the organization's employees.[66] The study utilizes an ecological framework that acknowledges the important role of managers as "gatekeepers" of policy who operate in a given microsystem with individuals bringing their own personalities and experience to the encounter within a particular context. The initiative was successful in increasing favorable views, which translated to increased use of FWAs by supervisees. Interestingly, managers who felt that their support of FWAs would improve their performance reviews were much more likely to increase use throughout the study. They also found that managers' attitudes about flexible work are malleable, and that experience managing flexible schedules led to more favorable attitudes over time. The same was not true, however, for location flexibility.[67]

Lastly, Earl and Taylor note the pressing need for more research on the day-to-day implementation of FWA aimed at retaining older workers. They conducted qualitative interviews with fifty-eight human resource managers across several labor sectors in Australia and focused on flexibility as a gender-conscious age management strategy. They found that human resource managers were conscious of age discrimination. They write that "materialization of benefits for older women workers seems to depend on the attitudes and capabilities of *their line managers*."[68]

## IMPLEMENTING FLEXIBLE WORK ARRANGEMENTS: THE VIEW OF LINE MANAGERS

In the last section of this chapter we present preliminary results of a study that aims to develop a rich source of qualitative data focused on the point of view of midlevel line supervisors to try to better understand barriers to implementation of FWA but also to understand why it succeeds when it succeeds. A particular organization's workplace flexibility program is primarily a statement that workplace flexibility is to be implemented at the discretion of line managers. Paperwork is available for negotiating a flexible work agreement that is to be signed not only by the supervisor and employee but at several levels up the chain. With an average employee age of fifty-five years, over the past ten years, the organization has been urging retirement through less generous retirement benefits after a certain date. The organization has around five hundred permanent and about twelve hundred contingent staff. The organization itself is highly decentralized with several major subunits, the leadership of which appear to have very different ideas about implementation of workplace flexibility.

Forty supervisors were randomly selected from a list of 140 supervisors across the organization. Email invitations were sent with an offer of a small incentive. Oral assent was obtained, and half-hour-long recorded interviews were conducted privately with each supervisor. Recordings were professionally transcribed and analyzed using traditional qualitative methods. Respondents had an average of seven years of tenure as supervisors and were supervising relatively small groups overall.

The interview protocol explained the aims of the study to be "understanding FWA for older workers." It is interesting to note that when the protocol was vetted through the human resources department, the phrase "workers with longer tenure in their careers" was suggested as preferable to "older workers," supporting Earl and Taylor's finding that human resources professionals are very conscious about age discrimination.[69] The protocol posed the following: "Have you ever had an employee with longer work tenure request a flexible work schedule, and by that I mean hours flexibility as well as days flexibility? If yes, were (are) there any problems with it? If no, what do you think makes the arrangement successful?" These questions were repeated for location flexibility. Based on the top barriers identified in the Pitt-Catsouphes et al. report[70] reviewed previously, a second set of questions asked supervisors to think about barriers to implementation: "In thinking about implementing flexible work policy, to what extent are the following concerns you might have—abuse of the policy? difficulties with supervising employees working in a flexible manner? loss of productivity? treating all employees equally? co-worker resentment? too time-consuming for you?" "When you have encountered these barriers, what strategies have you used to address them?"

### General Themes

There was a nearly unanimous sentiment that workplace flexibility is a privilege, not a right. As one supervisor said, "It's yours to lose." The responsibility was seen as being primarily the employees' to make sure the arrangement works. Putnam et al. have called for making workplace flexibility an employee right,[71] which would certainly be a significant policy development. Most supervisors also indicated that they themselves have very little location flexibility because they feel they have to be on-site to be able to do their job well. As one supervisor said, "We are the ones putting out the fires and need to be here to do it." Supervisors seemed very aware of the unit leadership's attitudes toward workplace flexibility and that the support or lack of support filtered down to them in terms of their comfort offering it to their staff.

## Succeeding at All Career Stages

Resonating with general findings in the literature, supervisors indicated that issues arising around FWA relate to workers at all career stages. One theme that emerged across several interviews was that when there is a lack of leadership support for workplace flexibility, supervisors took it upon themselves to offer flexibility on an ad hoc basis. All respondents felt very comfortable offering flexible start and end times around core hours of 10:00 a.m. and 3:00 p.m. (flextime). As one respondent said, it was easy in this way to "play the flex game." As others have found,[72] experience with FWA seemed to make a big difference for success. Those who had had it themselves in the past or had experience implementing it as supervisors were the strongest proponents. Supervisors with the most success indicated that communication was key. They emphasized the importance of creating a plan with clear expectations and then meeting regularly to review it and check in to see how it was going.

Several supervisors had staff with formal location flexibility. It was quite clear that for location flexibility to work, technology support was critical, such as Google Chat (an instant messaging service), video chat, call forwarding from work phone to cell, a centralized calendar, and even low-tech whiteboards on their door at work to say when they were working at home. As one respondent said, "With the right technology, remote work is not very different from on-site work." In line with other findings,[73] it was critical from the supervisor's point of view that success of the arrangement hinged on the employee's willingness to be flexible, for example, to come in to work on their day at home if needed.

## Barriers at All Career Stages

Technology was also seen as a potential barrier when it was not adequate. Supervisors talked about how much more they could do to facilitate location flexibility if the organization were willing to invest more in the infrastructure. Location flexibility, however, was the arrangement that supervisors perceived the least amount of support for from the organization's leadership. A second major barrier was the perception that, as one respondent said, "some jobs just can't flex." For example, some work involved using resources that could only be accessed directly on-site. These findings also resonate with prior studies.[74] Finally, several supervisors felt that many workers were daunted by the prospect of requesting and negotiating a formal agreement because of the required paperwork.

Interestingly, the common barriers of "abuse," "loss of productivity," "co-worker resentment," and "too much work" did not especially resonate. In terms of productivity, the feeling seemed to be it might be a concern but not necessarily unique to flexible work. None of the supervisors perceived coworker resentment as a major issue for them. And in terms of added workload, most said they handled that by "not sweating the details" and could tell pretty quickly if people were not productive.

### Succeeding with Workers Nearing Retirement

In terms of issues that relate specifically to workers "with longer tenure in their careers," there was what one respondent referred to as the "boomerang back" where workers reach an age of eligibility for retirement benefits, retire, and then *un*retire back to part-time work. In most cases the job was redefined to have many fewer duties than the career job. There were only a few instances of phased retirement that had been worked out at the initiative of the employee, and these seemed to be offered to highly valued employees. These findings resonate with those of Atkinson and Sandiford, who identify what they call role-based flexibility in which older workers are able to redefine their jobs to better suit their needs.[75]

### Barriers for Workers Nearing Retirement

In terms of barriers to implementing FWA for late-career workers, concerns about age discrimination came up when supervisors were explicitly instructed by the organization's human resources department *not to approach* late-career workers about retirement plans. A related issue was that succession planning is very much desired but almost never done. One respondent said, "You need the right combination of older employee ready to retire and new employee ready to take over." Several supervisors expressed that they thought there was, in some cases, a generation gap in use of the technology that enables remote work. Phased retirements, as noted, were only offered to highly valued employees as they are quite costly to the organization, which offers full benefits at half-time.

## CONCLUSION AND FUTURE DIRECTIONS

With the advent of population aging and policy focus on extending working lives, there is growing interest in creating age-friendly workplaces to attract and retain older workers. A rapidly growing research literature in this area attests to scholarly interest, and, as this chapter has suggested, governmental agencies and public and private policy organizations (e.g., SHRM, AARP, Sloan Foundation) are also playing an important role in helping set the agenda and creating and sharing resources for those on the front lines. As Rix has pointed out, however, we have a long way to go—in the U.S., little of this growing interest has been translated into formal policy initiatives and none made law.[76] Moreover, there is a risk of oversimplifying the task at hand. "Older workers" are as heterogeneous as any other population subgroup, and making one-size-fits-all policy is not likely to be successful.[77]

That said, the resources available to those interested in creating age-friendly workplaces are considerable (see Truxillo et al. for a review of workplace age interventions),[78] and novel approaches to encouraging age-friendly workplace policy are promising. One such example is the Age Smart Employers Award, an initiative of the Robert N. Butler Aging Center at Columbia University funded by the Sloan Foundation, that is awarded annually to employers in the New York City metropolitan area who are "engaging in AFW strategies such as workplace flexibility, recruitment to encourage older workers to apply, job restructuring, workplace health and safety, training, and alternative paths to retirement." The objective of the award is to stimulate interest in creating an AFW.[79] The organization RetirementJobs.com has sponsored a similar strategy, the Certified Age Friendly Employer program, in which employers demonstrate their commitment to AFWs by adhering to certain standards of recruitment and equality of opportunity for workers over age fifty. As competition for older workers grows, winning such awards and certifications may prove to be a powerful recruitment tool. In addition, to address the problem of low take-up of programs, employers may have to promote their AFW policies, for example, by using success stories to make the case to reluctant workers.[80]

## NOTES

1. Gwen G. Fisher, Dorey Chaffee, and Amanda Sonnega. 2016 "Retirement Timing: A Review and Agenda for Future Research." *Work, Aging, and Retirement* 2(2):230–61.

2. Society for Human Resource Management. 2015. "Preparing for an Aging Workforce: Executive Summary." Retrieved February 25, 2020 (https://www.shrm.org/hr-today/trends-and-forecasting/research-and-surveys/Documents/14-0765%20Executive%20Briefing%20Aging%20Workforce%20v4.pdf).

3. UN Department of Economic and Social Affairs, Population Division. 2017. "World Population Ageing 2017—Highlights." Retrieved February 25, 2020 (https://www.un.org/en/development/desa/population/publications/pdf/ageing/WPA2017_Highlights.pdf).

4. Organisation for Economic Co-operation and Development (OECD). 2019. "Ageing and Employment Policies: Working Better with Age." Retrieved February 25, 2020 (http://www.oecd.org/els/emp/Brochure%20OW%2028-08.pdf).

5. Kevin E. Cahill, Michael D. Giandrea, and Joseph F. Quinn. 2008. "Retirement Patterns and the Macroeconomy, 1992–2010: The Prevalence and Determinants of Bridge Jobs, Phased Retirement, and Reentry among Three Recent Cohorts of Older Americans." *The Gerontologist* 55(3):384–403.

6. Terry A. Beehr and Misty M. Bennett. 2015. "Working after Retirement: Features of Bridge Employment and Research Directions." *Work, Aging and Retirement* 1(1):112–28.

7. U.S. Senate, Special Committee on Aging. 2017. "America's Aging Workforce: Opportunities and Challenges." Retrieved February 25, 2020 (https://www.aging.senate.gov/imo/media/doc/Aging%20Workforce%20Report%20FINAL.pdf).

8. OECD, "Ageing and Employment Policies."

9. David Neumark and Joyce Song. 2013. "Do Stronger Age Discrimination Laws Make Social Security Reforms More Effective?" *Journal of Public Economics* 108:1–16.

10. Steven J. Haider and David S. Loughran. 2008. "The Effect of the Social Security Earnings Test on Male Labor Supply: New Evidence from Survey and Administrative Data." *Journal of Human Resources* 43(1):57–87.

11. Alan L. Gustman and Thomas L. Steinmeier. 2015. "Effects of Social Security Policies on Benefit Claiming, Retirement and Saving." *Journal of Public Economics* 129:51–62.

12. OECD, "Ageing and Employment Policies."

13. Henry J. Aaron and Jean Marie Callan. 2011. "Who Retires Early?" Chestnut Hill, MA: Center for Retirement Research, Boston College. CRR Working Paper 2011-10.

14. Philip Taylor. 2019. "Working Longer May Be Good Public Policy, but It Is Not Necessarily Good for Older People." *Journal of Aging and Social Policy* 31(2):99–105.

15. U.S. Senate, Special Committee on Aging, "America's Aging Workforce."

16. Ronald R. Loeppke et al. 2013. "Advancing Workplace Health Protection and Promotion for an Aging Workforce." *Journal of Occupational Environment Medicine* 55(5):500–6.

17. Philip Taylor, Louise Rolland, and Jing Zhou. 2017. "Retaining Australian Older Workers: A Literature Review." CSIRO-Monash Working Paper No. 2017-01.

18. U.S. Senate, Special Committee on Aging, "America's Aging Workforce."

19. U.S. Senate, Special Committee on Aging, "America's Aging Workforce."

20. Donald M. Truxillo, David M. Cadiz, and Leslie B. Hammer. 2015. "Supporting the Aging Workforce: A Review and Recommendations for Workplace Intervention Research." *Annual Review of Organizational Psychology and Organizational Behavior* 2(1):351–81.

21. U.S. Senate, Special Committee on Aging, "America's Aging Workforce."

22. Wan He and Luke Larsen. 2014. "Older Americans with a Disability: 2008–2012." U.S. Census Bureau. Retrieved February 25, 2020 (https://www.census.gov/content/dam/Census/library/publications/2014/acs/acs-29.pdf).

23. Loeppke et al., "Advancing Workplace Health Protection."

24. Amanda Sonnega et al. 2018. "A Comparison of Subjective and Objective Job Demands and Mismatch with Personal Resources as Predictors of Retirement Timing in a National U.S. Sample." *Work, Aging, and Retirement* 4(1):37–51.

25. Loeppke et al., "Advancing Workplace Health Protection."

26. AARP Public Policy Institute. 2015. "2015 Report: Caregiving in the U.S." Retrieved February 25, 2020 (https://www.aarp.org/content/dam/aarp/ppi/2015/caregiving-in-the-united-states-2015-report-revised.pdf).

27. Taylor, Rolland, and Zhou, "Retaining Australian Older Workers."

28. Julian C. Scholl et al. 2018. "Advancing Age-friendly Workplaces through the NIOSH National Center for Productive Aging." In *Handbook of Rehabilitation in Older Adults*, edited by Robert J. Gatchel et al. Cham, Switzerland: Springer Nature.

29. Scholl et al., "Advancing Age-friendly Workplaces."

30. Loeppke et al., "Advancing Workplace Health Protection."

31. Raphael Eppler-Hattab, Ilan Meshoulam, and Israel Doron. 2020. "Conceptualizing Age-friendliness in Workplaces: Proposing a New Multidimensional Model." *The Gerontologist* 60:12–21.

32. N. Renuga Nagarajan et al. 2019. "Defining Organizational Contributions to Sustaining an Ageing Workforce: A Bibliometric Review." *European Journal of Ageing* 16:337–61.

33. Loeppke et al., "Advancing Workplace Health Protection."

34. Scholl et al., "Advancing Age-friendly Workplaces," 73.

35. Nagarajan et al., "Defining Organizational Contributions."

36. Eppler-Hattab, Meshoulam, and Doron, "Conceptualizing Age-friendliness in Workplaces."

37. Scholl et al., "Advancing Age-friendly Workplaces."

38. James W. Grosch and Juliann C. Scholl. 2020. "Designing Age-friendly Workplaces: An Occupational Health Perspective." In *Current and Emerging Trends in Aging and Work*, edited by Sara J. Czaja et al. Cham, Switzerland: Springer Nature.

39. Evangelina Demerouti. 2014. "Design Your Own Job through Job Crafting." *European Psychologist* 19:237–47.

40. Hannes Zacher, Dorien T. A. M. Kooij, and Margaret E. Beier. 2018. "Active Aging at Work: Contributing Factors and Implications for Organizations." *Organizational Dynamics* 47:37–45.

41. Deborah Smeaton and Jane Perry. 2018. "Becoming an Age-friendly Employer: Evidence Report." Centre for Ageing Better. Retrieved February 25, 2020 (https://www.researchgate.net/publication/327622550_Becoming_an_age-friendly_employer_Evidence_report).

42. OECD, "Ageing and Employment Policies."

43. Scholl et al., "Advancing Age-friendly Workplaces."

44. Eppler-Hattab, Meshoulam, and Doron, "Conceptualizing Age-friendliness in Workplaces."
45. Jeffrey E. Hill et al. 2008. "Defining and Conceptualizing Workplace Flexibility." *Community, Work and Family* 11(2):149–63.
46. Boris B. Baltes et al. 1999. "Flexible and Compressed Workweek Schedules: A Meta-analysis of Their Effects on Work-related Criteria." *Journal of Applied Psychology* 84(4):496–513.
47. Jurg K. Siegenthaler and Andrea M. Brenner. 2001. "Flexible Work Schedules, Older Workers, and Retirement." *Journal of Aging and Social Policy* 12(1):19–34.
48. Barbara L. Rau and Gary A. Adams. 2005. "Attracting Retirees to Apply: Desired Organizational Characteristics of Bridge Employment." *Journal of Organization Behavior* 26:649–60.
49. John Ameriks et al. 2018. "Older Americans Would Work Longer If Jobs Were Flexible." NBER Working Paper No. 24008.
50. Richard W. Johnson. 2011. "Phased Retirement and Workplace Flexibility for Older Adults: Opportunities and Challenges." *Annals of the American Academy* 638:68–85.
51. Kevin E. Cahill, Jaquelyn B. James, and Marcie Pitt-Catsouphes. 2015. "The Impact of a Randomly-assigned Time and Place Management Initiative on Work and Retirement Expectations." *Work, Aging, and Retirement* 1(4):350–68.
52. Smeaton and Perry, "Becoming an Age-friendly Employer."
53. Society for Human Resource Management. 2014. "Leveraging Workplace Flexibility for Engagement and Productivity." Retrieved February 25, 2020 (https://www.shrm.org/hr-today/trends-and-forecasting/special-reports-and-expert-views/Documents/Leveraging-Workplace-Flexibility.pdf).
54. Society for Human Resource Management. 2012. "Flexible Work Arrangements: A Compliance Checklist." Retrieved February 25, 2020 (https://www.shrm.org/ResourcesAndTools/hr-topics/benefits/Pages/Flex_Compliance.aspx).
55. Smeaton and Perry, "Becoming an Age-friendly Employer."
56. OECD, "Ageing and Employment Policies."
57. Phyllis Moen, Erin L. Kelly, and Jack Lam. 2013. "Healthy Work Revisited: Do Changes in Time Strain Predict Well-being?" *Journal of Occupational Health Psychology* 18(2):157–72.
58. Linda L. Putnam, Karen K. Myers, and Bernadette M. Gaillard. 2014. "Examining the Tensions in Workplace Flexibility and Exploring Options for New Directions." *Human Relations* 67(4):413–40.
59. Eurofound. 2020. "Telework and ICT-based Mobile Work: Flexible Working in the Digital Age." New Forms of Employment Series, Publications Office of the European Union. Retrieved February 25, 2020 (http://www.bollettinoadapt.it/wp-content/uploads/2020/02/ef19032en_0.pdf).
60. Sarah A. Vickerstaff and Elaine Alden. 2015. "Negotiating Flexibility: Formality and Informality in the Management and Retention of Older Employees." *The Gerontologist* 55(S2):759.
61. Carol Atkinson and Peter Sandiford. 2016. "An Exploration of Older Worker Flexible Working Arrangements in Smaller Firms." *Human Resource Management Journal* 26(1):12–28.
62. Nicole Maestas et al. 2017. "Working Conditions in the United States: Results of the 2015 American Working Conditions Survey." Santa Monica, CA: RAND Corporation. Retrieved February 25, 2020 (https://www.rand.org/pubs/research_reports/RR2014.html).
63. Marcie Pitt-Catsouphes, Christina Matz-Costa, and Elyssa Besen. 2009. "Workplace Flexibility: Findings from the Age and Generations Study." *Issue Brief* 19. Chestnut Hill, MA: Sloan Center on Aging and Work, Boston College.
64. Marcie Pitt-Catsouphes et al. 2007. "The National Study Report: Phase II of the National Study of Business Strategy and Workforce Development." *Research Highlight* No. 04. Chestnut Hill, MA: Center on Aging and Work/Workplace Flexibility, Boston College.
65. Tay McNamara, Marcie Pitt-Catsouphes, and Christina Matz-Costa. 2012. "Access to and Utilization of Flexible Work Options." *Industrial Relations* 51(4):936–65.
66. Stephen Sweet, Marcie Pitt-Catsouphes, and Jacquelyn B. James. 2016. "Successes in Changing Flexible Work Arrangement Use: Managers and Work-unit Variation in a Financial Services Organization." *Work and Organizations* 43(1):75–109.
67. Stephen Sweet, Marcie Pitt-Catsouphes, and Jaquelyn B. James. 2017. "Manager Attitudes Concerning Flexible Work Arrangements: Fixed or Changeable?" *Community, Work and Family* 20(1):50–71.

68. Catherine Earl and Philip Taylor. 2015. "Is Workplace Flexibility Good Policy? Evaluating the Efficacy of Age Management Strategies for Older Women Workers." *Work, Aging and Retirement* 1(2):214–26.

69. Earl and Taylor, "Is Workplace Flexibility Good Policy?"

70. Pitt-Catsouphes et al., "National Study Report."

71. Putnam, Myers, and Gaillard, "Examining the Tensions in Workplace Flexibility."

72. Sweet, Pitt-Catsouphes, and James, "Successes in Changing Flexible Work Arrangement Use."

73. Pitt-Catsouphes, Matz-Costa, and Besen, "Workplace Flexibility."

74. Pitt-Catsouphes, Matz-Costa, and Besen, "Workplace Flexibility."

75. Atkinson and Sandiford, "Exploration of Older Worker Flexible Working Arrangements."

76. Sara E. Rix. 2016. "Working Late: Policy Relevance for Older Workers in the United States." *Australian Journal of Social Issues* 51(2):205–27.

77. Taylor, Rolland, and Zhou, "Retaining Australian Older Workers."

78. Truxillo, Cadiz, and Hammer, "Supporting the Aging Workforce."

79. Ruth Finkelstein. 2016. "Evidence from an Awards Strategy: Age Smart Employers." *The Gerontologist* 56(S3):454.

80. Pitt-Catsouphes, Matz-Costa, and Besen, "Workplace Flexibility."

## REFERENCES


Aaron, Henry J. and Jean Marie Callan. 2011. "Who Retires Early?" Chestnut Hill, MA: Center for Retirement Research, Boston College. CRR Working Paper 2011-10.

AARP Public Policy Institute. 2015. "2015 Report: Caregiving in the U.S." Retrieved February 25, 2020 (https://www.aarp.org/content/dam/aarp/ppi/2015/caregiving-in-the-united-states-2015-report-revised.pdf).

Ameriks, John, et al. 2018. "Older Americans Would Work Longer If Jobs Were Flexible." NBER Working Paper No. 24008.

Atkinson, Carol and Peter Sandiford. 2016. "An Exploration of Older Worker Flexible Working Arrangements in Smaller Firms." *Human Resource Management Journal* 26(1):12–28.

Baltes, Boris B., et al. 1999. "Flexible and Compressed Workweek Schedules: A Meta-analysis of Their Effects on Work-related Criteria." *Journal of Applied Psychology* 84(4):496–513.

Beehr, Terry A. and Misty M. Bennett. 2015. "Working after Retirement: Features of Bridge Employment and Research Directions." *Work, Aging and Retirement* 1(1):112–28.

Cahill, Kevin E., Michael D. Giandrea, and Joseph F. Quinn. 2008. "Retirement Patterns and the Macroeconomy 1992–2010: The Prevalence and Determinants of Bridge Jobs, Phased Retirement, and Reentry among Three Recent Cohorts of Older Americans." *The Gerontologist* 55(3):384–403.

Cahill, Kevin E., Jaquelyn B. James, and Marcie Pitt-Catsouphes. 2015. "The Impact of a Randomly-assigned Time and Place Management Initiative on Work and Retirement Expectations." *Work, Aging, and Retirement* 1(4):350–68.

Clarke, Sharon and Lynn Holdsworth. 2017. "Flexibility in the Workplace: Implication of Flexible Work Arrangements for Individuals, Teams, and Organizations." Advisory, Conciliation and Arbitration Service Research Paper.

Demerouti, Evangelina. 2014. "Design Your Own Job through Job Crafting." *European Psychologist* 19:237–47.

Earl, Catherine and Philip Taylor. 2015. "Is Workplace Flexibility Good Policy? Evaluating the Efficacy of Age Management Strategies for Older Women Workers." *Work, Aging and Retirement* 1(2):214–26.

Eppler-Hattab, Raphael, Ilan Meshoulam, and Israel Doron. 2020. "Conceptualizing Age-friendliness in Workplaces: Proposing a New Multidimensional Model." *The Gerontologist* 60:12–21.

Eurofound. 2020. "Telework and ICT-based Mobile Work: Flexible Working in the Digital Age." New Forms of Employment Series, Publications Office of the European Union.

Retrieved February 25, 2020 (http://www.bollettinoadapt.it/wp-content/uploads/2020/02/ef19032en_0.pdf).

Finkelstein, Ruth. 2016. "Evidence from an Awards Strategy: Age Smart Employers." *The Gerontologist* 56(S3):454.

Fisher, Gwen G., Dorey Chaffee, and Amanda Sonnega. 2016. "Retirement Timing: A Review and Agenda for Future Research." *Work, Aging, and Retirement* 2(2):230–61.

Grosch, James W. and Juliann C. Scholl. 2020. "Designing Age-friendly Workplaces: An Occupational Health Perspective." In *Current and Emerging Trends in Aging and Work*, edited by Sara J. Czaja et al. Cham, Switzerland: Springer Nature.

Gustman, Alan L. and Thomas L. Steinmeier. 2015. "Effects of Social Security Policies on Benefit Claiming, Retirement and Saving." *Journal of Public Economics* 129:51–62.

Haider, Steven J. and David S. Loughran. 2008. "The Effect of the Social Security Earnings Test on Male Labor Supply: New Evidence from Survey and Administrative Data." *Journal of Human Resources* 43(1):57–87.

He, Wan and Luke Larsen. 2014. "Older Americans with a Disability: 2008–2012." U.S. Census Bureau. Retrieved February 25, 2020 (https://www.census.gov/content/dam/Census/library/publications/2014/acs/acs-29.pdf).

Hill, Jeffrey E., et al. 2008. "Defining and Conceptualizing Workplace Flexibility." *Community, Work and Family* 11(2):149–63.

Johnson, Richard W. 2011. "Phased Retirement and Workplace Flexibility for Older Adults: Opportunities and Challenges." *Annals of the American Academy* 638:68–85.

Loeppke, Ronald R., et al. 2013. "Advancing Workplace Health Protection and Promotion for an Aging Workforce." *Journal of Occupational Environment Medicine* 55(5):500–6.

Maestas, Nicole, et al. 2017. "Working Conditions in the United States: Results of the 2015 American Working Conditions Survey." Santa Monica, CA: RAND Corporation. Retrieved February 25, 2020 (https://www.rand.org/pubs/research_reports/RR2014.html).

Matz-Costa, Christina and Marcie Pitt-Catsouphes. 2009. "Workplace Flexibility as an Organizational Response to the Aging of the Workforce: A Comparison of Nonprofit and For-profit Organizations." *Journal of Social Service Research* 36(1):68–80.

McNamara, Tay, Marcie Pitt-Catsouphes, and Christina Matz-Costa. 2012. "Access to and Utilization of Flexible Work Options." *Industrial Relations* 51(4):936–65.

Moen, Phyllis, Erin L. Kelly, and Jack Lam. 2013. "Healthy Work Revisited: Do Changes in Time Strain Predict Well-being?" *Journal of Occupational Health Psychology* 18(2):157–72.

Nagarajan, N. Renuga, et al. 2019. "Defining Organizational Contributions to Sustaining an Ageing Workforce: A Bibliometric Review." *European Journal of Ageing* 16:337–61.

Neumark, David and Joyce Song. 2013. "Do Stronger Age Discrimination Laws Make Social Security Reforms More Effective?" *Journal of Public Economics* 108:1–16.

Organisation for Economic Co-operation and Development (OECD). 2019. "Ageing and Employment Policies: Working Better with Age." Retrieved February 25, 2020 (http://www.oecd.org/els/emp/Brochure%20OW%2028-08.pdf).

Pitt-Catsouphes, Marcie, et al. 2007. "The National Study Report: Phase II of the National Study of Business Strategy and Workforce Development." *Research Highlight* No. 04. Chestnut Hill, MA: Center on Aging and Work/Workplace Flexibility, Boston College.

Pitt-Catsouphes, Marcie, Christina Matz-Costa, and Elyssa Besen. 2009. "Workplace Flexibility: Findings from the Age and Generation Study." *Issue Brief* 19. Chestnut Hill, MA: Sloan Center on Aging and Work, Boston College.

Putnam, Linda L., Karen K. Myers, and Bernadette M. Gaillard. 2014. "Examining the Tensions in Workplace Flexibility and Exploring Options for New Directions." *Human Relations* 67(4):413–40.

Rau, Barbara L. and Gary A. Adams. 2005. "Attracting Retirees to Apply: Desired Organizational Characteristics of Bridge Employment." *Journal of Organization Behavior* 26:649–60.

Rix, Sara E. 2016. "Working Late: Policy Relevance for Older Workers in the United States." *Australian Journal of Social Issues* 51(2):205–27.

Scholl, Julian C., et al. 2018. "Advancing Age-friendly Workplaces through the NIOSH National Center for Productive Aging." In *Handbook of Rehabilitation in Older Adults*, edited by Robert J. Gatchel et al. Cham, Switzerland: Springer Nature.

Siegenthaler, Jurg K. and Andrea M. Brenner. 2001. "Flexible Work Schedules, Older Workers, and Retirement." *Journal of Aging and Social Policy* 12(1):19–34.

Smeaton, Deborah and Jane Perry. 2018. "Becoming an Age-friendly Employer: Evidence Report." Centre for Ageing Better. Retrieved February 25, 2020 (https://www.researchgate.net/publication/327622550_Becoming_an_age-friendly_employer_Evidence_report).

Society for Human Resource Management. 2012. "Flexible Work Arrangements: A Compliance Checklist." Retrieved February 25, 2020 (https://www.shrm.org/ResourcesAndTools/hr-topics/benefits/Pages/Flex_Compliance.aspx).

Society for Human Resource Management. 2014. "Leveraging Workplace Flexibility for Engagement and Productivity." Retrieved February 25, 2020 (https://www.shrm.org/hr-today/trends-and-forecasting/special-reports-and-expert-views/Documents/Leveraging-Workplace-Flexibility.pdf).

Society for Human Resource Management. 2015. "Preparing for an Aging Workforce: Executive Summary." Retrieved February 25, 2020 (https://www.shrm.org/hr-today/trends-and-forecasting/research-and-surveys/Documents/14-0765%20Executive%20Briefing%20Aging%20Workforce%20v4.pdf).

Society for Human Resource Management. 2017. "Employee Benefits: Remaining Competitive in a Challenging Talent Market." Retrieved February 25, 2020 (https://www.shrm.org/hr-today/trends-and-forecasting/research-and surveys/Documents/2017%20Employee%20Benefits%20Report.pdf).

Sonnega, Amanda, et al. 2018. "A Comparison of Subjective and Objective Job Demands and Mismatch with Personal Resources as Predictors of Retirement Timing in a National U.S. Sample." *Work, Aging, and Retirement* 4(1):37–51.

Sweet, Stephen, Marcie Pitt-Catsouphes, and Jacquelyn B. James. 2016. "Successes in Changing Flexible Work Arrangement Use: Managers and Work-unit Variation in a Financial Services Organization." *Work and Organizations* 43(1):75–109.

Sweet, Stephen, Marcie Pitt-Catsouphes, and Jaquelyn B. James. 2017. "Manager Attitudes Concerning Flexible Work Arrangements: Fixed or Changeable?" *Community, Work and Family* 20(1):50–71.

Taylor, Philip. 2019. "Working Longer May Be Good Public Policy, but It Is Not Necessarily Good for Older People." *Journal of Aging and Social Policy* 31(2):99–105.

Taylor, Philip, Louise Rolland, and Jing Zhou. 2017. "Retaining Australian Older Workers: A Literature Review." CSIRO-Monash Working Paper No. 2017-01.

Truxillo, Donald M., David M. Cadiz, and Leslie B. Hammer. 2015. "Supporting the Aging Workforce: A Review and Recommendations for Workplace Intervention Research." *Annual Review of Organizational Psychology and Organizational Behavior* 2(1):351–81.

UN Department of Economic and Social Affairs, Population Division. 2017. "World Population Ageing 2017—Highlights." Retrieved February 25, 2020 (https://www.un.org/en/development/desa/population/publications/pdf/ageing/WPA2017_Highlights.pdf).

U.S. Senate, Special Committee on Aging. 2017. "America's Aging Workforce: Opportunities and Challenges." Retrieved February 25, 2020 (https://www.aging.senate.gov/imo/media/doc/Aging%20Workforce%20Report%20FINAL.pdf).

Vickerstaff Sarah A. and Elaine Alden. 2015. "Negotiating Flexibility: Formality and Informality in the Management and Retention of Older Employees." *The Gerontologist* 55(S2):759.

Zacher, Hannes, Dorien T. A. M. Kooij, and Margaret E. Beier. 2018. "Active Aging at Work: Contributing Factors and Implications for Organizations." *Organizational Dynamics* 47:37–45.

CHAPTER 12

# Tackling Ageism in the Workplace

Hannah J. Swift, Ben Steeden, and Georgina Randsley de Moura

## AGEISM DIRECTED TOWARD AND EXPERIENCED BY OLDER WORKERS

Many countries have encouraged policies to promote the labor market participation of older workers, who tend to be defined as those aged fifty and over.[1] Yet despite the existence of equality legislation that outlaws age discrimination in employment, ageism continues to be a core issue in the recruitment and retention of older workers. (See also chapter 3 and elsewhere in this volume.) Ageism is defined as the stereotyping of and discrimination against individuals or a group of individuals because of their age.[2] It can limit opportunities afforded to workers; influence interactions within the workplace; and result in avoidance, exclusion, or early exit from the labor market.[3,4] However, workers can also be affected by *self*-ageism, which is the application of negative age stereotypes to the self that can result in modified behavior, expectations, and performance-based outcomes.[5]

Although many employers consider their older workers to be a valuable asset and attribute to them many positive characteristics, including reliability, loyalty, and institutional memory,[6] these are often outweighed by negative stereotypes about older workers that underpin ageism in the workplace. Common perceptions in Western cultures are that older workers do not perform as well; are less productive, creative, and innovative; have lower motivation; are more resistant to change; are less able to learn; have a shorter job tenure; and are more costly compared to younger workers.[7,8,9] However, the prevalence of these stereotypes varies. For instance, they are more salient in industries with strong age norms, such as retail and advertising industries, where workforces are traditionally young, and in smaller companies rather than larger companies.[10]

These assumptions, which are largely unfounded by evidence, underpin discrimination and age bias against older workers because the strengths and abilities of older workers are overlooked, while more value is placed on positive traits and characteristics associated with younger workers.[11,12,13] For instance, evidence suggests that older workers tend to be judged less favorably compared with younger counterparts.[14,15] In contrast, younger workers benefit from assumptions that they are good at learning new skills and being creative, are better at using technology and social media, and are open to new ideas.[16] Abrams et al. demonstrated that two equally positive skill sets, one associated with younger people (good at learning new skills, being creative, using technology, making rapid decisions, being open to new ideas, using social media) and one associated with older people (good at settling arguments, understanding others' viewpoints, dealing with people politely, problem solving, being an effective complainer, using a library), can influence hiring preferences.[17] In three studies, participants of mixed ages were presented with profiles of two potential candidates. The candidates had similar qualifications, and neither had previous experience in the job. However, candidate A was presented as possessing the positive "old" traits while candidate B was presented with the positive "young" traits. In all studies, participants more often selected candidate B as a potential job candidate and estimated the age of this individual to be younger than candidate A, thereby demonstrating that age stereotypes or characteristics associated with older and younger people can influence hiring decisions, to the detriment of workers perceived to be older.

The final study revealed that the older-sounding profile was only preferred (equally to the younger-sounding profile) when the job position was presented as a subordinate role, whereas the younger-sounding profile was preferred when the role was presented as a supervisory or managerial position. The decision to hire the older-sounding profile for the subordinate role was mediated by the relative importance of the older attributes for the job and the relative favorability toward older traits. This supports the notion of pro-youth bias, even for leadership positions.

Some research suggests that this could be due to the preference for leadership potential in candidates, which has been associated with younger, but not older workers. For instance, Sun et al. found that when evaluators assessed candidates for a leadership role, they preferred candidates emphasizing the potential to be a good leader (leadership potential) over those with proven leadership performance.[18] In addition, they found that leadership potential candidates were perceived to be younger than those emphasizing leadership performance. Mediation analyses revealed that a preference for leadership potential was partly explained by a pro-youth bias, with participants preferring the leadership potential target partly because they were perceived to be younger. However, the idea that younger candidates might have an advantage when applying for leadership positions because they are perceived to have greater "potential" has not been replicated in the U.S., as Tormala et al. found no difference in the perceived age of leadership potential and leadership performance targets.[19] Sun et al. suggests that the contrast could be explained by a cultural difference in stereotypes of older and younger workers, their results reflecting Chinese cultural beliefs that potential is the property of youth,[20] whereas results from Tormala et al. reflected U.S. cultural beliefs that anyone can have potential.[21]

Conversely, research conducted by Hirschfeld and Thomas using archival data from 972 U.S. military officers found that older targets were perceived as having less observed leadership potential (OLP) than younger targets in evaluations from peers and observers.[22] Older candidates were also scored lower on tests of knowledge mastery, and this lack of mastery partly explained the relationship between age and perceived leadership potential. That is, candidate age was associated with less leadership potential partly due to lower perceived capability. Overall, the research suggests that a bias toward leadership potential is more likely to result in ageism toward older workers when there is lack of fit between stereotypes of older workers and the leadership role. Beyond suitability for leadership positions, assumptions made about decreasing potential and ability to learn with age also underpin other discriminatory practices within the workplace, such as lack of training opportunities.[23] (See also chapters 15 and 18.)

Perceived ageism, including lack of development opportunities to support and enhance career progression, can also provoke exit from an organization or the labor market altogether. For example, Thorsen et al. examined the association between ageism (defined as perceived fit, or lack of, and space for older workers within the organization) and older workers' retirement plans, while taking health and workability of the employee into account. Their study, which analyzed a representative sample of more than three thousand Danish employees, revealed that ageism, as well as lack of recognition, and lack of career development opportunities were associated with older male workers' plans to retire earlier.[24]

At the interpersonal level, ageism in the workplace can be expressed in the ways we talk to one another and how we communicate; for instance, it can take the form of under- or overaccommodation, and miscommunication.[25] It can include ageist discourse, such as jokes or teasing, expressing ageist attitudes (about the traits and characteristics of older workers, or about expectations and norms, e.g., people should retire when they reach a certain age), or communicating in an overly patronizing tone. Stereotypes regarding older workers underpin ageist discourse in the workplace. For instance, negative stereotypes regarding physical appearance or physical ability and health changes that are associated with aging are often the basis of hostile humor.[26] Stereotypes regarding older adults' cognitive abilities can also lead to inappropriate communication in intergenerational interactions, such as overaccommodation and infantilizing or dehumanizing speech.[27] Although much of this research is centered on speech within health and social care domains (e.g., care homes, hospitals, between caregivers and patients), it is also applicable to the workplace. The stereotype content model and the subsequent Behaviors from Intergroup Affect and Stereotypes (BIAS) map outline stereotypes denoting older adults as less competent but more warm and friendly than younger people. These result in feelings of pity and paternalistic prejudice, which in turn lead to behaviors, including overhelping or patronizing tones (known as active facilitation), or ignoring and avoidance behaviors (known as passive harm).[28,29]

Ageist language can also be present in third-party speech (e.g., comments about colleagues) and in attributions people make to age. Studies have shown that people erroneously use perceived age of people to inform evaluations of their performance. (See also chapter 13.) For instance, identical errors in memory and communication made by younger and older workers were perceived differently according to the age of the target.

Specifically, errors made by younger workers (aged thirty years) were perceived to be associated with "lack of effort," but with "lack of ability" when the worker was older (aged seventy years).[30,31] More recent research shows that older employees received more severe reprimands for poor performance than did their younger counterparts.[32]

Similar to other forms of prejudice and discrimination, the experience of ageism in the workplace has serious consequences, including reduced well-being, job satisfaction,[33,34] organizational commitment, and work engagement, and increased intentions to resign and retire,[35,36] but not all findings are consistent. In a sample of police officers from the UK, perceived age discrimination at work was associated with lower job satisfaction and commitment.[37] In a sample of eight hundred workers across the U.S., perceived age discrimination was associated with lower job satisfaction, but not job engagement or commitment.[38] (See also chapter 14.) In a study of Australian employees, aged forty-five years and over from three different organizations, perceived age discrimination was found to be negatively related to work engagement, while work engagement was associated with increased retirement age (i.e., intention to work longer). The authors suggest that experiences of ageism in the workplace lead to disengagement, which in turn increases intentions to exit or retire.[39]

Therefore, the research suggests that negative stereotypes regarding the perceived competence of older workers, their perceived potential, a lack of perceived "fit" with the organization, and a lack of respect and appreciation of older workers, are all important factors that reduce well-being and job satisfaction and lead to exclusion of older workers. The research reviewed here has shown that ageism on the grounds of perceived old age can manifest at the point of hiring and in the unequal provision of training opportunities, but also in the evaluation of older workers. Much of the research demonstrating age bias in the workplace shows how older adults are disadvantaged, evaluated, or treated differently in comparison with younger workers or younger targets.

## SELF-AGEISM IN THE WORKPLACE: SOCIAL PSYCHOLOGICAL APPROACHES TO TACKLING AGEISM IN THE WORKPLACE

It is clear that ageism on the grounds of perceived old age can take many forms, and much of the research reviewed thus far focuses on experiences of ageism in the workplace, or the ways in which age biases can lead to the differential treatment of older workers. However, being a target of age discrimination is only one way age stereotypes can have an impact in the workplace. The risks of ageism model draws upon the stereotype threat and stereotype embodiment literature to outline two other pathways through which negative age stereotypes can impact us all as we age (not just those perceived to belonging to the *old* age group).[40]

Stereotype threat is the fear of confirming a negative stereotype and involves fear of being judged negatively by others.[41] Age-based stereotype threat (ABST) transpires when age is the salient identity under threat due to corresponding negative age stereotypes. A recent review and meta-analysis has shown that under ABST, age stereotypes denoting older people as less competent than younger people have a detrimental impact on older adults' memory and cognitive performance, which in turn contributes to the self-fulfilling nature of age stereotypes.[42] For example, Abrams, Eller, and Bryant found that participants performed worse on cognitive tests when they were told that the purpose of the study was to explore age differences in memory, compared to being told the purpose was to explore individual differences.[43] Other research has shown that older participants performed worse on memory tests when task instructions mentioned memory compared to not mentioning memory,[44] or when an age-social comparison is made salient (e.g., participants told that performance on the test will be compared to younger participants taking part) versus no comparison.[45]

This suggests that contexts that evoke stereotype threat, such as training and test performance situations within the workplace, have the potential to put workers at risk of experiencing stereotype threat if the performance indicator is synonymous with a negative age stereotype.[46] Moreover, the wider stereotype threat literature suggests it can result in heightened anxiety,[47,48] disidentification and disengagement from stereotyped tasks or domains,[49] and reduced self-esteem and self-efficacy.[50] In practice, this means that workers may self-select and avoid engaging in tasks such as training where their performance may be judged negatively in terms of their perceived old age. This is a critical issue because training plays an important role in extending working lives; yet, there is a sharp decrease in participation in training once workers reach their mid-fifties.[51] (See also chapters 15, 17, and 18.)

One study by von Hippel, Kalokerinos, and Henry provides some evidence that stereotype threat experienced in the workplace is associated with lower job satisfaction and organizational commitment and increased intentions to resign.[52] Surveying 602 employees aged fifty to seventy-five years (mean age fifty-six) from a large Australian media company and 473 employees aged fifty to seventy-one years (mean age fifty-five) working in law enforcement, they measured the employees' experiences of stereotype threat, their attitudes toward their job, their work-related mental health, and their intentions to resign and retire. The study revealed that feelings of stereotype threat were associated with lower job satisfaction and organizational commitment, and increased work mental health issues and intentions to resign and retire. More recently, von Hippel and colleagues have demonstrated that age-based stereotype threat effects are experienced by both younger and older employees, but that older employees are more vulnerable to negative impacts on work outcomes, such as lower job satisfaction, commitment, well-being, and higher intentions to quit. This is because the older employees are less likely to appraise the stereotype threat as a challenge, and more likely to think over and ruminate when they experience stereotype threat.[53]

Stereotype threat has been shown to lead to underperformance in stereotyped domains that are relevant to workplace engagement and performance-based outcomes.[54] However, in addition to stereotype threat, the extent to which workers feel they fit within an organization can be informed by age stereotypes, prescriptive norms, self-perceptions, organizational identity, and the perceived age diversity within the organization.[55,56] That is, there is sometimes a perception that certain jobs should be held by employees of a certain age. Research suggests that when there is lack of perceived fit (e.g., when the perceived "correct" age of a person holding or applying for a particular job does not match the candidate's or existing worker's age) or lack of identity integration (when individuals perceive their age and the organizational age as incompatible), age stereotypes are more salient and more likely to influence individual decisions (e.g., when to retire, whether to apply for a job), influence organizational decision-making processes (e.g., hiring and firing), and make people more vulnerable to age-based stereotype threat.[57] A review of workplace stereotypes suggests that those favoring younger workers are particularly prevalent in certain industries, which are also considered to be "young" or have disproportionate number of younger workers, such as finance, insurance, advertising, retail, and information technology / computing.[58] In these industries, workers may consider themselves "too old" to apply for job positions or find themselves pushed out of the job earlier than they expected. It also could mean that workers in industries where age is a salient factor are more likely to experience threats to their identity if they are perceived as "too old," as posited by stereotype threat theory.[59]

Prescriptive norms describe ways and expectations surrounding how one should or should not behave. In the workplace, common phrases ("Should you be doing that at your age?" "Shouldn't you retire at your age?") indicate people's expectations of others based on age. Social psychological theory suggests that prescriptive stereotypes typically involve one group disproportionately targeting another, so as to foster some degree of social control or dominance and to maintain hierarchy.[60] In Western societies, middle-agers are perceived as holding highest social status followed by younger and then older people.[61,62] Therefore, older people adhering to prescriptive age norms can be seen as benefiting younger and middle-aged groups by maintaining social structures and hierarchies.

Relevant to the workplace and connected to descriptive stereotypes of older workers' decline in cognitive ability, younger and middle-aged workers are likely to perceive older workers' delayed retirement as limiting their own opportunities to enter the workplace or to progress in their careers. There is a common notion that there should be a natural transition or succession of resources and positions from older people to those who are younger. In one study, participants (who ranged in age) were asked to evaluate the competence and warmth of younger, middle-aged, and older targets who either violated the norm of succession or adhered to it. The study found that younger participants most often disrespected the older succession violator, and were more respectful of the older target who adhered to succession norms.[63] Similar results were found for evaluations of targets who violated other prescriptive age norms, such as older adults disproportionally consuming resources (consumption) or behaving or dressing in ways that are conventionally youth related (identity).[64] This research suggests that awareness of prescriptive stereotypes in the workplace could guide an individual's decisions about when to retire or exit the labor market in order to avoid a backlash from violating prescriptive norms.

In summary, the research suggests that awareness of negative age stereotypes regarding older workers can not only influence performance and job-based outcomes via stereotype threat processes but also the decisions people make about what jobs or roles are suitable depending on their age, and finally decisions about when to leave the labor market in order to adhere to prescriptive norms. These latter processes are examined less often since the focus of research tends to be on older workers who are the target of discrimination, but they are nevertheless important because they reflect the power of age stereotypes to influence behavior by their application to the self.[65,66]

There should be wider recognition that ageism is a barrier to policies that aim to extend working lives, as well as greater awareness of the consequences of exposure to stereotype threat in employment contexts, and also of how self-directed ageism can disadvantage workers as they age. In response to these challenges, employers could focus on monitoring and increasing age diversity in the workplace, both in recruitment and when providing opportunities for training, and on reducing age segregation. Supporting and promoting workplace intergenerational contact can help to reduce age separation, break down age stereotypes held by younger employees,[67] and help to reduce age-based stereotype threat effects via the reduction of anxiety and in-group bias.[68,69] Increasing older adults' access to and participation in educational opportunities and promoting lifelong learning strategies could also serve to reduce age segregation and change outdated stereotypes regarding declining ability to learn with age.

The evidence reviewed suggests that recruitment and selection are vulnerable to unconscious bias favoring younger over older workers.[70,71] In order to address and mitigate various types of bias in employment decisions, organizations increasingly offer training that aims to make unconscious bias conscious, focusing on characteristics such as gender, race, and age and encouraging fair treatment of stigmatized groups and equality in the workplace.[72,73] The training typically consists of an unconscious bias test and debrief of the results, education about the theories of prejudice and impact of unconscious bias, and techniques to mitigate its impact.

However, evidence regarding the impact of unconscious bias training on age bias in the workplace is limited. A recent review by Atewologun and colleagues of the effectiveness of unconscious bias training identified only two interventions focused on age bias. These interventions were linked with reduced implicit age bias, but there was no evidence that they raised awareness of such bias or led to behavioral change. Furthermore, unconscious bias training may lead to backfiring effects, whereby exposure to unconscious bias and stereotypes may encourage perceptions that they cannot be changed, serving to entrench the very biases the training seeks to overturn.[74] Further research is needed to assess whether unconscious bias training has any long-term effects in mitigating age bias in recruitment and selection, and whether its potential backfiring effects are outweighed by its benefits.

In line with the World Health Organization's focus on promoting age-friendly communities,[75] the creation of age-friendly workplaces has also been encouraged as a route to greater age equality on the job.[76,77] An age-friendly workplace has a work environment that explicitly addresses the physical and psychological safety of workers of all ages, especially older workers, aiming to create an inclusive workplace culture that values age diversity.[78,79,80] (See also chapters 7–11.) Although policies relating to fair treatment based on age are an integral part of this, they are not enough on their own to create an age-friendly workplace.[81] Organizational culture and workplace practices have been highlighted as essential levers in driving a workplace environment in which workers of all ages can excel and be valued.[82,83]

A recent review by Eppler-Hattab et al. aimed to better define age-friendly workplaces, highlighting aspects of organizational culture (the shared values and beliefs within an organization) and organizational climate (employees' experience of the policies and practices that are supported and encouraged).[84] Their model of an age-friendly workplace is grounded in a workplace culture that promotes fairness, equality, and respect for older workers through initiatives such as training and opportunities for positive intergenerational contact. Within this culture, policies and practices that promote lifelong learning, sustain employee well-being and skill development, adapt job roles to improve performance, and offer flexible working patterns that support work-life balance encourage an organizational climate in which workers of all ages are valued and evaluated on their skills and abilities rather than age-based assumptions.[85,86]

Although based on a review of the existing research literature, the Eppler-Hattab et al. model also reflects current industry best practice, as set out in guidelines from the Tripartite Alliance for Fair and Progressive Employment Practices that similarly promote practices such as job design, flexible working, and training and development as foundations for creating age-friendly workplaces.[87] Together, empirical research and industry best practice suggest that a range of interventions targeted at workplace culture and practice can create age-friendly conditions and reduce ageism in the workplace.[88,89] In this chapter, we also advocate that these interventions should not only focus on stereotypes applied to others to reduce discriminatory practices, but should also encompass greater awareness of self-ageism and how people apply stereotypes to themselves, which is not currently addressed by unconscious bias training.

A final, perhaps less well-known intervention is the use of mindfulness-based meditation practices for reducing bias and heuristic processing that rely erroneously on stereotypes. Mindfulness is a particular mode of conscious processing[90] defined by Brown and Ryan as "the state of being attentive to and aware of what is taking place in the present."[91] As a result, mindfulness involves a greater receptivity to internal and external stimuli as they occur. The evidence suggests that people in a higher state of mindfulness would be more aware and receptive to what affects themselves and others, and therefore less likely to display bias.[92]

Research has begun to understand the consequences of mindful-based practices on a range of organizational outcomes, including task performance and turnover intentions,[93,94] workplace well-being, and job satisfaction,[95] yet relatively little research has explored its potential to reduce biasing effects of age stereotypes, despite promising evidence.[96] For instance, Chen et al. investigated whether making people more mindful by increasing self-awareness reduced age bias. Sitting in front of a computer, participants read eight social judgments about a specific character. While doing this task, participants in the high self-awareness condition were able to see their own image in the computer screen, whereas participants in the low self-awareness condition saw images of a stranger. After reading the eight social judgments, half of the participants were then asked to read about a younger person and the other half about an older person. In each condition, participants were requested to make eight judgments about the last character they had been introduced to. Results showed that exposing people to age-related information was enough to activate age stereotypes and influence people's social judgment. However, the self-awareness manipulation, which was introduced to make people more mindful of the situation, dampened this effect. People who were in a high self-awareness condition were more sensitive to age information and also more aware of social norms against ageism, and therefore made fewer ageist judgments.[97]

Although these researchers did not directly use mindfulness as part of their manipulation, the literature suggests that increased self-awareness is the mechanism through which mindfulness should produce these effects.[98] However, Lueke and Gibson have shown that a ten-minute mindfulness meditation reduced implicit bias on the bases of race and age (measured using the implicit association test, IAT) of U.S. white college students compared to participants listening to a control audio describing historical events.[99] The mindfulness meditation is thought to limit the reliance on past associations in memory, reduce automatic processing, and increase focus on being nonjudgmental and open to thoughts and experiences in the present.[100] This is in line with the wider literature on bias reduction. Bargh suggests that the only way to control the effect of automatic bias on behavior and cognition is by becoming aware of such biases, that is, by bringing the unconscious into consciousness.[101] However, we have yet to see the impact of such an intervention tested and rolled out in organizational settings.

Overall this chapter outlines the ways in which ageism on the grounds of perceived old age can manifest in work and organizational settings. The majority of the research thus far tends to focus on age bias against older workers at the point of hiring, in the provision of learning, training and development opportunities, and ageism as a factor that pushes people out of the workplace and informs decisions to retire. However, negative age stereotypes regarding competence and ability to learn, but also prescriptive expectations about when people should retire, can also be applied by individuals to themselves with self-limiting consequences. The implications of this self-ageism are less widely researched, yet they serve as a reminder to look beyond ageism as a form of prejudice that harms older workers because they are targets of others' negative attitudes. Despite some promising interventions to tackle ageism by encouraging age-friendly workplace practices, including unconscious bias training, there is little exploration or evaluation of these in practice.

## NOTES

1. Roland Sigg and Valentina De-Luigi. 2007. "The Success of Policies Aimed at Extending Working Life." Pp. 55–58 in *Developments and Trends: Supporting Dynamic Social Security*. Geneva, Switzerland: International Social Security Association.
2. Dominic Abrams. 2010. "Processes of Prejudice: Theory, Evidence and Intervention." *Research Report* 56. London: EHRC.
3. Robert McCann and Howard Giles. 2002. "Ageism in the Workplace: A Communication Perspective." In *Ageism: Stereotyping and Prejudice Against Older Persons*, edited by Todd D. Nelson. Cambridge, MA: MIT Press.
4. Sannie Thorsen et al. 2012. "The Association between Psychosocial Work Environment, Attitudes towards Older Workers (Ageism) and Planned Retirement." *International Archives of Occupational and Environmental Health* 85(4):437–45. (https://doi.org/10.1007/s00420-011-0689-5).
5. Hannah J. Swift et al. 2017. "The Risks of Ageism Model: How Ageism and Negative Attitudes toward Age Can Be a Barrier to Active Aging." *Social Issues and Policy Review* 11(1):195–231. (https://doi.org/10.1111/sipr.12031).

6. Richard A. Posthuma and Michael A. Campion. 2009. "Age Stereotypes in the Workplace: Common Stereotypes, Moderators, and Future Research Directions." *Journal of Management* 35(1):158–88. (https://doi.org/10.1177/0149206308318617).

7. Paola Dordoni and Piergiorgio Argentero. 2015. "When Age Stereotypes Are Employment Barriers: A Conceptual Analysis and a Literature Review on Older Workers Stereotypes." *Ageing International* 40(4):393–412. (https://doi.org/10.1007/s12126-015-9222-6).

8. Sarah Harper et al. 2006. "Attitudes and Practices of Employers towards Ageing Workers: Evidence from a Global Survey on the Future of Retirement." *Ageing Horizons* 5:31–41.

9. Thomas W. H. Ng and Daniel C. Feldman. 2012. "Evaluating Six Common Stereotypes about Older Workers with Meta-analytical Data." *Personnel Psychology* 65:821–58. (https://doi.org/10.1111/peps.12003).

10. Posthuma and Campion, "Age Stereotypes in the Workplace."

11. Harper et al., "Attitudes and Practices of Employers."

12. Posthuma and Campion, "Age Stereotypes in the Workplace."

13. Ng and Feldman, "Evaluating Six Common Stereotypes."

14. Marc Bendick Jr., Charles W. Jackson, and J. Horacio Romero. 1996. "Employment Discrimination against Older Workers: An Experimental Study of Hiring Practices." *Journal of Aging and Social Policy* 8:25–46. (https://doi.org/10.1300/J031v08n04_03).

15. Lynn M. Shore, Jeanette N. Cleveland, and Caren B. Goldberg. 2003. "Work Attitudes and Decisions as a Function of Manager Age and Employee Age." *Journal of Applied Psychology* 88(3):529–37. (https://doi.org/10.1037/0021-9010.88.3.529).

16. Dominic Abrams, Hannah J. Swift, and Lisbeth Drury. 2016. "Old and Unemployable? How Age-based Stereotypes Affect Willingness to Hire Job Candidates." *Journal of Social Issues* 72:105–21. (https://doi.org/10.1111/josi.12158).

17. Abrams, Swift, and Drury, "Old and Unemployable?"

18. Xiaomin Sun et al. 2015. "A Cross-cultural Perspective on the Preference for Potential Effect: An Individual Participant Data (IPD) Meta-analysis Approach." *PLoS One* 10(3). (https://doi.org/10.1371/journal.pone.0124170).

19. Zakary L. Tormala, Jayson S. Jia, and Michael I. Norton. 2012. "The Preference for Potential." *Journal of Personality and Social Psychology* 103(4):567–83. (https://doi.org/10.1037/a0029227).

20. Sun et al., "Cross-cultural Perspective."

21. Tormala, Jia, and Norton, "Preference for Potential."

22. Robert R. Hirschfeld and Christopher H. Thomas. 2011. "Age- and Gender-based Role Incongruence: Implications for Knowledge Mastery and Observed Leadership Potential among Personnel in a Leadership Development Program." *Personnel Psychology* 64:661–92.

23. Harper et al., "Attitudes and Practices of Employers."

24. Thorsen et al., "Association between Psychosocial Work Environment."

25. McCann and Giles, "Ageism in the Workplace."

26. Patricia Andrew. 2012. "'Laughter Is the Best Medicine': The Construction of Old Age in Ageist Humor." Pp. 11–24 in *Language and Humour in the Media*, edited by Jan Chovanec and Isabel Ermida. Newcastle upon Tyne, England: Cambridge Scholars.

27. McCann and Giles, "Ageism in the Workplace."

28. Susan T. Fiske, et al. 2002. "A Model of (Often Mixed) Stereotype Content: Competence and Warmth Respectively Follow from Perceived Status and Competition." *Journal of Personality and Social Psychology* 82(6):878–902. (https://doi.org/10.1037/0022-3514.82.6.878).

29. Amy J. C. Cuddy, Susan T. Fiske, and Peter Glick. 2007. "The BIAS Map: Behaviors from Intergroup Affect and Stereotypes." *Journal of Personality and Social Psychology* 92(4):631–48. (https://doi.org/10.1037/0022-3514.92.4.631).

30. Joan T. Erber. 1989. "Young and Older Adults' Appraisal of Memory Failures in Young and Older Adult Target Persons." *Journal of Gerontology* 44(6):170–75. (https://doi.org/10.1093/geronj/44.6.P170).

31. Joan T. Erber and Sharon T. Rothberg. 1991. "Here's Looking at You: The Relative Effect of Age and Attractiveness on Judgments about Memory Failure." *Journal of Gerontology* 46(3):116–23. (https://doi.org/10.1093/geronj/46.3.P116).

32. Deborah E. Rupp, Stephen J. Vodanovich, and Marcus Crede. 2006. "Age Bias in the Workplace: The Impact of Ageism and Causal Attributions." *Journal of Applied Social Psychology* 36(6):1337–64.

33. Philip Taylor et al. 2013. "Everyday Discrimination in the Workplace, Job Satisfaction and Psychological Well-being: Age differences and Moderating Variables." *Ageing & Society* 33(7):1105–38.

34. Jamie L. Macdonald and Sheri R. Levy. 2016. "Ageism in the Workplace: The Role of Psychosocial Factors in Predicting Job Satisfaction, Commitment, and Engagement." *Journal of Social Issues* 72(1):169–90. (https://doi.org/https://doi.org/10.1111/josi.12161).

35. Piers H. Bayl-Smith and Barbara Griffin. 2014. "Age Discrimination in the Workplace: Identifying as a Late-career Worker and Its Relationship with Engagement and Intended Retirement Age." *Journal of Applied Social Psychology* 44(9):588–99. (https://doi.org/10.1111/jasp.12251).

36. Ed Snape and Tom Redman. 2003. "Too Old or Too Young? The Impact of Perceived Age Discrimination." *Human Resource Management Journal* 13(1):78–89. (https://doi.org/10.1111/j.1748-8583.2003.tb00085.x).

37. Tom Redman and Ed Snape. 2006. "The Consequences of Perceived Age Discrimination amongst Older Police Officers: Is Social Support a Buffer?" *British Journal of Management* 17(2):167–75. (https://doi.org/10.1111/j.1467-8551.2006.00492.x).

38. Macdonald and Levy, "Ageism in the Workplace."

39. Bayl-Smith and Griffin, "Age Discrimination in the Workplace."

40. Swift et al., "Risks of Ageism Model."

41. Claude M. Steele. 1997. "A Threat in the Air: How Stereotypes Shape Intellectual Identity and Performance." *American Psychologist* 52(6):613. (https://doi.org/10.1037/0003-066X.52.6.613).

42. Ruth A. Lamont, Hannah J. Swift, and Dominic Abrams. 2015. "A Review and Meta-analysis of Age-based Stereotype Threat: Negative Stereotypes, Not Facts, Do the Damage." *Psychology and Aging* 30:180–93. (https://doi.org/10.1037/a0038586).

43. Dominic Abrams, Anja Eller, and Jacqueline Bryant. 2006. "An Age Apart: The Effects of Intergenerational Contact and Stereotype Threat on Performance and Intergroup Bias." *Psychology and Aging* 23:691–702. (https://doi.org/10.1037/0882-7974.21.4.691).

44. Tamara A. Rahhal, Lynn Hasher, and Stanley J. Colcombe. 2001. "Instructional Manipulations and Age Differences in Memory: Now You See Them, Now You Don't." *Psychology and Aging* 16(4):697. (https://doi.org/10.1037//0882-7974.16.4.697).

45. Hannah J. Swift, Ruth A. Lamont, and Dominic Abrams. 2012. "Are They Half as Strong as They Used to Be? An Experiment Testing Whether Age-related Social Comparisons Impair Older People's Hand Grip Strength and Persistence." *BMJ Open*. (https://doi.org/10.1136/bmjopen-2012-001064).

46. Swift et al., "Risks of Ageism Model."

47. Hannah J. Swift, Dominic Abrams, and Sibila Marques. 2013. "Threat or Boost: Social Comparison Affects Older People's Performance Differently Depending on Task Domain." *Journals of Gerontology, Series B* 68:23–30. (https://doi.org/10.1093/geronb/gbs044).

48. Abrams, Eller, and Bryant, "An Age Apart."

49. Anna Woodcock et al. 2012. "The Consequences of Chronic Stereotype Threat: Domain Dis-identification and Abandonment." *Journal of Personality and Social Psychology* 103(4):635. (https://doi.org/10.1037%2Fa0029120).

50. Charlotte R. Pennington et al. 2016. "Twenty Years of Stereotype Threat Research: A Review of Psychological Mediators." *PLoS One* 11(1):e0146487. (https://doi.org/10.1371%2Fjournal.pone.0146487).

51. Sarah Vickerstaff, Wendy Loretto, and Philip J. White. 2007. "The Future for Older Workers: Opportunities and Constraints." Pp. 203–26 in *The Future for Older Workers: New Perspectives*, edited by Wendy Loretto, Sarah Vickerstaff, and Philip J. White. Bristol, UK: Policy Press.

52. Courtney von Hippel, Elise K. Kalokerinos, and Julie D. Henry. 2013. "Stereotype Threat among Older Employees: Relationship with Job Attitudes and Turnover Intentions." *Psychology and Aging* 28:17–27. (https://doi.org/10.1037/a0029825).

53. Courtney von Hippel, et al. 2018. "Age-based Stereotype Threat and Work Outcomes: Stress Appraisals and Rumination as Mediators." *Psychology and Aging*:68–84.

54. Elise K. Kalokerinos, Courtney von Hippel, and Hannes Zacher. 2014. "Is Stereotype Threat a Useful Construct for Organizational Psychology Research and Practice?" *Industrial and Organizational Psychology* 7:381–402. (https://doi.org/10.1111/iops.12167).

55. Posthuma and Campion, "Age Stereotypes in the Workplace."

56. Michael S. North and Susan T. Fiske. 2016. "Resource Scarcity and Prescriptive Attitudes Generate Subtle, Intergenerational Older-worker Exclusion." *Journal of Social Issues*, 72(1):122–45. (https://doi.org/10.1111/josi.12159).

57. Claudia Manzi et al. 2019. "Age-based Stereotype Threat and Negative Outcomes in the Workplace: Exploring the Role of Identity Integration." *European Journal of Social Psychology* 49(4):705–16.

58. Posthuma and Campion, "Age Stereotypes in the Workplace."

59. Manzi et al., "Age-based Stereotype Threat."

60. Michael S. North and Susan T. Fiske. 2013. "Act Your (Old) Age: Prescriptive, Ageist Biases over Succession, Consumption, and Identity." *Personality and Social Psychology Bulletin* 39(6):720–34. (https://doi.org/10.1177/0146167213480043).

61. Dominic Abrams et al. 2011. "Ageism in Europe: Findings from the European Social Survey." London: EURAGE/Age UK.

62. Teri A. Garstka et al. 2004. "How Young and Older Adults Differ in Their Responses to Perceived Age Discrimination." *Psychology and Aging* 19:326–35. (https://doi.org/10.1037/0882-7974.19.2.326).

63. North and Fiske, "Act Your (Old) Age."

64. North and Fiske, "Act Your (Old) Age."

65. Becca Levy. 2009. "Stereotype Embodiment." *Current Directions in Psychological Science* 18:332–36.

66. Swift et al., "Risks of Ageism Model."

67. Lisbeth Drury, Dominic Abrams, and Hannah J. Swift. 2016. "Evidence Review: Making Intergenerational Connections: What Are They, Why Do They Matter and How to Make More of Them." London: Age UK.

68. Abrams, Eller, and Bryant, "An Age Apart."

69. Dominic Abrams et al. 2008. "Threat Inoculation: Experienced and Imagined Intergenerational Contact Prevents Stereotype Threat Effects on Older People's Math Performance." *Psychology and Aging* 23:934–39. (https://doi.org/10.1037/a0014293).

70. Franciska Krings, Sabine Sczesny, and Annette Kluge. 2010. "Stereotypical Inferences as Mediators of Age Discrimination: The Role of Competence and Warmth." *British Journal of Management*:1–15. (https://doi.org/10.1111/j.1467-8551.2010.00721.x).

71. Abrams, Swift, and Drury, "Old and Unemployable?"

72. Sue Williamson and Meraiah Foley. 2018. "Unconscious Bias Training: The 'Silver Bullet' for Gender Equity?" *Australian Journal of Public Administration,* 77(3):355–59. (https://doi.org/10.1111/1467-8500.12313).

73. Doyin Atewologun, Tinu Cornish, and Fatima Tresh. 2018. "Unconscious Bias Training: An Assessment of the Evidence for Effectiveness." Manchester, UK: Equality and Human Rights Commission.

74. Atewologun, Cornish, and Tresh, "Unconscious Bias Training."

75. World Health Organization. 2007. "Global Age-friendly Cities: A Guide." Geneva, Switzerland: World Health Organization. (https://www.who.int/ageing/age_friendly_cities_guide/en/).

76. Age UK. 2019. "What Does It Mean to Be an Age-friendly Workplace?" (https://www.ageuk.org.uk/information-advice/work-learning/what-does-it-mean-to-be-an-age-friendly-workplace/).

77. Patrick Thomson. 2018. "Becoming an Age-friendly Employer." London: Centre for Ageing Better. (https://www.ageing-better.org.uk/sites/default/files/2018-09/Becoming-age-friendly-employer.pdf).

78. Age UK, "What Does It Mean to Be an Age-friendly Workplace?"

79. Allan B. de Guzman et al. 2014. "A Structural Equation Modeling of the Factors Affecting an Age-friendly Workplace." *Educational Gerontology* 40(6):387–400. (https://doi.org/10.1080/03601277.2013.802194).

80. Thomson, "Becoming an Age-Friendly Employer."

81. Raphael Eppler-Hattab, Ilan Meshoulam, and Israel Doron. 2019. "Conceptualizing Age-friendliness in Workplaces: Proposing a New Multidimensional Model." *The Gerontologist* 184. (https://doi.org/10.1093/geront/gny184).

82. Eppler-Hattab, Meshoulam, and Doron, "Conceptualizing Age-friendliness in Workplaces."

83. Thomson, "Becoming an Age-friendly Employer."

84. Eppler-Hattab, Meshoulam, and Doron, "Conceptualizing Age-friendliness in Workplaces."

85. Age UK, "What Does It Mean to Be an Age-Friendly Employer?"

86. Thomson, "Becoming an Age-friendly Employer."

87. Tripartite Alliance for Fair and Progressive Employment Practices (TAFEP). 2019. "Creating an Age-friendly Workplace (Employers)." (https://www.tal.sg/tafep/employment-practices/age-management/creating-age-friendly-workplace 20/09/2019).

88. Eppler-Hattab, Meshoulam, and Doron, "Conceptualizing Age-friendliness in Workplaces."

89. TAFEP, "Creating an Age-friendly Workplace."

90. Christopher P. Niemiec et al. 2010. "Being Present in the Face of Existential Threat: The Role of Trait Mindfulness in Reducing Defensive Responses to Mortality Salience." *Journal of Personality and Social Psychology* 99(2):344–65. (https://doi.org/10.1037/a0019388).

91. Kirk Warren Brown and Richard M. Ryan. 2003. "The Benefits of Being Present: Mindfulness and Its Role in Psychological Well-being." *Journal of Personality and Social Psychology* 84(4):822–48. (https://doi.org/10.1037/0022-3514.84.4.82212703651).

92. Adam Lueke and Bryan Gibson. 2016. "Brief Mindfulness Meditation Reduces Discrimination." *Psychology of Consciousness: Theory, Research, and Practice* 3(1):34–44. (https://doi.org/10.1037/cns0000081).

93. Erik Dane and Bradley J. Brummel. 2014. "Examining Workplace Mindfulness and Its Relations to Job Performance and Turnover Intention." *Human Relations* 67(1):105–28. (https://doi.org/10.1177/0018726713487753).

94. Erik Dane. 2011. "Paying Attention to Mindfulness and Its Effects on Task Performance in the Workplace." *Journal of Management* 37(4):997–1018. (https://doi.org/10.1177/0149206310367948).

95. Mehlika Saraç. 2020. "A Literature Review on Mindfulness at Work Places: Conceptualization, Measurement, and Outcomes." Pp. 55–71 in *Handbook of Research on Positive Organizational Behavior for Improved Workplace Performance*, edited by Elif Baykal. Hershey, PA: IGI Global. Retrieved September 20, 2019 (https://doi.org/10.4018/978-1-7998-0058-3.ch004).

96. Adam Lueke and Bryan Gibson. 2015. "Mindfulness Meditation Reduces Implicit Age and Race Bias: The Role of Reduced Automaticity of Responding." *Social Psychological and Personality Science* 6(3):284–91. (https://doi.org/10.1177/1948550614559651).

97. Yiwei Chen, Olivia Pethtel, and Xiaodong Ma. 2010. "Counteracting Age Stereotypes: A Self-awareness Manipulation." *Educational Gerontology*, 36(8):702–17. (https://doi.org/10.1080/03601270903534523).

98. David R. Vago and David A. Silbersweig. 2012. "Self-awareness, Self-regulation, and Self-transcendence (S-ART): A Framework for Understanding the Neurobiological Mechanisms of Mindfulness." *Frontiers in Human Neuroscience* 6:296. (https://doi.org/10.3389%2Ffnhum.2012.00296).

99. Lueke and Gibson, "Mindfulness Meditation."

100. Vago and Silbersweig, "Self-awareness, Self-regulation, and Self-transcendence (S-ART)."

101. John A. Bargh. 1997. "The Automaticity of Everyday Life." In *The Automaticity of Everyday Life: Advances in Social Cognition*, edited by Robert S. Wyer. Mahwah, NJ: Erlbaum.

## REFERENCES

Abrams, Dominic. 2010. "Processes of Prejudice: Theory, Evidence and Intervention." *Research Report* 56. London: EHRC.

Abrams, Dominic, et al. 2008. "Threat Inoculation: Experienced and Imagined Intergenerational Contact Prevent Stereotype Threat Effects on Older People's Math Performance." *Psychology and Aging* 23:934–39. (https://doi.org/10.1037/a0014293).

Abrams, Dominic, et al. 2011. "Ageism in Europe: Findings from the European Social Survey." London: EURAGE/Age UK.

Abrams, Dominic, Anja Eller, and Jacqueline Bryant. 2006. "An Age Apart: The Effects of Intergenerational Contact and Stereotype Threat on Performance and Intergroup Bias." *Psychology and Aging* 23:691–702. (https://doi.org/10.1037/0882-7974.21.4.691).

Abrams, Dominic, Hannah Swift, and Lisbeth Drury. 2016. "Old and Unemployable? How Age-based Stereotypes Affect Willingness to Hire Job Candidates." *Journal of Social Issues* 72:105–21. (https://doi.org/10.1111/josi.12158).

Age UK. 2019. "What Does It Mean to Be an Age-friendly Workplace?" (https://www.ageuk.org.uk/information-advice/work-learning/what-does-it-mean-to-be-an-age-friendly-workplace/).

Andrew, Patricia. 2012. "'Laughter Is the Best Medicine': The Construction of Old Age in Ageist Humor." Pp. 11–24 in *Language and Humour in the Media*, edited by Jan Chovanec and Isabel Ermida. Newcastle upon Tyne, England: Cambridge Scholars.

Atewologun, Doyin, Tinu Cornish, and Fatima Tresh. 2018. "Unconscious Bias Training: An Assessment of the Evidence for Effectiveness." Manchester, UK: Equality and Human Rights Commission.

Bargh, John A. 1997. "The Automaticity of Everyday Life." In *The Automaticity of Everyday Life: Advances in Social Cognition*, edited by Robert S. Wyer. Mahwah, NJ: Erlbaum.

Bayl-Smith, Piers H. and Barbara Griffin. 2014. "Age Discrimination in the Workplace: Identifying as a Late-career Worker and Its Relationship with Engagement and Intended Retirement Age." *Journal of Applied Social Psychology* 44(9):588–99. (https://doi.org/10.1111/jasp.12251).

Bendick Jr., Marc, Charles W. Jackson, and J. Horacio Romero. 1996. "Employment Discrimination against Older Workers: An Experimental Study of Hiring Practices." *Journal of Aging and Social Policy* 8:25–46. (https://doi.org/10.1300/J031v08n04_03).

Brown, Kirk Warren and Richard M. Ryan. 2003. "The Benefits of Being Present: Mindfulness and Its Role in Psychological Well-being." *Journal of Personality and Social Psychology* 84(4):822–48. (https://doi.org/10.1037/0022-3514.84.4.82212703651).

Chen, Yiwei, Olivia Pethtel, and Xiaodong Ma. 2010. "Counteracting Age Stereotypes: A Self-awareness Manipulation." *Educational Gerontology* 36(8):702–17. (https://doi.org/10.1080/03601270903534523).

Cuddy, Amy J. C., Susan T. Fiske, and Peter Glick. 2007. "The BIAS Map: Behaviors from Intergroup Affect and Stereotypes." *Journal of Personality and Social Psychology* 92(4):631–48. (https://doi.org/10.1037/0022-3514.92.4.631).

Dane, Erik. 2011. "Paying Attention to Mindfulness and Its Effects on Task Performance in the Workplace." *Journal of Management* 37(4):997–1018. (https://doi.org/10.1177/0149206310367948).

Dane, Erik and Bradley J. Brummel. 2014. "Examining Workplace Mindfulness and Its Relations to Job Performance and Turnover Intention." *Human Relations* 67(1):105–28. (https://doi.org/10.1177/0018726713487753).

de Guzman, Allan B., et al. 2014. "A Structural Equation Modeling of the Factors Affecting an Age-friendly Workplace." *Educational Gerontology* 40(6):387–400. (https://doi.org/10.1080/03601277.2013.802194).

Dordoni, Paola and Piergiorgio Argentero. 2015. "When Age Stereotypes Are Employment Barriers: A Conceptual Analysis and a Literature Review on Older Workers Stereotypes." *Ageing International* 40(4):393–412. (https://doi.org/10.1007/s12126-015-9222-6).

Drury, Lisbeth, Dominic Abrams, and Hannah J. Swift. 2016. "Evidence Review: Making Intergenerational Connections: What Are They, Why Do They Matter and How to Make More of Them." London: Age UK.

Eppler-Hattab, Raphael, Ilan Meshoulam, and Israel Doron. 2019. "Conceptualizing Age-friendliness in Workplaces: Proposing a New Multidimensional Model." *The Gerontologist* 184. (https://doi.org/10.1093/geront/gny184).

Erber, Joan T. 1989. "Young and Older Adults' Appraisal of Memory Failures in Young and Older Adult Target Persons." *Journal of Gerontology* 44(6):170–75. (https://doi.org/10.1093/geronj/44.6.P170).

Erber, Joan T. and Sharon T. Rothberg. 1991. "Here's Looking at You: The Relative Effect of Age and Attractiveness on Judgments about Memory Failure." *Journal of Gerontology* 46(3):116–23. (https://doi.org/10.1093/geronj/46.3.P116).

Fiske, Susan T., et al. 2002. "A Model of (Often Mixed) Stereotype Content: Competence and Warmth Respectively Follow from Perceived Status and Competition." *Journal of Personality and Social Psychology* 82(6):878–902. (https://doi.org/10.1037/0022-3514.82.6.878).

Garstka, Teri A., et al. 2004. "How Young and Older Adults Differ in Their Responses to Perceived Age Discrimination." *Psychology and Aging* 19:326–35. (https://doi.org/10.1037/0882-7974.19.2.326).

Harper, Sarah, et al. 2006. "Attitudes and Practices of Employers towards Ageing Workers: Evidence from a Global Survey on the Future of Retirement." *Ageing Horizons* 5:31–41.

Hirschfeld, Robert R. and Christopher H. Thomas. 2011. "Age- and Gender-based Role Incongruence: Implications for Knowledge Mastery and Observed Leadership Potential among Personnel in a Leadership Development Program." *Personnel Psychology* 64:661–92.

Kalokerinos, Elise K., Courtney von Hippel, and Hannes Zacher. 2014. "Is Stereotype Threat a Useful Construct for Organizational Psychology Research and Practice?" *Industrial and Organizational Psychology* 7:381–402. (https://doi.org/10.1111/iops.12167).

Krings, Franciska, Sabine Sczesny, and Annette Kluge. 2010. "Stereotypical Inferences as Mediators of Age Discrimination: The Role of Competence and Warmth." *British Journal of Management*:1–15. (https://doi.org/10.1111/j.1467-8551.2010.00721.x).

Lamont, Ruth A., Hannah J. Swift, and Dominic Abrams. 2015. "A Review and Meta-analysis of Age-based Stereotype Threat: Negative Stereotypes, Not Facts, Do the Damage." *Psychology and Aging* 30:180–93. (https://doi.org/10.1037/a0038586).

Levy, Becca. "Stereotype Embodiment." 2009. *Current Directions in Psychological Science* 18:332–36.

Lueke, Adam and Bryan Gibson. 2015. "Mindfulness Meditation Reduces Implicit Age and Race Bias: The Role of Reduced Automaticity of Responding." *Social Psychological and Personality Science* 6(3):284–91. (https://doi.org/10.1177/1948550614559651).

Lueke, Adam and Bryan Gibson. 2016. "Brief Mindfulness Meditation Reduces Discrimination." *Psychology of Consciousness: Theory, Research, and Practice* 3(1):34–44. (https://doi.org/10.1037/cns0000081).

Macdonald, Jamie L. and Sheri R. Levy. 2016. "Ageism in the Workplace: The Role of Psychosocial Factors in Predicting Job Satisfaction, Commitment, and Engagement." *Journal of Social Issues* 72(1):169–90. (https://doi.org/10.1111/josi.12161).

Manzi, Claudia, et al. 2019. "Age-based Stereotype Threat and Negative Outcomes in the Workplace: Exploring the Role of Identity Integration." *European Journal of Social Psychology* 49(4):705–16.

McCann, Robert and Howard Giles. 2002. "Ageism in the Workplace: A Communication Perspective." Pp. 163–200 in *Ageism: Stereotyping and Prejudice Against Older Persons*, edited by Todd D. Nelson. Cambridge, MA: MIT Press.

Ng, Thomas W. H. and Daniel C. Feldman. 2012. "Evaluating Six Common Stereotypes about Older Workers with Meta-analytical Data." *Personnel Psychology* 65:821–58. (https://doi.org/10.1111/peps.12003).

Niemiec, Christopher P., et al. 2010. "Being Present in the Face of Existential Threat: The Role of Trait Mindfulness in Reducing Defensive Responses to Mortality Salience." *Journal of Personality and Social Psychology* 99(2):344–65. (https://doi.org/10.1037/a0019388).

North, Michael S. and Susan T. Fiske. 2013. "Act Your (Old) Age: Prescriptive, Ageist Biases over Succession, Consumption, and Identity." *Personality and Social Psychology Bulletin* 39(6):720–34. (https://doi.org/10.1177/0146167213480043).

North, Michael S. and Susan T. Fiske. 2016. "Resource Scarcity and Prescriptive Attitudes Generate Subtle, Intergenerational Older-worker Exclusion." *Journal of Social Issues* 72(1):122–45. (https://doi.org/10.1111/josi.12159).

Pennington, Charlotte R., et al. 2016. "Twenty Years of Stereotype Threat Research: A Review of Psychological Mediators." *PloS One* 11(1):e0146487. (https://doi.org/10.1371%2Fjournal.pone.0146487).

Posthuma, Richard A. and Michael A. Campion. 2009. "Age Stereotypes in the Workplace: Common Stereotypes, Moderators, and Future Research Directions." *Journal of Management* 35(1):158–88. (https://doi.org/10.1177/0149206308318617).

Rahhal, Tamara A., Lynn Hasher, and Stanley J. Colcombe. 2001. "Instructional Manipulations and Age Differences in Memory: Now You See Them, Now You Don't." *Psychology and Aging* 16(4):697. (https://doi.org/10.1037//0882-7974.16.4.697).

Redman, Tom and Ed Snape. 2006. "The Consequences of Perceived Age Discrimination amongst Older Police Officers: Is Social Support a Buffer?" *British Journal of Management* 17(2):167–75. (https://doi.org/10.1111/j.1467-8551.2006.00492.x).

Rupp, Deborah E., Stephen J. Vodanovich, and Marcus Crede. 2006. "Age Bias in the Workplace: The Impact of Ageism and Causal Attributions." *Journal of Applied Social Psychology* 36(6):1337–64.

Saraç, Mehlika. 2020. "A Literature Review on Mindfulness at Work Places: Conceptualization, Measurement, and Outcomes." Pp. 55–71 in *Handbook of Research on Positive Organizational Behavior for Improved Workplace Performance*, edited by Elif Baykal. Hershey, PA: IGI Global. Retrieved September 20, 2019 (https://doi.org/10.4018/978-1-7998-0058-3.ch004).

Shore, Lynn M., Jeanette N. Cleveland, and Caren B. Goldberg. 2003. "Work Attitudes and Decisions as a Function of Manager Age and Employee Age." *Journal of Applied Psychology* 88(3):529–37. (https://doi.org/10.1037/0021-9010.88.3.529).

Sigg, Roland, and Valentina De-Luigi. 2007. "The Success of Policies Aimed at Extending Working Life." Pp. 51–59 in *Developments and Trends: Supporting Dynamic Social Security*. Geneva, Switzerland: International Social Security Association.

Snape, Ed and Tom Redman. 2003. "Too Old or Too Young? The Impact of Perceived Age Discrimination." *Human Resource Management Journal* 13(1):78–89. (https://doi.org/10.1111/j.1748-8583.2003.tb00085.x).

Steele, Claude M. 1997. "A Threat in the Air: How Stereotypes Shape Intellectual Identity and Performance." *American Psychologist* 52(6):613. (https://doi.org/10.1037/0003-066X.52.6.613).

Sun, Xiaomin, et al. 2015. "A Cross-cultural Perspective on the Preference for Potential Effect: An Individual Participant Data (IPD) Meta-analysis Approach." *PLoS One* 10(3). (https://doi.org/10.1371/journal.pone.0124170).

Swift, Hannah J., et al. 2017. "The Risks of Ageism Model: How Ageism and Negative Attitudes toward Age Can Be a Barrier to Active Aging." *Social Issues and Policy Review* 11(1):195–231. (https://doi.org/10.1111/sipr.12031).

Swift, Hannah J., Dominic Abrams, and Sibila Marques. 2013. "Threat or Boost: Social Comparison Affects Older People's Performance Differently Depending on Task Domain." *Journals of Gerontology, Series B* 68:23–30. (https://doi.org/10.1093/geronb/gbs044).

Swift, Hannah J., Ruth A. Lamont, and Dominic Abrams. 2012. "Are They Half as Strong as They Used to Be? An Experiment Testing Whether Age-related Social Comparisons Impair Older People's Hand Grip Strength and Persistence." *BMJ Open*. (https://doi.org/10.1136/bmjopen-2012-001064).

Taylor, Philip, et al. 2013. "Everyday Discrimination in the Workplace, Job Satisfaction and Psychological Well-being: Age Differences and Moderating Variables." *Ageing & Society* 33(7):1105–38.

Thomson, Patrick. 2018. "Becoming an Age-friendly Employer." London: Centre for Ageing Better. (https://www.ageing-better.org.uk/sites/default/files/2018-09/Becoming-age-friendly-employer.pdf).

Thorsen, Sannie, et al. 2012. "The Association between Psychosocial Work Environment, Attitudes towards Older Workers (Ageism) and Planned Retirement." *International Archives of Occupational and Environmental Health* 85(4):437–45. (https://doi.org/10.1007/s00420-011-0689-5).

Tormala, Zakary L., Jayson S. Jia, and Michael I. Norton. 2012. "The Preference for Potential." *Journal of Personality and Social Psychology* 103(4):567–83. (https://doi.org/10.1037/a0029227).

Tresh, Fatima, et al. 2019. "Endorsing and Reinforcing Gender and Age Stereotypes: The Negative Effect on Self-rated Leadership Potential for Women and Older Workers." *Frontiers in Psychology* 10. (https://doi.org/10.3389/fpsyg.2019.00688).

Tripartite Alliance for Fair and Progressive Employment Practices (TAFEP). 2019. "Creating an Age-friendly Workplace (Employers)." (https://www.tal.sg/tafep/employment-practices/age-management/creating-age-friendly-workplace 20/09/2019).

Vago, David R. and David A. Silbersweig. 2012. "Self-awareness, Self-regulation, and Self-transcendence (S-ART): A Framework for Understanding the Neurobiological Mechanisms of Mindfulness." *Frontiers in Human Neuroscience* 6:296. (https://doi.org/10.3389%2Ffnhum.2012.00296).

Vickerstaff, Sarah, Wendy Loretto, and Philip J. White. 2007. "The Future for Older Workers: Opportunities and Constraints." Pp. 203–26 in *The Future for Older Workers: New Perspectives*, edited by Wendy Loretto, Sarah Vickerstaff, and Philip J. White. Bristol, UK: Policy Press.

von Hippel, Courtney, et al. 2018. "Age-based Stereotype Threat and Work Outcomes: Stress Appraisals and Rumination as Mediators." *Psychology and Aging*:68–84. (https://doi.org/10.1037/pag0000308).

von Hippel, Courtney, Elise K. Kalokerinos, and Julie D. Henry. 2013. "Stereotype Threat among Older Employees: Relationship with Job Attitudes and Turnover Intentions." *Psychology and Aging* 28:17–27. (https://doi.org/10.1037/a0029825).

Williamson, Sue and Meraiah Foley. 2018. "Unconscious Bias Training: The 'Silver Bullet' for Gender Equity?" *Australian Journal of Public Administration* 77(3):355–59. (https://doi.org/10.1111/1467-8500.12313).

Woodcock, Anna, et al. 2012. "The Consequences of Chronic Stereotype Threat: Domain Dis-identification and Abandonment." *Journal of Personality and Social Psychology* 103(4):635. (https://doi.org/10.1037%2Fa0029120).

World Health Organization. 2007. "Global Age-friendly Cities: A Guide." Geneva, Switzerland: World Health Organization. (https://www.who.int/ageing/age_friendly_cities_guide/en/).

# PART III

# FACTORS INFLUENCING LABOR FORCE PARTICIPATION AT OLDER AGES

CHAPTER 13

# Older Workers and Job Performance

Elora C. Voyles and Michael P. Robinson

## OVERVIEW

This chapter examines three major components of aging and performance. As the mean age of the workforce has increased, there has been growing attention dedicated to understanding the relationship between job performance and worker age. This growing attention to age and performance has its roots in organizations' concerns for cost and productivity as well as stereotyped beliefs regarding job performance by age. Older workers face unique challenges in the workplace, including physical changes, cognitive changes, increased health problems, and interpersonal factors that may subsequently influence older worker performance.[1] Understanding the relationship between age and worker performance is important to researchers as evidenced by the four meta-analyses conducted on this topic.[2] Currently, there is little research on the perceptions of employers' attitudes and practices toward older workers.[3] This chapter will delve into the relationship between age and performance by examining three major components of aging and performance. The first section discusses the nuances of aging and explains the distinction between chronological age and functional age. The second section focuses on beliefs about older worker performance through an investigation of stereotypes and metastereotypes. The third section focuses on defining performance and productivity metrics. In addition, this section reviews and integrates research on the performance of actual older workers. The final sections integrate discrepancies between defined performance and beliefs about older worker performance and suggests accommodations, technological advances, and adjustments that can enhance it.

## DEFINING AGE

Before discussing the relationship between worker performance and age, the construct of age must be defined. Age can be defined and conceptualized in a variety of ways including chronological age and functional age. In addition, age can be defined in terms of subjective, cognitive, and contextual age.[4] Chronological age, functional age, subjective age, and then generational age will be defined in this chapter to give context to conceptualizations of older workers' performance. Chronological age is the most common way that age is defined in the research, and this chapter will follow this tendency by referring to age in terms of chronological age.

### Chronological Age versus Functional Age

Chronological age is a person's age according to the length of time since they were born. In contrast, functional age is based on health status and perceptions of health. (See also chapter 19.) For example, an employee may have a calendar age of fifty-four, but their health conditions and perceptions of their health may indicate a lower or higher functional age.[5] Chronological age is used most often in human resources management as well as research, but there are downsides to not accounting for the nuances of health status, lifestyle, and other contextual factors.[6]

### Subjective Age

Subjective age is defined as the perception that individuals have of their age. For example, an older worker may have the chronological age of sixty-five years, but subjectively they feel that they are younger.[7] It is important to note that subjective age is influenced by the environment in which older workers live and work.[8] When looking at subjective age, Rubin and Berntsen suggest that the lifespan-developmental view provides the best explanation of the discrepancy between subjective age and chronological age.[9] After age forty there is no increase in the discrepancy between chronological age and subjective age (it stays constant at 20 percent younger). Subjective age is an important factor that influences older workers' perceptions of their work demands and their ability to meet them.[10] In other words, older workers who felt that they were subjectively younger felt more capable of meeting the demands of their work. Much of the current research on older workers does not account for the influence of subjective age, but research by Kaliterna, Larsen, and Brkljacic indicates that subjective age is a relevant factor when studying older workers and performance.[11]

### Generations

In addition to conceptualizing age in terms of numbers and abilities, age is also defined in terms of generations. Broadly, generations are grouped by the concept of "birth cohorts" or people who were all born within a particular range of time.[12] The exact range of time for each generation varies slightly depending on the source. According to Van Rossem, baby boomers were born between 1946 and 1964. Generation X was born between 1965 and 1979, and Generation Y was born between 1980 and 2000. Generation Z was born after 2000, and the exact cutoff is debated but will likely be about 2020.[13] The idea of generations is based on historical and cultural influences that uniquely impact and influence different generations. Thus, the boundaries for the generation depend on factors such as international relations, technology, and social climate. However, there is debate as to whether the characteristics that are ascribed to different generational groups are due to current age and maturation or if the characteristics are unique to the generations. Both historical influences and current age can influence generation members' performance in the workplace. For example, Kowske, Rasch, and Wiley found small differences in work attitudes across generations when controlling for time period and age maturation.[14] Specifically, they found that millennials (Generation Y) had higher job satisfaction, job security, and satisfaction with recognition compared to older generations. However, while differences in job attitudes can influence job performance, it is important to note that the differences between Generation Y and the other generations was statistically very small.

The concept of age groups through generations can create perceptions of "in-groups and out-groups." Perceptions of disparate groups can promote *out-group homogeneity effects*, which are beliefs that differences within groups are smaller while differences between groups are larger than they are in reality. Out-group homogeneity can support stereotyping.[15] For example, the baby boomer generation's job performance is sometimes viewed as lower because of their advanced age.[16] However, the research on whether this stereotype is supported among workers of different age groups is mixed.

## STEREOTYPES AND METASTEREOTYPES

### Stereotypes

Broadly, age stereotypes are defined as one age group's belief about characteristics of another age group.[17] (See also chapter 9.) Negative stereotypes about older workers' performance suggest that they are less physically capable, less able to use technology, and more resistant to training.[18,19] Despite the variety of negative stereotypes targeting older workers, there are numerous positive stereotypes related to older workers' abilities and performance. The majority of stereotypes reported by younger and middle-aged workers were positive, 60 percent and 85 percent, respectively.[20] The content of these stereotypes included dependability, knowledge, and strong work ethic. Research has shown positive stereotypes are linked to greater perceptions of older workers' employability.[21]

### Metastereotypes

Metastereotypes refer to one's awareness or perception that other groups hold stereotypes regarding one's own group.[22] For example, metastereotyping occurs if an older worker believes that younger workers think older workers are incompetent with technology. Like stereotypes, metastereotypes can vary in content and valence.[23] In an investigation of stereotype content and metastereotype content, Finkelstein, Ryan, and King found a great degree of overlap between stereotypes and metastereotypes.[24] There is growing evidence concerning the influence of metastereotypes on intergenerational interactions, which likely have indirect effects on performance.[25] In addition, metastereotypes may also directly influence performance as metastereotypes are the first step toward stereotype threat in older workers.[26]

## Effects of Stereotypes and Metastereotypes

Stereotypes as well as metastereotypes can influence social interactions and self-beliefs in the workplace,[27] by affecting older workers in two ways: (a) influencing how older workers are treated by other people in the workplace, or (b) influencing older workers' self-beliefs that can subsequently impact their work behavior and performance.

Stereotypes can be used to justify discrimination against workers based on their age group.[28] Researchers suggest that negative stereotypes of older workers' abilities and performance are major barriers to attaining employment.[29] One study using profiles of job candidates with either young or old stereotypical descriptions found that 80 percent of the participants chose to hire the profile using the younger stereotypes. Past research on stereotypes has shown both positive and negative stereotypes regarding older workers' productivity.[30] In the case of memory, research evidence suggests that when older workers are forgetful, observers perceive memory failures as more serious and meaningful.[31]

Stereotypes can impact workers through stereotype threat that originates from an awareness of negative stereotypes regarding their group.[32,33] Stereotype threat ultimately leads to performance decrements as the result of feeling anxiety and preoccupation with negative stereotypes of one's group. The negative effects of stereotype threat have been demonstrated across a variety of groups, including black people, women, and older adults. For example, in a study of aging and stereotype threat, older participants were divided into two conditions: an experimental condition in which participants were informed that the study was about why older people are more likely to be implicated in an accident, and a neutral condition about reactions to driving.[34] The results showed that there were not any differences in the number of accidents in a simulated driving task, but older individuals in the stereotype threat condition committed more speeding infractions. Given the consistent findings in the stereotype threat literature, it is not surprising that exposure to negative stereotypes can impair older workers' performance. In addition, stereotype threat can impact organizational attitudes such as work engagement.[35]

Metastereotypes can influence whether older workers feel welcome and how likely they are to perform tasks that are in stereotyped domains for older workers.[36] Metastereotypes can also influence older workers' perceptions of their abilities at work. A diary study found that older workers' behaviors of conflict, avoidance, and engagement at work were influenced by affective reactions to age metastereotypes.[37]

Growing evidence shows the power of metastereotypes to influence behavior as well as performance. Researchers have also found physiological evidence of stress caused by negative age metastereotypes in older adults. Levy and colleagues found that participants exposed to negative metastereotypes exhibited higher levels of cardiovascular stress after exposure compared to older adults exposed to a positive or neutral metastereotype.[38] Physiological stress responses were further elevated after performing anxiety-inducing activities. Performing a cognitively demanding task requires many central processing executive resources; however, these same attentional, memory, problem-solving, and coordination areas are negatively impacted when cognitive resources are occupied with thoughts of threat and concerns with confirming negative stereotypes.[39] This diversion of cognitive resources is called cognitive load. Additional emotional load may impede functioning when necessary cognitive resources are withdrawn from neural areas and are instead dedicated to scanning for threats. Uncertainty may lead individuals experiencing threat to reduce their efforts and withdraw from taking risks on tasks.[40]

## ACTUAL JOB PERFORMANCE

Organizations employ a variety of metrics when considering older worker performance. According to Motowidlo and Kell, job performance is conceptualized as the organization's total expected value of the task-related behaviors that an employee performs within a specified period of time.[41] In addition to this broad definition, performance can be examined within the framework of task performance and contextual performance. *Task performance* includes behaviors that fulfill typical job duties outlined in a job description.[42] For example, task performance may include a list of cognitive work tasks and physical work tasks. *Contextual performance* refers to additional behaviors that benefit the organization but that may not be captured in a job description. For example, these contextual behaviors include motivating other employees, maintaining common areas at work, and providing a buffer for coworkers in times of stress. Contextual work behaviors can be positive with the performance of organizational citizenship behaviors (OCBs) or negative with counterproductive work behaviors (CWBs). According to Ng and Feldman, older workers may demonstrate increased contextual work performance due to years of experience.[43]

### Measures of Work Performance

Evaluation of older workers' performance may take place in a research lab setting or in a field setting such as an organization. Within lab settings, older worker performance has been examined using physical exercise, work computer simulations, and simulated shift work.[44] In a simulated shift-work study in which participants worked multiple twelve-hour work shifts in the lab across four days, researchers found that older workers performed consistently more poorly compared to younger workers. Interestingly, older workers performed much better during day shifts compared to their night shift performance. Compared to lab studies, there are relatively few field studies examining the relationship between age and worker performance. One field study examined age differences in errors of office workers. When comparing general performance, there was no significant relationship between age and performance. However, the researchers found that older workers made more errors than younger workers on cognitively taxing work.[45]

A recent meta-analysis examined ten dimensions of job performance—core task performance, creativity, performance in training programs, OCBs, safety performance, general CWBs, workplace aggression, on-the-job substance use, tardiness, and absenteeism—and found that there were only small correlations with age for some of the variables.[46] The results of the study showed that age was not typically associated with task performance, creativity, and training performance. The seven remaining dimensions were significantly related to age.

## Age-Related Changes in Cognitive, Physical, and Mental Abilities

As workers progress in age, they undergo a variety of changes that influence their cognitive, physical, and mental abilities.[47] Not surprisingly, some of these changes may directly impact older workers' performance on the job as well as indirectly impact work performance by influencing other factors such as physical health, social support, job demands, and burnout. Changes in cognition that occur with age include decreases in working memory, processing speed, and inhibitory function; however, crystallized knowledge remains intact. Not surprisingly, decreases in working memory capacity partially mediate the negative relationship between age and skill acquisition.[48] Overall physical condition deteriorates with increased age. Compared to younger workers, older workers also need more recovery time after physical exertion. In addition to cognitive and physical changes, older workers may also face changes to their psychological well-being. Some research has suggested decreased positive affect and increased negative affect with increased age.[49] However, compared to younger workers, a lower percent of older workers report major depressive symptoms.[50]

### COGNITIVELY DEMANDING WORK

The research on working older adults and cognitive abilities is somewhat mixed. A handful of studies have found no cognitive differences between older and younger workers;[51] many more have found a negative relationship between age and cognitive abilities.[52] According to Verhaegen and Salthouse, declines in processing and memory typically begin around age fifty,[53] yet older workers' performance is typically maintained.[54] One explanation is the compensation hypothesis: a study found that older bus drivers had fewer accidents despite decreased reaction times and visual acuity because they compensated by exercising more careful judgment and patience,[55] drawing on experience and crystallized intelligence.

When job applications include positive attributes of an older applicant, evaluators tend to view the older applicant as employable. However, in the absence of information, younger applicants are rated more positively than older applicants, particularly for physically demanding jobs, regardless of applicant qualities.[56]

### PHYSICAL WORK

When it comes to physically demanding work, as employees age, their bodies will begin to lose some of their natural strength making them susceptible to ailments and possible injuries. However, according to Norheim et al., older adults with high levels of fitness can maintain the capacity to perform physical tasks far longer than their sedentary counterparts.[57] Researchers suggest that improvements in technology for physical work will enable older workers to sustain performance in these occupations.[58] There is scant research on the influence of age on physically demanding work positions. Instead, much of the research posits that decreasing physical abilities lead to reduced performance. For example, Kenny and colleagues connected reduced physical capacities to increased work-related injuries.[59] Minimal research attention to the relationship between age and physical performance at work[60] may be in part due to the reduced number of physical labor jobs within the United States. In addition, it is likely that most jobs that rely heavily on physical labor do not include a large sample of older workers. An examination of workers' age and performance in a garment factory found that older workers perform better and with fewer accidents.[61] The authors suggested that the findings were related to the lighter physical demands of the garment factory positions as compared to other physical labor jobs. Most importantly, the data supported experience as a factor in older workers' performance. Within the United States, the increase in nonphysical jobs[62] represents greater opportunities for older workers.

### CONTEXTUAL WORK

Contextual work includes contributions and behaviors that influence the organization and its stakeholders.[63] Contextual work factors can include organizational citizenship behaviors (OCBs) and counterproductive work behaviors (CWBs), as mentioned above; interpersonal facilitation; and safety behavior.[64] OCBs were positively related to age, meaning that as age increased the practice of OCBs also increased, and while nontask related, these work behaviors are still beneficial to the organization.[65] In addition, older workers contribute to organizational citizenship by engaging in less absenteeism. Despite the increased incidence of disabilities in older workers, age is negatively associated with absenteeism.[66]

CWBs can result in reduced performance and increased costs for organizations. Examples of CWBs include using work time for nonwork tasks, stealing, sabotaging, instigating interpersonal conflicts, and other negative behaviors. Older aged workers engage in fewer CWBs as rated by supervisors and employee self-report ratings.[67] Within specific types of CWBs, older workers were less likely to engage in aggression.

## OLDER WORKERS AND NEW TECHNOLOGY

Older workers are frequently stereotyped as being inept at using technology.[68] (Also see chapters 15, 17, and 18.) Much of the research on older workers and technology has focused on contrasting training performance between older workers and young workers.[69] Based on this growing area of research, it seems that there is some merit to the stereotypes. Broadly speaking, older workers have performed less well in technology training studies compared to younger workers.[70] Researchers have found that older workers perform better in technology training when they have control over the amount of time spent on each concept within the training[71] and when the training is highly structured.[72]

## MOTIVATION AND PERFORMANCE

Motivation is defined as the force that stimulates the direction, intensity, and duration of goal-oriented behaviors. Previous research indicates a strong influence of work environment on older workers' motivation.[73] Motivation can influence performance and may be especially important for older workers' ability to persist despite age-related changes. Pervasive negative stereotypes suggest that older workers are lower in motivation compared to younger workers; however, few research studies have found support for this belief.[74] Most likely, there is no significant difference in workers' level of motivation; however, there are differences in what motivates older workers compared to other age groups.[75]

In order to enhance older workers' performance, it is important to examine motivation in older adults to better understand work factors that can make a difference. A meta-analysis examined the relationship between age and intrinsic motives, extrinsic motives, growth motives, social motives, and security motives of older adults.[76] *Intrinsic* motives are described as internal sources of motivation, such as satisfaction in the task itself, feelings of accomplishment, and interconnectedness with others.[77] *Extrinsic* motives relate to external sources of motivation that tend to be results from work rather than the work itself, for example, recognition and monetary rewards. *Growth* motives are enacted through challenging assignments that allow for gaining mastery. Motives based on social interactions and status are *social* motives. Lastly, *security* motives relate to factors such as job security and working conditions that affect the individual's perceptions of stability and safety. The results of the meta-analysis showed that age was positively related to intrinsic motives. Moreover, age was negatively related to growth motives and extrinsic motives. Generally, this indicates that older workers are more focused on the benefits of the work itself rather than on external rewards. Intrinsic motivation deserves close attention because older workers' willingness to continue working is positively correlated with intrinsic motivation.[78]

## OLDER WORKERS AND ACCOMMODATIONS

Some organizations may not be equipped to provide accommodations for an older workforce that is more likely to be affected by disabilities.[79] In fact, many older workers qualify for accommodations under Title I of the Americans with Disabilities Act (ADA).[80] This creates a fear that results in discrimination against the elderly, the fear that "if hired, older workers could become physically disabled or become injured and not be able to return to work."[81] In addition, confounding age and disability can make employers less likely to provide an accommodation.[82] Furthermore, workers who attribute their disability to natural aging are less likely to seek out workplace accommodations; in particular, workers older than sixty-one are less likely to request accommodations compared to slightly younger counterparts. Older workers who were more knowledgeable about ADA accommodations were more likely to request accommodations. The provision of accommodations for disabilities at work enables older workers to continue working longer.[83] Not surprisingly, providing needed accommodations can enable older workers to maintain performance despite aging-related changes.[84]

### Time and Place Alternatives

One of the popular workplace trends that emerged in the early 2000s was the flexibility of telework. (See also chapter 11.) Working from a distance may provide older workers needed flexibility that may encourage them to stay in the workforce longer.[85] For example, telework may enable older workers to better manage their own health as well as caregiving responsibilities.

In addition to telework, flexible arrangements in the workplace may be beneficial for older workers, including job rotation (release from certain tasks), part-time hours, and temporary leave options.[86] Interviews with older workers reveal that flexible work options are highly valued and at times necessary in order for older workers to remain in their current work positions.[87] One of the key benefits to flexible work arrangements is increased long-term retention while providing customized solutions for older workers.

## RECOMMENDATIONS FOR ORGANIZATIONS WITH OLDER WORKERS

By and large, organizations are currently not providing needed support to older workers.[88] (See also chapters 7, 8, 10, and 16.) Researchers note that compared to younger workers, older worker performance is more dependent on available resources.[89] Older workers face stereotypes and metastereotypes, changing abilities, and performance demands, all of which can impact their well-being, performance, and intention to remain in the workforce. As the workforce ages in the coming years, it becomes increasingly important for organizations to ensure that older workers get the organizational resources they need in order to perform their best. Organizations need to develop policies to foster positive intergenerational interactions in order to reduce negative stereotypes and metastereotypes. These policies could include age-diversity training, education, actively promoting a culture of age acceptance, and social support to mitigate worker exhaustion and negative work outcomes.

Directly related to performance, organizations need to examine the strengths of their older workers in order to design tasks and work that maximize their strengths. Task performance can be further enhanced by engaging older workers' intrinsic motivation and removing barriers that primarily impact older workers experiencing changes to their cognitive and physical abilities. Older workers would also benefit from the availability of flexibility in time and place of work, enabling them to adapt schedules to fit their needs.

## CONCLUSION

With the aging of workforces worldwide, it is becoming increasingly important to understand how aging relates to work performance. Specifically, researchers and practitioners would benefit from a greater understanding of potential moderators in the relationship between age and worker performance.[90] What is clear is that organizations will retain and encourage higher performance levels from older employees by adapting to their needs.

## NOTES

1. Stephen M. Popkin et al. 2008. "Age Is More Than Just a Number: Implications for an Aging Workforce in the US Transportation Sector." *Applied Ergonomics* 39(5):542–49.

2. Glenn M. McEvoy and Wayne F. Cascio. 1989. "Cumulative Evidence of the Relationship between Employee Age and Job Performance. *Journal of Applied Psychology* 74(1):11; Thomas W. H. Ng and Daniel C. Feldman. 2008. "The Relationship of Age to Ten Dimensions of Job Performance." *Journal of Applied Psychology* 93(2):392; Michael C. Sturman. 2003. "Searching for the Inverted U-shaped Relationship between Time and Performance: Meta-analyses of the Experience / Performance, Tenure / Performance, and Age / Performance Relationships." *Journal of Management* 29(5):609–40; David A. Waldman and Bruce J. Avolio. 1986. "A Meta-analysis of Age Differences in Job Performance." *Journal of Applied Psychology* 71(1):33.

3. Wendy Loretto and Phil White. 2006. "Employers' Attitudes, Practices and Policies towards Older Workers." *Human Resource Management Journal* 16(3):313–30.

4. Alexander R. Schwall, 2012. "Defining Age and Using Age-relevant Constructs." Pp. 169–86 in *The Oxford Handbook of Work and Aging*, edited by Jerry W. Hedge and Walter C. Borman. Oxford: Oxford University Press.

5. Wendy Koolhaas et al. 2011. "Towards a Sustainable Healthy Working Life: Associations between Chronological Age, Functional Age and Work Outcomes." *European Journal of Public Health* 22(3):424–29.

6. Schwall, "Defining Age."

7. David C. Rubin and Dorthe Berntsen. 2006. "People over Forty Feel 20% Younger Than Their Age: Subjective Age across the Lifespan." *Psychonomic Bulletin & Review* 13(5):776–80. (https: / / doi.org / 10.3758 / BF03193996).

8. Maria C. W. Peeters and Hetty van Emmerik. 2008. "An Introduction to the Work and Well-being of Older Workers: From Managing Threats to Creating Opportunities." *Journal of Managerial Psychology* 23(4):353–63.

9. Rubin and Berntsen, "People over Forty."

10. Ljiljana Kaliterna, Zrjezdana P. Larsen, and Tihana Brkljacic. 2002. "Chronological and Subjective Age in Relation to Work Demands: Survey of Croatian Workers." *Experimental Aging Research* 28(1):39–49.

11. Kaliterna, Larsen, and Brkljacic, "Chronological and Subjective Age."

12. Annick H. D. Van Rossem. 2019. "Generations as Social Categories: An Exploratory Cognitive Study of Generational Identity and Generational Stereotypes in a Multigenerational Workforce." *Journal of Organizational Behavior* 40(4):434–55.

13. Van Rossem, "Generations as Social Categories."

14. Brenda J. Kowske, Rena Rasch, and Jack Wiley. 2010. "Millennials' (Lack of) Attitude Problem: An Empirical Examination of Generational Effects on Work Attitudes." *Journal of Business and Psychology* 25(2):265–79.

15. Thalia Vrantsidis and William A. Cunningham. April 10, 2019. "The Effect of Knowledge about a Group on Perceived Group Variability and Certainty about Stereotype-based Inferences." *OSF Preprints*. (https: / / doi.org / 10.31219 / osf.io / 84fua).

16. Richard A. Posthuma and Michael A. Campion. 2009. "Age Stereotypes in the Workplace: Common Stereotypes, Moderators, and Future Research Directions." *Journal of Management* 35(1):158–88.

17. Pascale Peters et al. 2019. "Please Don't Look at Me That Way: An Empirical Study into the Effects of Age-based (Meta-) Stereotyping on Employability Enhancement among Supermarket Workers." *Frontiers in Psychology* 10:249.

18. Kerstin Isaksson and Gunn Johansson. 2000. "Adaptation to Continued Work and Early Retirement Following Downsizing: Long-term Effects and Gender Differences." *Journal of Occupational and Organizational Psychology* 73(2):241–56; Laura Riolli-Saltzman and Fred Luthans. 2001. "After the Bubble Burst: How Small High-tech Firms Can Keep in Front of the Wave." *Academy of Management Perspectives* 15(3):114–24.

19. Donatienne Desmette and Mathieu Gaillard. 2008. "When a 'Worker' Becomes an 'Older Worker': The Effects of Age-related Social Identity on Attitudes towards Retirement and Work." *Career Development International* 13(2):168–85.

20. Lisa M. Finkelstein, Katherine M. Ryan, and Eden B. King. 2013. "What Do the Young (Old) People Think of Me? Content and Accuracy of Age-based Meta-stereotypes." *European Journal of Work and Organizational Psychology* 22(6):633–57.

21. Anne C. Kroon et al. 2016. "Poles Apart: The Processing and Consequences of Mixed Media Stereotypes of Older Workers." *Journal of Communication* 66(5):811–33. (https://doi.org/10.1111/jcom.12249).

22. Jacquie D. Vorauer, Kelley J. Main, and Gordon B. O'Connell. 1998. "How Do Individuals Expect to Be Viewed by Members of Lower Status Groups? Content and Implications of Meta-stereotypes." *Journal of Personality and Social Psychology* 75(4):917.

23. Finkelstein, Ryan, and King, "What Do the Young (Old) People Think of Me?"

24. Finkelstein, Ryan, and King, "What Do the Young (Old) People Think of Me?"

25. Lisa M. Finkelstein et al. June 2019. "A Daily Diary Study of Responses to Age Meta-stereotypes." *Work, Aging and Retirement*. (https://doi.org/10.1093/workar/waz005).

26. Elora C. Voyles, Lisa Finkelstein, and Eden King. 2014. "A Tale of Two Theories: Stereotype Threat and Meta-stereotypes." *Industrial and Organizational Psychology* 7(3):419–22.

27. Finkelstein, Ryan, and King, "What Do the Young (Old) People Think of Me?"

28. Christian S. Crandall et al. 2011. "Stereotypes as Justifications of Prejudice." *Personality and Social Psychology Bulletin* 37(11):1488–98.

29. OECD. 2006. *Live Longer, Work Longer*. Ageing and Employment Policies. Paris: OECD Publishing. (https://doi.org/10.1787/9789264035881-en).

30. Hendrik P. Van Dalen, Kène Henkens, and Joop Schippers. 2010. "Productivity of Older Workers: Perceptions of Employers and Employees." *Population and Development Review* 36(2):309–30.

31. Laura L. Carstensen and Christine R. Hartel, eds. 2006. "When I'm 64." Committee on Aging Frontiers in Social Psychology, Personality, and Adult Developmental Psychology. *Board on Behavioral, Cognitive, and Sensory Sciences, Division of Behavioral and Social Sciences and Education.* Washington, DC: National Research Council/The National Academies Press.

32. Claude M. Steele and Joshua Aronson. 1995. "Stereotype Threat and the Intellectual Test Performance of African Americans." *Journal of Personality and Social Psychology* 69(5):797.

33. Mélanie Joanisse, Sylvain Gagnon, and Mihnea Voloaca. 2013. "The Impact of Stereotype Threat on the Simulated Driving Performance of Older Drivers." *Accident Analysis & Prevention* 50:530–38.

34. Carol T. Kulik, Sanjeewa Perera, and Christina Cregan. 2016. "Engage Me: The Mature-age Worker and Stereotype Threat." *Academy of Management Journal* 59(6):2132–56.

35. Kulik, Perera, and Cregan, "Engage Me."

36. Finkelstein, Ryan, and King, "What Do the Young (Old) People Think of Me?"

37. Finkelstein, Ryan, and King, "What Do the Young (Old) People Think of Me?"

38. Becca R. Levy et al. 2000. "Reducing Cardiovascular Stress with Positive Self-stereotypes of Aging." *Journals of Gerontology Series B: Psychological Sciences and Social Sciences* 55(4):P205–213.

39. Toni Schmader and Sian Beilock. 2012. "An Integration of Processes That Underlie Stereotype Threat." Pp. 34–50 in *Stereotype Threat: Theory, Process, and Application*, edited by Michael Inzlicht and Toni Schmader. Oxford, UK: Oxford Scholarship Online.

40. Schmader and Beilock, "Integration of Processes."

41. Stephan J. Motowidlo and Harrison J. Kell. 2012. "Job Performance." *Handbook of Psychology, 2nd Edition*:12.

42. Walter C. Borman and Stephan J. Motowidlo. 1993. "Expanding the Criterion Domain to Include Elements of Contextual Performance." *Personnel Selection in Organizations*. San Francisco: Jossey-Bass:71.

43. Ng and Feldman, "Relationship of Age to Ten Dimensions of Job Performance."

44. Mark P. Cote et al. 2014. "Reference Values for Physical Performance Measures in the Aging Working Population." *Human Factors* 56(1):228–42.

45. Kamal Birdi, Janet Pennington, and Dieter Zapf. 1997. "Ageing and Errors in Computer-based Work: An Observational Field Study." *Journal of Occupational and Organizational Psychology* 70(1):35–47.

46. Ng and Feldman, "Relationship of Age to Ten Dimensions of Job Performance."

47. Peeters and van Emmerik, "Introduction to the Work and Well-being of Older Workers."

48. Kristen M. Kennedy, Ty Partridge, and Naftali Raz. 2008. "Age-related Differences in Acquisition of Perceptual-motor Skills: Working Memory as a Mediator." *Aging, Neuropsychology, and Cognition* 15(2):165–83.

49. Martin Pinquart. 2001. "Age Differences in Perceived Positive Affect, Negative Affect, and Affect Balance in Middle and Old Age." *Journal of Happiness Studies* 2(4):375–405. (https://doi:10.1023/A:1013938001116).

50. Carolyn S. Dewa et al. 2004. "Nature and Prevalence of Mental Illness in the Workplace." *Healthcare Papers* 5(2):12–25.

51. Daniele Artistico, Daniel Cervone, and Lina Pezzuti. 2003. "Perceived Self-efficacy and Everyday Problem Solving among Young and Older Adults." *Psychology and Aging,* 18(1):68; Paula Brough et al. 2011. "Comparisons of Cognitive Ability and Job Attitudes of Older and Younger Workers." *Equality, Diversity and Inclusion: An International Journal* 30(2):105–26; Jaeyeop Chung et al. 2015. "A Study on the Relationships between Age, Work Experience, Cognition, and Work Ability in Older Employees Working in Heavy Industry." *Journal of Physical Science* 27(1):155–57.

52. Kennedy, Partridge and Raz, "Age-related Differences"; Sunghan Kim, Lynn Hasher, and Rose T. Zacks. 2007. "Aging and a Benefit of Distractibility." *Psychonomic Bulletin & Review* 14(2):301–5; Matthew G. Rhodes. 2004. "Age-related Differences in Performance on the Wisconsin Card Sorting Test: A Meta-Analytic Review." *Psychology & Aging,* 19(3):482–94. (https://doi-org.libproxy.siue.edu/10.1037/0882-7974.19.3.482).

53. Paul Verhaeghen and Timothy A. Salthouse. 1997. "Meta-analyses of Age–cognition Relations in Adulthood: Estimates of Linear and Non-linear Age Effects and Structural Models." *Psychological Bulletin* 122(3):231.

54. Brough et al., "Comparisons of Cognitive Ability."

55. Roy J. Shepard, Erich Prien, and Garry L. Hughes. 1988. "Age Restrictions on Bus Driver Selection." *Journal of Human Ergology* 17:119–38.

56. Lisa M. Finkelstein, Michael J. Burke, and Manbury S. Raju. 1995. "Age Discrimination in Simulated Employment Contexts: An Integrative Analysis." *Journal of Applied Psychology* 80(6):652.

57. Kristoffer Norheim et al. 2019. "Physical-work Ability and Chronic Musculoskeletal Complaints Are Related to Leisure-time Physical Activity: Cross-sectional Study among Manual Workers Aged 50–70 years." *Scandinavian Journal of Public Health* 47. (https://doi.org/10.1177/1403494819839533).

58. Ng and Feldman, "Relationship of Age to Ten Dimensions of Job Performance."

59. Glen P. Kenny et al. 2008. "Physical Work Capacity in Older Adults: Implications for the Aging Worker." *American Journal of Industrial Medicine* 51(8):610–25.

60. Seymour Giniger, Angelo Dispenzieri, and Joseph Eisenberg. 1983. "Age, Experience, and Performance on Speed and Skill Jobs in an Applied Setting." *Journal of Applied Psychology* 68(3):469.

61. Giniger, Dispenzieri, and Eisenberg, "Age, Experience, and Performance,"

62. Marlene Lee and Mark Mather. 2008. "U.S. Labor Force Trends." United States, Population Reference Bureau. *Population Bulletin* 63(2):1–18.

63. Borman and Motowidlo, "Expanding the Criterion Domain."

64. Suzanne J. Peterson and Barry K. Spiker. 2005. "Establishing the Positive Contributory Value of Older Workers: A Positive Psychology Perspective." *Organizational Dynamics* 34(2):153–67; Ng and Feldman, "Relationship of Age to Ten Dimensions of Job Performance."

65. Dennis W. Organ. 1997. "Organizational Citizenship Behavior: It's Construct Clean-up Time." *Human Performance* 10(2):85–97.

66. Nicole Maestas, Kathleen J. Mullen, and Stephanie Rennane. 2018. "Absenteeism and Presenteeism among American Workers." Washington, DC: NBER.

67. Ng and Feldman, "Relationship of Age to Ten Dimensions of Job Performance."

68. Finkelstein, Ryan, and King, "What Do the Young (Old) People Think of Me?"

69. Tracy C. McCausland et al. 2015. "The Technological Age: The Effects of Perceived Age in Technology Training." *Journal of Business and Psychology* 30(4):693–708. (https://doi.org/10.1007/s10869-014-9390-5).

70. Jamye M. Hickman, Wendy A. Rogers, and Arthur D. Fisk. 2007. "Training Older Adults to Use New Technology." *Journals of Gerontology* 62B:77–84; Lisa Jenkins and William J. Hoyer. 2000. "Instance-based Automaticity and Aging: Acquisition, Reacquisition, and Long-term Retention." *Psychology and Aging* 15:551–65; Stephan J. Westerman and D. R. Davies. 2000. "Acquisition and Application of New Technology Skills: The Influence of Age." *Occupational Medicine* 50:478–82. (https://doi.org/10.1093/occmed/50.7.478).

71. Natalie Wolfson, Thomas Cavanagh, and Kurt Kraiger. 2014. "Older Adults and Technology-based Instruction: Optimizing Learning Outcomes and Transfer." *Academy of Management Learning and Education* 13:26–44. (https://doi.org/10.5465/amle.2012.0056).

72. Natalie Wolfson and Kurt Kraiger. 2014. "Cognitive Aging and Training: The Role of Instructional Coherence and Advance Organizers." *Experimental Aging Research*, 40:164–86. (https://doi.org/10.1080/0361073X.2014.882206).

73. Peter T. Van Den Berg. 2011. "Characteristics of the Work Environment Related to Older Employees' Willingness to Continue Working: Intrinsic Motivation as a Mediator." *Psychological Report* 109:174–86.

74. Carlos-Maria Alcover and Gabriela Topa. 2018. "Work Characteristics, Motivational Orientations, Psychological Work Ability and Job Mobility Intentions of Older Workers." *PLoS One* 13(4):e0195973.

75. Ilke Inceoglu, Jesse Segers, and Dave Bartram. 2012. "Age-related Differences in Work Motivation." *Journal of Occupational and Organizational Psychology* 85(2):300–29.

76. Dorien Kooij et al. 2011. "Age and Work-related Motives: Results of a Meta-analysis." *Journal of Organizational Behavior* 32:197–225. (https://doi.org/10.1002/job.665).

77. Kooij et al., "Age and Work-related Motives."

78. Van Den Berg, "Characteristics of the Work Environment."

79. Shengli Dong. 2018. "Assessing Workplace Accommodation Requests among Older Workers." *Rehabilitation Counseling Bulletin* 61(2):101–11; Robert O. Hansson et al. 1997. "Successful Aging at Work: Annual Review, 1992–1996: The Older Worker and Transitions to Retirement." *Journal of Vocational Behavior* 51(2):202–33.

80. Dong, "Assessing Workplace Accommodation Requests."

81. Malcolm Sargeant. 2008. "Older Workers and the Need for Reasonable Accommodation." *International Journal of Discrimination and the Law.* 9(3):163–180. (https://doi.org/10.1177/135822910800900303).

82. Julie Ann McMullin and Kim M. Shuey. 2006. "Ageing, Disability and Workplace Accommodations." *Ageing & Society* 26(6):831–47.

83. Marsha L. Ellison et al. 2003. "Patterns and Correlates of Workplace Disclosure among Professionals and Managers with Psychiatric Conditions." *Journal of Vocational Rehabilitation* 18(1):3–13.

84. Phillip D. Rumrill et al. 1998. "Situational Assessment of the Accommodation Needs of Employees Who Are Visually Impaired." *Journal of Visual Impairment & Blindness* 92(1):42–54.

85. Joseph Sharit et al. 2009. "The Employability of Older Workers as Teleworkers: An Appraisal of Issues and an Empirical Study." *Human Factors and Ergonomics in Manufacturing* 19(5):457–77.

86. Carol Atkinson and Peter Sandiford. 2016. "An Exploration of Older Worker Flexible Working Arrangements in Smaller Firms." *Human Resource Management Journal* 26(1):12–28.

87. Atkinson and Sandiford, "An Exploration."

88. Lynzee Head et al. 2006. "Barriers to Evidence-based Practice in Accommodations for an Aging Workforce." *Work* 27:391–96.

89. Brough et al., "Comparisons of Cognitive Ability."

90. Margaret E. Beier and Ruth Kanfer. 2013. "Work Performance and the Older Worker." Pp. 97–117 in *The SAGE Handbook of Aging, Work and Society*, edited by John Field, Ronald J. Burke, and Cary L. Cooper. Thousand Oaks, CA: SAGE.

## REFERENCES


Alcover, Carlos-Maria and Gabriela Topa. 2018. "Work Characteristics, Motivational Orientations, Psychological Work Ability and Job Mobility Intentions of Older Workers." *PLoS One* 13(4):e0195973.

Artistico, Daniele, Daniel Cervone, and Lina Pezzuti. 2003. "Perceived Self-efficacy and Everyday Problem Solving among Young and Older Adults." *Psychology and Aging* 18(1):68.

Atkinson, Carol and Peter Sandiford. 2016. "An Exploration of Older Worker Flexible Working Arrangements in Smaller Firms." *Human Resource Management Journal* 26(1):12–28.

Beier, Margaret E. and Ruth Kanfer. 2013. "Work Performance and the Older Worker." Pp. 97–117 in *The SAGE Handbook of Ageing and Society*, edited by John Field, Ronald J. Burke, and Cary L. Cooper. Thousand Oaks, CA: SAGE.

Birdi, Kamal, Janet Pennington, and Dieter Zapf. 1997. "Ageing and Errors in Computer-based Work: An Observational Field Study." *Journal of Occupational and Organizational Psychology* 70(1):35–47.

Borman, Walter C. and Stephan J. Motowidlo. 1993. "Expanding the Criterion Domain to Include Elements of Contextual Performance." *Personnel Selection in Organizations*. San Francisco: Jossey-Bass:71.

Brough, Paula, et al. 2011. "Comparisons of Cognitive Ability and Job Attitudes of Older and Younger Workers." *Equality, Diversity and Inclusion: An International Journal* 30(2):105–26.

Carstensen, Laura L. and Christine R. Hartel, eds. 2006. "When I'm 64." Committee on Aging Frontiers in Social Psychology, Personality, and Adult Developmental Psychology. *Board on Behavioral, Cognitive, and Sensory Sciences, Division of Behavioral and Social Sciences and Education*. Washington, DC: National Research Council / The National Academies Press.

Chung, Jaeyeop, et al. 2015. "A Study on Relationships between Age, Work Experience, Cognition, and Work Ability in Older Employees Working in Heavy Industry." *Journal of Physical Therapy Science* 27(1):155–57.

Cote, Mark P., et al. 2014. "Reference Values for Physical Performance Measures in the Aging Working Population." *Human Factors* 56(1):228–42.

Crandall, Christian S., et al. 2011. "Stereotypes as Justifications of Prejudice." *Personality and Social Psychology Bulletin* 37(11):1488–98.

Dalecki, Marc, et al. 2017. "Age-related Operator Deficits in a Realistic Instrument-control Task: Assessment of Possible Motor, Cognitive and Mental Causes." *International Journal of Industrial Ergonomics* 59:100–7.

Desmette, Donatienne and Mathieu Gaillard. 2008. "When a 'Worker' Becomes an 'Older Worker': The Effects of Age-related Social Identity on Attitudes toward Retirement and Work." *Career Development International* 13(2):168–85.

Dewa, Carolyn S., et al. 2004. "Nature and Prevalence of Mental Illness in the Workplace." *Healthcare Papers* 5(2):12–25.

Dong, Shengli. 2018. "Assessing Workplace Accommodation Requests among Older Workers." *Rehabilitation Counseling Bulletin* 61(2):101–11.

Ellison, Marsha L., et al. 2003. "Patterns and Correlates of Workplace Disclosure among Professionals and Managers with Psychiatric Conditions." *Journal of Vocational Rehabilitation* 18(1):3–13.

Finkelstein, Lisa M., et al. June 2019. "A Daily Diary Study of Responses to Age Meta-stereotypes." *Work, Aging and Retirement*. (https://doi.org/10.1093/workar/waz005).

Finkelstein, Lisa M., Michael J. Burke, and Manbury S. Raju. 1995. "Age Discrimination in Simulated Employment Contexts: An Integrative Analysis." *Journal of Applied Psychology* 80(6):652.

Finkelstein, Lisa M., Katherine M. Ryan, and Eden B. King. 2013."What Do the Young (Old) People Think of Me? Content and Accuracy of Age-based Meta-stereotypes." *European Journal of Work and Organizational Psychology* 22(6):633–57.

Giniger, Seymour, Angelo Dispenzieri, and Joseph Eisenberg. 1983. "Age, Experience, and Performance on Speed and Skill Jobs in an Applied Setting." *Journal of Applied Psychology* 68(3):469.

Hansson, Robert O., et al. 1997. "Successful Aging at Work: Annual Review, 1992–1996: The Older Worker and Transitions to Retirement." *Journal of Vocational Behavior* 51(2):202–33.

Head, Lynzee, et al. 2006. "Barriers to Evidence-based Practice in Accommodations for an Aging Workforce." *Work* 27(4):391–96.

Hickman, Jamye M., Wendy A. Rogers, and Arthur D. Fisk. 2007. "Training Older Adults to Use New Technology." *Journals of Gerontology* 62B:77–84.

Inceoglu, Ilke, Jesse Segers, and Dave Bartram. 2012. "Age-related Differences in Work Motivation." *Journal of Occupational and Organizational Psychology* 85(2):300–29.

Isaksson, Kerstin and Gunn Johansson. 2000. "Adaptation to Continued Work and Early Retirement Following Downsizing: Long-term Effects and Gender Differences." *Journal of Occupational and Organizational Psychology* 73(2):241–56.

Jenkins, Lisa and William J. Hoyer. 2000. "Instance-based Automaticity and Aging: Acquisition, Reacquisition, and Long-term Retention." *Psychology and Aging* 15:551–65.

Joanisse, Mélanie, Sylvain Gagnon, and Mihnea Voloaca. 2013. "The Impact of Stereotype Threat on the Simulated Driving Performance of Older Drivers." *Accident Analysis & Prevention* 50:530–38.

Kaliterna, Ljiljana, Zrjezdana P. Larsen, and Tihana Brkljacic. 2002. "Chronological and Subjective Age in Relation to Work Demands: Survey of Croatian Workers." *Experimental Aging Research* 28(1):39–49.

Kennedy, Kristen M., Ty Partridge, and Naftali Raz. 2008. "Age-related Differences in Acquisition of Perceptual-motor Skills: Working Memory as a Mediator." *Aging, Neuropsychology, and Cognition* 15(2):165–83.

Kenny, Glen P., et al. 2008. "Physical Work Capacity in Older Adults: Implications for the Aging Worker." *American Journal of Industrial Medicine* 51(8):610–25.

Kim, Sunghan, Lynn Hasher, and Rose T. Zacks. 2007. "Aging and a Benefit of Distractibility." *Psychonomic Bulletin & Review* 14(2):301–5.

Kooij, Dorien, et al. 2011. "Age and Work-related Motives: Results of a Meta-analysis." *Journal of Organizational Behavior* 32:197–225. (https://doi.org/10.1002/job.665).

Koolhaas, Wendy, et al. 2011. "Towards a Sustainable Healthy Working Life: Associations between Chronological Age, Functional Age and Work Outcomes." *European Journal of Public Health* 22(3):424–29.

Kowske, Brenda J., Rena Rasch, and Jack Wiley. 2010. "Millennials' (Lack of) Attitude Problem: An Empirical Examination of Generational Effects on Work Attitudes." *Journal of Business and Psychology* 25(2):265–79.

Kroon, Anne C., et al. 2016. "Poles Apart: The Processing and Consequences of Mixed Media Stereotypes of Older Workers." *Journal of Communication* 66(5):811–33. (https://doi.org/10.1111/jcom.12249).

Kulik, Carol T. 2014. "Spotlight on the Context: How a Stereotype Threat Framework Might Help Organizations to Attract and Retain Older Workers." *Industrial and Organizational Psychology: Perspectives on Science and Practice* 7(3):456–61. (https://doi.org/10.1111/iops.12180).

Kulik, Carol T., Sanjeewa Perera, and Christina Cregan. 2016. "Engage Me: The Mature-age Worker and Stereotype Threat." *Academy of Management Journal* 59(6):2132–56.

Lee, Marlene and Mark Mather. 2008. "U.S. Labor Force Trends." United States, Population Reference Bureau. *Population Bulletin*, 63(2):1–18.

Levy, Becca R., et al. 2000. "Reducing Cardiovascular Stress with Positive Self-stereotypes of Aging." *Journals of Gerontology Series B: Psychological Sciences and Social Sciences* 55(4):P205–213.

Lord, Robert L. 2002. "Traditional Motivation Theories and Older Engineers." *Engineering Management Journal* 1(3):3–7.

Loretto, Wendy and Phil White. 2006. "Employers' Attitudes, Practices and Policies towards Older Workers." *Human Resource Management Journal* 16(3):313–30.

Maestas, Nicole, Kathleen J. Mullen, and Stephanie Rennane. 2018. "Absenteeism and Presenteeism among American Workers." Washington, DC: NBER.

McCausland, Tracy C., et al. 2015. "The Technological Age: The Effects of Perceived Age in Technology Training." *Journal of Business and Psychology* 30(4):693–708. (https://doi.org/10.1007/s10869-014-9390-5).

McEvoy, Glenn M. and Wayne F. Cascio. 1989. "Cumulative Evidence of the Relationship between Employee Age and Job Performance." *Journal of Applied Psychology* 74(1):11–17.

McMullin, Julie Ann and Kim M. Shuey. 2006. "Ageing, Disability and Workplace Accommodations." *Ageing & Society* 26(6):831–47.

Motowidlo, Stephan J. and Harrison J. Kell. 2012. "Job Performance." *Handbook of Psychology, Second Edition*:12.

Munir, Fehmidah, et al. 2009. "Self-management of Health Behaviors among Older and Younger Workers with Chronic Illness." *Patient Education and Counseling* 77(1):109–15.

Ng, Thomas W. H. and Daniel C. Feldman. 2008. "The Relationship of Age to Ten Dimensions of Job Performance." *Journal of Applied Psychology* 93(2):392.

Ng, Thomas W. H. and Daniel C. Feldman. 2013. "How Do Within-person Changes Due to Aging Affect Job Performance?" *Journal of Vocational Behavior* 83:500–13. (https://doi.org/10.1016/j.jvb.2013.07.007).

Norheim, Kristoffer, et al. 2019. "Physical-work Ability and Chronic Musculoskeletal Complaints Are Related to Leisure-time Physical Activity: Cross-sectional Study among Manual Workers Aged 50–70 Years." *Scandinavian Journal of Public Health* 47. (https://doi.org/10.1177/1403494819839533).

OECD. 2006. *Live Longer, Work Longer*. Ageing and Employment Policies. Paris: OECD Publishing. (https://doi.org/10.1787/9789264035881-en).

Organ, Dennis W. 1997. "Organizational Citizenship Behavior: It's Construct Clean-up Time." *Human Performance* 10(2):85–97.

Peeters, Maria C. W. and Hetty van Emmerik. 2008. "An Introduction to the Work and Well-being of Older Workers: From Managing Threats to Creating Opportunities." *Journal of Managerial Psychology* 23(4):353–63.

Peters, Pascale, et al. 2019. "Please Don't Look at Me That Way: An Empirical Study into the Effects of Age-based (Meta-)Stereotyping on Employability Enhancement among Supermarket Workers." *Frontiers in Psychology* 10:249.

Peterson, Suzanne J. and Barry K. Spiker. 2005. "Establishing the Positive Contributory Value of Older Workers: A Positive Psychology Perspective." *Organizational Dynamics* 34(2):153–67.

Pinquart, Martin. 2001. "Age Differences in Perceived Positive Affect, Negative Affect, and Affect Balance in Middle and Old Age." *Journal of Happiness Studies* 2(4):375–405. (https://doi:10.1023/A:1013938001116).

Popkin, Stephen M., et al. 2008. "Age Is More Than Just a Number: Implications for an Aging Workforce in the U.S. Transportation Sector." *Applied Ergonomics* 39(5):542–49.

Posthuma, Richard A. and Michael A. Campion. 2009. "Age Stereotypes in the Workplace: Common Stereotypes, Moderators, and Future Research Directions." *Journal of Management* 35(1):158–88.

Reid, Kathryn and Drew Dawson. 2001. "Comparing Performance on a Simulated 12-hour Shift Rotation in Young and Older Subjects." *Occupational and Environmental Medicine* 58(1):58–62.

Rhodes, Matthew G.. 2004. "Age-related Differences in Performance on the Wisconsin Card Sorting Test: A Meta-analytic Review." *Psychology and Aging* 19(3):482–94. (https://doi.org/10.1037/0882-7974.19.3.482).

Riolli-Saltzman, Laura and Fred Luthans. 2001. "After the Bubble Burst: How Small High-tech Firms Can Keep in Front of the Wave." *Academy of Management Perspectives* 15(3):114–24.

Rodríguez-Cifuentes, Francisco, Jesús Farfán, and Gabriela Topa. 2018. "Older Worker Identity and Job Performance: The Moderator Role of Subjective Age and Self-efficacy." *International Journal of Environmental Research and Public Health* 15:2731. (https://doi.org/10.3390/ijerph15122731).

Rubin, David C. and Dorthe Berntsen. 2006. "People over Forty Feel 20% Younger Than Their Age: Subjective Age Across the Lifespan." *Psychonomic Bulletin & Review* 13(5):776–80. (https://doi.org/10.3758/BF03193996).

Rumrill, Phillip D., et al. 1998. "Situational Assessment of the Accommodation Needs of Employees Who Are Visually Impaired." *Journal of Visual Impairment & Blindness* 92(1):42–54.

Sargeant, Malcolm. 2008. "Older Workers and the Need for Reasonable Accommodation." *International Journal of Discrimination and the Law* 9(3):163–80. (https://doi.org/10.1177/1358229108 00900303).

Schmader, Toni and Sian Beilock. 2012. "An Integration of Processes That Underlie Stereotype Threat." Pp. 34–50 in *Stereotype Threat: Theory, Process, and Application*, edited by Michael Inzlicht and Toni Schmader. Oxford, UK: Oxford Scholarship Online.

Schwall, Alexander R. 2012. "Defining Age and Using Age-relevant Constructs." Pp. 169–86 in *The Oxford Handbook of Work and Aging*, edited by Jerry W. Hedge and Walter C. Borman. Oxford: Oxford University Press.

Sharit, Joseph, et al. 2009. "The Employability of Older Workers as Teleworkers: An Appraisal of Issues and an Empirical Study." *Human Factors and Ergonomics in Manufacturing* 19(5):457–77.

Shepard, Roy J., Erich Prien, and Garry L. Hughes. 1988. "Age Restrictions on Bus Driver Selection." *Journal of Human Ergology* 17:119–38.

Stamov-Roßnagel, Christian and Guido Hertel. 2010. "Older Workers' Motivation: Against the Myth of General Decline." *Management Decision* 48(6):894–906.

Steele, Claude M. and Joshua Aronson. 1995. "Stereotype Threat and the Intellectual Test Performance of African Americans." *Journal of Personality and Social Psychology* 69(5):797.

Sturman, Michael C. 2003. "Searching for the Inverted U-shaped Relationship between Time and Performance: Meta-analyses of the Experience/Performance, Tenure/Performance, and Age/Performance Relationships." *Journal of Management* 29(5):609–40.

Toomey, Eileen C. and Cort W. Rudolph. 2017. "Age-conditional Effects in the Affective Arousal, Empathy, and Emotional Labor Linkage: Within-person Evidence from an Experience Sampling Study." *Work, Aging and Retirement* 4(2):145–60.

Toossi, Mitra. 2006. "A New Look at Long-term Labor Force Projections to 2050." U.S. Bureau of Labor Statistics. *Monthly Labor Review* 129:19–39.

Van Dalen, Hendrik P., Kène Henkens, and Joop Schippers. 2010. "Productivity of Older Workers: Perceptions of Employers and Employees." *Population and Development Review* 36(2):309–30.

Van Den Berg, Peter T. 2011. "Characteristics of the Work Environment Related to Older Employees' Willingness to Continue Working: Intrinsic Motivation as a Mediator." *Psychological Reports* 109:174–86.

Van Rossem, Annick H. D. 2019. "Generations as Social Categories: An Exploratory Cognitive Study of Generational Identity and Generational Stereotypes in a Multigenerational Workforce." *Journal of Organizational Behavior* 40(4):434–55.

Verhaeghen, Paul and Timothy A. Salthouse. 1997. "Meta-analyses of Age–cognition Relations in Adulthood: Estimates of Linear and Non-linear Age Effects and Structural Models." *Psychological Bulletin* 122(3):231.

Vorauer, Jacquie D., Kelley J. Main, and Gordon B. O'Connell. 1998. "How Do Individuals Expect to Be Viewed by Members of Lower Status Groups? Content and Implications of Meta-stereotypes." *Journal of Personality and Social Psychology* 75(4):917.

Voyles, Elora C., Lisa Finkelstein, and Eden King. 2014. "A Tale of Two Theories: Stereotype Threat and Meta-stereotypes." *Industrial and Organizational Psychology* 7(3):419–22.

Vrantsidis, Thalia and William A. Cunningham. April 10, 2019. "The Effect of Knowledge about a Group on Perceived Group Variability and Certainty about Stereotype-based Inferences." *OSF Preprints*. (https://doi.org/10.31219/osf.io/84fua).

Waldman, David A. and Bruce J. Avolio. 1986. "A Meta-analysis of Age Differences in Job Performance." *Journal of Applied Psychology* 71(1):33.

Westerman, Steve J. and D. R. Davies. 2000. "Acquisition and Application of New Technology Skills: The Influence of Age." *Occupational Medicine* 50:478–82. (https://doi.org/10.1093/occ med/50.7.478).

Wolfson, Natalie, Thomas Cavanagh, and Kurt Kraiger. 2013. "Older Adults and Technology-based Instruction: Optimizing Learning Outcomes and Transfer." *Academy of Management Learning and Education* 13(1):26–44. (https://doi.org/10.5465/amle.2012.0056).

Wolfson, Natalie and Kurt Kraiger. 2014. "Cognitive Aging and Training: The Role of Instructional Coherence and Advance Organizers." *Experimental Aging Research* 40:164–86. (https://doi.org/10.1080/0361073X.2014.882206).

CHAPTER 14

# Productive Engagement among Older Workers

Yi Wang, Takashi Amano, and Kara A. Carter

## PRODUCTIVE AGING—BACKGROUND

The age distribution of the world's population is changing. Societies face huge challenges in providing economic support and health care to burgeoning older populations as the size of the younger population shrinks. Most discussions about aging societies focus on these major challenges, as they only consider the burden of older adults on the economy and health/social care system. Such discussions do not consider the "other side" of the story—the tremendous value of the demographic shifts. Older adults are living longer and, in general, healthier lives. In many developed countries, males and females at age sixty-five can expect to live at least another twenty to twenty-five years, respectively.[1] Additionally, education levels are increasing for each subsequent cohort of older adults.[2] In sum, the human capital of the aging population is growing, and this human capital needs to be viewed as an asset to be used to address issues associated with population aging.[3,4]

The emerging topic of "productive engagement in later life" (also known as "productive aging") is based on the assumption that societies cannot afford to dismiss the human capital of the older population. While there is no universally agreed upon definition, the terms "productive aging" and "productive engagement" represent a value and attitude shift away from older adults as burdens to older adults as contributors. The capacity of older adults can be engaged in activities that make economic and social contributions to society—working, volunteering, caregiving, and grandparenting—activities that produce goods and services, whether paid for or not. Engagement can lead to multiple positive ends: offsetting the financial strains of an aging population, contributing to the betterment of society, and maintaining the health of older adults.[5]

In fact, it is argued that there will be increased demand for older adults in these roles in future years. The labor supply in certain industries in the U.S. will demand longer working lives as the number of younger workers shrinks.[6] Growing social problems and reduced public expenditures will require increased volunteerism. Greater numbers of the oldest old will demand a larger force of caregivers. Thus, our society may require the productive engagement of older adults who perform a variety of valued functions.

## THEORETICAL DEVELOPMENTS AND UNDERLYING VALUES

The term "productive aging" was first introduced in 1983 by Robert Butler, a preeminent American geriatrician and the first director of the National Institute on Aging. Butler argued that we should transform retirement by extending work life and by expanding volunteer roles for the benefit of society as well as the individual.[7] He drew attention to the capacity of older adults and to the valued contributions they made to their families and communities.[8] A decade earlier, he pointed out in his award-winning book *Why Survive? Being Old in America*[9] that older Americans were unjustly labeled "unproductive" and viewed as incompetent and useless. He noted that the potential contributions of older adults were being limited by ageist attitudes, outdated organizational structures, and ineffective policies. With the productive aging concept, Butler started an advocacy movement among gerontologists and researchers to debunk the myth of a useless, incompetent older population. What followed was a period of knowledge production that documented the involvement of older adults as workers, formal volunteers, informal helpers, caregivers, and grandparents. This work served to challenge the negative images of aging that prevailed in U.S. society.[10]

The advocacy agenda began to shift to a more defined research agenda, as illustrated by the work of Bass, Caro, and Chen and Sherraden, Morrow-Howell, and Hinterlong. Bass and his colleagues offered a definition of productive aging that included engagement in activities that produced goods and services, paid or unpaid; and they included capacity-building activities, such as education and training. They also identified antecedents of participation in these activities: individual factors (motivation, attitude, gender), situational factors (roles, responsibilities, health, family situation), environmental factors (economy, culture, cohort), and social policy factors (employment policies, pensions, programs). They concluded that increasing the participation of older adults in activities that have economic value to society can best be achieved through policies, rules, and regulations.[11]

Sherraden and his colleagues furthered the development of a research agenda on productive aging. They offered a definition of productive engagement, including working, volunteering, and caregiving; and they advanced the idea that institutional capacity, social policies, and program development should be targeted to increase the productive involvement of older adults. They proposed that productive engagement is a function of both individual and institutional capacity.[12] As individual capacity grows in society, it is largely affected by sociodemographic factors and is less amenable to interventions, whereas social policies and programs from the federal to the organizational level can be modified to increase institutional capacity. Such policy level changes could ultimately increase participation in productive activities.

Some gerontologists express concern about the concept of productive aging. They fear that older adults will be judged by their ability or inability to be productive. They fear that older adults with low resources, both health and economic, may be expected to volunteer or work. Those older adults who have been disadvantaged across the life course, like women and ethnic minorities, may be further marginalized in later life when they continue to face discrimination in access to or support for productive engagement. (See also chapters 3–6.) In light of these concerns, it is important to articulate core values that guide the development of productive participation of older adults. As Morrow-Howell and Wang have suggested,[13] policies and programs should enhance engagement, not lead to exploitation. There should be opportunity for engagement, not obligation. There should be recognition and support for unpaid work, like caregiving. All older adults, across various levels of health, education, and income, should be included. In sum, the productive aging concept should, at heart, be about creating abundant opportunity and choices for productive engagement in later life and supporting older adults in these valued roles for benefit to the individual, the family, and society. The aim is to tap the growing human capital of aging societies, not to exploit older adults.

## OLDER WORKERS IN THE UNITED STATES

The number of older adults in the American workforce is growing. According to the U.S. Department of Labor, the labor force participation rate for those who were fifty-five years and over was 22.4 percent in 2016, and the rate increased for the twentieth consecutive year.[14] Given that the civilian labor force participation rate for the total population remained lower after the 2008 recession for more than a decade,[15] this figure shows an eloquent increase of older workers. In general, older workers with more health, education, income, and financial literacy work longer.[16]

The aging of the workforce is expected to continue. There is uncertainty about which industrial sectors will have labor shortages, but it appears that there will be a demand for longer working lives with the drop in the number of younger workers.[17] The percentage of workers who feel very confident in their ability to live comfortably in retirement remains low at just 17 percent.[18] American workers expect to work longer, for financial security as well as for personal meaning.[19]

While Americans are staying in the formal workforce longer, there is a trend toward more gradual withdrawal, with older workers stepping down to part-time work and transitional arrangements. (See also chapter 22.) There is also an increase in career switching, with older adults looking for different work in the last part of their working lives. These jobs tend to be lower paying, less demanding, and more flexible.[20] Despite the need and desire to work longer, older workers face certain challenges. For example, ongoing professional development and retraining is necessary to remain competitive, yet opportunities might not be readily available. (See also chapters 15 and 18.) Further, despite evidence that older workers are more experienced, loyal, and dependable than younger workers, American employers do not appear committed to older-worker-friendly environments; and there is still quite a bit of ageism and age discrimination in the workplace.[21] (See also chapters 11 and 12.)

Much research has focused on working, volunteering, and caregiving/grandparenting as *independent* topics, whereas this chapter focuses on the engagement in productive activities *among older workers*. Specifically, we review engagement types and patterns, determinants and motives, and benefits and outcomes. We also explore the gender and age differences in such engagement. The chapter aims to provide an overview of productive engagement among older individuals who participate in the labor force and also to shed light on future directions for supporting older workers engaging in productive activities outside of employment.

## ENGAGEMENT ACTIVITIES AMONG OLDER WORKERS

At the outset, operational definitions of productive engagement must be articulated. What types of engagement or what activities are considered productive? There is a lack of consistency in the literature; both broad and narrow definitions have been used by researchers. As stated above, productive activities at the narrowest level are defined as activities that produce goods and services, whether paid for or not, including working, formal and informal volunteering, and caregiving.[22] A broader definition also included capacity-building activities, such as education and training.[23]

Formal volunteering includes activities supported by an agency or formal organization, while informal volunteering includes mutual aid and neighboring. (See also chapter 24.) Caregiving involves helping others who require assistance because of an illness or disability and includes spousal caregiving and caregiving to family members or friends. (See also chapter 20.) These activities of work, volunteering, and caregiving can be assigned dollar values. For example, in the U.S., the estimated economic value of unpaid contributions was approximately $470 billion in 2017, up from an estimated $450 billion in 2009.[24,25] The approximate value of older adults' formal volunteering activities was $78 billion in 2017.[26] In sum, these activities have tremendous economic value that is quite easy to assess.

Instead of separating the productive activities and treating them independently, the authors used theoretical perspectives explained below (e.g., activity substitution / complement theory, role accumulation theory, role enhancement / strain / conflict theory) to review the multiple productive roles of older workers and to examine the antecedents as well as impacts of multiple productive roles on the well-being of older workers. The next section adopts a relatively broad definition of productive aging and reviews older workers' productive engagement in (1) formal and informal volunteering, and (2) caregiving and grandparenting.

### Older Workers and Volunteering

Formal volunteering refers to an activity undertaken willingly by an individual at no or minimal pay (like a stipend), directed toward community needs, and structured by an organization. The U.S. Bureau of Labor Statistics estimates that 23.5 percent of American adults aged sixty-five years and older volunteer commit more volunteer hours than younger workers.[27,28] Older adults with more human and social capital are more likely to volunteer—those with more education, more income, and more social connections. Those with fewer personal resources and those of ethnic minority status in the U.S. are less likely to undertake formal volunteering.[29] Health issues may also be a significant barrier to volunteer engagement.[30] Informal volunteering (sometimes called mutual aid or neighboring) is unpaid service that people provide on a more casual basis, outside any bureaucratized system. Compared to formal volunteers, informal volunteers are more likely to be older adults of lower socioeconomic status and diverse ethnic backgrounds.[31]

It has long been debated whether the relationship between paid work and formal volunteering is a trade-off or complementary. One theory that supports the former is *activity substitution*.[32,33] This theory posits that older adults engage in volunteering activity as a substitute for reduced roles in their employment, such as retirement. This premise was supported by some early empirical evidence indicating the negative relationship between time spent for paid work and time spent for volunteering among older adults.[34] However, some studies also suggest that activity substitution theory may not explain some aspects of the dynamic and complex relationship between employment and volunteering. For example, Mutchler and colleagues specify that the association between employment status and hours of volunteering was observed only among older adults who did not volunteer prior to retirement, and the relationship was not observed among those who engaged in volunteering before their retirement.[35] In addition, more recent empirical studies have found contradictory results for activity substitution theory. For example, Butrica and colleagues found that the onset of work resulted in a higher likelihood of volunteering than did the cessation of work.[36] McNamara and Gonzales showed no association between employment status and engagement and cessation of volunteering.[37] These findings imply that although it may be true that people are more likely to spend more time for volunteering after they fully or partially retire from paid work, engagement in volunteering may be more complex than just a substitution for paid work.

The other perspective regarding the relationship between paid work and volunteering sees volunteering as *complementary* to paid work. *Activity complement theory* regards volunteering activity as an extension of paid work.[38,39] According to this theory, employment status helps older workers to engage in volunteer activities because workers develop and maintain social resources through employment. Some empirical studies have supported this theory. For example, Tang showed that older adults who were not retired or partially retired were more likely to volunteer than those who fully retired or were not working. This study also revealed that being in employment transition was not associated with engagement or disengagement in volunteering activities.[40] These findings indicate that social networks embedded in the workplace may provide channels to volunteering among older workers and that older workers maintain those channels through transition from full employment to partial or full retirement. Another important implication of activity complement theory is that the workplace may be conducive to recruitment of older volunteers. McNamara and Gonzales suggest that gaining flexibility of working conditions for older workers may be an important strategy for recruiting older volunteers.[41] In addition, although not explicitly posited, if the relationship between paid work and volunteering is complementary, it can be assumed that engaging in volunteering may be associated with prolonged employment. For example, Lancee and Radl showed that formal social participation including volunteering delayed labor force withdrawal.[42] However, as Tang observed, the relationship between paid work and volunteering is dynamic and complex and depends on various factors.[43] Future studies are needed to clarify the dynamic and complex nature of volunteering among older workers.

Another aspect of volunteering among older workers is the health benefits for those who engage in both paid work and volunteering. According to *role accumulation theory*, people who have multiple roles may experience better well-being because role accumulation may provide personal and social resources.[44,45,46] Some empirical evidence supports the joint effect of paid work and volunteering on health-related outcomes. Hao found that older adults who engaged in both paid work and volunteering had lower depressive symptoms over time than those who did not engage in either activity.[47] This study further specified that the joint effect could be observed only when older adults had full-time (not part-time) work, lower level (fewer than one hundred hours per year) of volunteering, and concurrent participation in both paid work and volunteering over the study period. However, some studies have reported contradictory results. For example, Potočnik and Sonnentag revealed that volunteering was associated with better quality of life among retirees but not among older employees in Germany.[48] Additionally, Pavlova and Silbereisen showed that volunteering was related to better coping with occupational uncertainty among younger workers but not among older workers.[49] As suggested in Hao,[50] role accumulation may not be beneficial for all workers and volunteers since multiple roles may contain role constraints. Again, further studies are needed to gain better understanding of the joint effects of paid work and volunteering.

Finally, the difference between informal and formal volunteering has been understudied. In most studies, volunteering includes both forms. However, according to Mutchler, Burr, and Caro, formal and informal volunteering are structured differently.[51] They also found no association between paid work and informal volunteering. Since the detailed relationship between working and informal volunteering has not been well documented, future studies are needed to articulate whether the joint effect of working and informal volunteering differs from formal volunteering.

## Older Workers and Caregiving

A substantial proportion of the older population requires assistance in daily activities. According to a recent study reporting nationally representative data, nearly one-half of older adults, or eighteen million people, had difficulty or received help in the last month with daily activities.[52] With the rapid growth in absolute number and relative size of this age group, older adults' need for assistance will only increase. While many older adults are care recipients, numerous older adults are care providers, furnishing assistance to their spouses, parents, disabled adult children, grandchildren, and friends. Such care, known as activities of daily living, includes bathing, dressing, and grooming. Additional care, known as instrumental activities of daily living, includes the tasks necessary to maintain safety and independence. These include household tasks of meal preparation, shopping, bill paying, as well as arrangement of medical appointments, transportation, and medication compliance. The health and social care system of the U.S. depends heavily upon the labor provided by these caregivers.

The typical caregiver in the U.S. is a woman, aged forty-nine years. The average age of caregivers is increasing: 19 percent of caregivers are over age sixty-five, and 34 percent are between the ages of fifty and sixty-four years.[53] The average age of caregivers is expected to increase further with the aging of the baby boom generation. For the younger adult caregiver, the care recipient is more likely to be a parent, but with older caregivers, spousal caregiving is more prevalent. Among older caregivers age sixty-five and above, 70 percent are caring for a spouse while 42 percent are caring for parents or parents-in-law.[54]

Another form of caregiving in later life is grandparenting. Grandparenting is a traditional role for older adults, but recent trends in American society have led to growing rates of custodial grandparenting. The number of multigenerational households in the U.S. is increasing. In 2012, 4.2 million American households (3 percent of total households) contained children under age eighteen and their grandparents. Additionally, 10 percent of American children are living with their grandparents, and 2.7 million grandparents are providing primary caregiving to grandchildren.[55] Clearly, the contributions of older adults as primary caregivers to young grandchildren should be recognized and supported to achieve maximize positive outcomes for the children as well as the older adults.[56] According to the American Community Survey of the U.S. Census Bureau, there are about seventy million grandparents in the U.S., with an annual inflow of about two million. Most of the grandparents have grandchildren before retirement,[57] leading to an increased number of older Americans balancing work and grandparenting.

Therefore, it is important to understand the dynamic between caregiver and worker roles as we advance in years because the demand for caregiving by older adults is rising at a time when efforts that seek to extend paid employment are being made in response to shrinking labor pools. Theoretical perspectives that shed light on the associations between caregiving and paid work include *role theory*, specifically, two opposing perspectives on multiple roles: role *enhancement* and role *strain*. According to the role enhancement perspective, multiple-role occupancy offers the individual many avenues to resources not otherwise available to those without multiple roles.[58] The alternative perspective, role strain, emphasizes the cost to an individual associated with occupying multiple roles.[59] Stemming from a scarcity hypothesis, the notion of role strain posits that people do not have enough time or resources to adequately fulfill their multiple roles.[60] The role strain perspective has been widely used in studies on caregiving. The onset of caregiving is believed to be a key period, as it places demands on older individuals who are still participating in the labor force. The conflict between multiple roles can take a toll on health outcomes when caregiving responsibilities make it difficult for older employees to maintain healthy behaviors.[61]

Similar to the role strain perspective, the *microeconomic perspective* frames the relationship between caregiving and paid work as a question of time allocation. It is believed that individuals seek to maximize "utility," which can be derived from pecuniary (e.g., earnings from paid employment) and nonpecuniary roles (e.g., the "emotional returns" of caregiving).[62] When facing caregiving demand, individuals have to make decisions to allocate their limited time, energy, and resources. Individuals may choose to reduce their working hours or exit paid employment altogether; the decision depends on the marginal utility of paid work.[63] Therefore, compared with workers receiving low wages, workers receiving high wages are less likely to replace hours of employment with caregiving because of the greater amount of lost earnings.[64]

The growing literature on caregiving and extended work life has produced mixed results. Some studies find a negative association between caregiving and paid work,[65,66] some find a positive association,[67,68] and still others find a small effect or none.[69,70] The explanation for the positive association is that in addition to the pecuniary form of utility (i.e., wages), work may also provide *non*pecuniary forms of reward, such as self-esteem, support from coworkers, or enjoyment,[71] and may offer a respite from caregiving responsibilities.[72] On the other hand, due to the negative effects of caregiving on health,[73] caregiving responsibilities may subsequently lead to early labor market exit.[74]

To date, research focused on the effect of work, volunteering, or caregiving on health outcomes of older adults has produced mixed support for either perspective. For example, as summarized by Matz-Costa and her colleagues,[75] studies have found that the associations between disengagement from paid work and well-being in later life range from negative relationship,[76] to no relationship,[77] to positive relationship.[78] As for the impact of caregiving, findings are relatively consistent. Studies suggested that caregiving had a negative effect on well-being, particularly when extensive amounts of care were required.[79] Therefore, it is argued that it is not "the number of roles" that matters to health or well-being; it is one's experience of the roles, the "role quality"[80] that can differentially affect outcomes.[81] Specifically, the associations varied according to the experienced reciprocity between efforts spent and rewards received. Reciprocal exchange (i.e., balance between perceived effort and perceived reward) was associated with positive well-being, whereas nonreciprocal exchange (i.e., imbalance between perceived effort and perceived reward) was associated with negative well-being.[82,83]

## COMPARISONS BY AGE AND GENDER

As posited by *activity substitution theory*, some may replace roles and social resources lost through retirement by engaging in volunteering. Given that sixty-five is commonly considered retirement age, it may seem reasonable to assume that age is an important indicator of engagement in volunteering; however, not all studies agree. According to the U.S. Bureau of Labor Statistics, groups of thirty-five- to forty-four-year-olds and forty-five- to fifty-four-year-olds were more likely to engage in volunteering than other groups (28.9 percent and 28.0 percent, respectively, compared with 23.5 percent of people who were sixty-five years or older).[84] Moreover, retirement age may not be an important indicator of engagement in volunteering. Komp, Tilburg, and Van Groenou tested six hypotheses concerning the direct effect of age on volunteer engagement: age may be an important indicator because of natural withdrawal from society (disengagement theory); cohort effect; selection effect (those who live longer tend to engage in volunteering); retirement increases opportunities; retirement decreases opportunities; and health issues.[85] Their results suggest that all six of the hypotheses should be rejected, and the authors recommend that age should not be a primary criterion for recruiting volunteers.

Nevertheless, age may be an important factor of benefits people receive from volunteering. Some studies reported that benefits of volunteering, such as higher life satisfaction,[86] fewer depressive symptoms,[87] and physical health,[88] were more salient for older adults than younger adults. Those results can be explained by *compensatory theory*, as Okun et al. indicate.[89] The compensatory theory posits that the role given by volunteering enhances psychosocial resources and could be protective against diminished health and resources. In the study, Okun et al. showed that the relationship between volunteering and positive affect and resilience was strengthened as the number of chronic health conditions increased. Since people tend to have more chronic conditions and fewer resources as they age, volunteering may be more beneficial to older adults than younger adults. Future studies should further examine whether this moderation by health conditions is dependent on the type of health issue.

The above argument may be applicable to the joint effects of employment and volunteering. For example, Van Willigen found an association between volunteering and higher life satisfaction among older workers but not among younger workers.[90] This result suggests that older workers who are more susceptible to health issues than younger workers may receive more benefit from volunteer engagement. It should be noted, however, that this argument may not be applicable to occupational benefits of joint effects such as skill and knowledge acquisition and supports for occupational hardships. As noted, Pavlova and Silbereisen showed that volunteering among workers fostered coping with occupational uncertainty among younger workers but not among older workers.[91]

In sum, age may not be an important indicator of volunteer engagement or of the benefits that come from volunteering. Individual characteristics and situations of older workers should be noted when recruiting and supporting volunteer engagement among this population. Future studies should focus on the complex relationship between employment, volunteer engagement, and health issues rather than just focusing on chronological age.

Gender difference in the share of caregiving responsibilities has been well documented. In the United States, the bulk of care to aging family members is provided by middle-aged and older women, and that trend is projected to grow from its current twenty to twenty-two million women to thirty-seven to forty million by 2050.[92] Concurrently, older women now participate in the labor force at a rate higher than ever before, with statistics indicating that over 60 percent of women aged fifty-five years and older are actively engaged in the labor force.[93] These two demographic trends suggest that an increasing number of older women simultaneously embrace the roles of caregiving and working in the U.S.

Caregiving responsibilities not only affect a woman's work life,[94] but also take a toll on a caregiver's physical and psychological well-being. The latter has been very well documented. Research that investigated the interaction of the dual roles among older women indicates that they tend to experience frequent interruptions at work (e.g., late arrival, early departure, absence) due to caregiving responsibilities.[95,96,97] A report from the Sloan Center on Aging & Work indicates significant differences in the experiences of women with elder care responsibilities and those with other dependent care responsibilities.[98] Women who provided care to an older person reported having less access to flexible work options, receiving less support from their supervisors, and having less job security than did those who provided childcare or other dependent care.

In spite of the growth in the number of older working caregivers of both sexes, working female caregivers may sacrifice more economically. According to a report by MetLife Mature Market Institute, ten million caregivers aged fifty and above lose an estimated $3 trillion in wages, pensions, retirement funds, and benefits.[99] The total costs are higher for working women who are caregivers than for working men. With many older adults juggling work and caregiving, further research is needed to increase understanding of how best to improve the lives of older adults who are both in the labor force and family caregivers.

## CONCLUSION

Motivated by an underlying assumption that societies cannot afford to dismiss the growing, untapped human capital of the aging population, the concept of "productive engagement" proposes to include older workers as part of the solutions to challenges associated with population aging. This chapter summarized the theoretical development and definition of productive aging. The chapter also reviewed current knowledge about older adults' engagement in three primary productive activities (i.e., working, volunteering, and caregiving), specifically, the prevalence, determinants, health benefits, and economic value of the engagement.

The discussion revealed that formal volunteering and caregiving are two major activities undertaken by older workers. Formal volunteering can be complementary to employment, buffering negative effects of reduction of social roles and social network through the transition from full employment to full retirement. Health benefits of the joint effect of working and volunteering may exist, but further studies are needed to understand the complex relationship between health and productive engagement. Caregiving among older workers, on the other hand, may compete with staying longer in the workforce. Health and psychological costs and/or benefits of caregiving are dependent on a caregiver's personal experiences.

Finally, this chapter explored age and gender differences. It found the joint health benefits of employment and volunteering may be more salient for older workers than for younger workers, thus strategies to engage older workers need attention. Since typical caregivers are middle-aged women, caregiving affects women's work life and health more than men's. Considering the economic values of caregiving, supports for women within the workplace and for their health are necessary.

## NOTES

1. Wan He, Daniel Goodkind, and Paul Kowal. 2016. *An Aging World: 2015. International Population Reports.* National Institute on Aging. Washington, DC: U.S. Census Bureau. (https://www.census.gov/library/publications/2016/demo/P95-16-1.html).

2. Kevin Kinsella and Wan He. 2009. *An Aging World: 2009. International Population Reports.* National Institute on Aging. Washington, DC: U.S. Census Bureau. (https://www.census.gov/prod/2009pubs/p95-09-1.pdf).

3. Nancy Morrow-Howell. 2010. "Volunteering in Later Life: Research Frontiers." *Journals of Gerontology, Series B* 65(4):461.

4. Jennifer C. Greenfield. 2010. "An Overview of Informal Caregiving among Families in the U.S.: Who Are the Caregivers and How Are They Chosen?" Unpublished paper.

5. Nancy Morrow-Howell, James Hinterlong, and Michael Sherraden. 2001. *Productive Aging: Concepts and Challenges*. Baltimore: Johns Hopkins University Press.

6. T. Alan Lacey and Benjamin Wright. 2009. "Employment Outlook: 2008–18: Occupational Employment Projections to 2018." Washington, DC: Bureau of Labor Statistics. *Monthly Labor Review* 132:82. (https://stats.bls.gov/opub/mlr/2009/11/art5full.pdf).

7. Robert N. Butler. 1997. "Living Longer, Contributing Longer." *JAMA* 278(16):1372–73.

8. Robert N. Butler and Herbert P. Gleason. 1985. *Productive Aging*. New York: Springer.

9. Robert N. Butler. 1975. *Why Survive? Being Old in America.* New York: Harper & Row.

10. Morrow-Howell, Hinterlong, and Sherraden, *Productive Aging.*

11. Scott A. Bass, Francis G. Caro, and Yung-Ping Chen. 1993. *Achieving a Productive Aging Society.* Westport, CT: Auburn House.

12. Michael Sherraden, Nancy Morrow-Howell, and James Hinterlong. 2001. "Productive Aging: Theoretical Choices and Directions," P. 260 in *Productive Aging: Concepts and Challenges*, edited by Nancy Morrow-Howell, James Hinterlong, and Michael Sherraden. Baltimore: Johns Hopkins University Press.

13. Nancy Morrow-Howell and Yi Wang. 2013. "Productive Engagement of Older Adults: Elements of a Cross-cultural Research Agenda." *Ageing International* 38(2):159–70.

14. U.S. Department of Labor. 2016. "Civilian Labor Force Participation Rate."

15. Mitra Toossi and Elka Torpey. May 2017. "Older Workers: Labor Force Trends and Career Options." *Career Outlook.* U.S. Department of Labor.

16. Ernest Gonzales. 2010. "Working Longer: A Survey of Issues." Working Paper. Washington University in St. Louis: Center for Social Development.

17. Peter Cappelli. 2003. "Will There Really Be a Labor Shortage?" *Organizational Dynamics* 3(32):221–33.

18. Employee Benefit Research Institute. 2018. *2018 Retirement Confidence Survey.* Washington, DC: EBRI/Greenwald. (https://www.ebri.org/docs/default-source/rcs/1_2018rcs_report_v5mgachecked.pdf?sfvrsn=e2e9302f_2).

19. Michael Smyer and Marcie Pitt-Catsouphes. 2007. "The Meanings of Work for Older Workers." *Generations* 31(1):23–30.

20. Richard W. Johnson, Janette Kawachi, and Erik K. Lewis. 2009. *Older Workers on the Move: Recareering in Later Life.* AARP Public Policy Institute. Washington, DC. (http://webarchive.urban.org/uploadedpdf/1001272_olderworksonthmove.pdf).

21. David J. Ekerdt. 2010. "Frontiers of Research on Work and Retirement." *Journals of Gerontology Series B: Psychological Sciences and Social Sciences* 65(1):69–80.

22. Sherraden, Morrow-Howell, and Hinterlong, "Productive Aging."

23. Bass, Caro, and Chen, *Achieving a Productive Aging Society.*

24. Susan C. Reinhard et al. July 2015. "Valuing the Invaluable: 2015 Update." *Insight on the Issues*. Washington, DC: AARP Public Policy Institute. (https://www.aarp.org/content/dam/aarp/ppi/2015/valuing-the-invaluable-2015-update-new.pdf).

25. Susan C. Reinhard et al. November 2019. "Valuing the Invaluable: 2019 Update." *Insight on the Issues*. Washington, DC: AARP Public Policy Institute.

26. Corporation for National & Community Service. May 16, 2017. "Older Americans Provide Services Valued at $78 Billion to U.S. Economy." Senior Corps. Washington, DC.; John Foster-Bey, Nathan Dietz, and Robert Grimm. 2007. *Keeping Baby Boomers Volunteering: A Research Brief on Volunteer Retention and Turnover.* Washington, DC: Corporation for National & Community Service.

27. U.S. Department of Labor. February 25, 2016. "Volunteering in the United States—2015." Bureau of Labor Statistics. *News Release.* (https://www.bls.gov/news.release/pdf/volun.pdf).

28. Corporation for National & Community Service. November 15, 2016. "New Report: Service Unites Americans; Volunteers Give Service Worth $184 Billion." Washington, DC.

29. Marc A. Musick and John Wilson. 2003. "Volunteering and Depression: The Role of Psychological and Social Resources in Different Age Groups." *Social Science & Medicine* 56(2):259–69.

30. Fengyan Tang, Nancy Morrow-Howell, and Eunhee Choi. 2010. "Why Do Older Adult Volunteers Stop Volunteering?" *Ageing & Society* 30(5):859–78.

31. Iris Carlton-LaNey. 2006. "'Doing the Lord's Work': African American Elders' Civic Engagement." *Generations* 30(4):47–50.

32. Jan E. Mutchler, Jeffrey A. Burr, and Francis G. Caro. 2003. "From Paid Worker to Volunteer: Leaving the Paid Workforce and Volunteering in Later Life." *Social Forces* 81(4):1267–93.

33. Fengyan Tang. 2016. "Retirement Patterns and Their Relationship to Volunteering." *Nonprofit and Voluntary Sector Quarterly* 45(5):910–30.

34. Mutchler, Burr, and Caro, "From Paid Worker to Volunteer."

35. Mutchler, Burr, and Caro, "From Paid Worker to Volunteer."

36. Barbara A. Butrica, Richard W. Johnson, and Sheila R. Zedlewski. 2009. "Volunteer Dynamics of Older Americans." *Journals of Gerontology Series B: Psychological Sciences and Social Sciences* 64(5):644–55.

37. Tay K. McNamara and Ernest Gonzales. 2011. "Volunteer Transitions among Older Adults: The Role of Human, Social, and Cultural Capital in Later Life." *Journals of Gerontology Series B: Psychological Sciences and Social Sciences* 66(4):490–501.

38. Tang, "Retirement Patterns."

39. Maria K. Pavlova and Rainer K. Silbereisen. 2012."Participation in Voluntary Organizations and Volunteer Work as a Compensation for the Absence of Work or Partnership? Evidence from Two German Samples of Younger and Older Adults." *Journals of Gerontology Series B: Psychological Sciences and Social Sciences* 67(4):514–24.

40. Tang, "Retirement Patterns."

41. McNamara and Gonzales, "Volunteer Transitions among Older Adults."

42. Bram Lancee and Jonas Radl. 2012. "Social Connectedness and the Transition from Work to Retirement." *Journals of Gerontology Series B: Psychological Sciences and Social Sciences* 67(4):481–90.

43. Tang, "Retirement Patterns."

44. Phyllis Moen, Donna Dempster-McClain, and Robin M. Williams Jr. 1992. "Successful Aging: A Life-Course Perspective on Women's Multiple Roles and Health." *American Journal of Sociology* 97(6):1612–38.

45. Sam D. Sieber. 1974. "Toward a Theory of Role Accumulation." *American Sociological Review* 39(4):567–78.

46. Yanni Hao. 2008. "Productive Activities and Psychological Well-being among Older Adults." *Journals of Gerontology Series B: Psychological Sciences and Social Sciences* 63(2):S64–S72.

47. Hao, "Productive Activities."

48. Kristina Potočnik and Sabine Sonnentag. 2013. "A Longitudinal Study of Well-being in Older Workers and Retirees: The Role of Engaging in Different Types of Activities." *Journal of Occupational and Organizational Psychology* 86(4):497–521.

49. Pavlova and Silbereisen, "Participation in Voluntary Organizations."

50. Hao, "Productive Activities."

51. Mutchler, Burr, and Caro, "From Paid Worker to Volunteer."

52. Vicki A. Freedman and Brenda C. Spillman. 2014. "Disability and Care Needs among Older Americans." *Milbank Quarterly* 92(3):509–41.

53. AARP. 2015. *Caregiving in the U.S.* National Alliance for Caregiving. (https://www.aarp.org/content/dam/aarp/ppi/2015/caregiving-in-the-united-states-2015-report-revised.pdf).

54. AARP, *Caregiving in the U.S.*

55. AARP, *Caregiving in the U.S.*

56. Denise Burnette. August 9–11, 2011. "Supporting Grandparents as Family Caregivers." Paper presented at the Productive Aging in China: Towards Evidence Based Practice and Policy Conference. Peking University, China.

57. Peter Rupert and Giulio Zanella. 2018. "Grandchildren and Their Grandparents' Labor Supply." *Journal of Public Economics* 159:89–103.

58. Phillip A. Rozario, Nancy Morrow-Howell, and James E Hinterlong. 2004. "Role Enhancement or Role Strain: Assessing the Impact of Multiple Productive Roles on Older Caregiver Well-Being." *Research on Aging* 26(4):413–28.

59. Moen, Dempster-McClain, and Williams, "Successful Aging."

60. Ada C. Mui. 1992. "Caregiver Strain among Black and White Daughter Caregivers: A Role Theory Perspective." *The Gerontologist* 32(2):203–12.

61. Marcie Pitt-Catsouphes, Jacquelyn B. James, and Christina Matz-Costa. 2015. "Workplace-based Health and Wellness Programs: The Intersection of Aging, Work, and Health." *The Gerontologist* 55(2):262–70.

62. C. Katharina Spiess and A. Ulrike Schneider. 2003. "Interactions between Care-giving and Paid Work Hours among European Midlife Women, 1994 to 1996." *Ageing & Society* 23(1):41–68.

63. Ewan Carr et al. 2016. "The Association between Informal Caregiving and Exit from Employment among Older Workers: Prospective Findings from the U.K. Household Longitudinal Study." *Journals of Gerontology: Series B* 73(7):1253–62.

64. Fiona Carmichael, Susan Charles, and Claire Hulme. 2010. "Who Will Care? Employment Participation and Willingness to Supply Informal Care." *Journal of Health Economics* 29(1):182–90.

65. Carmichael, Charles, and Hulme, "Who Will Care?"

66. Andreas Kotsadam. 2011. "Does Informal Eldercare Impede Women's Employment? The Case of European Welfare States." *Feminist Economics* 17(2):121–44.

67. Derek King and Linda Pickard. 2013. "When Is a Carer's Employment at Risk? Longitudinal Analysis of Unpaid Care and Employment in Midlife in England." *Health & Social Care in the Community* 21(3):303–14.

68. Bettina Kubicek et al. 2010. "Work and Family Characteristics as Predictors of Early Retirement in Married Men and Women." *Research on Aging* 32(4):467–98.

69. Andrew Leigh. 2010. "Informal Care and Labor Market Participation." *Labour Economics* 17(1):140–49.

70. Ann Mooney, June Statham, and Antonia Simon. 2002. *The Pivot Generation: Informal Care and Work after Fifty*. Bristol, UK: Policy.

71. Fiona Carmichael and Susan Charles. 2003. "The Opportunity Costs of Informal Care: Does Gender Matter?" *Journal of Health Economics* 22(5):781–803.

72. Mooney, Statham, and Simon, *Pivot Generation*.

73. Martin Pinquart and Silvia Sörensen. 2003. "Differences between Caregivers and Non-caregivers in Psychological Health and Physical Health: A Meta-analysis." *Psychology and Aging* 18(2):250.

74. Rogier Van Rijn et al. 2014. "Influence of Poor Health on Exit from Paid Employment: A Systematic Review." *Occupational and Environmental Medicine* 71(4):295–301.

75. Christina Matz-Costa et al. April 2014. "Differential Impact of Multiple Levels of Productive Activity Engagement on Psychological Well-being in Middle and Later Life." *The Gerontologist* 54(2):277–89.

76. Dhaval Dave, Inas Rashad, and Jasmina Spasojevic. 2006. *The Effects of Retirement on Physical and Mental Health Outcomes*. Cambridge, MA: National Bureau of Economic Research.

77. Claudia Thomas, Michaela Benzeval, and Stephen A. Stansfeld. 2005. "Employment Transitions and Mental Health: An Analysis from the British Household Panel Survey." *Journal of Epidemiology & Community Health* 59(3):243–49.

78. Gill Mein et al. 2003. "Is Retirement Good or Bad for Mental and Physical Health Functioning? Whitehall II Longitudinal Study of Civil Servants." *Journal of Epidemiology & Community Health* 57(1):46–49.

79. Matz-Costa et al., "Differential Impact."

80. Rosalind C. Barnett and Janet Shibley Hyde. 2001. "Women, Men, Work, and Family: An Expansionist Theory." *American Psychologist* 56(10):781.

81. Matz-Costa et al., "Differential Impact."

82. Anne McMunn et al. 2009. "Participation in Socially-Productive Activities, Reciprocity and Well-being in Later Life: Baseline Results in England." *Ageing & Society* 29(5):765–82.

83. Morten Wahrendorf, Olaf von dem Knesebeck, and Johannes Siegrist. 2006. "Social Productivity and Well-being of Older People: Baseline Results from the Share Study." *European Journal of Ageing* 3(2):67–73.

84. Mary Meghan Ryan. 2015. *Handbook of U.S. Labor Statistics: Employment, Earnings, Prices, Productivity, and Other Labor Data*. 18th ed. Lanham, MD: Bernan.

85. Kathrin Komp, Theo Van Tilburg, and Marjolein Broese Van Groenou. 2012. "Age, Retirement, and Health as Factors in Volunteering in Later Life." *Nonprofit and Voluntary Sector Quarterly* 41(2):280–99.

86. Marieke Van Willigen. 2000. "Differential Benefits of Volunteering across the Life Course." *Journals of Gerontology, Series B: Psychological Sciences and Social Sciences* 55(5):S308–S18.

87. Musick and Wilson, "Volunteering and Depression."

88. Nancy Morrow-Howell et al. 2003. "Effects of Volunteering on the Well-being of Older Adults." *Journals of Gerontology, Series B: Psychological Sciences and Social Sciences* 58(3):S137–S45.

89. Morris A. Okun et al. 2011. "Does the Relation between Volunteering and Well-being Vary with Health and Age?" *International Journal of Aging & Human Development* 72(3):265–87.

90. Van Willigen, "Differential Benefits of Volunteering."

91. Pavlova and Silbereisen, "Participation in Voluntary Organizations."

92. Kim Parker and Eileen Patten. 2013. "The Sandwich Generation." *Pew Research: Social and Demographic Trends.*

93. Judith R. Gordon et al. 2012. "Balancing Caregiving and Work: Role Conflict and Role Strain Dynamics." *Journal of Family Issues* 33(5):662–89.

94. Meredith B. Lilly, Audrey Laporte, and Peter C. Coyte. 2007. "Labor Market Work and Home Care's Unpaid Caregivers: A Systematic Review of Labor Force Participation Rates, Predictors of Labor Market Withdrawal, and Hours of Work." *Milbank Quarterly* 85(4):641–90.

95. Julian Barling et al. 1994. "Predictors and Outcomes of Elder-care-based Interrole Conflict." *Psychology and Aging* 9(3):391.

96. Rosalind C. Barnett. 2005. "Ageism and Sexism in the Workplace." *Generations* 29(3):25–30.

97. Chizuko Wakabayashi and Katharine M. Donato. 2005. "The Consequences of Caregiving: Effects on Women's Employment and Earnings." *Population Research and Policy Review* 24(5):467–88.

98. Marcie Pitt-Catsouphes, Christina Matz-Costa, and Elyssa Besen. 2009. "Workplace Flexibility: Findings from the Age & Generations Study." Chestnut Hill, MA: Sloan Center on Aging & Work. *Issue Brief* 19:2–3.

99. MetLife Mature Market Institute. 2011. *The MetLife Study of Caregiving Costs to Working Caregivers: Double Jeopardy for Baby Boomers Caring for Their Parents.* Westport, CT: MetLife Mature Market Institute. (https://www.caregiving.org/wp-content/uploads/2011/06/mmi-caregiving-costs-working-caregivers.pdf).

## REFERENCES


AARP. 2015. *Caregiving in the U.S.* National Alliance for Caregiving. (https://www.aarp.org/content/dam/aarp/ppi/2015/caregiving-in-the-united-states-2015-report-revised.pdf).

Barling, Julian, et al. 1994. "Predictors and Outcomes of Elder-care-based Interrole Conflict." *Psychology and Aging* 9(3):391.

Barnett, Rosalind C. 2005. "Ageism and Sexism in the Workplace." *Generations* 29(3):25–30.

Barnett, Rosalind C. and Janet Shibley Hyde. 2001. "Women, Men, Work, and Family: An Expansionist Theory." *American Psychologist* 56(10):781.

Bass, Scott A., Francis G. Caro, and Yung-Ping Chen. 1993. *Achieving a Productive Aging Society.* Westport, CT: Auburn House.

Burnette, Denise. August 9–11, 2011. "Supporting Grandparents as Family Caregivers." Paper presented at the Productive Aging in China: Towards Evidence Based Practice and Policy Conference. Peking University, China.

Butler, Robert N. 1975. *Why Survive? Being Old in America.* New York: Harper & Row.

Butler, Robert N. 1997. "Living Longer, Contributing Longer." *JAMA* 278(16):1372–73.

Butler, Robert N. and Herbert P. Gleason. 1985. *Productive Aging.* New York: Springer.

Butrica, Barbara A., Richard W. Johnson, and Sheila R. Zedlewski. 2009. "Volunteer Dynamics of Older Americans." *Journals of Gerontology Series B: Psychological Sciences and Social Sciences* 64(5):644–55.

Cappelli, Peter. 2003. "Will There Really Be a Labor Shortage?" *Organizational Dynamics* 3(32):221–33.

Carlton-LaNey, Iris. 2006. "'Doing the Lord's Work': African American Elders' Civic Engagement." *Generations* 30(4):47–50.

Carmichael, Fiona and Susan Charles. 2003. "The Opportunity Costs of Informal Care: Does Gender Matter?" *Journal of Health Economics* 22(5):781–803.
Carmichael, Fiona, Susan Charles, and Claire Hulme. 2010. "Who Will Care? Employment Participation and Willingness to Supply Informal Care." *Journal of Health Economics* 29(1):182–90.
Carr, Ewan, et al. 2016. "The Association between Informal Caregiving and Exit from Employment among Older Workers: Prospective Findings from the U.K. Household Longitudinal Study." *Journals of Gerontology: Series B* 73(7):1253–62.
Corporation for National & Community Service. November 15, 2016. "New Report: Service Unites Americans; Volunteers Give Service Worth $184 Billion." Washington, DC.
Corporation for National & Community Service. May 16, 2017. "Older Americans Provide Services Valued at $78 Billion to U.S. Economy." Senior Corps. Washington, DC.
Corporation for National & Community Service. 2019. "Demographics." Washington, DC. (https://www.nationalservice.gov/serve/via/demographics).
Dave, Dhaval, Inas Rashad, and Jasmina Spasojevic. 2006. *The Effects of Retirement on Physical and Mental Health Outcomes.* Cambridge, MA: National Bureau of Economic Research.
Ekerdt, David J. 2010. "Frontiers of Research on Work and Retirement." *Journals of Gerontology Series B: Psychological Sciences and Social Sciences* 65(1):69–80.
Employee Benefit Research Institute. 2018. *2018 Retirement Confidence Survey.* Washington, DC: EBRI/Greenwald. (https://www.ebri.org/docs/default-source/rcs/1_2018rcs_report_v5mgachecked.pdf?sfvrsn=e2e9302f_2).
Foster-Bey, John, Nathan Dietz, and Robert Grimm. 2007. *Keeping Baby Boomers Volunteering: A Research Brief on Volunteer Retention and Turnover.* Washington, DC: Corporation for National & Community Service.
Freedman, Vicki A. and Brenda C. Spillman. 2014. "Disability and Care Needs among Older Americans." *Milbank Quarterly* 92(3):509–41.
Gonzales, Ernest. 2010. "Working Longer: A Survey of Issues." Working Paper. Washington University in St. Louis: Center for Social Development.
Gordon, Judith R., et al. 2012. "Balancing Caregiving and Work: Role Conflict and Role Strain Dynamics." *Journal of Family Issues* 33(5):662–89.
Greenfield, Jennifer C. 2010. "An Overview of Informal Caregiving among Families in the U.S.: Who Are the Caregivers and How Are They Chosen?" Unpublished paper.
Hao, Yanni. 2008. "Productive Activities and Psychological Well-being among Older Adults." *Journals of Gerontology Series B: Psychological Sciences and Social Sciences* 63(2):S64–S72.
He, Wan, Daniel Goodkind, and Paul Kowal. 2016. *An Aging World: 2015. International Population Reports.* National Institute on Aging. Washington, DC: U.S. Census Bureau. (https://www.census.gov/library/publications/2016/demo/P95-16-1.html).
Johnson, Richard W., Janette Kawachi, and Erik K. Lewis. 2009. *Older Workers on the Move: Recareering in Later Life.* AARP Public Policy Institute. Washington, DC. (http://webarchive.urban.org/uploadedpdf/1001272_olderworksonthmove.pdf).
King, Derek and Linda Pickard. 2013. "When Is a Carer's Employment at Risk? Longitudinal Analysis of Unpaid Care and Employment in Midlife in England." *Health & Social Care in the Community* 21(3):303–14.
Kinsella, Kevin and Wan He. 2009. *An Aging World: 2008. International Population Reports.* National Institute on Aging. Washington, DC: U.S. Census Bureau. (https://www.census.gov/prod/2009pubs/p95-09-1.pdf).
Komp, Kathrin, Theo Van Tilburg, and Marjolein Broese Van Groenou. 2012. "Age, Retirement, and Health as Factors in Volunteering in Later Life." *Nonprofit and Voluntary Sector Quarterly* 41(2):280–99.
Kotsadam, Andreas. 2011. "Does Informal Eldercare Impede Women's Employment? The Case of European Welfare States." *Feminist Economics* 17(2):121–44.
Kubicek, Bettina, et al. 2010. "Work and Family Characteristics as Predictors of Early Retirement in Married Men and Women." *Research on Aging* 32(4):467–98.
Lacey, T. Alan and Benjamin Wright. 2009. "Employment Outlook: 2008–18: Occupational Employment Projections to 2018." Washington, DC: Bureau of Labor Statistics. *Monthly Labor Review* 132:82. (https://stats.bls.gov/opub/mlr/2009/11/art5full.pdf).

Lancee, Bram and Jonas Radl. 2012. "Social Connectedness and the Transition from Work to Retirement." *Journals of Gerontology Series B: Psychological Sciences and Social Sciences* 67(4):481–90.

Leigh, Andrew. 2010. "Informal Care and Labor Market Participation." *Labour Economics* 17(1):140–49.

Lilly, Meredith B., Audrey Laporte, and Peter C. Coyte. 2007. "Labor Market Work and Home Care's Unpaid Caregivers: A Systematic Review of Labor Force Participation Rates, Predictors of Labor Market Withdrawal, and Hours of Work." *Milbank Quarterly* 85(4):641–90.

Matz-Costa, Christina, et al. April 2014. "Differential Impact of Multiple Levels of Productive Activity Engagement on Psychological Well-being in Middle and Later Life." *The Gerontologist* 54(2):277–89.

McMunn, Anne, et al. 2009. "Participation in Socially-Productive Activities, Reciprocity and Well-being in Later Life: Baseline Results in England." *Ageing & Society* 29(5):765–82.

McNamara, Tay K. and Ernest Gonzales. 2011. "Volunteer Transitions among Older Adults: The Role of Human, Social, and Cultural Capital in Later Life." *Journals of Gerontology Series B: Psychological Sciences and Social Sciences* 66(4):490–501.

Mein, Gill, et al. 2003. "Is Retirement Good or Bad for Mental and Physical Health Functioning? Whitehall II Longitudinal Study of Civil Servants." *Journal of Epidemiology & Community Health* 57(1):46–49.

MetLife Mature Market Institute. 2011. *The MetLife Study of Caregiving Costs to Working Caregivers: Double Jeopardy for Baby Boomers Caring for Their Parents.* Westport, CT: MetLife Mature Market Institute. (https://www.caregiving.org/wp-content/uploads/2011/06/mmi-caregiving-costs-working-caregivers.pdf).

Moen, Phyllis, Donna Dempster-McClain, and Robin M. Williams Jr. 1992. "Successful Aging: A Life-Course Perspective on Women's Multiple Roles and Health." *American Journal of Sociology* 97(6):1612–38.

Mooney, Ann, June Statham, and Antonia Simon. 2002. *The Pivot Generation: Informal Care and Work after Fifty.* Bristol, UK: Policy.

Morrow-Howell, Nancy. 2010. "Volunteering in Later Life: Research Frontiers." *Journals of Gerontology, Series B* 65(4):461–69.

Morrow-Howell, Nancy, et al. 2003. "Effects of Volunteering on the Well-being of Older Adults." *Journals of Gerontology, Series B: Psychological Sciences and Social Sciences* 58(3):S137–S45.

Morrow-Howell, Nancy, James Hinterlong, and Michael Sherraden. 2001. *Productive Aging: Concepts and Challenges.* Baltimore: Johns Hopkins University Press.

Morrow-Howell, Nancy and Yi Wang. 2013. "Productive Engagement of Older Adults: Elements of a Cross-cultural Research Agenda." *Ageing International* 38(2):159–70.

Mui, Ada C. 1992. "Caregiver Strain among Black and White Daughter Caregivers: A Role Theory Perspective." *The Gerontologist* 32(2):203–12.

Musick, Marc A. and John Wilson. 2003. "Volunteering and Depression: The Role of Psychological and Social Resources in Different Age Groups." *Social Science & Medicine* 56(2):259–69.

Mutchler, Jan E., Jeffrey A. Burr, and Francis G. Caro. 2003. "From Paid Worker to Volunteer: Leaving the Paid Workforce and Volunteering in Later Life." *Social Forces* 81(4):1267–93.

Okun, Morris A., et al. 2011. "Does the Relation between Volunteering and Well-being Vary with Health and Age?" *International Journal of Aging & Human Development* 72(3):265–87.

Parker, Kim, and Eileen Patten. 2013. "The Sandwich Generation." *Pew Research: Social and Demographic Trends.*

Pavlova, Maria K. and Rainer K. Silbereisen. 2012. "Participation in Voluntary Organizations and Volunteer Work as a Compensation for the Absence of Work or Partnership? Evidence from Two German Samples of Younger and Older Adults." *Journals of Gerontology Series B: Psychological Sciences and Social Sciences* 67(4):514–24.

Pinquart, Martin and Silvia Sörensen. 2003. "Differences between Caregivers and Noncaregivers in Psychological Health and Physical Health: A Meta-analysis." *Psychology and Aging* 18(2):250.

Pitt-Catsouphes, Marcie, Christina Matz-Costa, and Elyssa Besen. 2009. "Workplace Flexibility: Findings from the Age & Generations Study." Chestnut Hill, MA: Sloan Center on Aging & Work. *Issue Brief* 19:2–3.

Pitt-Catsouphes, Marcie, Jacquelyn B. James, and Christina Matz-Costa. 2015. "Workplace-based Health and Wellness Programs: The Intersection of Aging, Work, and Health." *The Gerontologist* 55(2):262–70.

Potočnik, Kristina and Sabine Sonnentag. 2013. "A Longitudinal Study of Well-being in Older Workers and Retirees: The Role of Engaging in Different Types of Activities." *Journal of Occupational and Organizational Psychology* 86(4):497–521.

Reinhard, Susan C., et al. July 2015. "Valuing the Invaluable: 2015 Update." *Insight on the Issues*. Washington, DC: AARP Public Policy Institute. (https://www.aarp.org/content/dam/aarp/ppi/2015/valuing-the-invaluable-2015-update-new.pdf).

Reinhard, Susan C., et al. November 2019. "Valuing the Invaluable: 2019 Update." *Insight on the Issues*. Washington, DC: AARP Public Policy Institute.

Rozario, Philip A., Nancy Morrow-Howell, and James E Hinterlong. 2004. "Role Enhancement or Role Strain: Assessing the Impact of Multiple Productive Roles on Older Caregiver Well-being." *Research on Aging* 26(4):413–28.

Rupert, Peter and Giulio Zanella. 2018. "Grandchildren and Their Grandparents' Labor Supply." *Journal of Public Economics* 159:89–103.

Ryan, Mary Meghan, ed. 2015. *Handbook of U.S. Labor Statistics: Employment, Earnings, Prices, Productivity, and Other Labor Data.* 18th ed. Lanham, MD: Bernan.

Sherraden, Michael, Nancy Morrow-Howell, and James Hinterlong. 2001. "Productive Aging: Theoretical Choices and Directions." Pp. 260–84 in *Productive Aging: Concepts and Challenges*, edited by Nancy Morrow-Howell, James Hinterlong, and Michael Sherraden. Baltimore: Johns Hopkins University Press.

Sieber, Sam D. 1974. "Toward a Theory of Role Accumulation." *American Sociological Review* 39(4):567–78.

Smyer, Michael and Marcie Pitt-Catsouphes. 2007. "The Meanings of Work for Older Workers." *Generations* 31(1):23–30.

Spiess, C. Katharina and A. Ulrike Schneider. 2003. "Interactions between Care-giving and Paid Work Hours among European Midlife Women, 1994 to 1996." *Ageing & Society* 23(1):41–68.

Tang, Fengyan. 2016. "Retirement Patterns and Their Relationship to Volunteering." *Nonprofit and Voluntary Sector Quarterly* 45(5):910–30.

Tang, Fengyan, Nancy Morrow-Howell, and Eunhee Choi. 2010. "Why Do Older Adult Volunteers Stop Volunteering?" *Ageing & Society* 30(5):859–78.

Thomas, Claudia, Michaela Benzeval and Stephen A. Stansfeld. 2005. "Employment Transitions and Mental Health: An Analysis from the British Household Panel Survey." *Journal of Epidemiology & Community Health* 59(3):243–49.

Toossi, Mitra and Elka Torpey. May 2017. "Older Workers: Labor Force Trends and Career Options." *Career Outlook.* U.S. Department of Labor.

U.S. Department of Labor. February 25, 2016. "Volunteering in the United States—2015." Bureau of Labor Statistics. *News Release*. (https://www.bls.gov/news.release/pdf/volun.pdf).

Van Rijn, Rogier M., et al. 2014. "Influence of Poor Health on Exit from Paid Employment: A Systematic Review." *Occupational and Environmental Medicine* 71(4):295–301.

Van Willigen, Marieke. 2000. "Differential Benefits of Volunteering across the Life Course." *Journals of Gerontology, Series B: Psychological Sciences and Social Sciences* 55(5):S308–S18.

Wahrendorf, Morten, Olaf von dem Knesebeck, and Johannes Siegrist. 2006. "Social Productivity and Well-being of Older People: Baseline Results from the Share Study." *European Journal of Ageing* 3(2):67–73.

Wakabayashi, Chizuko and Katharine M. Donato. 2005. "The Consequences of Caregiving: Effects on Women's Employment and Earnings." *Population Research and Policy Review* 24(5):467–88.

CHAPTER 15

# Self-Management of Career and Retirement

## Issues of Competence and Dyscompetence

Harvey L. Sterns and Anthony A. Sterns

### OVERVIEW

"I have said many times I will do this job as long as I can do it full steam. When I can't that will be the time when I'll step down." This 2018 quote from Justice Ruth Bader Ginsberg is the major theme of this chapter. People may have the opportunity to work longer, although few have a lifetime appointment. The decision to work longer may be because a person enjoys the involvement or needs to work longer for financial reasons or some combination of both reasons. The opportunity to continue to work beyond what was considered the perceived normative retirement age of sixty-five has been evolving. More individuals are continuing full-time work or part-time work in the same career or in a new career or in a bridge job before retirement. (See also chapters 21 and 22.) Many people continue to perform well and continue to work, and others choose a planned retirement. Some individuals may no longer be able to perform at an acceptable level and have to work in some altered capacity, either with different responsibilities or in a new role elsewhere. Maintaining competence is the key determinant of performance success. Nonperformance may be the reason a person needs to stop working, to choose less demanding employment, or to retire.[1]

## DEFINING COMPETENCE AND DYSCOMPETENCE

Competence is defined as one's total ability to deal with the work environment. Lawton and Nahemow proposed the ecological model of aging as an interaction between the person and environment.[2] The model had individual competence on one axis and environmental "press" on the other axis. When an individual's capability is challenged by the demands of the environment and performance is high, this falls in what we call the area of maximum performance. High capability with unchallenging, perhaps boring and unstimulating work results in marginal performance. If the environmental press is high but capability is insufficient and performance is low, the result may be maladaptive performance. Adaptation within the environmental press model can enhance a person's capabilities through increases in knowledge or skill level—in other words, education and training. Adaptation can also reduce job demand by providing a tool (e.g., computer) or support (e.g., team members) or improvement in the work environment (e.g., ergonomic workstation).

Competence is measured by the level of a person's knowledge, skills, and abilities. Operationally, competence determines the fit between a job's demands and the skills required to do the job. This is referred to as the person-job fit.[3] The degree of person-job fit has explanatory value for understanding the motivation of a person to decide to manage the fit or tolerate the lack of fit. Using this model, there is a clear sense of why a person might like or dislike their work (e.g., too hard, too easy, not a good fit). We illustrate this model using competence and job demand in figure 15.1. From the perspective of remaining in the position, a person is likely to want to stay if the challenge and the

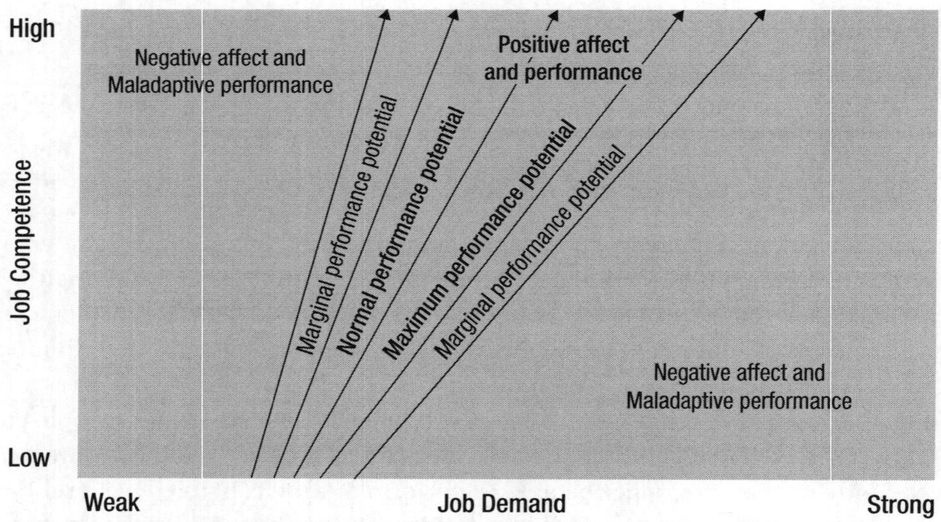


**FIGURE 15.1.** The Job Demand Model of Performance. Note: The more competent the individual, the wider the range of job situations in which a sense of comfort will be experienced and performance acceptable (top middle of the figure). Less competent individuals (left and right of the figure) are more likely to feel boredom (left) or stress (right) as a result of a mismatch with job demands.
*Source:* Sterns, H. and Sterns, A., 2020.

fit are good. If too easy perhaps, or especially if too hard or not a good fit, the person will leave—if that is an option. From a longitudinal perspective, if the job was a good fit early in a person's career but is no longer a good fit in the later stages of the career, this becomes the reason to leave or retire.

Dyscompetence is the opposite state of competence. It does not imply that workers were never competent, rather that they once were competent and are no longer due to a change in the knowledge or skills required for their positions. It can also describe a situation in which workers are capable of doing a good job, but the job is no longer needed (e.g., card punch machine repair technician).

Dyscompetence is typically an issue for highly knowledge-focused professions or highly skill-focused professions.[4] When and why decreases in performance exist and what factors are responsible for changes in performance need to be better understood. Remediation of substandard performance needs to be understood as well. Competence is possessing the requisite skills and abilities to perform effectively in the scope of professional practice. Establishing competence is usually done with criterion-referenced testing in which test takers demonstrate a set of competencies at a minimally required level or higher. Examples include the test required to enter legal practice (e.g., bar exam), medical practice (e.g., board certification), or nursing (e.g., NCLEX test).

Dyscompetence occurs when a worker fails to maintain acceptable standards in one or more areas of professional practice. Much of the discussion with regard to careers has been focused on physicians, nurses, and dentists. Medical professionals, challenged by the increasing and changing knowledge of medical practice, genetics, and pharmaceuticals, are expected to remain up to date; if such updating is not maintained, dyscompetence eventually occurs. Similarly, people in professions such as dancing or professional sports who can no longer compete at the highest level must at some point make the decision to retire. These challenges can apply to an aging workforce in general. Then again, work experience may lead to accommodations that allow workers to stay productive and minimize errors and injuries.

Balancing competence and dyscompetence and accurately and efficiently measuring such states are key challenges of organizational science and human resource management. How and when to carry out these assessments and how to incorporate both between-person variance and within-person variance over time is connected to how we view the employee over time and exactly what we mean by the term *older worker*.

## APPROACHES TO DEFINING THE OLDER WORKER

There are six definitions of the term *older worker*: chronological, functional, psychosocial, organizational, lifespan developmental, and psychology of work.[5] *Chronological* age is the earliest and most common approach to defining older workers. The Age Discrimination in Employment Act (ADEA) of 1967 and its 1978 and 1986 amendments define an older worker as any individual aged forty and over who is still an active worker.[6] Chronological age has been favored by courts in the assessment of individual performance capacity. Chronological age has consistently been supported as a bona fide occupational qualification (BFOQ) when reasonably related to job performance.

The BFOQ affords an opportunity to establish an age limit, if the case can be made that certain age-related changes would impair an employee's ability to perform the required skills of the job.

Commercial airline pilots, for example, are still subject to mandatory retirement, now at sixty-five, raised from sixty, based on their chronological age. Airline pilots are tested biannually and must pass a physical test, so they are monitored closely to ensure that their performance meets expectations. Typical workers receive annual performance appraisals, and these contain elements of skill and knowledge evaluation. Good appraisals, such as "360" assessments from subordinates, peers, and superiors, will include guidance on those skills that are excellent, those that are adequate, and those that need improvement. Often, however, the organization leaves corrective action related to maintaining or adding competencies at the discretion of the employee. Over time, those skills that need improvement and go unaddressed can accumulate, and the fit becomes increasingly problematic for the person and the organization.

*Functional* age focuses on the individual's performance when assigning an age. Functional age is presented as a single index that combines assessments based on biological and psychological changes. These take into account the range of abilities as well as changes in skill, wisdom, and experience that may either increase or decrease in the individual. The index is an indication of how the person performs compared to the average individual of a given age. So, we would say that a specific fifty-year-old who can run a mile as fast as the average twenty-five-year-old has a functional age of twenty-five. Two ways of judging functional age are physical abilities analysis and functional capacity assessment. These assessments require validation and age norming and are used more often for research or for very high-performance standards, such as the pilot qualifications previously mentioned, or for first responders who have important physical and endurance requirements to ensure the safety of themselves and their teammates. Professional competence evolves out of this definition as the ability to function effectively at the profession's essential tasks. That is, specific knowledge and technical skills provide the ability to solve the types of problems encountered within the profession at a measurable level indicating success.

*Psychosocial* definitions of older workers come from societal norms and social perceptions of older workers. When workers are seen as "older," the attitudes of others toward them and the implications for personnel decisions of the label "older worker" are central issues within this view. Research has shown considerable change in organizations' opinions about older workers—revealing both negative and positive perceptions. Research in the 1970s and 1980s found that negative perceptions about older workers included being regarded as more difficult to train, less receptive to technological changes, more accident prone, less promotable, and less motivated. On the positive side, older adults were perceived as more dependable, cooperative, conscientious, consistent, and knowledgeable. In the 1990s, perceptions shifted such that a sizeable minority of older workers desired to continue working.[7] More recently, older workers are seen as likely to continue working, due in equal parts to a desire to be active and to financial necessity.

Stereotypes of older workers remain.[8] On the negative side, older workers are still viewed as having less flexibility, less energy, disinterest in training, and greater health problems. Positive stereotypes depict them as very loyal and reliable employees. These attitudes can influence whether workers get opportunities and encouragement to maintain competencies related to the job. Professional competence here depends on the intellectual ability, personality traits, motivation, attitudes, and values of the individual that facilitate its development and ongoing maintenance.

According to Smyer and Pitt-Catsouphes at the Center on Aging & Work, Boston College, one of the dimensions in which workers can be viewed is through a generational lens.[9] Each cohort is not only similar in age but has also been exposed to significant historical events that may alter views or values expressed in the workplace. Examples include the technological savvy of millennials (born between 1981 and 1999) who grew up with easy access to computers and the internet, or baby boomers (born between 1946 and 1964) who had an expectation of lifelong employment and a sense of loyalty that is likely not present in more recent generations.

Managers should avoid misusing the generational lens and overgeneralizing certain characteristics of a "generation" to all members of the cohort instead of treating each employee as an individual. In addition, they should be aware that different views, values, or work ethics can cause conflict in the workplace when responsibilities require team interaction and collaboration. The relational pattern of resilience is pertinent here as older workers must count on positive peer interactions and support to maintain a successful work environment. Another interesting aspect of this perspective is that competence and dyscompetence may be viewed differently by each generation. It is more a matter of each cohort ascribing different weights to aspects of performance than of cohorts focusing on completely different aspects. The different emphasis on task execution and components of performance can give a diverse workforce a positive robustness, and it can also be expressed negatively as divisiveness.

The *organizational* approach to age focuses on understanding the roles of individuals in an organization and the impact of the mix of ages of personnel on the organization as a whole. This perspective emphasizes expertise, seniority, and tenure rather than age per se. An organization is considered old when the average age of its members is older. For example, a start-up software company may have an average age in the thirties with employee tenures of less than one year, whereas an established manufacturing company may have an average age of forty-five and tenures of fifteen years or more. As the average age of personnel increases, attitudinal and financial demands on the organization may change. This approach is most concerned with the nature of and interactions within the organization. The mix of cognitive and physical requirements determined by the activities of personnel as a whole is the important consideration when examining the impact of aging on workers in an organization. For the start-up, software languages and programming are apt to change quickly, whereas in manufacturing environments the change is often more gradual, with rare discontinuous sudden changes.

The *lifespan* orientation combines each of the above approaches with an understanding that people are dynamic and that behavioral change occurs over the entire working life of individuals. This approach emphasizes recognition of substantial individual differences as individuals age.[10] Individuals are influenced by normative, age-graded biological and environmental developments (physical and cognitive changes as one ages); normative, history-graded factors (generational events); and nonnormative occurrences unique to every individual. These normative and nonnormative changes interact to influence and steer an individual's career path. Over time, these influences determine the strengths and limitations, the skills and experience that individuals bring to their organizational roles. They determine the level of motivation an individual has to be engaged with a job and to ensure that existing skills are maintained and new opportunities pursued. Each worker begins with different potentials and each person will improve, achieve, and decline uniquely.

Finally, the *psychology of work* perspective on age goes beyond the traditional approaches of industrial/organizational and vocational psychology.[11] It formally considers the impact of social barriers that prevent individuals from fully achieving their potential. It focuses on the realities of working life as they are experienced, whether or not an individual is pursuing a hierarchical self-managed career. According to this perspective, the person is operating in an environment where fit and achievement are not a primary concern; instead, more basic needs of day-to-day survival dominate. This perspective is particularly helpful for understanding those individuals who are challenged by a poor regional economy, disability or addictions, or work limitations due to care of children, spouse, or older loved ones.

Professional competence is demonstrated by job performance. (See also chapter 13.) Supervisory personnel typically assess a person's level of competence by observational and assessment procedures associated with licensure or recertification. These involve evaluating a sample of the professional's behavior (performance) via tests, simulation tasks, or proof of continued training (e.g., continuing education units).

These six definitions of older workers will be affected by the degree to which the impact of future technological changes, employment opportunities, and incentives to remain in the workforce are understood and interpreted. The definitions also cast light on how competence is defined, maintained, and assessed. Also to be considered is whether an individual is on a career track or experiences a disconnected series of jobs over the lifetime of work. Individuals with greater educational attainment are better able to adapt and succeed financially over their working lifetimes. Regardless, effective interventions can be tailored when these issues are appropriately considered.

Each of the six approaches emphasizes a unique viewpoint and produces recommendations for interventions specific to that perspective. The chronological definition emphasizes legal issues. Functional age perspectives emphasize the capacity of the worker, both physically and cognitively, and measurement of that capacity. Psychosocial perspectives require methods for monitoring the attitudes of individuals and determining perceived norms in organizations and in industry. Organizational perspectives focus on the management of human resources and require measures of productivity and efficiency. The lifespan perspective and the psychology of working perspective remind us to look for individual differences and to be cautious of overgeneralizing. These six perspectives must each be considered in turn as assessments of productivity and functionality are weighed and policies and practices are determined regarding older workers.

In order to understand the role of aging on the productivity of a workforce (the advantages and the limitations of aging's impact on individual workers), the tasks involved in a job must be well defined and understood. Defining formally what is required of the person doing the job is determined by a process known as job analysis.

Job analysis is the methodology for the development of a job description. The job description documents the knowledge, skills, and abilities required of an individual to perform the job successfully. In other words, the job analysis provides the criteria for defining and measuring the competencies needed to perform the job. The level of a person's competence in relation to the job's demand contributes to how long he or she will work and influences the decision to retire.

## THE SELF-MANAGEMENT MODEL OF CAREER AND RETIREMENT

Many people now can choose how long they will work and when they will retire. Others may find themselves laid off or having to accept a buyout much earlier than expected, resulting in the search for new employment. All too frequently, older adults are unable to build up sufficient resources in a defined contribution plan to retire or are part of an industry where defined benefit plans were not protected, and retirement income is far below what was anticipated. The choice to retire can be gradual or sudden depending on the planning, the opportunities presented, and crises encountered.

In this section, we employ the lens of self-management to examine the challenges faced by midlife and older workers seeking to continue working.[12] As organizations transition to flatter, more streamlined, more technological- and automation-focused configurations, ongoing job restructuring often requires retraining or may lead to job obsolescence. Present and future older workers are increasingly pressed to take active involvement in and responsibility for career management. One may want to continue in a present job since reemployment may not be possible in challenging economic periods, such as experienced in the early 2010s. Another may want to leverage recent training and switch positions or employment, switching being easier in times of labor shortages, such as experienced in the early 2020s.

Decisions regarding career and updating are based on many dimensions. Individuals can move in or out of the work role. We propose a multidimensional model for self-management of retirement that incorporates continued retraining and extended time working.[13]

## EVOLVING FROM AN EARLY RETIREMENT MESSAGE TO A "WORK FOR PURPOSE" PERSPECTIVE

A person's self-concept is influenced by many factors in consideration of retirement issues (see figure 15.2). First, there is the understanding of our past selves and what values, preferences, and desires are based in our past. This is countered and complemented by our future selves—the possibility of new lifestyles, new living environments, new friends, new actions or options; or the decision to live in the same community but carry out a new set of life activities outside of work in a familiar environment. Three factors are important here: an understanding of change and an awareness of the passage of time; the amount of perceived control that we have about

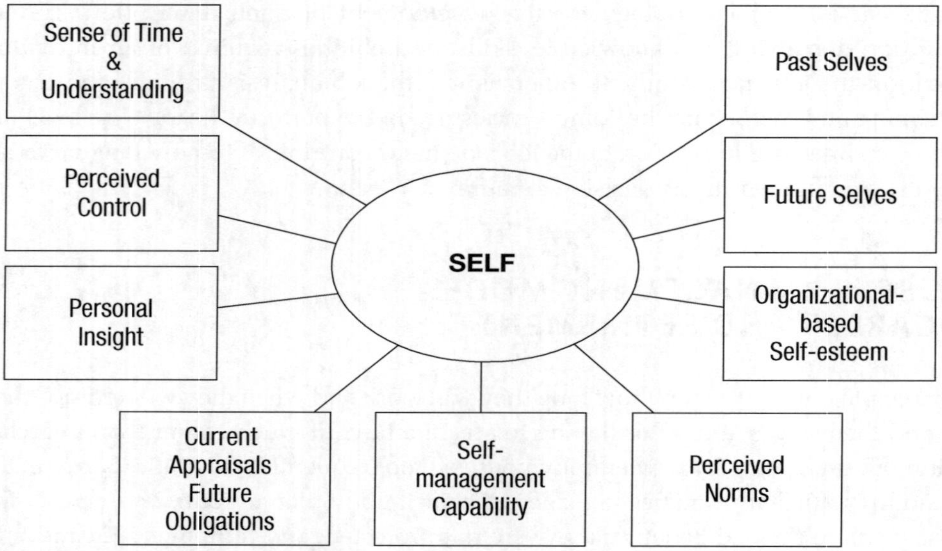


**FIGURE 15.2.** Influences on Self
*Source:* Sterns, H. and Kaplan, J., 2003.

our lives at the personal level in relation to our work and nonwork roles; and personal insight—how well we understand ourselves, our motivations, our personal desires, our work approaches, our relations to family, friends and organizations. Self-study, education, and counseling may aid this process.

Figure 15.3 focuses on the work environment. Briefly, this involves self-evaluation of the employment situation. The older worker needs to learn how he or she is viewed

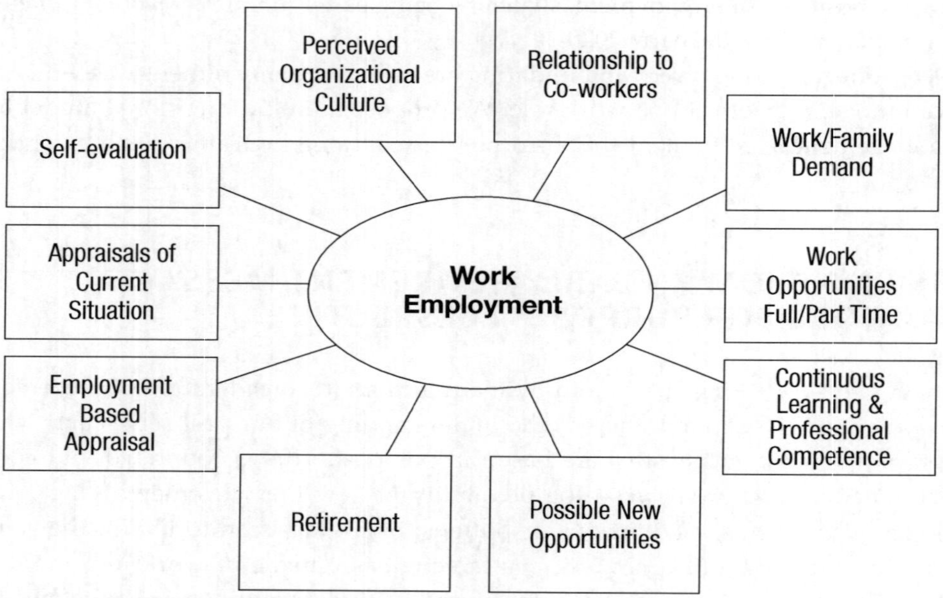


**FIGURE 15.3.** Work Influences
*Source:* Sterns, H. and Kaplan, J., 2003.

by supervisors, what the outcomes of performance appraisals are, where perceived growth opportunities exist within the organization, and how other later-career employees have been treated. Part of this process leads to recognizing one's personal strengths and weaknesses and one's approach to meeting assignments, deadlines, and so forth.

Figure 15.4 focuses on marriage and other significant relationships that can influence decisions regarding work and retirement. One of the benefits of formal retirement education is that husbands and wives or significant others can engage in planning exercises that often help to create awareness. Family relationships may become more important and become a major influence in self-management of retirement. For instance, caregiving responsibility for parents or spouse may be a major concern. (See chapter 20.) In many cases, an employee may choose or feel forced to retire in order to provide care to loved ones, while admitting that he or she did not expect retirement to become a major caregiving experience. Corporate eldercare services have been available for over two decades to assist employees who have care responsibilities.

Figure 15.5 relates to what keeps people in their home communities, those aspects of community that are important to providing a meaningful context and sense of belonging. Much of the classical retirement literature has focused on these dimensions of community. What is important here is how these dimensions relate to our self-concept and how this influences our decisions to continue to work or retire. Some individuals feel alienated by their community relationships and wish to reestablish themselves in a new community context. Others may have more than one residence and move back and forth between the new and the old empowered by both locations, and still others totally enjoy being a part of roles and involvements that are long standing. Self-concept is influenced in many of the above-described ways. What is essential is the ability to bridge from the individual level to the broader work and societal context.

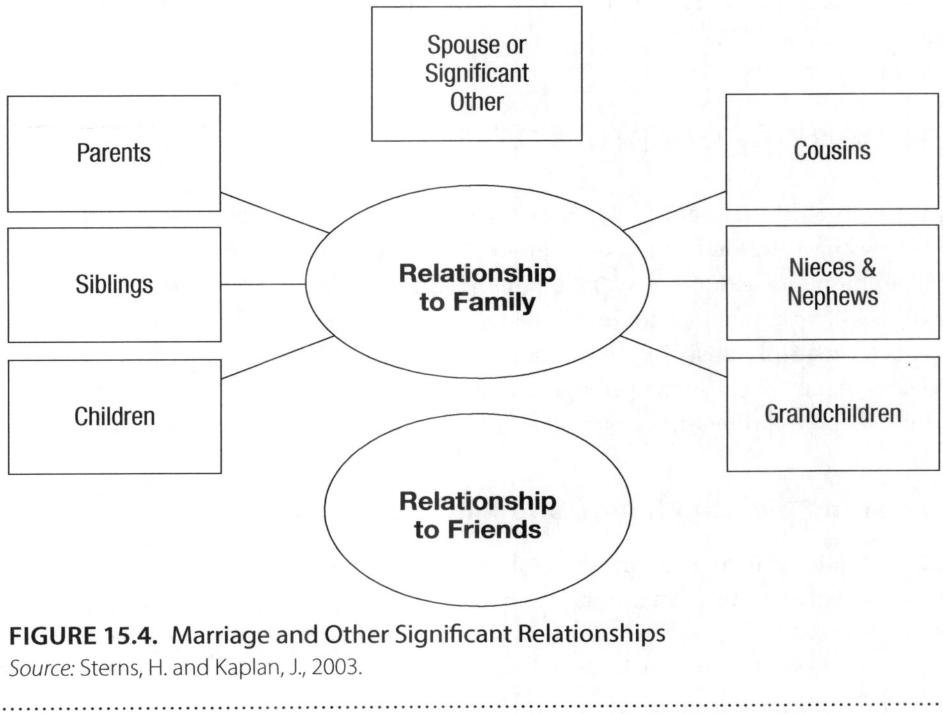


**FIGURE 15.4.** Marriage and Other Significant Relationships
*Source:* Sterns, H. and Kaplan, J., 2003.

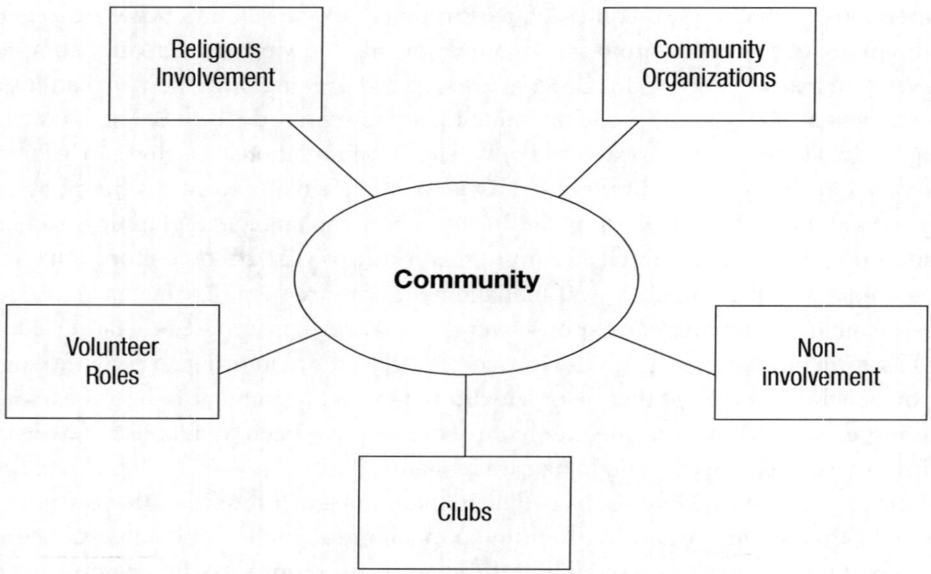


**FIGURE 15.5.** Community Influences
*Source:* Sterns, H. and Kaplan, J., 2003.

From an organizational perspective, it is important for managers and executives to have a clear understanding of what it means for adult and older workers to keep working longer in terms of planning, training, and knowledge management. Managers must not be driven by negative stereotypes when considering which approaches will retain the embedded knowledge of older adult workers, particularly the best workers. Equally important is training and retraining workers to ensure they are fully competent and have the requisite skills to continue to perform well in their jobs. (See also chapters 17 and 18.)

## FACTORS REINFORCING WORKING LONGER

Continuing to work in later life depends on a combination of factors—the organization providing support in the form of accommodations for meeting the physical and biological requirements of extended work life, as well as the older adult having continuing motivation to work, whether internal satisfaction derived from pleasurable interactions and impact, or simply ensuring that food, safety, and shelter needs are met. Work often plays a strong part in self-perception and in social connection, and it may offer the most important social relationships a person has and as a result wants to maintain.

### Age-Related Physical Change and Functional Capacity

Age and job performance are generally unrelated.[14] General performance of older workers is less of an issue than the ability to maintain skill competency when responding to highly frequent changes, such as increases in mobile and cloud-based technologies. Extensive research shows that learning capabilities do not significantly decline with age.[15] The factors that drive age-related decline in older workers (e.g., sensory decline) provide guidance on appropriate ergonomic interventions an organization may utilize to support extending the length of time older workers remain on the job.

## Changes in Health and Rehabilitation

Because health is one of several variables affecting the functional capacity of older persons, it is important to know what decades of research can teach us about it. (See also chapter 19.) What aspects of health are used for measuring disability and its impact on work life? Health may be defined in several ways. One perspective is that of total well-being and absence of disease. However, distinguishing between chronic and acute disease reminds us that functional capacity is not directly tied to the presence of disease or impairment. Heart disease, cancer, lung and liver disease, and stroke are major conditions that increase with age. Other disabling conditions that affect people in all age groups include arthritis, deformities or orthopedic impairments, hearing and speech impairments, and intellectual disability. These disabilities may limit the kind of work an individual can do, but they need not prevent work altogether.

Disability—defined by the inability to perform one or more major life activities—affected more than 11 percent of Americans in 2002 and 14 percent in 2018. This means that forty-six million people have functional limitations that prevent them from working, attending school, or maintaining a household.[16] Still, large numbers of middle-aged and older persons with disabilities are able to work, and an increasing number continues to do so. Although older persons (over age sixty-five) have more health problems than middle-aged persons (ages forty-five to sixty-four), there are no major differences between the age groups in terms of work performance. Health patterns do differ by gender, with women reporting more problems overall than men. The health status of older Hispanics and blacks is poorer than that of older whites. Older black women and men are disadvantaged in terms of their health status, especially older black men.

The majority of people aged forty-five years and older report no functional limitations from chronic conditions. While two-thirds of those aged forty-five and older rate their health as good or excellent, the remaining third report health limitations leading to some level of impairment. Ten percent of those aged forty-five years and older categorize themselves as unable to work or do housework as a result of having a chronic condition.

Health status has been a frequent theme in studies about leaving the workforce. In general, declining health over time, as well as the onset of new health conditions, has been found to be positively related to earlier retirement. The development of chronic health issues may make individuals more aware of the realities of aging.[17]

## Age-Related Cognitive Changes in Performance

There are real complexities in the relationship between cognitive change and maintaining work ability.[18] There are also very different concerns from the perspective of the organization and the perspective of someone self-managing his or her career. Industrial gerontology first concerned itself with research on age changes in intelligence, memory, and learning. More recent efforts are looking at changes over the lifespan in effortful and automatic processing and the development and maintenance of expertise. Let's consider how professional knowledge and well-practiced job skills are affected by changes in cognitive ability as men and women reach the last stages of their career.

Recent dynamic approaches have produced mental models reflecting great diversity and individual change in adult and older adult workers. These models help illuminate how well-researched declines in motor and perceptual speed can be offset by the combined positive effects of increased knowledge, added skills, and practice from doing work daily. This phenomenon provides guidance on possible workplace interventions and accommodations that will support functioning and work behaviors despite changes in abilities and health that become disabilities and chronic conditions.

## Changes in Intelligence

Over sixty years of gerontological research has provided important information regarding intellectual ability, learning, and memory. Major longitudinal studies have shown that most individuals maintain stable intellectual functioning well into the seventies and beyond.[19] Unless there is a major health problem, most people remain at the same level of intellectual ability up to very late life.

Recent evidence has demonstrated that plasticity and modifiability in brain function normally remain intact throughout a person's working career.[20] In cases where adults must divide attention and process complex information, evidence does find performance declining with age. While information-processing capacity and efficiency of processing may be affected by aging, most job situations do not involve maximal levels of performance. Thus, most adult and older adult workers can continue to perform satisfactorily. For many work-related cognitive abilities, there is no age variation across the working years.

## Prolonging Productivity of Workers across the Lifespan

Designing a workplace that supports older workers in their efforts to remain updated and competent is one important application of motivation research. The design of training opportunities and methods should be age sensitive. When employers are sensitive and take into account age-related changes of older workers, this clears the way for supportive actions and accommodations that lead to greater success in training and updating.

Equipment, particularly mobile devices such as smartphones and tablets, can assist older workers in adopting compensatory behaviors and support monitoring of them. These can serve as "cognitive prosthetics" to help older workers adapt to changing demands of work tasks.[21] Other modifications such as cues about monitoring oneself for safety reasons can also have a substantial impact on older workers.

By redesigning training, a deeper degree of learning the material may be achieved if the training design reduces distractions detrimentally affecting allocation of working memory to learning new information related to job tasks. Such redesign will have greater impact on older trainees when these important age-related factors are accounted for and should lead to increases in feelings of trainability and job performance competency.

More attention should also be placed on information exchange interfaces and the user experience between workers and information systems, now referred to as UX. Organizations should evaluate and understand the underlying cognitive subsystem of the man-machine system to ensure a proper match between employee and information system as this may have a differential impact on older adults. More attention should be paid in UX experimentation to the inclusion of older workers so that any age-related changes are designed out. All these suggested modifications will ensure that the organization and the work environment are supportive of maintaining competence.

## FACTORS REINFORCING THE DECISION TO RETIRE

Another reason people are working longer is that the Social Security Act was amended in 1983 by gradually increasing "full retirement age" from sixty-five to sixty-seven years of age. The change was meant to preserve the solvency of the Social Security Trust Funds—because people are living longer and many are in better health, they can remain in the workforce and pay into the system for longer periods of time. Individuals can still choose to retire as early as age sixty-two with a reduction in payment to offset the longer time they will receive payments. They can also opt to delay retirement after reaching "full retirement age" and receive increased payments. However, the age for Medicare eligibility remains sixty-five, and waiting longer may lead to higher costs for Parts B and D. Even if a person is still employed and has health insurance, he or she must sign up at age sixty-five to lock in benefits.

In addition to changes in Social Security's benefit calculation rules, companies have made a steady shift away from providing *defined benefits* plans (pension based on years of service and salary level, now available to about 22 percent of workers) to offering *defined contribution* plans (pension based on money contributed by the worker plus some level of contribution by the employer), with the expectation that retirees will bear the costs of their health care insurance. Both changes have extended the average person's work life and changed how and when that person will retire. The world of work has evolved from one that incentivized early retirement to one that, in many cases, discourages it.

Retirement is increasingly identified as much more than a one-time event and is instead conceptualized as a lifespan / life course *transition* to which an individual adjusts; adjustment may have a variable nonlinear course. (See also chapter 21.) The lifespan / life course perspective has been suggested as ideal for capturing the entirety of the retirement transition experience in which older workers may go from full-time employment to any one of a variety of retirement options available today. The transition may also range from uneventful change to disabling crisis. In sum, retirement has become more individualized and has evolved from total withdrawal from the workforce to gradual retreat, often accompanied by continued active involvement in the world of work.

## CONCLUSION

Organizations and individuals self-managing their careers have to cope with many changes in the occupational environment. Organizations need to take responsibility for maintaining competence, while individuals need to ensure that their competence matches job demands in order to maintain acceptable or better performance.

The changes occurring as workers age have not been adequately explored. We know that many older adults experience declines in physical, sensory, and, to some extent, facets of cognitive abilities; yet for some individuals there may be no significant age-related decline across most of the adult lifespan. We do not know how these declines affect performance at work, for example, and how performance can be ameliorated through effective ergonomic and information system interface designs. Also unclear is the extent to which organizations today, and organizations with nearly twice as many older workers in the near future, will focus on, monitor, and act on these issues.

Despite recommendations about ergonomic interventions to assist in ameliorating age-related decline factors (e.g., providing visual sound maps or transcripts to account for hearing sensitivity declines), only a few studies have tested whether those ergonomic interventions actually make a difference for older employees. Thus, greater efforts to understand the real impact of ergonomic interventions for older adults in the workplace is recommended as an important area for future research.

An additional work-related issue to be considered is stress in the workplace. Sources of stress at work may include task-related factors like information overload, equipment underload, and deficiencies of equipment and information system interface design; interpersonal factors like overcrowding; environmental factors (e.g., noise, heat, lighting, dirt, and squalor); and personal threats to physical safety, economic security, or self-esteem. In dealing with stress, individuals can call upon long-standing mediating factors, such as personality, attitude, and coping skills. These help reduce the subjective or perceived effects of stressors.

Not only does stress have physical manifestations, but performance and job satisfaction may also be sacrificed. Controlling sources of stress such as task design and environment will bolster older workers' ability to withstand stress and increase the area of positive affect and performance. Research on how to best arm older workers who are vulnerable to the effects of stress should be another focus for future research. This topic is especially relevant when older workers are likely to enter into a second career, for example, taking an entrepreneurial role in small business or industry or a "bridge" job that is similar to the former primary career. (See also chapters 22 and 23.)

The psychological characteristics of the job must also be considered. The workplace should be designed to best promote health for older adults (e.g., implementation of a "wellness" program). Additionally, the job should be designed to promote mental stimulation, autonomy, and room for development.

Finally, it is important to address the quality of the lives of those individuals who have lived with a disability, who have been ignored or forgotten as a result of social class, or as a result of racism, sexism, ageism, or other forms of social oppression.[22] There continues to be an ongoing need to develop employment-based approaches and programs that help older adults achieve a more successful and fulfilling work experience. It should never be considered too late to provide skills to disadvantaged individuals at any time or any age. Such programs should support continued employment, provide new knowledge and skills, and provide the global self-management wherewithal to support ongoing work, contributions through volunteerism, and execution of successful later-life leisure pursuits and retirement.

In conclusion, the combination of changing demographics with an increasingly sophisticated workplace puts greater emphasis on ergonomic and technological interventions in workspace design to extend the work life of older adults who desire to participate in the workforce. More empirical research in this area is greatly needed in order to understand and meet the needs of an aging workforce.

## NOTES

1. William J. Rothwell et al. 2008. *Working Longer: New Strategies for Managing, Training, and Retaining Older Workers.* New York: American Management Association.
2. M. Powell Lawton and Lucille Nahemow. 1973. "Ecology and the Aging Process." Pp. 619–74 in *The Psychology of Adult Development and Aging*, edited by Carl Eisdorfer and M. Powell Lawton. Washington, DC: American Psychological Association. (https://doi.org/10.1037/10044-020).
3. Ruth Kanfer. 2009. "Work and Older Adults. Motivation and Performance." Pp. 209–31 in *Aging and Work: Issues and Implications in a Changing Landscape*, edited by Sara J. Czaja and Joseph Sharit. Baltimore: Johns Hopkins University Press.
4. Betsy W. Williams. 2005. "Risk of Physician Impairment and/or Dyscompetence in an Aging Health Care Workforce." Pp. 165–87 in *Annual Review of Gerontology and Geriatrics.* Vol. 25, *Aging Healthcare Workforce Issues*, edited by Toni Miles and L. L. D. Antonio Furino. New York: Springer.
5. Harvey L. Sterns and Anthony A. Sterns. 2013. "Approaches to Aging and Working." Pp. 160–84 in *The Oxford Handbook of the Psychology of Working*, edited by David L. Blustein. New York: Oxford University Press.
6. Harvey L. Sterns, Dennis Doverspike, and Greta A. Lax. 2005. "The Age Discrimination in Employment Act." Pp. 256–93 in *Employment Discrimination Litigation: Behavioral, Quantitative, and Legal Perspectives*, edited by F. S. Landy. San Francisco: Jossey-Bass.
7. Harvey L. Sterns and Anthony A. Sterns. 1995. "Health and the Employment Capability of Older Americans." Pp. 10–34 in *Older and Active*, edited by Scott A. Bass. New Haven, CT: Yale University Press.
8. Richard A. Posthuma and Michael A. Campion. 2009. "Age Stereotypes in the Workplace: Common Stereotypes, Moderators, and Future Research Directions." *Journal of Management* 35:158–88.
9. Michael Smyer and Marcie Pitt-Catsouphes. 2007. "The Meanings of Work for Older Workers." *Generations* 31(1):23–30.
10. Catherine E. Bowen, Martin G. Noack, and Ursula M. Staudinger. 2011. "Aging in the Work Context." Pp. 263–77 in *Handbook of the Psychology of Aging*, 7th ed., edited by K. Warner Schaie and Sherry L. Willis. Boston: Academic.
11. David L. Blustein et al. 2008. "The Psychology of Working: A New Framework for Counseling Practice and Public Policy." *Career Development Quarterly* 56:294–308.
12. Harvey L. Sterns and Jerome Kaplan. 2003. "Self-management of Career and Retirement." Pp. 188–213 in *Retirement: Current Research and Future Directions*, edited by Terry A. Beehr and Gary A. Adams. New York: Springer.
13. Harvey L. Sterns. 1986. "Training and Retraining Adult and Older Workers." Pp. 93–113 in *Age, Health, and Employment*, edited by J. E. Birren and J. Livingston. Englewood Cliffs, NJ: Prentice-Hall.

14. Jeanette N. Cleveland et al. 2019. "Lifespan Perspectives on Job Performance, Performance Appraisal/Management and Creative Performance." Pp. 291–321 in *Work across the Lifespan*, edited by Boris B. Baltes, Cort W. Rudolph, and Hannes Zacher. London: Elsevier Science.

15. Harvey L. Sterns and A. Katherine Harrington. 2019. "Lifespan Perspectives on Learning and Training." Pp. 323–40 in *Work across the Lifespan*, edited by Boris B. Baltes, Cort W. Rudolph, and Hannes Zacher. London: Elsevier Science.

16. Antje Schmitt and Dana Unger. 2019. "Lifespan Perspectives on Occupational Health." Pp. 369–93 in *Work across the Lifespan*, edited by Boris B. Baltes, Cort W. Rudolph, and Hannes Zacher. London: Elsevier Science.

17. Harvey L. Sterns and Margaret H. Huyck. 2001. "Midlife and Work." Pp. 447–86 in *Handbook of Midlife Development*, edited by Margie E. Lachman. New York: John Wiley & Sons.

18. Gwenith G. Fisher, Marisol Chacon, and Dorey S. Chaffee. 2019. "Theories of Cognitive Aging and Work." Pp. 17–36 in *Work across the Lifespan*, edited by Boris B. Baltes, Cort W. Rudolph, and Hannes Zacher. London: Elsevier Science.

19. K. Warner Schaie. 2011. "Historical Influences on Aging and Behavior." Pp. 263–77 in *Handbook of the Psychology of Aging*, 7th ed., edited by K. Warner Schaie and Sherry L. Willis. Boston: Academic.

20. Diane E. Papalia et al. 2009. *Desarrollo Del Adulto Y Vejez*. Spanish ed. Mexico: McGraw-Hill.

21. Anthony A. Sterns. 2005. "Evaluation of a Curriculum Design and Program to Train Older Adults to Use Personal Digital Assistants." *The Gerontologist* 45:828–34.

22. Blustein et al., "Psychology of Working."

## REFERENCES


Blustein, David L., et al. 2008. "The Psychology of Working: A New Framework for Counseling Practice and Public Policy." *Career Development Quarterly* 56:294–308.

Bowen, Catherine E., Martin G. Noack, and Ursula M. Staudinger. 2011. "Aging in the Work Context." Pp. 263–77 in *Handbook of the Psychology of Aging*, 7th ed., edited by K. Warner Schaie and Sherry L. Willis. Boston: Academic.

Cleveland Jeanette N., et al. 2019. "Lifespan Perspectives on Job Performance, Performance Appraisal/Management and Creative Performance." Pp. 291–321 in *Work across the Lifespan*, edited by Boris Baltes, Cort W. Rudolph, and Hannes Zacher. London: Elsevier Science.

Fisher, Gwenith G., Marisol Chacon, and Dorey S. Chaffee. 2019. "Theories of Cognitive Aging and Work." Pp. 17–36 in *Work across the Lifespan*, edited by Boris Baltes, Cort W. Rudolph, and Hannes Zacher. London: Elsevier Science.

Kanfer, Ruth. 2009. "Work and Older Adults. Motivation and Performance." Pp. 209–31 in *Aging and Work: Issues and Implications in a Changing Landscape*, edited by Sara J. Czaja and Joseph Sharit. Baltimore: Johns Hopkins University Press.

Lawton, M. Powell and Lucille Nahemow. 1973. "Ecology and the Aging Process." Pp. 619–74 in *The Psychology of Adult Development and Aging*, edited by Carl Eisdorfer and M. Powell Lawton. Washington, DC: American Psychological Association. (https://doi.org/10.1037/10044-020).

Papalia, Diane E., et al. 2009. *Desarrollo Del Adulto Y Vejez*. Spanish ed. Mexico: McGraw-Hill.

Posthuma, Richard A. and Michael A. Campion. 2009. "Age Stereotypes in the Workplace: Common Stereotypes, Moderators, and Future Research Directions." *Journal of Management* 35:158–88.

Rothwell, William J., et al. 2008. *Working Longer: New Strategies for Managing, Training, and Retaining Older Workers*. New York: American Management Association.

Schaie, K. Warner. 2011. "Historical Influences on Aging and Behavior." Pp. 263–77 in *Handbook of the Psychology of Aging*, 7th ed., edited by K. Warner Schaie and Sherry L. Willis. Boston: Academic.

Schmitt, Antje and Dana Unger. 2019. "Lifespan Perspectives on Occupational Health." Pp. 369–93 in *Work across the Lifespan*, edited by Boris Baltes, Cort W. Rudolph, and Hannes Zacher. London: Elsevier Science.

Smyer, Michael and Marcie Pitt-Catsouphes. 2007. "The Meanings of Work for Older Workers." *Generations* 31(1):23–30.

Sterns, Anthony A. 2005. "Evaluation of a Curriculum Design and Program to Train Older Adults to Use Personal Digital Assistants." *The Gerontologist* 45:828–34.

Sterns, Harvey L. 1986. "Training and Retraining Adult and Older Workers." Pp. 93–113 in *Age, Health, and Employment*, edited by J. E. Birren and J. Livingston. Englewood Cliffs, NJ: Prentice-Hall.

Sterns, Harvey L., Dennis Doverspike, and Greta A. Lax. 2005. "The Age Discrimination in Employment Act." Pp. 256–93 in *Employment Discrimination Litigation: Behavioral, Quantitative, and Legal Perspectives*, edited by F. S. Landy. San Francisco: Jossey-Bass.

Sterns, Harvey L. and A. Katherine Harrington. 2019. "Lifespan Perspectives on Learning and Training." Pp. 323–40 in *Work across the Lifespan*, edited by Boris Baltes, Cort W. Rudolph, and Hannes Zacher. London: Elsevier Science.

Sterns, Harvey L. and Margaret H. Huyck. 2001. "Midlife and Work." Pp. 447–86 in *Handbook of Midlife Development*, edited by Margie E. Lachman. New York: John Wiley & Sons.

Sterns, Harvey L. and Jerome Kaplan. 2003. "Self-management of Career and Retirement." Pp. 188–213 in *Retirement: Current Research and Future Directions*, edited by Terry A. Beehr and Gary A. Adams. New York: Springer.

Sterns, Harvey L. and Anthony A. Sterns. 1995. "Health and the Employment Capability of Older Americans." Pp. 10–34 in *Older and Active*, edited by Scott A. Bass. New Haven, CT: Yale University Press.

Sterns, Harvey L. and Anthony A. Sterns. 2013. "Approaches to Aging and Working." Pp. 160–84 in *The Oxford Handbook of the Psychology of Working*, edited by David L. Blustein. New York: Oxford University Press.

Williams, Betsy W. 2005. "Risk of Physician Impairment and/or Dyscompetence in an Aging Health Care Workforce." Pp. 165–87 in *Annual Review of Gerontology and Geriatrics*. Vol. 25, *Aging Healthcare Workforce Issues*, edited by Toni Miles and L. L. D. Antonio Furino. New York: Springer.

CHAPTER 16

# Older Workers' Self-Management and Sustainable Employability at Work

## Lessons Learned from Science and Practice

Annet de Lange, Trude Furunes, and Anne-Marijie Buckens

### Case Report 1: Nurse Angela Baker

*Angela Baker (fifty years old) has been active as a nurse for more than twenty-five years in eldercare, a profession she had wanted to practice since childhood. Caring for others (her mother, grandmother, the neighbors) gave her life a sense of meaning. After her college education in nursing, she was lucky to get started right away within an elderly care institution. She enjoyed working there until she was twenty-five. By obtaining new training certificates in specialized elderly care, other types of jobs also came within reach. She saw more complex forms of care as a new challenge (self-development). In her opinion, the past twenty-five years have really flown by. She was happy to work as part of an enthusiastic team. Recently, however, she has started to experience pressure from increased administrative duties, absence of sick colleagues, and merger with another institution (reorganization). Angela wonders (self-reflection) how she can better manage the caregiving tasks at work, increased administrative pressure, and caregiving at home where she provides informal care for her eighty-eight-year-old mother. Angela says: "A period of leave or sabbatical would enable me to care for my sick mother, but I don't want to abandon my team at work. The department, with an increasing number of patients, is already so busy and colleagues are regularly sick." Her supervisor recently indicated in a development interview that given her private situation, Angela may take a short period of care leave (an available HR practice), but there is unfortunately not much room for adjusting schedules, given the dropout of colleagues. Angela and her supervisor make a plan together and discuss it with the team. Angela feels somewhat relieved. The proposed leave period and the support and confidence of her supervisor and team provide her with a feeling of being valued at work, but she fears that the leave will not be sufficient for the long-term care she needs to provide for her mother. Practically speaking, there are few options for adjustments or job crafting after return from her leave.*

## OVERVIEW

The global labor force participation rate* shows that the number of older workers has increased significantly during the past decade, and many countries face a so-called graying workforce with relatively more older than younger workers.[1] For example, 2020 statistics from OECD countries (figure 16.1) show that 82.6 percent of adults aged fifty-five-plus were working in Iceland in 2019 compared to 69.7 percent in the Netherlands, 63.8 percent in the United States of America, and 33.7 percent in Turkey. As a result, employers face a challenge: how to enhance a sustainable working life for older workers like Angela Baker in the above case report?[2] It is not surprising that the concept of successful aging at work has become a popular research topic, attracting theoretical as well as conceptual research attention.

For example, Kooij conceptualizes successful aging at work from a sustainability perspective and argues that a continuous *person-job fit* between the changing person and changing work is required for employees to be able to maintain their health, motivation, and work ability, and thus age successfully at work.[3] On the other hand, Zacher and colleagues point to a more process-based definition focusing on elements of self-management and adaptation of aging workers across time.[4] More specifically, they argue that personal resources, active regulation of behavior and optimal investment of resources,[5] maintenance of the (perceived) capacity to influence the environment, and focusing on positive events and experiences[6] enable individuals to age successfully across the lifespan. Finally, according to de Lange and Kooij, successful aging at work can be defined as the proactive maintenance or adaptive recovery (after loss) to high(er) levels of (subjective) health, vitality, work capacity, employability and motivation to continue working, and at the same time creating or maintaining a fit with the work environment.[7] In other words, successful aging at work is the self-management process of workers necessary to become and remain employable during the life course, indicating that employees are able to pro-actively recover and improve over time through self-management skills and actions, and with support or interventions from the work environment.

This chapter discusses the importance of proactive self-management of aging workers at work and possible intervention methods (based on insights of science as

*The labor force participation rate is based on "the sum of all workers who are employed or actively seeking employment divided by the total noninstitutionalized, civilian working-age population." https://www.investopedia.com/terms/p/participationrate.asp.

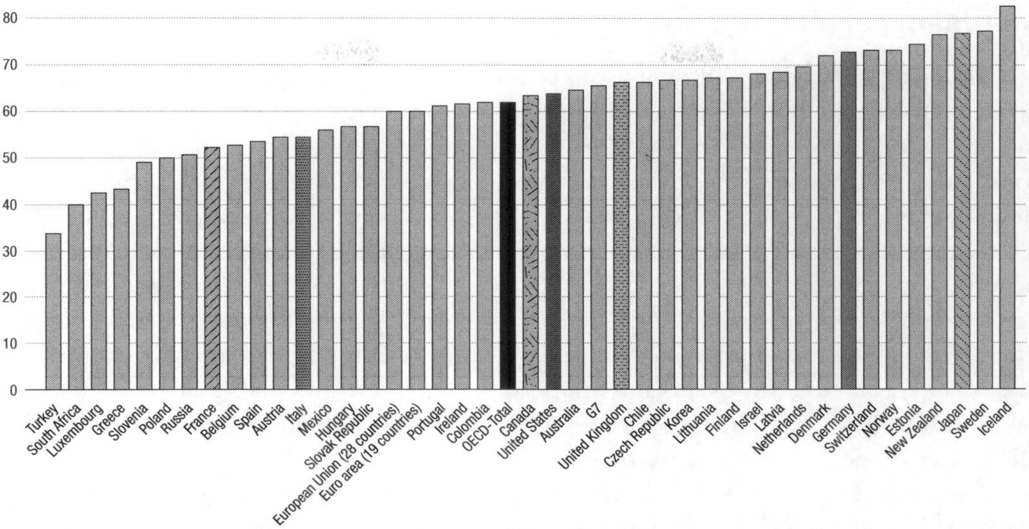


**FIGURE 16.1.** OECD Employment Rates for Workforce Aged 55–64 Years

well as practical experience). We take an integrative perspective including information from the psychosocial job design literature (self-management literature) but will also highlight relevant insights from human resource management and leadership studies on how leaders can play an important role in sustaining employees' self-management and employability.

## SELF-MANAGEMENT AND SUSTAINABLE EMPLOYABILITY: AN INTEGRATIVE PERSPECTIVE

*Sustainable employability* has often been measured as work ability,[8] vitality,[9] and employability.[10] As these capacities relate to human strengths, health, and motivation in organizations, they are considered crucial for employees to remain and perform at work.[11] While work ability represents the health component of sustainable work ability, vitality represents the motivational component, demonstrated by high levels of energy and mental resilience while working, and the willingness to invest effort in one's work and persist even in the face of difficulties.[12] Employability refers to individuals' ability to adequately fulfill work in current and future jobs, inside and outside the current organization.[13] Although the opportunity to retain or find work might also depend on labor market characteristics, it is generally noted that individuals' characteristics, such as self-management at work, abilities, skills, and knowledge, contribute to employability and labor market participation. Organizations and managers can facilitate and support self-management of aging workers by providing the right conditions and by implementing interventions that, for example, actively focus on improving the self-management skills and capacities of older employees. In the next section, we will address definitions of self-management at work and, subsequently, highlight the different ways self-management can be improved within the workplace.

## Self-Management at Work

There are many different definitions of self-management. Some definitions emphasize psychological topics such as self-awareness, self-image, self-analysis, self-control, attention, and choice processes,[14] while other definitions place more emphasis on behavioral areas that people can or cannot control, such as health behavior, learning, and development.[15] For example, Lorig and Holman showed that people can distinguish the following self-management tasks: select new goals or challenges and formulate relevant actions to reach those goals (e.g., "I want to live a healthier life" or "I will acquire new skills to start a new profession"); make decisions (e.g., "I am going to go to fitness after work"); maintain and apply resources (e.g., "I know which physical, mental, cognitive, and social resources I can use on and off the job"); enter into and maintain interpersonal relationships (e.g., "I will develop a relevant professional network through LinkedIn"); and follow up and sustain actions over time.[16]

Self-management at work therefore involves a complex psychological process that has interfaces with concepts such as "self-determination"[17] and "self-efficacy" (personal effectiveness).[18] Self-determination is the extent to which an individual feels that he or she can initiate and regulate actions at work to maintain a fit with the work environment (in terms of required knowledge, skills, motivation, and physical and mental well-being). "Self-efficacy" (or self-effectiveness) is the individual's confidence that he or she can (continue to) perform certain tasks at work. Self-management (also known as "human agency")[19] of workers implies that workers know themselves well, can manage themselves, and can (learn to) change or adapt themselves within and outside the work context to be able to stay connected to the work environment. As a result, self-management has cognitive, affective, and behavioral elements.[20] Based on the aforementioned line of reasoning, de Lange developed the following psychological multidimensional definition of self-management at work.[21] (See also figure 16.2.)

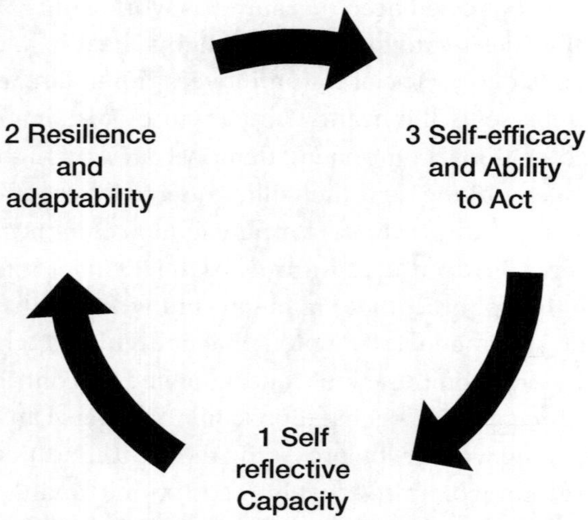


**FIGURE 16.2.** Self-Management at Work: A Psychological Multidimensional Concept with Cognitive, Affective, and Behavioral Elements

*Source:* de Lange, A., 2019.

*Self-management at work* is the extent to which a worker:

- **has self-reflective capacity.** This means that a worker is cognitively self-aware; knows what he or she wants and can do to develop a meaningful self-image at work over time (has self-insights, has a clear self-concept); can make an analysis of available goals, self-regulatory strategies, and rewards; and can develop an action plan to achieve and maintain a desired (future) goal or self-image at work. Subsequently, the worker can monitor and evaluate progress in personal development and the alignment or fit with the work environment over time (can achieve self-monitoring and self-evaluation).
- **knows resilience and adaptive capacity.** This means that a worker can adapt his or her own cognitions or ideas, emotions, and behavior in a changing context; has the capacity to change or adapt; and is capable of self-development and self-improvement across time.[22]
- **is self-effective and able to act.** The worker can effectively convert goals into concrete follow-up steps, behavior, or actions and therefore can successfully implement action plan(s). As a result, a worker is able to apply self-management when he or she makes optimal use of the demands and resources that the work and home environment have to offer. The worker takes the initiative to adapt or develop behavior to fit personal capabilities and level of resilience in a dynamic work context.[23,24]

## A Multifactorial Life Course-Based Psychological Perspective on Self-Management at Work

Relatively few theories are available in work and organizational psychology that focus on the relationship between self-management and successful aging at work across time. Moreover, little research has focused on a positive approach or on empowerment of aging workers (e.g., seeing older workers as potential talent) to sustain or improve their level of employability at work. Strong points in the aging process at work have received little attention. At the beginning of the twenty-first century, however, clinical psychologist Martin Seligman, together with an important network of psychologists (including Mihaly Csikszentmihalyi)[25] introduced the term *positive psychology*. More attention was paid in this theoretical tradition to the importance of positive emotions, meaning-making processes, positive thoughts, and intrapersonal as well as interpersonal resources for self-management at work, aimed at progress, growth, and development of human behavior in organizations.

Based on positive psychological theory, de Lange's multifactorial model of successful aging at work[26] (see figure 16.3) postulates that sustainable employability of workers over time is a result of the (changing) dynamics between the contextual workload and individual self-management capacity across the life course.[27] Every profession and every practical context has its own unique proximal and distal demands as well as possible proximal and distal resources. "Proximal" means factors that are close to or can be perceived and experienced directly by the worker. "Distal" means factors further away from the worker, but still affecting worker outcomes. In the case report of Angela Baker presented previously, the contextual demand at work is, for example, the reported administrative workload, but Angela also reports support from her supervisor in looking at her double-duty caregiving tasks and being able to take additional leave (job resource, human resource practice). The level of experienced contextual workload can, in this respect, be explained by the combination of the contextual proximal and distal demands and the proximal and distal resources in relation to the self-management skills and strategies of a worker. If the contextual workload meets the self-management capacity of a worker, he or she will experience a fit with the work environment.[28,29]

A person-environment fit and a fulfilled psychological contract are important positive predictors for sustainable employability during the life course.[30] It is important that the motivation, knowledge, and skills of the employee match the work context in the sense of the requirements set by the job, also labeled as a demand-abilities fit. Secondly, the attitude and motivation of the employee (such as self-determination and sense of purpose) must match the work context in the sense of the provided job challenges and resources and, for example, task significance that the work generates. In the latter case we speak of a needs-supply fit. The needs of the worker and the supply from the work match.

Figure 16.3, the multifactorial model, builds upon earlier models like the job-demands-resources model[31] but expands it by distinguishing self-management skills and strategies of aging workers in and outside of the work environment and including the influence of lifespan changes as possible moderators.

Shanahan and Macmillan give the following definition of life course: "the age-graded sequence of roles, opportunities, constraints, and events that shape the biography from birth to death."[32] Positive and negative life course events over time influence the way in which individuals develop. By ordering and summarizing events in stories and our thoughts, we give them a positive or negative meaning. Azevedo, Martins, and Maia state: "Human beings are time-binding, storytelling creators, whose lives themselves are situated in time, as time-binding narratives—past, present, future."[33] *Life events* can refer to important moments in life, such as a birth, obtaining a diploma, a marriage. They can also refer to periods or conditions—such as a period as a spouse, or after a divorce—versus experiences and perceptions of (missed) opportunities and events during the life course: "I would like to have children"; "I want to enjoy my children more"; "I want a loving partner." Life course perceptions are therefore not only about development over time but can also be about the (desired) interaction with others and the environment during the life course.[34]

Life events are based on periods and the subjective meaning given to it, positive or negative. In our case, Angela Baker experienced the reported double-duty caregiving tasks as more taxing across time, in combination with the increased proximal workload in the health care institution. Research by Pak and colleagues shows that life course events are very diverse in terms of type of event and impact, and they influence perceived sustainable employability at work.[35] In addition, negative assessment of a life event can go hand in hand with reduced employability, for example, through reduced personal resources for self-management. It is therefore important to pay attention to the self-reflection processes and emotional meaning-making processes of life events and how these processes affect reported self-efficacy at work, and reported person-work fit.

The unique changes that workers experience during the life course can progress gradually but can also be experienced abruptly. Normative life course changes apply to

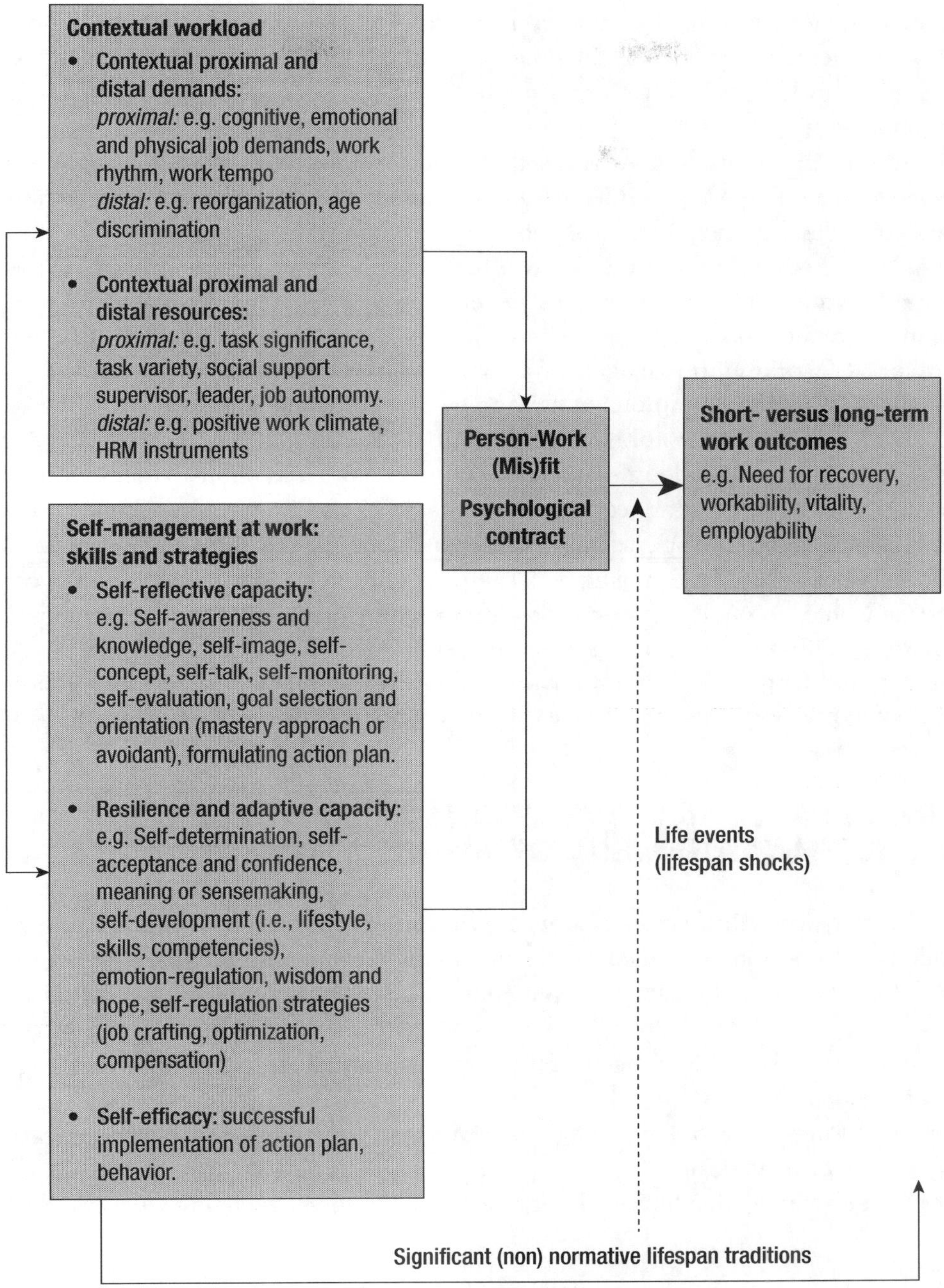


**FIGURE 16.3.** Multifactorial Model
*Source:* de Lange, A., 2019.

many employees, such as menopause for women and the decrease in physical reserves among employees after the age of fifty. Nonnormative influences occur more by chance, such as winning the lottery or having an accident.[36] In this context, researchers also refer to meaningful life events or transitions, such as birth or marriage, the death of a loved one, the start and end of a career, or the start of caregiving roles. Life shocks are life course changes or transitions that occur unexpectedly and have a high impact or are emotionally demanding, such as the death of a child.[37] Life events that are evaluated as negative or shocking will have larger depleting effects on the self-management skills and strategies of workers.

Ward-Griffin and colleagues show that female nurses with more intensive forms of dual care (care at work and informal care at home) reported negative effects in their employability levels, such as reduced chances of promotion, an increased risk of overloading, and a reduced work capacity over time.[38] In their study, three different types of informal care conditions and the nurses' experienced burden or load were distinguished through self-reflection and group sessions. Namely, the nurses could distinguish: "making it work," "working to manage," and "living on the edge" caregiving situations. In the "making it work" condition, caregivers were able to manage the caregiving load themselves by asking others for help. As a result, nurses with informal care duties experienced minimal so-called double-duty caregiving at work and home. Nurses who were "working to manage" experienced caregiving tasks as more taxing, resulting in work-life imbalance and more work problems. The most burdensome double-duty-caregiving condition was the "living on the edge." Their double caregiving situation had become too burdensome (too many expectations in work and private life both internally and externally and little to no support), and they experienced reduced mental and physical well-being and feared to drop out soon. In the next section, we will address possible work-related interventions to improve self-management at work of aging adults.

## WORK-RELATED INTERVENTIONS TO IMPROVE THE SELF-MANAGEMENT OF AGING WORKERS

In this section we will discuss evidence-based interventions to strengthen the self-management of workers in relation to sustainable employability.[39] (See figure 16.3.) Three interventions that create or implement are:

1. healthy work design that meets and fosters the self-management capacity of aging workers;
2. the use of human resource management practices to build self-management capacity of aging workers; and
3. the influence of leadership behavior at work in empowering aging workers.

### Design of Healthy Work and Job Crafting

Healthy work design is characterized by a balance between contextual job demands and job resources. Working for a prolonged time in a situation with an imbalance (too-high task demands combined with insufficient resources, such as autonomy and social support) leads to the development of mental and physical complaints and increased risk of reduced employability over time. Self-management and sustainable employability is therefore a topic that needs to be interpreted within a certain context. For example, the work context of nurse Angela Baker (described in the case report at the beginning of the chapter) can be characterized by a relatively high workload and reduced job resource options (due to colleagues dropping out, reorganizations, and a high administrative workload). The design of active and healthy jobs in which task requirements are balanced with resources is therefore of great importance to enable self-management and maintaining a fit with the work environment.

*Job crafting*: Job crafting as a technique can be used to sustain employability and create a better fit with the work environment. Job crafting refers to ways in which workers utilize opportunities to adapt to or change their work environment to develop an improved fit with their self-management capacity.[40,41] Self-regulatory actions can include a worker adjusting his or her own cognitive view or beliefs of the work tasks, focusing on the positive elements of the work (*cognitive crafting*); actively changing the task or selecting other tasks (*task crafting*); and creating meaningful social interactions at work and seeking to work only with a nice supervisor (*relational crafting*). According to the selection, optimization, and compensation (SOC) model of Baltes et al., sustainable employability is possible through the use of the right self-management strategy: *selection* (focusing on specific work tasks), *optimization* (making ergonomic adjustments to the work setting), or *compensation* (taking more time for a cognitive task). To be able to age successfully, older people will show more compensatory behavior or look for other possibilities by, for example, finding tasks that are physically less intensive or by creating recovery options. In this way they retain their sense of control and positive self-image.[42]

Similarly, the motivational theory of lifespan development[43] shows that individuals strive to exercise continuous control over their environment during their life cycle to make it more in line with their own wishes, personal projects, or life goals, the so-called *primary control capacity*. In contrast, *secondary control* processes focus more in crafting the self to bring oneself or one's self-management skills more in line with environmental demands. The two processes together are proposed to optimize an individual's sense of control and human agency. Primary control strategies aimed at compensation are, for example, external aids, such as help from others or technical aids that workers can use at work. Secondary control strategies focus on adjusting their dedication or energy in a work task. Individuals increase their dedication to reach a work goal, for example, by imagining how happy they will be when the goal is achieved and by repeating that they can achieve the goal. Secondary control strategies aimed at compensation with regard to the preferred life- or work-related goals can include workers accepting and mentally detaching from unattainable goals and protecting themselves by comparing themselves with others who are worse off.

Kooij and colleagues tested the effect of a job-crafting intervention and found that participation in a job-crafting workshop was effective in relation to "strength-based crafting or strengthening self-management skills," aligning the work with their own self-management strengths and talents.[44] The intervention was aimed at adjusting the job to personal strengths and interests, and older workers who participated and crafted the job toward their strengths revealed positive results for demands-abilities and needs-supplies fit. Unexpectedly, participating in the job-crafting intervention did not influence job crafting toward interests.

## Human Resource Management (HRM)

A growing body of research pays attention to the role of HR practices in sustaining older adults at work.[45] (See also chapters 7, 8, and 10.) For example, Kooij and colleagues formulated four bundles of HR practices—*developmental, maintenance, utilization,* and *accommodative* practices—based on the aforementioned selection, optimization, and compensation model.[46] (See table 16.1.) The SOC model suggests that employees allocate their resources in line with four major life goals, namely, growth, maintenance, recovery, and the regulation of loss. If HR practices are bundled according to these employee life goals, research has shown that employees will use HR practices that fit their goals and see these practices as one coherent set. First, developmental practices aim to aid workers in improving their performance (e.g., training and promotion). These practices are mainly related to advancement and satisfy the need for growth and development. As such they are important job resources, which can help employees generate additional personal self-management related skills. For example, de Lange and colleagues showed that employees gained job resources like autonomy after receiving a promotion.[47] As developmental practices are classified as job resources and can help workers generate additional personal self-management based skills, we argue that they will be beneficial for successful aging at work. In line with this expectation, the review of Pak et al. revealed significant relations between developmental practices and work outcomes like employability and work motivation.[48]

Second, HR maintenance practices help workers to sustain their performance in spite of (age-related) loss of resources (e.g., declines in physical capabilities). These practices are mainly focused on security and protection of personal resources (e.g., health). Examples of maintenance practices are health checks and performance appraisals. Maintenance practices can help individuals increase their job and personal resources. For example, ergonomic adjustments made to the workplace can reduce the number of work-related physical disorders. Moreover, the review of Pak et al. showed that maintenance practices (especially health promotion) were significantly positively associated with work ability.[49]

Third, utilization practices tap the experience, knowledge, and competencies of older workers (e.g., mentoring roles and participation in decision-making), thus optimizing their personal resources. These practices can be used to assist workers in regaining performance after having experienced a drop in performance. They usually make use of lateral development in which job demands that do not fit the coping resources of the employee are replaced by other demands that fit better with the existing personal resources of the individual. For example, through mentoring, an older worker is better able to use such resources as knowledge and skills of the company and the profession. Nonetheless, the current evidence on association between utilization practices and work outcomes like work ability, employability, and motivation to work is still inconclusive and deserves more research attention to draw stronger conclusions.

Fourth, accommodative practices (e.g., demotions and exemption from overtime) are used when an employee can no longer regain previous levels of performance and needs to be assisted in functioning at a lower level. This type of practice helps to regulate the loss of employee resources. To illustrate, a worker who had a burnout can be offered a demotion to a less challenging position, thereby reducing strain and allowing the employee to continue working until retirement age. Earlier research has found that accommodative practices like workplace rehabilitation, reducing the number of working hours, and getting exemptions from evening and night work were found to have a positive effect on work ability.

An overview of all HR practices that are included in the different bundles can be found in table 16.1.[50,51,52]

When Van der Mark-Reeuwijk et al. reviewed evidence-based interventions to prolong working lives of older workers, they found seven interventions that are relevant: (1) career development workshops; (2) health promotion at work, such as yoga, fitness, availability of free fruit; (3) preventive consultation with a company doctor; (4) online health risk assessment; (5) mental coaching by phone; (6) regular exercise; and (7) tai chi.[53] In general, these interventions seem to have small, positive effects. For example, studies showed significant positive changes: a reduction in the need for recovery, improved work capacity, and reduced absenteeism and dropouts from work. In addition, job resources such as autonomy, social support, feedback, and leadership, but also HRM practices such as health promotion and stimulating career counseling, have strong positive effects in predicting indicators of sustainable employability (measured as work ability, employability, and motivation to continue working).

The design of a healthy working environment and HR interventions are therefore important tools that employers can use to enhance the self-management of workers during the life course. Another powerful factor in sustaining self-management and sustainable employability is leadership and behavior toward aging workers.

**TABLE 16.1.** Overview of HR Practices Supporting Older Worker Self-Management

| *Accommodative Practices* | *Utilization Practices* | *Maintenance Practices* | *Developmental Practices* |
|---|---|---|---|
| Long career break<br>Early retirement<br>Reduction of tasks and/or responsibilities | Participation<br>Task enrichment (knowledge transfer) | Flexible benefits<br>Performance pay<br>Compressed workweek<br>Health promotion | Career planning<br>Promotion |
| Additional leave | (Partial) change in tasks or responsibilities | Ergonomic adjustments to the workplace | Continuous training or instruction on the job |
| Demotion | | Adjustments to work tasks due to illness | |
| Retirement<br>Exemption from working overtime/night shifts<br>Reduced workload | | | |

*Source:* de Lange, A., Kooij, D., and van der Heijden, B., 2015.

## Leadership: Health-Promoting Leadership as Important Factor

Leadership can influence person-environment fit of subordinates (see figure 16.3). While there are many definitions of leadership, most see leadership as a process whereby a leader through intentional influence guides, structures, and facilitates activities and relationships within a group or an organization, that is, motivating and inspiring his or her employees to work for a common goal.[54] Although the terms *leadership* and *management* are sometimes used interchangeably, leadership refers to "one to one" (dyadic leadership) or "one to many" (leadership). Management, on the other hand, concerns the organization of work, that is, planning and controlling work activities, focusing on administration and task achievement. When it comes to categorizing leadership styles or approaches, some researchers use the label "leadership," and others use "management."

Leadership theories are dynamic, and new theories have been developed over time,[55] without rejecting former theories. If so, how do different approaches to leadership interact? The contingency theory suggests that leadership is situational, and that there is no single right way to lead because it depends on the situation of the followers (e.g., their self-management skills), the person-work fit (e.g., work ability, vitality, and employability), and the dyadic relationship between leader and follower. This means that a style effective in one situation may not be effective in a different situation.

Because leadership is relational, the dyadic relationship between a manager and his or her subordinates is central to developing sustainable employability. For instance, research on dyadic relationships based on leader-member-exchange theory (LMX) suggests that leaders unaware of the ongoing development of dyadic relationships will automatically form strong relationships with a small number of employees (in-group) and weaker relationships with the remaining group of followers (out-group). The assumption is that in-group members are highly committed and more likely to get interesting work tasks, get invited into networks, and so forth, and the leader uses internal attribution to explain success of the project (due to the knowledgeable employee) or failure (due to external circumstances). In contrast, out-group members are expected to do what is in their work contract, and the leader will most likely use external attribution to explain failure of the project (due to the employee's incompetence) or success (due to external circumstances).

Dyadic leadership theory suggests that the dyad relationship between leaders and their members, rated from the employee perspective, may influence workers' well-being. Furunes et al. found that followers with a weak relationship to their closest supervisor were more prone to be stressed and to experience bullying and age discrimination, as well as negative affectivity.[56] Older workers may be particularly vulnerable. Few studies have investigated whether particular approaches to leadership may be more fruitful in terms of sustaining older workers' employability.

Research suggests that some leadership styles may be better suited to addressing and adapting to workers' diverse expectations and needs. *Transformational* leaders are found to highly prioritize their relationship with their followers and to show individualized consideration in order to meet followers' needs for empowerment, personal growth, self-efficacy, and achievement.[57] Transformational leadership correlates positively with both individual and organizational outcomes. A meta-review suggests that transformational leadership can predict many positive and negative aspects of employee well-being;[58] nonetheless, evidence is blurred. When it comes to employee health, Nielsen and Daniels suggest that there may also be negative effects of transformational leadership.[59] Because transformational leaders have high expectations, employees may perform beyond their own capacities, which may have long-term negative health consequences (e.g., longer sick leave). Due to these limitations of the transformational leadership approach, researchers have looked into new approaches to leadership, which both directly and indirectly focus on employees' physical and mental health.

A systematic review suggests that health-promoting leadership adds value to transformational leadership.[60] Health-promoting leadership is defined as the process of creating a culture for health-promoting workplaces and values that inspire and motivate employees to participate in such a development.[61] Health-promoting leadership is considered to be a promising path to not only sustaining employee health, but also building organizational capacity and resilience,[62] that is, a holistic workplace strategy. The health-promoting leader actively engages in promoting employees' health, takes responsibility for action, maintains open communication, and accommodates employees' participation in change processes.

A recent study by Furunes et al. of health-promoting leadership in a nursing context suggests certain characterizing qualities, including autonomy, role clarity and the relevant level of job demands, the possibility of participating in decision-making, getting support from colleagues, and developing one's skills and competence.[63] A health-promoting leader in the health context is described as being attentive, taking action, and communicating openly. Nurses expect their leaders to care about and invest in their professional development. This study contributed to the health-promoting leadership literature by showing that nurses expect their leaders to foster meaningfulness in their daily work. Meaningfulness is found to be of particular importance for health professionals in coping with high quantitative and emotional demands[64] and may buffer burnout or other negative employee outcomes.

Moreover, Furunes and colleagues suggest that health-promoting leadership concerns both core leadership tasks and core leadership behavior.[65] Core leadership tasks are short-term (demanding immediate action), medium-term, and long-term tasks. Short-term tasks include giving feedback to employees and handling sick leave. Medium-term activities include building an organizational culture for health promotion, through building trust, care, and health awareness. Long-term activities are the leadership tasks related to encouraging employees' sense of coherence. Sense of coherence refers to the degree that employees feel that their work (situation) is meaningful and manageable, and whether they understand the whole. Health-promoting leader behavior includes being attentive, authentic, curious, and courageous.

How, then, does health-promoting leadership contribute to sustaining older workers' employability? Drawing again on a study of nurses,[66] we learn that meaningfulness is one of the main motivations to continue working. Meaningfulness is related to making a difference for patients and their families, and the nurse-patient relationship is considered the most meaningful. Nursing is a profession where many leave the profession early, hence older, experienced nurses are likely to be resilient and have developed coping mechanisms that make stressful situations manageable and comprehensible. This may be partly due to the individual's self-management strategies, but could also be facilitated by the leader or closest supervisor through health-promoting leader behavior and/or human resource management activities. Nurses mention that self-efficacy and reliance on one's own judgment increase with work experience, thus making them more prone to staying on the job. One dilemma addressed was the increase in job demands, compromising quality of care. For example, extreme time pressure might make it impossible for the nurses to fulfill work tasks to the professional standard they aspired to, thus compromising their ethical standards. Leaders need to understand that nurses' motivation to continue working is based on making a difference for patients (meaningfulness or self-determination), mastering the job (self-efficacy), and mentoring younger colleagues (generativity motives).

## INSIGHTS FROM PRACTICE: SELF-MANAGEMENT CHALLENGES OF UNEMPLOYED OLDER WORKERS

We will end this chapter with reflections of director Anne-Marije Buckens based on her practical work in 50 Company, an agency that specializes in reskilling and retraining fifty-plus workers who want to change careers or are unemployed and searching for new work. (See case report 2.)

### Case Report 2: Unemployed Peter Finds a New Job—The Outcome of Untagging, Talent Scouting, and Self-Management in Practice

*One day Peter (age fifty-five) came to 50 Company for help. Peter had worked as a pathologist but could no longer perform his work due to arthrosis in his hands. His profession was so specific that he had no idea what other professions he could practice. We helped Peter untag and stripped him of all labels that fit the pathologist-anatomist profession.*

*Peter talked about what his position entailed and what tasks his work mainly consisted of. Contrary to what we assumed at first, Peter's job consisted mainly of communication. Peter said that he is good at bringing complicated news in an emotional context to patients' relatives. Peter proudly told about the moments he looks back with satisfaction, and where he made a difference with his communication skills.*

*An important part of Peter's new talent profile was "communicating in difficult situations." We examined professions where this element was essential. Peter found a new job as a counselor*

**TOP 10 TWENTY-FIRST CENTURY SKILLS**

1. Complex problem solving
2. Critical thinking
3. Creativity
4. People management
5. Coordinating with others
6. Emotional intelligence
7. Judgment and decision-making
8. Service orientation
9. Negotiation
10. Cognitive flexibility

*for victim assistance. He does what he has been good at for years, communicating in difficult situations. He did not have to retrain and can use the competencies that he has had for years.*

## RETAINING OR GETTING A NEW JOB AS A FIFTY-PLUS WORKER: INSIGHTS FROM PRACTICE

In the dynamic labor market, mainly through robotization and technological innovation, reskilling, training, and lifelong education in twenty-first-century skills have become crucial to remain employable and attractive for employers (see textbox above). However, a large group of older adults has received insufficient training and is unable to meet the requested competence profile of employers searching for new applicants. Moreover, just like Peter, older workers are unaccustomed to taking self-reflection time to determine their ideal self-concept at work or reflecting upon and evaluating the strengths, talents, and weaknesses in their work functioning.

### From Untagging to Talent Scouting, Talent Development across the Life Course

During educational and vocational training and working life, aging workers receive numerous tags (e.g., good in math or language). These tags largely determine the choices workers make in their careers but often do not capture all possible talents or self-management strengths of older workers. To create more sustainable careers across the life course, science as well as practice show that we need to untag workers and invest more time in self-reflection, talent scouting, and development, thus expanding self-management skills and capabilities across the life course.

### Checklist for Finding a New Job as an Older Worker

In summary, the practical case reports as well as relevant empirical research reveal that the following self-management skills and capabilities are important to take into account if an older worker is to remain employable across time: self-reflective capacity, resilience, and adaptability, as well as self-efficacy at work. We will end with a checklist older workers can use to reflect upon their self-management and employability at work:

1. *Self-reflective capacity*: Take enough time to reflect on your possible future work self and possible strengths, talents, or weaknesses in relation to your work functioning. Do you have enough resilience to change your career view, to job craft and create a new career path, or to take up new training? Do you have enough self-efficacy, or do you need coaching to successfully implement formulated action plan(s)? Map your knowledge, skills, personality traits, motives, ambition, and added value to an organization according to the principle of untagging and talent scouting and talent development (see case report 2).
2. *Resilience and adaptability*: Determine which future-proof professions and functions match your profile, talents, and self-management skills and capabilities, and take

up new training. Do not fear change. Being fifty-plus means that you have a lot of life experience and possible wisdom. Your patience, trust, attitude, and life wisdom are very attractive for an employer.

3. Write a labor market pitch in which you explain to the new employer what added value you can offer to the organization.
4. Determine which network contacts can help you acquire your new job, and, via LinkedIn, get in touch with those people.
5. *Self-efficacy*: Work on your personal branding based on positive storytelling via the internet. Build a personal brand by posting business-, professional-, and work-related expressions in the form of blogs, vlogs, interviews, and opinion pieces.
6. Don't be fooled that after the age of fifty you are no longer attractive to employers. You are as attractive or unattractive, young or old, as you present yourself. Make sure you have a good story and let it count. Make sure you develop a positive self-concept, self-talk, and learn to reflect positively about yourself.
7. Don't be too modest in your presentation. State what you are good at, what your passion and ambition is.
8. When finding an appropriate job, be able to further craft the job (in terms of relations with supervisors and colleagues, tasks, possible human resource management practices) so it fits your own self-management talents or strengths.

## NOTES

1. OECD. 2020. "Employment Rate by Age Group (Indicator)." Retrieved February 23, 2020 (https://doi.org/10.1787/084f32c7-en).

2. Annet H. de Lange, Dorien T. A. M. Kooij, and Beatrice I. J. M. van der Heijden. 2015. "Human Resource Management and Sustainability at Work across the Lifespan: An Integrative Perspective." Pp. 50–79 in *Facing the Challenges of a Multi-age Workforce: A Use-inspired Approach*, edited by Lisa M. Finkelstein et al. New York: Routledge.

3. Dorien T. A. M. Kooij. 2015. "Successful Aging at Work: The Active Role of Employees." *Work, Aging and Retirement* 1(4):309–19. (https://doi.org/10.1093/workar/wav018).

4. Hannes Zacher, Dorien T. A. M. Kooij, and Margaret E. Beier. 2018. "Active Aging at Work." *Organizational Dynamics* 47(1):37–45.

5. Paul B. Baltes and Margret M. Baltes. 1990. "Psychological Perspectives on Successful Aging: The Model of Selective Optimization with Compensation." Pp. 1–34 in *Successful Aging: Perspectives from the Behavioral Sciences*, edited by Paul B. Baltes and Margret M. Baltes. New York: Cambridge University Press.

6. Laura L. Carstensen, Derek M. Isaacowitz, and Susan T. Charles. 1999. "Taking Time Seriously: A Theory of Socioemotional Selectivity." *American Psychologist* 54(3):165–81. (https://doi.org/10.1037/0003-066X.54.3.165).

7. Annet H. de Lange and Dorien T. A. M. Kooij. 2019. "Successful Aging at Work: A Positive Psychological Perspective." *Tijdschrift voor Positieve Psychologie* 3:27–34.

8. Monika E. von Bonsdorff et al. 2011. "Work Strain in Midlife and 28-year Work Ability Trajectories." *Scandinavian Journal of Work, Environment & Health* 37(6):455–63. (https://doi.org/10.5271/sjweh.3177).

9. Arnold B. Bakker and Evangelia Demerouti. 2017. "Job Demands–Resources Theory: Taking Stock and Looking Forward." *Journal of Occupational Health Psychology* 22(3):273–85. (https://doi.org/10.1037/ocp0000056).

10. Beatrice I. J. M. van der Heijden et al. 2009. "Age Effects on the Employability–Career Success Relationship." *Journal of Vocational Behavior* 74(2):156–64. (https://doi.org/10.1016/j.jvb.2008.12.009).

11. Judith H. Semeijn et al. 2015. "Sustainable Labor Participation and Sustainable Careers." Pp. 146–60 in *Handbook of Research on Sustainable Careers*, edited by Ans De Vos and Beatrice I. J. M. van der Heijden. Cheltenham, UK: Edward Elgar. (https://doi.org/10.4337/9781782547037.00015).

12. Wilmar B. Schaufeli, Arnold B. Bakker, and Marisa Salanova. 2006. "The Measurement of Work Engagement with a Short Questionnaire: A Cross-national Study." *Educational and Psychological Measurement* 66(4):701–16. (https://doi.org/10.1177/0013164405282471).

13. Semeijn et al., "Sustainable Labor Participation."

14. Carl E. Thoresen and Michael J. Mahoney. 1974. *Behavioral Self-control*. New York: Holt, Rinehart & Winston.

15. Kate R. Lorig and Halsted Holman. 2003. "Self-management Education: History, Definition, Outcomes, and Mechanisms." *Annals of Behavioral Medicine* 26(1):1–7.

16. Lorig and Holman, "Self-management Education." (https://doi.org/10.1207/S15324796ABM2601_01).

17. Renu Burr and John L. Cordery. 2001. "Self-management Efficacy as a Mediator of the Relation between Job Design and Employee Motivation." *Human Performance* 14:27–44. (https://doi.org/10.1207/S15327043HUP1401_03).

18. Albert Bandura. 2006. "Toward a Psychology of Human Agency." *Perspectives on Psychological Science* 1(2):164–80. (https://doi/pdf/10.1111/j.1745-6916.2006.00011).

19. Bandura, "Toward a Psychology of Human Agency."

20. Sandy K. Piderit. 2000. "Rethinking Resistance and Recognizing Ambivalence: A Multidimensional View of Attitudes toward an Organizational Change." *Academy of Management Review* 25(4):783–94. (https://pdfs.semanticscholar.org/8b38/ade01f69aab5e3b6511544c6f4be58d0c084.pdf).

21. Annet H. de Lange. 2019. *Successful Aging at Work. Psychological Perspectives on Self-management and Sustainable Employability across the Lifespan*. Heerlen, Netherlands: Open Universiteit: Bureau Ketel.

22. de Lange, *Successful Aging at Work*.

23. Karen Van Dam, Tanja Bipp, and Joris Van Ruysseveldt. 2015. "The Role of Employee Adaptability, Goal Striving and Proactivity for Sustainable Careers." Pp. 190–204 in *Handbook of Research on Sustainable Careers*, edited by Ans de Vos and Beatrice van der Heijden. Cheltenham, UK: Edward Elgar.

24. de Lange, *Successful Aging at Work*.

25. Martin E. P. Seligman and Mihaly Csikszentmihalyi. 2014. "Positive Psychology: An Introduction." Pp. 279–98 in *Flow and the Foundations of Positive Psychology: The Collected Works of Mihaly Csikszentmihalyi*, edited by Mihaly Csikszentmihalyi. Dordrecht, Netherlands: Springer.

26. de Lange, *Successful Aging at Work*.

27. Frank Van Dijk et al. 1990. "Re-evaluation of the Workload and Work Capacity Model." *Tijdschrift Sociale Gezondheidszorg* 68:3–10.

28. P. Matthijs Bal et al. 2008. "Psychological Contract Breach and Job Attitudes: A Meta-analysis of Age as a Moderator." *Journal of Vocational Behavior* 72(1):143–58. (https://doi.org/10.1016/j.jvb.2007.10.005).

29. Jeffrey R. Edwards. 2007. "The Relationship between Person-environment Fit and Outcomes: An Integrative Theoretical Framework." Pp. 209–58 in *Perspectives on Organizational Fit*, edited by Cheri Ostroff and Timothy A. Judge. San Francisco: Jossey-Bass.

30. P. Matthijs Bal and Tim Vantilborgh. 2019. "Lifespan Perspectives on Psychological Contracts." Pp. 455–74 in *Work across the Lifespan*, edited by Boris B. Baltes, Cort W. Rudolph, and Hannes Zacher. London: Elsevier.

31. Arnold B. Bakker, Danyang Du, and Daantje Derks. 2019. "Major Life Events in Family Life, Work Engagement, and Performance: A Test of the Work-home Resources Model." *International Journal of Stress Management* 26(3):238–49. (https://doi.org/10.1037/str0000108).

32. Michael Shanahan and Ross Macmillan. 2008. *Biography and the Sociological Imagination*. New York: Norton.

33. Vanessa Azevedo, Carla Martins, and Angela Maia. 2018. "Life Experiences throughout the Lifespan: What Do People Say (or Not) about Them?" *Journal of Adult Development* 25(2):69–85. (https://doi.org/10.1007/s10804-017-9277-6).

34. Duane F. Alwin. 2012. "Integrating Varieties of Life Course Concepts." *Journals of Gerontology, Series B: Psychological Sciences & Social Sciences* 67(2):206–20. (https://doi.org/10.1093/geronb/gbr146).

35. Karen Pak et al. Under review, 2020. "The Perceived Influence of Career Shocks on One's Career: A Qualitative Study among Older Workers." *Career Development Quarterly*.

36. John C. Cavanaugh and Fredda Blanchard-Fields. 2018. *Neuroscience as a Basis for Adult Development and Aging*. 8th ed. Boston: Cengage.

37. Azevedo, Martins, and Maia, "Life Experiences."

38. Catherine Ward-Griffin et al. 2010. "Double-duty Caregiving: Women in the Health Professions." *Canadian Journal on Aging* 24(4):379–94. (https://doi.org/10.1353/cja.2006.0015).

39. de Lange, Kooij, and van der Heijden, "Human Resource Management."

40. Maria Tims and Arnold Bakker. 2010. "Job Crafting: Towards a New Model of Individual Job Redesign." *SA Journal of Industrial Psychology* 36:1–9. (https://doi.org.10.4102/sajip.v36i2.841).

41. Amy Wrzesniewski and Jane E. Dutton. 2001. "Crafting a Job: Revisioning Employees as Active Crafters of Their Work." *Academy of Management Review* 26:179–201. (http://www.jstor.org/stable/259118).

42. Darya Moghimi et al. 2017. "The Selection, Optimization, and Compensation Model in the Work Context: A Systematic Review and Meta-analysis of Two Decades of Research." *Journal of Organizational Behavior* 38(2):247–75. (https://doi.org/10.1002/job.2108).

43. Jutta Heckhausen, Carsten Wrosch, and Richard Schulz. 2010. "A Motivational Theory of Life-span Development." *Psychological Review* 117(1):32–60. (https://doi.org/10.1037/a0017668).

44. Dorien T. A. M. Kooij et al. 2017. "Job Crafting towards Strengths and Interests: The Effects of a Job Crafting Intervention on Person-job Fit and the Role of Age." *Journal of Applied Psychology* 102(6):971–81. (https://doi.org/10.1037/apl0000194).

45. Karen Pak et al. 2019. "Human Resource Management and the Ability, Motivation and Opportunity to Continue Working: A Review of Quantitative Studies." *Human Resource Management Review* 29(3):336–52. (https://doi.org/10.1016/j.hrmr.2018.07.002).

46. Dorien T. A. M. Kooij et al. 2014. "Managing Aging Workers: A Mixed Methods Study on Bundles of HR Practices for Aging Workers." *International Journal of Human Resource Management* 25(15):2192–212. (https://doi.org/10.1080/09585192.2013.872169).

47. Annet H. de Lange, Hans De Witte, and Guy Notelaers. 2008. "Should I Stay or Should I Go? Examining Longitudinal Relations among Job Resources and Work Engagement for Stayers versus Movers." *Work & Stress* 22(3):201–23. (https://doi.org/10.1080/02678370802390132).

48. Pak et al., "Human Resource Management."

49. Pak et al., "Human Resource Management."

50. Pak et al., "Human Resource Management."

51. Kooij et al., "Managing Aging Workers."

52. de Lange, Kooij, and van der Heijden, "Human Resource Management."

53. Kerstin Van der Mark-Reeuwijk et al. September 2019. "Health and Prolonging Working Lives: An Advisory Report of the Health Council of the Netherlands." *Scandinavian Journal of Work, Environment & Health* 45(5):514–19. (https://doi.org/10.5271/sjweh.3828).

54. Gary Yukl and William L. Gardner. 2019. *Leadership in Organizations*. 9th ed. Harlow, England: Pearson.

55. Abdulaziz Al-Sawai. 2013. "Leadership of Healthcare Professionals: Where Do We Stand?" *Oman Medical Journal* 28(4):285–87. (https://doi.org/10.5001/omj.2013.79).

56. Trude Furunes et al. 2015. "Do Low-quality Leader-member Relationships Matter for Subordinates? Evidence from Three Samples on the Validity of the Norwegian LMX Scale." *Nordic Journal of Working Life Studies* 5(2):71–82. (https://doi.org/10.19154/njwls.v5i2.4794).

57. Irfanulla Khan and Allah Nawaz. 2016. "The Leadership Styles and Employees Performance: A Review." *Gomal University Journal of Research* 32(2):144–50. (https://pdfs.semanticscholar.org/56e8/a90ea2952da4e92b4b92964c93dddda913e4.pdf).

58. Kara A. Arnold. 2017. "Transformational Leadership and Employee Psychological Well-being: A Review and Directions for Future Research." *Journal of Occupational Health Psychology* 22(3):381–93. (https://doi.org/10.1037/ocp0000062).

59. Karina Nielsen and Kevin Daniels. 2016. "The Relationship between Transformational Leadership and Follower Sickness Absence: The Role of Presenteeism." *Work & Stress* 30(2):193–208. (https://doi.org/10.1080/02678373.2016.1170736).

60. Kristin Akerjordet et al. 2018. "Health-promoting Leadership: An Integrative Review and Future Research Agenda." *Journal of Advanced Nursing* 74(2):1505–16. (https://doi.org/10.1111/jan.13567).

61. Andrea Eriksson. 2017. "Management and Leadership Approaches to Health Promotion and Sustainable Workplaces: A Scoping Review." *Societies* 7(2):14. (https://doi.org/10.3390/soc7020014).

62. Aaron Antonovsky. 1996. "The Salutogenic Model as a Theory to Guide Health Promotion." *Health Promotion International* 11(1):11–18. (https://doi.org/10.1093/heapro/11.1.11).

63. Trude Furunes, Anita Kaltveit, and Kristin Akerjordet. 2018. "Health-promoting Leadership: A Qualitative Study from Experienced Nurses' Perspective." *Journal of Clinical Nursing* 27(23–24):4290–301. (https://doi.org/10.1111/jocn.14621).

64. Trude Furunes, Ida Grindland, and Kristin Akerjordet. Submitted for publication, 2020. "Health-promoting Leadership: Core Tasks and Leader Behaviour."

65. Furunes, Kaltveit, and Akerjordet, "Health-promoting Leadership: A Qualitative Study from Experienced Nurses' Perspective."

66. Furunes, Kaltveit, and Akerjordet, "Health-promoting Leadership: A Qualitative Study."

## REFERENCES

Akerjordet, Kristin, et al. 2018. "Health-promoting Leadership: An Integrative Review and Future Research Agenda." *Journal of Advanced Nursing* 74(2):1505–16. (https://doi.org/10.1111/jan.13567).

Al-Sawai, Abdulaziz. 2013. "Leadership of Healthcare Professionals: Where Do We Stand?" *Oman Medical Journal* 28(4):285–87. (https://doi.org/10.5001/omj.2013.79).

Alwin, Duane F. 2012. "Integrating Varieties of Life Course Concepts." *Journals of Gerontology, Series B: Psychological Sciences & Social Sciences* 67(2):206–20. (https://doi.org/10.1093/geronb/gbr146).

Antonovsky, Aaron. 1996. "The Salutogenic Model as a Theory to Guide Health Promotion." *Health Promotion International* 11(1):11–18. (https://doi.org/10.1093/heapro/11.1.11).

Arnold, Kara A. 2017. "Transformational Leadership and Employee Psychological Well-being: A Review and Directions for Future Research." *Journal of Occupational Health Psychology* 22(3):381–93. (https://doi.org/10.1037/ocp0000062).

Azevedo, Vanessa, Carla Martins, and Angela Maia. 2018. "Life Experiences throughout the Lifespan: What Do People Say (or Not) about Them?" *Journal of Adult Development* 25(2):69–85. (https://doi.org/10.1007/s10804-017-9277-6).

Bakker, Arnold B., Danyang Du,, and Daantje Derks. 2019. "Major Life Events in Family Life, Work Engagement, and Performance: A Test of the Work-home Resources Model." *International Journal of Stress Management* 26(3):238–49. (https://doi.org/10.1037/str0000108).

Bakker, Arnold B. and Evangelia Demerouti. 2017. "Job Demands–Resources Theory: Taking Stock and Looking Forward." *Journal of Occupational Health Psychology* 22(3):273–85. (https://doi.org/10.1037/ocp0000056).

Bal, P. Matthijs, et al. 2008. "Psychological Contract Breach and Job Attitudes: A Meta-analysis of Age as a Moderator." *Journal of Vocational Behavior* 72(1):143–58. (https://doi.org/10.1016/j.jvb.2007.10.005).

Bal, P. Matthijs and Tim Vantilborgh. 2019. "Lifespan Perspectives on Psychological Contracts." Pp. 455–74 in *Work across the Lifespan*, edited by Boris B. Baltes, Cort W. Rudolph, and Hannes Zacher. London: Elsevier.

Baltes, Paul B. and Margret M. Baltes. 1990. "Psychological Perspectives on Successful Aging: The Model of Selective Optimization with Compensation." Pp. 1–34 in *Successful Aging: Perspectives from the Behavioral Sciences*, edited by Paul B. Baltes and Margret M. Baltes. New York: Cambridge University Press.

Bandura, Albert. 2006. "Toward a Psychology of Human Agency." *Perspectives on Psychological Science* 1(2):164–80. (https://doi/pdf/10.1111/j.1745-6916.2006.00011).

Burr, Renu and John L. Cordery. 2001. "Self-management Efficacy as a Mediator of the Relation between Job Design and Employee Motivation." *Human Performance* 14(1):27–44. (https://doi.org/10.1207/S15327043HUP1401_03).

Carstensen, Laura L., Derek M. Isaacowitz, and Susan T. Charles. 1999. "Taking Time Seriously: A Theory of Socioemotional Selectivity." *American Psychologist* 54(3):165–81. (https://doi.org/10.1037/0003-066X.54.3.165).

Cavanaugh, John C. and Fredda Blanchard-Fields. 2018. *Neuroscience as a Basis for Adult Development and Aging*. 8th ed. Boston: Cengage.

de Lange, Annet H. 2019. *Successful Aging at Work. Psychological Perspectives on Self-management and Sustainable Employability across the Lifespan*. Heerlen, Netherlands: Open Universiteit: Bureau Ketel.

de Lange, Annet H., Hans De Witte, and Guy Notelaers. 2008. "Should I Stay or Should I Go? Examining Longitudinal Relations among Job Resources and Work Engagement for Stayers versus Movers." *Work & Stress* 22(3):201–23. (https://doi.org/10.1080/02678370802390132).

de Lange, Annet H. and Dorien T. A. M. Kooij. 2019. "Successful Aging at Work: A Positive Psychological Perspective." *Tijdschrift voor Positieve Psychologie* 3:27–34.

de Lange, Annet H., Dorien T. A. M. Kooij, and van der Heijden, Beatrice I. J. M. 2015. "Human Resource Management and Sustainability at Work across the Lifespan: An Integrative Perspective." Pp. 50–79 in *Facing the Challenges of a Multi-age Workforce: A Use-inspired Approach*, edited by Lisa M. Finkelstein et al. New York: Routledge.

Edwards, Jeffrey R. 2007. "The Relationship between Person-environment Fit and Outcomes: An Integrative Theoretical Framework." Pp. 209–58 in *Perspectives on Organizational Fit*, edited by Cherie Ostroff and Timothy A. Judge. San Francisco: Jossey-Bass.

Eriksson, Andrea, et al. 2017. "Management and Leadership Approaches to Health Promotion and Sustainable Workplaces: A Scoping Review." *Societies* 7(2):14. (https://doi.org/10.3390/soc7020014).

Furunes, Trude, et al. 2015. "Do Low-quality Leader-member Relationships Matter for Subordinates? Evidence from Three Samples on the Validity of the Norwegian LMX Scale." *Nordic Journal of Working Life Studies* 5(2):71–87. (https://doi.org/10.19154/njwls.v5i2.4794).

Furunes, Trude, Ida Grindland, and Kristin Akerjordet. Submitted for publication, 2020. "Health-promoting Leadership: Core Tasks and Leader Behaviour."

Furunes, Trude, Anita Kaltveit, and Kristin Akerjordet. 2018. "Health-promoting Leadership: A Qualitative Study from Experienced Nurses' Perspective." *Journal of Clinical Nursing* 27(23-24):4290–301. (https://doi.org/10.1111/jocn.14621).

Heckhausen, Jutta, Carsten Wrosch, and Richard Schulz. 2010. "A Motivational Theory of Life-span Development." *Psychological Review* 117(1):32–60. (https://doi.org/10.1037/a0017668).

Khan, Irfanullah and Allah Nawaz. 2016. "The Leadership Styles and the Employees Performance: A Review." *Gomal University Journal of Research* 32(2):144–50. (https://pdfs.semanticscholar.org/56e8/a90ea2952da4e92b4b92964c93dddda913e4.pdf).

Kooij, Dorien T. A. M. 2015. "Successful Aging at Work: The Active Role of Employees." *Work, Aging and Retirement* 1(4):309–19. (https://doi.org/10.1093/workar/wav018).

Kooij, Dorien T. A. M., et al. 2014. "Managing Aging Workers: A Mixed Methods Study on Bundles of HR Practices for Aging Workers." *International Journal of Human Resource Management* 25(15):2192–212. (https://doi.org/10.1080/09585192.2013.872169).

Kooij, Dorien T. A. M., et al. 2017. "Job Crafting towards Strengths and Interests: The Effects of a Job Crafting Intervention on Person-job Fit and the Role of Age." *Journal of Applied Psychology* 102(6):971–81. (https://doi.org/10.1037/apl0000194).

Lorig, Kate R. and Halsted Holman. 2003. "Self-management Education: History, Definition, Outcomes, and Mechanisms." *Annals of Behavioral Medicine* 26(1):1–7. (https://doi.org/10.1207/S15324796ABM2601_01).

Moghimi, Darya, et al. 2017. "The Selection, Optimization, and Compensation Model in the Work Context: A Systematic Review and Meta-analysis of Two Decades of Research." *Journal of Organizational Behavior* 38(2):247–75. (https://doi.org/10.1002/job.2108).

Nielsen, Karina and Kevin Daniels. 2016. "The Relationship between Transformational Leadership and Follower Sickness Absence: The Role of Presenteeism." *Work & Stress* 30(2):193–208. (https://doi.org/10.1080/02678373.2016.1170736).

OECD. 2020. "Employment Rate by Age Group (Indicator)." Retrieved February 23, 2020 (https://doi.org/10.1787/084f32c7-en).

Pak, Karen, et al. 2019. "Human Resource Management and the Ability, Motivation and Opportunity to Continue Working: A Review of Quantitative Studies." *Human Resource Management Review* 29(3):336–52. (https://doi.org/10.1016/j.hrmr.2018.07.002).

Pak, Karen, et al. Under review, 2020. "The Perceived Influence of Career Shocks on One's Career: A Qualitative Study among Older Workers." *Career Development Quarterly.*

Piderit, Sandy K. 2000. "Rethinking Resistance and Recognizing Ambivalence: A Multidimensional View of Attitudes toward an Organizational Change." *Academy of Management Review* 25(4):783–94. (https://pdfs.semanticscholar.org/8b38/ade01f69aab5e3b6511544c6f4be58d0c084.pdf).

Schaufeli, Wilmar B., Arnold B. Bakker, and Marisa Salanova. 2006. "The Measurement of Work Engagement with a Short Questionnaire: A Cross-national Study." *Educational and Psychological Measurement* 66(4):701–16. (https://doi.org/10.1177/0013164405282471).

Seligman, Martin E. P. and Mihaly Csikszentmihalyi. 2014. "Positive Psychology: An Introduction." Pp. 279–98 in *Flow and the Foundations of Positive Psychology: The Collected Works of Mihaly Csikszentmihalyi*, edited by Mihaly Csikszentmihalyi. Dordrecht, Netherlands: Springer.

Semeijn, Judith, et al. 2015. "Sustainable Labor Participation and Sustainable Careers." Pp. 146–60 in *Handbook of Research on Sustainable Careers*, edited by Ans De Vos and Beatrice I. J. M. van der Heijden. Cheltenham, UK: Edward Elgar. (https://doi.org/10.4337/9781782547037.00015).

Shanahan, Michael and Ross Macmillan. 2008. *Biography and the Sociological Imagination.* New York: Norton.

Thoresen, Carl E. and Michael J. Mahoney. 1974. *Behavioral Self-control.* New York: Holt, Rinehart & Winston.

Tims, Maria and Arnold B. Bakker. 2010. "Job Crafting: Towards a New Model of Individual Job Redesign." *SA Journal of Industrial Psychology* 36:1–9. (https://doi.org.10.4102/sajip.v36i2.841).

Van Dam, Karen, Tanja Bipp, and Joris Van Ruysseveldt. 2015. "The Role of Employee Adaptability, Goal Striving and Proactivity for Sustainable Careers." Pp. 190–204 in *Handbook of Research on Sustainable Careers*, edited by Ans De Vos and Beatrice van der Heijden. Cheltenham, UK: Edward Elgar.

van der Heijden, Beatrice I. J. M., et al. 2009. "Age Effects on the Employability–Career Success Relationship." *Journal of Vocational Behavior* 74(2):156–64. (https://doi.org/10.1016/j.jvb.2008.12.009).

Van der Mark-Reeuwijk, Kerstin G., et al. 2019. "Health and Prolonging Working Lives: An Advisory Report of the Health Council of the Netherlands." *Scandinavian Journal of Work, Environment & Health* 45(5):514–19. (https://doi.org/10.5271/sjweh.3828).

Van Dijk, Frank, et al. 1990. "Re-evaluation of the Workload and Work Capacity Model." *Tijdschrift Sociale Gezondheidszorg* 68:3–10.

Von Bonsdorff, Monica E., et al. 2011. "Work Strain in Midlife and 28-year Work Ability Trajectories." *Scandinavian Journal of Work, Environment & Health* 37(6):455–63. (https://doi.org/10.5271/sjweh.3177).

Ward-Griffin, Catherine, et al. 2010. "Double-duty Caregiving: Women in the Health Professions." *Canadian Journal on Aging* 24(4):379–94. (https://doi.org/10.1353/cja.2006.0015).

Wrzesniewski, Amy and Jane E. Dutton. 2001. "Crafting a Job: Revisioning Employees as Active Crafters of Their Work." *Academy of Management Review* 26:179–201. (http://www.jstor.org/stable/259118).

Yukl, Gary and William L. Gardner. 2019. *Leadership in Organizations*. 9th ed. Harlow, England: Pearson.

Zacher, Hannes, Dorien T. A. M. Kooij, and Margaret E. Beier. 2018. "Active Aging at Work." *Organizational Dynamics* 47(1):37–45.

CHAPTER 17

# Emerging Technologies, the Aging Workforce, and the Future of Work

Margaret E. Beier and Meghan K. Davenport

Technology promises to change the landscape of work in the twenty-first century. According to some experts, virtually no aspect of work is exempt from the impact of technological innovation: from the types of jobs available to where and when work gets done, even the definition of an "employee" is now up for debate. It is indeed difficult to predict how technology will impact the workplace in the coming decades, but history can provide a useful precedent for what the future might hold, particularly given that forecasts about the future of work leading to sparse jobs and plentiful leisure time echo those voiced on the cusp of the Industrial Revolution. Of course, past forecasts did not account for innovation concurrent with the Industrial Revolution that led to new jobs and new industries, a phenomenon that is likely to recur in the workplace throughout the twenty-first century. Indeed, according to many experts, work will be plentiful into the near future. But, similar to the shift in the types of jobs available from agrarian to manufacturing during the Industrial Revolution, the technological revolution promises to shift the types of jobs from manufacturing to knowledge.[1]

Concurrent with technological innovation are demographic shifts in the labor force. Globally, people are living longer and having fewer children. By the year 2030, the number of people over fifty years old will be unprecedented in virtually all European and Asian countries.[2] In the U.S., the number of people age sixty-five or older is expected to exceed the number of children under the age of eighteen by 2030. These trends affect the availability of workers, and by 2020, 23 percent of workers in the U.S. are expected to be sixty-five and older, compared to just 12 percent in 1990.[3] Many older workers will be in so-called encore careers or bridge employment—indeed, one in five new entrepreneurs in the U.S. is aged fifty-five to sixty-five—most likely because they prefer to remain engaged in work for its psychological benefits.[4] Yet many workers will need to continue working for financial reasons, particularly given increased life expectancies and, in the U.S., increased reliance on defined contribution plans instead of company-managed pension plans.[5] Regardless of why they continue working, older workers will need to engage with the type of work available—work that will be significantly impacted by technological innovation.

The purpose of this chapter is to examine these two converging societal phenomena: the aging of the labor force and the proliferation of technology in the workplace. We try not to focus on any individual technology because technology moves so quickly that any specific application we describe may be obsolete before we finish writing. Rather, we focus on characteristics and affordances of technology and their impact on the experiences of older workers in the workplace of the future.

## WORKPLACE AGING

Perhaps the only uniform thing about aging is that everyone ages differently. Although there are normative trends in aging such as declines in some traits and abilities and increases in others, there is extreme variability in the ways in which people age. Looking strictly at their trait and ability profiles, some fifty-year-olds will resemble seventy-year-olds, while others more resemble thirty-year-olds. One implication of this variability is that there is typically not a single age at which a person is considered an "older worker." Although it is useful to describe normative trends in aging—and we discuss these below—we acknowledge that individual experiences will vary depending on myriad factors such as genetics, health, and the resources one has available throughout life.[6]

The aging process has been described as one of "loss, gain, reorganization, and exchange."[7] *Loss* refers to age-related declines in abilities associated with reasoning through novel problems, including working-memory abilities. *Gains* refer to increases in the knowledge gained through life experiences. Although losses in reasoning and memory abilities are indeed salient to many older workers, declines in these abilities can be considered adaptive in that as people age, there are fewer completely novel situations that might require raw reasoning/memory ability to navigate. This is because people *gain* experiences across a wide array of situations through the lifespan that they bring to bear to navigate their daily lives. Indeed, knowledge gained through experience—work, educational, or any lived experience—can be considered the essential element of adult intellect.[8]

*Reorganization* and *exchange* refer to changes in non-ability traits such as affect and motivation.[9] Socioemotional selectivity theory (SST) describes how goals tend to shift from being achievement focused when people are relatively younger to socioemotional (i.e., making connections with others) as people age.[10] This implies that older workers may be more oriented toward relationships with other people—mentoring and connecting with others—than they will be toward working to obtain their next promotion.

The dynamic experiences of aging described above point to the benefits of engaging older workers (e.g., their knowledge, interpersonal skills), but also suggest that older workers may have more difficulty constantly updating their skills and abilities in the face of rapidly changing technology. Moreover, age will affect older worker motivation and self-efficacy for technology-related tasks (self-efficacy defined as a person's perception that he or she can successfully accomplish a task).[11] For instance, declines in memory abilities are likely salient to older people, who may have reduced self-efficacy for skills updating when the material to be learned appears novel and complex. This lowered self-efficacy is likely to negatively affect motivation for developing technological skills and reduce persistence in such activities in the face of difficulty. Without a strategy for designing technology and technological training with older workers in mind, the constant skills updating necessary in the workplace of the future may disadvantage older workers.[12] (See also chapters 15 and 18.)

## EMERGING TECHNOLOGY

The past century has seen a shift from the industrial era, which was focused on the procurement of physical resources and mass production, to the digital era, which is focused on the generation of products via data, information, and knowledge delivered in digital format. Within the digital era, which began around 1950 or so with mainframe computers, technology has evolved to a period of ubiquitous computing, in which technology permeates all aspects of work and life. Ubiquitous computing is defined as technology that enables "people to access and control their environments at any time and from anywhere."[13] A benefit of ubiquitous computing is that it provides workers unprecedented control and autonomy over where and when work gets done. It also provides opportunities for increased productivity by making information and the ability to communicate with one another possible twenty-four hours a day, seven days a week.

Communication technologies such as Slack and Skype for Business enable workers to connect electronically in a way that is designed to be more instantaneous and conversational than email, taking the place of watercooler quips and/or walking over to someone's desk and asking a quick question that does not merit an email. These technologies enable teams to work efficiently regardless of their physical proximity, facilitating remote work and collaboration across physical office locations. An important by-product of ubiquitous technologies that support business processes is the data generated when people are constantly plugged into their devices. The hardware (mobile devices, laptops, GPS systems) and applications/programs (email, Skype, Slack, Zoom, Hangouts, etc.) generate unprecedented amounts of data on human behavior, including location, communication patterns, and performance, that can be used to automate the tasks of daily life and work through artificial intelligence (AI). These data can also be used to customize delivery of information to individuals based on patterns of behavior exhibited in the past. Consumers shopping online have experienced customized marketing messages based on prior searches and purchases. The ethics of the type of constant behavioral monitoring associated with ubiquitous computing, and implications for worker privacy, are still up for debate, and this debate is outside the scope of this chapter.[14] Rather, we describe characteristics of technology and how they affect older workers (for better or worse).

Table 17.1 shows the characteristics of technology we feel are most relevant to the aging workforce, the relationship between the technology and job demands and

**TABLE 17.1.** Characteristics and Affordances of Emerging Technologies, Their Impact on Job Demands and Resources, and Age-related Considerations

| *Technology Characteristics and Affordances* | *Notable Characteristics* | *Impact on Job Demands and Resources* | *Age-Related Considerations* |
|---|---|---|---|
| Ubiquitous computing | Enables access to information anytime and anyplace. | Increased job autonomy. Permits workers to decide when, where, and how to work.<br>Increases decision stress.<br>Blurs the line between work and leisure.<br>Reduces opportunity for supervisory and/or coworker support. | Older workers might benefit from autonomy because it can provide flexibility at work.<br>Flexibility may increase the appeal of working longer if workers can reduce hours and/or work remotely instead of retiring.<br>Isolation and lack of social support might be more detrimental to older adults than it is to younger workers. |
| Automation | Offloads standardized/routine tasks to technology rather than relying on humans.<br>Not all routinized tasks are easily automated. Tasks that require fine motor coordination and manipulation of nonstandard objects are difficult/impossible for machines as of 2020. | Reduces the need to perform cognitively and physically tedious tasks.<br>Potentially increases the complexity of jobs.<br>Creates a need for complementary skills like complex decision-making and social skills. | Older workers are particularly susceptible to strain and injury from physically demanding jobs, meaning that automation can help them stay working longer.<br>Older workers have the interpersonal skills that automation cannot replace.<br>Reskilling that might be necessary as jobs change due to automation is tougher for older workers. |
| Interactive, adaptive, and feedback affordances | ***Interactive:*** when a system presents new information in response to actions initiated by the user.<br>***Adaptive***: when a system presents information contingent on the characteristics of the user.<br>System-driven ***feedback*** is immediate and unbiased. | Adaptive and interactive systems can make some tasks easier.<br>Feedback allows errors to be detected and corrected fairly and without bias.<br>All are affordances that can facilitate learning and engagement. | Older workers can use interactive and adaptive technology to gain information that might help compensate for age-related declines.<br>Automated feedback facilitates learning outside of official training environments, which is especially helpful for older workers given potential low training self-efficacy and perceptions of lack of trainability. |
| Intelligent agents and robots | Intelligent agents can learn, pursue goals, and interact socially without human control. | Robots reduce the need for humans to perform tasks that require physical strength and endurance.<br>Humans and robots can work side by side instead of a human needing to control the robot.<br>Robots will need to function as members of teams, meaning that psychological processes like trust, psychological contracts, and social support will be sought from robot teammates. | Reduction in physical job demands makes more jobs accessible to older workers.<br>If the introduction of robot coworkers decreases the availability of socioemotional motivating factors in the workplace, older adults might be more likely to opt out of working longer. |

resources,[15] and considerations for older workers. This list of technological characteristics and affordances is not meant to be exhaustive, but it was derived from our research on the impact of technology on jobs, learning, and aging and represents our best thinking about what is most relevant to aging workers.[16] Affordances are properties of technology that facilitate an activity by a human agent.[17] Technological affordances are thus the ways in which technology interacts with people to support human endeavors. Job demands and resources, which are central to work design theories, describe demands as the aspects of a job that require sustained physical or psychological effort. Job resources are the physical or psychological aspects of a job that support workers in achieving work-related goals, that reduce the burden associated with job demands, and/or that stimulate personal growth and development.[18]

### *Ubiquitous Computing*

The main characteristic of ubiquitous computing is that it enables access to technology anyplace and anytime, such as current mobile devices (smartphones and tablets) that provide powerful computing in small portable packages.[19] The portability of computing affects job demands and resources, most directly perhaps, through the autonomy it affords to workers to decide when and how they are going to work.[20] Job autonomy is typically considered a job resource, a characteristic of work that will reduce job demands and/or stimulate growth and development.[21] For example, the autonomy associated with ubiquitous computing provides flexibility to workers in terms of when they work. This flexibility allows workers to deal with nonwork demands (e.g., health and family) during work hours, but usually requires workers to make up missed work during hours they might normally reserve for leisure. Autonomy associated with where to work can also be useful to workers even when they do not have much autonomy about when. For example, there is an array of programs that permit communication and videoconference calls, where team members can engage in projects from anywhere in the world.[22] Research has supported the benefits of remote work, particularly in terms of increased autonomy leading to job satisfaction, job performance, reduced turnover intentions, and lowered job stress.[23] Furthermore, research suggests that the flexibility afforded by technology is particularly desirable to older workers.[24] Flexibility, particularly when paired with working fewer hours overall, can provide a means through which older workers can retain the psychological and financial benefits of working without the strain of having to report to an office and of adhering to a full-time schedule.

Although job autonomy may be considered a job resource to the extent that it promotes productivity and motivation, too much autonomy may burden workers and cause stress.[25] On the most basic level, decisions about where, how, and when to work impose the burden of actually making—and taking responsibility for—these decisions. The responsibility for decision-making adds a level of complexity in terms of prioritizing tasks that may be particularly problematic for workers who are not good at imposing structure on the work environment.[26] Increased job autonomy may also be associated with lower levels of other workplace resources such as managerial and coworker support and general social support.[27] Remote workers typically do not interact face-to-face with other people in the workplace, and this reduced communication may impact workers' ability to build relationships that may be instrumental (e.g., receiving informal help on a work-related project or feedback to improve one's performance) or interpersonal (e.g., developing long-lasting friendships that endure beyond the workplace).[28] Indeed, research suggests that intensive remote work (i.e., more than 2.5 days a week of telecommuting) harmed relationships among coworkers.[29] And although workplace relationships may seem trivial compared to task work, researchers have linked work relationships to job satisfaction, turnover intentions, burnout, organizational commitment, and subjective performance ratings.[30]

Workplace social interaction may be particularly important for older workers. Both theory and research suggest that age is positively related to a desire to pursue socioemotional versus achievement goals as described above,[31] which implies that the isolation associated with remote work arrangements will be less attractive to older workers. As such, the benefit of autonomy that remote work provides will be offset by a reduction in the network of colleagues one interacts with during the workday. This reduced social network may have an unforeseen but perilous impact on maintaining social support that can sustain people through work and retirement. Rates of loneliness are increasing among adults over forty-five, and those who indicate that they are lonely are also more likely to report that electronic communication afforded by the internet makes them feel more (not less) lonely.[32] Moreover, loneliness has been linked to both mental and physical health concerns for people of all ages,[33] but older adults are particularly at risk.[34] To date, however, very little research has examined the value of workplace relationships for subjective well-being and loneliness, and the impact of technology on the development of social relationships, particularly for older workers.

Warr's vitamin model[35] provides an interesting lens through which to examine autonomy at work. The vitamin model proposes that some job resources might, like vitamins, be problematic in large doses. For instance, as described above, job autonomy may be considered a job resource to the extent it promotes productivity and motivation.[36] Research on the vitamin model shows a curvilinear relationship between autonomy and job satisfaction, job stress, and engagement with work, suggesting that too much autonomy can be as problematic as too little.[37]

One concrete, and technology-relevant, example of the vitamin model and ubiquitous computing is related to the use of email in business and personal interactions. Over the past twenty years, email has become an essential component of work for most workers regardless of industry. It has many benefits including saving time and providing an electronic paper trail that makes tracking past communication easy. With the proliferation of mobile devices (laptops, phones, and tablets), email can be accessed anywhere, anytime, increasing workplace autonomy. But the sheer volume of email and ease of access are not without cost. As of 2019, the average office worker receives 121 emails per day (a number apt to be much larger for some workers), and this average is expected to increase as the number of people using email increases.[38] In addition to the volume of emails, the length of messages, the unpredictability of tasks associated with the messages, the interruption and task switching demanded by responding to email (particularly if messages are related to both work and personal affairs), and the pressure to respond quickly, all add to the stress associated with email.[39] Consider that 50 percent of people report checking email while in bed and 40 percent report checking it in the bathroom, places that have historically been nonwork zones for good reason. These disturbing statistics suggest that workers feel a constant need to be available and engaged in work, which can impair worker ability to recover from work and can leave workers feeling isolated and burned out.[40]

## Automation

Automation removes the need for humans to engage in a process by offloading it to technological systems. At work, automation has the potential to replace jobs currently filled by human workers, particularly those with highly repetitive and routine tasks. However, it is likely that most jobs cannot be replaced entirely; rather, automation will replace job tasks that are cognitively or physically tedious, which may have the advantage of making jobs more interesting and accidents less likely.[41] Automation is particularly interesting for physical jobs that require static physical strength, such as lifting heavy objects, endurance, repetitive physical tasks, and balance, as such jobs can be hard on older workers.[42] Automating these physically demanding aspects of jobs will lead to fewer injuries, which may help workers remain in the workplace for longer. For instance, one Japanese company is building innovative lumbar support robots that can help ease the physical difficulties of caregiving, such as lifting a patient, thereby helping medical staff work longer without fear of strain and injury.[43]

The benefits of automation are countered with speculation that it will replace jobs in industrialized economies over the coming decades, leaving many without work.[44] These predictions even go so far as to decry the end of work and the introduction of a basic income to provide for the all-leisure class.[45] Although automation will likely replace some jobs, not all jobs are at risk and the threat is not imminent. Even state-of-the-art automated systems are currently unable to handle some repetitive and routine job tasks, particularly those involving nonstandard objects and unique requests. For example, robots routinely work alongside humans at Amazon warehouses, where they move about the warehouses retrieving standard-sized bins filled with product. They deliver these bins to workers who then select merchandise from the bins to fulfill unique orders.[46] As of this writing, robots have neither the manual dexterity to handle individual merchandise nor the ability to do quality control checks for each order. Robots do, however, have the endurance to cover large distances in the warehouses and lift heavy bins without rest. The ability of robots to handle these routine but challenging physical tasks makes jobs more interesting and less physically challenging for human workers. In this case, automation also makes human jobs safer and may permit aging workers to work longer before retirement.

Despite fears about the overall scarcity of work in future decades, technological innovation has historically created jobs for people who have the skills that complement technology.[47] For example, automated systems cannot adapt to ambiguity and unpredictability, make complex decisions, or understand the human psyche enough to effectively relate to, motivate, or support subordinates, colleagues, or customers. Forecasters predict that interpersonal skills will be in high demand in the workplace of the future,[48] which will put older adults at an advantage.[49]

One stark implication of the pace of technological innovation is that workers will thrive in the workplace of the future only if they are willing and able to continually retool and avoid skill obsolescence,[50] which may negatively affect older workers for two reasons. First, age is negatively related to learning in training and positively related to time in training, particularly when the information to be learned is completely novel.[51] Although little is known about the best approaches for training older workers relative to their ability profile (although see Beier and colleagues' review)[52] training that links new learning to well-learned routines will benefit older learners. Indeed, research suggests that older workers can and do learn new skills in training when the training interventions are designed with the unique needs of older learners in mind.[53]

The second reason that the constant need for skills updating may disadvantage older workers is the perception that managers, coworkers, and older workers themselves may have that older workers cannot learn new information.[54] Perpetuated by managers and coworkers, these perceptions will limit opportunities for continuous development afforded to older workers. When they are perpetuated by older workers themselves, these perceptions will decrease older worker motivation and self-efficacy for training.[55] In summary, perceptions about inflexibility of skill development, particularly as they affect opportunities for development, motivation, and self-efficacy, will make older workers more vulnerable to skill obsolescence and thus unemployment relative to younger workers. More research is needed to understand how to best design training interventions for older workers, and how to mitigate negative stereotypes about older worker inflexibility and inability to learn. (See also chapters 12 and 13.)

## Interactive, Adaptive, and Feedback Affordances

Technology that is interactive, adaptive, and that provides immediate and accurate feedback can affect how people do their jobs, and perhaps most importantly, it can affect continuous learning and development on the job.[56] *Interactivity* occurs when a system presents new information in response to actions initiated by the user. For example, word processing programs interact with users when users are saving or opening files. A system is *adaptive* when it presents information contingent on the characteristics of the user. Adaptive systems, for example, automatically adjust to user knowledge, habits, and preferences (e.g., presenting content of appropriate difficulty based on prior performance in a training program). System-driven *feedback* is generally immediate and unbiased, such as when word processing programs immediately redline spelling and grammatical errors. Although it is true that human supervisors and trainers can also provide experiences that are interactive, adaptive, and that include feedback, the advantage of technology is that it is scalable.

Adaptive and interactive technologies permit older workers to compensate for age-related changes in physical and mental abilities described above.[57] For example, font size can be adjusted on computer screens to accommodate older eyes. Interactive prompts in an electronic user manual can boost older worker memory when assisting a customer in solving a complex problem. In essence, interactive and adaptive technology accounts for the vast diversity in human aging.

Technological affordances have mainly been studied in the context of learning and development. A review of this literature is beyond the scope of this chapter (although see a review by Beier).[58] We will mention, however, that because technological affordances can be embedded in everyday work processes, they can facilitate learning and development in relatively unobtrusive ways. That is, workers need only to engage in normal work activities with systems that are interactive, adaptive, and that provide feedback to maximize learning and development, which may reduce the need for more formal training interventions like classroom training.[59] Embedding these affordances into technology may thus serve to decrease motivational barriers for skills updating, as learning and development becomes part of a daily routine. All of this is speculative, however, since there is very little research on the impact of technology on training and development in organizations,[60] and even less on the impact of technology on learning for mature workers.[61] Given the rapidity with which technology is increasing the landscape of work in the coming decades, the aging of the global workforce, and the importance of constant skills updating for all workers, this is an area for future research.

## Intelligent Agents and Robots

Artificial intelligence (AI) typically refers to the ability of a computer system to perform tasks that normally require human intelligence, such as perception (visual and speech recognition), decision-making, and most recently writing and creating.[62] AI is embedded in many of the features described above, particularly as related to adaptive systems and customization. However, recent innovation in AI has changed the nature of the human-technology relationship from one in which the human controls technology to one in which the human may work alongside an intelligent agent to complete a task. Intelligent agents are autonomous entities that can engage in goal directed actions, learn, and respond to their environments without being controlled by a human operator.[63] Intelligent agents can be extremely simple, such as thermostats that adjust to ambient temperatures, or they can be more complex, such as robots that engage in a sequence of actions to meet a goal.[64]

Workplace teams currently (and will increasingly in the future) comprise robots and human members that interact and rely on one another to complete job tasks. Researchers have begun to examine how this type of team composition will impact important psychological processes, such as the psychological contract (i.e., an implicit understanding that fosters trust among team members and improves motivation and performance).[65,66] But much more research is needed to answer questions about, for example, how job functions should be allocated among robots and humans, trust in human-robot teams, and fears about robots replacing human workers.[67] There are also ethical considerations associated with the use of intelligent agents that require additional thought and research (e.g., who is responsible for the actions of intelligent agents acting autonomously?).[68] There is even less research in this area focused on experiences of older workers. We speculate that, to the extent that robots can offset some of the physical demands of a job as any automated system can, such as heavy lifting and repetitive physical tasks, robots have the potential to extend the working life of older workers by reducing the likelihood of injury. However, working alongside robots rather than people may not satisfy workers' desire for socioemotional connection, which may be more salient to older workers' experiences.[69] The extent to which robots might be developed to provide instrumental and emotional support, and the extent to which robot-human interactions can replace human-to-human contact and friendship, however, is a question for future research.

## Additional Considerations

Above we described how age-related trajectories in abilities, goals, and attitudes might interface with emerging technologies to affect worker engagement, performance, preference for training and development activities, and motivation to continue working longer. There are, however, additional ways in which emerging technologies will affect the experiences of older workers in the future. These issues are more general than any one specific technology but span across the features and affordances described in table 17.1. Specifically, we consider (a) the interface between an aging applicant pool and HR functions related to selection, and (b) age considerations in adopting new technologies.

## Age, Technology, and HR Functions

Beyond the ways in which industry-specific technologies might shift the work of an individual, such as a new machine or a new records-management system that a person must learn, organizations are increasingly making use of emerging technologies to streamline, automate, and inform their HR processes. One example of this is increased technology use in selection processes. Resume screening is often automated, which is particularly useful given that organizations can receive literally thousands of online applications per job. An AI-trained system designed to identify key elements from resumes in order to determine which candidates are considered by a human HR professional can save countless hours of work. Once a candidate is selected to move forward in the hiring process, the next step might be a work sample or test, such as a personality or cognitive ability test, which are often administered online. And even though organizations are fast adopting technologies to support HR processes, little is known about how these processes will affect older workers.

On the one hand, technology promises to reduce bias in selection because it makes decisions less susceptible to human error by taking the human out of the decision-making process. On the other hand, technology might introduce different biases[70] and it may codify existing biases. AI, for example, learns its algorithms based on existing data.[71] If existing data are biased, resulting algorithms will also be biased. Consider, for example, an algorithm used to predict job performance in a selection system that is based on incumbent performance ratings that favor—for no other reason than stereotypes and biases—younger employees over older. We use selection as the example above, but the same concerns apply to an array of HR functions like recruitment and training. Consider, for example, an algorithm that displays job ads online only to users who most closely resemble job incumbents rather than a diverse array of potential applicants. In sum, using AI-based selection systems that organizations cannot understand or explain may negatively impact older workers' opportunities and put organizations at risk of litigation. It will be important for organizational scientists, particularly those working in HR practices, to better understand the impact of technology and particularly AI on HR functions in the twenty-first century.

### Age and Adopting New Technology

When a new technology is introduced in the workplace, management may expect that employees will immediately buy in, appreciating the potential for increased productivity and functionality that the product affords. However, in order for employees to adopt a technology, they must develop a level of trust in the technology, feeling confident that it will allow them to be successful at their job.[72] Otherwise, workers may continue to use a previous, now outdated technology with which they feel comfortable, or create workarounds using processes that they trust.[73] The unified theory of acceptance and use of technology (UTAUT) consolidates previous theory on technology adoption.[74] According to UTAUT, social influence, performance expectancy, and effort expectancy impact whether a person intends to use a new technology. Intention and facilitating conditions in the environment that support technology adoption determine whether workers will ultimately engage.

Studies of UTAUT across the age range of working adults found that older workers' intention to use new technology was more impacted by effort expectancy and social influence, while younger workers' intention to use was more impacted by performance expectancy.[75] The results of this research are in line with known age-related shifts in motivation based on perceptions of the amount of effort required to reach a given level of performance,[76] and shifts away from achievement toward socioemotional goals, as discussed above.[77] This research also highlights the potential for interventions to affect technology use for older workers. That is, facilitating conditions, such as providing tech support for PC users, were more predictive of new technology use for older versus younger people. The notion that older workers may be dissuaded from using technology by perceptions of effort are supported by research that finds that computer self-efficacy and computer anxiety mediate the negative relationship between age and technology adoption.[78] In other words, there is nothing inherent about age that affects the likelihood of technology use. Rather, it is the cognitive and motivational factors that are associated with age that should be the focus of organizational interventions directed at adopting new technology.

## FUTURE DIRECTIONS AND CONCLUSION

Although we cannot know the technological changes that will most impact the experience of work for older workers, we do know that for many of the technologies described above, the future is already here. Organizational scientists can and should conduct research now to understand how the confluence of technological innovation and workplace aging will impact the workplace of the future. We hope that the discussion above has piqued our readers' interest in myriad research questions related to technology and workplace aging. Here, we highlight four main areas of future research that we find most compelling (table 17.2).

**TABLE 17.2. Future Research Directions for Emerging Technology and the Aging Workforce**

| *Theme* | *Guiding Questions* |
|---|---|
| Changing job demands and resources in the twenty-first-century workplace | Do technology-related changes in job demands and resources impact the performance, retirement intentions, and job attitudes of aging workers?<br>Will the shift away from repetitive, physically demanding jobs impact older adults? Will older workers be able to capitalize on newly created jobs that demand different skills? How will the types of jobs available in the twenty-first century differentially impact older adults of varying education and income levels? |
| Social support and well-being in the workplace | Can robots be successfully integrated into the workplace without sacrificing the social support that is critically important, especially for older workers?<br>How can jobs be designed to take advantage of technology without the negative implications of constantly being "on"? Does the lack of work-life separation afforded by ubiquitous computing affect older and younger workers differently? |
| Training design for older adults | Can training be designed to mitigate age-related stereotypes and negative self-attitudes?<br>How can organizations ensure that training opportunities are extended to all workers regardless of age?<br>Can technology be leveraged to provide more effective training to older adults, and more generally to workers across ability and experience levels?<br>How can workplace training be reimagined as an integrated part of the workday, instead of a stand-alone event? Will this reimagining remove motivational barriers to training and development? |
| Implications of technology-driven HR practices for older workers | Can organizations ensure that algorithms for hiring, training, and compensation that are derived from existing company data do not simply perpetuate systemic biases, including biases against older workers?<br>How can technology promote equity and assist HR departments in their efforts to comply with the law, as opposed to being a mechanism that creates inequity and legal issues for organizations? |

First, and perhaps most generally, we have described the ways in which technology will change job demands and job resources. We know little, however, about how age interacts with these job characteristics to continue to engage older workers. Some research has indicated that flexible work arrangements are particularly beneficial and desirable for older workers,[79] but perhaps not if these arrangements come with increased demands associated with ubiquitous computing. We thus call for more research that examines how changes in job demands and resources associated with technology are likely to affect an aging workforce in terms of performance, retirement intentions, and job attitudes.

Second, the increased use of technology-supported communication and the use of intelligent agents in teams will decrease the amount of person-to-person contact for all workers, which may increase worker isolation and lead to negative health outcomes, particularly for older workers. We currently know very little, however, about the extent to which technology-supported communication can serve as a useful proxy for face-to-face communication or about how human-robot teams will operate. Investigating person-robot team dynamics and the extent to which person-to-person communication is necessary for worker mental health, particularly for older workers, is another area needing research attention.

Third, as described above, technology promises to adapt to the unique needs of workers, which can benefit older workers in performing their jobs and in their learning and development. We know little, however, about how best to design training interventions to meet the unique needs of older workers. Much more research is needed to understand how best to design formal training interventions for older learners (e.g., how to adapt structure and instructions to boost learner performance and self-efficacy),[80] and how to embed developmental opportunities into everyday work so older learners perceive them as less effortful.[81] As part of this effort, it will be useful to more fully examine how age-related stereotypes affect motivation for training and development, and whether embedded developmental opportunities facilitated by technology mitigate these stereotypes.

Fourth, technology is already changing how employees are selected, from technology-facilitated interviews via phone or Skype to initial resume reviews using AI. Given the convenience of these approaches, organizations are moving ahead with changes to HR processes without the benefit of input from organizational scientists. It is, however, imperative that organizational scientists study how HR processes are changing, and how these changes might affect those most vulnerable in society, including older workers.

This is an exciting time to study workplace aging. Technology promises to change the landscape of work in the twenty-first century and the experience of work for older workers in ways that we cannot imagine today. Some of these changes will certainly benefit the aging workforce, and others will not. Here we have highlighted some of the technological features and affordances we feel are most relevant to workplace aging but acknowledge that our list is incomplete and may prove obsolete in short order given the rapidity at which innovation is changing the workplace. Only time will tell. What we know for certain, however, is that organizational scientists have an opportunity to influence the experience of work in ways that benefit workers, organizations, and society, and we recommend they take it.

## NOTES

1. David H. Autor. August 2015. "Why Are There Still So Many Jobs? The History and Future of Workplace Automation." *Journal of Economic Perspectives* 29(3):3–30. (https://doi.org/10.1257/jep.29.3.3).
2. Wan He, Daniel Goodkind, and Paul Kowal. March 2016. "An Aging World: 2015." International Population Reports. U.S. Department of Commerce, Washington, DC: U.S. Census Bureau.
3. Paul H. Irving and Anusuya Chatterjee. 2014. "The Rise of a Mature World: By the Numbers." Pp. xxv–xxxii in *The Upside of Aging: How Long Life Is Changing the World of Health, Work, Innovation, Policy, and Purpose*, edited by Paul H. Irving and Rita Beamish. Hoboken, NJ: John Wiley & Sons.

4. Mo Wang and Connie R. Wanberg. 2017. "100 Years of Applied Psychology Research on Individual Careers: From Career Management to Retirement." *Journal of Applied Psychology* 102(3):546–63. (https://doi.org/10.1037/apl0000143).

5. Veronica M. Dendinger, Gary A. Adams, and Jamie D. Jacobson. 2005. "Reasons for Working and Their Relationship to Retirement Attitudes, Job Satisfaction and Occupational Self-efficacy of Bridge Employees." *International Journal of Aging and Human Development* 61(1):21–35. (https://doi.org/10.2190/K8KU-46LH-DTW5-44TU).

6. John C. Cavanaugh and Fredda Blanchard-Fields. 2010. *Adult Development and Aging*. Boston: Cengage Learning.

7. Ruth Kanfer and Phillip L. Ackerman. July 2004. "Aging, Adult Development, and Work Motivation." *Academy of Management Review* 29(3):440. (https://doi.org/10.2307/20159053).

8. Phillip L. Ackerman. 2000. "Domain-specific Knowledge as the 'Dark Matter' of Adult Intelligence: Gf/Gc, Personality and Interest Correlates." *Journals of Gerontology Series B: Psychological Sciences and Social Sciences* 55(2):69–84. (http://dx.doi.org/10.1093/geronb/55.2.p69).

9. Kanfer and Ackerman, "Aging."

10. Laura L. Carstensen, Derek M. Isaacowitz, and Susan T. Charles. March 1999. "Taking Time Seriously. A Theory of Socio-emotional Selectivity." *American Psychologist* 54:165–81. (https://doi.org/10.1037/0003-066X.54.3.165).

11. Albert Bandura. 1982. "Self-efficacy Mechanism in Human Agency." *American Psychologist* 37:122–47.

12. W. Jackeline Torres, Brittany C. Bradford, and Margaret E. Beier. 2019. "Technology and the Aging Worker: A Review and Agenda for Future Research." Pp. 608–40 in *The Cambridge Handbook of Technology and Employee Behavior*, edited by Richard N. Landers. New York: Cambridge University Press.

13. Wayne F. Cascio and Ramiro Montealegre. 2016. "How Technology Is Changing Work and Organizations." *Annual Review of Organizational Psychology and Organizational Behavior* 3(1):353. (https://doi.org/10.1146/annurev-orgpsych-041015-062352).

14. Jonathan P. West and James S. Bowman. July 2016. "Electronic Surveillance at Work: An Ethical Analysis." *Administration & Society* 48(5):628–51. (https://doi.org/10.1177/0095399714556502).

15. Evangelia Demerouti et al. 2001. "The Job Demands-resources Model of Burnout." *Journal of Applied Psychology* 86(3):499–512. (https://doi.org/10.1037/0021-9010.86.3.499).

16. Torres, Bradford, and Beier, "Technology and the Aging Worker."

17. Donald A. Norman. 2013. *The Design of Everyday Things*. Rev. and expanded ed. New York: Basic Books.

18. Demerouti et al., "Job Demands-resources Model of Burnout."

19. Cascio and Montealegre, "How Technology Is Changing Work and Organizations."

20. Evangelia Demerouti et al. 2014. "New Ways of Working: Impact on Working Conditions, Work-family Balance, and Well-being." Pp. 123–41 in *The Impact of ICT on Quality of Working Life*, edited by Christian Korunka and Peter Hoonakker. Dordrecht, Netherlands: Springer. (https://doi.org/10.1007/978-94-017-8854-0_8).

21. Demerouti et al., "Job Demands-resources Model of Burnout."

22. Scott Wharton. July 20, 2018. "Is Videoconferencing Still the Future?" *Yale Insights: Ideas from the Yale School of Management* (blog). (https://insights.som.yale.edu/insights/is-videoconferencing-still-the-future).

23. Ravi S. Gajendran and David A. Harrison. 2007. "The Good, the Bad, and the Unknown about Telecommuting: Meta-analysis of Psychological Mediators and Individual Consequences." *Journal of Applied Psychology* 92(6):1524–41. (https://doi.org/10.1037/0021-9010.92.6.1524).

24. Cheryl Paullin. 2014. "The Aging Workforce: Leveraging the Talents of Mature Employees." SHRM Foundation's Effective Practice Guidelines Series. (http://www.shrm.org/about/foundation/products/Documents/Aging%20Workforce%20EPG-FINAL.pdf).

25. Peter Warr. 2013. "Jobs and Job-holders: Two Sources of Happiness and Unhappiness." Pp. 733–50 in *The Oxford Handbook of Happiness*, edited by Susan A. David, Ilona Boniwell, and Amanda Conley Ayers. New York: Oxford University Press.

26. Bettina Kubicek, Matea Paškvan, and Johanna Bunner. 2017. "The Bright and Dark Sides of Job Autonomy." Pp. 45–63 in *Job Demands in a Changing World of Work*, edited by Christian Korunka

and Bettina Kubicek. Cham, Switzerland: Springer International. (https://doi.org/10.1007/978-3-319-54678-0_4).

27. Warr, "Jobs and Job-holders."

28. Amy E. Colbert, Joyce E. Bono, and Radostina K. Purvanova. 2016. "Flourishing via Workplace Relationships: Moving beyond Instrumental Support." *Academy of Management Journal* 59(4):1199–1223. (https://doi.org/10.5465/amj.2014.0506).

29. Gajendran and Harrison, "The Good, the Bad, and the Unknown."

30. Stephen E. Humphrey, Jennifer D. Nahrgang, and Frederick P. Morgeson. 2007. "Integrating Motivational, Social, and Contextual Work Design Features: A Meta-analytic Summary and Theoretical Extension of the Work Design Literature." *Journal of Applied Psychology* 92(5):1332–56. (https://doi.org/10.1037/0021-9010.92.5.1332); Adam M. Grant and Sharon K. Parker. 2009. "Redesigning Work Design Theories: The Rise of Relational and Proactive Perspectives." *Academy of Management Annals* 3(1):317–75. (https://doi.org/10.1080/19416520903047327).

31. Carstensen, Isaacowitz, and Charles, "Taking Time Seriously."

32. Colette Thayer and G. Oscar Anderson. September 24, 2018. "Loneliness and Social Connections: A National Survey of Adults 45 and Older." AARP Research. (https://doi.org/10.26419/res.00246.001).

33. John T. Cacioppo and William Patrick. 2008. *Loneliness: Human Nature and the Need for Social Connection*. New York: Norton.

34. Julianne Holt-Lunstad et al. March 2015. "Loneliness and Social Isolation as Risk Factors for Mortality: A Meta-analytic Review." *Perspectives on Psychological Science: A Journal of the Association for Psychological Science* 10(2):227–37. (https://doi.org/10.1177/1745691614568352).

35. Warr, "Jobs and Job-holders."

36. Robert A. Karasek. June 1979. "Job Demands, Job Decision Latitude, and Mental Strain: Implications for Job Redesign." *Administrative Science Quarterly* 24(2):285. (https://doi.org/10.2307/2392498).

37. Kubicek, Paškvan, and Bunner, "Bright and Dark Sides of Job Autonomy"; Peter B. Warr. October 1990. "Decision Latitude, Job Demands, and Employee Well-being." *Work & Stress* 4(4):285–94. (https://doi.org/10.1080/02678379008256991).

38. Heinz Tschabitscher. June 27, 2019. "Everything You Always Wanted to Know about Email." Lifewire: 19 Fascinating Email Facts. (https://www.lifewire.com/how-many-emails-are-sent-every-day-1171210).

39. Demerouti et al., "New Ways of Working."

40. David G. Allen, Robert W. Renn, and Rodger W. Griffeth. 2003. "The Impact of Telecommuting Design on Social Systems, Self-regulation, and Role Boundaries." *Research in Personnel and Human Resources Management* 1:125–63. (https://doi.org/10-02T00:00:00Z); Nitya Chawla et al. June 2019. "Unplugging or Staying Connected? Examining the Nature, Antecedents, and Consequences of Profiles of Daily Recovery Experiences." *Journal of Applied Psychology* 105(1). (https://doi.org/10.1037/apl0000423).

41. Miguel Paredes. 2018. "Can Artificial Intelligence Help Reduce Human Medical Errors? Two Examples from ICUs in the US and Peru." Washington, DC: Technology Policy Institute (https://techpolicyinstitute.org/wp-content/uploads/2018/02/Paredes-Can-Artificial-Intelligence-help-reduce-human-medical-errors-DRAFT.pdf).

42. Joanne O. Crawford et al. 2010. "The Health Safety and Health Promotion Needs of Older Workers." *Occupational Medicine* 60(3):184–92. (https://doi.org/10.1093/occmed/kqq028).

43. Don Lee. July 25, 2019. "Desperate for Workers, Aging Japan Turns to Robots for Healthcare." *Los Angeles Times*. (https://www.latimes.com/world-nation/story/2019-07-25/desperate-for-workers-aging-japan-turns-to-robots-for-healthcare).

44. Carl Benedikt Frey and Michael A. Osborne. 2017. "The Future of Employment: How Susceptible Are Jobs to Computerisation?" *Technological Forecasting and Social Change* 114:254–80. (https://doi.org/10.1016/j.techfore.2016.08.019).

45. Catherine Clifford. 2018. "Elon Musk: Free Cash Handouts 'Will Be Necessary' If Robots Take Humans' Jobs." Make It. (https://www.cnbc.com/2018/06/18/elon-musk-automated-jobs-could-make-ubi-cash-handouts-necessary.html).

46. Nick Wingfield. September 10, 2017. "As Amazon Pushes Forward with Robots, Workers Find New Roles." *New York Times*, Technology. (https://www.nytimes.com/2017/0f9/10/technology/amazon-robots-workers.html).

47. Autor, "Why Are There Still So Many Jobs?"

48. Margaret E. Beier, Jackeline Torres, and Daniel J. Beal. In press. "Workplace Aging and Jobs in the 21st Century." To appear in *New and Emerging Topics in Aging and Work*, edited by Sara J. Czaja, Joseph Sharit, and Jacqueline B. James. New York: Springer.

49. Thomas M. Hess, Nicole L. Osowski, and Christina M. Leclerc. 2005. "Age and Experience Influences on the Complexity of Social Inferences." *Psychology and Aging* 20(3):447–59. (https://doi.org/10.1037/0882-7974.20.3.447).

50. Cascio and Montealegre, "How Technology Is Changing Work and Organizations."

51. Jean E. Kubeck et al. 1996l "Does Job-related Training Performance Decline with Age?" *Psychology and Aging* 11:92–107.

52. Margaret E. Beier, Mark S. Teachout, and Cody B. Cox. 2012. "The Training and Development of an Aging Workforce." Pp. 436–53 in *The Oxford Handbook of Work and Aging*, edited by Walter C. Borman and Jerry W. Hedge. New York: Oxford University Press. (https://doi.org/10.1093/oxfordhb/9780195385052.013.0138).

53. Judith Scully Callahan, D. Scott Kiker, and Tom Cross. 2003. "Does Method Matter? A Meta-analysis of the Effects of Training Method on Older Learner Training Performance." *Journal of Management* 29:663–80.

54. Richard A. Posthuma and Michael A. Campion. 2009. "Age Stereotypes in the Workplace: Common Stereotypes, Moderators, and Future Research Directions." *Journal of Management* 35(1):158–88. (https://doi.org/10.1177/0149206308318617).

55. Kanfer and Ackerman, "Aging"; Margaret E. Beier et al. 2019. "Cognition, Motivation, and Lifespan Development." In *Work across the Lifespan*, edited by Boris B. Baltes, Cort W. Rudolph, and Hannes Zacher. New York: Elsevier Academic Press. (https://doi.org/10.1016/B978-0-12-812756-8.00007-4).

56. Margaret E. Beier. 2019. "The Impact of Technology on Workforce Skill Learning." Thinking Forward. (https://smartech.gatech.edu/handle/1853/61063); Committee on How People Learn II. 2018. *How People Learn II: Learners, Contexts, and Cultures*. Washington, DC: National Academies Press. (https://doi.org/10.17226/24783).

57. Kanfer and Ackerman, "Aging."

58. Beier, "Impact of Technology."

59. Margaret E. Beier, Jackeline Torres, and Jaqueline M. Gilberto. 2017. "Continuous Development throughout a Career: A Lifespan Perspective on Autonomous Learning." Pp. 179–200 in *Autonomous Learning in the Workplace*, edited by Jill E. Ellingson and Raymond A. Noe. SIOP Organizational Frontiers Series. New York: Routledge/Taylor & Francis Group.

60. Kenneth G. Brown, Steven D. Charlier, and Abigail Pierotti. 2012. "E-learning at Work: Contributions of Past Research and Suggestions for the Future." Pp. 89–114 in *The International Review of Industrial and Organizational Psychology*, vol. 27, edited by Gerard P. Hodgkinson and J. Kevin Ford. Hoboken, NJ: John Wiley & Sons. (https://doi.org/10.1002/9781118311141).

61. Beier, Teachout, and Cox, "Training and Development."

62. IBM. September 11, 2015. "The Quest for AI Creativity." IBM Cognitive—What's Next for AI? (http://www.ibm.com/watson/advantage-reports/future-of-artificial-intelligence/ai-creativity.html); Parag Jain et al. July 18, 2017. "Story Generation from Sequence of Independent Short Descriptions." *ArXiv:1707.05501 [Cs]*. (http://arxiv.org/abs/1707.05501).

63. Jeffrey Heer. February 5, 2019. "Agency plus Automation: Designing Artificial Intelligence into Interactive Systems." *Proceedings of the National Academy of Sciences* 116(6):1844–50. (https://doi.org/10.1073/pnas.1807184115).

64. Sarah Bankins and Paul Formosa. 2020. "When AI Meets PC: Exploring the Implications of Workplace Social Robots and a Human-robot Psychological Contract." *European Journal of Work and Organizational Psychology* 29(2):215–29. (https://doi.org/10.1080/1359432X.2019.1620328).

65. Denise M. Rousseau. 1989. "Psychological and Implied Contracts in Organizations." *Employee Responsibilities and Rights Journal* 2(2):121–39. (https://doi.org/10.1007/BF01384942).

66. Bankins and Formosa, "When AI Meets PC."

67. Cascio and Montealegre, "How Technology Is Changing Work and Organizations."

68. David J. Gunkel. July 19, 2017. "Mind the Gap: Responsible Robotics and the Problem of Responsibility." *Ethics and Information Technology*. (https://doi.org/10.1007/s10676-017-9428-2).

69. Alap Kshirsagar et al. 2019. "Monetary-incentive Competition between Humans and Robots: Experimental Results." In *2019 14th ACM/IEEE International Conference on Human-Robot Interaction*. Daegu, South Korea: IEEE:95–103. (https://doi.org/10.1109/HRI.2019.8673201).

70. Nikki Blacksmith, Jon C. Willford, and Tara S. Behrend. 2016. "Technology in the Employment Interview: A Meta-analysis and Future Research Agenda." *Personnel Assessment and Decisions* 2(1):2.

71. Jeffrey Dastin. October 9, 2018. "Amazon Scraps Secret AI Recruiting Tool That Showed Bias against Women." Reuters. (https://www.reuters.com/article/us-amazon-com-jobs-automation-insight/amazon-scraps-secret-ai-recruiting-tool-that-showed-bias-against-women-id....).

72. Ji-Hwan Lee and Chi-Hoon Song. 2013. "Effects of Trust and Perceived Risk on User Acceptance of a New Technology Service." *Social Behavior and Personality: An International Journal* 41(4):587–97. (https://doi.org/10.2224/sbp.2013.41.4.587).

73. Jason J. Saleem et al. 2009. "Exploring the Persistence of Paper with the Electronic Health Record." *International Journal of Medical Informatics* 78(9):618–28. (https://doi.org/10.1016/j.ijmedinf.2009.04.001).

74. Viswanath Venkatesh et al. 2003. "User Acceptance of Information Technology: Toward a Unified View." *MIS Quarterly* 27(3):425–78. (https://doi.org/10.2307/30036540).

75. Venkatesh et al., "User Acceptance."

76. Beier et al., "Cognition"; Kanfer and Ackerman, "Aging."

77. Carstensen, Isaacowitz, and Charles, "Taking Time Seriously."

78. Sara J. Czaja et al. 2006. "Factors Predicting the Use of Technology: Findings from the Center for Research and Education on Aging and Technology Enhancement (Create)." *Psychology and Aging* 21(2):333–52. (https://doi.org/10.1037/0882-7974.21.2.333).

79. Donald M. Truxillo, D. A. Cadiz, and Jennifer R. Rineer. 2012. "Designing Jobs for an Aging Workforce: An Opportunity for Occupational Health." *Contemporary Occupational Health Psychology: Global Perspectives on Research and Practice* 2:109–25.

80. Madeline Carter and Margaret E. Beier. August 2010. "The Effectiveness of Error Management Training with Working-aged Adults." *Personnel Psychology* 63(3):641–75. (https://doi.org/10.1111/j.1744-6570.2010.01183.x).

81. Beier, Torres, and Gilberto, "Continuous Development"; Kanfer and Ackerman, "Aging."

## REFERENCES


Ackerman, Phillip L. 2000. "Domain-specific Knowledge as the 'Dark Matter' of Adult Intelligence: Gf/Gc, Personality and Interest Correlates." *Journals of Gerontology Series B: Psychological Sciences and Social Sciences* 55(2):69–84. (http://dx.doi.org/10.1093/geronb/55.2.p69).

Allen, David G., Robert W. Renn, and Rodger W. Griffeth. 2003. "The Impact of Telecommuting Design on Social Systems, Self-regulation, and Role Boundaries." *Research in Personnel and Human Resources Management* 1:125–63. (https://doi.org/10-02T00:00:00Z).

Autor, David H. August 2015. "Why Are There Still So Many Jobs? The History and Future of Workplace Automation." *Journal of Economic Perspectives* 29(3):3–30. (https://doi.org/10.1257/jep.29.3.3).

Bandura, Albert. 1982. "Self-efficacy Mechanism in Human Agency." *American Psychologist* 37:122–47.

Bankins, Sarah and Paul Formosa. 2020. "When AI Meets PC: Exploring the Implications of Workplace Social Robots and a Human-robot Psychological Contract." *European Journal of Work and Organizational Psychology* 29(2):215–29. (https://doi.org/10.1080/1359432X.2019.1620328).

Beier, Margaret E. 2019. "The Impact of Technology on Workforce Skill Learning." Thinking Forward. (https://smartech.gatech.edu/handle/1853/61063).

Beier, Margaret E., et al. 2019. "Cognition, Motivation, and Lifespan Development." In *Work across the Lifespan*, edited by Boris B. Baltes, Cort W. Rudolph, and Hannes Zacher. New York: Elsevier Academic Press. (https://doi.org/10.1016/B978-0-12-812756-8.00007-4).

Beier, Margaret E., Mark S. Teachout, and Cody B. Cox. 2012. "The Training and Development of an Aging Workforce." Pp. 436–53 in *The Oxford Handbook of Work and Aging*, edited by Walter C. Borman and Jerry W. Hedge. New York: Oxford University Press. (https://doi.org/10.1093/oxfordhb/9780195385052.013.0138).

Beier, Margaret E., Jackeline Torres, and Daniel J. Beal. In press. "Workplace Aging and Jobs in the 21st Century." To appear in *New and Emerging Topics in Aging and Work*, edited by Sara J. Czaja, Joseph Sharit, and Jacqueline B. James. New York: Springer.

Beier, Margaret E., Jackeline Torres, and Jaqueline M. Gilberto. 2017. "Continuous Development throughout a Career: A Lifespan Perspective on Autonomous Learning." Pp. 179–200 in *Autonomous Learning in the Workplace*, edited by Jill E. Ellingson and Raymond A. Noe. SIOP Organizational Frontiers Series. New York: Routledge/Taylor & Francis Group.

Blacksmith, Nikki, Jon C. Willford, and Tara S. Behrend. 2016. "Technology in the Employment Interview: A Meta-analysis and Future Research Agenda." *Personnel Assessment and Decisions* 2(1):2.

Brown, Kenneth G., Steven D. Charlier, and Abigail Pierotti. 2012. "E-learning at Work: Contributions of Past Research and Suggestions for the Future." Pp. 89–114 in *The International Review of Industrial and Organizational Psychology*, vol. 27, edited by Gerard P. Hodgkinson and J. Kevin Ford. Hoboken, NJ: John Wiley & Sons. (https://doi.org/10.1002/9781118311141).

Cacioppo, John T. and William Patrick. 2008. *Loneliness: Human Nature and the Need for Social Connection*. New York: Norton.

Callahan, Judith Scully, D. Scott Kiker, and Tom Cross. 2003. "Does Method Matter? A Meta-analysis of the Effects of Training Method on Older Learner Training Performance." *Journal of Management* 29:663–80.

Carstensen, Laura L., Derek M. Isaacowitz, and Susan T. Charles. March 1999. "Taking Time Seriously: A Theory of Socio-emotional Selectivity." *American Psychologist* 54:165–81. (https://doi.org/10.1037/0003-066X.54.3.165).

Carter, Madeline and Margaret E. Beier. August 2010. "The Effectiveness of Error Management Training with Working-aged Adults." *Personnel Psychology* 63(3):641–75. (https://doi.org/10.1111/j.1744-6570.2010.01183.x).

Cascio, Wayne F. and Ramiro Montealegre. 2016. "How Technology Is Changing Work and Organizations." *Annual Review of Organizational Psychology and Organizational Behavior* 3(1):349–75. (https://doi.org/10.1146/annurev-orgpsych-041015-062352).

Cavanaugh, John C. and Fredda Blanchard-Fields. 2010. *Adult Development and Aging*. Boston: Cengage Learning.

Chawla, Nitya, et al. June 2019. "Unplugging or Staying Connected? Examining the Nature, Antecedents, and Consequences of Profiles of Daily Recovery Experiences." *Journal of Applied Psychology* 105(1). (https://doi.org/10.1037/apl0000423).

Clifford, Catherine. 2018. "Elon Musk: Free Cash Handouts 'Will Be Necessary' If Robots Take Humans' Jobs." Make It. (https://www.cnbc.com/2018/06/18/elon-musk-automated-jobs-could-make-ubi-cash-handouts-necessary.html).

Colbert, Amy E., Joyce E. Bono, and Radostina K. Purvanova. 2016. "Flourishing via Workplace Relationships: Moving beyond Instrumental Support." *Academy of Management Journal* 59(4):1199–1223. (https://doi.org/10.5465/amj.2014.0506).

Committee on How People Learn II. 2018. *How People Learn II: Learners, Contexts, and Cultures*. Washington, DC: National Academies Press. (https://doi.org/10.17226/24783).

Crawford, Joanne O., et al. 2010. "The Health Safety and Health Promotion Needs of Older Workers." *Occupational Medicine* 60(3):184–92. (https://doi.org/10.1093/occmed/kqq028).

Czaja, Sara J., et al. 2006. "Factors Predicting the Use of Technology: Findings from the Center for Research and Education on Aging and Technology Enhancement (Create)." *Psychology and Aging* 21(2):333–52. (https://doi.org/10.1037/0882-7974.21.2.333).

Dastin, Jeffrey. October 9, 2018. "Amazon Scraps Secret AI Recruiting Tool That Showed Bias against Women." Reuters. (https://www.reuters.com/article/us-amazon-com-jobs-automation-insight/amazon-scraps-secret-ai-recruiting-tool-that-showed-bias-against-women-id....).

Demerouti, Evangelia, et al. 2001. "The Job Demands-resources Model of Burnout." *Journal of Applied Psychology* 86(3):499–512. (https://doi.org/10.1037/0021-9010.86.3.499).

Demerouti, Evangelia et al. 2014. "New Ways of Working: Impact on Working Conditions, Work-family Balance, and Well-being." Pp. 123–41 in *The Impact of ICT on Quality of Working Life*, edited by Christian Korunka and Peter Hoonakker. Dordrecht, Netherlands: Springer. (https://doi.org/10.1007/978-94-017-8854-0_8).

Dendinger, Veronica M., Gary A. Adams, and Jamie D. Jacobson. 2005. "Reasons for Working and Their Relationship to Retirement Attitudes, Job Satisfaction and Occupational Self-efficacy of Bridge Employees." *International Journal of Aging and Human Development* 61(1):21–35. (https://doi.org/10.2190/K8KU-46LH-DTW5-44TU).

Frey, Carl Benedikt and Michael A. Osborne. 2017. "The Future of Employment: How Susceptible Are Jobs to Computerisation?" *Technological Forecasting and Social Change* 114:254–80. (https://doi.org/10.1016/j.techfore.2016.08.019).

Gajendran, Ravi S. and David A. Harrison. 2007. "The Good, the Bad, and the Unknown about Telecommuting: Meta-analysis of Psychological Mediators and Individual Consequences." *Journal of Applied Psychology* 92(6):1524–41. (https://doi.org/10.1037/0021-9010.92.6.1524).

Grant, Adam M. and Sharon K. Parker. 2009. "Redesigning Work Design Theories: The Rise of Relational and Proactive Perspectives." *Academy of Management Annals* 3(1):317–75. (https://doi.org/10.1080/19416520903047327).

Gunkel, David J. July 19, 2017. "Mind the Gap: Responsible Robotics and the Problem of Responsibility." *Ethics and Information Technology*. (https://doi.org/10.1007/s10676-017-9428-2).

He, Wan, Daniel Goodkind, and Paul Kowal. March 2016. "An Aging World: 2015." International Population Reports. U.S. Department of Commerce, Washington, DC: U.S. Census Bureau.

Heer, Jeffrey. February 5, 2019. "Agency plus Automation: Designing Artificial Intelligence into Interactive Systems." *Proceedings of the National Academy of Sciences* 116(6):1844–50. (https://doi.org/10.1073/pnas.1807184115).

Hess, Thomas M., Nicole L. Osowski, and Christina M. Leclerc. 2005. "Age and Experience Influences on the Complexity of Social Inferences." *Psychology and Aging* 20(3):447–59. (https://doi.org/10.1037/0882-7974.20.3.447).

Holt-Lunstad, Julianne, et al. March 2015. "Loneliness and Social Isolation as Risk Factors for Mortality: A Meta-analytic Review." *Perspectives on Psychological Science: A Journal of the Association for Psychological Science* 10(2):227–37. (https://doi.org/10.1177/1745691614568352).

Humphrey, Stephen E., Jennifer D. Nahrgang, and Frederick P. Morgeson. 2007. "Integrating Motivational, Social, and Contextual Work Design Features: A Meta-analytic Summary and Theoretical Extension of the Work Design Literature." *Journal of Applied Psychology* 92(5):1332–56. (https://doi.org/10.1037/0021-9010.92.5.1332).

IBM. September 11, 2015. "The Quest for AI Creativity." IBM Cognitive—What's Next for AI? (http://www.ibm.com/watson/advantage-reports/future-of-artificial-intelligence/ai-creativity.html).

Irving, Paul H. and Anusuya Chatterjee. 2014. "The Rise of a Mature World: By the Numbers." Pp. xxv–xxxii in *The Upside of Aging: How Long Life Is Changing the World of Health, Work, Innovation, Policy, and Purpose*, edited by Paul H. Irving and Rita Beamish. Hoboken, NJ: John Wiley & Sons.

Jain, Parag, et al. July 18, 2017. "Story Generation from Sequence of Independent Short Descriptions." *ArXiv:1707.05501 [Cs]*. (http://arxiv.org/abs/1707.05501).

Kanfer, Ruth and Phillip L. Ackerman. July 2004. "Aging, Adult Development, and Work Motivation." *Academy of Management Review* 29(3):440–58. (https://doi.org/10.2307/20159053).

Karasek, Robert A. June 1979. "Job Demands, Job Decision Latitude, and Mental Strain: Implications for Job Redesign." *Administrative Science Quarterly* 24(2):285. (https://doi.org/10.2307/2392498).

Kshirsagar, Alap et al. 2019. "Monetary-incentive Competition between Humans and Robots: Experimental Results." In *2019 14th ACM/IEEE International Conference on Human-Robot Interaction*. Daegu, South Korea: IEEE:95–103. (https://doi.org/10.1109/HRI.2019.8673201).

Kubeck, Jean E. et al. 1996. "Does Job-related Training Performance Decline with Age?" *Psychology and Aging* 11:92–107.

Kubicek, Bettina, Matea Paškvan, and Johanna Bunner. 2017. "The Bright and Dark Sides of Job Autonomy." Pp. 45–63 in *Job Demands in a Changing World of Work*, edited by Christian Korunka and Bettina Kubicek. Cham, Switzerland: Springer International. (https://doi.org/10.1007/978-3-319-54678-0_4).

Lee, Don. July 25, 2019. "Desperate for Workers, Aging Japan Turns to Robots for Healthcare." *Los Angeles Times*. (https://www.latimes.com/world-nation/story/2019-07-25/desperate-for-workers-aging-japan-turns-to-robots-for-healthcare).

Lee, Ji-Hwan and Chi-Hoon Song. 2013. "Effects of Trust and Perceived Risk on User Acceptance of a New Technology Service." *Social Behavior and Personality: An International Journal* 41(4):587–97. (https://doi.org/10.2224/sbp.2013.41.4.587).

Norman, Donald A. 2013. *The Design of Everyday Things*. Rev. and expanded ed. New York: Basic Books.

Paredes, Miguel. 2018. "Can Artificial Intelligence Help Reduce Human Medical Errors? Two Examples from ICUs in the US and Peru." Washington, DC: Technology Policy Institute (https://techpolicyinstitute.org/wp-content/uploads/2018/02/Paredes-Can-Artificial-Intelligence-help-reduce-human-medical-errors-DRAFT.pdf).

Paullin, Cheryl. 2014. "The Aging Workforce: Leveraging the Talents of Mature Employees." SHRM Foundation's Effective Practice Guidelines Series. (http://www.shrm.org/about/foundation/products/Documents/Aging%20Workforce%20EPG-FINAL.pdf).

Posthuma, Richard A. and Michael A. Campion. 2009. "Age Stereotypes in the Workplace: Common Stereotypes, Moderators, and Future Research Directions." *Journal of Management* 35(1):158–88. (https://doi.org/10.1177/0149206308318617).

Rousseau, Denise M. 1989. "Psychological and Implied Contracts in Organizations." *Employee Responsibilities and Rights Journal* 2(2):121–39. (https://doi.org/10.1007/BF01384942).

Saleem, Jason J., et al. 2009. "Exploring the Persistence of Paper with the Electronic Health Record." *International Journal of Medical Informatics* 78(9):618–28. (https://doi.org/10.1016/j.ijmedinf.2009.04.001).

Thayer, Colette and G. Oscar Anderson. September 24, 2018. "Loneliness and Social Connections: A National Survey of Adults 45 and Older." AARP Research. (https://doi.org/10.26419/res.00246.001).

Torres, W. Jackeline, Brittany C. Bradford, and Margaret E. Beier. 2019. "Technology and the Aging Worker: A Review and Agenda for Future Research." Pp. 608–40 in *The Cambridge Handbook of Technology and Employee Behavior*, edited by Richard N. Landers. New York: Cambridge University Press.

Truxillo, Donald M., D. A. Cadiz, and Jennifer R. Rineer. 2012. "Designing Jobs for an Aging Workforce: An Opportunity for Occupational Health." *Contemporary Occupational Health Psychology: Global Perspectives on Research and Practice* 2:109–25.

Tschabitscher, Heinz. June 27, 2019. "Everything You Always Wanted to Know about Email." Lifewire: 19 Fascinating Email Facts. (https://www.lifewire.com/how-many-emails-are-sent-every-day-1171210).

Venkatesh, Viswanath, et al. 2003. "User Acceptance of Information Technology: Toward a Unified View." *MIS Quarterly* 27(3):425–78. (https://doi.org/10.2307/30036540).

Wang, Mo and Connie R. Wanberg. 2017. "100 Years of Applied Psychology Research on Individual Careers: From Career Management to Retirement." *Journal of Applied Psychology* 102(3):546–63. (https://doi.org/10.1037/apl0000143).

Warr, Peter. 2013. "Jobs and Job-holders: Two Sources of Happiness and Unhappiness." Pp. 733–50 in *The Oxford Handbook of Happiness*, edited by Susan A. David, Ilona Boniwell, and Amanda Conley Ayers. New York: Oxford University Press.

Warr, Peter B. October 1990. "Decision Latitude, Job Demands, and Employee Well-being." *Work & Stress* 4(4):285–94. (https://doi.org/10.1080/02678379008256991).

West, Jonathan P. and James S. Bowman. July 2016. "Electronic Surveillance at Work: An Ethical Analysis." *Administration & Society* 48(5):628–51. (https://doi.org/10.1177/0095399714556502).

Wharton, Scott. July 20, 2018. "Is Videoconferencing Still the Future?" *Yale Insights: Ideas from the Yale School of Management* (blog). (https://insights.som.yale.edu/insights/is-videoconferencing-still-the-future).

Wingfield, Nick. September 10, 2017. "As Amazon Pushes Forward with Robots, Workers Find New Roles." *New York Times*, Technology. (https://www.nytimes.com/2017/0f9/10/technology/amazon-robots-workers.html).

# CHAPTER 18

# Living Longer, Working Longer, Learning Longer

Phyllis A. Cummins, Peter Riley Bahr, and Takashi Yamashita

## LIFE EXPECTANCY AND EXTENDED WORK LIFE

Slowing population growth over the past decade, largely due to declining birth rates,[1] will require increased labor force participation for all age groups in the coming decades if the United States is to remain competitive in the global economy. Countries throughout the world have implemented policies to encourage increased participation in the labor force at older ages. Pension reforms, such as linking the retirement age to increases in life expectancy, have been implemented in some countries, and early retirement programs are being eliminated. A retirement age of sixty-seven is now quite common.[2]

Older adults, those ages fifty-five and older, represent an increasingly important segment of the U.S. workforce. Individuals are continuing to work at older ages for many reasons, including shifts from defined benefit to defined contribution retirement plans, increases in Social Security's full retirement age, improved health,[3] and low returns on investments in recent years that have slowed the growth of retirement accounts.[4] Increased life expectancy has also been a factor in longer working lives. Between 1959 and 2016, life expectancy in the U.S. increased by nine years to seventy-nine years.[5]

## THE FUTURE OF THE U.S. LABOR FORCE

The age structure of the labor force in the U.S. has changed in recent decades, with older age groups representing a greater proportion of the labor force. By 2028, the fifty-five and older age group is projected to represent more than 25 percent of the civilian labor force compared to 12 percent in 1998.[6] Between 1998 and 2028, the overall labor force participation rate (LFPR) is projected to decline from 67 percent to 61 percent, but participation rates are projected to increase for both the fifty-five-to-sixty-four (increasing from 59 percent in 1998 to 68 percent in 2028) and the sixty-five-to-seventy-four (increasing from 18 percent in 1998 to 33 percent) age groups.[7]

There are substantial differences in LFPR between males and females. Participation rates for males aged fifty-five to sixty-four have remained relatively stable for the past two decades at about 70 percent and are expected to remain stable through 2050. Participation rates for females ages fifty-five to sixty-four are projected to continue increasing for the next several decades, growing from 59 percent in 2018 to about 65 percent in 2050.[8,9] LFPR in 2018 varied by both sex and country. In figures 18.1 and 18.2, we compare LFPR for males and females in the U.S. with several geographically diverse, developed nations. The average LFPR for member countries of the Organisation for Economic Co-operation and Development (OECD) for males aged fifty-five to sixty-four was 73 percent, while it was 55 percent for females in the same age group.[10] At 71 percent, males aged fifty-five to sixty-four in the U.S. have a lower participation rate as compared to the OECD average and also lower than any of the comparison countries. By contrast, with a 24 percent participation rate, males aged sixty-five and older in the U.S. have a higher participation rate than the OECD average and all comparison countries except Japan. Participation rates for older females are higher than the OECD average for both the fifty-five-to-sixty-four and the sixty-five-plus age groups.[11,12] Encouraging continued work at older ages has many benefits, both to the individual through increased financial security[13] and to society by maintaining or increasing economic growth.[14]

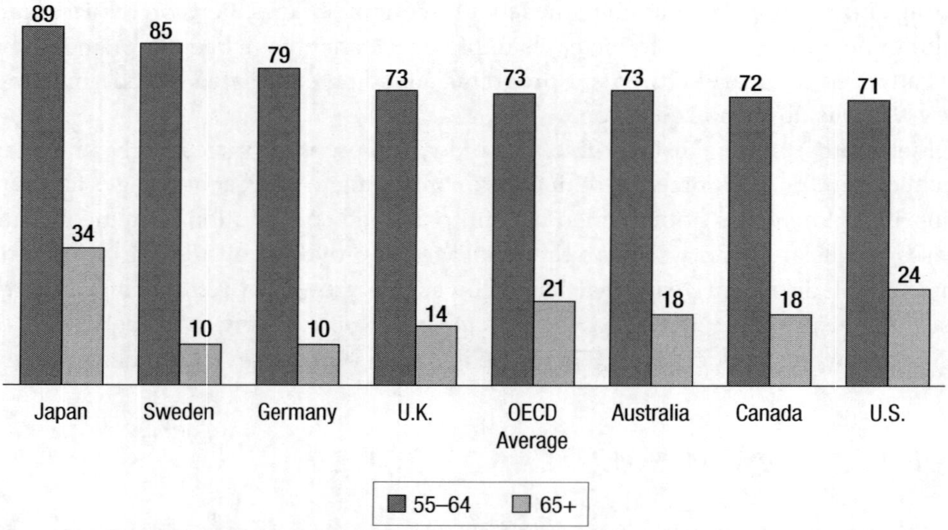


**FIGURE 18.1.** Labor Force Participation Rates, Males Ages 55–64 and 65+ (%)
*Source:* International Labor Organization, Labor Force Participation Rate by Sex and Age—ILO Modeled Estimates, July 2019—Annual. Retrieved January 23, 2020, from https://www.ilo.org/shinyapps/bulkexplorer11/?lang=en&segment=indicator&id=EAP_2WAP_SEX_AGE_RT_A.

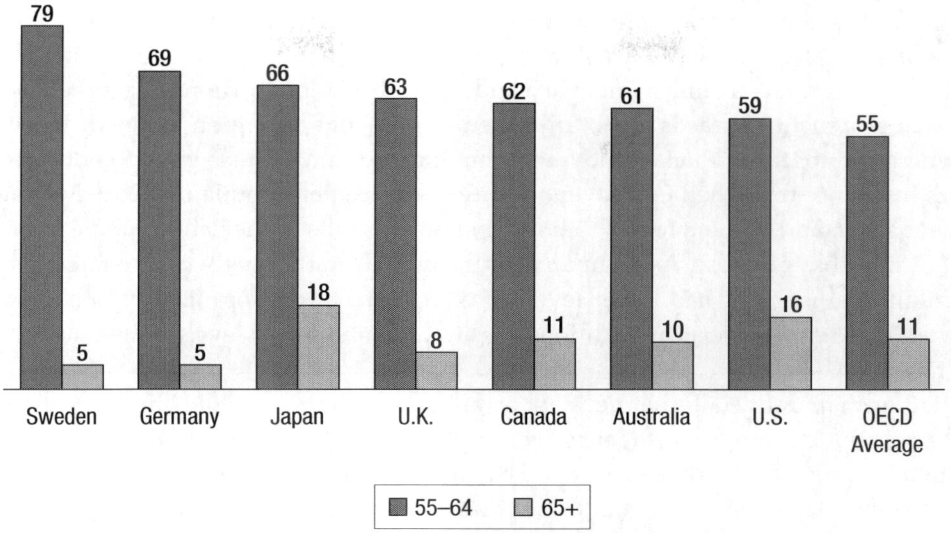


**FIGURE 18.2.** Labor Force Participation Rates, Females Ages 55–64 and 65+ (%)
*Source:* International Labor Organization, Labor Force Participation Rate by Sex and Age—ILO Modeled Estimates, July 2019—Annual. Retrieved January 23, 2020, from https://www.ilo.org/shinyapps/bulkexplorer11/?lang=en&segment=indicator&id=EAP_2WEX_AGE_RT_A.

## Physically Demanding Work

Workers in physically demanding jobs are sometimes unable to continue working at older ages and often are faced with an early exit from the labor market. In 2014, more than eight million older adults reported working in physically demanding jobs, and, due to the aging of the baby boomer cohort, that number is likely to continue increasing.[15] Unlike individuals holding jobs that are less physically demanding, older adults in physically demanding jobs often are forced into early retirement despite the desire and need to remain in the workforce.[16] In addition, many physically demanding jobs are under the threat of being replaced with automation. As a result, a significant number of older adults are at risk of unemployment, presenting a conflict between the ability to work and having the skills necessary for a job that is less physically demanding.[17] Generally, older adults in physically demanding jobs are less likely to be working in skilled occupations or to be college educated.[18] These concerns elevate the importance of identifying new ways of adapting the workplace for older adult workers and providing reskilling opportunities. There is a great need for education and training that equips older adults to enter new career paths that are stable and less physically demanding. (See also chapters 8, 10, 15, 17, 25, and 26.)

## Alternative Work Arrangements

Alternative work arrangements are becoming more common among middle-aged and older adults, placing them at increased risk of financial insecurity as they age.

Those employed in nontraditional work arrangements, sometimes referred to as "informal workers," are especially at risk for inadequate retirement savings. Definitions of nontraditional work arrangements vary widely, as do the proportions of workers with these employment characteristics, all depending on the definition utilized. Using a definition for nontraditional employment that includes individuals who do not receive health insurance from their employer or participate in a pension plan, in 2019 Munnell, Sanzenbacher, and Walters found that nearly half of adults in their fifties and early sixties fall into that category. As compared to those with traditional work arrangements, nontraditional workers had lower levels of education; were more likely to be female; and had more chronic health conditions, less wealth, and lower levels of income.[19] (See also chapters 2–6.)

Rather than define alternative work arrangements by receipt of benefits, Katz and Krueger included temporary agency workers, on-call workers, contract workers, and independent contractors or freelancers. They found that, in 2015, 26 percent of workers ages fifty-five to seventy-five met one of those criteria as compared to 14 percent in 2005, representing the largest increase of all age groups. This increase may be due to job loss during the Great Recession, which resulted in workers seeking alternative work arrangements due to the unavailability of traditional work.[20]

Regardless of the definition used, however, it is clear that a substantial portion of adults over age fifty are employed in alternative work arrangements and that the proportion has grown in recent years. Reskilling, a process that allows adults an opportunity to gain or update skills and education, can be used by middle-aged and older adults to prepare for new occupations. Reskilling provides them with qualifications sought by employers and potentially affords more leverage in employment arrangements.

## EDUCATIONAL ATTAINMENT AND THE WORKFORCE

Recognizing the need for increased educational attainment in the U.S., the Lumina Foundation established a goal that 60 percent of adults ages twenty-five to sixty-four have a postsecondary degree, such as an associate degree or professional certificate, by 2025. As of 2017, less than 48 percent had such a credential. Thus far, more than forty states have established attainment goals in general alignment with Lumina's goals for postsecondary education.[21] Older adults are a heterogeneous group who may require different types of recruiting methods, support systems, and program structures than do younger students, which will necessitate postsecondary institutions changing to meet the needs of students rather than expecting students to adapt to existing processes and structures.

Adults generally recognize the importance of credential attainment and ongoing skill upgrading. Nearly 90 percent of adults currently in the labor force believe it will be either important or essential for them to participate in training and acquire new skills over their career to remain employable.[22] Despite this recognition, low-skilled and older workers may be reluctant to participate in learning activities due to a lack of understanding of the financial benefits, limited availability of programs to meet their needs, or a fear of returning to the classroom.[23,24]

## DIGITAL SKILLS IN TECHNOLOGY-ADVANCED ECONOMIES

Rapid technological advances in a global economy have increased the importance of continuous skill upgrading and development over the life course. Participation in learning activities reduces the risk of low-skilled workers being limited to poor-quality jobs or unemployment,[25] and it allows workers to remain in the labor force at older ages.[26] Digital skills have become essential in both blue-collar and white-collar jobs, but many low-skill older workers lack the computer, problem-solving and teamwork skills required by today's employers.[27] In recent years, the proportion of jobs requiring minimal digital skills has declined, while jobs requiring medium- and high-level digital skills continue to increase—of new jobs created between 2010 and 2016, almost two-thirds required advanced digital skills. In addition, earnings are higher for occupations requiring high- and medium-skill levels.[28]

The term "digital natives"[29] has been used to describe individuals who grew up using computers and are assumed to be more technologically adept. In contrast, the term "digital immigrants" refers to those who entered adulthood before the use of digital technologies became widespread. As "digital immigrants," older adults would be expected to face additional obstacles to using technology.[30] However, existing evidence belies the existence of a simple dichotomy between older and traditional-age students, and students who did not grow up using computers can acquire digital skills later in life. Wang and colleagues propose the concept of "digital fluency" as an alternative to the immigrant/native metaphor.[31] Longitudinal data suggest that older adults become successful technology learners over time,[32] but they often learn at a slower rate and may be initially intimidated by new technologies.[33]

## HOW WILL OLDER WORKERS BE IMPACTED BY AUTOMATION?

While job automation and possible impacts of aging populations are often discussed, the potential magnitude of the impacts across age groups is still unclear.[34] As such, we provide here the estimated numbers and proportions of jobs at the risk of automation by age groups for the U.S. workforce.

### Methods

Data for 2019 were obtained from the U.S. Bureau of Labor Statistics (BLS) Current Population Survey (CPS),[35] the primary data source for national labor statistics in the United States. We also adopted the published risks of automation. Frey and Osborne used the standard occupational classification system codes and various data sources, to estimate the risk of automation for six major and twenty-two subcategories of 702 occupations.[36] Although the estimated risk is not associated with a specific time period, Frey and Osborne[37] suggest that it will take place over a ten-to-twenty-year time period. Per the occupational classification in the BLS, seventeen occupations were excluded due to the unavailability of the estimated risks. The CPS 2019 data show that there are 157.5 million employed persons. In this study, we focus on 156.0 million (99.0 percent) of them after excluding the aforementioned seventeen occupations. The risks of each occupation were manually matched to the CPS data, and jobs at risk of automation were individually computed. The estimated numbers of jobs at risk were aggregated by the six major and twenty-two subindustries. It should be noted that the margin of estimation errors could not be estimated with available information, and, therefore, interpretation requires caution.

### Results

Overall, nearly half (48 percent) of the jobs were classified as at risk of automation for the next ten to twenty years, which is equivalent to approximately seventy-five million jobs. Four major industries including "service," "sales and office," "natural resources, construction and maintenance," and "production, transportation, and material moving" had greater risks at 60–75 percent compared to "management, business, and financial operations" and "professional and related" occupations (14–27 percent). Given the size differences of industries at higher risk, "service," "sales and office," and "production, transportation, and material moving" seem to have more significant impacts (when combined, over fifty-three million jobs at risk) on the job market than others. The proportions of jobs at risk were fairly equally distributed across age groups, which is consistent with the findings of Belbase and Eschtruth.[38] Future older workers (age fifty-five and older in ten to twenty years, or those ages thirty-five to fifty-four in 2019) may face roughly twenty-nine million jobs being replaced by automation. Given potentially large estimation errors, seventy-five million jobs may not be actually replaced. However, even if just half of them (thirty-eight million, or roughly one in four jobs) were automated, the impacts on the job market and workforce would be enormous. Adults with lower levels of education are most at risk for job loss due to automation,[39] and may require reskilling to remain in the labor force.

## LIFELONG LEARNING AND ADULT EDUCATION

In previous sections of this chapter, we discussed the importance of continuous learning over the life course to ensure that individuals have skills required by employers so that they can remain in the labor force at older ages if they desire or need to do so. Hijzen and Schwellnus identify two main functions of adult learning: "equipping workers with job-related skills that match employers' needs and raise workers' productivity, employability and earnings; and helping people acquire foundation skills (for example in literacy and numeracy) which are essential to support lifelong learning, even if they may have less immediate returns."[40]

Lifelong learning, sometimes referred to as adult education and training, can take many forms. Consistent with the Commission of the European Communities, we define lifelong learning as "all purposeful learning activity, undertaken on an ongoing basis with the aim of improving knowledge, skills and competence."[41] There are three categories of learning activities: formal (learning that takes place in education and training institutions and leads to recognized credentials and diplomas), nonformal (learning that takes place in educational and training settings, including the workplace, but does not typically lead to a formalized credential), and informal (learning that takes place in everyday life and is not necessarily intentional and may not even be recognized by the individuals themselves as contributing to their knowledge and skills; it can include reading a book or a newspaper).[42] It is more common for middle-aged and older adults to participate in nonformal and informal learning activities as compared to formal activities.

## PARTICIPATION IN ADULT EDUCATION AND TRAINING

The Program for the International Assessment of Adult Competencies (PIAAC) is a skills assessment survey organized by the OECD and implemented by each participating country. PIAAC's goal is to assess and compare basic skills, including literacy, numeracy, and problem-solving skills in technology-rich environments. Assessment focuses on "cognitive and workplace skills necessary for successful participation in the twenty-first-century society and the global economy."[43] Approximately forty countries have participated in the PIAAC skills assessments with data collection taking place in most countries between 2011 and 2014.[44] A complex sampling method provided nationally representative data. In addition to the skills assessment, the survey included an extensive background questionnaire addressing basic demographic information along with information regarding the development and maintenance of skills, such as participation in various types of adult education and training programs, employment status, and income.[45]

In this section, we descriptively compare associations among literacy proficiency levels, employment, and participation in adult education and training of adults in the United States with adults in Australia, Canada, Germany, Japan, Sweden, and the United Kingdom. These countries were selected based on their geographic diversity, level of economic development, and availability of PIAAC data. The adult education and training (AET) measure we used for these descriptive analyses includes formal and nonformal education, both job related and non-job related. We also examine participation in AET-based employment status and high versus low literacy skills. For the data analysis, we used the OECD PIAAC Data Explorer[46] and the National Center for Education Statistics PIAAC Data Explorer.[47]

PIAAC defines literacy as "understanding, evaluating, using and engaging with written text to participate in society, to achieve one's goals and to develop one's knowledge and potential."[48] Literacy scores range from 0 to 500 and have been divided into proficiency levels ranging from below level 1 to level 5.[49] Lower-skill proficiency levels are associated with lower levels of earnings and education[50] and with poorer health.[51]

We compared literacy proficiency levels by country for the fifty-five-to-sixty-five age group (see figure 18.3). Japan has the lowest proportion (12 percent) of respondents scoring at or below level 1, whereas Germany had the greatest proportion (24 percent), followed closely by the U.S. and Canada (both 23 percent). As compared to the average of all jurisdictions that participated in PIAAC, all the countries we analyzed had lower

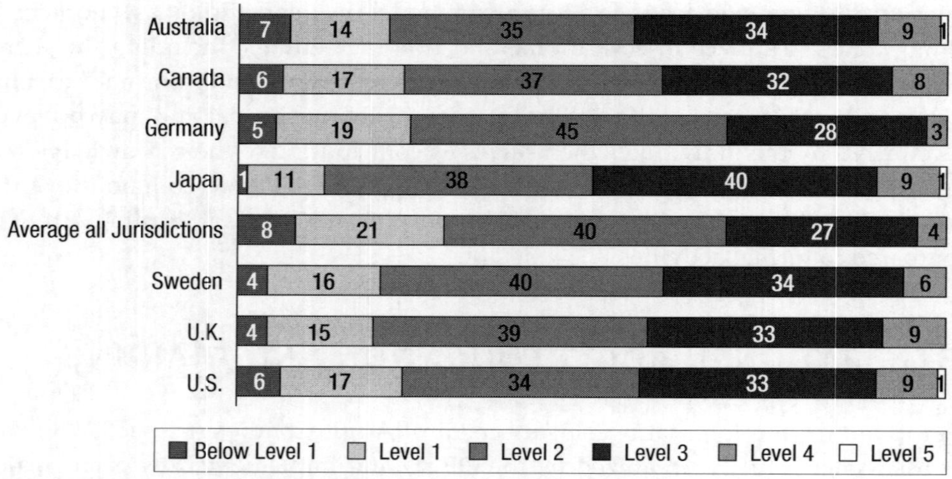


**FIGURE 18.3.** Literacy Levels by Country, Ages 55–65 (%).

*Source:* OECD, "OECD Skills Surveys: PIAAC Data Explorer," https://piaacdataexplorer.oecd.org/ide/idepiaac/dataset.aspx., 2020; National Center for Education Statistics, "PIAAC Data Explorer."

*Note:* Canada, Germany, Average of all Jurisdictions, Sweden, and the UK had <.5% at level 5.

proportions scoring at or below level 1. In terms of higher skill levels, Japan had the greatest proportion scoring in the three highest skill levels (50 percent), which was substantially more than any of the comparison countries. In the United States, 43 percent scored in the three highest literacy proficiency levels.

While older adults in the U.S. had smaller percentages than the average of all jurisdictions scoring at or below level 1 in literacy, there are still a meaningful number of individuals in those categories that raises concern about older adults' preparedness for increasingly complex and technologically advanced workplaces. To some extent, this is confirmed by examining the proportion of employed older adults by skill level. In all the countries analyzed, there were meaningful differences in employment for low- versus high-skilled adults. To illustrate, for adults ages fifty-five to sixty-five in the U.S., 75 percent of those who had literacy proficiency scores at levels 4 and 5 were employed as compared to 50 percent of those with literacy proficiency scores at and below level 1. The comparison countries had similar patterns.

Figure 18.4 provides data on AET participation by age group. In most of the comparison countries, AET participation declined with age, and, in all countries, the fifty-five-to-sixty-five age group had the lowest participation rate. Of the countries examined, the U.S. had the highest participation rate (50 percent) for the fifty-five-to-sixty-five age group while Sweden had the highest participation rate for all other age groups. Adults in the fifty-five-to-sixty-five age group for all comparison countries had AET participation rates equal to or higher than the OECD average.

Next, we examined AET participation comparing the highest (levels 4 and 5) with the lowest (below level 1 and level 1) proficiency skill levels for ages fifty-five to sixty-five. In all countries, there were substantial differences in AET participation based

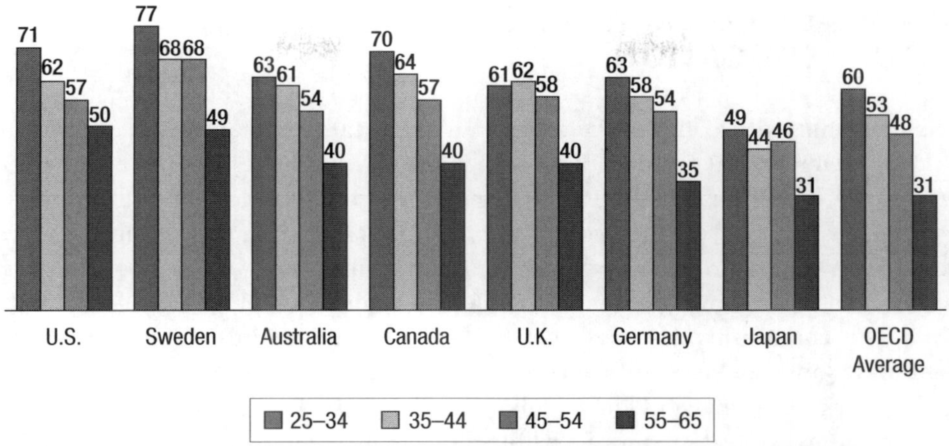


**FIGURE 18.4.** Adult Education and Training Participation by Age Group and Country (%)
*Source:* OECD, "OECD Skills Surveys: PIAAC Data Explorer," https://piaacdataexplorer.oecd.org/ide/idepiaac/dataset.aspx., 2020; National Center for Education Statistics, "PIAAC Data Explorer."

on skill proficiency. For example, in the U.S., 72 percent of those who had the highest skill levels participated in AET, whereas only 33 percent in the lowest skill proficiency levels participated.

Finally, we compared AET participation by employment status for the fifty-five-to-sixty-five age group. Due to sample size limitations for the unemployed group, we were limited to comparing the U.S. with Canada and all participating jurisdictions. In all cases, the employed group had the highest rates of AET participation, followed by the unemployed. The U.S. had the highest participation rates for all three groups (64 percent employed, 47 percent unemployed, and 22 percent for not in the labor force). Without an employer to provide opportunities for AET, the unemployed must rely on their own funds, on publicly sponsored employment programs, or on programs funded by nonprofit organizations. The same is true for those not in the labor force. Providing AET opportunities for the unemployed and those not in the labor force could expedite reemployment and result in some returning to the labor force.

In summary, the 23 percent of older adults in the U.S. with low literacy skills are more likely than the high skilled to be at risk of either being unemployed or out of the labor force, which can result in heightened risk of income insecurity in retirement years. Increased AET participation by low-skilled adults could give them skills desired by employers and improve their economic outlook. Lack of participation in AET occurs for multiple reasons, including fear of returning to the classroom, exam anxiety, and lack of funding.[52] Projected increases in job loss due to automation, which will be especially consequential for low-skilled adults,[53] necessitates policy changes in the provision of adult training opportunities. The Nordic countries are recognized for providing educational opportunities to adults of all ages and serve as a model for other countries.[54] Future research that identifies creative and successful models of adult education are needed to support policy changes.

## THE ROLE OF COMMUNITY COLLEGES IN ADULT EDUCATION

Although community colleges have been an important part of U.S. economic and workforce development for decades, more recently they have become a key source for employee reskilling and skill upgrading to provide employers with a globally competitive workforce.[55,56] Most community colleges have open admissions policies, comparatively low tuition, convenient geographic location, and a focus on community needs, which make them the preferred choice for older adults.[57] Another advantage of community colleges over four-year public institutions is shorter-term credentialing options, such as occupational certificates. Because older adults are likely to work full-time and have family obligations, shorter programs of study with fewer interruptions are more feasible;[58] optimally they result in upgraded skills and career advancement. Research has consistently confirmed earnings gains from obtaining a community college certificate especially in STEM, nursing, and construction.[59,60] Community college programs increasingly include a work-experience component (e.g., internship, co-op, clinical, or apprenticeship)[61] which allows students to see what an actual job involves while, at the same time, improving the likelihood of immediate job placement upon graduation.

Workers with a high school education or less are most at risk of job loss due to technology advances.[62] Most good jobs (i.e., jobs that pay self-sustaining wages), which Carnevale and colleagues define as $35,000 or more per year for those up to age forty-five, and $45,000 or more per year for workers ages forty-five and older, require education beyond high school, such as a postsecondary certificate or an associate degree.[63] Since 1991, good jobs requiring only a high school diploma have declined by 1 million, whereas good jobs for associate degree holders increased by 3.2 million over the same period.[64] In coming years, continued technological advances and automation will require workers of all ages to critically assess their own skills and credentials to ensure that they remain employable.

The majority of middle-aged and older adults who return to college enroll at a community college rather than a baccalaureate institution, and most enroll on a part-time basis.[65] In this section we draw on key findings from a research project undertaken by Drs. Cummins and Bahr and funded by the Institute of Education Sciences (grant # R305A160156). The research took place between July 2016 and June 2020. Using administrative data on all public postsecondary institutions in Ohio from the Ohio Longitudinal Data Archive (OLDA), maintained by the Ohio Educational Research Center (OERC),[66] and qualitative data from focus groups and key informant interviews at three case study colleges, our mixed-methods project focused on adults ages forty to sixty-four who enrolled in a community college in Ohio. The investigation is unique in focusing on this older age group. Prior research has typically lumped into a single group of adult learners all students who are twenty-five years of age and older, not differentiating the needs, experiences, and barriers to education among older students.

## WHY DO MID- AND LATER-LIFE STUDENTS RETURN TO COLLEGE?

We identified multiple reasons why mid- and later-life students (MLLs) enroll at a community college. We categorize them as *reactive, proactive,* and *beyond reactive or proactive.* Reactive reasons can be described as freeing (they finally can) or compelling (they suddenly must). Family status changes can be either freeing or compelling and were a common reason mentioned by focus group participants. A newly empty nest or the end of caregiving responsibilities for an aging parent were "freeing" reasons discussed by several MLLs as the motivation for returning to school. Examples of compelling changes include divorce and death or illness of a spouse or partner, which often result in the need for new or additional sources of income and acquisition of new skills.

Not all enrollments take place in reaction to changes or immediate financial pressures. Many students enroll proactively, perhaps in anticipation of an impending challenge, sometimes age associated, such as declining health and the need for less physically demanding work. Students also reported job precarity due to changing technologies and concern for job loss.

Rather than enrolling for reactive or proactive reasons, some wanted to serve as a role model for their grandchildren, while others sought to learn for personal interest or development, or to aid entrepreneurial ambitions. Understanding reasons why students enroll can inform marketing and recruiting efforts to ensure that this segment of the potential student population is aware of educational opportunities.

## SIMILARITIES AND DIFFERENCES BETWEEN YOUNGER ADULT STUDENTS AND MLLS

As noted previously, most research lumps adult students into a single group aged twenty-five and older. Educational goals and challenges may differ for a thirty-year-old and a fifty-year-old student. For example, a fifty-year-old is more likely to enroll for personal interest reasons, and the thirty-year-old is more likely to seek an associate degree.

Younger students and MLLs may share some challenges to enrolling or staying in college, such as balancing classroom demands with other life interests and responsibilities. However, MLLs face unique challenges, like gap years between previous education and current learning endeavors so that changes in classroom/learning technology can leave them at a disadvantage. Another concern is academic readiness and the ability to succeed in the classroom. Many MLLs experience greater family demands than their younger peers, and working full-time and attending classes in the evening often limits access to student support services and academic advising, typically available only during normal business hours. Lastly, a common concern of focus group participants was their remaining time in the labor force. An MLL might have only ten or fifteen years, or even less time, until expected retirement. As they reinvent themselves, they want a new occupation that will be long lasting and enjoyable, with minimal risk of skill obsolescence. To increase the likelihood of success, it is important that community college faculty and staff understand the differences between young and older adult students and offer supportive services to meet the needs of all students.

## ARE OLDER LEARNERS AIMING TO COMPLETE POSTSECONDARY CREDENTIALS?

Using OLDA data, we found that the fraction of newly enrolled community college students between fall 2007 and winter 2011 who reported that they were pursuing job-related goals, particularly job-related goals that do not result in a postsecondary credential, rose rapidly with students' age at college entry.[67] About one in thirteen students (8 percent) who were seventeen to nineteen years old when they entered community college were taking a few courses to upgrade work-related skills or train for a new job, as opposed to seeking a postsecondary degree or certificate. Among students twenty to twenty-nine years of age, it was about one in seven (14 percent). Approximately one in four students (23 percent) who were thirty to forty-nine years of age were seeking a noncredential, job-related goal, as were almost one in three students (31 percent) who were fifty to sixty-four years old.

Still, a large percentage of students of all ages, including older students, were aiming for a postsecondary credential, whether a certificate, associate degree, or baccalaureate degree. This included the vast majority of students seventeen to nineteen years of age (87 percent) and in their twenties (80 percent). In addition, more than two-thirds (70 percent) of students in their thirties and forties were seeking a postsecondary credential, and more than half (55 percent) of students in their fifties and early sixties.

## IS THERE A DISPARITY IN GRADUATION RATES BETWEEN OLDER AND YOUNGER LEARNERS?

Given the differences in goals across age groups, one would expect that older students would be somewhat less likely to complete postsecondary credentials than their younger peers, but the achievement gaps were greater than anticipated. Students in their thirties and forties were 19 percent less likely to complete a postsecondary credential within six years than were students seventeen to nineteen years of age, while students in their fifties and sixties were 24 percent less likely to graduate than were students in the seventeen-to-nineteen age group.

To examine this finding more closely, we estimated a series of multilevel regression models analyzing the association between age, gender, and the likelihood of graduating from college within six years, while controlling for differences by age and gender in the distribution of self-reported academic goals, previous college experience in a four-year postsecondary institution, first-year financial aid, and race/ethnicity. The purpose was to assess the magnitude of the gaps in attainment between older and younger learners after accounting for other potentially relevant correlated differences between them, especially differences in academic goal. Said another way, we asked, how large are the expected differences in graduation rates between students of different ages who are otherwise similar in their goals and other characteristics? We distinguished between three types of postsecondary credentials that students might earn, namely, a postsecondary certificate or an associate degree from an Ohio public community college, or a baccalaureate degree from an Ohio public four-year institution.

We found that, even after accounting for differences in goals and other factors, older students—especially older males—faced a marked disadvantage relative to younger peers in the likelihood of completing a baccalaureate degree within six years, and increasingly so with greater age at community college entry. Moreover, the gaps in the likelihood of completing a baccalaureate degree between older and younger students likely were even larger than they appeared because the data included only baccalaureate degrees awarded by Ohio's public four-year institutions. Younger students transferring to out-of-state four-year institutions at a higher rate than older students likely undercounted baccalaureate degree completion by younger students, making the gap in baccalaureate attainment between older and younger students appear smaller than it is in reality.

With respect to the likelihood of completing a postsecondary certificate, older students had a modest edge over younger students, and this advantage increased with age but was more evident among older females than among older males. Older females, but not older males, had a stronger likelihood of completing an associate degree than did their younger peers, though this advantage peaked among women in their forties and declined thereafter.

## WHAT IS THE ROLE OF ACADEMIC MOMENTUM IN COLLEGE COMPLETION AMONG OLDER LEARNERS?

One potential avenue for improving the likelihood of graduating for older students, which, in light of the findings discussed above, may be especially important for older males, is strengthening their early academic progress, sometimes referred to as momentum. Evidence indicates that students who make early academic progress, building momentum toward a postsecondary credential, are more likely to graduate.[68] In short, getting students started off strong increases their chances of persisting and completing college.

That said, momentum may look differently for older students than for younger students.[69] Taking a heavier first-year course credit load, which is associated with better outcomes among younger students, might be deleterious to older students' efforts to balance work, family, and school, and hurt their chances of staying in college to complete a credential.[70] Alternatively, early progress in the form of completing key milestones, such as college math or college English, might be especially important for older students as a hedge against changes (specifically increases) in work or family demands that impede academic progress later on. It also may reinforce adult students' academic self-efficacy, their belief that they can succeed in college.

To investigate how momentum differs for older versus younger students, we used multilevel regression analysis to examine how the relationships between five measures of early academic progress and the three aforementioned indicators of college completion measured over six years (earning a postsecondary certificate or associate degree from an Ohio public community college or a baccalaureate degree from an Ohio public four-year institution) differ depending on a student's age.[71] The five measures of momentum, all assessed in students' first year in community college, were: cumulative number of credits earned in Ohio community colleges (a measure of the intensity of enrollment); number of days enrolled in Ohio community colleges (a measure of the continuity of enrollment); the proportion of credits attempted that were completed with a passing grade (i.e., credit success rate); whether a student completed a college-level math course successfully; and whether a student completed a college-level English course successfully.

We found that the number of days that students enrolled in community college in the first year was a moderately stronger predictor of completing a postsecondary certificate among older students than it was among their younger peers, and more so for adult women than adult men. In other words, with respect to certificates, older students appear to benefit somewhat more from continuous enrollment than do younger students. However, the relationships between the other four aspects of momentum and the likelihood of certificate completion did not differ significantly with age.

Completing college math in the first year was a stronger predictor of associate degree completion for older students than for younger students, and to a greater degree for adult men than for adult women. Achieving this particular milestone early appears to be an especially important step toward an associate degree for older learners. Relative to students in their late teens or early twenties, number of days enrolled also was a stronger predictor of associate degree completion for adult students into their forties, with an especially pronounced relationship among adult women.

Completing college math in the first year was a strong predictor of baccalaureate degree completion, but the relationship declined in magnitude with age rather than increasing, in contrast to what was observed with associate degree completion. Our findings suggested that the other aspects of momentum played relatively smaller roles in the likelihood of baccalaureate degree completion, and the relationships did not vary greatly across the spectrum of ages found in community colleges.

Collectively, the evidence suggests that adult students do build momentum differently than their younger peers in some respects. In particular, early completion of college math and continuity of enrollment in the first year seem to be especially important for older students' chances of completing a certificate or associate degree.

In other respects, older learners and younger learners are more alike than different. For example, the number of credits completed in the first year in community college was a positive predictor of all three outcomes—certificate, associate degree, and baccalaureate degree—but the differences between older and younger students in these relationships were modest, indicating that this aspect of momentum is important for students of all ages. As stakeholders aim to narrow the completion gap between older and younger students, understanding differences in how older and younger students build momentum toward a postsecondary credential will be key to developing effective strategies.

## CONCLUSION

Older adults will be an increasingly important component of the American labor force. For the nation to remain competitive in a technologically advanced global economy, continuous skill upgrades of its workforce will be critical. Some level of digital skills will continue to be necessary for most jobs, and jobs requiring medium to high digital skills will continue to increase. Adults with lower levels of education and skills will be at a particular disadvantage as an increasing number of jobs are automated. Nearly half of all jobs are at risk for automation over the next two to three decades.

Participation in adult education and training is lower for older age groups than younger. In addition, older adults with lower levels of literacy skills are less likely to participate in adult education and training as compared to those with higher levels of literacy skills. Because older adults with low skills are at risk for job loss in times of economic downturns, access to reskilling will be necessary for them to remain employable. Community colleges provide middle-aged and older adults with opportunities for reskilling, but historically they have focused on traditional-age students, under age twenty-five.

MLLs tend to hold different academic goals than their younger counterparts. They are more likely to enroll to upgrade skills and less likely to seek a credential. Community colleges are known to have low attainment rates for all age groups. One potential way to improve completion rates for MLLs is to provide academic support and advising that increases their momentum toward postsecondary credentials, including helping them maintain continuous enrollment and complete college-level coursework in foundational subjects, such as math.

## NOTES

Acknowledgments: The research reported here was partially supported by the Institute of Education Sciences, U.S. Department of Education, through Grants R305A160156 and R305A170183 to Miami University. The opinions expressed are those of the authors and do not represent views of the institute or the U.S. Department of Education.

1. William H. Frey. January 2020. "The 2010s May Have Seen the Slowest Population Growth in U.S. History, Census Data Show: A 2020 Census Preview of Population and Congressional Reappointment." Washington, DC: Brookings.
2. OECD. 2017. *Pensions at a Glance 2017*. Paris: OECD:21–22.
3. Courtney Coile. May 2018. "Working Longer in the U.S.: Trends and Explanations." NBER Working Paper No. 24576. Cambridge, MA: National Bureau of Economic Research:1, 13.
4. Vanya Horneff, Raimond Maurer, and Olivia S. Mitchell. 2018. "How Persistent Low Expected Returns Alter Optimal Life Cycle Saving, Investment, and Retirement Behavior." Cambridge, MA: National Bureau of Economic Research:2.
5. Steven H. Woolf and Heidi Schoomaker. 2019. "Life Expectancy and Mortality Rates in the United States, 1959–2017." *JAMA* 322(20):1996.
6. U.S. Bureau of Labor Statistics. 2019. "Employment Projections: Civilian Labor Force, by Age, Sex, Race, and Ethnicity." Labor Force Statistics from the Current Population Survey. Washington, DC. (https://www.bls.gov/emp/tables/civilian-labor-force-summary.htm).

7. U.S. Bureau of Labor Statistics, "Employment Projections."

8. U.S. Bureau of Labor Statistics, "Employment Projections."

9. Mitra Toossi. 2016. "A Look at the Future of the U.S. Labor Force to 2050." Washington, DC: *Monthly Labor Review*. Washington, DC: Bureau of Labor Statistics. Unpublished detailed tables were provided to P. Cummins by M. Toossi through a personal communication.

10. OECD. 2018. "OECD Statistics." (https://stats.oecd.org/).

11. OECD, "OECD Statistics."

12. International Labour Organization. July 2019. "Labour Force Participation Rate by Sex and Age—ILO Modelled Estimates." (https://www.ilo.org/shinyapps/bulkexplorer13/?lang=en&segment=indicator&id=EAP_2WAP_SEX_AGE_RT_A).

13. Alicia H. Munnell. 2015. "Falling Short: The Coming Retirement Crisis and What to Do About It." No. 2015-7. Chestnut Hill, MA: Center for Retirement Research, Boston College.

14. Nicole Maestas, Kathleen J. Mullen, and David Powell. 2016. "The Effect of Population Aging on Economic Growth, the Labor Force and Productivity." Cambridge, MA: National Bureau of Economic Research:31–32.

15. Cherrie Bucknor and Dean Baker. 2016. "Still Working Hard: An Update on the Share of Older Workers in Physically Demanding Jobs." No. 2016-04. Washington, DC: Center for Economic and Policy Research:1, 7.

16. David Neumark and Joanne Song. 2012. "Barriers to Later Retirement: Increases in the Full Retirement Age, Age Discrimination, and the Physical Challenges of Work." *SSRN Electronic Journal*:3. (https://doi.org/10.2139/ssrn.2188363).

17. Anek Belbase and Andrew D. Eschtruth. 2020. "How Will Emerging Computers Affect Older Workers by 2040?" Issue Brief No. 2020-1. Chestnut Hill, MA: Center for Retirement Research, Boston College. (https://crr.bc.edu/briefs/how-will-emerging-computers-affect-older-workers-by-2040/).

18. David M. Cutler, Ellen Meara, and Seth Richards-Shubik. 2013. "Health and Work Capacity of Older Adults: Estimates and Implications for Social Security Policy." *SSRN Electronic Journal*:16. (https://doi.org/10.2139/ssrn.2577858).

19. Alicia H. Munnell, Geoffrey T. Sanzenbacher, and Abigail N. Walters. 2019. "How Do Older Workers Use Nontraditional Jobs?" Working Paper No. 2019-12. Chestnut Hill, MA: Center for Retirement Research, Boston College:1–2.

20. Lawrence F. Katz and Alan B. Krueger. 2019. "The Rise and Nature of Alternative Work Arrangements in the United States, 1995–2015." *ILR Review* 72(2):396, 399.

21. Lumina Foundation. 2019. "A Stronger Nation: Learning beyond High School Builds American Talent." Indianapolis, IN:3, 5.

22. Pew Research Center. 2016. "The State of American Jobs." Washington, DC: Pew Research Center:4.

23. Didier Fouarge, Trudie Schils, and Andries De Grip. 2013. "Why Do Low-educated Workers Invest Less in Further Training?" *Applied Economics* 45(18):2595.

24. Thomas Zwick. 2011. "Why Training Older Employees Is Less Effective." Mannheim:11. (https://doi.org/10.2139/ssrn.1886428).

25. Alexander Hijzen and Cyrille Schwellnus. 2018. *Good Jobs for All in a Changing World of Work: The OECD Jobs Strategy*. Paris: OECD :1.

26. Mark Keese. 2006. *Live Longer, Work Longer.* Paris: OECD:1–2.

27. Paul Osterman. 2019. "Employment and Training for Mature Adults: The Current System and Moving Forward." Washington, DC: Brookings: 409.

28. Mark Muro et al. 2017. "Digitalization and the American Workforce." Metropolitan Policy Program. Washington, DC: Brookings:15, 21.

29. Marc Prensky. 2001. "Digital Natives, Digital Immigrants." *On the Horizon* 9(5):1.

30. Prensky, "Digital Natives," 1–2.

31. Emily Wang, Michael D. Myers, and David Sundaram, 2013. "Digital Natives and Digital Immigrants: Towards a Model of Digital Fluency." *Business & Information Systems Engineering* 5(6):409.

32. Sergio Sayago, Paula Forbes, and Josep Blat. 2013. "Older People Becoming Successful ICT Learners over Time: Challenges and Strategies through an Ethnographical Lens." *Educational Gerontology* 39(7):543.

33. Neil Charness. 2006. "Work, Older Workers, and Technology." *Generations* 30(2):28.

34. Philip Taylor and Warwick Smith. 2017. "What's Age Got to Do with It? Towards a New Advocacy on Ageing and Work." Melbourne, Australia:19.

35. U.S. Bureau of Labor Statistics, "Employment Projections."

36. Carl Benedikt Frey and Michael Osborne. 2013. "The Future of Employment." Oxford, UK: Martin Programme on Technology and Employment:31.

37. Frey and Osborne, "Future of Employment," 31.

38. Belbase and Eschtruth, "Emerging Computers," 4.

39. Frey and Osborne, "Future of Employment," 48.

40. Hijzen and Schwellnus, *Good Jobs for All*, 252.

41. Commission of the European Communities. 2000. "A Memorandum on Lifelong Learning." Lisbon, Portugal: European Commission: 3.

42. Commission of the European Communities, "Memorandum on Lifelong Learning."

43. Madeline Goodman et al. 2013. "Literacy, Numeracy, and Problem Solving in Technology-rich Environments among U.S. Adults: Results from the Program for the International Assessment of Adult Competencies 2012. First Look." Washington, DC: National Center for Education Statistics:1.

44. OECD. 2020b. "OECD Skills Surveys: PIAAC 1st Cycle." https://www.oecd.org/skills/piaac/about/piaac1stcycle/.

45. OECD. 2010. "PIAAC Background Questionnaire (Ms Version 2.1 D.D. 15-12-2010)." B-13.

46. OECD. 2020a. "OECD Skills Surveys: PIAAC Data Explorer." (https://piaacdataexplorer.oecd.org/ide/idepiaac/dataset.aspx).

47. National Center for Education Statistics. 2017. "PIAAC Data Explorer." (https://nces.ed.gov/surveys/piaac/ideuspiaac/).

48. OECD. 2012. "Literacy, Numeracy and Problem Solving in Technology-rich Environments: Framework for the OECD Survey of Adult Skills." Paris: OECD:3–3, 1.

49. Goodman et al., "Literacy, Numeracy, and Problem Solving." Additional details for literacy tasks descriptions for each proficiency level are provided in Exhibit B-1, II-3, B-3.

50. Eric A. Hanushek et al. 2015. "Returns to Skills around the World: Evidence from PIAAC." *European Economic Review* 73:103–30.

51. Sujay Kakarmath et al. 2018. "Association between Literacy and Self-rated Poor Health in 33 High- and Upper Middle-income Countries." *International Journal of Public Health* 63(2):218.

52. Phyllis A. Cummins, Suzanne Kunkel, and Ryan Michael Walker. 2015. "Adult Education and Training Programs for Older Adults in the U.S.: National Results and Cross-national Comparisons Using PIAAC Data." Paper Commissioned by American Institutes for Research:24, 25. (https://static1.squarespace.com/static/51bb74b8e4b0139570ddf020/t/55de28c6e4b0daf2d66f69ea/1440622790514/Cummins_Kunkel_Walker_PIAAC.pdf).

53. Frey and Osborne, "Future of Employment," 543.

54. Kjell Rubenson and Richard Desjardins. 2009. "The Impact of Welfare State Regimes on Barriers to Participation in Adult Education: A Bounded Agency Model." *Adult Education Quarterly* 59(3):187–207.

55. Paul Osterman and Andrew Weaver. 2016. "Community Colleges and Employers: How Can We Understand Their Connection?" *Industrial Relations: A Journal of Economy and Society* 55(4):523–45.

56. Daniel C. Hickman and William W. Olney. 2011. "Globalization and Investment in Human Capital." *ILR Review* 64(4):654–72.

57. David Baime and Sandy Baum. 2016. "Community Colleges: Multiple Missions, Diverse Student Bodies, and a Range of Policy Solutions." Washington, DC: Urban Institute:2.

58. Thomas Bailey. 2018. "Responding to Divergent Trends: Vocational and Transfer Education at Community Colleges." *Change: The Magazine of Higher Learning* 50(3–4):115.

59. Clive Belfield and Thomas Bailey. 2017. "The Labor Market Returns to Sub-baccalaureate College: A Review." A Capsee Working Paper. Center for Analysis of Postsecondary Education and Employment. New York: Teachers College, Columbia University:13, 24.

60. Eric Bettinger and Adela Soliz. 2016. "Returns to Vocational Credentials: Evidence from Ohio's Community and Technical Colleges." A Capsee Working Paper. New York: Teachers College, Columbia University:15, 16.

61. Rooney Columbus. January 2019. "Non-degree Credentials, Work-based Learning, and the American Working Class." Washington, DC: American Enterprise Institute:17.

62. Frey and Osborne, "Future of Employment," 15, 16.

63. Anthony P. Carnevale et al. 2018. "Good Jobs That Pay Without a BA." Washington, DC: Georgetown University Center on Education and the Workforce: 2.

64. Carnevale et al., "Good Jobs," 2.

65. U.S. Department of Education, and National Center for Education Statistics. 2018. "Table 303.30: Total Fall Enrollment in Degree-granting Postsecondary Institutions, by Level and Control of Institution, Attendance Status, and Sex of Student: Selected Years, 1970 through 2027." In *Digest of Education Statistics.* Washington, DC.

66. The Ohio Longitudinal Data Archive (OLDA) is a project of the Ohio Education Research Center (oerc.osu.edu) and provides researchers with centralized access to administrative data. The OLDA is managed by The Ohio State University's CHRR (chrr.osu.edu) in collaboration with Ohio's state workforce and education agencies (ohioanalytics.gov), with those agencies providing oversight and funding. For information on OLDA sponsors, see http://chrr.osu.edu/projects/ohio-longitudinal-data-archive.

67. The sample discussed in this section was limited to students enrolling in community college as undergraduates, excluding dual-enrolled high school students. Students who had previously enrolled in a public four-year institution in Ohio were retained in (not excluded from) the sample, but students were excluded if, in their first year in community college, a majority of their credits were taken in a public four-year institution. We also excluded students who earned zero credits in their first year in community college.

68. Xueli Wang. 2017. "Toward a Holistic Theoretical Model of Momentum for Community College Student Success." Pp. 259–308 in *Higher Education: Handbook of Theory and Research*, edited by Michael B. Paulsen. Cham, Switzerland: Springer International.

69. Juan Carlos Calcagno et al. 2007. "Stepping Stones to a Degree: The Impact of Enrollment Pathways and Milestones on Older Community College Student Outcomes." *Research in Higher Education* 48(7):796–97.

70. Peter Riley Bahr, Claire Boeck, and Phyllis Cummins. Forthcoming. "Strengthening Outcomes of Adult Students in Community Colleges." In *Higher Education: Handbook of Theory and Research*. Cham, Switzerland: Springer.

71. Peter Riley Bahr, et al. N.d. "Less Is More, or Is It? Differences by Age in Relationships Between Academic Momentum and College Completion."

## REFERENCES


Administrations on Aging. 2017. "A Profile of Older Americans: 2017." (https://acl.gov/sites/default/files/Aging%20and%20Disability%20in%20America/2018OlderAmericansProfile.pdf).

Bahr, Peter Riley, et al. N.d. "Less Is More, or Is It? Differences by Age in Relationships between Academic Momentum and College Completion."

Bahr, Peter Riley, Claire Boeck, and Phyllis Cummins. Forthcoming. "Strengthening Outcomes of Adult Students in Community Colleges." In *Higher Education: Handbook of Theory and Research*. Cham, Switzerland: Springer.

Bailey, Thomas. 2018. "Responding to Divergent Trends: Vocational and Transfer Education at Community Colleges." *Change: The Magazine of Higher Learning* 50(3–4):113–16.

Baime, David and Sandy Baum. 2016. "Community Colleges: Multiple Missions, Diverse Student Bodies, and a Range of Policy Solutions." Washington, DC: Urban Institute.

Belbase, Anek and Andrew D. Eschtruth. 2020. "How Will Emerging Computers Affect Older Workers by 2040?" Issue Brief No. 2020-1. Chestnut Hill, MA: Center for Retirement Research, Boston College. (https://crr.bc.edu/briefs/how-will-emerging-computers-affect-older-workers-by-2040/).

Belfield, Clive and Thomas Bailey. 2017. "The Labor Market Returns to Sub-baccalaureate College: A Review." A Capsee Working Paper. Center for Analysis of Postsecondary Education and Employment. New York: Teachers College, Columbia University.

Bettinger, Eric and Adela Soliz. 2016. "Returns to Vocational Credentials: Evidence from Ohio's Community and Technical Colleges." A Capsee Working Paper. New York: Teachers College, Columbia University.

Bucknor, Cherrie and Dean Baker. 2016. "Still Working Hard: An Update on the Share of Older Workers in Physically Demanding Jobs." No. 2016-04. Washington, DC: Center for Economic and Policy Research.

Calcagno, Juan Carlos, et al. 2007. "Stepping Stones to a Degree: The Impact of Enrollment Pathways and Milestones on Older Community College Student Outcomes." *Research in Higher Education* 48(7):775–801.

Carnevale, Anthony P., et al. 2018. "Good Jobs That Pay without a BA." Washington, DC: Georgetown University Center on Education and the Workforce.

Charness, Neil. 2006. "Work, Older Workers, and Technology." *Generations* 30(2):25–30.

Coile, Courtney. May 2018. "Working Longer in the U.S.: Trends and Explanations." NBER Working Paper No. 24576. Cambridge, MA: National Bureau of Economic Research.

Columbus, Rooney. January 2019. "Non-degree Credentials, Work-based Learning, and the American Working Class." Washington, DC: American Enterprise Institute.

Commission of the European Communities. 2000. "A Memorandum on Lifelong Learning." Lisbon, Portugal: European Commission.

Cummins, Phyllis A., Suzanne Kunkel, and Ryan Michael Walker. 2015. "Adult Education and Training Programs for Older Adults in the U.S.: National Results and Cross-national Comparisons Using PIAAC Data." Paper commissioned by American Institutes for Research. (https://static1.squarespace.com/static/51bb74b8e4b0139570ddf020/t/55de28c6e4b0daf2d66f69ea/1440622790514/Cummins_Kunkel_Walker_PIAAC.pdf).

Cutler, David M., Ellen Meara, and Seth Richards-Shubik. 2013. "Health and Work Capacity of Older Adults: Estimates and Implications for Social Security Policy." *SSRN Electronic Journal*. (https://doi.org/10.2139/ssrn.2577858).

Fouarge, Didier, Trudie Schils, and Andries De Grip. 2013. "Why Do Low-educated Workers Invest Less in Further Training?" *Applied Economics* 45(18):2587–601.

Frey, Carl Benedikt and Michael Osborne. 2013. "The Future of Employment." Oxford, UK: Martin Programme on Technology and Employment.

Frey, William H. January 2020. "The 2010s May Have Seen the Slowest Population Growth in U.S. History, Census Data Show: A 2020 Census Preview of Population and Congressional Reappointment." Washington, DC: Brookings.

Goodman, Madeline, et al. 2013. "Literacy, Numeracy, and Problem Solving in Technology-rich Environments among U.S. Adults: Results from the Program for the International Assessment of Adult Competencies 2012. First Look." Washington, DC: National Center for Education Statistics.

Hanushek, Eric A., et al. 2015. "Returns to Skills around the World: Evidence from PIAAC." *European Economic Review* 73:103–30.

Hickman, Daniel C. and William W. Olney. 2011. "Globalization and Investment in Human Capital." *ILR Review* 64(4):654–72.

Hijzen, Alexander and Cyrille Schwellnus. 2018. *Good Jobs for All in a Changing World of Work: The OECD Jobs Strategy*. Paris: OECD.

Horneff, Vanya, Raimond Maurer, and Olivia S Mitchell. 2018. "How Persistent Low Expected Returns Alter Optimal Life Cycle Saving, Investment, and Retirement Behavior." Cambridge, MA: National Bureau of Economic Research.

International Labour Organization. July 2019. "Labour Force Participation Rate by Sex and Age—ILO Modelled Estimates." (https://www.ilo.org/shinyapps/bulkexplorer11/?lang=en&segment=indicator&id=EAP_2WAP_SEX_AGE_RT_A).

Kakarmath, Sujay, et al. 2018. "Association between Literacy and Self-rated Poor Health in 33 High- and Upper Middle-income Countries." *International Journal of Public Health* 63(2):213–22.

Katz, Lawrence F. and Alan B. Krueger. 2019. "The Rise and Nature of Alternative Work Arrangements in the United States, 1995–2015." *ILR Review* 72(2):382–416.

Keese, Mark. 2006. *Live Longer, Work Longer.* Paris: OECD.

Lumina Foundation. 2019. "A Stronger Nation: Learning beyond High School Builds American Talent." Indianapolis, IN.

Maestas, Nicole, Kathleen J. Mullen, and David Powell. 2016. "The Effect of Population Aging on Economic Growth, the Labor Force and Productivity." Cambridge, MA: National Bureau of Economic Research.

Munnell, Alicia H. 2015. "Falling Short: The Coming Retirement Crisis and What to Do about It." No. 2015-7. Chestnut Hill, MA: Center for Retirement Research, Boston College.

Munnell, Alicia H., Geoffrey T. Sanzenbacher, and Abigail N. Walters. 2019. "How Do Older Workers Use Nontraditional Jobs?" Working Paper No. 2019-12. Chestnut Hill, MA: Center for Retirement Research, Boston College.

Muro, Mark, et al. 2017. "Digitalization and the American Workforce." Metropolitan Policy Program. Washington, DC: Brookings.

National Center for Education Statistics. 2017. "PIAAC Data Explorer." (https://nces.ed.gov/surveys/piaac/ideuspiaac/).

Neumark, David and Joanne Song. 2012. "Barriers to Later Retirement: Increases in the Full Retirement Age, Age Discrimination, and the Physical Challenges of Work." *SSRN Electronic Journal*. (https://doi.org/10.2139/ssrn.2188363).

OECD. 2010. "PIAAC Background Questionnaire (Ms Version 2.1 D.D. 15-12-2010)."

OECD. 2012. "Literacy, Numeracy and Problem Solving in Technology-rich Environments: Framework for the OECD Survey of Adult Skills." Paris: OECD.

OECD. 2017. *Pensions at a Glance 2017.* Paris: OECD. (https://doi.org/10.1787/pension_glance-2017-en).

OECD. 2018. "OECD Statistics." (https://stats.oecd.org/).

OECD. 2020a. "OECD Skills Surveys: PIAAC Data Explorer." (https://piaacdataexplorer.oecd.org/ide/idepiaac/dataset.aspx).

OECD. 2020b. "OECD Skills Surveys: PIAAC 1st Cycle." (https://www.oecd.org/skills/piaac/about/piaac1stcycle/).

Osterman, Paul. 2019. "Employment and Training for Mature Adults: The Current System and Moving Forward." Washington, DC: Brookings.

Osterman, Paul and Andrew Weaver. 2016. "Community Colleges and Employers: How Can We Understand Their Connection?" *Industrial Relations: A Journal of Economy and Society* 55(4):523–45.

Pew Research Center. 2016. "The State of American Jobs." Washington, DC: Pew Research Center.

Prensky, Marc. 2001. "Digital Natives, Digital Immigrants." *On the Horizon* 9(5).

Rubenson, Kjell and Richard Desjardins. 2009. "The Impact of Welfare State Regimes on Barriers to Participation in Adult Education: A Bounded Agency Model." *Adult Education Quarterly* 59(3):187–207.

Saetermoe, Carrie L., et al. 2017. "Critical Race Theory as a Bridge in Science Training: The California State University, Northridge Build Poder Program." *BMC Proceedings* 11(Suppl 12):21.

Sayago, Sergio, Paula Forbes, and Josep Blat. 2013. "Older People Becoming Successful ICT Learners over Time: Challenges and Strategies through an Ethnographical Lens." *Educational Gerontology* 39(7):527–44.

Taylor, Philip and Warwick Smith. 2017. "What's Age Got to Do with It? Towards a New Advocacy on Ageing and Work." Melbourne, Australia.

Toossi, Mitra. 2016. "A Look at the Future of the U.S. Labor Force to 2050." *Monthly Labor Review.* Washington, DC: Bureau of Labor Statistics:19–39.

U.S. Bureau of Labor Statistics. 2019. "Employment Projections: Civilian Labor Force, by Age, Sex, Race, and Ethnicity." Labor Force Statistics from the Current Population Survey. Washington, DC. (https://www.bls.gov/emp/tables/civilian-labor-force-summary.htm).

U.S. Department of Education, and National Center for Education Statistics. 2018. "Table 303.30: Total Fall Enrollment in Degree-granting Postsecondary Institutions, by Level and Control of Institution, Attendance Status, and Sex of Student: Selected Years, 1970 through 2027." In *Digest of Education Statistics*. Washington, DC.

Wang, Emily, Michael D. Myers, and David Sundaram. 2013. "Digital Natives and Digital Immigrants: Towards a Model of Digital Fluency." *Business & Information Systems Engineering* 5(6):409–19.

Wang, Xueli. 2017. "Toward a Holistic Theoretical Model of Momentum for Community College Student Success." Pp. 259–308 in *Higher Education: Handbook of Theory and Research*, edited by Michael B. Paulsen. Cham, Switzerland: Springer International.

Woolf, Steven H. and Heidi Schoomaker. 2019. "Life Expectancy and Mortality Rates in the United States, 1959–2017." *JAMA* 322(20):1996–2016.

Zwick, Thomas. 2011. "Why Training Older Employees Is Less Effective." Mannheim. (https://doi.org/10.2139/ssrn.1886428).

# PART IV

# DETERMINANTS OF EMPLOYEE WELL-BEING

CHAPTER 19

# Resilience, Need Fulfillment, and Well-Being in Older Workers

Katherine D. King and Christine Rutledge Smith

All individuals will face hardship in life, but there are certain challenges that more typically come with entry into older adulthood. Stressors such as increased caregiving demands, illness, deaths of loved ones, and more begin to amass. In the workplace, older adults may experience age discrimination or find that the skills they relied on to be successful in the past are no longer in demand. Although older adults tend to possess strong coping skills, these difficulties nonetheless test their resilience.

Resilience is commonly understood as the capacity for individuals to achieve positive adaptation after serious difficulties.[1] Manning and Bouchard interviewed older adults and observed a recurring theme that they called resilient identity, defined as "the outcome of the processes through which one identifies their abilities to reframe problems while recognizing the possibilities for growth and expansion that managing hardships can offer."[2] Individuals with a resilient identity seemed to have developed it early in life as a result of childhood adversity. One interviewee remarked:

> I am resilient but I am not a superhero. I guess for me it's about being able to withstand and overcome all the obstacles in life and to keep doing this, every day, moving along and forward. It's ordinary living, part of just what life entails. It's not really magical.[3]

Resilience was indeed once thought to be a feature of only extraordinary individuals, but it is now seen as a common response to difficult life stressors. In research on the development of resiliency in children, there has been focus on key protective systems, such as "individual capabilities, social supports and relationships, and protections embedded in religions, community, and other cultural systems."[4] This chapter explores these psychosocial elements as they operate in the lives of older workers, and how employment intersects with resilience and well-being.

Resilience involves positive outcomes after hardship, but what exactly does a good outcome look like? In this chapter, we argue that a positive outcome occurs when an individual returns to some degree of *well-being* after hardship. Well-being has been explored in multiple ways, with early psychological theory focused on the absence of psychological illness.[5] More contemporary research has looked at possession of positive personality traits,[6] presence of stable and strong relationships,[7] self-reported subjective well-being,[8] or subjective vitality.[9] Researchers in positive psychology suggest the subcategories of *hedonic* and *eudemonic* well-being to delineate between states of positive emotion and a sense of meaning, respectively.[10]

Each of these definitions offers a useful lens through which to consider well-being, but they lack a comprehensive view of the full range of human experience. In order to understand whether someone is experiencing well-being, we argue that it is important to look at fulfillment of basic necessities, subjective experience, and loftier goals such as purpose and meaning. For this reason, we define well-being as the degree to which an individual has fulfilled fundamental human needs. In particular, we use the needs framework defined by Maslow.[11] He posits that individuals have a hierarchy of needs that begins with basic physiological needs. Once met, the individual moves to higher-order needs such as love, belongingness, esteem, and ultimately self-actualization. Although the initial hierarchical structure that Maslow proposed has been called into question,[12] his delineation remains a useful, holistic, and comprehensive catalog of the needs that individuals seek to fulfill in life.

Each need articulated by Maslow has the potential of being fulfilled through employment, and can subsequently contribute to an individual's overall well-being.[13] There are many ways that Maslow's needs may be fulfilled, and the places people look for need fulfillment will vary between individuals and within individuals across time. In his seminal work on vocational development, Donald Super[14] proposed that career choice was not an event but instead a process, and that it varies from person to person due to individual differences. At different points in life, a person may take on a variety of roles (e.g., homemaker, student, worker, grandparent). The interplay between these roles and one's career choice is a salient factor in career selection. For an older worker who may have multiple life roles, an important aspect of well-being may be to negotiate these roles in a way that aligns with one's identity and purpose at the time, which may shift over the lifespan depending on these various occupied roles.

Employment potentially allows an individual to contribute to the broader social good, and the temperament and unique values of the individual will determine how much he or she pursues need fulfillment through work. For instance, an older worker may have had her need for belonging fulfilled by a circle of friends, but as friends have begun to pass away she may choose to continue to work to feel a sense of belonging among her coworkers. In this chapter, we argue that work settings are a reasonable place where older adults may go to meet their needs and consider factors that may influence whether they are ultimately fulfilled.

## WHO IS AN OLDER WORKER?

The term "older worker" does not have a single definition. One common perception is that an older worker is one who is approaching or continuing to work past full retirement age. The U.S. government describes "full retirement age" as "the age at which a person may first become entitled to full or unreduced retirement benefits."[15] Depending on one's birth year, this could be between the ages of sixty-five and sixty-seven, although a person can retire as early as age sixty-two and qualify for reduced benefits.

It is common to hear the word "old" uttered to describe workers who are younger than full retirement age, and U.S. policy is not consistent in its definition. The Age Discrimination in Employment Act of 1967 protects employees age forty and above from being discriminated against on the basis of training, promotion, hiring, or terms of employment,[16] thus delineating people forty years and above as a protected older working population vulnerable to ageist bias. The Older Americans Act of 1965 (OAA), an act funding community-based social services to the elderly and supporting elder abuse prevention, defines "older individual" as someone age sixty or older.[17] Additionally, the AARP (formerly the American Association of Retired Persons), a nonprofit organization offering benefits and publications to aging populations, allows membership to people fifty and above.[18] Research studies have also begun to group older adults into smaller age categories, for example, "young old" (sixty to sixty-nine), "middle old" (seventy to seventy-nine), and "very old" (eighty-plus).[19] Age has also been broken down into several categories including psychological age (how old one feels or acts), chronological age (years since birth), social age (role within family, e.g., grandparent), and biological age (e.g., function of physiological systems).[20]

It is also possible that others define the older worker not by age but rather by stereotypical characteristics of older adults, such as physical features (e.g., gray hair), visible markers of illness or disability (e.g., use of a cane), temperament (e.g., grouchy), perceived cognitive deficits (e.g., reduced memory), or family roles (e.g., being a grandparent). In one study,[21] older adults were rated according to ageist stereotypes about emotional resilience. In this study, participants were given a set of adjectives and shown photographs of a young male worker, a young female worker, an older male worker, and an older female worker. The older workers were rated to be less flexible, adaptable, and well balanced and more rigid, uncontrollable, and inflexible. These ageist stereotypes directly contradict findings that older adults tend to be better able to handle demanding and emotional situations when compared to their younger counterparts.[22] (See also chapters 12 and 13.)

Each definition of older adults, and older workers, is limited. Bowen, Noack, and Staudinger state "to describe 'older workers' as a homogenous social group can be misleading given the increasing diversity of age trajectories. Furthermore, there is no dichotomy between 'older' and 'younger' workers."[23] For the purpose of this chapter, the older worker will be defined as any person who is nearing the age criterion for any government or social service program, any person who may be vulnerable to age discrimination, and men and women who may be subjectively experiencing aspects of aging and consider themselves to be in this category.

## NEED FULFILLMENT

Maslow's need framework includes physiological, safety, love, belonging, esteem, and self-actualization needs. An individual can be said to experience well-being to the extent that each of these needs is met.[24] The following section explores factors which may contribute to each need being met through older workers' employment experiences.

### Physiological and Safety Needs

Survival and safety needs are frequently met through the financial compensation that work provides, and our success as a species has hinged on the ability of our ancestors to engage in productive labor.[25] At present, many older workers may need to work beyond statutory retirement age in order to supplement their pension. In 2016, the United States Bureau of Labor Statistics cited that 23.6 percent of people between the age of sixty-five and seventy-four participated in the labor force.[26] In a 2014 AARP study, one in every three of these workers (between the ages of sixty-five and seventy-four) said that the most significant reason they work is funding their living expenses.[27] In the United States, Social Security benefits are calculated based on lifetime earnings. A person also must have worked for ten years in order to qualify for benefits.[28] In 2019, the average monthly Social Security benefit paid to a retiree is $1,461.[29] For perspective, this is equal to $17,500 annually or a full-time hourly wage of $9.13. For reference, the federal hourly minimum wage according to the U.S. Department of Labor is $7.25, which has remained unchanged since 2009.[30] (See also chapters 2 and 21.)

Safety needs drive people to avoid instability, danger, pain, chaos, illness, or abuse and instead seek unthreatening, orderly, respectful, healthy, peaceful, and "good" environments. The ways in which individuals attempt to fulfill these needs are varied, but employment supports attainment of each of them. People will be motivated to work in order to afford shelter in a safe neighborhood, to obtain adequate health care, to maintain financial independence, or even as an escape from an abusive home environment. Further, elder abuse is unfortunately a prevalent occurrence in the United States, as it is estimated to impact 10 percent of Americans over the age of sixty-five.[31] It is characterized by physical, verbal, sexual, and psychological abuse; neglect; and financial exploitation. Many people thus may continue to work past retirement to avoid making themselves vulnerable to abuse, neglect, or manipulation by caregivers, acquaintances, or strangers.

Continued employment also allows one to build savings and thus financial security, which can contribute to an individual's sense of safety, security, and well-being overall.[32] The routines and predictability of some work settings can also enhance a sense of order and stability in life and potentially provide the physical activity and cognitive stimulation necessary to maintain good health.

Maslow writes that people can get stuck in the search to fulfill safety needs, particularly people who are neurotic. Such individuals may be more alert to danger and may engage in avoidant or ritualistic safety behaviors in order to evade potentially hazardous or unstable situations. Maslow argues that neurotic people may arrange their lives so that there is no danger, and they will tend to prefer what is familiar. Thus, there may be such a subset of older workers who continue to work solely to avoid the fear and anxiety that arises when contemplating retirement.

People do not always have personal choice in their career trajectories. This may be due to lack of financial resources; inadequate access to education; lack of role models; labor market trends; and discriminatory employment practices influenced by ageism, sexism, racism, and other sources of bias.[33] In such circumstances, individuals may find themselves in poor-quality jobs. These jobs, particularly those with multiple psychosocial stressors, may lead to negative health consequences as bad as those experienced by unemployed individuals.[34]

Some work settings have the potential to protect individuals from hardship, while others confer risk to our health and well-being.[35] Brough and colleagues[36] elucidate features of both psychologically healthy and unhealthy workplaces. The former healthy environments pay attention to work-family balance, employee development, health and safety, and employee involvement. In contrast, the latter unhealthy workplaces are characterized by poor supervisor and coworker support, excessive workload, role stress, and high demand coupled with low control or autonomy.

## Love and Belonging

While many individuals seek independence, Maslow also argues that individuals have a need for love. He defines this need as encompassing belongingness and affection, stating that "[people] will hunger for affectionate relations with people in general, namely for a place in [their] group, and [they] will strive with great intensity to achieve this goal."[37] He also notes that both receiving and giving love are essential to having this need fulfilled. Given the propensity for older adults' social circles to decrease due to losses of family and friends, maintaining social connection later in life becomes even more integral to resilience and well-being. Many work settings can facilitate this as they involve frequent contact with other individuals, making it a potential constant in people's lives that reliably links them to others.[38] The relational theory of working asserts that all aspects of work life are experienced within, influenced by, and understood in the context of relationships.[39] While there are individuals who have difficulty finding rewarding relationships at work, or who may experience harsh treatment, isolation, and alienation,[40] many others find meaningful social connection among colleagues.

Although it may seem that work relationships are purely transactional, many workers report peer relationships at work, including acquaintances, friends, close friends, and even best friends.[41] Friendships in the workplace are different from colleague relationships because friendships typically develop by choice and also involve people seeing each other "as 'whole persons' rather than as packages of discrete attributes or mere role occupants."[42] Workplaces may potentially facilitate the development of closeness through frequent communication, daily interaction for extended time periods, collaboration within potentially high-stress situations, enduring similar challenges (e.g., working for a challenging supervisor, downsizing), and engaging in team work toward shared goals. In some cases, there may be shared values or interests that lead people to work for the same organization or pursue the same career. The corporate culture of some workplaces may also encourage cultivating bonds among employees.

Sewdas and colleagues[43] conducted a qualitative study in the Netherlands exploring reasons why older workers may pursue employment past retirement age. In their results, participants noted social connection as a reason to continue working. Older individuals with nonworking partners often felt pulled to retire early. In couples where one partner continued working, the other partner also wished to continue working. One participant stated, "It is no fun sitting at home alone."[44] Individuals without romantic partners may benefit from the social opportunities that many work settings provide. One such unpartnered participant in the study stated, "I am living alone and I like it if I can go somewhere where I can see and meet people, such as my colleagues."[45]

Kram and Isabella[46] discuss *special relationships* among coworkers. These relationships are the most intimate type of work-related peer relationship. Within them, personal disclosures and dilemmas from all domains of life are shared. These relationships require years to develop, are rare, and involve deep bonding and emotional support. When these relationships are formed, people report a greater sense of belongingness in their jobs.

*Continuity theory* suggests that people need only to continue their usual level of social engagement in order to maintain a sense of well-being later in life.[47] Therefore, if a person was a solitary individual who enjoyed infrequent social connection early in life, then continuing this pattern of social engagement may be satisfying later as well. On the other hand, if a person is highly socially engaged, he or she will likely be satisfied only by continuing in a similar manner. Thus, one motivator for continued employment among older workers may simply be to maintain the same frequency and quality of social activity.

There is mutual influence between work and family life. Work demands and experiences can shape aspects of home life, such as when there is spillover of job stress into the home context. Alternatively, family needs, demands, and expectations can have a profound influence on our work opportunities, choices, and trajectories. Of particular relevance to older workers are the potential influences of caregiving demands (e.g., spousal caregiving or caregiving for younger generations), retirement of one's domestic partner, and familial beliefs about the appropriateness of continued job skill training and professional involvement in older age. For cultures in which family and community values are emphasized, selecting a field of work may also be a result of familial or communal expectations,[48] thus facilitating group identity and social contribution.[49]

## Esteem

According to Maslow, esteem needs are related to an individual's desire to have a "high evaluation of themselves, for self-respect, or self-esteem, and for the esteem of others."[50] Self-esteem includes feeling good about oneself, having a sense of identity, and a positive self-evaluation. Each of these can be strongly connected to one's role in the sphere of work. Employment is one way in which individuals achieve a personally meaningful sense of identity. It has been said that "people's capacity to engage in meaningful occupations provides the key to being not just a person but a *particular* person."[51] Identity can be discovered and shaped by membership in groups.[52] By performing actions, utilizing personal agency, and engaging in meaningful activities, people develop their sense of self.[53] These actions will contribute to group dynamics within the workplace. Workplace social groups may share common attitudes, feelings, or values that go on to shape workplace culture, which has further and more far-reaching effects on the values and behavior of those in the environment.[54]

One way in which employment can contribute to older workers' self-esteem is through achievement. It has been found that older workers' motivations for achievement tend to vary considerably from what is observed in younger workers. While younger workers tend to focus on extrinsically driven performance goals, financial goals, or task-based goals in order to feel better about themselves, older workers tend to be motivated to achieve by obtaining intrinsically driven mastery and competence goals.[55] Older workers may also continue employment in order to maintain their skills and abilities,[56] which then buoys self-esteem.

In the lives of older workers, how one thinks and feels about one's age and aging can be an important factor in self-esteem and its influence on employment. *Subjective age* reflects the age at which one feels oneself to be. Montepare and Lachman[57] obtained the subjective age identities of participants by asking them to name the age that best corresponded to how they felt, how they looked, the age of people whose interests and activities were most like theirs, and the age they felt they would like to be. Results showed that adults in middle and later life tended to report younger age identities, and that differences between one's subjective age and actual age were associated with decreased life satisfaction and more fears of aging.

Subjective age is also not a static entity, and its daily variations seem to correlate with daily well-being.[58] When faced with an experience of age discrimination, some older adults may preserve their well-being by adopting a younger subjective age.[59] Evidence has also been found that subjective age may integrate information gained from social and biological cues.[60] In this study, individuals with higher subjective age were more likely to report experiences of age discrimination. Further, higher subjective age was linked to physiological markers such as lower pulmonary and muscular function, and higher waist circumference. Lower subjective age was related to better peak expiratory flow, stronger grip strength, and lower waist circumference.

Nagy, Johnston, and Hirschi[61] explored the influence of subjective age on older workers' engagement in crafting a work environment that is a good fit for themselves. As individuals develop across the lifespan, job crafting is a way that workers can continue to optimize their work environment to their changing interests and abilities. For instance, a worker who was previously engaged in manual labor may begin to do more administrative work as physical strength declines. One meta-analysis suggests that individuals do engage in less job crafting as they get older.[62] Nagy, Johnston, and Hirschi found that individuals who report feeling younger than their chronological age tended to engage in job crafting at a significantly higher level even when controlling for other factors such as health, autonomy, and chronological age. They also found that engaging in job crafting predicted work meaningfulness. (See also chapters 9, 11, and 16.)

Internalized ageism occurs when an older adult has come to believe age-based stereotypes about him- or herself. (See also chapter 12.) This can have real-world consequences in the workplace. For instance, if older workers believe they can no longer learn new things due to their age, then they will not volunteer for further job skills training that would contribute to workplace success. Having an *older worker identity* (OWI) indicates that an individual puts him- or herself in a category with other older adults in the workplace and has internalized negative beliefs and stereotypes about this group, for instance, seeing oneself as having lower motivation, being more resistant to change, or performing more poorly overall.[63] Rodríguez-Cifuentes, Farfán, and Topa[64] found that individuals may age more successfully at work if they actively manage their subjective age. In their study, they found a negative relationship between OWI and task performance. OWI had a negative influence on performance, but subjective age and self-efficacy moderated the degree of this influence.

Romaioli and Contarello[65] describe self-sabotaging rhetoric in the minds of older adults. In particular, they explore the attitude that many older individuals have that they are "too old for" (TOF) a variety of possible activities. This attitude is influenced by a broader social construction of aging as a time of diminishment and loss. It creates a chasm between what might otherwise be considered a desirable goal and what people feel is feasible to achieve in their older years. The TOF narrative is self-sabotaging and self-limiting. It influences people to reject or avoid certain activities, which may in fact be fulfilling and achievable should the person engage in them. In a content analysis of older adults' narratives, the authors observed TOF rhetoric to be associated with four themes: declining physical energy, the impossibility of making valid plans for the future, a lack of initiative to take part in social activities, and a perceived limitation of their capacity to learn. While this rhetoric may influence many domains of an individual's life, most important for the current chapter is the way in which it may lead older adults to cease pursuing new employment ventures, job skills training, deepening of expertise, and other activities that can lead to more success and fulfillment at work.

Some unexpected results were also found regarding TOF rhetoric. For instance, some interviewees expressed concern about becoming too old to do something in the future, and this seemed to help motivate them to take action in the present. Some older adults also seemed to use a TOF narrative as a way of encouraging themselves to relax their ambitions in favor of acceptance and contentedness. According to the authors, "many difficult realities . . . are generated by ideas that are shared and taken for granted, and that change can be promoted by involving people in generating, exploring and implementing alternative constructions."[66] Some older individuals in their study articulated counternarratives to TOF rhetoric, including the importance of willpower, consistency, rising to challenges, duty, passion, eternal youth, and successful aging.

TOF rhetoric may also influence employers, colleagues, and family members of older workers and undergird a variety of ageist assumptions, making it more difficult to obtain esteem from others. If an older worker's supervisor believes an individual is too old to learn a new computer program, the worker may then not be given appropriate training. An older worker seeking to return to school for a career change may be dissuaded by a spouse or adult child who believes they are too old to do so.

Another way to obtain esteem from others is to be valued and appreciated for your contributions. Feeling valued at work is correlated with better mental and physical health[67] and may inspire people to continue to work past statutory retirement age.[68] Additionally, feeling valued by an employer may make employees more satisfied, motivated, and engaged when compared to those who do not feel valued at work. Feeling valued at work also has the potential to counteract age discrimination, ageism, and stereotyping that occurs inside and outside of the workplace, thus increasing the older worker's self-esteem. Having power, influence, and social status at work, or being regarded as an expert or leader, can also demonstrate to individuals that they have others' esteem in the workplace.

Independence is valued to varying degrees by culture and is a strongly held value in the current cohort of older Americans. Studies have demonstrated that the majority of older people wish to "age in place," meaning that they wish to remain in their communities, be independent, be able to transport themselves, and avoid being institutionalized.[69] For those with such values, independence can facilitate self-esteem as it staves off feelings of vulnerability and dependency.

## Self-Actualization

Maslow uses the term "self-actualization" to describe the drive to live toward one's own unique potential. Eudaimonia, a state of well-being, has been said to occur when people live most concordant with their most deeply held values. In this state, a person may feel most alive and authentic.[70] This kind of eudemonic well-being has also been referred to as "flourishing"[71] and can result in many positive aspects of self-concept including self-acceptance, authenticity, purpose in life, effective functioning toward one's potential, and relating to the self positively. Eudemonic well-being can be thought to include both living in accordance with one's true identity as well as transcending the self in service to a greater good. In fact, a revision to Maslow's original hierarchy of needs lists transcendence as the highest need, existing beyond even self-actualization.

For older workers, finding meaning in one's work could be the deciding factor between choosing to continue employment versus choosing to retire. Meaning in work can be highly subjective and relies less on the external qualities of the job and more on the fit between the individual and the work tasks and environment. An individual's cultural background can be an influence on the chosen employment trajectory. Our socioeconomic and cultural background shapes how central work is to our lives,[72] how much meaning we seek from our work, and what is considered an "honest day's work." Meaningful work tends to correlate with greater job satisfaction, increased motivation, and organizational commitment.[73] Several theories of meaningful work have been advanced. Chalofsky[74] proposes that it entails: (1) sense of self (e.g., bringing one's full self to work, having a sense of life purpose that connects to one's work); (2) sense of work (e.g., the opportunity to carry out a sense of purpose through one's work tasks); and (3) sense of balance (e.g., balancing work and personal roles). And Schnell and colleagues[75] found several characteristics that predicted meaning in work, including: (1) significance of work tasks (e.g., required duties are experienced as meaningful); (2) work-role fit (e.g., identity and job duties are well matched); (3) sociomoral climate (e.g., open, appreciative, and collaborative); and (4) having an organizational self-transcendent orientation (e.g.. commitment to values of organization in a prosocial manner).

In a 2019 MetLife research study, 72 percent of workers over the age of fifty-three perceived their job as contributing to a sense of purpose.[76] When asked what "purpose" means to them, these older workers stated not only regular accomplishment of tasks, but also doing meaningful work, feeling passionate about their work, and creating value. The last definition of purpose, "creating value," relates to the second component of eudemonic well-being, which is transcending the self, service toward others, and generativity. Erikson[77] proposes that one of the primary needs in later adulthood is generativity, which involves creating a lasting impact on the world through creative and productive acts, such as raising children, making art, or contributing to advancements in one's profession. Generativity can be motivated by both selfish and selfless desires.[78] Finding a generative meaning in one's work may lead to continued employment, though generativity may also make people less likely to continue employment and instead pursue postretirement volunteerism, civic engagement, or family care.[79]

As older workers achieve success in their jobs, they may fear leaving their position due to "question[ing] whether their successors can be relied on to respect the monument that took them so long to build."[80] These monuments can be large or small scale, and also can be both abstract (such as forming a company, a policy, a team culture, or a theory) or tangible (such as a piece of equipment, a patent, or a computer system). Whatever they are, they represent an important contribution in the mind of the older worker, and anyone who has made such a contribution through hard work may wish to avoid "passing the baton" to a successor and thus continue working well into older adulthood. The transfer of experience and knowledge from older to younger workers has been found to be an important employment value,[81] and some older workers have reported that the opportunity to provide mentorship is part of what inspires them to continue working.[82]

## CONCLUSION

Employment is not a guaranteed pathway to well-being for older workers, but it is also an essential consideration and key influence on psychological health.[83] Further, although it is known that work satisfaction is linked to life satisfaction,[84] the workplace is frequently ignored as an important domain of life.[85] This chapter has described resilience, defined older workers, and emphasized a variety of psychosocial aspects of resilience and well-being among older workers. We have focused largely on how Maslow's catalog of human needs offers a useful framework for considering potential dimensions of well-being. We close here by offering some suggestions for older adults themselves, as well as for their employers.

For older workers, we recommend a proactive approach to job crafting as a crucial way to age successfully at work. Bringing together literature on lifespan and organizational psychology, Kooij[86] identifies numerous potential proactive behaviors that would support an older worker in continuing to work later in life. These activities include engaging in health-promoting activities to stay physically well, negotiating changes to job duties to better reflect strengths and accommodate weaknesses, and asking for increased flexibility, among many others. Kooij also discusses the theory of selective optimization with compensation[87] in the context of successful aging at work. Here, selection involves focusing on the most important work-related goals, and optimization includes practicing skills that are most relevant to goal achievement. Engaging in compensation for areas of difficulty can be done by seeking help from others, using technical aids, or managing impressions to maximize the visibility of success.

Carstensen and colleagues[88] hold that an individual's future time perspective will influence the choice of activities. Believing the remaining time in life is small will lead to greater selectivity in allocating time and spending social and emotional resources. In contrast, believing there is still significant time ahead in life will make for less selective and broader investment of social and emotional energies. We suggest older workers consider this theory in the context of need fulfillment as described in this chapter. As individuals begin to sense less time remaining in life, we theorize it would be beneficial to focus on those activities that fulfill important and highly valued needs. If employment continues to be an activity where needs of physiological wellness, safety, esteem, love, belongingness, self-actualization, or transcendence are met, then continued employment may well be just what the doctor ordered.

We remind employers that work settings that are perceived as engaging and interesting, and where employers hire and retain older workers, can inspire older workers to continue employment later in life.[89] The American Psychological Association[90] found that 80 percent of individuals aged fifty-five and older stated that they simply enjoyed their work. Additionally, "work-life fit" was cited as the second highest retention factor for those above age fifty-five. Work-life fit involves the match between an employee and many aspects of the work environment and is sometimes called person-environment fit.[91] This type of fit occurs when a person subjectively perceives a good "match" with the organization, and when cognitive beliefs, such as personal values, match those of the organization.

It is incumbent on organizations wishing to retain or attract older workers to pay attention to the strengths and values held by these individuals. It is also important to be direct and articulate about the mission of the institution and to encourage older workers to find synergies between their personal values and those of the organization. Employers may focus too much on how to accommodate possible limitations of older workers and allot insufficient time and effort for creating a working environment that is free of ageist bias, that allows the strengths of older workers to be harnessed, and that provides the meaning and purpose that will inspire individuals to continue their work. Although we have primarily focused on older workers in this chapter, we also remind employers that the work setting is a place where all individuals can seek and obtain fulfillment of the full range of human needs.

## NOTES

1. Ann S. Masten. 2001. "Ordinary Magic: Resilience Processes in Development." *American Psychologist* 56(3):227–38. (https://doi.org/10.1037/0003-066x.56.3.227).

2. Lydia K. Manning and Lauren Bouchard. 2019. "Encounters with Adversity: A Framework for Understanding Resilience in Later Life." *Aging & Mental Health*:4. (https://doi.org/10.1080/13607863.2019.1594162).

3. Manning and Bouchard, "Encounters with Adversity."

4. Ann S. Masten and Margaret O'Dougherty Wright. 2010. "Resilience over the Lifespan: Developmental Perspectives on Resistance, Recovery, and Transformation." P. 222 in *Handbook of Adult Resilience*, edited by John W. Reich, Alex J. Zautra, and John Stuart Hall. New York: Guilford.

5. Richard M. Ryan and Edward L. Deci. 2001. "On Happiness and Human Potentials: A Review of Research on Hedonic and Eudaimonic Well-being." *Annual Review of Psychology* 52(1):141–66. (https://doi.org/10.1146/annurev.psych.52.1.141).

6. Kennon M. Sheldon et al. 1997. "Trait Self and True Self: Cross-role Variation in the Big-five Personality Traits and Its Relations with Psychological Authenticity and Subjective Well-being." *Journal of Personality and Social Psychology* 73(6):1380–93. (https://doi.org/10.1037//0022-3514.73.6.1380).

7. Roy F. Baumeister and Mark R. Leary. 1995. "The Need to Belong: Desire for Interpersonal Attachments as a Fundamental Human Motivation." *Psychological Bulletin* 117(3):497–529. (https://doi.org/10.1037/0033-2909.117.3.497).

8. Ed Diener and Martin E. P. Seligman. 2004. "Beyond Money: Toward an Economy of Well-being." *Psychological Science in the Public Interest* 5(1):1–31. (https://doi.org/10.1111/j.0963-7214.2004.00501001.x).

9. Richard M. Ryan and Christina Frederick. 1997. "On Energy, Personality, and Health: Subjective Vitality as a Dynamic Reflection of Well-being." *Journal of Personality* 65(3):529–65. (https://doi.org/10.1111/j.1467-6494.1997.tb00326.x).

10. Alan S. Waterman. 1993. "Two Conceptions of Happiness: Contrasts of Personal Expressiveness (Eudaimonia) and Hedonic Enjoyment." *Journal of Personality and Social Psychology* 64(4):678–91. (https://doi.org/10.1037//0022-3514.64.4.678).

11. Abraham H. Maslow. 1970. *Motivation and Personality*. 2nd ed. New York: Harper & Row.

12. Mahmoud A. Wahba and Lawrence G. Bridwell. 1973. "Maslow Reconsidered: A Review of Research on the Need Hierarchy Theory." *Academy of Management Proceedings* 1:514–20. (https://doi.org/10.5465/ambpp.1973.4981593).

13. Robert W. Lent and Steven D. Brown. 2013. "Understanding and Facilitating Career Development in the 21st Century." Pp. 1–26 in *Career Development and Counseling: Putting Theory and Research to Work*, 2nd ed., edited by Steven D. Brown and Robert W. Lent. Hoboken, NJ: John Wiley & Sons.

14. Donald E. Super. 1990. "A Life-span, Life-space Approach to Career Development." Pp. 197–261 in *Career Choice and Development: Applying Contemporary Theories in Practice*, 2nd ed., edited by Duane Brown and Linda Brooks. San Francisco: Jossey-Bass.

15. U.S. Social Security Administration. N.d. *Benefits Planner: Retirement*. Retrieved August 1, 2019 (https://www.ssa.gov/planners/retire/agereduction.html).

16. U.S. Department of Labor. N.d. *Age Discrimination Act of 1975*. Office of the Assistant Secretary for Administration & Management. Retrieved August 1, 2019 (https://www.dol.gov/agencies/oasam/regulatory/statutes/age-discrimination-act).

17. U.S. Department of Health and Human Services. November 8, 2017. *Older Americans Act*. Administration for Community Living. (https://acl.gov/about-acl/authorizing-statutes/older-americans-act).

18. AARP. N.d. "AARP." Retrieved August 1, 2019 (https://www.aarp.org/).

19. Daniel E. Forman et al. 1992. "PTCA in the Elderly: The 'Young-old' versus the 'Old-old.'" *Journal of the American Geriatrics Society* 40(1):19–22. (https://doi.org/10.1111/j.1532-5415.1992.tb01823.x).

20. Judith E. Phillips, Kristine J. Ajrouch, and Sarah Hillcoat-Nalletamby. 2010. *Key Concepts in Social Gerontology*. Thousand Oaks, CA: SAGE:12–13.

21. Cornelia Rauschenbach, Anja S. Göritz, and Guido Hertel. 2012. "Age Stereotypes about Emotional Resilience at Work." *Educational Gerontology* 38(8):511–19. (https://doi.org/10.1080/03601277.2011.567187).

22. James J. Gross et al. 1997. "Emotion and Aging: Experience, Expression, and Control." *Psychology and Aging* 12(4):590–99. (https://doi.org/10.1037//0882-7974.12.4.590).

23. Catherine E. Bowen, C. Martin G. Noack, and Ursula M. Staudinger. 2011. "Aging in the Work Context." P. 264 in *Handbook of the Psychology of Aging*, 7th ed., edited by K. Warner Schaie and Sherry L. Willis. Amsterdam, Netherlands: Elsevier Science & Technology. (https://doi.org/10.1016/b978-0-12-380882-0.00017-6).

24. Don Gorman. 2010. "Maslow's Hierarchy and Social and Emotional Well-being." *Aboriginal and Islander Health Worker Journal* 33(5):1–13. (https://eprints.usq.edu.au/6830/4/Gorman_AIHWJ_V34N1_2010_AV.pdf).

25. David L. Blustein. 2008. "The Role of Work in Psychological Health and Well-being: A Conceptual, Historical, and Public Policy Perspective." *American Psychologist* 63(4):228–40. (https://doi.org/10.1037/0003-066x.63.4.228).

26. U.S. Social Security Administration. N.d. *Your Retirement Benefit: How It's Figured.* Retrieved August 1, 2019 (https://www.ssa.gov/pubs/EN-05-10070.pdf).

27. Mark Miller. February/March 2015. "Take This Job and Love It!" *AARP the Magazine.* (https://www.aarp.org/work/working-after-retirement/info-2015/work-over-retirement-happiness.html).

28. U.S. Social Security Administration, *Your Retirement Benefit.*

29. AARP. October 10, 2018. "The Maximum Social Security Benefit Explained." (https://www.aarp.org/retirement/social-security/questions-answers/maximum-ss-benefit/).

30. U.S. Department of Labor. N.d. *Minimum Wage.* Retrieved September 16, 2019 (https://www.dol.gov/general/topic/wages/minimumwage).

31. U.S. Department of Health and Human Services. N.d. *Statistics and Data.* Administration for Community Living, National Center on Elder Abuse (NCEA). Retrieved August 1, 2019 (https://ncea.acl.gov/What-We-Do/Research/Statistics-and-Data.aspx).

32. Richard G. Netemeyer et al. 2017. "How Am I Doing? Perceived Financial Well-being, Its Potential Antecedents, and Its Relation to Overall Well-being." *Journal of Consumer Research* 45(1):68–89. (https://doi.org/10.1093/jcr/ucx109).

33. American Psychological Association. 2016. "Professional Practice Guidelines for Integrating the Role of Work and Career into Psychological Practice." (https://www.apa.org/practice/guidelines/role-work-career).

34. Dorothy H. Broom et al. 2006. "The Lesser Evil: Bad Jobs or Unemployment? A Survey of Mid-aged Australians." *Social Science & Medicine* 63(3):575–86. (https://doi.org/10.1016/j.socscimed.2006.02.003).

35. Jane L. Swanson. 2012. "Work and Psychological Health." Pp. 3–27 in *APA Handbook of Counseling Psychology*, edited by Nadya A. Fouad, Jean A. Carter, and Linda M. Subich. Washington, DC: American Psychological Association.

36. Paula Brough et al. 2009. *Workplace Psychological Health: Current Research and Practice.* Cheltenham, England: Edward Elgar.

37. Maslow, *Motivation and Personality*, 381.

38. David L. Blustein. 2006. *The Psychology of Working: A New Perspective for Career Development, Counseling, and Public Policy*. Mahwah, NJ: Lawrence Erlbaum.

39. David L. Blustein. 2011. "A Relational Theory of Working." *Journal of Vocational Behavior* 79(1):1–17. (https://doi.org/10.1016/j.jvb.2010.10.004).

40. Donna E. P. Schultheiss. 2006. "The Interface of Work and Family Life." *Professional Psychology: Research and Practice* 37(4):334–41. (https://doi.org/10.1037/0735-7028.37.4.334).

41. Patricia M. Sias and Daniel J. Cahill. 1998. "From Co-workers to Friends: The Development of Peer Friendships in the Workplace." *Western Journal of Communication* 62(3):273–99. (https://doi.org/10.1080/10570319809374611).

42. Paul H. Wright. 1978. "Toward a Theory of Friendship Based on a Conception of Self." *Human Communication Research* 4(3):199. (https://doi.org/10.1111/j.1468-2958.1978.tb00609.x).

43. Ranu Sewdas et al. 2017. "Why Older Workers Work beyond the Retirement Age: A Qualitative Study." *BMC Public Health* 17(1). (https://doi.org/10.1186/s12889-017-4675-z).

44. Sewdas et al., "Why Older Workers Work," 5.

45. Sewdas et al., "Why Older Workers Work," 5.

46. Kathy E. Kram and Lynn A. Isabella. 1985. "Mentoring Alternatives: The Role of Peer Relationships in Career Development." *Academy of Management Journal* 28(1):110–32. (https://doi.org/10.5465/256064).

47. Robert C. Atchley. 2003. "Why Most People Cope Well with Retirement." Pp. 123–38 in *Mental Wellness in Aging: Strengths-based Approaches*, edited by Judah L. Ronch and Joseph A. Goldfield. Baltimore: Health Professions.

48. Nadya A. Fouad and Neeta Kantamneni. 2008. "Contextual Factors in Vocational Psychology: Intersections of Individual, Group, and Societal Dimensions." Pp. 408–25 in *Handbook of Counseling Psychology*, 4th ed., edited by Steven D. Brown and Robert W. Lent. Hoboken, NJ: John Wiley & Sons.

49. Lent and Brown, "Understanding and Facilitating Career Development."

50. Maslow, *Motivation and Personality*, 381.

51. Linsey Howie, Michelle Coulter, and Susan Feldman. January 2004. "Crafting the Self: Older Persons' Narratives of Occupational Identity." *American Journal of Occupational Therapy* 58(4):447. (https://doi.org/10.5014/ajot.58.4.446).

52. Henri Tajfel and John C. Turner. 1979. "An Integrative Theory of Intergroup Conflict." Pp. 33–37 in *The Social Psychology of Intergroup Relations*, edited by William G. Austin and Stephen Worchel. Monterey, CA: Brooks/Cole.

53. Charles H. Christiansen. January 1999. "Defining Lives: Occupation as Identity; An Essay on Competence, Coherence, and the Creation of Meaning." *American Journal of Occupational Therapy* 53(6):547–58. (https://doi.org/10.5014/ajot.53.6.547).

54. Edgar H. Schein and Peter Schein. 2016. *Organizational Culture and Leadership*. 5th ed. San Francisco: Jossey-Bass.

55. Ruth Kanfer and Phillip L. Ackerman. 2004. "Aging, Adult Development, and Work Motivation." *Academy of Management Review* 29(3):440–58. (https://doi.org/10.2307/20159053).

56. Annet H. de Lange et al. 2010. "Dominant Achievement Goals of Older Workers and Their Relationship with Motivation-related Outcomes." *Journal of Vocational Behavior* 77(1):118–25. (https://doi.org/10.1016/j.jvb.2010.02.013).

57. Joann M. Montepare and Margie E. Lachman. 1989. "'You're Only as Old as You Feel': Self-perceptions of Age, Fears of Aging, and Life Satisfaction from Adolescence to Old Age." *Psychology and Aging* 4(1):73–78. (https://doi.org/10.1037//0882-7974.4.1.73).

58. Bibiana M. Armenta et al. 2018. "Dynamic, Not Stable: Daily Variations in Subjective Age Bias and Age Group Identification Predict Daily Well-being in Older Workers." *Psychology and Aging* 33(4):559–71. (https://doi.org/10.1037/pag0000263).

59. Bibiana M. Armenta et al. 2017. "Feeling Younger and Identifying with Older Adults: Testing Two Routes to Maintaining Well-being in the Face of Age Discrimination." *Plos One* 12(11):1–21. (https://doi.org/10.1371/journal.pone.0187805).

60. Angela R. Sutin, Stephan Yannick, and Antonio Terracciano. April 2015. "How Old Do You Feel? The Role of Age Discrimination and Biological Aging in Subjective Age." *Plos One* 10(3). (https://doi.org/10.1371/journal.pone.0119293).

61. Noemi Nagy, Claire S. Johnston, and Andreas Hirschi. 2019. "Do We Act as Old as We Feel? An Examination of Subjective Age and Job Crafting Behaviour of Late Career Employees." *European Journal of Work and Organizational Psychology* 28(3):373–83. (https://doi.org/10.1080/1359432x.2019.1584183).

62. Cort W. Rudolph et al. 2017. "Job Crafting: A Meta-analysis of Relationships with Individual Differences, Job Characteristics, and Work Outcomes." *Journal of Vocational Behavior* 102:112–38. (https://doi.org/10.1016/j.jvb.2017.05.008).

63. Enrica N. Ruggs et al. April 2014. "Selection Biases That Emerge When Age Meets Gender." *Journal of Managerial Psychology* 29(8):1028–43. (https://doi.org/10.1108/jmp-07-2012-0204).

64. Francisco Rodríguez-Cifuentes, Jesús Farfán, and Gabriela Topa. 2018. "Older Worker Identity and Job Performance: The Moderator Role of Subjective Age and Self-efficacy." *International Journal of Environmental Research and Public Health* 15(12):2731. (https://doi.org/10.3390/ijerph15122731).

65. Diego Romaioli and Alberta Contarello. March 2019. "'I'm Too Old for . . .' Looking into a Self-sabotage Rhetoric and Its Counter-narratives in an Italian Setting." *Journal of Aging Studies* 48:25–32. (https://doi.org/10.1016/j.jaging.2018.12.001).

66. Romaioli and Contarello, "I'm Too Old," 26.

67. American Psychological Association. August 28, 2012. "Work-life Fit and Enjoying What They Do Top the List of Reasons Why Employees Stay on the Job, New APA Survey Finds." News release. (https://www.apa.org/news/press/releases/2012/08/work-life).

68. G. Lennart van der Zwaan, et al. 2019. "The Role of Personal Characteristics, Work Environment and Context in Working beyond Retirement: A Mixed-methods Study." *International Archives of Occupational and Environmental Health* 92:535–49. (https://doi.org/10.1007/s00420-018-1387-3).

69. National Conference of State Legislatures and the AARP Public Policy Institute. 2011. *Aging in Place: A State Survey of Livability Policies and Practices.* (https://assets.aarp.org/rgcenter/ppi/liv-com/aging-in-place-2011-full.pdf).

70. Waterman, "Two Conceptions of Happiness."

71. Carol D. Ryff and Burton Singer. 1998. "The Contours of Positive Human Health." *Psychological Inquiry* 9(1):1–28. (https://doi.org/10.1207/s15327965pli0901_1).

72. Blustein, *Psychology of Working.*

73. Michael F. Steger et al. 2013. "Engaging in Work Even When It Is Meaningless: Positive Affective Disposition and Meaningful Work Interact in Relation to Work Engagement." *Journal of Career Assessment* 21(2):348–61. (https://doi.org/10.1177/1069072712471517).

74. Neal Chalofsky. 2003. "An Emerging Construct for Meaningful Work." *Human Resource Development International* 6(1):69–83. (https://doi.org/10.1080/1367886022000016785).

75. Tatjana Schnell, Thomas Höge, and Edith Pollet. 2013. "Predicting Meaning in Work: Theory, Data, Implications." *Journal of Positive Psychology* 8(6):543–54. (https://doi.org/10.1080/17439760.2013.830763).

76. MetLife. 2019. *Thriving in the New Work-life World: MetLife's 17th Annual U.S. Employee Benefit Trends Study.* (https://www.metlife.com/content/dam/metlifecom/us/ebts/pdf/MetLife-Employee-Benefit-Trends-Study-2019.pdf).

77. Erik H. Erikson. 1950. *Childhood and Society.* New York: Norton.

78. Dan P. McAdams and Regina Lopata Logan. 2004. "What Is Generativity?" Pp. 15–31 in *The Generative Society: Caring for Future Generations,* edited by Ed de St. Aubin, Dan P. McAdams, and Tae-Chang Kim. Washington, DC: American Psychological Association. (http://dx.doi.org/10.1037/10622-002).

79. Ulrike Fasbender et al. March 2015. "The Meaning of Work for Post-retirement Employment Decisions." *Work, Aging and Retirement*:12–23. (https://doi.org/10.1093/workar/wav015).

80. Manfred F. R. Kets de Vries. February 26, 2014. "The Dark Side of Retirement." *Harvard Business Review.* (https://hbr.org/2014/02/the-dark-side-of-retirement).

81. Michál E. Mor-Barak. 1995. "The Meaning of Work for Older Adults Seeking Employment: The Generativity Factor." *International Journal of Aging and Human Development* 41(4):325–44. (https://doi.org/10.2190/vgtg-epk6-q4bh-q67q).

82. van der Zwaan et al., "Role of Personal Characteristics," 535–49.

83. American Psychological Association, "Professional Practice Guidelines."

84. Swanson, "Work and Psychological Health."

85. American Psychological Association, "Professional Practice Guidelines."

86. Dorien T. A. M. Kooij. October 2015. "Successful Aging at Work: The Active Role of Employees." *Work, Aging and Retirement* 1(4):309–19. (https://doi.org/10.1093/workar/wav018).

87. Paul B. Baltes and Margret M. Baltes. 1990. "Psychological Perspectives on Successful Aging: The Model of Selective Optimization with Compensation." Pp. 1–34 in *Successful Aging: Perspectives from the Behavioral Sciences,* edited by Paul B. Baltes and Margret M. Baltes. New York: Cambridge University Press.

88. Laura L. Carstensen, Derek M. Isaacowitz, and Susan T. Charles. March 1999. "Taking Time Seriously: A Theory of Socioemotional Selectivity." *American Psychologist* 54(3):165–81. (https://doi.org//10.1037//0003-066X.54.3.165).

89. van der Zwaan et al., "Role of Personal Characteristics," 535–49.

90. American Psychological Association, "Work-life Fit."

91. Steven D. Caldwell, David M. Herold, and Donald B. Fedor. 2004. "Toward an Understanding of the Relationships among Organizational Change, Individual Differences, and Changes in Person-environment Fit: A Cross-level Study." *Journal of Applied Psychology* 89(5):868–82. (https://doi.org/10.1037/0021-9010.89.5.868).

## REFERENCES


AARP. N.d. "AARP." Retrieved August 1, 2019 (https://www.aarp.org/).

AARP. October 10, 2018. "The Maximum Social Security Benefit Explained." (https://www.aarp.org/retirement/social-security/questions-answers/maximum-ss-benefit/).

American Psychological Association. March 8, 2012. "APA Survey Finds Feeling Valued at Work Linked to Well-being and Performance." News release. (https://www.apa.org/news/press/releases/2012/03/well-being).

American Psychological Association. August 28, 2012. "Work-life Fit and Enjoying What They Do Top the List of Reasons Why Employees Stay on the Job, New APA Survey Finds." News release. (https://www.apa.org/news/press/releases/2012/08/work-life).

American Psychological Association. 2016. "Professional Practice Guidelines for Integrating the Role of Work and Career into Psychological Practice." (https://www.apa.org/practice/guidelines/role-work-career).

Armenta, Bibiana M., et al. 2017. "Feeling Younger and Identifying with Older Adults: Testing Two Routes to Maintaining Well-being in the Face of Age Discrimination." *Plos One* 12(11):1–21. (https://doi.org/10.1371/journal.pone.0187805).

Armenta, Bibiana M., et al. 2018. "Dynamic, Not Stable: Daily Variations in Subjective Age Bias and Age Group Identification Predict Daily Well-being in Older Workers." *Psychology and Aging* 33(4):559–71. (https://doi.org/10.1037/pag0000263).

Atchley, Robert C. 2003. "Why Most People Cope Well with Retirement." Pp. 123–38 in *Mental Wellness in Aging: Strengths-based Approaches*, edited by Judah L. Ronch and Joseph A. Goldfield. Baltimore: Health Professions.

Baltes, Paul B. and Margret M. Baltes. 1990. "Psychological Perspectives on Successful Aging: The Model of Selective Optimization with Compensation." Pp. 1–34 in *Successful Aging: Perspectives from the Behavioral Sciences*, edited by Paul B. Baltes and Margret M. Baltes. New York: Cambridge University Press.

Baumeister, Roy F. and Mark R. Leary. 1995. "The Need to Belong: Desire for Interpersonal Attachments as a Fundamental Human Motivation." *Psychological Bulletin* 117(3):497–529. (https://doi.org/10.1037//0033-2909.117.3.497).

Blustein, David L. 2006. *The Psychology of Working: A New Perspective for Career Development, Counseling, and Public Policy.* Mahwah, NJ: Lawrence Erlbaum.

Blustein, David L. 2008. "The Role of Work in Psychological Health and Well-being: A Conceptual, Historical, and Public Policy Perspective." *American Psychologist* 63(4):228–40. (https://doi.org/10.1037/0003-066x.63.4.228).

Blustein, David L. 2011. "A Relational Theory of Working." *Journal of Vocational Behavior* 79(1):1–17. (https://doi.org/10.1016/j.jvb.2010.10.004).

Bowen, Catherine E., C. Martin G. Noack, and Ursula M. Staudinger. 2011. "Aging in the Work Context." Pp. 263–77 in *Handbook of the Psychology of Aging*, 7th ed., edited by K. Warner Schaie and Sherry L. Willis. Amsterdam, Netherlands: Elsevier Science & Technology. (https://doi.org/10.1016/B978-0-12-380882-0.00017-6).

Broom, Dorothy H., et al. 2006. "The Lesser Evil: Bad Jobs or Unemployment? A Survey of Mid-aged Australians." *Social Science & Medicine* 63(3):575–86. (https://doi.org/10.1016/j.socscimed.2006.02.003).

Brough, Paula, et al. 2009. *Workplace Psychological Health: Current Research and Practice.* Cheltenham, England: Edward Elgar.

Caldwell, Steven D., David M. Herold, and Donald B. Fedor. 2004. "Toward an Understanding of the Relationships among Organizational Change, Individual Differences, and Changes in Person-environment Fit: A Cross-level Study." *Journal of Applied Psychology* 89(5):868–82. (https://doi.org/10.1037/0021-9010.89.5.868).

Carstensen, Laura L., Derek M. Isaacowitz, and Susan T. Charles. March 1999. "Taking Time Seriously: A Theory of Socioemotional Selectivity." *American Psychologist* 54(3):165–181. (https://doi.org/10.1037//0003-066X.54.3.165).

Chalofsky, Neal. 2003. "An Emerging Construct for Meaningful Work." *Human Resource Development International* 6(1):69–83. (https://doi.org/10.1080/1367886022000016785).

Christiansen, Charles H. January 1999. "Defining Lives: Occupation as Identity; An Essay on Competence, Coherence, and the Creation of Meaning." *American Journal of Occupational Therapy* 53(6):547–58. (https://doi.org/10.5014/ajot.53.6.547).

de Lange, Annet H., et al. 2010. "Dominant Achievement Goals of Older Workers and Their Relationship with Motivation-related Outcomes." *Journal of Vocational Behavior* 77(1):118–25. (https://doi.org/10.1016/j.jvb.2010.02.013).

de Vries, Manfred F. R. Kets. February 26, 2014. "The Dark Side of Retirement." *Harvard Business Review.* (https://hbr.org/2014/02/the-dark-side-of-retirement).

Diener, Ed and Martin E. P. Seligman. 2004. "Beyond Money: Toward an Economy of Well-being." *Psychological Science in the Public Interest* 5(1):1–31. (https://doi.org/10.1111/j.0963-7214.2004.00501001.x).

Erikson, Erik H. 1950. *Childhood and Society.* New York: Norton.

Fasbender, Ulrike, et al. March 2015. "The Meaning of Work for Post-retirement Employment Decisions." *Work, Aging and Retirement*:12–23. (https://doi.org/10.1093/workar/wav015).

Forman, Daniel E., et al. 1992. "PTCA in the Elderly: The 'Young-old' versus the 'Old-old.'" *Journal of the American Geriatrics Society* 40(1):19–22. (https://doi.org/10.1111/j.1532-5415.1992.tb01823.x).

Fouad, Nadya A. and Neeta Kantamneni. 2008. "Contextual Factors in Vocational Psychology: Intersections of Individual, Group, and Societal Dimensions." Pp. 408–25 in *Handbook of Counseling Psychology*, 4th ed., edited by Steven D. Brown and Robert W. Lent. Hoboken, NJ: John Wiley & Sons.

Gorman, Don. 2010. "Maslow's Hierarchy and Social and Emotional Well-being." *Aboriginal and Islander Health Worker Journal* 33(5):1–13. (https://eprints.usq.edu.au/6830/4/Gorman_AIHWJ_V34N1_2010_AV.pdf).

Gross, James J., et al. 1997. "Emotion and Aging: Experience, Expression, and Control." *Psychology and Aging* 12(4):590–99. (https://doi.org/10.1037//0882-7974.12.4.590).

Howie, Linsey, Michelle Coulter, and Susan Feldman. January 2004. "Crafting the Self: Older Persons' Narratives of Occupational Identity." *American Journal of Occupational Therapy* 58(4):446–54. (https://doi.org/10.5014/ajot.58.4.446).

Kanfer, Ruth, and Phillip L. Ackerman. 2004. "Aging, Adult Development, and Work Motivation." *Academy of Management Review* 29(3):440–58. (https://doi.org/10.2307/20159053).

Kooij, Dorien T. A. M. October 2015. "Successful Aging at Work: The Active Role of Employees." *Work, Aging and Retirement* 1(4):309–19. (https://doi.org/10.1093/workar/wav018).

Kram, Kathy E. and Lynn A. Isabella. 1985. "Mentoring Alternatives: The Role of Peer Relationships in Career Development." *Academy of Management Journal* 28(1):110–32. (https://doi.org/10.5465/256064).

Lent, Robert W. and Steven D. Brown. 2013. "Understanding and Facilitating Career Development in the 21st Century." Pp. 1–26 in *Career Development and Counseling: Putting Theory and Research to Work*, 2nd ed., edited by Steven D. Brown and Robert W. Lent. Hoboken, NJ: John Wiley & Sons.

Manning, Lydia K. and Lauren Bouchard. 2019. "Encounters with Adversity: A Framework for Understanding Resilience in Later Life." *Aging & Mental Health*:1–8. (https://doi.org/10.1080/13607863.2019.1594162).

Maslow, Abraham H. 1970. *Motivation and Personality*. 2nd ed. New York: Harper & Row.

Masten, Ann S. 2001. "Ordinary Magic: Resilience Processes in Development." *American Psychologist* 56(3):227–38. (https://doi.org/10.1037/0003-066x.56.3.227).

Masten, Ann S. and Margaret O'Dougherty Wright. 2010. "Resilience over the Lifespan: Developmental Perspectives on Resistance, Recovery, and Transformation." Pp. 213–37 in *Handbook of Adult Resilience*, edited by John W. Reich, Alex J. Zautra, and John Stuart Hall. New York: Guilford.

McAdams, Dan P. and Regina Lopata Logan. 2004. "What Is Generativity?" Pp. 15–31 in *The Generative Society: Caring for Future Generations*, edited by Ed de St. Aubin, Dan P. McAdams, and Tae-Chang Kim. Washington, DC: American Psychological Association. (http://dx.doi.org/10.1037/10622-002).

MetLife. 2019. *Thriving in the New Work-life World: MetLife's 17th Annual U.S. Employee Benefit Trends Study*. (https://www.metlife.com/content/dam/metlifecom/us/ebts/pdf/MetLife-Employee-Benefit-Trends-Study-2019.pdf).

Miller, Mark. February/March 2015. "Take This Job and Love It!" *AARP the Magazine*. (https://www.aarp.org/work/working-after-retirement/info-2015/work-over-retirement-happiness.html).

Montepare, Joann M. and Margie E. Lachman. 1989. "'You're Only as Old as You Feel': Self-perceptions of Age, Fears of Aging, and Life Satisfaction from Adolescence to Old Age." *Psychology and Aging* 4(1):73–78. (https://doi.org/10.1037//0882-7974.4.1.73).

Mor-Barak, Michál E. 1995. "The Meaning of Work for Older Adults Seeking Employment: The Generativity Factor." *International Journal of Aging and Human Development* 41(4):325–44. (https://doi.org/10.2190/vgtg-epk6-q4bh-q67q).

Nagy, Noemi, Claire S. Johnston, and Andreas Hirschi. 2019. "Do We Act as Old as We Feel? An Examination of Subjective Age and Job Crafting Behaviour of Late Career Employees." *European Journal of Work and Organizational Psychology* 28(3):373–83. (https://doi.org/10.1080/1359432x.2019.1584183).

National Conference of State Legislatures and the AARP Public Policy Institute. 2011. *Aging in Place: A State Survey of Livability Policies and Practices*. (https://assets.aarp.org/rgcenter/ppi/liv-com/aging-in-place-2011-full.pdf).

Netemeyer, Richard G, et al. 2017. "How Am I Doing? Perceived Financial Well-being, Its Potential Antecedents, and Its Relation to Overall Well-being." *Journal of Consumer Research* 45(1):68–89. (https://doi.org/10.1093/jcr/ucx109).

Phillips, Judith E., Kristine J. Ajrouch, and Sarah Hillcoat-Nalletamby. 2010. *Key Concepts in Social Gerontology*. Thousand Oaks, CA: SAGE.

Rauschenbach, Cornelia, Anja S. Göritz, and Guido Hertel. 2012. "Age Stereotypes about Emotional Resilience at Work." *Educational Gerontology* 38(8):511–19. (https://doi.org/10.1080/03601277.2011.567187).

Rodríguez-Cifuentes, Francisco, Jesús Farfán, and Gabriela Topa. 2018. "Older Worker Identity and Job Performance: The Moderator Role of Subjective Age and Self-efficacy." *International Journal of Environmental Research and Public Health* 15(12):2731. (https://doi.org/10.3390/ijerph15122731).

Romaioli, Diego and Alberta Contarello. March 2019. "'I'm Too Old for . . .' Looking into a Self-sabotage Rhetoric and Its Counter-narratives in an Italian Setting." *Journal of Aging Studies* 48:25–32. (https://doi.org/10.1016/j.jaging.2018.12.001).

Rudolph, Cort W., et al. 2017. "Job Crafting: A Meta-analysis of Relationships with Individual Differences, Job Characteristics, and Work Outcomes." *Journal of Vocational Behavior* 102:112–38. (https://doi.org/10.1016/j.jvb.2017.05.008).

Ruggs, Enrica N., et al. April 2014. "Selection Biases That Emerge When Age Meets Gender." *Journal of Managerial Psychology* 29(8):1028–43. (https://doi.org/10.1108/jmp-07-2012-0204).

Ryan, Richard M. and Edward L. Deci. 2001. "On Happiness and Human Potentials: A Review of Research on Hedonic and Eudaimonic Well-being." *Annual Review of Psychology* 52(1):141–66. (https://doi.org/10.1146/annurev.psych.52.1.141).

Ryan, Richard M. and Christina Frederick. 1997. "On Energy, Personality, and Health: Subjective Vitality as a Dynamic Reflection of Well-being." *Journal of Personality* 65(3):529–65. (https://doi.org/10.1111/j.1467-6494.1997.tb00326.x).

Ryff, Carol D. and Burton Singer. 1998. "The Contours of Positive Human Health." *Psychological Inquiry* 9(1):1–28. (https://doi.org/10.1207/s15327965pli0901_1).

Schein, Edgar H. and Peter Schein. 2016. *Organizational Culture and Leadership*. 5th ed. San Francisco: Jossey-Bass.

Schnell, Tatjana, Thomas Höge, and Edith Pollet. 2013. "Predicting Meaning in Work: Theory, Data, Implications." *Journal of Positive Psychology* 8(6):543–54. (https://doi.org/10.1080/17439760.2013.830763).

Schultheiss, Donna E. P. 2006. "The Interface of Work and Family Life." *Professional Psychology: Research and Practice* 37(4):334–41. (https://doi.org/10.1037/0735-7028.37.4.334).

Sewdas, Ranu, et al. 2017. "Why Older Workers Work beyond the Retirement Age: A Qualitative Study." *BMC Public Health* 17(1). (https://doi.org/10.1186/s12889-017-4675-z).

Sheldon, Kennon M., et al. 1997. "Trait Self and True Self: Cross-role Variation in the Big-five Personality Traits and Its Relations with Psychological Authenticity and Subjective Well-being." *Journal of Personality and Social Psychology* 73(6):1380–93. (https://doi.org/10.1037//0022-3514.73.6.1380).

Sias, Patricia M. and Daniel J. Cahill. 1998. "From Co-workers to Friends: The Development of Peer Friendships in the Workplace." *Western Journal of Communication* 62(3):273–99. (https://doi.org/10.1080/10570319809374611).

Steger, Michael F., et al. 2013. "Engaging in Work Even When It Is Meaningless: Positive Affective Disposition and Meaningful Work Interact in Relation to Work Engagement." *Journal of Career Assessment* 21(2):348–61. (https://doi.org/10.1177/1069072712471517).

Super, Donald E. 1990. "A Life-span, Life-space Approach to Career Development." Pp. 197–261 in *Career Choice and Development: Applying Contemporary Theories in Practice*, 2nd ed., edited by Duane Brown and Linda Brooks. San Francisco: Jossey-Bass.

Sutin, Angela R., Stephan Yannick, and Antonio Terracciano. April 2015. "How Old Do You Feel? The Role of Age Discrimination and Biological Aging in Subjective Age." *Plos One* 10(3). (https://doi.org/10.1371/journal.pone.0119293).

Swanson, Jane L. 2012. "Work and Psychological Health." Pp. 3–27 in *APA Handbook of Counseling Psychology*, edited by Nadya A. Fouad, Jean A. Carter, and Linda M. Subich. Washington, DC: American Psychological Association.

Tajfel, Henri and John C. Turner. 1979. "An Integrative Theory of Intergroup Conflict." Pp. 33–37 in *The Social Psychology of Intergroup Relations*, edited by William G. Austin and Stephen Worchel. Monterey, CA: Brooks/Cole.

U.S. Department of Health and Human Services. N.d. *Statistics and Data*. Administration for Community Living. National Center on Elder Abuse (NCEA). Retrieved August 1, 2019 (https://ncea.acl.gov/What-We-Do/Research/Statistics-and-Data.aspx).

U.S. Department of Health and Human Services. November 8, 2017. *Older Americans Act*. Administration for Community Living. (https://acl.gov/about-acl/authorizing-statutes/older-americans-act).

U.S. Department of Labor. N.d. *Age Discrimination Act of 1975*. Office of the Assistant Secretary for Administration & Management. Retrieved August 1, 2019 (https://www.dol.gov/agencies/oasam/regulatory/statutes/age-discrimination-act).

U.S. Department of Labor. N.d. *Minimum Wage*. Retrieved September 16, 2019 (https://www.dol.gov/general/topic/wages/minimumwage).

U.S. Department of Labor. May 29, 2019. *Labor Force Participation Rate for Workers Age 75 and Older Projected to Be over 10 percent by 2026*. U.S. Bureau of Labor Statistics. (https://www.bls.gov/opub/ted/2019/labor-force-participation-rate-for-workers-age-75-and-older-projected-to-be-over-10-percent-by-2026.htm).

U.S. Social Security Administration. N.d. *Benefits Planner: Retirement*. Retrieved August 1, 2019 (https://www.ssa.gov/planners/retire/agereduction.html).

U.S. Social Security Administration. N.d. *Your Retirement Benefit: How It's Figured*. Retrieved August 1, 2019 (https://www.ssa.gov/pubs/EN-05-10070.pdf).

van der Zwaan, G. Lennart, et al. 2019. "The Role of Personal Characteristics, Work Environment and Context in Working beyond Retirement: A Mixed-methods Study." *International Archives of Occupational and Environmental Health* 92:535–49. (https://doi.org/10.1007/s00420-018-1387-3).

Wahba, Mahmoud A. and Lawrence G. Bridwell. 1973. "Maslow Reconsidered: A Review of Research on the Need Hierarchy Theory." *Academy of Management Proceedings* 1:514–20. (https://doi.org/10.5465/ambpp.1973.4981593).
Waterman, Alan S. 1993. "Two Conceptions of Happiness: Contrasts of Personal Expressiveness (Eudaimonia) and Hedonic Enjoyment." *Journal of Personality and Social Psychology* 64(4):678–91. (https://doi.org/10.1037//0022-3514.64.4.678).
Wright, Paul H. 1978. "Toward a Theory of Friendship Based on a Conception of Self." *Human Communication Research* 4(3):196–207. (https://doi.org/10.1111/j.1468-2958.1978.tb00609.x).

CHAPTER 20

# Aging, Work, and Caregiving

## Current Knowledge and Directions for Future Research

Sarah E. Patterson and Andrew Arche

### OVERVIEW

This chapter focuses on midlife and older adults ages fifty and older, a part of the life course associated with many different and co-occurring life processes and transitions. We highlight the intersection of working and caregiving at these ages because demographic changes in health and life expectancy lead to shifting experiences of aging, work, and care. For instance, life expectancy in the U.S. is increasing over each decade and continues to increase in most other places around the world (though in the U.S. it has stagnated in recent years).[1] Currently, one out of every seven adults in the U.S. is aged sixty-five or older, but by 2040, the rate of adults ages sixty-five and older is expected to be one out of every five adults in the U.S.[2] Although we mainly focus on the U.S., we also consider rates of caregiving and work among mid- and later-life adults internationally in order to understand the variability in experiences around the world.

Mid- and later-life older adults are extending their years of employment, including full-time work.[3] Among European countries tracked by the Organisation for Economic Co-operation and Development (OECD), on average, over half (61.4 percent) of adults ages fifty-five to sixty-four are employed, with the U.S. falling at about average with 63.7 percent of adults ages fifty-five to sixty-five being employed.[4] Although traditionally, most older adults are expected to retire from employment around age sixty-five,[5] these trends are shifting as older adults have started to participate in other forms of "retirement." These can include gradual retirement, where an older adult may take a "bridge job" or a new job after retiring from the job they worked in for a long career; phased retirement, which includes continuing to work for the same employer but part-time; or "unretirement," where an older adult returns to work in a full capacity after formally retiring.[6] (See also chapters 21 and 22.)

Rates of caregiving generally increase with age and rates of providing family care are highest among middle- and older-age adults.[7,8] In Europe, providing any care to another family member or friend is high among younger adults, who are mostly caring for children, but rises again in midlife (between ages fifty and sixty-five), when caregiving for other family members, including aging parents, spouses or partners, and adult children, increases.[9] In the U.S., two-thirds of family caregivers are sixty years or older.[10]

As older adults extend their years of employment, and rates of caregiving naturally increase during mid- and later life, aging adults may increase their chances of having dual work and caregiver roles. Caregivers often work at similar rates compared to non-caregivers in the U.S. (54.6 percent versus 64.4 percent, respectively).[11] Balancing mid-to-later-life care and work responsibilities may have varying consequences for older worker outcomes compared to their younger counterparts. For instance, although a review of the literature finds few effects on employment from caregiving, these studies often include adults across the life course.[12] When focusing on middle age and older adults in the U.S., providing high rates of time and financial transfers to aging parents is associated with retiring early,[13] and among fully retired older adults ages sixty-two and older, providing care for a spouse is associated with a reduction in the likelihood of unretirement or returning to work after retirement.[14]

## VARIATIONS IN TYPES OF CAREGIVING ROLES IN MID- TO LATER LIFE

The types of care that mid- and later-life adults provide to their family members vary and can have unequal influence on work patterns depending on who the caregiver is in relation to who is being cared for. Among adults ages fifty and older, partners and spouses are often the frontline caregivers, but adult children are the second most common provider of care.[15] Grandchild care is a common form of care provided by mid-to-later-life adults compared to younger counterparts, especially as life expectancy is extended and family members remain alive for longer periods of other family members' lives.[16] Mid-to-later-life adults are also more likely to be "sandwiched" between the activities of caregiving for someone else, or multiple people, and work, creating an even more complex balancing act between work and care responsibilities.[17]

Who receives care is also associated with the type and timing of care needs provided.[18] The broadest type of care that mid-to-later-life adults may provide includes "transfers" to other family members or friends; these types of exchanges are also most common because they are typically what most population level surveys track. Transfers can include general time spent helping with needs, financial transfers or loans, and providing emotional support.[19] Other more specific tasks that caregivers may provide include helping with household activities (e.g., paying bills, helping with laundry; also referred to as instrumental activities of daily living or "IADLs") and helping with personal care activities (e.g., bathing or dressing) and mobility (together, these two categories are more commonly referred to as activities of daily living or "ADLs") that are fundamental for living independently.[20]

Among nonmedical roles and functions, a family caregiver may serve as an "attendant," helping the care receiver with self-care, giving administrative help with IADLs, providing companionship and emotional support, or serving as a driver or facilitating transportation. Medical roles and functions may be more complex, ranging from advocating for the care receiver to providing direct medical care.[21] Stopping and starting, or transitioning into and out of care, may be more common than long bouts of care, depending on the care receiver and other care characteristics,[22,23] but few surveys track trends in care over the life course.

The person receiving care and the type of care matter for the worker's ability to balance responsibilities. For instance, in a nationally representative study of British midlife adults (ages fifty and fifty-five), providing more personal care for a parent figure and a higher number of hours of any care are both associated with exiting employment.[24] More broadly, among European adults ages fifty to seventy, providing daily care for an older adult—a parent, parent-in-law, stepparent, or grandparent—is associated with a reduction in both the likelihood of employment and the number of work hours. In contrast, providing care weekly or even less frequently than weekly is not associated with employment status.[25] Being the primary caregiver reduces the likelihood of working but does not have the same effect for secondary caregivers,[26] and greater intensity of care is associated with lower rates of work overall.[27] Thus, it is important that studies include both aspects of the care provided as well as specifics about work in order to fully capture how mid- and later-life adults are balancing both responsibilities.

## COSTS AND BENEFITS OF BALANCING CARE AND WORK

Providing family care is associated with high financial costs for caregivers. On average, informal care in the U.S. is valued at $412 billion annually; that number rises to $522 billion when accounting for caregivers who are sixty-five and older.[28] Some direct estimates of care provided by family members show that, for instance, in the UK, a woman in her midfifties spends around $164,726 on caregiving over two years, which is roughly the equivalent of two years in a retirement home.[29] Working caregivers also have lower wages than non-caregivers, but this may be due in part to the need for flexibility in their work.[30] Whatever the impetus for working in low-wage work, however, aging caregivers may need to work longer into the life course to gain financial stability for their own aging needs.

In addition to direct financial costs of care, there are indirect "opportunity costs" that may be incurred from providing care during mid- and later life, including forgoing other activities like work or leisure. Generally, caregiving has a negative effect on employment, and the more caregiving one does, the more likely the effects on work are to be negative; however, it can depend on the worker's age. As an example, an employed caregiver aged fifty who is balancing care for an aging parent alongside helping an adult child may incur more direct and opportunity costs to their career and financial security compared to a retired individual aged sixty-five with the same care responsibilities. For instance, in the UK, caregivers ages fifty to sixty-four are at the highest risk of leaving the workplace,[31] and both men and women who provide high-intensity care in Canada are more likely to retire before sixty-five compared to working caregivers who give low amounts of care.[32] In an attempt to balance their own financial needs and providing care, older workers may seek part-time employment; however, availability of and support for part-time work are limited as often these jobs suffer from a lack of stability and benefits.[33] Caregivers who spend more than twenty hours a week caring may retire early or even exit the workforce completely.[34]

Another type of cost to workers providing care can be the toll on their mental and physical well-being from managing dual roles alongside their own aging processes. Combining work and care may lead to positive emotional outcomes for the care provider, including providing a sense of purpose or strengthening the relationship with the care receiver, but a majority of the literature finds negative effects on mental well-being from providing care. For instance, providing care can have negative implications for mental health, including higher levels of depression or difficulty,[35,36] and older caregivers report fewer positive outcomes from providing care compared to younger caregivers.[37] Working caregivers have higher levels of emotional stress, and the negative effects persist the longer they spend combining roles.[38]

Combining caregiving and work can also affect the physical well-being of caregivers, yet a majority of the literature focuses on mental health outcomes, with little understanding of direct physical health outcomes.[39] It may be difficult to tease apart physical effects from mental health effects as they often go hand in hand, and rates of physical disability increase with age, making it more difficult to pinpoint causal effects.[40] Recent scholarship on European adults aged fifty and older finds that transitioning into a care role, where one provides intense personal care for a spouse, is associated with negative effects on physical health (defined in this study as "frailty") for both men and women.[41] Importantly, retirees who provide caregiving have less frailty than employed older adults who do so, and though not explicitly tested in this article, the results suggest that work and care can be intertwined in their influence on an older adult's health outcomes.

## GENDER AND THE DYNAMICS OF CAREGIVING

The gender dynamics of caregiving start to shift around middle age with a higher percentage of men providing care to family members compared to younger men; additionally, caregiving rates among mid- and later-life adults start to look alike for men and women, depending on the type of care assessed. Even though rates become similar among older adults, women are more likely than men in middle age to be caregiving for two or more family members,[42] and these gendered patterns are found across a variety of countries.[43,44] In the U.S., specifically, mid- and later-life adults are staying in the labor force longer at the same time that they are increasing their rates of care.

Care rates among mid-to-later-life adults are associated with work patterns that vary by gender. Women who provide care are more likely to be retired or not working, but women today continue higher rates of care even when employed than previous cohorts of women.[45] Patterns by gender vary by location. For instance, among middle-age women in Australia, transitions into care roles are not associated with being employed, in that less time in paid labor is not associated with increasing rates of care; however, increasing rates of care are later associated with declines in employment even after accounting for sociodemographic and health characteristics.[46] Even if not leaving the labor force completely, midlife women who provide caregiving, especially help with personal care or household tasks, reduce the hours they work. If they are providing a lot of care, they reduce their work hours by as much as ten hours per week, or five hundred hours per year.[47]

Gendered patterns in employment also vary by care characteristics. For instance, in Canada, high-intensity caregivers, those who provide fifteen hours or more of care, are more likely to be fully retired compared to other caregivers, with similar rates for fully retired men (45 percent) and women (46 percent). However, men who give low-intensity care are more likely to return to work compared to women.[48] Among British midlife adults, more intense care tasks are associated with fewer work hours for men, but not for women.[49] Combining multiple care roles with work may compound effects on employment. Women providing sandwiched care, between an adult and a grandchild, are more likely to work part-time or not at all compared to men.[50]

Caregiving is an underexplored mechanism in the association between gender and uneven work outcomes seen among mid- and later-life adults. Women provide care earlier and more often throughout the life course,[51] which has consequences for their own aging and long-term outcomes. Providing care earlier in the life course is associated with lower household income, which further disadvantages women down the line.[52] Women over the age of sixty-two who assume the role of a caregiver for a frail parent are unlikely to return to the labor force once caregiving is over, and these women are also less likely to receive full-time job offers in the future.[53] Women are also unlikely to find a flexible work schedule (such as part-time) to help them with their caring, thus compromising their ability to return to the workforce.[54] In addition, baby boom generation women providing caregiving earn less on average than their male counterparts.[55] All of these different outcomes taken together—the ability to remain in the labor force, the ability to work part-time if needed, and wages—can unevenly affect women's own aging needs in mid- and later life.

The ability to juggle work and care responsibilities can also have unequal financial and health consequences for men and women. Female caregivers who lack financial stability experience greater rates of declining mental health compared to well-off counterparts.[56] Mid- and later-life (ages fifty to seventy) daughters who provide caregiving to parents have higher rates of depression when the parent is in poor health compared to those with healthy parents; sons, however, have no significant increase in depression scores when a parent is in poor health compared to being in good health.[57] Women who provide high levels of ADL care are significantly more likely to experience emotional burden, compared to caregivers who provide low levels of ADL care.[58]

Although women comprise a large portion of caregivers across the life course, the proportion of men providing care increases over the life course.[59] Because research on older men providing care at later life stages is nascent, research on men's care patterns at other points in the life course can provide insights. In a study of adults younger than age fifty who provide care, men who are responsible for double-duty caregiving—that is, who work in the care industry as well as provide care for an aging parent—are likely to report a higher incidence of emotional burnout but less primary stress and higher job satisfaction with more control over their schedules.[60] In contrast, Cook et al. have found that among adults who provide high monthly hours of care, men are significantly more likely than women to experience emotional burden whereas women are more likely to experience positive emotions.[61]

## THE CAREGIVING EXPERIENCE VARIES BY RACE AND ETHNICITY

In the U.S., the proportion of racially and ethnically diverse Americans over age sixty-five is increasing over time.[62] Although non-Hispanic white adults are the majority of caregivers, often this is a by-product of the racial composition of the U.S. as well as the samples within surveys. Our understanding of how rate and patterns of balancing care vary by race and ethnicity is emerging (we address the lack of research on work, race/ethnicity, and care in the future research section). Although some studies find few differences in care rates by race and ethnicity,[63] a majority of scholarship does find variability. For instance, black female caregivers are significantly more likely than white female caregivers to provide more hours giving intense IADL and ADL care, although there is no significant difference in high IADL caring between white and Hispanic women.[64] As for men, caregivers who are either black or Hispanic are significantly more likely to provide high rates of IADL care compared to white men who provide care.[65] Among older adults needing care, black older adults were more likely to be lacking a caregiver compared to white older adults, while Hispanic older adults were less likely to have no caregiver compared to white older adults. Further, Hispanic older adults are more likely to receive help from a spouse or other family member, with their care coming from many sources compared to whites.[66] Among the limited data available on American Indians, in a study of more than five thousand American Indian adults residing on two Lakota Sioux reservations in the Northern Plains and one community in the Southwest, while some general patterns of care persist (e.g., women are more likely to provide care than men), important cultural differences emerge, like the importance of cultural identity and traditional healing practices in the caregiving relationship.[67]

Different ethnic groups may experience caregiving in different ways. White caregivers who provide both many hours per month and high levels of help with ADLs report more negative emotional burden relative to black caregivers, who are more likely to report positive emotions.[68] A majority of studies that focus on work, care, and racial/ethnic differences use smaller, focused methods. In an interview with employees ages thirty and older, at the University of California, Berkeley, white, Asian, and Hispanic employees reported higher levels of role strain compared to black employees.[69]

## SOCIAL, ECONOMIC, AND GEOGRAPHIC CONTEXT AND WORK-CARE BALANCE

Socioeconomic status may be another important dimension to aid our understanding of work and care patterns and the degree to which they balance. Women with lower socioeconomic status are more likely to be informal caregivers than those who have wealth.[70] Providing care can have negative implications for one's own financial well-being. Adults who provide care more than twenty hours per week are 25 percent more likely to live in poverty, 27 percent more likely to receive public assistance, and 46 percent more likely to receive Medicaid up to eight years following the caregiving experience.[71] Importantly, caregiving in tandem with work may perpetuate a vicious cycle of high-intensity caregiving and low income among older adults, who are particularly vulnerable due to their own aging and retirement needs.

Another socioeconomic dimension along which balancing care and work may vary for older adults is by rural and urban locations. Rural areas tend to be smaller in population and may have less access to resources and supports like hospitals or formal care help. Rural caregivers who work give five fewer hours of care per week compared to urban caregivers.[72] Urban and rural caregivers ages fifty-five and older report more physical barriers than younger caregivers do. Rural caregivers are more likely than their urban counterparts to report difficulty owing to providing care.[73]

## SUPPORTS FOR WORKING CAREGIVERS

In order to talk about supports for working caregivers, we must first address social norms of care, which have the potential to influence social policies and the supports available to working caregivers. Generally, there are strong norms for the family to serve as the main caretakers of other family members, and this norm is especially strong in the U.S. where families rather than outside institutional help (e.g., government or private providers) are expected to take on caregiving responsibilities for aging family members. Although many feel that family members should provide care for other members, attitudes toward supports for those balancing care and work are mixed. In a nationally representative U.S. study about attitudes toward various policy solutions for family members caring for an ill or disabled member, Americans were most supportive of providing tax credits for caregivers, followed by time off from work. The least supported measure was direct payment to caregivers.[74] These attitudes translate to patterns of care and work. In a study of twenty-one European countries, women in nations with stronger norms of family care were less likely to remain attached to the labor force when balancing care responsibilities, whereas women in nations with weaker "family as caregiver" norms were more likely to do so.[75]

Supports for working caregivers can take on a variety of forms, including both private (e.g., employer-based) and public (i.e., national or state policy-based) solutions. The rates at which working caregivers have access to these policies, however, is generally mixed. In the UK, about half of employees report that their workplace has a flexible working arrangement and 83 percent of employers say they offer flexible work.[76] The United States in particular does not have a federal system that supports caregivers[77] and lags behind other nation-states in terms of available programs for caregivers.[78] Formal paid leave would benefit older workers who are balancing providing care, but current policy is usually unpaid.[79]

The Family and Medical Leave Act (FMLA) is one policy in the U.S. available to some caregivers. With up to twelve weeks of unpaid leave available, workers can provide care for a child or ill adult. There is no national policy for paid leave. However, national legislation for *paid* leave—through the Family and Medical Insurance Leave Act, an addendum to FMLA—is being considered,[80] and some states including California, New Jersey, Rhode Island, New York, and Washington have or will implement paid leave for caregivers. These policies allow family caregivers up to six weeks paid leave per year. California was the first state to implement the program in 2004. The California Paid Family Leave Program (CA-PFL) replaced 55 percent of a worker's weekly earnings up to a maximum benefit of $1,216 per week in 2018. Analysis of the outcome of the program for middle-age women who work and provide care shows that the likelihood of continuing work increased with the CA-PFL but only among caregivers who were early middle aged, near poor, and who had the highest level of education.[81]

The U.S. Congress passed the Recognize, Assist, Include, Support, and Engage (RAISE) Family Caregivers Act in 2018 in order to establish a national strategy to acknowledge and assist family caregivers. This legislation is aimed at developing policy initiatives, infrastructure, and programming for family caregivers. State-level responses have ranged from eliminating Medicaid wait lists for home- and community-based services for older adults in Tennessee to providing grants to nonprofits in the community in Minnesota.[82]

Workplace supports may matter more for particular groups of workers, including older adults, women, and part-time workers, who may be more likely to be in precarious work situations and more vulnerable to negative outcomes from balancing work and care. Often supports for working caregivers vary widely depending on the position of the worker within the employment hierarchy.[83] Urban caregivers have more access to workplace benefits than rural caregivers, including the ability to telecommute (24.9 percent versus 9.7 percent), have access to support programs (25.8 percent versus 15.2 percent), and have paid leave (34.1 percent versus 17.7 percent).[84]

Support for working caregivers can also come from colleagues or family. A study of employed caregivers in fifty different organizations in the Netherlands shows that caregivers who feel supported—by colleagues and supervisors—are more likely to report positive work outcomes.[85] Working caregivers who receive informal support from family and friends have better outcomes compared to caregivers who do not feel supported.[86] Caregivers may also receive support from other family members, including financial support.[87] This informal support may be just as important for working caregivers' outcomes as formal policies.

A lack of supports for working caregivers costs about $29 million annually in lost productivity in the U.S., and caregivers themselves spend over $2,000 on "unreimbursed out-of-pocket expenses associated with caregiving."[88] Families may choose to give informal care because they are unable to find formal services, lack knowledge of how to access them, and lack knowledge of eligibility. Many caregivers report unreliable services, poor planning and organization on the program's end, insignificant visits (in that they were too short), a lack of having enough volunteers, a lack of compensation, and reduced support for employment and transport.[89]

## FUTURE RESEARCH ON FAMILY CAREGIVING BY OLDER WORKERS

Mid-to-later-life adults who are providing care are also balancing their own aging and well-being while they balance both work and care responsibilities. (See also chapter 19.) This is an important topic as aging adults continue on in the labor force for longer periods at the exact same time that their rates of caregiving increase in the life course. There is a rich and robust set of literature on the topic of work and caregiving, but through our review, we identify some areas of potential future research to better understand the experience of mid- and later-life workers, specifically, who are also providing care for family members or friends. We focus on both substantive topics as well as methodological advances that can be made.

Considering that mid- to later life is an important life course transition in and of itself, whether workers are deciding to retire or remain in the workforce has important implications for the working caregiver as well as for those who may receive care from them. A majority of the research focuses on coarse measures of work characteristics, like being employed at all and the number of hours of work. This gives us some insights; however, it is currently unclear from the literature how more nuanced aspects of the workplace influence the balance of work and care, or even the decision to remain at (or even increase) work despite or in light of care responsibilities. This could include aspects like the flexibility to leave work if a family caregiving emergency arises, or perceptions of coworkers' support for balancing work and care.

Another example of this gap in the literature surrounds the type of workers we study and the lack of detailed aspects of their work life. For instance, working in the nursing industry alongside providing "sandwiched care" between an adult and child may create "triple duty" for some older adults where they are providing care in multiple locations across the day for multiple people at work and at home.[90] Yet we have little information on the intensity of some work aspects, like care duties, and the direct effect on the ability to manage care duties at home. In addition, a majority of our current knowledge of balancing work and care often focuses on professional workers, with less understanding about lower-wage workers or workers who may be balancing heavy "care" work like retail jobs or teaching, alongside providing care at home, or those who have labor-intensive work like construction or manufacturing that is bounded by typical work hours. In addition, with the rise in precarious work, like contract and temporary work (e.g., Uber driving), we know very little about how these jobs, with potentially more flexibility but also more precarity, allow or do not allow people to balance care and work responsibilities. (See also chapter 5.) Professional workers tend to be more advantaged in their access to supports, so this is a major oversight in our knowledge of how workers achieve balance. This is also important because although the rates of employed caregivers are similar in both blue- and white-collar jobs, working women who provide care are more likely to be in service jobs than men.[91]

Taking it one step further, more research should focus on the balance between these decisions and factors that caregivers take into consideration when making a decision, such as whether they account for their aging needs and financial well-being. For instance, if working caregivers have only been in the labor force a short time and therefore would not have built up enough savings to retire, they may continue working alongside caring, or if they leave the labor force to care, this may affect their own well-being down the line. Similarly, we also currently have little detailed information about transitions into and out of care and work roles. Transitions into caregiving can affect well-being; yet, due to limitations in availability of longitudinal data, we also have to rely on loose measurement of these transitions, often based on the waves of data collected. Newer work suggests that the transitions into and out of care roles can affect physical well-being outcomes,[92] highlighting the importance of understanding transitions of these roles especially as they become more complex with newer types of work status like *un*retirement.

These gaps regarding care, work, and transitional information in the substantive literature also point to methodological gaps. One limitation of current population-level surveys is that they often focus mainly on one aspect, either work or caregiving, and few surveys inquire about why respondents have made a change in one arena or the other. Considering that caregiving is a large part of working-age adults' lives, surveys should strive to provide detailed information about *both* care and work responsibilities, as well as other factors regarding the working caregiver's own future. Currently, qualitative work is able to fill many of these knowledge gaps by providing insights into the specific details and work and care characteristics that some population-level datasets cannot.

Future research could also better integrate information about men's changing caregiving and work balance, especially among older men who are more likely than their younger counterparts to report caregiving. Although there is a growing set of literature on men's caregiving in general, we find few studies that focus on the effect of caregiving on men's potential early retirement or later financial burden. Similarly, as women enter and remain in the labor force longer and at older ages, it is important to understand how the changing nature of their employment is or is not associated with caregiving and related outcomes. Future research could investigate how providing for one person, compared to multiple people (multigenerational or sandwiched care) may compound combining work and care, especially "newer" forms of care like grandchild care. This is especially important with respect to gender as women are more likely to care for multiple family members over the life course.

More research should strive to gain insight into patterns of care and work among diverse populations. The bulk of our current knowledge about caregiving and work among middle- and later-life adults focuses on white, non-Hispanic samples, and among studies that do include other racial and ethnic populations, a majority of the scholarship on care does not dive into issues of balancing work and care responsibilities specifically. (See also chapter 6.) As the aging U.S. population becomes increasingly diverse, it is important to understand group variation in care and work patterns. To this end, more work on American Indians, immigrants, and other groups should be done. As an example, in a study of Pueblo caregivers, qualitative work is leveraged to craft measures that show how Pueblo caregivers define "caregiving burden" differently from the way most research does.[93] Qualitative work can dive deep into smaller, hidden populations that may be missed in large population-level datasets, but this is an opportunity for population scientists to work to understand caregiving from perspectives previously difficult to measure.

Furthermore, the LGBT+ population is a growing proportion of both the aging and caregiving population; both groups may face a different set of issues when making work and care decisions. This is an emerging field of study. For instance, in recent qualitative work among midlife gay men and lesbian women, intergenerational relationships with other family members are characterized by diverse experiences of support, strain, and ambivalence.[94] As another example, in a qualitative study of transgender older adults in Canada, although the respondents had a diverse set of experiences of aging, one of the main concerns that emerged was the lack of support from families and community members. Respondents felt a connection within the LGBT+ community but felt as if transgender people were not welcome in broader community spaces.[95] Overall, more studies should be conducted in order to better understand experiences of balancing care and work among mid- and later-life LGBT+ adults.

Finally, more research should focus on supports used, as well as desired, by working caregivers at both home and work. It is critical to understand which provisions for working caregivers are most successful. The current literature suggests that it is informal supports, like feeling supported by coworkers or family, that have greater influence on caregiver outcomes compared to more formal programs that may be hard to access; however, these outcomes may be moderated by other caregiver characteristics. For instance, support from family and friends is associated with better health for black caregivers who care for someone with dementia, but formal support utilization is associated with worse health for Mexican Americans who provide care for an older adult with dementia.[96] Even when policies are implemented, some programs lack sufficient resources to fully support caregivers, so future research should also focus on the tipping point of when and how programs can be fruitful. Future research should also directly address how policies and solutions have unequal results for different groups, including those differing by gender, race/ethnicity, and citizenship, as well as occupation and industry.[97] In addition, countries offer various programs and solutions for helping caregivers balance work and care, but this makes it difficult to track down what has been done and to compare outcomes.[98]

Overall, we need a better understanding of mid- and later-life workers who balance care in the grand scheme of their entire life course and the effect of dual responsibilities on aging and well-being, particularly among diverse populations.[99] Taking a life course perspective will advance our understanding of any association between earlier life experiences of aging, work, and caregiving and mid- and later-life balancing of care and work, as well as how mid- and later-life specific transitions, like retirement or losing a spouse, are associated with work and care patterns. Through identifying and researching these topics and issues, we can better create support networks and policies that benefit working caregivers and those who receive care from them.

## NOTES

Acknowledgments: Thank you to Vicki Freedman for comments. This work was supported by a National Institute on Aging of the National Institutes of Health Postdoctoral Traineeship (T32AG000221). The content is solely the responsibility of the authors and does not necessarily represent the official views of the National Institutes of Health.

1. World Bank. N.d. "Life Expectancy at Birth, Total (Years)." Retrieved March 1, 2020 (https://data.worldbank.org/indicator/SP.DYN.LE00.IN).
2. Administration on Aging. April 2017. "Profile of Older Americans." Administration for Community Living:3–4. (https://acl.gov/sites/default/files/Aging%20and%20Disability%20in%20America/2017OlderAmericansProfile.pdf).
3. U.S. Bureau of Labor Statistics. 2008. "More Seniors Working Full Time." *TED: Economics Daily*. Retrieved March 1, 2020 (https://www.bls.gov/opub/ted/2008/aug/wk1/art03.htm).
4. Organisation for Economic Co-operation and Development (OECD). 2019. "Employment Rate by Age Group." Retrieved March 1, 2020 (https://data.oecd.org/emp/employment-rate-by-age-group.htm).
5. Nancy Morrow-Howell et al. January 2015. "Increasing Productive Engagement in Later Life." Grand Challenges for Social Work Initiative. (https://openscholarship.wustl.edu/cgi/viewcontent.cgi?article=1784&context=csd_research).
6. Fengyan Tang, Eunhee Choi, and Rachel Goode. 2013. "Older Americans Employment and Retirement." *Ageing International* 38(1):84. (https://doi.org/10.1007/s12126-012-9162-3).
7. Alison Dixley, Rachel Boughey, and Alison Herrington. September 2019. "Informal Carers and Employment: Summary Report of a Systematic Review," 9. (https://dera.ioe.ac.uk/34161/1/Informal_Carers_and_Employment.pdf).
8. Sarah E. Patterson and Rachel Margolis. 2019. "The Demography of Multigenerational Caregiving: A Critical Aspect of the Gendered Life Course." *Socius: Sociological Research for a Dynamic World* 5:6. (https://doi.org/10.1177/2378023119862737).
9. Patterson and Margolis, "Demography of Multigenerational Caregiving," 9.
10. Vicki A. Freedman and Jennifer L. Wolff. Forthcoming. "The Changing Landscape of Family Caregiving in the United States." In *Caregiving Leave*, edited by Isabelle Sawhill and Betsey Stevenson. Washington, DC: AEI/Bookings.
11. Freedman and Wolff, "Changing Landscape of Family Caregiving."
12. Meredith B. Lilly, Audrey Laporte, and Peter C. Coyte. 2007. "Labor Market Work and Home Care's Unpaid Caregivers: A Systematic Review of Labor Force Participation Rates, Predictors of Labor Market Withdrawal, and Hours of Work." *Milbank Quarterly* 85(4):646–48. (https://doi.org/10.1016/j.jhealeco.2010.08.007).
13. Rachel R. Stoiko and JoNell Strough. 2019. "His and Her Retirement: Effects of Gender and Familial Caregiving Profiles on Retirement Timing." *International Journal of Aging and Human Development* 89(2):146. (https://doi.org/10.1177/0091415018780009).
14. Ernest Gonzales, Yeonjung Lee, and Celeste Brown. 2017. "Back to Work? Not Everyone. Examining the Longitudinal Relationships between Informal Caregiving and Paid Work after Formal Retirement." *Journals of Gerontology, Series B: Psychological Sciences and Social Sciences* 72(3):534–36. (https://doi.org/10.1093/geronb/gbv095).
15. Jennifer L. Wolff et al. 2016. "A National Profile of Family and Unpaid Caregivers Who Assist Older Adults with Health Care Activities." *JAMA Internal Medicine* 176(3):377. (https://doi.org/10.1001/jamainternmed.2015.7664).
16. Athina Vlachantoni et al. February 2019. "Caught in the Middle in Mid-life: Provision of Care across Multiple Generations." *Ageing & Society*:17–18. (https://doi.org/10.1017/S0144686X19000047).
17. Denys Dukhovnov and Emilio Zagheni. 2015. "Who Takes Care of Whom in the United States? Time Transfers by Age and Sex." *Population and Development Review* 41(2):202–4. (https://doi.org/10.1111/j.1728-4457.2015.00044.x).
18. Freedman and Wolff, "Changing Landscape of Family Caregiving."

19. Patterson and Margolis, "Demography of Multigenerational Caregiving," 3.

20. Freedman and Wolff, "Changing Landscape of Family Caregiving."

21. Freedman and Wolff, "Changing Landscape of Family Caregiving."

22. Janneke Berecki-Gisolf et al. 2008. "Transitions into Informal Caregiving and out of Paid Employment of Women in Their 50s." *Social Science and Medicine* 67(1):126. (https://doi.org/10.1016/j.socscimed.2008.03.031).

23. Freedman and Wolff, "Changing Landscape of Family Caregiving."

24. Madelin Gomez-Leon et al. 2019. "The Dynamics of Social Care and Employment in Midlife." *Ageing & Society* 39(2):398. (https://doi.org/10.1017/S0144686X17000964).

25. Nicola Ciccarelli and Arthur Van Soest. 2018. "Informal Caregiving, Employment Status and Work Hours of the 50+ Population in Europe." *De Economist* 166(3):384. (https://doi.org/10.1007/s10645-018-9323-1).

26. Ha Trong Nguyen and Luke Brian Connelly. January 2014. "The Effect of Unpaid Caregiving Intensity on Labour Force Participation: Results from a Multinomial Endogenous Treatment Model." *Social Science and Medicine* 100:120. (https://doi.org/10.1016/j.socscimed.2013.10.031).

27. Meredith B. Lilly, Audrey Laporte, and Peter C. Coyte. 2010. "Do They Care Too Much to Work? The Influence of Caregiving Intensity on the Labour Force Participation of Unpaid Caregivers in Canada." *Journal of Health Economics* 29(6):900. (https://doi.org/10.1016/j.jhealeco.2010.08.007).

28. Amalavoyal V. Chari et al. 2015. "The Opportunity Costs of Informal Elder-care in the United States: New Estimates from the American Time Use Survey." *Health Services Research* 50(3):877. (https://doi.org/10.1111/1475-6773.12238).

29. Meghan M. Skira. 2015. "Dynamic Wage and Employment Effects of Elder Patient Care." *International Economic Review* 56(1):89. (https://doi.org/10.1111/iere.12095).

30. Berecki-Gisolf et al., "Transitions into Informal Caregiving," 125.

31. Caroline Glendinning et al. 2009. "Care Provision within Families and Its Socio-economic Impact on Care Providers across the European Union." University of York, Social Policy Research Unit, Heslington, York, UK.

32. Josephine C. Jacobs et al. February 2014. "Caregiving Intensity and Retirement Status in Canada." *Social Science and Medicine* 102:80. (https://doi.org/10.1016/j.socscimed.2013.11.051).

33. Nancy Morrow-Howell, Ernest Gonzales, and Christina Matz-Costa. September 2016. "Policy Recommendations for Meeting the Grand Challenge to Advance Long and Productive Lives." Grand Challenges for Social Work Initiative:1–2. (https://openscholarship.wustl.edu/cgi/viewcontent.cgi?article=1784&context=csd_research).

34. Margaret M. Moussa. 2019. "The Relationship Between Elder Care-giving and Labor Force Participation in the Context of Policies Addressing Population Ageing: A Review of Empirical Studies Published between 2006 and 2016." *Ageing & Society* 39(6):1305. (https://doi.org/10.1017/S0144686X18000053).

35. Judith Bom et al. 2019. "The Impact of Informal Caregiving for Older Adults on the Health of Various Types of Caregivers: A Systematic Review." *The Gerontologist* 59(5):e629–42. (https://doi.org/10.1093/geront/gny137).

36. I-Fen Lin, Holly R. Fee, and Hsueh-Scheng Wu. 2012. "Negative and Positive Caregiving Experience: A Closer Look at the Intersection of Gender and Relationship." *Family Relations* 61(2):343–58. (https://doi.org/10.1111/j.1741-3729.2011.00692.x).

37. Sarah K. Cook, Lauren Snellings, and Steven A. Cohen. 2018. "Socioeconomic and Demographic Factors Modify Observed Relationship between Caregiving Intensity and Three Dimensions of Quality of Life in Informal Adult Children Caregivers." *Health and Quality of Life Outcomes* 16(169):8. (https://doi.org/10.1186/s12955-018-0996-6).

38. Margaret L. Longcare et al. 2017. "Work Impact and Emotional Stress among Informal Caregivers for Older Adults." *Journals of Gerontology, Series B: Psychological Sciences and Social Sciences* 72(3):525–28. (https://doi.org/10.1093/geronb/gbw027).

39. Jan M. Bauer and Alfonso Sousa-Poza. 2015. "Impacts of Informal Caregiving on Caregiver Employment, Health, and Family." *Journal of Population Ageing* 8(3):129. (https://doi.org/10.1007/s12062-015-9116-0).

40. Martin Pinquart and Silvia Sörenson. 2007. "Correlates of Physical Health of Informal Caregivers: A Meta-analysis." *Journals of Gerontology, Series B: Psychological Sciences and Social Sciences* 62(2):131. (https://doi.org/10.1093/geronb/62.2.P126).

41. Damiano Uccheddu et al. 2019. "The Pains and Reliefs of the Transitions into and out of Spousal Caregiving. A Cross-national Comparison of the Health Consequences of Caregiving by Gender." *Social Science and Medicine* 240:6. (https://doi.org/10.1016/j.socscimed.2019.112517).

42. Patterson and Margolis, "Demography of Multigenerational Caregiving," 6.

43. Dukhovnov and Zagheni, "Who Takes Care of Whom," 204.

44. Patterson and Margolis, "Demography of Multigenerational Caregiving," 10.

45. Eliza K. Pavalko and Joseph D. Wolfe. 2016a. "Do Women Still Care? Cohort Changes in US Women's Care for the Ill or Disabled." *Social Forces* 94(3):1373. (https://doi.org/10.1093/sf/sov101).

46. Berecki-Gisolf et al., "Transitions into Informal Caregiving," 125–26.

47. Courtney H. Van Houtven, Norma B. Coe, and Meghan M. Skira. 2013. "The Effect of Informal Care on Work and Wages." *Journal of Health Economics* 32(1):249. (https://doi.org/10.1016/j.jhealeco.2012.10.006).

48. Jacobs et al., "Caregiving Intensity and Retirement Status," 78.

49. Gomez-Leon et al., "Dynamics of Social Care and Employment," 398–99.

50. Vlachantoni et al., "Caught in the Middle in Mid-life," 19.

51. Patterson and Margolis, "Demography of Multigenerational Caregiving," 6–10.

52. Lee et al., "Vicious Cycle of Parental Caregiving," 428–29.

53. Skira, "Dynamic Wage and Employment Effects," 87–89.

54. Skira, "Dynamic Wage and Employment Effects," 64.

55. Rebecca Glauber. 2019. "The Wage Penalty for Parental Caregiving: Has It Declined over Time?" *Journal of Marriage and Family* 81(2):424. (https://doi.org/10.1111/jomf.12555).

56. Chizuko Wakabayashi and Katherine M. Donato. 2006. "Does Caregiving Increase Poverty among Women in Later Life? Evidence from the Health and Retirement Survey." *Journal of Health and Social Behavior* 47(3):266–67. (https://doi.org/10.1177/002214650604700305).

57. Dörte Heger. 2017. "The Mental Health of Children Providing Care to Their Elderly Parent." *Health Economics*, 26(12):1622. (https://doi.org/10.1002/hec.3457).

58. Cook et al., "Socioeconomic and Demographic Factors," 8.

59. Patterson and Margolis, "Demography of Multigenerational Caregiving," 6–9.

60. Nicole DePasquale et al. 2018. "Double- and Triple-duty Caregiving Men: An Examination of Subjective Stress and Perceived Schedule Control." *Journal of Applied Gerontology* 37(4): 474–78. (https://doi.org/10.1177/0733464816641391).

61. Cook et al., "Socioeconomic and Demographic Factors," 8.

62. Administration on Aging, "Profile of Older Americans," 5.

63. Eliza K. Pavalko and Joseph D. Wolfe. 2016b. "Unpaid Care Work." Pp. 181–203 in *Gerontology: Changes, Challenges, and Solutions*, edited by Madonna Harrington Meyer and Elizabeth A. Daniele. Santa Barbara, CA: Praeger.

64. Steven A. Cohen et al. 2019. "Differences within Differences: Gender Inequalities in Caregiving Intensity Vary by Race and Ethnicity in Informal Caregivers." *Journal of Cross-Cultural Gerontology* 34:252. (https://doi.org/10.1007/s10823-019-09381-9).

65. Cohen et al., "Differences within Differences," 252.

66. Terry Y. Lum. 2005. "Understanding the Racial and Ethnic Differences in Caregiving Arrangements." *Journal of Gerontological Social Work* 45(4):14. (https://doi.org/10.1300/J083v45n04).

67. R. Turner Goins et al. 2011. "Adult Caregiving among American Indians: The Role of Cultural Factors." *The Gerontologist* 51(3):314–18. (https://doi.org/10.1093/geront/gnq101).

68. Cook et al., "Socioeconomic and Demographic Factors," 8.

69. Karen I. Fredriksen-Goldsen and Nancy Farwell. 2005. "Dual Responsibilities among Black, Hispanic, Asian, and White Employed Caregivers." *Journal of Gerontological Social Work* 43(4):35. (https://doi.org/10.1300/J083v43n04).

70. Yeonjung Lee et al. 2015. "The Vicious Cycle of Parental Caregiving and Financial Well-being: A Longitudinal Study of Women." *Journals of Gerontology, Series B: Psychological Sciences and Social Sciences* 70(3):429. (https://doi.org/10.1093/geronb/gbu001).

71. Wakabayashi and Donato, "Does Caregiving Increase Poverty," 268.

72. Carrie Henning-Smith and Megan Lahr. 2019. "Rural-urban Difference in Workplace Supports and Impacts for Employed Caregivers." *Journal of Rural Health* 35(1):51. (https://doi.org/10.1111/jrh.12309).

73. Erin D. Bouldin et al. 2018. "Financial and Health Barriers and Caregiving-related Difficulties among Rural and Urban Caregivers." *Journal of Rural Health* 34(3):267. (https://doi.org/10.1111/jrh.12273).

74. Merril Silverstein and Tonya M. Parrott. 2001. "Attitudes toward Government Policies That Assist Informal Caregivers: The Link between Personal Troubles and Public Issues." *Research on Aging* 23(3):369. (https://doi.org/10.1177/0164027501233004).

75. Manuela Naldini, Emmanuele Pavolini, and Cristina Solera. 2016. "Female Employment and Elderly Care: The Role of Care Policies and Culture in 21 European Countries." *Work, Employment and Society* 30(4):607. (https://doi.org/10.1177/0950017015625602).

76. Carers UK. November 2012. "Sandwich Caring: Combining Childcare with Caring for Older or Disabled Relatives." Retrieved December 2019 (http://www.carersuk.org/for-professionals/policy/policy-library/sandwich-caring).

77. Charlotte Muller and Oleg Volkov. 2009. "Older Women: Work and Caregiving in Conflict? A Study of Four Countries." *Social Work in Health Care* 48(7):675. (https://doi.org/10.1080/00981380902921732).

78. Bauer and Sousa-Poza, "Impacts of Informal Caregiving," 129.

79. Morrow-Howell et al., "Policy Recommendations," 1–2.

80. National Partnership for Women & Families. February 2019. "The Family and Medical Insurance Leave Act (The FAMILY Act)." (https://www.nationalpartnership.org/our-work/resources/economic-justice/coalition/family-act-faq.pdf).

81. Ji Young Kang et al. 2019. "The Effect of California's Paid Family Leave Program on Employment among Middle-aged Female Caregivers." *The Gerontologist* 59(6):1096. (https://doi.org/10.1093/geront/gny105).

82. Jennifer Aufill, Julia Burgdorf, and Jennifer Wolff. June 2019. "In Support of Family Caregivers: A Snapshot of Five States." Milbank Memorial Fund. (https://www.milbank.org/wp-content/uploads/2019/06/MMF_Caregiver_Report_6.19.pdf).

83. Dixley et al., "Informal Carers and Employment," 9.

84. Henning-Smith and Lahr, "Rural-urban Difference," 52.

85. Inger Plaisier, Marjolein I. Broese van Groenou, and Saskia Keuzenkamp. 2015. "Combining Work and Informal Care: The Importance of Caring Organisations." *Human Resource Management Journal* 25(2):277. (https://doi.org/10.1111/1748-8583.12048).

86. Dixley et al., "Informal Carers and Employment," 14.

87. Thomas J. Durant and Ollie G. Christian. 2006. "Caregiving to Aging Parents." *Forum on Public Policy*. (https://www.forumonpublicpolicy.com/archive07/durant.pdf).

88. Durant and Christian, "Caregiving to Aging Parents," 2.

89. Nicola Brimblecombe et al. 2018. "Barriers to Receipt of Social Care Services for Working Carers and the People They Care For in Times of Austerity." *Journal of Social Policy* 47(2):227–30. (https://doi.org/10.1017/S0047279417000277).

90. DePasquale et al., "Double- and Triple-duty Caregiving Men," 467.

91. Pavalko and Wolfe, "Unpaid Care Work," 193.

92. Uccheddu et al., "Pains and Reliefs," 1–9.

93. Robert John et al. 2001. "Toward the Conceptualization and Measurement of Caregiver Burden among Pueblo Indian Family Caregivers." *The Gerontologist* 41(2):217. (https://doi.org/10.1093/geront/41.2.210).

94. Corinne Reczek. 2014. "The Intergenerational Relationships of Gay Men and Lesbian Women." *Journals of Gerontology, Series B: Psychological Sciences and Social Sciences* 69(6):915. (https://doi.org/10.1093/geronb/gbu042).

95. Celeste Pang, Gloria Gutman, and Brian de Vries. 2019. "Later Life Care Planning and Concerns of Transgender Older Adults in Canada." *International Journal of Aging and Human Development* 89(1):48. (https://doi.org/10.1177/0091415019843520).

96. Sunshine M. Rote et al. 2019. "Caregiving across Diverse Populations: New Evidence from the National Study of Caregiving and Hispanic EPESE." *Innovation in Aging* 3(2):8. (https://doi.org/10.1093/geroni/igz033).

97. Morrow-Howell et al., "Increasing Productive Engagement," 9.

98. Bauer and Sousa-Poza, "Impacts of Informal Caregiving," 129.

99. Morrow-Howell et al., "Increasing Productive Engagement," 1–2.

## REFERENCES


Administration on Aging. April 2017. "Profile of Older Americans." Administration for Community Living. (https://acl.gov/sites/default/files/Aging%20and%20Disability%20in%20America/2017OlderAmericansProfile.pdf).

Aufill, Jennifer, Julia Burgdorf, and Jennifer Wolff. June 2019. "In Support of Family Caregivers: A Snapshot of Five States." Milbank Memorial Fund. (https://www.milbank.org/wp-content/uploads/2019/06/MMF_Caregiver_Report_6.19.pdf).

Bauer, Jan M. and Alfonso Sousa-Poza. 2015. "Impacts of Informal Caregiving on Caregiver Employment, Health, and Family." *Journal of Population Ageing* 8(3):113–45. (https://doi.org/10.1007/s12062-015-9116-0).

Berecki-Gisolf, Janneke, et al. 2008. "Transitions into Informal Caregiving and out of Paid Employment of Women in Their 50s." *Social Science and Medicine* 67(1):122–27. (https://doi.org/10.1016/j.socscimed.2008.03.031).

Bom, Judith, et al. 2019. "The Impact of Informal Caregiving for Older Adults on the Health of Various Types of Caregivers: A Systematic Review." *The Gerontologist* 59(5):e629–42. (https://doi.org/10.1093/geront/gny137).

Bouldin, Erin D., et al. 2018. "Financial and Health Barriers and Caregiving-related Difficulties among Rural and Urban Caregivers." *Journal of Rural Health* 34(3):263–74. (https://doi.org/10.1111/jrh.12273).

Brimblecombe, Nicola, et al. 2018. "Barriers to Receipt of Social Care Services for Working Carers and the People They Care For in Times of Austerity." *Journal of Social Policy* 47(2):215–33. (https://doi.org/10.1017/S0047279417000277).

Carers UK. November 2012. "Sandwich Caring: Combining Childcare with Caring for Older or Disabled Relatives." Retrieved December 2019 (http://www.carersuk.org/for-professionals/policy/policy-library/sandwich-caring).

Chari, Amalavoyal V., et al. 2015. "The Opportunity Costs of Informal Elder-care in the United States: New Estimates from the American Time Use Survey." *Health Services Research* 50(3):871–82. (https://doi.org/10.1111/1475-6773.12238).

Ciccarelli, Nicola, and Arthur Van Soest. 2018. "Informal Caregiving, Employment Status and Work Hours of the 50+ Population in Europe." *De Economist* 166(3):363–96. (https://doi.org/10.1007/s10645-018-9323-1).

Cohen, Steven A., et al. 2019. "Differences within Differences: Gender Inequalities in Caregiving Intensity Vary by Race and Ethnicity in Informal Caregivers." *Journal of Cross-Cultural Gerontology* 34(3):245–63. (https://doi.org/10.1007/s10823-019-09381-9).

Cook, Sarah K., Lauren Snellings, and Steven A. Cohen. 2018. "Socioeconomic and Demographic Factors Modify Observed Relationship between Caregiving Intensity and Three Dimensions of Quality of Life in Informal Adult Children Caregivers." *Health and Quality of Life Outcomes* 16(169):1–12. (https://doi.org/10.1186/s12955-018-0996-6).

DePasquale, Nicole, et al. 2018. "Double- and Triple-duty Caregiving Men: An Examination of Subjective Stress and Perceived Schedule Control." *Journal of Applied Gerontology* 37(4):464–92. (https://doi.org/10.1177/0733464816641391).

Dixley, Alison, Rachel Boughey, and Alison Herrington. September 2019. "Informal Carers and Employment: Summary Report of a Systematic Review." (https://dera.ioe.ac.uk/34161/1/Informal_Carers_and_Employment.pdf).

Dukhovnov, Denys, and Emilio Zagheni. 2015. "Who Takes Care of Whom in the United States? Time Transfers by Age and Sex." *Population and Development Review* 41(2):183–206. (https://doi.org/10.1111/j.1728-4457.2015.00044.x).

Durant, Thomas J. and Ollie G. Christian. 2006. "Caregiving to Aging Parents." *Forum on Public Policy*. (https://www.forumonpublicpolicy.com/archive07/durant.pdf).

Fredriksen-Goldsen, Karen I. and Nancy Farwell. 2005. "Dual Responsibilities among Black, Hispanic, Asian, and White Employed Caregivers." *Journal of Gerontological Social Work* 43(4):25–44. (https://doi.org/10.1300/J083v43n04_03).

Freedman, Vicki A. and Jennifer L. Wolff. Forthcoming. "The Changing Landscape of Family Caregiving in the United States." In *Caregiving Leave*, edited by Isabelle Sawhill and Betsey Stevenson. Washington, DC: AEI/Brookings.

Glauber, Rebecca. 2019. "The Wage Penalty for Parental Caregiving: Has It Declined over Time?" *Journal of Marriage and Family* 81(2):415–33. (https://doi.org/10.1111/jomf.12555).

Glendinning, Caroline, et al. 2009. "Care Provision within Families and Its Socio-economic Impact on Care Providers across the European Union." University of York, Social Policy Research Unit, Heslington, York, UK.

Goins, R. Turner, et al. 2011. "Adult Caregiving among American Indians: The Role of Cultural Factors." *The Gerontologist* 51(3):310–20. (https://doi.org/10.1093/geront/gnq101).

Gomez-Leon, Madelin, et al. 2019. "The Dynamics of Social Care and Employment in Mid-life." *Ageing & Society* 39(2):381–408. (https://doi.org/10.1017/S0144686X17000964).

Gonzales, Ernest, Yeonjung Lee, and Celeste Brown. 2017. "Back to Work? Not Everyone. Examining the Longitudinal Relationships between Informal Caregiving and Paid Work after Formal Retirement." *Journals of Gerontology, Series B: Psychological Sciences and Social Sciences* 72(3):532–39. (https://doi.org/10.1093/geronb/gbv095).

Heger, Dörte. 2017. "The Mental Health of Children Providing Care to Their Elderly Parent." *Health Economics* 26(12):1617–29. (https://doi.org/10.1002/hec.3457).

Henning-Smith, Carrie and Megan Lahr. 2019. "Rural-urban Difference in Workplace Supports and Impacts for Employed Caregivers." *Journal of Rural Health* 35(1):49–57. (https://doi.org/10.1111/jrh.12309).

Jacobs, Josephine C., et al. February 2014. "Caregiving Intensity and Retirement Status in Canada." *Social Science and Medicine* 102:74–82. (https://doi.org/10.1016/j.socscimed.2013.11.051).

John, Robert, et al. 2001. "Toward the Conceptualization and Measurement of Caregiver Burden among Pueblo Indian Family Caregivers." *The Gerontologist* 41(2):210–19. (https://doi.org/10.1093/geront/41.2.210).

Kang, Ji Young, et al. 2019. "The Effect of California's Paid Family Leave Program on Employment among Middle-aged Female Caregivers." *The Gerontologist* 59(6):1092–102. (https://doi.org/10.1093/geront/gny105).

Lee, Yeonjung, et al. 2015. "The Vicious Cycle of Parental Caregiving and Financial Well-being: A Longitudinal Study of Women." *Journals of Gerontology, Series B: Psychological Sciences and Social Sciences* 70(3):425–31. (https://doi.org/10.1093/geronb/gbu001).

Lee, Yeonjung and Fengyan Tang. 2015. "More Caregiving, Less Working: Caregiving Roles and Gender Difference." *Journal of Applied Gerontology* 34(4):465–83. (https://doi.org/10.1177/0733464813508649).

Lilly, Meredith B., Audrey Laporte, and Peter C. Coyte. 2007. "Labor Market Work and Home Care's Unpaid Caregivers: A Systematic Review of Labor Force Participation Rates, Predictors of Labor Market Withdrawal, and Hours of Work." *Milbank Quarterly* 85(4):641–90. (https://doi.org/10.1111/j.1468-0009.2007.00504.x).

Lilly, Meredith B., Audrey Laporte, and Peter C. Coyte. 2010. "Do They Care Too Much to Work? The Influence of Caregiving Intensity on the Labour Force Participation of Unpaid Caregivers in Canada." *Journal of Health Economics* 29(6):895–903. (https://doi.org/10.1016/j.jhealeco.2010.08.007).

Lin, I-Fen, Holly R. Fee, and Hsueh-sheng Wu. 2012. "Negative and Positive Caregiving Experiences: A Closer Look at the Intersection of Gender and Relationships." *Family Relations* 61(2):343–58. (https://doi.org/10.1111/j.1741-3729.2011.00692.x).

Longcare, Margaret L., et al. 2017. "Work Impact and Emotional Stress among Informal Caregivers for Older Adults." *Journals of Gerontology, Series B: Psychological Sciences and Social Sciences* 72(3):522–31. (https://doi.org/10.1093/geronb/gbw027).

Lum, Terry Y. 2005. "Understanding the Racial and Ethnic Differences in Caregiving Arrangements." *Journal of Gerontological Social Work* 45(4):3–21. (https://doi.org/10.1300/J083v45n04_02).

Morrow-Howell, Nancy, et al. January 2015. "Increasing Productive Engagement in Later Life." Grand Challenges for Social Work Initiative. (https://grandchallengesforsocialwork.org/wp-content/uploads/2015/03/Productive-Engagement-3.24.15.pdf).

Morrow-Howell, Nancy, Ernest Gonzales, and Christina Matz-Costa. September 2016. "Policy Recommendations for Meeting the Grand Challenge to Advance Long and Productive Lives." Grand Challenges for Social Work Initiative. (https://openscholarship.wustl.edu/cgi/viewcontent.cgi?article=1784&context=csd_research).

Moussa, Margaret M. 2019. "The Relationship between Elder Care-giving and Labor Force Participation in the Context of Policies Addressing Population Ageing: A Review of Empirical Studies Published between 2006 and 2016." *Ageing & Society* 39(6):1281–1310. (https://doi.org/10.1017/S0144686X18000053).

Muller, Charlotte and Oleg Volkov. 2009. "Older Women: Work and Caregiving in Conflict? A Study of Four Countries." *Social Work in Health Care* 48(7):665–95. (https://doi.org/10.1080/00981380902921732).

Naldini, Manuela, Emmanuele Pavolini, and Cristina Solera. 2016. "Female Employment and Elderly Care: The Role of Care Policies and Culture in 21 European Countries." *Work, Employment and Society* 30(4):607–30. (https://doi.org/10.1177/0950017015625602).

National Partnership for Women & Families. February 2019. "The Family and Medical Insurance Leave Act (The FAMILY Act)." (https://www.nationalpartnership.org/our-work/resources/economic-justice/coalition/family-act-faq.pdf).

Nguyen, Ha Trong and Luke Brian Connelly. January 2014. "The Effect of Unpaid Caregiving Intensity on Labour Force Participation: Results from a Multinomial Endogenous Treatment Model." *Social Science and Medicine* 100:115–22. (https://doi.org/10.1016/j.socscimed.2013.10.031).

Organisation for Economic Co-operation and Development (OECD). 2019. "Employment Rate by Age Group." *OECD Data*. Retrieved March 1, 2020 (https://data.oecd.org/emp/employment-rate-by-age-group.htm).

Pang, Celeste, Gloria Gutman, and Brian de Vries. 2019. "Later Life Care Planning and Concerns of Transgender Older Adults in Canada." *International Journal of Aging and Human Development* 89(1):39–56. (https://doi.org/10.1177/0091415019843520).

Patterson, Sarah E. and Rachel Margolis. 2019. "The Demography of Multigenerational Caregiving: A Critical Aspect of the Gendered Life Course." *Socius: Sociological Research for a Dynamic World* 5:1–19. (https://doi.org/10.1177/2378023119862737).

Pavalko, Eliza K. and Joseph D. Wolfe. 2016a. "Do Women Still Care? Cohort Changes in US Women's Care for the Ill or Disabled." *Social Forces* 94(3):1359–84. (https://doi.org/10.1093/sf/sov101).

Pavalko, Eliza K. and Joseph D. Wolfe. 2016b. "Unpaid Care Work." Pp. 181–203 in *Gerontology: Changes, Challenges, and Solutions*, edited by Madonna Harrington Meyer and Elizabeth A. Daniele. Santa Barbara, CA: Praeger:.

Pinquart, Martin and Silvia Sörensen. 2007. "Correlates of Physical Health of Informal Caregivers: A Meta-analysis." *Journals of Gerontology, Series B: Psychological Sciences and Social Sciences* 62(2):126–37. (https://doi.org/10.1093/geronb/62.2.P126).

Plaisier, Inger, Marjolein I. Broese van Groenou, and Saskia Keuzenkamp. 2015. "Combining Work and Informal Care: The Importance of Caring Organisations." *Human Resource Management Journal* 25(2):267–80. (https://doi.org/10.1111/1748-8583.12048).

Reczek, Corinne. 2014. "The Intergenerational Relationships of Gay Men and Lesbian Women." *Journals of Gerontology, Series B: Psychological Sciences and Social Sciences* 69(6):909–19. (https://doi.org/10.1093/geronb/gbu042).

Rote, Sunshine M., et al. 2019. "Caregiving across Diverse Populations: New Evidence from the National Study of Caregiving and Hispanic EPESE." *Innovation in Aging* 3(2):1–11. (https://doi.org/10.1093/geroni/igz033).

Silverstein, Merril, and Tonya M. Parrott. 2001. "Attitudes toward Government Policies That Assist Informal Caregivers: The Link between Personal Troubles and Public Issues." *Research on Aging* 23(3):349–74. (https://doi.org/10.1177/0164027501233004).

Skira, Meghan M. 2015. "Dynamic Wage and Employment Effects of Elder Parent Care." *International Economic Review* 56(1):63–93. (https://doi.org/10.1111/iere.12095).

Stoiko, Rachel R. and Jo Nell Strough. 2019. "His and Her Retirement: Effects of Gender and Familial Caregiving Profiles on Retirement Timing." *International Journal of Aging and Human Development* 89(2):131–50. (https://doi.org/10.1177/0091415018780009).

Tang, Fengyan, Eunhee Choi, and Rachel Goode. 2013. "Older Americans Employment and Retirement." *Ageing International* 38(1):82–94. (https://doi.org/10.1007/s12126-012-9162-3).

Uccheddu, Damiano, et al. June 2019. "The Pains and Reliefs of the Transitions into and out of Spousal Caregiving: A Cross-national Comparison of the Health Consequences of Caregiving by Gender." *Social Science and Medicine* 240:1–9. (https://doi.org/10.1016/j.socscimed.2019.112517).

U.S. Bureau of Labor Statistics. 2008. "More Seniors Working Full Time." *TED: Economics Daily*. Retrieved March 1, 2020 (https://www.bls.gov/opub/ted/2008/aug/wk1/art03.htm).

Van Houtven, Courtney H., Norma B. Coe, and Meghan M. Skira. 2013. "The Effect of Informal Care on Work and Wages." *Journal of Health Economics* 32(1):240–52. (https://doi.org/10.1016/j.jhealeco.2012.10.006).

Vlachantoni, Athina, et al. February 2019. "Caught in the Middle in Mid-life: Provision of Care across Multiple Generations." *Ageing & Society*:1–21. (https://doi.org/10.1017/S0144686X19000047).

Wakabayashi, Chizuko and Katharine M. Donato. 2006. "Does Caregiving Increase Poverty among Women in Later Life? Evidence from the Health and Retirement Survey." *Journal of Health and Social Behavior* 47(3):258–74. (https://doi.org/10.1177/002214650604700305).

Wolff, Jennifer L., et al. 2016. "A National Profile of Family and Unpaid Caregivers Who Assist Older Adults with Health Care Activities." *JAMA Internal Medicine* 176(3):372–79. (https://doi.org/10.1001/jamainternmed.2015.7664).

World Bank. N.d. "Life Expectancy at Birth, Total (Years)." Databank. Retrieved March 1, 2020 (https://data.worldbank.org/indicator/SP.DYN.LE00.IN).

# PART V

# AS THE EXPERIENCE OF AGING CHANGES, SO TOO DOES RETIREMENT

CHAPTER 21

# The Changing Landscape of Retirement

Helen Dennis and Kelly Ann Marnfeldt

## RETIREMENT HISTORY HIGHLIGHTS

In the past century, the changing nature of work significantly impacted retirement. As society moved from the agricultural to the industrial period, workers moved from farms to cities without savings or community ties and consequently held on to their jobs as long as possible. Simultaneously, society became obsessed with progress and looked for obstacles that would impede such efforts; older workers were targeted.[1] The anti-aging message was elevated by Dr. William Osler, one of Johns Hopkins Hospital's most respected physicians, who declared in his 1905 retirement speech, "Men over 40 were comparatively useless to society with their inelastic minds" and "men over the age of 60 were completely useless, . . . a drain [that] should be retired."[2]

Retirement and age discrimination became important at the same time and not by coincidence.[3] Retirement was used by employers to restructure their workforces while addressing the "impulse towards inefficiency,"[4] valuing the impersonal and egalitarian nature of retirement. The Social Security Act of 1935 further advanced retirement by providing the opportunity to cease working while receiving income. Corporate pension plans did the same.[5]

In contrast to financial incentives to retire, the Age Discrimination in Employment Act of 1967 allowed older workers to continue working with protection from age discrimination. (See chapter 12 and elsewhere in this volume.) The legislation was the most significant and formal announcement of ageism in the workplace, protecting employees between the ages of forty and sixty-five from forced retirement.[6] In 1987, the age cap was lifted, allowing employees to determine the timing of their retirement while also giving them the option to continue working. Retirement was no longer a fixed point in time for most occupations.

The age of retirement has been influenced by eligibility for Social Security, private pensions, and life expectancy as well as the preferences and aspirations of older workers. Historically, men's retirement age has slowly decreased from just over sixty-five in 1982 to 63.9 in 2013.[7] Women's retirement age sharply increased from fifty-three in the early 1960s to 61.9 in 2013, possibly because of the increase in women's participation in the labor force.[8] In 2019, the average retirement age for men was sixty-four and for women, sixty-two.[9]

## RETIREMENT OR A NEW LIFE STAGE

Retirement has no single definition; it comes in many forms and can occur many times. Most often it refers to ceasing work for pay, although that definition has been considered insufficient,[10] given the increasing number of retirees who work for pay and even move on to second and third careers. Individuals are considered retired if they receive a pension or describe themselves as retired,[11] although one can continue to work and also receive Social Security.

Retirement was long considered part of a linear life course consisting of about twenty-five years of learning, followed by three to four decades of work ending with retirement, a time to rest and relax. The four phases have been succinctly referred to as learning, working, resting, and dying with increased longevity extending that rest time.[12] The linear model has been challenged by midlife and older adults seeking opportunities for continuous renewal and reinvention—a cyclical model of later life interspersing work, learning, and leisure in no particular order.[13]

Mature adults need a new map of life "characterized by purpose, contribution and commitment,"[14] one that does not define the problem as longevity. The actual problem is "living in a culture designed for lives half as long as the ones we have."[15] To address this dissonance, in 2018 the Stanford Center on Longevity launched a five-year initiative called "The New Map of Life,"[16] convening architects, academics, scientists, executives, educators, and others charged with envisioning what vibrant long lives would look like. Retirement is part of that vision.

The new life stage has no agreed-upon name, no set beginning or end, and no rites of passage and faces a culture that seems in denial that it even exists.[17] It is so new that gerontologists, psychologists, anthropologists, and other social scientists employ different terminology. For example, Stanford's Longevity Center calls this stage Act IV;[18] social scientists at Boston College refer to it as the X Revolution;[19] developmental psychologist and psychoanalyst Erik Erikson called it the stage of generativity, while Ken Dychtwald, CEO and founder of Age Wage, named it "middlescense";[20] geriatricians Louise Aronson and William Thomas call it elderhood.[21,22] Encore.org naturally favors "encore," and author Abigail Trafford touts the "bonus years."[23] A word was invented by Bernice Bratter and Helen Dennis—Renewment™—a unique combination of retirement and renewal.[24]

In some instances, expectations for the new life stage have exceeded the actual retirement experience. The financial services industry is apt to oversell retirement in advertisements, presenting it as a form of positive aging in which retirees are depicted as healthy and loving newfound freedom from work. Retirement savings are discussed as opportunities for leisure consumption, avoiding portrayals of retirement as a potential period of illness, loss, or financial insecurity and paying less attention to medical or long-term care expenses or funding income for survivors.[25]

## DETERMINANTS OF RETIREMENT

### Economics

The overarching determinant of retirement ease is economic status, a challenge for 13 percent of non-retirees in their sixties who have no retirement savings, and for those whose savings are inadequate. Baby boomers have the highest savings rate of $144,000 compared to Generation X at $64,000 and millennials at $23,000.[26] Prior to the pandemic in January 2020, retirees reported a sense of financial security. Over three-quarters (77 percent) indicated confidence in having enough money for a comfortable retirement.[27]

### Corporate Policies

Corporate policies on retirement have been influenced by ageist attitudes of employers toward older workers, despite the fact that most of the myths have been debunked.[28] The pervasiveness of ageist stereotypes (e.g., older people can't handle new technology and are resistant to change) is part of what keeps employers from providing them with education and skills training.[29] Management's stance regarding experienced workers has been largely limited to offering early retirement incentives, rather than being geared toward maintaining and fostering an active older workforce.[30]

The reality that is already upon employers—that older workers comprise the fastest-growing age group in the labor force—is expected to continue well into the future. Employers can no longer take for granted that workers will work "X" number of years and then retire at an expected age. While corporate policies must include comprehensive retirement preparation, training, and education, they must also include strategies for managing and developing the older workforce that is already in place.[31] (See also chapters 7, 8, and 10.)

Rather than making an abrupt exit from the labor force, older workers often prefer to transition into retirement. (See also chapters 11, 22, and 24.) Yet fewer than 40 percent of employers have policies that accommodate the transitioning worker, such as encore career options, flextime hours, phased retirement, succession planning, and lateral or even downward mobility to take on a less strenuous position within the company.[32] Despite older workers saying they want options that are strongly aligned with phased retirement, only 14 percent of employers plan to implement formal policies for it, with 11 percent citing lack of employee interest as a reason for ignoring the practice.[33]

Even though phased retirement has been shown to have net positive benefits for employers and employees, lack of clarity in the "nondiscrimination provisions and employment-related discrimination laws" is another obstacle to embracing formal policies.[34] Employers say the two biggest challenges to implementing phased retirement policies in the near future are misalignment with workforce strategy (42 percent) and difficulty of administration (32 percent),[35] which might imply the fear of age discrimination litigation. (See chapter 12.)

## Incentives for Early Retirement

The timing of retirement is dependent upon a variety of both positive and negative determinants, sometimes referred to as "push/pull" factors, that accumulate across the life course.[36] Scharn and colleagues found as many as forty-nine individual "determinants of retirement timing for modern industrialized countries," such as social factors and work characteristics, which indicates a highly individualized and nuanced process.[37] On the "pull" side of the equation, having autonomy over one's time emerges as a common theme. Men and women alike report that spending time with or taking care of grandchildren is a big driver,[38] as is spending time with an already-retired spouse, working on hobby projects, or doing volunteer work.[39]

On the negative end of the spectrum, poor health is a common push factor of early retirement, particularly among black and Hispanic workers.[40] Black workers who retire before age sixty-five have greater concern about health compared to whites who are more likely to have retired early, at least in part, because they wanted to do things other than work.[41] In addition, women and people in manual labor jobs are overrepresented among those who take early exit from the workforce for health reasons.[42] Other negative influencers include the challenges of doing shift work, the absence of employee appreciation by workplace managers, lack of social support, and incompetence among coworkers.[43] While some research shows that low job satisfaction can be a push factor,[44] others found it to be insignificant[45] and outweighed by the impact of poor health on an early retirement decision.[46]

Aside from negative push factors that are more individual in nature, early retirement is sometimes spurred by unanticipated events, often referred to as "shocks," which include significant changes to a person's health, employment, family, or financial situation.[47] (See also chapter 19.) The shock with the greatest probability of prompting an early retirement is being unable to find work after a job loss, followed by having a parent move in, having a spouse retire, and, finally, worsening health.[48] While job loss is likely to precipitate early retirement, poor health happens on a much more frequent basis to more people.[49] In one study, 40 percent of retirees age sixty-two and younger and 30 percent of retirees ages sixty-two to sixty-four indicate poor health as a factor in their retirement decision, whereas lack of work was a contributing factor for 20 percent of early retirees.[50]

## Incentives to Delay Retirement

Just as there are forces at play for choosing early retirement, there are also corresponding drivers to remain on the job beyond normal retirement age. As discussed above, at one time work and retirement were binary; individuals either worked or were retired but not at the same time. That model has changed. Seventy percent of preretirees indicate they want to work during their retirement years.[51] Their motivation to work is not only for a paycheck but also for emotional, social, and intellectual rewards, making work an integral part of the retirement experience.

A nationally representative sample survey by Merrill Lynch & Age Wave[52] identified four types of "working retirees": "Driven Achievers" (15 percent), "Caring Contributors" (33 percent), "Life Balancers" (24 percent), and "Earnest Earners" (28 percent). While 42–54 percent of achievers, contributors, and balancers felt prepared for retirement, only 4 percent of earnest earners felt financially ready. The majority of respondents (62 percent) said their top reason for continuing to work was to stay mentally active, a motivator that was twice as important to them as money. The study also revealed that staying physically active (46 percent), maintaining social connections (42 percent), and maintaining a sense of identity (36 percent) ranked next in order of importance over and above money (31 percent), and wanting new challenges fell just below that at 30 percent. It should be noted that 43 percent of the earnest earners who continued to work in order to meet financial obligations were far less satisfied with their jobs than the other types of retirees and also reported higher levels of frustration and feelings of regret over having to work. On the other end of the spectrum, 79 percent of the driven achievers were not only highly satisfied with their jobs, they also reported feeling "at the top of their game."

Outside of personal and financial reasons, positive psychosocial dynamics in the workplace can influence whether an employee is incentivized to continue working during the retirement-eligible years.[53] Generous job resources that "stimulate personal growth, learning and development and contribute towards the achievement of work goals or reduce job demands" and offer high levels of job control (i.e., "decision latitude, decision authority, autonomy, predictability of work, influence at work and flexibility of work hours/place") make later retirement more likely.[54]

As we have seen, retirement is not always permanent. Once retired, individuals frequently return to work, either for an employer or for themselves, possibly as entrepreneurs. (See also chapter 23.) Once retired, individuals between ages fifty-five and eighty-five who return to work are often referred to as "unretired." The concept of unretirement is based on the assumption that a better educated and healthy workforce can continue to earn income in the retirement years, create wealth, and, if entrepreneurs, address pressing issues facing society.[55] A study from the RAND Corporation indicates a sizeable portion of the U.S. population unretires by design, not because of unexpected circumstances.[56]

Older entrepreneurs, in particular, continue to work longer than people who work for traditional employers[57] for at least two reasons—(1) difficulty extricating themselves from their business after owning it for a long time, feeling psychologically attached to it, and (2) lack of preparation when finances, business valuation, or strategic concepts are unaligned with their intention to retire.[58]

Older adults continue to work in new ways that fulfill the desire for purpose and in some cases, income. In 2009, Marc Freedman, CEO and founder of Encore.org, introduced the "encore career," "forging a new hybrid between the spirit of service and the practicality of continued income."[59] (See also chapter 24.) An encore career embraces purpose, passion, a paycheck, and giving back for the greater good, providing an opportunity for adults age fifty and older to be productively engaged in work that has social impact as well as personal meaning. A survey in 2014 reported that more than 4.5 million Americans ages fifty to seventy were enjoying their second career and 21 million were planning to start one within the next five years.[60]

## EVOLUTION OF RETIREMENT PLANNING, LIFE PLANNING, AND RETIREMENT COACHING

Traditionally, retirement planning meant helping individuals create a financial plan that would lead to financial security as well as accommodate their lifestyle. In 1968, Woodrow Hunter at the University of Michigan added the *non*financial dimension to retirement planning, teaching older adults how to get the most out of their retirement years. Retirement planning, including both financial and nonfinancial topics, was the purview of consulting firms, publishing companies, and advocacy organizations such as AARP. A big shift occurred in the 1970s when corporate human resource departments assumed the role of retirement planners and educators, presenting not only information about pensions, estate planning, Social Security, and Medicare but also health, housing, and leisure opportunities.

With increased awareness of an aging population, massive layoffs, and early retirements in the 1980s, a more holistic approach evolved called life planning. The National Endowment for Financial Education defines it as "(1) a process of helping people focus on the true values and motivations of their lives; (2) determining the goals and objectives they have as they see their lives develop; (3) using these values, motivations, goals and objectives to guide the planning process and provide a framework for making choices and decisions in life that have financial and non-financial implications and consequences."[61]

Around 2000, retirement coaching came on the scene, helping clients develop a plan for the mental, social, physical, and spiritual changes that often take place during retirement. Retirement coaches come from diverse backgrounds—social work, psychotherapy, counseling, financial planning, executive coaching, and gerontology. Although no license or degree is required, most coaches go through training to meet professional standards, such as the Certified Professional Retirement Coach program.[62]

The changing nature of retirement planning takes into account longer lives as well as the aspirations and expectations of pre-retirees. The progression from retirement planning to life planning and retirement coaching acknowledges the holistic dimensions of the retirement experience. Whether developing a plan independently or with a professional, the use of time emerges as a priority.

### Retirees' Use of Time

Americans sixty years and older spend a significant part of their time on leisure activities, averaging seven hours a day. They spend almost half of that time watching television or videos, spending over four hours daily in front of a screen. Additionally, they spend more than eight hours a day sleeping, three hours on chores or errands, over one hour for eating, and another hour on personal activities such as grooming or health care. As figure 21.1 shows, screen time has increased as older adults have become more

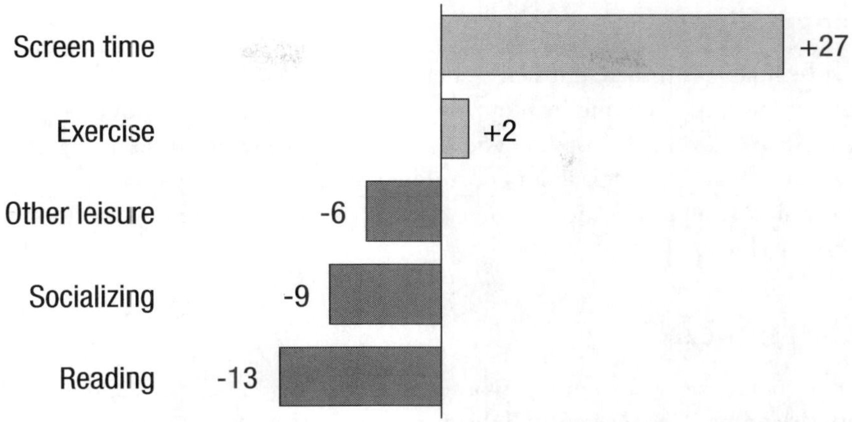


**FIGURE 21.1.** Change in Daily Time Use 2005–2015 (Minutes), for People 60 and Older

*Source:* Pew Research Center analysis of 2003–2006 and 2014–2017 American Time Use Survey (IPUMS).

digitally savvy. Internet usage has increased dramatically, whereas time spent on recreational activities such as reading or socializing has slightly decreased.[63]

Retirees highly value the freedom experienced in their new life stage—the flexibility to do what they want to do and when to do it, balancing health, free time, and emotional well-being. Many say enjoyable experiences are more important than things. Relationships are highly regarded; the person they spend time with is more important than the activity they share. Almost one out of four retirees volunteer in some capacity, which translates to 1.9 billion hours of services worth $45.5 billion in contributions.[64] They are motivated to give back and make a difference in their churches, organizations, communities, and wherever there is a need. However, although "many in their fifties and sixties view traditional retirement as the perfect time to seek refuge from a complicated world," for others "the mere notion of retirement strikes fear in their very hearts."[65]

Retirees counteract the open-endedness of retirement with routine, conveying a sense of competence and discipline conforming to the ideals of active aging.[66] One study described retirees as practiced in accounting for their time.[67] Even when not working, they measure themselves according to the standards and criteria of work.[68]

Retirees also undertake short-term employment for extra income, to pay bills, or just to try something different.[69] Over four hundred thousand older adults participate in the online gig economy. Benefits include opportunities for social interaction, avoiding interviews and the risks of age discrimination, and the flexibility of combining retirement activities with paid work.[70]

Retirees are returning to work for former employers as independent contractors to meet labor shortages in sectors such as health care, finance, insurance, and other industries.[71] The Aerospace Corporation in El Segundo, California, a federally funded research and development center, lets retirees work part-time as "casual" workers, while continuing to receive salary and benefits if they work fewer than one thousand hours per plan year.[72] In 2005 and 2017, older workers were more likely to be independent contractors than any other age group.[73]

## Select Populations

Disparities based on race, ethnicity, social class, and a myriad of other factors are well documented and systemic in our culture. These disparities follow people across the life course and don't disappear when someone reaches retirement age. (See also chapters 3–6.) In fact, age itself is an enormous barrier that creates disadvantages and obstacles for almost all populations. Three groups disproportionately affected in retirement are highlighted.

### GENDER DIFFERENCES

Labor participation rates among women steadily increased during the last half of the twentieth century, leveling off slightly in the twenty-first.[74] Women have always worked at nearly every age, whether in a paid, underpaid, or unpaid capacity, but what is different now is that women working in older age are primarily working full-time, regardless of the type of employment.[75] Over the decades, as women gained more and more access to education, they were gradually able to move up in the workplace creating greater job satisfaction, which, in turn, has made women want to continue working into their later years.[76] While job satisfaction is important to women in deciding whether to retire, single and married women whose significant other also continues to work into older age are more likely to want to keep working as well.[77]

The gender wage gap undoubtedly plays a role in women's financial security throughout their lives, so it's no surprise that women's feeling of security and financial readiness for retirement differs from men's. Additional factors that disproportionately influence women's retirement readiness over time are longer life expectancy, lower wages, parenting and family caregiving, and lack of access to or inadequate retirement benefits.[78]

### LESBIAN, GAY, BISEXUAL, AND TRANSGENDER WORKERS

For all the progress that has been made toward ensuring equal rights and access to resources for lesbian, gay, bisexual, and transgender (LGBT) citizens in recent years, there is still much work to be done, particularly for older LGBT people. A 2018 survey of LGBT Americans aged forty-five and older found that there still is a lot of fear about growing older that leaves LGBT people feeling vulnerable about discrimination in housing, health care, and long-term care.[79] As a result, older LGBT people feel disproportionately vulnerable when it comes to retirement. A 2014 survey of LGBT people aged forty-five to seventy-five by the advocacy group SAGE Advocacy & Services for LGBT Elders found respondents twice as concerned as their non-LGBT counterparts about having to work long past age sixty-five to cover living expenses in retirement,[80] outliving retirement savings, and not being able to handle an unexpected emergency.[81]

### ELDER ORPHANS

The term "elder orphans" is referred to in gerontological circles as "aged, community-dwelling individuals who are socially and/or physically isolated, without an available known family member or designated surrogate or caregiver."[82] An alternative term "solo agers" was recently introduced by author and life planning coach Sarah Zeff Geber.[83] Geriatricians, gerontologists, retirement planners, and others concerned about older adults aging alone are focused on the "acute" issues solo agers may face, such as making plans for what would happen should they need legal guardianship or become incapacitated with no one to advocate for them. These are important for most older adults, but perhaps more urgent for solo agers. The most up-to-date advice for potential solo agers contemplating retirement is that they should (1) acknowledge that they will likely need to save more money than non-solo agers; (2) consider multiple scenarios regarding the level of support they may need as they age in terms of health and cognition; (3) consider looking at options for housing, such as cohousing or a continuing care retirement community; (4) investigate the value of purchasing long-term care insurance; (5) carefully vet the people they appoint to take over their care and finances; and (6) build and maintain social networks throughout their retirement years.[84]

## PERSPECTIVES ON THE FUTURE

People who reach retirement age with adequate income from sources such as Social Security, pensions, and savings should be able to fund their retirement needs. In addition to having adequate income, maintaining good health and having social connections and a sense of purpose will increase their chances of living a fulfilling and secure retirement. Yet the financial aspect of this scenario is virtually nonexistent for a significant number of individuals. The reduction in pensions along with steadily growing income and wealth disparities over the last few decades mean most American workers of any age have little or no retirement savings (those between fifty-five and sixty-four have less than a year's worth of income in a savings account).[85] (See also chapter 2.)

Adding to this preexisting condition, the unthinkable occurred in 2020 when COVID-19 upended all sense of normalcy. *New York Times* columnist David Brooks refers to the virus as "The First Invasion of America" where existential security disappears as we undergo "a more permanent shift in national consciousness, a reconstruction of meaning, symbols, values and narratives."[86] The institution of retirement cannot escape this invasion.

According to one of the earliest surveys on retirement confidence during the pandemic, only 23 percent of workers felt confident they would have an adequate amount of money to retire; fewer than half had fully recovered from the Great Recession.[87] Unprepared before the pandemic,[88] millions may be facing the reality they no longer will be able to afford to retire when they want to, if at all. Furthermore, the lack of sufficient income may lessen opportunities for independent living as the number of aging parents living with adult children is dramatically rising.[89]

The pandemic likely will affect retirement timing, depending on individual circumstances. The average age of retirement will increase if older adults work longer for income by continuing with their current job, finding a new position, or becoming self-employed. Conversely, the retirement age may decrease if retirement-eligible workers lose their jobs or find working remotely a poor fit. It also is possible that older workers have found the stay-at-home experience to be a "dress rehearsal" for early retirement.

The unknown impact of COVID-19 has provoked anxiety and fear across the globe with many unanswered questions about health, economic survival, relationships, and even death that separately or collectively can lead to anxiety, depression, and other mental health problems. Amid the unknowns and hardships, the pandemic has forced people to become more reflective, focusing on what is essential and nonessential to their lives, including the value of social connection for a sense of well-being and belonging. One of the lessons learned from the pandemic is that the systemic social and economic problems facing America can no longer be ignored.

No matter how the new normal is defined, existing retirement issues will remain or become exacerbated if problems associated with health care, employment, housing, and transportation as well as age, gender, and race discrimination are not addressed. Although these issues affect all Americans, older adults are disproportionately affected. The following changes are recommended to address systemic problems as well as those exacerbated by the pandemic:

1. Recognize retirees and all older adults as contributors, problem solvers, and assets to society.
2. Provide adequate health care for all older adults.
3. Eliminate all discrimination by age, gender identity, and race that prevents a dignified, meaningful, and secure retirement.
4. Provide financial planning opportunities and solutions, regardless of income or wealth.
5. Establish employment opportunities in later life, including flexible work options.
6. Develop corporate policies and programs that advance retirement planning, both financial and nonfinancial.
7. Support the proliferation of age-friendly communities that ensure adequate housing, transportation, social services, and civic engagement.
8. Increase research on the needs of solo retirees.

Despite the global catastrophe, society has an opportunity to define what matters and emphasize an essential life value that is a basis of change—caring for and about one another. Let's remember that tragedy can lead to innovation, a coming together with a shared sense of humanity.

## NOTES

1. William Graebner. 1980. *A History of Retirement: The Meaning and Function of an American Institution. 1885–1978.* New Haven, CT: Yale University Press:35.
2. Graebner, *History of Retirement*, 4.
3. Graebner, *History of Retirement*, 53.
4. Graebner, *History of Retirement*, 53.
5. Seattle Times Staff. December 31, 2013. "A Brief History of Retirement: It's a Modern Idea." *Seattle Times*. (https://www.seattletimes.com/nation-world/a-brief-history-of-retirement-its-a-modern-idea/).

6. Helen Dennis and Kathryn Thomas. 2007. "Ageism in the Workplace." *Generations: Journal of the American Society on Aging* 31(1):84–89.

7. Alicia H. Munnell. March 2015. "The Average Retirement Age—An Update." *Issue in Brief* 15-4. Chestnut Hill, MA: Center for Retirement Research, Boston College. (https://crr.bc.edu/wp-content/uploads/2015/03/IB_15-4_508_rev.pdf).

8. Munnell, "Average Retirement Age."

9. Mark Mather, Paola Scommenga, and Lillian Kilduff, July 15, 2019. "Fact Sheet: Aging in the United States." Washington, DC: Population Reference Bureau. (https://www.prb.org/aging-unitedstates-fact-sheet/).

10. Iwona Mendryk. 2017. "Retirement Age: Preferences of Employees Representing Various Age Groups." *Economics & Sociology* 10(4):32. (https://doi.org/10.14254/2071-789x.2017/10-4/3).

11. Mendryk, "Retirement Age," 31.

12. Paul Irving. 2014. *The Upside of Aging: How Long Life Is Changing the World of Health, Work, Innovation, Policy, and Purpose.* Hoboken, NJ: John Wiley & Sons:69.

13. Ken Dychtwald and Daniel J. Kadlec. 2005. *The Power Years: A User's Guide to the Rest of Your Life.* Hoboken, NJ: John Wiley & Sons:7.

14. Marc Freedman. 2011. *The Big Shift: Navigating the New Stage beyond Midlife.* New York: PublicAffairs:11.

15. Laura L. Carstensen. November 29, 2019. "We Need a Major Redesign of Life." *Washington Post.* (https://www.washingtonpost.com/opinions/we-need-a-major-redesign-of-life/2019/11/29/a63daab2-1086-11ea-9cd7-a1becbc82f5e_story.html).

16. Stanford Center on Longevity. September 2018. "A New Map of Life." Stanford, CA. (https://longevity.stanford.edu/a-new-map-of-life/).

17. Freedman, *Big Shift*, 15.

18. Freedman, *Big Shift*, 82.

19. Jacquelyn B. James et al. 2012. *Just Do It? . . . Maybe Not! Insights on Activity in Later Life from the Life & Times in an Aging Society Study*. Chestnut Hill, MA: Sloan Center on Aging & Work, Boston College. (https://www.bc.edu/content/dam/files/research_sites/agingandwork/pdf/publications/EAWA_JustDoIt.pdf).

20. Dychtwald and Kadlec, *Power Years*, 7.

21. Louise Aronson. 2019. *Elderhood: Redefining Aging, Transforming Medicine, Reimagining Life.* New York: Bloomsbury:8.

22. William H. Thomas. 2004. *What are Old People For? How Elders Will Save the World.* St. Louis, MO: VanderWyk & Burnham:126.

23. Abigail Trafford. 2003. *My Time: Making the Most of the Rest of Your Life.* New York: Basic Books.

24. Bernice Bratter and Helen Dennis. 2008. *Project Renewment: The First Retirement Model for Career Women.* New York: Simon & Schuster:1.

25. David Ekerdt and Evelyn Clark. 2001. "Selling Retirement in Financial Planning Advertisements." *Journal of Aging Studies* 15(1):55–68. (https://doi.org/10.1016/s0890-4065(00)00016-5).

26. Catherine Collinson, Patti Rowey, and Heidi Cho. May 2020. "Retirement Security amid COVID-19: The Outlook of Three Generations; 20th Annual Transamerica Retirement Survey of Workers." Los Angeles: Transamerica Center for Retirement Studies. (https://transamericacenter.org/docs/default-source/retirement-survey-of-workers/tcrs2020_sr_retirement_security_amid_covid-19.pdf).

27. Jack Van Derhi. March 7, 2019. "Retirement Savings Shortfalls: Evidence from EBRI's 2019 Retirement Security Projection Model." Employee Benefit Research Institute:4. (https://www.shrm.org/ResourcesAndTools/hr-topics/benefits/Documents/EBRI_IB_410_Feb15_RSShrtfls.pdf).

28. Thomas W. Ng and Daniel C. Feldman. 2012. "Evaluating Six Common Stereotypes about Older Workers with Meta-analytical Data." *Personnel Psychology* 65(4):821–58. (https://doi.org/10.1111/peps.12003).

29. Carole B. Cox. 2015. *Social Policy for an Aging Society: A Human Rights Perspective.* New York: Springer:101.

30. Kène Henkens et al. 2017. "What We Need to Know about Retirement: Pressing Issues for the Coming Decade." *The Gerontologist* 58(5):808. (https://doi.org/10.1093/geront/gnx095).

31. Society for Human Resource Management (SHRM). January 16, 2020. "Employing Older Workers." (https://www.shrm.org/resourcesandtools/tools-and-samples/toolkits/pages/employingolderworkers.aspx).

32. Catherine Collinson, Patti Rowey, and Heidi Cho. December 2019. "19th Annual Transamerica Retirement Survey: A Compendium of Findings about U.S. Workers." Los Angeles: Transamerica Center for Retirement Studies. (https://transamericacenter.org/retirement-research/19th-annual-retirement-survey).

33. Robert Clark et al. 2019. "Employer Concerns and Responses to an Aging Workforce." NBER Working Paper No. 25572. Cambridge, MA: National Bureau of Economic Research. (https://doi.org/10.3386/w25572).

34. U.S. Government Accountability Office. 2017. "Older Workers: Phased Retirement Programs, Although Uncommon, Provide Flexibility for Workers and Employers." U.S. Government Accountability Office. (https://www.gao.gov/assets/690/685324.pdf).

35. Clark, "Employer Concerns and Responses," 10.

36. Hanne De Preter, Dorien Van Looy, and Dimitri Mortelmans. 2013. "Individual and Institutional Push and Pull Factors as Predictors of Retirement Timing in Europe: A Multilevel Analysis." *Journal of Aging Studies* 27(4):299–307. (https://doi.org/10.1016/j.jaging.2013.06.003).

37. Micky Scharn et al. 2018. "Domains and Determinants of Retirement Timing: A Systematic Review of Longitudinal Studies." *BMC Public Health* 18(1083):12. (https://doi.org/10.1186/s12889-018-5983-7).

38. De Preter, Van Looy, and Mortelmans, "Individual and Institutional Push and Pull Factors," 302–3.

39. Tilja I. Van den Berg, Leo A. Elders, and Alex Burdorf. 2010. "Influence of Health and Work on Early Retirement." *Journal of Occupational and Environmental Medicine* 52(6):581. (https://doi.org/10.1097/jom.0b013e3181de8133).

40. Federal Reserve System. May 2019. "The Fed—Retirement." Board of Governors of the Federal Reserve System. (https://www.federalreserve.gov/publications/2019-economic-well-being-of-us-households-in-2018-retirement.htm).

41. Federal Reserve System, "The Fed—Retirement."

42. Clare E. Edge, Anna M. Cooper, and Margaret Coffey. 2017. "Barriers and Facilitators to Extended Working Lives in Europe: A Gender Focus." *Public Health Reviews* 38(2):10. (https://doi.org/10.1186/s40985-017-0053-8).

43. Van den Berg, Elders, and Burdorf, "Influence of Health and Work," 578.

44. Van den Berg, Elders, and Burdorf, "Influence of Health and Work," 578.

45. De Preter, Van Looy, and Mortelmans, "Individual and Institutional Push and Pull Factors," 300.

46. Peter Browne et al. April 2018. "The Relationship between Workplace Psychosocial Environment and Retirement Intentions and Actual Retirement: A Systematic Review." *European Journal of Ageing* 16(1):74.

47. Debra S. Dwyer and Jianting Hu. 2000. "Retirement Expectations and Realizations: The Role of Health Shocks and Economic Factors." Pp. 274–83 in *Forecasting Retirement Needs and Retirement Wealth*, edited by Olivia S. Mitchell, P. Brett Hammond, and Anna M. Rappaport. Philadelphia: University of Pennsylvania Press.

48. Munnell, "Average Retirement Age."

49. Munnell, "Average Retirement Age."

50. Federal Reserve System, "The Fed—Retirement."

51. Age Wave. 2014. "Work in Retirement: Myths and Motivations, Career Reinventions and the New Retirement Workscape." *Age Wave—The World's Leader in Understanding the Effects of an Aging Population on the Marketplace, the Workplace and Our Lives.* (https://agewave.com/wp-content/uploads/2016/07/2014-ML-AW-Work-in-Retirement_Myths-and-Motivations.pdf).

52. Age Wave, "Work in Retirement," 13.

53. Browne et al, "Relationship between Workplace Psychosocial Environment," 76.

54. Browne et al., "Relationship between Workplace Psychosocial Environment." 74.

55. Chris Farrell. 2014. *Unretirement: How Baby Boomers Are Changing the Way We Think about Work, Community, and the Good Life*. New York: Bloomsbury:21.

56. Nicole Maestas. 2007. "Back to Work: Expectations and Realizations of Work after Retirement." Santa Monica, CA: RAND Corporation. (https://www.rand.org/pubs/working_papers/WR196-2.html).

57. Johan Klaesson, Esteban Lopez, and Özge Öner. 2017. "Who Works Longer—and Why? Regional and Individual Characteristics in the Timing of Retirement." *Tijdschrift voor Economische en Sociale Geografie* 109(3):357. (https://doi.org/10.1111/tesg.12295).

58. Nancy Forster-Holt. 2013. "Entrepreneur as 'End'repreneur: The Intention to Retire." *Small Business Institute Journal* 9(2):29–42.

59. Marci Alboher. 2013. *The Encore Career Handbook: How to Make a Living and a Difference in the Second Half of Life*. New York: Workman:viii.

60. Encore.org. 2014. *Encore Careers: The Persistence of Purpose*. (https://encore.org/wp-content/uploads/files/2014EncoreResearchOverview.pdf).

61. Helen Dennis. 2002. "The Retirement Planning Specialty." *Generations: Journal of the American Society on Aging* 26(2):57.

62. Dorian Mintzer. February 23, 2018. "How to Become a Certified Retirement Coach." *Revolutionize Retirement*. (https://revolutionizeretirement.com/certified-retirement-coach/).

63. Gretchen Livingston. 2019. "Americans 60 and Older Are Spending More Time in Front of Their Screens Than a Decade Ago." Washington, DC: Pew Research Center. (https://www.pewresearch.org/fact-tank/2019/06/18/americans-60-and-older-are-spending-more-time-in-front-of-their-screens-than-a-decade-ago/).

64. Corporation for National and Community Service. 2015. "Older Adults (Age 65+)." (https://www.nationalservice.gov/vcla/demographic/older-adults-age-65).

65. Chip Conley. 2018. *Wisdom at Work: The Making of a Modern Elder*. New York: Currency:155.

66. David Ekerdt and Catheryn Koss. 2015. "The Task of Time in Retirement." *Ageing and Society* 36(6):1295–1311. (https://doi.org/10.1017/s0144686x15000367).

67. Ekerdt and Koss, "Task of Time in Retirement," 1306.

68. Ekerdt and Koss, "Task of Time in Retirement," 1307.

69. Mia Taylor. March 13, 2020. "Retirement in the Age of Uber: Can Gig Economy Workers Ever Call It Quits?" *The Simple Dollar*. (https://www.thesimpledollar.com/make-money/retirement-in-the-uber-era/).

70. Eleanor Laise. May 5, 2017. "Retirees, Survive and Thrive in the Gig Economy." *Kiplinger*. (https://www.kiplinger.com/article/retirement/T012-C000-S004-survive-and-thrive-in-the-gig-economy.html).

71. Kerry Hannon. November 9, 2018. "Retired Workers Are Going Back to Former Employers." Washington, DC: AARP. (https://www.aarp.org/work/job-search/info-2018/how-to-boomerang-to-old-job.html).

72. Aerospace Corporation. 2017. *Aerospace Employees' Retirement Plan for Participants in the New Combined Retirement Program—AERP 2*. (https://retirees.aerospace.org/files/2017/06/AERP2-20117.pdf).

73. Eileen Applebaum, Arne Kalleberg, and Hye Jin Rho. February 28, 2019. "Nonstandard Work Arrangements and Older Americans, 2005–2017." Washington, DC: Economic Policy Institute. (https://www.epi.org/publication/nonstandard-work-arrangements-and-older-americans-2005-2017/).

74. Mitra Toossi and Teresa L. Morisi. July 18, 2017. "Women in the Workforce before, during, and after the Great Recession." *Spotlight on Statistics*. U.S. Bureau of Labor Statistics. (https://www.bls.gov/spotlight/2017/women-in-the-workforce-before-during-and-after-the-great-recession/home.htm).

75. Claudia Goldin and Lawrence F. Katz. September 2016. "Women Working Longer: Facts and Some Explanations." NBER Working Paper No. 22607. Cambridge, MA: National Bureau of Economic Research. (https://doi.org/ 10.3386/w22607).

76. Goldin and Katz, "Women Working Longer."

77. Goldin and Katz, "Women Working Longer."

78. Collinson, Rowey, and Cho, "19th Annual Transamerica Retirement Survey."

79. Angela Houghton. March 2018. "Maintaining Dignity: A Survey of LGBT Adults Age 45 and Older." Washington, DC: AARP. (https://doi.org/10.26419/res.00217.001).

80. SAGE Advocacy and Services for LGBT Elders. 2014. "Out & Visible: The Experiences and Attitudes of Lesbian, Gay, Bisexual and Transgender Older Adults, Ages 45–75." *Advocating for LGBT Seniors | Fighting for LGBT Rights—SAGE:* 15. (https://www.sageusa.org/wp-content/uploads/2018/05/sageusa-out-visible-lgbt-market-research-full-report.pdf).

81. SAGE Advocacy and Services for LGBT Elders, "Out & Visible."

82. Maria T. Carney et al. 2016. "Elder Orphans Hiding in Plain Sight: A Growing Vulnerable Population." *Current Gerontology and Geriatrics Research*:1–11. (https://doi.org/10.1155/2016/4723250).

83. Richard Eisenberg. October 11, 2018. "Sara Zeff Geber: Offering Retirement Advice for Solo Agers." *Next Avenue*. (https://www.nextavenue.org/sara-zeff-geber/).

84. Anna M. Rappaport. 2019. "Retirement Success and Elder Orphans." Society of Actuaries. (https://www.soa.org/globalassets/assets/files/resources/essays-monographs/2019-family-structure/2019-family-structure-rappaport-orphans.pdf).

85. Bureau of Labor Statistics, U.S. Department of Labor. October 2, 2018. "The Economics Daily: 51 Percent of Private Industry Workers Had Access to Only Defined Contribution Retirement Plans on the Internet." U.S. Bureau of Labor Statistics. (https://www.bls.gov/opub/ted/2018/51-percent-of-private-industry-workers-had-access-to-only-defined-contribution-retirement-plans-march-2018.htm?view_full).

86. David Brooks. May 21, 2020. "The First Invasion of America." *New York Times*.

87. Collinson, Rowey, and Cho, "Retirement Security amid COVID-19."

88. Alessandra Malito. May 14, 2020. "What Does the Government Need to Do to Help Retirement Savers through the COVID-19 Crisis?" *MarketWatch*. (https://www.marketwatch.com/story/what-does-the-government-need-to-do-to-help-retirement-savers-through-the-covid-19-crisis-2020-05-14?mod=alessandra-malito).

89. Charlotte Cowles. May 2, 2020. "My Retirement Plan Is You: Americans without Retirement Savings Are Increasingly Moving In with Their Millennial Children." *New York Times*. (https://www.nytimes.com/2020/05/02/business/Parents-retirement-moving-in-millennials.html).

## REFERENCES

Aerospace Corporation. 2017. *Aerospace Employees' Retirement Plan for Participants in the New Combined Retirement Program—AERP 2*. (https://retirees.aerospace.org/files/2017/06/AERP2-20117.pdf).

Age Wave. 2014. "Work in Retirement: Myths and Motivations, Career Reinventions and the New Retirement Workscape." *Age Wave—The World's Leader in Understanding the Effects of an Aging Population on the Marketplace, the Workplace and Our Lives*. (https://agewave.com/wp-content/uploads/2016/07/2014-ML-AW-Work-in-Retirement_Myths-and-Motivations.pdf).

Alboher, Marci. 2013. *The Encore Career Handbook: How to Make a Living and a Difference in the Second Half of Life*. New York: Workman.

Applebaum, Eileen, Arne Kalleberg, and Hye Jin Rho. February 28, 2019. "Nonstandard Work Arrangements and Older Americans, 2005–2017." Washington, DC: Economic Policy Institute. (https://www.epi.org/publication/nonstandard-work-arrangements-and-older-americans-2005-2017/).

Aronson, Louise. 2019. *Elderhood: Redefining Aging, Transforming Medicine, Reimagining Life*. New York: Bloomsbury.

Bratter, Bernice and Helen Dennis. 2008. *Project Renewment: The First Retirement Model for Career Women*. New York: Simon & Schuster.

Brooks, David. May 21, 2020. "The First Invasion of America." *New York Times*.

Brown, Jennifer E., Joelle Saad-Lessler, and Diane Oakley. 2018. *Retirement in America: Out of Reach for Working Americans?* National Institute on Retirement Security. (https://www.nirsonline.org/wp-content/uploads/2018/09/SavingsCrisis_Final.pdf).

Browne, Peter, et al. April 2018. "The Relationship between Workplace Psychosocial Environment and Retirement Intentions and Actual Retirement: A Systematic Review." *European Journal of Ageing* 16(1):73–82.

Bureau of Labor Statistics, U.S. Department of Labor. October 2, 2018. "The Economics Daily: 51 Percent of Private Industry Workers Had Access to Only Defined Contribution Retirement Plans on the Internet." U.S. Bureau of Labor Statistics. (https://www.bls.gov/opub/ted/2018/51-percent-of-private-industry-workers-had-access-to-only-defined-contribution-retirement-plans-march-2018.htm?view_full).

Carney, Maria T., et al. 2016. "Elder Orphans Hiding in Plain Sight: A Growing Vulnerable Population." *Current Gerontology and Geriatrics Research*:1–11. (https://doi.org/10.1155/2016/4723250).

Carstensen, Laura L. November 29, 2019. "We Need a Major Redesign of Life." *Washington Post*. (https://www.washingtonpost.com/opinions/we-need-a-major-redesign-of-life/2019/11/29/a63daab2-1086-11ea-9cd7-a1becbc82f5e_story.html).

Choi, Soon K. and Ilan H. Meyer. 2016. *LGBT Aging: A Review of Research Findings, Needs, and Policy Implications*. Los Angeles: Williams Institute. (https://williamsinstitute.law.ucla.edu/wp-content/uploads/LGBT-Aging-Aug-2016.pdf).

Clark, Robert, et al. 2019. "Employer Concerns and Responses to an Aging Workforce." NBER Working Paper No. 25572. Cambridge, MA: National Bureau of Economic Research. (https://doi.org/10.3386/w25572).

Collinson, Catherine, Patti Rowey, and Heidi Cho. December 2019. "19th Annual Transamerica Retirement Survey: A Compendium of Findings about U.S. Workers." Los Angeles: Transamerica Center for Retirement Studies. (https://transamericacenter.org/retirement-research/19th-annual-retirement-survey).

Collinson, Catherine, Patti Rowey, and Heidi Cho. May 2020. "Retirement Security amid COVID-19: The Outlook of Three Generations; 20th Annual Transamerica Retirement Survey of Workers." Los Angeles: Transamerica Center for Retirement Studies. (https://transamericacenter.org/docs/default-source/retirement-survey-of-workers/tcrs2020_sr_retirement_security_amid_covid-19.pdf).

Conley, Chip. 2018. *Wisdom at Work: The Making of a Modern Elder*. New York: Currency.

Corporation for National and Community Service. 2015. "Older Adults (Age 65+)." (https://www.nationalservice.gov/vcla/demographic/older-adults-age-65).

Cowles, Charlotte. May 2, 2020. "My Retirement Plan Is You: Americans without Retirement Savings Are Increasingly Moving In with Their Millennial Children." *New York Times*. (https://www.nytimes.com/2020/05/02/business/Parents-retirement-moving-in-millennials.html).

Cox, Carole B. 2015. *Social Policy for an Aging Society: A Human Rights Perspective*. New York: Springer.

Dennis, Helen. 2002. "The Retirement Planning Specialty." *Generations: Journal of the American Society on Aging* 26(2):55–60.

Dennis, Helen and Kathryn Thomas. 2007. "Ageism in the Workplace." *Generations: Journal of the American Society on Aging* 31(1):84–89.

De Preter, Hanne, Dorien Van Looy, and Dimitri Mortelmans. 2013. "Individual and Institutional Push and Pull Factors as Predictors of Retirement Timing in Europe: A Multilevel Analysis." *Journal of Aging Studies* 27(4):299–307. (https://doi.org/10.1016/j.jaging.2013.06.003).

Dwyer, Debra S. and Jianting Hu. 2000. "Retirement Expectations and Realizations: The Role of Health Shocks and Economic Factors." Pp. 274–83 in *Forecasting Retirement Needs and Retirement Wealth*, edited by Olivia S. Mitchell, P. Brett Hammond, and Anna M. Rappaport. Philadelphia: University of Pennsylvania Press.

Dychtwald, Ken and Daniel J. Kadlec. 2005. *The Power Years: A User's Guide to the Rest of Your Life*. Hoboken, NJ: John Wiley & Sons.

Edge, Clare E., Anna M. Cooper, and Margaret Coffey. 2017. "Barriers and Facilitators to Extended Working Lives in Europe: A Gender Focus." *Public Health Reviews* 38(2):1–27. (https://doi.org/10.1186/s40985-017-0053-8).

Eisenberg, Richard. October 11, 2018. "Sara Zeff Geber: Offering Retirement Advice for Solo Agers." *Next Avenue*. (https://www.nextavenue.org/sara-zeff-geber/).

Ekerdt, David. April 22, 2018. "In Defense of the Not-so-busy Retirement." *Wall Street Journal*. (https://www.wsj.com/articles/in-defense-of-the-not-so-busy-retirement-1524449520).

Ekerdt, David and Evelyn Clark. 2001. "Selling Retirement in Financial Planning Advertisements." *Journal of Aging Studies* 15(1):55–68. (https://doi.org/10.1016/s0890-4065(00)00016-5).

Ekerdt, David and Catheryn Koss. 2015. "The Task of Time in Retirement." *Ageing and Society* 36(6):1295–311. (https://doi.org/10.1017/s0144686x15000367).

Encore.org. 2014. *Encore Careers: The Persistence of Purpose*. (https://encore.org/wp-content/uploads/files/2014EncoreResearchOverview.pdf).

Farrell, Chris. 2014. *Unretirement: How Baby Boomers Are Changing the Way We Think about Work, Community, and the Good Life*. New York: Bloomsbury.

Federal Reserve System. May 2019. "The Fed—Retirement." Board of Governors of the Federal Reserve System. (https://www.federalreserve.gov/publications/2019-economic-well-being-of-u s-households-in-2018-retirement.htm).

Forster-Holt, Nancy. 2013. "Entrepreneur as 'End'repreneur: The Intention to Retire." *Small Business Institute Journal* 9(2):29–42.

Freedman, Marc. 2008. *Encore: Finding Work That Matters in the Second Half of Life*. New York: PublicAffairs.

Freedman, Marc. 2011. *The Big Shift: Navigating the New Stage beyond Midlife*. New York: PublicAffairs.

Fry, Richard. January 31, 2018. "More U.S. Adults Now Share Their Living Space." Washington, DC: Pew Research Center. (https://www.pewresearch.org/fact-tank/2018/01/31/more-adults-now-share-their-living-space-driven-in-part-by-parents-living-with-their-adult-children/).

Goldin, Claudia and Lawrence F. Katz. September 2016. "Women Working Longer: Facts and Some Explanations." NBER Working Paper No. 22607. Cambridge, MA: National Bureau of Economic Research. (https://doi.org/ 10.3386/w22607).

Graebner, William. 1980. *A History of Retirement: The Meaning and Function of an American Institution, 1885–1978*. New Haven, CT: Yale University Press.

Hannon, Kerry. November 9, 2018. "Retired Workers Are Going Back to Former Employers." Washington, DC: AARP. (https://www.aarp.org/work/job-search/info-2018/how-to-boomerang-to-old-job.html).

Henkens, Kène, et al. 2017. "What We Need to Know about Retirement: Pressing Issues for the Coming Decade." *The Gerontologist* 58(5):805–12. (https://doi.org/10.1093/geront/gnx095).

Houghton, Angela. March 2018. "Maintaining Dignity: A Survey of LGBT Adults Age 45 and Older." Washington, DC: AARP. (https://doi.org/10.26419/res.00217.001).

Irving, Paul. 2014. *The Upside of Aging: How Long Life Is Changing the World of Health, Work, Innovation, Policy, and Purpose*. Hoboken, NJ: John Wiley & Sons.

James, Jacquelyn B., et al. 2012. *Just Do It? . . . Maybe Not! Insights on Activity in Later Life from the Life & Times in an Aging Society Study*. Chestnut Hill, MA: Sloan Center on Aging & Work, Boston College. (https://www.bc.edu/content/dam/files/research_sites/agingandwork/pdf/publications/EAWA_JustDoIt.pdf).

Klaesson, Johan, Esteban Lopez, and Özge Öner. 2017. "Who Works Longer—and Why? Regional and Individual Characteristics in the Timing of Retirement." *Tijdschrift voor Economische en Sociale Geografie* 109(3):350–70. (https://doi.org/10.1111/tesg.12295).

Laise, Eleanor. 2017. "Retirees, Survive and Thrive in the Gig Economy." *Kiplinger*. Last modified May 5, 2017 (https://www.kiplinger.com/article/retirement/T012-C000-S004-survive-and-thrive-in-the-gig-economy.html).

Livingston, Gretchen. 2019. "Americans 60 and Older Are Spending More Time in Front of Their Screens Than a Decade Ago." Washington, DC: Pew Research Center. (https://www.pewresearch.org/fact-tank/2019/06/18/americans-60-and-older-are-spending-more-time-in-front-of-their-screens-than-a-decade-ago/).

Maestas, Nicole. 2007. "Back to Work: Expectations and Realizations of Work after Retirement." Santa Monica, CA: RAND Corporation. (https://www.rand.org/pubs/working_papers/WR196-2.html).

Malito, Alessandra. May 14, 2020. "What Does the Government Need to Do to Help Retirement Savers through the COVID-19 Crisis?" *MarketWatch*. (https://www.marketwatch.com/story/what-does-the-government-need-to-do-to-help-retirement-savers-through-the-covid-19-crisis-2020-05-14?mod=alessandra-malito).

Mather, Mark, Paola Scommenga, and Lillian Kilduff. July 15, 2019. "Fact Sheet: Aging in the United States." Washington, DC: Population Reference Bureau. (https://www.prb.org/aging-unitedstates-fact-sheet/).

McKernan, Signe-Mary, Caroline Ratcliffe, and C. Eugene Steuerle. December 2, 2015. "Wealth Inequalities." Washington, DC: Urban Institute. (https://www.urban.org/policy-centers/cross-center-initiatives/inequality-and-mobility/projects/wealth-inequalities).

Mendryk, Iwona. 2017. "Retirement Age: Preferences of Employees Representing Various Age Groups." *Economics & Sociology* 10(4):29–40. (https://doi.org/10.14254/2071-789x.2017/10-4/3).

Mintzer, Dorian. February 23, 2018. "How to Become a Certified Retirement Coach." *Revolutionize Retirement.* (https://revolutionizeretirement.com/certified-retirement-coach/).

Morrissey, Monique. March 3, 2016. "The State of American Retirement: How 401(k)s Have Failed Most American Workers." Washington, DC: Economic Policy Institute. (https://www.epi.org/publication/retirement-in-america).

Munnell, Alicia H. March 2015. "The Average Retirement Age—An Update." *Issue in Brief* 15-4. Chestnut Hill, MA: Center for Retirement Research, Boston College. (https://crr.bc.edu/wp-content/uploads/2015/03/IB_15-4_508_rev.pdf).

National Institute on Aging. April 23, 2019. "Social Isolation, Loneliness in Older People Pose Health Risks." (https://www.nia.nih.gov/news/social-isolation-loneliness-older-people-pose-health-risks).

Ng, Thomas W. and Daniel C. Feldman. 2012. "Evaluating Six Common Stereotypes about Older Workers with Meta-analytical Data." *Personnel Psychology* 65(4):821–58. (https://doi.org/10.1111/peps.12003).

Rappaport, Anna M. 2019. "Retirement Success and Elder Orphans." Society of Actuaries. (https://www.soa.org/globalassets/assets/files/resources/essays-monographs/2019-family-structure/2019-family-structure-rappaport-orphans.pdf).

Reynolds, Susan S. November 25, 2010. "Book Review: 'Composing a Further Life.'" *Los Angeles Times.* (https://www.latimes.com/archives/la-xpm-2010-nov-25-la-et-book-20101125-story.html).

Ruffenach, Glenn. July 5, 2019. "What People Do in Retirement, Hour by Hour." *Wall Street Journal.* (https://www.wsj.com/articles/what-people-do-in-retirement-hour-by-hour-11562338744).

SAGE Advocacy and Services for LGBT Elders. 2014. "Out & Visible: The Experiences and Attitudes of Lesbian, Gay, Bisexual and Transgender Older Adults, Ages 45–75." *Advocating for LGBT Seniors | Fighting for LGBT Rights—SAGE.* (https://www.sageusa.org/wp-content/uploads/2018/05/sageusa-out-visible-lgbt-market-research-full-report.pdf).

Scharn, Micky, et al. 2018. "Domains and Determinants of Retirement Timing: A Systematic Review of Longitudinal Studies." *BMC Public Health* 18(1083):1–14. (https://doi.org/10.1186/s12889-018-5983-7).

Seattle Times Staff. December 31, 2013. "A Brief History of Retirement: It's a Modern Idea." *Seattle Times.* (https://www.seattletimes.com/nation-world/a-brief-history-of-retirement-its-a-modern-idea/).

Society for Human Resource Management (SHRM). January 16, 2020. "Employing Older Workers." (https://www.shrm.org/resourcesandtools/tools-and-samples/toolkits/pages/employingolderworkers.aspx).

Stanford Center on Longevity. September 2018. "A New Map of Life." Stanford, CA. (https://longevity.stanford.edu/a-new-map-of-life/).

Taylor, Mia. March 13, 2020. "Retirement in the Age of Uber: Can Gig Economy Workers Ever Call It Quits?" *The Simple Dollar.* (https://www.thesimpledollar.com/make-money/retirement-in-the-uber-era/).

Templer, Andrew, Marjorie Armstrong-Stassen, and Julian Cattaneo. 2010. "Antecedents of Older Workers' Motives for Continuing to Work." *Career Development International* 15(5):479–500. (https://doi.org/10.1108/13620431011075349).

Thomas, William H. 2004. *What Are Old People For? How Elders Will Save the World.* St. Louis, MO: VanderWyk & Burnham.

Thomas, William H. 2015. *Second Wind: Navigating the Passage to a Slower, Deeper, and More Connected Life*. New York: Simon & Schuster.

Toossi, Mitra and Teresa L. Morisi. July 18, 2017. "Women in the Workforce before, during, and after the Great Recession." *Spotlight on Statistics*. U.S. Bureau of Labor Statistics. (https://www.bls.gov/spotlight/2017/women-in-the-workforce-before-during-and-after-the-great-recession/home.htm).

Trafford, Abigail. 2003. *My Time: Making the Most of the Rest of Your Life*. New York: Basic Books.

U.S. Government Accountability Office. 2017. "Older Workers: Phased Retirement Programs, Although Uncommon, Provide Flexibility for Workers and Employers." U.S. Government Accountability Office. (https://www.gao.gov/assets/690/685324.pdf).

Van den Berg, Tilja I., Leo A. Elders, and Alex Burdorf. 2010. "Influence of Health and Work on Early Retirement." *Journal of Occupational and Environmental Medicine* 52(6):576–83. (https://doi.org/10.1097/jom.0b013e3181de8133).

Van Derhi, Jack. March 7, 2019. "Retirement Savings Shortfalls: Evidence from EBRI's 2019 Retirement Security Projection Model." Employee Benefit Research Institute. (https://www.shrm.org/ResourcesAndTools/hr-topics/benefits/Documents/EBRI_IB_410_Feb15_RSShrtfls.pdf).

Weisman, Mary-Lou. March 21, 1999. "The History of Retirement, from Early Man to A.A.R.P." *New York Times*. (http://libproxy.usc.edu/login?url=https://search-proquest-com.libproxy1.usc.edu/docview/431142202?accountid=14749).

Ybema, Jan F., et al. 2014. "Study on Transitions in Employment, Ability and Motivation (STREAM): The Design of a Four-year Longitudinal Cohort Study among 15,118 Persons Aged 45 to 64 Years." *British Journal of Medicine and Medical Research* 4(6):21–28.

CHAPTER 22

# Bridge Employment

Karen Pak and Mo Wang

## OVERVIEW

The population and workforces of most Western countries are aging as fertility rates decline, life expectancies rise, and the retirement of the large baby boom cohort is under way.[1] This combination of demographic trends is putting pressure on pension systems all over the world[2] and is expected to lead to long-term labor shortages.[3] To cope with the resulting pension costs, governments have raised the mandatory retirement age[4] and simultaneously seek ways to persuade individuals to work beyond the retirement age. As a result, research interest in bridge employment has increased over the past decades.[5] Bridge employment is seen as an important way to reduce pressure on pension systems and to reduce labor shortages.[6] Furthermore, bridge employment is becoming increasingly common among retirees as it provides them with a more gradual transition into retirement.[7] For example, data from the Health and Retirement Study (HRS) in the United States revealed that 47 percent of older workers engaged in postretirement employment.[8] Three subpopulations can be found among retirees in the United States during the first six years of their retirement—namely, those who stayed in full retirement (43.1 percent), those who remained in bridge employment (14.8 percent), and those who moved in and out of bridge employment (42.2 percent).[9] In Europe, the prevalence of bridge employment is generally lower, ranging from 0.8 percent in Spain to 13.5 percent in Greece.[10] However, in all countries, the participation rates of bridge employment have been increasing.[11,12]

By easing the transition from work to retirement, bridge employment can make retirement a less disruptive life event.[13] Over the lifespan, individuals are likely to face several major life events such as retirement.[14] Empirical studies that examine major life events in relation to work outcomes are scarce,[15] and to our knowledge no study to date has examined major life events in relation to bridge employment. However, as major life events can cause resource depletion and influence career decisions, they are likely to impact the decision to engage in bridge employment.[16] In line with continuity theory,[17] stability in the work domain provided by bridge employment might help retirees become more resilient should major life events occur in a later-life stage (e.g., becoming ill or losing a loved one). On the other hand, following role theory, major life events such as becoming a grandparent or having one's spouse retire might "pull" retirees toward full retirement and into other roles (e.g., caregiver).[18]

## DEFINING BRIDGE EMPLOYMENT

"Bridge employment" is an arrangement whereby employees gradually transfer from paid employment to full retirement.[19] It refers to paid work, often part-time, that older workers engage in after they retire from their main job before proceeding to full retirement.[20] Bridge employment is commonly divided in two main categories, namely, *career bridge employment* and *bridge employment in another field*.[21] Career bridge employment refers to individuals remaining at work in the same field or industry they worked in during the majority of their career. In line with this categorization, previous studies found that the different types of bridge employment relate differently to a variety of correlates.[22,23,24] Other distinctions that are made with regard to bridge employment are: flexible bridge employment (work reductions for the current employer) versus contingent bridge employment (sporadic employment for the current employer or other employers);[25] career bridge employment (continued work in the same field or industry) versus organizational bridge employment (continued work for the same employer);[26] and self-employed versus wage/salary-based bridge employment.[27]

## THEORIES RELATED TO BRIDGE EMPLOYMENT

Bridge employment can be studied from a variety of theoretical perspectives. In this chapter we will zoom in on three of these perspectives that we believe to be particularly beneficial for the study of major life events in relation to bridge employment. They are role theory,[28] continuity theory,[29] and a process model of successful aging at work.[30]

### Role Theory

Role theory[31] treats the retirement process as a process in which one experiences role loss and role transition. This theory states that through involvement in a specific (work) role, the identity belonging to this role starts to affect people's behavior and decisions.[32] When people retire, they tend to lose their work identity and transition to the retiree role. How this transition is experienced depends on how the work role was valued. When work was unpleasant (e.g., due to high workload, low salary, or unpleasant work relations), the loss of the work role may be seen as desirable, whereas workers who see their job as pleasant are likely to experience more stress and disruption due to the loss of the job role.[33] The transition from one role to the other can be made easier by maintaining the work identity (i.e., engaging in bridge work) or by becoming active in new roles (e.g., volunteering). Based on role theory, we therefore assume that work characteristics during the career and engagement in roles other than the work role will influence the decision to engage in bridge employment. Furthermore, we assume that major life events that make role domains outside of work salient will have a negative impact on the decision to engage in bridge employment. For example, if a retiree's spouse becomes ill, the caregiving role might replace the work role for the retiree. However, major life events that threaten nonwork roles might place more importance on the work role. For example, after a divorce or the death of a partner, the role of spouse being lost makes the employee role more valuable to protect.

### Continuity Theory

Continuity theory[34] suggests that older individuals aim to avoid psychological distress caused by the disruption of internal and external structures. Continuity refers in this case to the consistency of patterns over time and the accommodation of change without it becoming a stressful experience. Disruption of internal and external structures after retirement can be minimized by relying on the resources (e.g., educational level, financial status, and health) that have been accumulated over one's working life. In line with this theory, it is suggested that negative consequences of retirement can be avoided when social contacts and lifestyle from before the retirement are maintained.[35] Indeed, major life events can cause resource loss,[36] which threatens continuity in lifestyle. In line with continuity theory, engaging in bridge employment could minimize the negative consequences of major life events as it allows individuals to maintain lifestyle resources.

### A Process Model of Successful Aging at Work

Kooij and colleagues argue in their process model of successful aging at work that people will age successfully at work (i.e., have high ability and motivation to continue working) and subsequently engage in bridge employment if they are able to maintain or restore their person-environment fit by making effective use of self-regulation strategies. (See also chapter 15.) (Mis)fit can occur when (age-related) changes such as deterioration of physical abilities or major life events take place within the person (i.e., micro level) or at work (i.e., meso and macro level).[37] In line with this process model, we expect that bridge employment results from effective use of self-regulation strategies during the aging process.

## ANTECEDENTS OF BRIDGE EMPLOYMENT

The vast majority of research into bridge employment focuses on its antecedents.[38] These antecedents can be divided into variables relating to: (1) the individual, (2) the job, (3) the family, and (4) the socioeconomic context.[39,40] In this chapter we will also discuss a fifth type of antecedent that can occur at the individual, job, or family level—major life events.

First, with regard to individual attributes, previous studies found that retirees who were younger, male, and in good health and who received more years of education were more likely to engage in bridge employment than to retire.[41,42,43,44] Moreover, job-seeking self-efficacy of retirees is positively related to bridge employment.[45] Another important antecedent of bridge employment on the individual level is a person's motivational orientation. Previous research shows that retirees with high levels of *communion striving* (i.e., having a high propensity to direct goals toward improving relationships with others) and *generativity striving* (i.e., having a high propensity to direct goals toward knowledge sharing with people from younger generations) were more likely to engage in bridge employment.[46,47] Those with high levels of communion striving were also more likely to work more hours in bridge employment.[48] Furthermore, it was found that older males with high levels of status striving were more likely to engage in bridge employment, but this was not the case for older females with high levels of status striving.[49] Another important antecedent of bridge employment at the individual level is retirement planning. Retirees who did not think much about their retirement were more likely to engage in bridge employment,[50] whereas the more certain retirees were about their retirement plans, the more likely they were to fully retire.[51] Additionally, bridge employment appears to be common across all retirees with different levels of wealth.[52] However, retirees with low levels of wealth were less likely to transfer into self-employment and more likely to transfer into full-time bridge jobs.

Second, with regard to job-level antecedents, retirees with higher *job satisfaction* (i.e., the degree to which one is satisfied with the job) and *job involvement* (i.e., the degree to which one is inclined to continue working even when there is no financial necessity) in their preretirement jobs were more likely to engage in career bridge employment compared to full retirement.[53,54] Furthermore, retirees who experienced less stress in their preretirement jobs were more likely to engage in career bridge employment compared to bridge employment in another field or full retirement.[55,56] Additionally, those individuals who did well in their preretirement jobs and liked their preretirement jobs were more likely to engage in career bridge employment compared to bridge jobs in another field.[57] Furthermore, the degree to which an employee is committed to the organization appears to be a predictor of bridge employment for the same employer,[58] whereas career commitment was a predictor of career bridge employment,[59,60] Additionally, retirees were found to rate job ads featuring flexible work arrangements and equal employment opportunities as more attractive, whereas training and mentoring opportunities did not impact the attractiveness of the bridge employment opportunity.[61] It is important to note, however, that not all retirees seeking to engage in bridge employment were able to secure such a position. Older adults who had experienced involuntary retirement were especially unsuccessful in finding a bridge employment position.[62] Finally, managers are generally not eager to hire retirees, but their chances of getting hired increase when the organization faces labor shortages or when the retiree applies for a position similar to his or her career job.[63] The prevalence of bridge work is very similar among public- and private-sector workers, but public-sector workers engaged more often in part-time work after retirement compared to private-sector employees.[64]

Third, with regard to family-level variables, retirees with a spouse who was still working and dependent children at home were more likely to accept bridge employment.[65] Moreover, marital and family satisfaction do not impact the decision to accept bridge employment.[66,67] However, retirees who received social support for job seeking from their family and friends were more likely to engage in active job seeking for bridge employment.[68]

Fourth, with regard to societal-level variables, using data from sixteen European countries, Dingemans and colleagues found that retirees had a lower likelihood of engaging in bridge employment in countries with higher expenditures on pensions.[69] Furthermore, they found that in countries where there were strong norms regarding extended work life, engagement in bridge employment was more likely.[70]

Fifth, major life events in older age that occur at the individual, job, or family level may also be important antecedents of bridge employment. Major life events can be categorized as normative transitions, such as marriage or retirement; meaningful changes, such as a promotion or the birth of a (grand)child; and major individual experiences, such as death of a loved one.[71] Given the late life development stage, meaningful changes and major individual experiences are more likely to be associated with one's decision to engage in bridge employment. For example, in collective cultures, birth of a grandchild may prompt older adults to retire fully so that they can help out and meet the cultural expectation of the grandparenting role.[72] Indeed, it is conceivable that major life events can affect the decision to engage in bridge employment through influencing many of the individual-level (e.g., health), job-level (e.g., work-family conflict), and family-level (e.g., caregiving) predictors of engagement in bridge employment.

## OUTCOMES OF BRIDGE EMPLOYMENT

The majority of research on bridge employment has focused on the antecedents of bridge employment, and the outcomes of bridge employment have been largely overlooked.[73] However, two types of outcomes of bridge employment have received some attention: health and life satisfaction. In line with findings from the job loss and reemployment literature, it is expected that bridge employment will be beneficial for health outcomes.[74,75] Indeed, employees engaged in bridge employment reported fewer physical diseases and functional limitations than those who were fully retired.[76,77] Further, employees engaged in career bridge employment reported better mental health. These findings suggest that bridge employment is beneficial for one's health.

With regard to postretirement life satisfaction, mixed results are found. Whereas one study found that engaging in bridge employment had a positive influence on retirement satisfaction and life satisfaction,[78] another study showed that those who transitioned into full retirement had higher life satisfaction than those who remained in the workforce and the life satisfaction of those who involuntarily retired was lower than those who retired voluntarily or remained in the workforce.[79] This seems to indicate that it is better for life satisfaction not to engage in bridge employment. A third study offered a more nuanced understanding, wherein life satisfaction increased for bridge employees who were driven by intrinsic enjoyment goals, and it decreased for bridge employees who were driven by financial need.[80] These different effects for employees based on the reason for engaging in bridge employment can explain why such contradictory results were found in the previous two studies. Moreover, research shows that bridge employment could partially buffer the negative consequences of involuntary retirement on life satisfaction. The authors suggest that by engaging in bridge employment these retirees regained control over their work and thereby could ensure some form of continuity.[81]

Finally, to our knowledge only one study has examined what organizations could do to maintain work outcomes of bridge employees over time. More specifically, this study examined the extent to which human resource practices and social support mattered for work outcomes (i.e., work engagement, health, and work ability) of bridge employees. The researchers found that social support had beneficial effects on the work outcomes of bridge employees, whereas maintenance and development human resource practices, such as the opportunity to take part in the decision-making of the company and in training, had no effect.[82]

## DISCUSSION AND FUTURE DIRECTIONS

In this section we discuss the theoretical implications of bridge employment research and provide some avenues for future research. First, as previously mentioned, major life events have the potential to impact a number of factors that can shape retirees' bridge employment decisions. Therefore, these normative and nonnormative transitional events may have important implications for understanding bridge employment. However, studies that examine the influence of major life events in relation to work outcomes are quite rare.[83] To our knowledge, no study to date has examined the influence of major life events on bridge employment decisions or bridge employment experiences. This appears to be a fruitful avenue for future research.

Second, in line with the notion of cumulative advantage and disadvantage (see also chapters 3–6), those workers who are doing well during their career also appear to do well in bridge employment.[84,85] They are more likely to engage in bridge employment and when they do, they experience more benefits than less advantaged employees. In particular, those with better health, more years of education, and higher job satisfaction are more open to and successful in engaging in bridge employment.[86] Further, bridge employment appears to have positive outcomes for those whose bridge employment decision is driven by intrinsic enjoyment, but negative outcomes for those whose bridge employment decision is driven by financial need.[87] This suggests that bridge employment can potentially widen even further the well-being gap between retirees with good socioeconomic status and retirees with poor socioeconomic status. Major life events such as a divorce or bankruptcy that influence the socioeconomic status of an individual are therefore potential risk factors that might negatively impact not only the work experiences of an individual but postretirement experiences as well. More research is needed to examine how changes in socioeconomic status impact postretirement experiences.

Third, socioemotional selectivity theory[88] (SST) and selection optimization compensation (SOC) theory[89] provide insights into development over the lifespan and can be used to gauge desired work characteristics for bridge jobs. SST suggests that as one ages, motives shift from a focus on gains to a focus on affective rewards. Therefore, older workers are expected to place more importance on meaningful social interactions. Consequently, they have higher levels of generativity and higher needs for social intimacy as well as social embeddedness.[90] As noted earlier, generativity motives are therefore an important reason for engaging in bridge work.[91] Therefore, it is expected that job elements that promote socioemotional goals will be attractive to retirees.

However, Adams and Rau found that retirees did not rate job ads that mentioned mentoring opportunities as more attractive.[92] Therefore, research is needed on how employers should integrate and act on these socioemotional goals in order to attract retirees. Moreover, SOC theory suggests that in order to age successfully, people should aim to maximize age-related increases and minimize age-related losses. Accordingly, older individuals are less likely to invest in growth, while focusing more on maintenance and the regulation of loss. As a result, training is not likely to make bridge jobs more attractive, whereas maintenance and accommodative practices are expected to be more desirable. Indeed, Adams and Rau found that employment ads mentioning workplace flexibility made these jobs more desirable to retirees; conversely, ads that mentioned training were not considered to be desirable.[93] More research is needed to determine how a broader range of maintenance and accommodative practices affect the attractiveness of jobs for bridge employees.

Fourth, the majority of research on bridge employment has been conducted in the United States, with several exceptions using data from Canada, Europe, and Australia. However, studies on bridge employment in South America, Asia, and Africa are still very rare. The research of Dingemans and colleagues showed that country-level variables such as expenditure on pensions and country norms on working past the retirement age were important factors influencing the decision to engage in bridge employment.[94] Therefore, the current body of research, which has mostly taken a Western perspective, may not generalize to non-Western countries. To achieve more comprehensive understanding of the antecedents and outcomes of bridge employment, future research will benefit from data collection in non-Western countries.

## NOTES

1. United Nations. 2017. *World Population Prospects: The 2017 Revision, Key Findings and Advance Tables.* UN Department of Economic and Social Affairs.
2. Mikael Stattin. 2005. "Retirement on Grounds of Ill Health." *Occupational and Environmental Medicine* 62(2):135–40. (https://doi.org/10.1136/oem.2004.015669).
3. Thomas W. Ng and Daniel C. Feldman. March 2008. "The Relationship of Age to Ten Dimensions of Job Performance." *Journal of Applied Psychology* 93(2):392–423. (https://doi.org/10.1037/0021-9010.93.2.392).
4. United Nations, *World Population Prospects.*
5. Kenneth S. Shultz and Mo Wang. April 2011. "Psychological Perspectives on the Changing Nature of Retirement." *American Psychology* 66(3):170–9. (https://doi.org/10.1037/a0022411).
6. Nicole Maestas and Julie Zissimopoulos. 2010. "How Longer Work Lives Ease the Crunch of Population Aging." *Journal of Economic Perspectives* 24(1):139–60. (https://doi.org/10.1257/jep.24.1.139).
7. Joseph F. Quinn. 2010. "Work, Retirement, and the Encore Career: Elders and the Future of the American Workforce." *Generations* 34(3):45–55.
8. Robin L. Pleau. 2010. "Gender Differences in Postretirement Employment." *Research on Aging* 32(3):267–303. (https://doi.org/10.1177/0164027509357706).
9. Mo Wang and David Chan. 2011. "Mixture Latent Markov Modeling: Identifying and Predicting Unobserved Heterogeneity in Longitudinal Qualitative Status Change." *Organizational Research Methods* 14(3):411–31. (https://doi.org/10.1177/1094428109357107).

10. Gabriela Topa et al. 2014. "Bridge Employment Quality and Its Impact on Retirement Adjustment: A Structural Equation Model with Share Panel Data." *Economic and Industrial Democracy* 35(2):225–44. (https://doi.org/10.1177/0143831x12475242).

11. Kevin E. Cahill, Michael D. Giandrea, and Joseph F. Quinn. 2013. "Retirement Patterns and the Macroeconomy, 1992–2010: The Prevalence and Determinants of Bridge Jobs, Phased Retirement, and Reentry among Three Recent Cohorts of Older Americans." *The Gerontologist* 55(3):384–403. (https://doi.org/10.1093/geront/gnt146).

12. Dawn Alley and Eileen Crimmins. 2007. "The Demography of Aging and Work." Pp. 31–48 in *Aging and Work in the 21st Century*, edited by Kenneth Shultz and Gary Adams. New York: Psychology Press.

13. Mo Wang. 2007. "Profiling Retirees in the Retirement Transition and Adjustment Process: Examining the Longitudinal Change Patterns of Retirees' Psychological Well-being." *Journal of Applied Psychology* 92(2):455–47. (https://doi.org/10.1037/0021-9010.92.2.455).

14. Paul B. Baltes. 1987. "Theoretical Propositions of Life-span Developmental Psychology: On the Dynamics between Growth and Decline." *Developmental Psychology* 23(5):611–26. (https://doi.org/10.1037%2F0012-1649.23.5.611).

15. Jari J. Hakanen and Arnold B. Bakker. 2017. "Born and Bred to Burn Out: A Life-course View and Reflections on Job Burnout." *Journal of Occupational Health Psychology* 22(3):354–64. (https://doi.org/10.1037/ocp0000053).

16. Jos Akkermans, Scott E. Seibert, and Stefan T. Mol. 2018. "Tales of the Unexpected: Integrating Career Shocks in the Contemporary Careers Literature." *South African Journal of Industrial Psychology* 44(1):1–10. (https://doi.org/10.4102/sajip.v44i0.1503).

17. Robert C. Atchley. 1989. "A Continuity Theory of Normal Aging." *The Gerontologist* 29(2):183–90. (https://doi.org/10.1093/geront/29.2.183).

18. Blake E. Ashforth. 2001. *Role Transitions in Organizational Life: An Identity-based Perspective*. Mahwah, NJ: Erlbaum.

19. Kenneth S. Shultz. 2003. "Bridge Employment: Work after Retirement." Pp. 214–41 in *Retirement: Reasons, Processes, and Results*, edited by Gary Adams and Terry Beehr. New York: Springer.

20. Terry A. Beehr and Misty M. Bennett. 2015. "Working after Retirement: Features of Bridge Employment and Research Directions." *Work, Aging and Retirement* 1(1):112–28. (https://doi.org/10.1093/workar/wau007).

21. Mo Wang et al. 2008. "Antecedents of Bridge Employment: A Longitudinal Investigation." *Journal of Applied Psychology* 93(4):818–30. (https://doi.org/10.1037/0021-9010.93.4.818).

22. Wang et al., "Antecedents of Bridge Employment."

23. Kirsten T. Gobeski and Terry A. Beehr. 2009. "How Retirees Work: Predictors of Different Types of Bridge Employment." *Journal of Organizational Behavior* 30(3):401–25. (https://doi.org/10.1002/job.547).

24. Monika E. Von Bonsdorff et al. 2009. "The Choice between Retirement and Bridge Employment: A Continuity Theory and Life Course Perspective." *International Journal of Aging and Human Development* 69(2):79–100. (https://doi.org/10.2190/AG.69.2.a).

25. Sugumar Mariappanadar. 2013. "Do Retirement Anxieties Determine Bridge Employment Preference? A Study among Pre-retirees in the Australian Construction Industry." *Personnel Review* 42(2):176–204. (https://doi.org/10.1108/00483481311309375).

26. Yujie Zhan, Mo Wang, and Xiang Yao. 2013. "Domain Specific Effects of Commitment on Bridge Employment Decisions: The Moderating Role of Economic Stress." *European Journal of Work and Organizational Psychology* 22(3):362–75. (https://doi.org/10.1080/1359432x.2012.762763).

27. Gerry Kerr and Marjorie Armstrong-Stassen. 2011. "The Bridge to Retirement: Older Workers' Engagement in Post-career Entrepreneurship and Wage-and-salary Employment." *Journal of Entrepreneurship* 20(1):55–76. (https://doi.org/10.1177/097135571002000103).

28. Ashforth, *Role Transitions*.

29. Atchley, "Continuity Theory of Normal Aging."

30. Dorien T.A.M. Kooij et al. 2019. "Successful Aging at Work: A Process Model to Guide Future Research and Practice." *Industrial and Organizational Psychology: Perspectives on Science and Practice* 13(3):35–65.

31. Ashforth, *Role Transitions*.

32. Ashforth, *Role Transitions*.

33. Janet L. Barnes-Farrell. 2003. "Beyond Health and Wealth: Attitudinal and Other Influences on Retirement Decision-making." Pp. 159–87 in *Retirement: Reasons, Processes, and Results*, edited by Gary Adams and Terry Beehr. New York: Springer.

34. Atchley, "Continuity Theory of Normal Aging."

35. Heather E. Quick and Phyllis Moen. 1998. "Gender, Employment and Retirement Quality: A Life Course Approach to the Differential Experiences of Men and Women." *Journal of Occupational Health Psychology* 3(1):44–64. (https://doi.org/10.1037/1076-8998.3.1.44).

36. Karen Pak et al. Under review. "The Perceived Influence of Career Shocks on One's Career: A Qualitative Study among Older Workers."

37. Kooij et al., "Successful Aging at Work."

38. Beehr and Bennett, "Working after Retirement."

39. Yujie Zhan and Mo Wang. 2015. "Retirement and Bridge Employment: People, Context and Time." Pp. 230–49 in *Facing the Challenges of a Multi-age Workforce: A Use-inspired Approach*, edited by Lisa Finkelstein et al. New York: Routledge.

40. Mo Wang and Kenneth S. Shultz. 2010. "Employee Retirement: A Review and Recommendations for Future Investigation." *Journal of Management* 36(1):172–206. (https://doi.org/10.1177/0149206309347957).

41. Wang et al., "Antecedents of Bridge Employment."

42. Barnes-Farrell, "Beyond Health and Wealth."

43. Seongsu Kim and Daniel C. Feldman. 2000. "Working in Retirement: The Antecedents of Bridge Employment and Its Consequences for Quality of Life in Retirement." *Academy of Management Journal* 43(6):1195–210. (https://doi.org/10.2307/1556345).

44. Gabriela Topa et al. 2009. "Antecedents and Consequences of Retirement Planning and Decision-making: A Meta-analysis and Model." *Journal of Vocational Behavior* 75(1):38–55. (https://doi.org/10.1016/j.jvb.2009.03.002).

45. Chanjira Pengcharoen and Kenneth S. Shultz. 2010. "The Influences on Bridge Employment Decisions." *International Journal of Manpower* 31(3):322–36. (https://doi.org/10.1108/01437721011050602).

46. Kerr and Armstrong-Stassen, "Bridge to Retirement."

47. Yujie Zhan, Mo Wang, and Junqi Shi. 2015. "Retirees' Motivational Orientations and Bridge Employment: Testing the Moderating Role of Gender." *Journal of Applied Psychology* 100(5):1319–31. (https://doi.org/10.1037/a0038731).

48. Zhan, Wang, and Shi, "Retirees' Motivational Orientations and Bridge Employment."

49. Zhan, Wang, and Shi, "Retirees' Motivational Orientations and Bridge Employment."

50. Wang et al., "Antecedents of Bridge Employment."

51. Pengcharoen and Shultz, "Influences on Bridge Employment Decisions."

52. Kevin E. Cahill, Michael D. Giandrea, and Joseph F. Quinn. 2017. "To What Extent Is Gradual Retirement a Product of Financial Necessity?" *Work, Aging and Retirement* 3(1):25–54. (https://doi.org/10.1093/workar/waw027).

53. Wang et al., "Antecedents of Bridge Employment."

54. Pengcharoen and Shultz, "Influences on Bridge Employment Decisions."

55. Wang et al., "Antecedents of Bridge Employment."

56. Gobeski and Beehr, "How Retirees Work."

57. Gobeski and Beehr, "How Retirees Work."

58. Zhan, Wang, and Yao, "Domain Specific Effects of Commitment."

59. Zhan, Wang, and Yao, "Domain Specific Effects of Commitment."

60. Barbara L. Rau and Gary A. Adams. 2005. "Attracting Retirees to Apply: Desired Organizational Characteristics of Bridge Employment." *Journal of Organizational Behavior* 26(6):649–60. (https://doi.org/10.1002/job.330).

61. Rau and Adams, "Attracting Retirees to Apply."

62. Ellen Dingemans, Kène Henkens, and Hanna van Solinge. 2015. "Access to Bridge Employment: Who Finds and Who Does Not Find Work after Retirement?" *The Gerontologist* 56(4):630–40. (https://doi.org/10.1093/geront/gnu182).

63. Kasia Karpinska, Kène Henkens, and Joop Schippers. 2011. "The Recruitment of Early Retirees: A Vignette Study of the Factors That Affect Managers' Decisions." *Ageing & Society* 31(4):570–89. (https://doi.org/10.1017/s0144686x10001078).

64. Joseph F. Quinn, Kevin E. Cahill, and Michael D. Giandrea. 2019. "Transitions from Career Employment among Public- and Private-sector Workers." *Journal of Pension Economics & Finance*:1–20. (https://doi.org/10.3386/w25003).

65. Kim and Feldman, "Working in Retirement."

66. Wang et al., "Antecedents of Bridge Employment."

67. Pengcharoen and Shultz, "Influences on Bridge Employment Decisions."

68. Gary Adams and Barbara Rau. 2004. "Job Seeking among Retirees Seeking Bridge Employment." *Personnel Psychology* 57(3):719–44. (https://doi.org/10.1111/j.1744-6570.2004.00005.x).

69. Ellen Dingemans, Kène Henkens, and Hanna van Solinge. 2017. "Working Retirees in Europe: Individual and Societal Determinants." *Work, Employment and Society* 31(6):972–91. (https://doi.org/10.1177/0950017016664677).

70. Jule Specht, Boris Egloff, and Stefan C. Schmukle. 2011. "Stability and Change of Personality across the Life Course: The Impact of Age and Major Life Events on Mean-level and Rank-order Stability of the Big Five." *Journal of Personality and Social Psychology* 101(4):862–82. (https://doi.org/10.1037/a0024950).

71. Specht, Egloff, and Schmukle, "Stability and Change of Personality."

72. Barbara Griffin, Vanessa Loh, and Beryl Hesketh. 2013. "A Mental Model of Factors Associated with Subjective Life Expectancy." *Social Science & Medicine* 82:79–86. (https://doi.org/10.1016/j.socscimed.2013.01.026).

73. Shultz, "Bridge Employment."

74. Luana Giatti, Sandhi M. Barreto, and Cibele C. César. 2010. "Unemployment and Self-rated Health: Neighborhood Influence." *Social Science & Medicine* 71(4):815–23. (https://doi.org/10.1016/j.socscimed.2010.05.021).

75. Andreas Lundin et al. 2014. "Unemployment and Coronary Heart Disease among Middle-aged Men in Sweden: 39,243 Men Followed for 8 Years." *Occupational Environmental Medicine* 71(3):183–88. (https://doi.org/10.1136/oemed-2013-101721).

76. Yujie Zhan et al. 2009. "Bridge Employment and Retirees' Health: A Longitudinal Investigation." *Journal of Occupational Health Psychology* 14(4):374–89. (https://doi.org/10.1037/a0015285).

77. Alley and Crimmins, "Demography of Aging and Work."

78. Kim and Feldman, "Working in Retirement."

79. Douglas A. Hershey and Kène Henkens. 2013. "Impact of Different Types of Retirement Transitions on Perceived Satisfaction with Life." *The Gerontologist* 54(2):232–44. (https://doi.org/10.1093/geront/gnt006).

80. Karpinska, Henkens, and Schippers, "Recruitment of Early Retirees."

81. Karpinska, Henkens, and Schippers, "Recruitment of Early Retirees."

82. Klaske N. Veth et al. 2018. "Bridge over an Aging Population: Examining Longitudinal Relations among Human Resource Management, Social Support, and Employee Outcomes among Bridge Workers." *Frontiers in Psychology* 9:574. (https://doi.org/10.3389/fpsyg.2018.00574).

83. Arnold B. Bakker, Danyang Du, and Daantje Derks. 2018. "Major Life Events in Family Life, Work Engagement, and Performance: A Test of the Work-home Resources Model." *International Journal of Stress Management* 26(3):238–49. (https://doi.org/10.1037/str0000108).

84. Stephen Crystal and Dennis Shea. 1990a. "Cumulative Advantage, Cumulative Disadvantage, and Inequality among Elderly People." *The Gerontologist* 30(4):437–43. (https://doi.org/10.1093/geront/30.4.437).

85. Stephen Crystal and Dennis Shea. 1990b. "The Economic Well-being of the Elderly." *Review of Income and Wealth* 36(3):227–47. (https://doi.org/10.1111/j.1475-4991.1990.tb00302.x).

86. Beehr and Bennett, "Working after Retirement."

87. Karpinska, Henkens, and Schippers, "Recruitment of Early Retirees."

88. Laura L. Carstensen. 1995. "Evidence for a Life-span Theory of Socioemotional Selectivity." *Current Directions in Psychological Science* 4(5):151–56. (https://doi.org/10.1111/1467-8721.ep11512261).

89. Paul B. Baltes, Ursula M. Staudinger, and Ulman Lindenberger. 1999. "Lifespan Psychology: Theory and Application to Intellectual Functioning." *Annual Review of Psychology* 50(1):471–507. (https://doi.org/10.1146/annurev.psych.50.1.471).

90. Frieder R. Lang and Laura L. Carstensen. 2002. "Time Counts: Future Time Perspective, Goals, and Social Relationships." *Psychology and Aging* 17(1):125–39. (https://doi.org/10.1037/0882-7974.17.1.125).

91. Zhan and Wang, "Retirement and Bridge Employment."

92. Dingemans, Henkens, and van Solinge, "Working Retirees in Europe."

93. Dingemans, Henkens, and van Solinge, "Working Retirees in Europe."

94. Specht, Egloff, and Schmukle, "Stability and Change of Personality."

## REFERENCES

Adams, Gary and Barbara Rau. 2004. "Job Seeking among Retirees Seeking Bridge Employment." *Personnel Psychology* 57(3):719–44. (https://doi.org/10.1111/j.1744-6570.2004.00005.x).

Akkermans, Jos, Scott E. Seibert, and Stefan T. Mol. 2018. "Tales of the Unexpected: Integrating Career Shocks in the Contemporary Careers Literature." *South African Journal of Industrial Psychology* 44(1):1–10. (https://doi.org/10.4102/sajip.v44i0.1503).

Alley, Dawn and Eileen Crimmins. 2007. "The Demography of Aging and Work." Pp. 31–48 in *Aging and Work in the 21st Century*, edited by Kenneth Shultz and Gary Adams. New York: Psychology Press.

Ashforth, Blake E. 2001. *Role Transitions in Organizational Life: An Identity-based Perspective.* Mahwah, NJ: Erlbaum.

Atchley, Robert C. 1989. "A Continuity Theory of Normal Aging." *The Gerontologist* 29(2):183–90. (https://doi.org/10.1093/geront/29.2.183).

Bakker, Arnold B., Danyang Du, and Daantje Derks. 2018. "Major Life Events in Family Life, Work Engagement, and Performance: A Test of the Work-home Resources Model." *International Journal of Stress Management* 26(3):238–49. (https://doi.org/10.1037/str0000108).

Baltes, Paul B. 1987. "Theoretical Propositions of Life-span Developmental Psychology: On the Dynamics between Growth and Decline." *Developmental Psychology* 23(5):611–26. (https://doi.org/10.1037%2F0012-1649.23.5.611).

Baltes, Paul B., Ursula M. Staudinger, and Ulman Lindenberger. 1999. "Lifespan Psychology: Theory and Application to Intellectual Functioning." *Annual Review of Psychology* 50(1):471–507. (https://doi.org/10.1146/annurev.psych.50.1.471).

Barnes-Farrell, Janet L. 2003. "Beyond Health and Wealth: Attitudinal and Other Influences on Retirement Decision-making." Pp. 159–87 in *Retirement: Reasons, Processes, and Results*, edited by Gary Adams and Terry Beehr. New York: Springer.

Beehr, Terry A. and Misty M. Bennett. 2015. "Working after Retirement: Features of Bridge Employment and Research Directions." *Work, Aging and Retirement* 1(1):112–28. (https://doi.org/10.1093/workar/wau007).

Cahill, Kevin E., Michael D. Giandrea, and Joseph F. Quinn. 2013. "Retirement Patterns and the Macroeconomy, 1992–2010: The Prevalence and Determinants of Bridge Jobs, Phased Retirement, and Reentry among Three Recent Cohorts of Older Americans." *The Gerontologist* 55(3):384–403. (https://doi.org/10.1093/geront/gnt146).

Cahill, Kevin E., Michael D. Giandrea, and Joseph F. Quinn. 2017. "To What Extent Is Gradual Retirement a Product of Financial Necessity?" *Work, Aging and Retirement* 3(1):25–54. (https://doi.org/10.1093/workar/waw027).

Carstensen, Laura L. 1995. "Evidence for a Life-span Theory of Socioemotional Selectivity." *Current Directions in Psychological Science* 4(5):151–56. (https://doi.org/10.1111/1467-8721.ep11512261).

Crystal, Stephen and Dennis Shea. 1990a. "Cumulative Advantage, Cumulative Disadvantage, and Inequality among Elderly People." *The Gerontologist* 30(4):437–43. (https://doi.org/10.1093/geront/30.4.437).

Crystal, Stephen and Dennis Shea. 1990b. "The Economic Well-being of the Elderly." *Review of Income and Wealth* 36(3):227–47. (https://doi.org/10.1111/j.1475-4991.1990.tb00302.x).

Dingemans, Ellen, Kène Henkens, and Hanna van Solinge. 2015. "Access to Bridge Employment: Who Finds and Who Does Not Find Work after Retirement?" *The Gerontologist* 56(4):630–40. (https://doi.org/10.1093/geront/gnu182).

Dingemans, Ellen, Kène Henkens, and Hanna van Solinge. 2017. "Working Retirees in Europe: Individual and Societal Determinants." *Work, Employment and Society* 31(6):972–91. (https://doi.org/10.1177/0950017016664677).

Giatti, Luana, Sandhi M. Barreto, and Cibele C. César. 2010. "Unemployment and Self-rated Health: Neighborhood Influence." *Social Science & Medicine* 71(4):815–23. (https://doi.org/10.1016/j.socscimed.2010.05.021).

Gobeski, Kirsten T. and Terry A. Beehr. 2009. "How Retirees Work: Predictors of Different Types of Bridge Employment." *Journal of Organizational Behavior* 30(3):401–25. (https://doi.org/10.1002/job.547).

Griffin, Barbara, Vanessa Loh, and Beryl Hesketh. 2013. "A Mental Model of Factors Associated with Subjective Life Expectancy." *Social Science & Medicine* 82:79–86. (https://doi.org/10.1016/j.socscimed.2013.01.026).

Hakanen, Jari J. and Arnold B. Bakker. 2017. "Born and Bred to Burn Out: A Life-course View and Reflections on Job Burnout." *Journal of Occupational Health Psychology* 22(3):354–64. (https://doi.org/10.1037/ocp0000053).

Hershey, Douglas A. and Kène Henkens. 2013. "Impact of Different Types of Retirement Transitions on Perceived Satisfaction with Life." *The Gerontologist* 54(2):232–44. (https://doi.org/10.1093/geront/gnt006).

Jones, David A. and Barbara R. McIntosh. 2010. "Organizational and Occupational Commitment in Relation to Bridge Employment and Retirement Intentions." *Journal of Vocational Behavior* 77(2):290–303. (https://doi.org/10.1016/j.jvb.2010.04.004).

Karpinska, Kasia, Kène Henkens, and Joop Schippers. 2011. "The Recruitment of Early Retirees: A Vignette Study of the Factors That Affect Managers' Decisions." *Ageing & Society* 31(4):570–89. (https://doi.org/10.1017/s0144686x10001078).

Kerr, Gerry and Marjorie Armstrong-Stassen. 2011. "The Bridge to Retirement: Older Workers' Engagement in Post-career Entrepreneurship and Wage-and-salary Employment." *Journal of Entrepreneurship* 20(1):55–76. (https://doi.org/10.1177/097135571002000103).

Kim, Seongsu and Daniel C. Feldman. 2000. "Working in Retirement: The Antecedents of Bridge Employment and Its Consequences for Quality of Life in Retirement." *Academy of Management Journal* 43(6):1195–210. (https://doi.org/10.2307/1556345).

Kooij, Dorien T. A. M., et al. 2019. "Successful Aging at Work: A Process Model to Guide Future Research and Practice." *Industrial and Organizational Psychology: Perspectives on Science and Practice* 13(3):35–65.

Lang, Frieder R. and Laura L. Carstensen. 2002. "Time Counts: Future Time Perspective, Goals, and Social Relationships." *Psychology and Aging* 17(1):125–39. (https://doi.org/10.1037/0882-7974.17.1.125).

Lundin, Andreas, et al. 2014. "Unemployment and Coronary Heart Disease among Middle-aged Men in Sweden: 39,243 Men Followed for 8 Years." *Occupational Environmental Medicine* 71(3):183–88. (https://doi.org/10.1136/oemed-2013-101721).

Maestas, Nicole and Julie Zissimopoulos. 2010. "How Longer Work Lives Ease the Crunch of Population Aging." *Journal of Economic Perspectives* 24(1):139–60. (https://doi.org/10.1257/jep.24.1.139).

Mariappanadar, Sugumar. 2013. "Do Retirement Anxieties Determine Bridge Employment Preference? A Study among Pre-retirees in the Australian Construction Industry." *Personnel Review* 42(2):176–204. (https://doi.org/10.1108/00483481311309375).

Ng, Thomas W. and Daniel C. Feldman. March 2008. "The Relationship of Age to Ten Dimensions of Job Performance." *Journal of Applied Psychology* 93(2):392–423. (https://doi.org/10.1037/0021-9010.93.2.392).

Pak, Karen, et al. Under review. "The Perceived Influence of Career Shocks on One's Career: A Qualitative Study among Older Workers."

Pengcharoen, Chanjira and Kenneth S. Shultz. 2010. "The Influences on Bridge Employment Decisions." *International Journal of Manpower* 31(3):322–36. (https://doi.org/10.1108/01437721011050602).

Pleau, Robin L. 2010. "Gender Differences in Postretirement Employment." *Research on Aging* 32(3):267–303. (https://doi.org/10.1177/0164027509357706).

Quick, Heather E. and Phyllis Moen. 1998. "Gender, Employment and Retirement Quality: A Life Course Approach to the Differential Experiences of Men and Women." *Journal of Occupational Health Psychology* 3(1):44–64. (https://doi.org/10.1037/1076-8998.3.1.44).

Quinn, Joseph F. 2010. "Work, Retirement, and the Encore Career: Elders and the Future of the American Workforce." *Generations* 34(3):45–55.

Quinn, Joseph F., Kevin E. Cahill, and Michael D. Giandrea. 2019. "Transitions from Career Employment among Public- and Private-sector Workers." *Journal of Pension Economics & Finance*:1–20. (https://doi.org/10.3386/w25003).

Rau, Barbara L. and Gary A. Adams. 2005. "Attracting Retirees to Apply: Desired Organizational Characteristics of Bridge Employment." *Journal of Organizational Behavior* 26(6):649–60. (https://doi.org/10.1002/job.330).

Shultz, Kenneth S. 2003. "Bridge Employment: Work after Retirement." Pp. 214–41 in *Retirement: Reasons, Processes, and Results*, edited by Gary Adams and Terry Beehr. New York: Springer.

Shultz, Kenneth S. and Mo Wang. April 2011. "Psychological Perspectives on the Changing Nature of Retirement." *American Psychology* 66(3):170–79. (https://doi.org/10.1037/a0022411).

Specht, Jule, Boris Egloff, and Stefan C. Schmukle. 2011. "Stability and Change of Personality across the Life Course: The Impact of Age and Major Life Events on Mean-level and Rank-order Stability of the Big Five." *Journal of Personality and Social Psychology* 101(4):862–82. (https://doi.org/10.1037/a0024950).

Stattin, Mikael. 2005. "Retirement on Grounds of Ill Health." *Occupational and Environmental Medicine* 62(2):135–40. (https://doi.org/10.1136/oem.2004.015669).

Topa, Gabriela, et al. 2009. "Antecedents and Consequences of Retirement Planning and Decision-making: A Meta-analysis and Model." *Journal of Vocational Behavior* 75(1):38–55. (https://doi.org/10.1016/j.jvb.2009.03.002).

Topa, Gabriela, et al. 2014. "Bridge Employment Quality and Its Impact on Retirement Adjustment: A Structural Equation Model with Share Panel Data." *Economic and Industrial Democracy* 35(2):225–44. (https://doi.org/10.1177/0143831x12475242).

United Nations. 2017. *World Population Prospects: The 2017 Revision, Key Findings and Advance Tables.* UN Department of Economic and Social Affairs.

Veth, Klaske N., et al. 2018. "Bridge over an Aging Population: Examining Longitudinal Relations among Human Resource Management, Social Support, and Employee Outcomes among Bridge Workers." *Frontiers in Psychology* 9:574. (https://doi.org/10.3389/fpsyg.2018.00574).

Von Bonsdorff, Monika E., et al. 2009. "The Choice between Retirement and Bridge Employment: A Continuity Theory and Life Course Perspective." *International Journal of Aging and Human Development* 69(2):79–100. (https://doi.org/10.2190/AG.69.2.a).

Wang, Mo. 2007. "Profiling Retirees in the Retirement Transition and Adjustment Process: Examining the Longitudinal Change Patterns of Retirees' Psychological Well-being." *Journal of Applied Psychology* 92(2):455–74. (https://doi.org/10.1037/0021-9010.92.2.455).

Wang, Mo, et al. 2008. "Antecedents of Bridge Employment: A Longitudinal Investigation." *Journal of Applied Psychology* 93(4):818–30. (https://doi.org/10.1037/0021-9010.93.4.818).

Wang, Mo and David Chan. 2011. "Mixture Latent Markov Modeling: Identifying and Predicting Unobserved Heterogeneity in Longitudinal Qualitative Status Change." *Organizational Research Methods* 14(3):411–31. (https://doi.org/10.1177/1094428109357107).

Wang, Mo and Kenneth S. Shultz. 2010. "Employee Retirement: A Review and Recommendations for Future Investigation." *Journal of Management* 36(1):172–206. (https://doi.org/10.1177/0149206309347957).

Zhan, Yujie, et al. 2009. "Bridge Employment and Retirees' Health: A Longitudinal Investigation." *Journal of Occupational Health Psychology* 14(4):374–89. (https://doi.org/10.1037/a0015285).

Zhan, Yujie and Mo Wang. 2015. "Retirement and Bridge Employment: People, Context and Time." Pp. 230–49 in *Facing the Challenges of a Multi-age Workforce: A Use-inspired Approach,* edited by Lisa Finkelstein et al. New York: Routledge.

Zhan, Yujie, Mo Wang, and Junqi Shi. 2015. "Retirees' Motivational Orientations and Bridge Employment: Testing the Moderating Role of Gender." *Journal of Applied Psychology* 100(5):1319–31. (https://doi.org/10.1037/a0038731).

Zhan, Yujie, Mo Wang, and Xiang Yao. 2013. "Domain Specific Effects of Commitment on Bridge Employment Decisions: The Moderating Role of Economic Stress." *European Journal of Work and Organizational Psychology* 22(3):362–75. (https://doi.org/10.1080/1359432x.2012.762763).

CHAPTER 23

# Senior Entrepreneurship

## The Twenty-First Century's Most Underrated Economic Engine

Elizabeth Isele

### OVERVIEW

Senior entrepreneurship is not an oxymoron, and the "experienced economy" is not just a sound bite. I know. I first coined the term "senior entrepreneurship" and launched SeniorEntrepreneurshipWorks.com back in 2012 at the experienced age of seventy. My goal was to disrupt the pervasive negative stereotype of aging as a period of decline and dependency and transform it through education, programs, new public policy, and research into an unprecedented twenty-first-century opportunity to boost social and economic prosperity worldwide.

Senior Entrepreneurship Works grew into the Global Institute of Experienced Entrepreneurship (GIEE). And, for the past eight years, I have been crisscrossing the globe, convening dynamic summits of world leaders in government, universities, and the private sector to raise awareness of and activate the power of experience. Older adults are not a social expenditure, but rather an investment in terms of present and future capabilities. Part of that investment should be to meet the urgent need to build an ecosystem of innovative collaborations and new pathways through technology and inclusion to equip older individuals with the skills and resources they need to optimize and sustain an "experienced economy."

## WHY SENIOR ENTREPRENEURSHIP? WHY NOW?

When governments confront the global aging phenomenon, they are often overwhelmed by the challenges, especially the cost, of health care, pensions, welfare, and other social programs needed to address demographic projections. But thinking about older generations primarily as a liability obscures how much they can be an *asset*.

With our unparalleled, twenty-first-century gift of twenty, thirty, forty-plus years of extended longevity, we're all entrepreneurs. We're all thinking out of the box because there is no box. There's no grand design or even a road map for what to do next to add life to those extended years.

The traditional concept of work as a career job before retiring on a comfortable pension no longer exists. (See also chapter 21.) After decades of accruing information and skills, we are now at a point in our lives where we have an opportunity to distill all that experience into actionable steps to live the next decades of our lives meaningfully and productively. Seniors around the globe are proactively creating new lives, optimizing their life and work experience in nontraditional career paths, and creating businesses of their own—from micro- to multimillion-dollar ventures—in unprecedented numbers.

## SEISMIC DEMOGRAPHIC SHIFTS

The aging population is the world's largest, fastest-growing, untapped natural resource. With approximately 16 percent of the world's population aged fifty-five years or older today, entrepreneurial activity directly affects more than 1.2 billion people. This impact will grow as the world population continues to age and life expectancy increases. According to the WHO *World Report on Ageing and Health*,[1] the number of people over the age of sixty is expected to double by 2050.

And with longevity increasing, we should measure age in future potential rather than the chronology of lived years, argues Sergei Scherbov, director of demographic analysis for the Wittgenstein Centre for Demography and Global Human Capital and speaker at the UN Forum on Aging in Bangkok in February 2019 and the International Policy Forum on the Silver Economy at Chatham House, London, in July 2019.

These seismic shifts affect individuals, communities, governments, and private-sector organizations as they seek to address challenges related to health care, housing, work, pensions, and retirement. All these factors seem to suggest the aging population is a burden for society, but GIEE is turning this negative trend around by helping society understand the ways in which experience can be a competitive advantage. Innovation does not decline with age. Research demonstrates that older workers can actually be more innovative than their younger counterparts.[2] One explanation is that it takes time for education and work experience to settle in our brain and trigger new ideas about better ways of doing things.

Although the media image of an entrepreneur is a tech-savvy youth in a hoodie working in his garage,[3] the Kauffman Index of Startup Activity found that the highest rate of entrepreneurial activity in the U.S. over the past fifteen years was among the fifty-five-to-sixty-four age group.[4] Similarly, a 2014 Merrill Lynch study, "Work in

Retirement: Myths and Motivations,"[5] found that older employees who have no intention of retiring were three times more likely than young people to become entrepreneurs and launch their own businesses.

We're entering a new era, and it's about an "experienced economy" where fifty-plus-year-old entrepreneurs are building new businesses faster than any other group, creating jobs, and driving prosperity for people of all ages. Forget rocking chairs—fifty-plus-year-olds are rocking the global economy.

## DATA REVEAL THE IMPACT OF SENIOR ENTREPRENEURSHIP

Thanks to technology and access to capital through such mechanisms as crowdfunding, it has never been an easier time to start a business. The challenge lies in operationalizing and scaling up that business. And crowdfunding is about much more than money. One of its greatest assets is the ability to focus-group test a product or service at minimal cost. If, for example, a business idea is posted on a crowdfunding site and no one is willing to contribute a dollar or two, clearly that idea is a bust. There's no market for it. Countless hours and dollars can be saved by jettisoning the idea and moving on to another.

Senior entrepreneurs are a huge untapped resource. Not only do they know how to connect the dots in their trove of experience, but they know what has worked and what hasn't. Moreover, they know how to take initiative, can spot an opportunity, and are eager to engage in creative problem solving, turning ideas into actions with people of all ages. This is not just wishful thinking. Data collected worldwide by GIEE demonstrates the impact of senior entrepreneurship in the workforce. For example:

- Entrepreneurial activity among the over-fifties has increased by more than 50 percent since 2008, and they're almost twice as likely to establish successful companies than those between ages twenty and thirty-four.[6]
- A sixty-year-old start-up founder is three times as likely as a thirty-year-old founder to launch a successful start-up and is 1.7 times as likely to found a start-up that winds up in the top 0.1 percent of all companies.[7]
- Entrepreneurs aged fifty and older are two to three times more likely to form a new business, creating jobs for others, than they are to be involved in the gig economy.[8]
- Five years after start-up, 70 percent of ventures established by senior entrepreneurs are still in operation, compared to just 28 percent of enterprises launched by younger entrepreneurs.[9]
- More financial institutions worldwide, such as AIB Dublin (the largest funding source for entrepreneurs in Ireland), are deciding that the numbers of seniors who wish to start businesses is good business; data collected on their success rates are positive indicators of the new market opportunity. "This is a unique lending group, deserving of specific consideration in lending, that accounts for the maturity and seasoning of people 50+," states the bank's executive vice president of strategy and enablement.[10]
- Under the United Nations' standard assumption that a working life ends at sixty-five, forcing aging populations to retire instead of tapping into their experience

could cut growth rates in parts of the world by one-third and then by one-half over the coming years.[11]

- The Federal Reserve Bank's "Growing Grassroots Entrepreneurial Ecosystems" is focusing on senior entrepreneurs to boost rural economic development in the U.S.[12]
- A recent study from the UPS Store found that nearly two in five Americans regret not starting the small business of their dreams, and nearly 54 percent of Americans would rather start a business than retire.[13]
- In the U.S., senior entrepreneurs are not depleting entitlement programs, as they are often portrayed as doing.[14] Today, they contribute more than $120 billion in federal taxes annually to support federal programs.
- Babson College's study *The State of Small Business in America* found that more than half of all U.S. small-business owners were aged fifty and older in 2016—up from 46 percent in 2007,[15] and it is well documented that small businesses are the largest net contributor of new jobs in the U.S.

Senior entrepreneurship has another significant economic impact. There is increasing evidence that older people who remain engaged in life, feel productive, and know that their opinions are valued stay healthier. A 2016 study of nearly three thousand people, published in the *Journal of Epidemiology and Community Health,* suggested that working even one more year beyond retirement age was associated with a 9–11 percent lower risk of dying during the eighteen-year study period, regardless of health.[16] And a 2015 study of eighty-three thousand older adults over fifteen years, published in the CDC journal *Preventing Chronic Disease,* suggested that people who worked past age sixty-five were about three times more likely to report being in good health and about half as likely to have serious health problems, compared with people who retired.[17]

Senior entrepreneurship is not just a U.S. phenomenon: fifty-plus-year-olds worldwide are launching more start-ups than any other cohort. The UK, Ireland,[18] and Australia[19] are leading the way, and the European Union has determined that senior enterprise is key[20] to achieving its 2020 economic growth goals. In Japan, which has the largest and fastest growing aging population in the world, the government is supporting university innovation centers, (public/private) business incubators, and special finance programs to support older entrepreneurs. The intergenerational incubator in Oita, Japan is one of the finest and more successful in the world.

As Marko Curavic, head of industry and entrepreneurship for the EU Commission, said at GIEE's Brussels Summit on Senior Entrepreneurship in March 2015:

> The real point is that we are all living longer and better and healthier lives, and the concept of retiring to a sort of eternal vacation—or the idea of being deemed to be "taking a job from a younger person"—is an idea from a time gone past. More and more, seniors are seeking renewed purpose, have ideas they want to bring to life, and are looking to retirement as a time of new opportunity and [he emphasized] fun!
>
> These are some of the reasons that the European Commission has been targeting senior entrepreneurs and senior mentors for new entrepreneurs as important groups to help rekindle the spirit of entrepreneurship across Europe.

> Our Entrepreneurship 2020 Action Plan, which was adopted about two years ago by our twenty-eight Member States, specifically mentions senior entrepreneurs as one of the groups who are often overlooked.

## WHY THE SURGE IN SENIOR ENTREPRENEURSHIP?

*Entrepreneuring never gets old!* An entrepreneur can be anyone, anytime, anywhere. Technology and medical advances are driving invention and, thereby, our abilities to live longer, actively, independently, and healthier than ever before. Across the world, people aged fifty-plus are asking what they can do with this windfall. Companies are urgently asking how they can stop the "brain drain," and governments fear a flood of retirements will bankrupt their social benefits programs. Understanding the value of senior entrepreneurship, devising ways to raise awareness, and creating programs to activate the potential of experience across generations represents an unprecedented opportunity to boost workplace engagement, productivity, and profitability and accelerate successful new business start-ups.

Former senator Claire McCaskill, ranking member of the U.S. Senate Special Committee on Aging, shared the following thoughts at GIEE's Washington, DC, Summit on Senior Entrepreneurship in March 2015:

> There isn't any age limit on entrepreneurial dreams and success. Some of the most dynamic, innovative businesses started in Missouri in the past decade have been built by seniors. And we need these older entrepreneurs to succeed if we're going to continue making economic headway in my state and across the nation. I'd like to think that in my work-life I've shown the younger crowd a thing or two, and I know many of today's senior entrepreneurs are doing the same.

Seniors are flocking to the start-up arena for a variety of reasons. Some are fulfilling a lifelong dream, others have lost their jobs and do not see reemployment in their future, and some enter the entrepreneurship arena accidentally.

Baby boomers are vastly unprepared to underwrite another fifteen to twenty-five years of life. A Pew Research Report[21] sadly notes that six in ten of those aged fifty to sixty-one say they may have to postpone retirement.[22] Northwestern Mutual's 2018 Planning & Progress Study[23] revealed that 78 percent of Americans are worried about not having enough money for retirement. Their concerns are well founded, for 21 percent of Americans have nothing saved and another 10 percent have less than $5,000 tucked away.[24]

At age sixty-four-plus, Robert Gray was laid off after working forty years as an industry analyst and computer storage systems designer. "It was ironic," he said, "because as an industry analyst I was paid to forecast future trends and, while I had been thinking about retiring, I had not forecast that the decision would be taken out of my hands." It took his Cornell University reunion of sixty-five former members of the Cornell Radio Guild, who were entrepreneurial innovators in the early 1960s, to ignite his light bulb moment.

He was shocked at the loss of skills and expertise among all the attendees who had also been "involuntarily retired," and he determined to do something about it. He rebooted the veteran techies by creating a cooperative called Aha!, where they would build travel apps for iPhones to replace the weighty books carried all over the world. The irony, of course, is that these handheld apps were built by techies whose first computers filled an entire room.

Whereas Gray's start-up was purpose driven, Mandy Aftel's was accidental. She had had a successful thirty-year career as a therapist in Berkeley, California, when she realized she wanted to write a book. She decided to make the main character a perfumer and, like any good author, dutifully began her research. She became so enthralled with the art and history of making perfume that she registered for a class to learn how to mix fragrances. She discovered a hidden talent for creating luxurious natural scents, and that's how her company, Aftelier Perfumes, began. (Aftelier is Aftel's spin on the French word *atelier*, meaning an artist's studio or workshop.)

She eschews anything synthetic and hand-blends each perfume from her collection of unique natural essences. Business is booming for the seventy-two-year-old Aftel. Many of her perfumes are packaged in antique French bottles, and they sell for upwards of $150 for a quarter ounce. Her custom blends sell for $2,000 per half ounce. *Vogue* calls her "one of the fragrance industry's most creative thinkers," and *Forbes* named her one of the top seven bespoke perfumers in the world. Not bad for an accidental entrepreneur!

## SENIORS BRING ADVANTAGES TO THE ENTREPRENEURIAL TABLE

Today's older and bolder entrepreneurs with their wealth of life and work experience have much to offer. They have accumulated considerable social and human capital—an extensive network; greater workforce experience; and well-honed communication, management, and human resource skills. Financial rewards beyond making ends meet is not a high motivation for starting a business. Their goals focus more on autonomy and self-actualization, on realizing creativity, capabilities, potential, and wanting to feel active, useful, and valuable. They also have a strong desire to create a better, more sustainable environment for their families and communities (as evidenced by several of the senior entrepreneurs highlighted in this chapter).

Innovation is much more than having an idea. Real innovation is recognizing the value of that idea and operationalizing it. It takes experience, skill, and risk, and we have found seniors less risk averse than young people when faced with uncertainty. Seniors have tried and failed at many things in their lifetimes and know when to let go of an idea and pivot to another way to achieve their desired solution. Resilience is one of their greatest assets. (See also chapter 19.)

Seniors often possess five character traits that Tiffany Shlain highlights as key to innovation and survival in her inspiring minidocumentary *The Adaptable Mind*:[25]

- *Curiosity*—They thrive on learning and making new discoveries.
- *Creativity*—They find solutions by making unlikely connections drawn from their experience.

- *Initiative*—They are proactive, positive, practical optimists eager to solve problems; their life experience of knowing what works and what doesn't is a huge advantage over those who've spent little time testing new ideas.
- *Multidisciplinary*—Entrepreneurs are not all cut from the same mold, nor do they have every skill needed for success. Whether innovators, developers, or executors, experienced individuals reach out to others from multiple disciplines, age groups, and backgrounds to test and fine-tune their ideas. One of Shlain's most memorable lines in the movie is, "Instead of multi-tasking, we should be multi-asking."
- *Empathy*—Be it selling an idea, product, or service, empathy is key. What Maya Angelou said about her stories is telling: "I've learned that people will forget what you said, people will forget what you did, but people will never forget how you made them feel." The ability to sense motives and feelings of others grows stronger throughout life and enhances the ability to communicate effectively face-to-face as well as via any form of social media.

## GOOD NEWS FOR OLDER ENTREPRENEURS FROM NEUROSCIENTISTS

In *The Secret Life of the Grown-Up Brain*, Barbara Straunch reminds us that the aging brain can grow and learn: "The brain, as it traverses middle age, gets better at recognizing the central idea, the big picture. If kept in good shape, the brain can continue to build pathways that help its owner recognize patterns and, as a consequence, see significance and even solutions much faster than a young person can."[26]

Asked to name the ideal age to retire, neuroscientist Daniel Levitin replied, "Never!"[27] In *Successful Aging*,[28] Levitin says that one of the most important predicates to successful aging is openness to new experience, new ideas, and new ways of doing things. Their ability to extract patterns—to see similarities in circumstances and situations—can lead to better decision-making and better problem solving in general.[29] All of this indicates that innovative, experience-driven entrepreneurship is good for seniors' brain health and well-being—not just for the economy.

## OLDER WOMEN AS ENTREPRENEURS

While our focus, thus far, has been on both men and women, it's important to draw particular attention to older women as entrepreneurs. In the majority of countries today, there are more older female entrepreneurs than male. Women are generally paid less and have often had to take a break in their careers to care for children or parents, thus negatively impacting any savings and/or pensions they might have and making their retirement needs quite different from men's. Moreover, almost 70 percent of married women will outlive their spouses by an average of five years.[30] In today's new longevity economy, women can expect to live fifteen to forty years beyond the traditional retirement age.

One of the best-kept secrets in economic development is the power of older, female entrepreneurs in both rural and urban areas and in developing and developed countries to boost social and economic prosperity, locally and globally. Older women have an innate entrepreneurial mindset. Though they often do not think of themselves as entrepreneurs, they have been thinking and acting entrepreneurially—improvising—for much of their lives to make sure their families have care, food, and shelter. The lack of recognition for older women is due, in no small part, to a pervasive negative perception of aging, which combined with sexism tends to make them invisible. This is not just about gender equality. So many people are focused on the World Economic Forum's dire prediction that it will take more than 250 years for women to achieve economic parity that they miss the huge, unprecedented economic opportunity right in front of them!

Qualitative data gathered by GIEE in interviews with senior entrepreneurs and policy makers highlight some of the inherent strengths that equip older women to excel at entrepreneurship. Older women are highly motivated both socially and politically to challenge injustices, protect their communities, and improve the environment. They have a fierce desire to continue contributing, to be relevant and economically self-reliant. Their diverse, reliable base of marketable skills as employees, teachers, caregivers, crisis managers, homemakers, educators, and financial wizards for businesses and households (to name just a few) can be applied to a plethora of new opportunities.

Two women, one in rural Wisconsin in the U.S. and one in Australia's Northern Territory, are prime examples of resourceful senior entrepreneurs who are driving economic growth and social benefits for their communities.

Jill Kerttula's "involuntary retirement" and unsuccessful search for a new job at age fifty-eight prompted her to explore whether the fiber art she loved doing as a hobby could generate income. She decided to risk investing $1,000 in a special sewing machine and began to design and reconstruct sweaters at her home in Wisconsin and sell them on Etsy, the world's largest online marketplace for handmade goods. Her unique sweaters found an audience. Selling at $300 and up, Kerttula's profit margins were significant. Key to her success is low overhead. She works from her home, has only one employee, and takes the finished sweaters to the local post office herself for shipping. Her cost of goods is minimal as she sources her fabrics at charity-based resale shops. Kerttula takes pride in saving materials that otherwise may have been destined for landfills. She says, "All my suppliers are chosen for their philanthropy and good works in hope of also keeping my business eco-friendly and socially responsible."

Kerttula was reluctant to call herself an entrepreneur until the economic impact she was creating in her rural community was pointed out to her: the suppliers from whom she purchases her fabrics and sewing materials, the employee she is paying, the postal service delivering her products, the internet provider connecting her to a virtual marketplace, even the gas she purchases to handle these tasks. It is a small but valuable supply chain that is boosting prosperity locally.

Karen Sheldon started her career as a chef at the remote Barrow Creek Roadhouse, about 174 miles north of Alice Springs in Australia's Northern Territory. She'd never cooked before but had a desire to learn and an understanding boss. Even more valuable, she was mentored by a group of local indigenous women who whetted her appetite for Aboriginal culture and local flavors. She went on to open her own restaurant, which she called the "Dolly Pot" after a tool the local miners used. It became an iconic, award-winning restaurant, and she went on to build a catering business that eventually grew to eleven locations across Australia. Sheldon was able to convert this success into tangible benefits for her local community. At the age of sixty, she launched the territory's first Vocational Training and Employment Centre, where she provides training for indigenous job seekers. Three years ago, in her midseventies, she founded Saltbush Mob, which worked with the Department of Health to develop a therapeutic program, case management model, and aftercare program that provides cost-effective, results-driven, and sustainable solutions to the territory's alcohol abuse problems.

Community-based economic development is driven by entrepreneurs like Kerttula and Sheldon, and the world can no longer afford to miss tapping into the potential of this overlooked demographic.

## HOW TO HARNESS THE INDIVIDUAL AND COLLECTIVE EXPERIENCE OF OLDER ADULTS TO BOOST PROSPERITY FOR ALL AGES

As a society we can offset this wasted potential by doing the following:

- Energizing communities to foster a senior entrepreneurship approach to economic development.
- Networking stakeholders to build supportive ecosystems and migrate those operating in an informal economy into the formal economy, so they become part of the solution rather than part of the problem.
- Creating space (ecosystems) for senior entrepreneurship and innovation.
- Stimulating robust investment in senior entrepreneurs.
- Developing senior entrepreneurship education programs, including intergenerational programs.
- Generating new research initiatives to document the social, environmental, and economic impact of senior entrepreneurship to help generate new public policy.

Creating grassroots entrepreneurial ecosystems is key, but that will only happen when different sectors realize the economic impact (what's in it for them) and work collaboratively to support this new cohort of entrepreneurs.

For the past eight years, GIEE has been hosting global forums from Australia to Chile, Ireland to Istanbul, Brussels to Japan, and points in between, convening cross-sector groups of key thought leaders with the power to make transformative change happen. The more diverse the leaders the better because true innovation occurs at the points where unique disciplines intersect. Framing the challenges of reengineering the twenty-first-century workforce through our ET&A (Entrepreneurial Thought and Action) solutions' lens, GIEE draws upon the experience and brainpower in the room to identify needs, opportunities, and best practices to create concrete takeaways, including action steps to ensure value and make a real impact in business and entrepreneurship, public policy, research, and academic arenas. The senior entrepreneurship summit GIEE hosted within the Amplify Festival, the largest corporate innovation learning platform in Australia and New Zealand, explored cutting-edge thinking, disruptive technologies, and emerging trends that impact business. (To learn more, including the origins of the program, go to http://www.experieneurship.com.)

## SENIOR ENTREPRENEURSHIP EDUCATION PROGRAMS

Many entrepreneurship courses are available to help people of any age launch and grow a business, but few are specifically designed to develop an entrepreneurial mindset and help seniors translate their experience into the skills needed to create and grow a business. GIEE developed the Experience Incubator to help seniors, many of whom are intimidated by the word "entrepreneur," understand how they have been thinking and acting entrepreneurially all their lives, so it's not a great leap to think of themselves as entrepreneurs today. The blended curriculum, specifically designed for adult learners, demystifies entrepreneurship beginning with a session called "Decoding Your Entrepreneurial History Decade by Decade."

One workshop participant shared her "red bicycle" story, describing how she created and scaled a weed-pulling business at age seven. A neighbor spotted her pulling weeds for a penny each in her own yard and offered her a penny to pull the weeds in his yard. She then took her wagon to the neighbor on the other side and got that neighbor to sign up for a penny a weed, too. Next, she ventured down her entire block with her wagon, gathering new customers along the way. Before long, she had saved enough money to buy the red bicycle she'd been eyeing for months. She came home, hitched her wagon to the red bike, and pedaled across the street to the next block and the next. Almost everyone signed up for her weed-pulling business, and by the time she reached age eight she had the entire neighborhood sewn up. Talk about building a business and scaling it through her neighbor-to-neighbor relationships. She had never thought of herself as an entrepreneur, but the class recognized she was a natural.

Google launched one of GIEE's Experience Incubators at its London Campus in 2015, and it became one of the "Top 10 Trending Voices" at Google. Francis Bacon said, "Knowledge is power," but GIEE recognizes the *dynamic process of learning* as even more powerful.[31]

In 2010, when sixty-six-year-old Paul Tasner decided he wanted to start his own pulp manufacturing business, he joined Dominican University's Venture Greenhouse, an incubator for social and environmental entrepreneurs in his community of San Rafael, California. He said, "There are tons of incubators out there, but many are just places where entrepreneurs can hang their hats and share war stories. I had a lot of experience but none in business ownership, so I was looking for real hands-on mentorship from seasoned professionals and like-minded environmentalists."

After working on the idea at the Greenhouse for a year, Tasner launched PulpWorks Inc. Tasner takes great pride in saying the company turns people's garbage into safe, planet-friendly products for protective packaging and countless other products. Today, PulpWorks Inc. is a million-dollar, triple-bottom-line, business-to-business venture, rooted at the crossroads of sustainable packaging, green architecture, and urban job creation. (To watch Paul Tasner's TED talk on his journey from employee to entrepreneur, go to https://www.ted.com/talks/paul_tasner_how_i_became_an_entrepreneur_at_66?utm_campaign=tedspread&utm_medium=referral&utm_source=tedcomshare.)

## ADVOCACY AND PUBLIC POLICY

GIEE advocates locally and globally, successfully spearheading new public policy that recognizes fifty-plus-year-olds as assets, not liabilities, and supports fifty-plus inclusion in the workforce and entrepreneurship. In February 2014, GIEE helped design the U.S. Senate's first ever hearing on the growing trend of older Americans starting their own businesses. The joint Senate committee hearing "In Search of a Second Act: The Challenges and Advantages of Senior Entrepreneurship" was hosted by the chairs of the Senate Small Business and Entrepreneurship Committee and the Senate Special Committee on Aging. GIEE and three other witnesses testified on ways to reduce barriers for senior entrepreneurs; outlined various initiatives, such as creating access to training and capital for senior business owners; described the impact of the Affordable Care Act on senior entrepreneurs; demonstrated senior entrepreneurs' impact on the overall economy; and pointed out the need to expand policy and programs.

As a result, Maine senator Susan Collins is drafting new legislation regarding seniors being allowed to use their unemployment benefits for entrepreneurship education and start-up seed money. New legislation regarding banking policy and improved access to capital is also being explored, as well as a number of other items to support senior business start-ups. The entire hearing can be seen on C-SPAN, where it was the most viewed of any previous Senate hearing.[32]

## RESEARCH

It is essential to design, collect, analyze, and communicate quantitative as well as qualitative research to document the social and economic impact of senior entrepreneurship and to substantiate and drive forward key efforts to support it. GIEE's current senior entrepreneurship research collaborations include partnerships with the University of Michigan's Institute for Social Research and its Ross School of Business, including the Center for Venture Capital and Private Equity; the Ewing Marion Kauffman Foundation; Babson College; GEM (Global Entrepreneurship Monitor); and U.S. Federal Reserve Bank.

Still, entrepreneurship at older ages remains a relatively understudied area despite its important implications for older adults' financial security and global economic growth. There is a great need to understand the entrepreneurial arc regarding ideation, opportunity identification, sustainability, growth, and exit strategy/business transition for the fifty-plus-year-old entrepreneur. Further, even though more financial institutions worldwide are seeing the numbers of seniors who wish to start businesses as a good investment and are tracking evidence of their success rates, the single most prolific entrepreneurs—seniors themselves—receive the least start-up and scalable growth funding (and this has been exacerbated in the COVID-19 pandemic).

## CONCLUSION

Corporations pushing older employees into retirement prematurely fail to understand the grievous impact on employee engagement, knowledge transfer, productivity, and entrepreneurship. Governments worldwide panic, thinking that millions of seniors will bankrupt their treasuries. As a society we have diminished the value of experience and perpetrated a brain drain, the scope of which is socially and economically devastating. We must spread the insights of practical visionaries such as António Guterres, secretary general of the United Nations, who said at the 2019 United Nations International Day of Older People, "We must find more ways to help older individuals continue to contribute. They are key to achieving our Sustainable Development Goals!"

Speaking of visionaries, one of the most inspiring stories about transforming personal and professional experience into a purposeful enterprise is Arlene Blum's. In 2007 at age sixty-two, Blum, a biochemist and world-class mountaineer, founded the Green Science Policy Institute[33] to eliminate toxic chemicals such as Tris (the flame-retardant chemical that was being used in children's pajamas) and regulate PFAS waste (per- and polyfluoroalkyl substances) to protect human and ecological health. Earlier in her career, in the 1970s, Blum had led the first all-women's American team to reach the 26,500-foot summit of Nepal's Annapurna I, one of the highest and most difficult peaks in the Himalayas. She also co-led the first women's team to climb Denali; completed the Great Himalayan Traverse across the mountain regions of Bhutan, Nepal, and India; and hiked the length of the European Alps with her infant daughter. Arlene Blum is the author of *Annapurna: A Woman's Place*[34] and *Breaking Trail: A Climbing Life*.[35]

Blum says, "Part of what we do is promote safer alternatives because there are many non-toxic ways to make products fire-safe. Working with an international coalition, we have already stopped the passage of a dozen new flammability standards that would have led to the use of hundreds of millions of pounds of potentially toxic flame-retardant chemicals in consumer household electronics and other products around the world." She admits her crusading work can be exhausting, which is saying a lot given her mountaineering. When asked what advice she would offer others who would like to enter the environmental enterprise arena, Blum said, "There's much work to be done, and I always recommend the same advice I use for climbing a mountain." Her tips:

- *Define your goals.* Determine what you want to do and visualize the summit.
- *Prepare for the expedition.* Before launching an enterprise, get your finances in order.
- *Select a winning team.* Choose people you'd trust with your life.
- *Be passionate.* Make certain you have the enthusiasm, persistence, and the physical, mental, and emotional fitness required for the long climb.

Anyone who still thinks global aging is a problem should think again. Today's senior entrepreneurs are breaking stereotypes and, as the twenty-first century's new economic engines, they are boosting prosperity for people of all ages locally and globally. Entrepreneuring trumps aging!

## EPILOGUE

As I write this chapter, COVID-19 has plunged the world into a devastating global crisis. Thousands of people have died worldwide, and there is no end in sight. One of the most pernicious side effects of the pandemic is the way it has exacerbated age bias. When older adults are depicted as vulnerable and sometimes even disposable, positive aging is set back exponentially. I call it "COVID-ageism." We still have a long way to go in advancing senior business start-ups, and COVID-19 has compounded a situation that was already wanting. Seniors, who have weathered many crises in their lifetimes, have much-needed wisdom and resilience to share. We ignore their experience at our peril. With humanity at a virus-induced crossroads, we can use it to get back to "normal" or we can use it to accelerate change. Let's choose change!

## NOTES

1. World Health Organization. September 30, 2015. *World Report on Ageing and Health*. Geneva: WHO.
2. Pierre Azoulay et al. April 2018. "Age and High-growth Entrepreneurship." Cambridge, MA: National Bureau of Economic Research. Working Paper No. 24489. (https://ssrn.com/abstract=3158929).
3. Carmine Gallo. February 2018. "New Studies Reveal the Ideal Age to Start a Business, and It's Not in Your 20s." *Inc.* (https://www.inc.com).
4. Ewing Marion Kauffman Foundation et al. May 1, 2017. "2017 Kauffman Index of Startup Activity: National Trends." (https://ssrn.com/abstract=2974462 or http://dx.doi.org/10.2139/ssrn.2974462).
5. Merrill Lynch/Age Wave. 2014. "Work in Retirement: Myths and Motivations/Career Reinventions and the New Retirement Workscape." Merrill Lynch Retirement Study, conducted in partnership with Age Wave. (https://agewave.com/wp-content/uploads/2016/07/2014-ML-AW-Work-in-Retirement_Myths-and-Motivations.pdf).
6. Thomas Schøtt et al. 2017. "GEM Special Report on Senior Entrepreneurship 2017." Global Entrepreneurship Research Association. (www.gemconsortium.org).
7. Azoulay et al., "Age and High-growth Entrepreneurship."
8. Understanding America Study (UAS) 165. 2020. "Entrepreneurship and the Understanding America Study: A Research Collaboration among the University of Michigan's Institute for Social Research, the Ross School of Business, and GIEE." Funded by the Ewing Marion Kauffman Foundation (RG-201806-4444).
9. Halima Khan. February 2013. "Five Hours a Day: Systemic Innovation for an Ageing Population." Nesta.org. (https://media.nesta.org.uk/documents/five_hours_a_day_jan13.pdf).
10. John Irwin, EVP of Strategy and Enablement, AIB Bank, Dublin, stated this after attending the GIEE Senior and Intergenerational Entrepreneurship Forum in Dublin, Ireland. February 2015.
11. The Economist. April 26, 2014. "Demography, Growth and Inequality: Age Invaders." Briefing. (https://www.economist.com/briefing/2014/04/26/age-invaders).
12. Dell Gines and Elizabeth Isele. August 2019. "Six Steps to Aid Older Rural Entrepreneurs." The Federal Reserve Bank of Kansas City. *Community Connections*. (https://www.kansascityfed.org/publications/community/connections/articles/2019/q12019/senior.%20rural%20entrepreneurs).
13. UPS Store. 2019. "Inside Small Business." Annual survey. (https://www.theupsstore.com/insidesmallbusiness and https://www.theupsstore.com/File%20Library/theupsstore/pr/full-results-isb-survey-2019.pdf).

14. Janet Adamy and Paul Overberg. June 2018. "Growth in Retiring Baby Boomers Strains U.S. Entitlement Programs." *Wall Street Journal.* (https://www.wsj.com/articles/retiring-baby-boomers-leave-the-u-s-with-fewer-workers-to-support-the-elderly-1529553660).

15. Babson College Report. 2016. *The State of Small Business in America 2016.* (https://www.babson.edu/media/babson/site-assets/content-assets/images/news/announcements/goldman-10ksb-report-2016.pdf).

16. Harvard Health Letter. June 2018. "Working Later in Life Can Pay Off in More Than Just Income." (https://www.health.harvard.edu/staying-healthy/working-later-in-life-can-pay-off-in-more-than-just-income).

17. Harvard Health Letter, "Working Later in Life."

18. Anna Pilkova, Marian Holienka, and Jan Rehak. April 2014. "Senior Entrepreneurship in the Perspective of European Entrepreneurial Environment." *Procedia Economics and Finance* 12:523–32. (https://doi.org/10.1016/S2212-5671(14)00375-X).

19. Alex Maritz, Roxanne Zolin, Gerrit De Waal, et al. 2015. "Senior Entrepreneurship in Australia: Active Ageing and Extending Working Lives." *International Journal of Organizational Innovation*:1–39.

20. Pilkova, Holienka, and Rehak, "Senior Entrepreneurship."

21. Pew Research Center. May 2009. *Different Age Groups, Different Recessions.* Social and Demographic Trends Report. Washington, DC. (https://www.pewsocialtrends.org/2009/05/14/different-age-groups-different-recessions/).

22. Pew Research Center, *Different Age Groups, Different Recessions.*

23. Northwestern Mutual. 2018. Planning & Progress Study. (https://news.northwesternmutual.com/2018-05-08-1-In-3-Americans-Have-Less-Than-5-000-In-Retirement-Savings).

24. Northwestern Mutual, Planning & Progress Study.

25. Tiffany Shlain (author and director) and Sawyer Steele (author and producer). 2016. "The Adaptable Mind." A Let it Ripple Film Studio minidocumentary. YouTube video, 11:02. (https://www.youtube.com/watch?v=937iCwJd3fI).

26. Barbara Straunch. 2010. *The Secret Life of the Grown-up Brain: The Surprising Talents of the Middle-aged Mind.* New York: Viking.

27. Daniel Levitin. February 2020. "What Is the Ideal Age to Retire? Never!" Ideas at TED.com. (https://ideas.ted.com/what-is-the-ideal-age-to-retire-never-according-to-a-neuroscientist/).

28. Daniel Levitin. 2020. *Successful Aging: A Neuroscientist Explores the Power and Potential of Our Lives.* New York: Dutton.

29. Levitin, *Successful Aging.*

30. Chris Taylor. January 2012. "Why Boomer Widows Are Financially at Risk." Reuters. (https://www.reuters.com/article/us-widows-financial/why-boomer-widows-are-financially-at-risk-idUSTRE80J1FQ20120120).

31. Examples of senior entrepreneurship education programs: One of the first, developed in 2012, was SeniorEnterprise.ie in Dublin, Ireland, sponsored by the EU's INTERREG IVB NWE and the Princes Fund in the UK. Another was the Dare to Dream New Venture Incubator for Older Adults in Israel. In 2015, the European Union hosted its first Senior Enterprise Summit in Barcelona, Spain, and now is expanding its senior enterprise training "labs" throughout member countries and creating semiannual "best practice" forums for lab directors. SeniorPlanet, which originated in New York City, has expanded to Denver, San Antonio, and Palo Alto. The Oita Prefectural Intergenerational Start-Up Center in Japan has members reaching into their nineties who are thriving.

32. U.S. Senate, Special Committee on Aging Hearing. February 2014. "In Search of a Second Act: The Challenges and Advantages of Senior Entrepreneurship." (https://www.aging.senate.gov/hearings/watch?hearingid=8DD9C8C7-5056-A032-52B5-5CEC26CDDCDC).

33. The Green Science Policy Institute. N.d. Berkeley, CA. (https://greensciencepolicy.org/).

34. Arlene Blum. 1980. *Annapurna: A Woman's Place.* New York: Random House.

35. Arlene Blum. 2005. *Breaking Trail: A Climbing Life.* New York: Scribner.

## REFERENCES


Adamy, Janet and Paul Overberg. June 2018. "Growth in Retiring Baby Boomers Strains U.S. Entitlement Programs." *Wall Street Journal.* (https://www.wsj.com/articles/retiring-baby-boomers-leave-the-u-s-with-fewer-workers-to-support-the-elderly-1529553660).

Akola, E. June 22–25, 2008. "Entrepreneurship at Later Life—Intentions, Motivations and Perceptions of Entrepreneurship among Aging Populations." In 2008 International Council for Small Business World Conference Proceedings. Halifax, Canada.

Amoros, José E. and Neils Bosma. 2013. *2013 Global Report: Fifteen Years of Assessing Entrepreneurship across the Globe.* London, UK: Global Entrepreneurship Monitor.

Azoulay, Pierre, et al. April 2018. "Age and High-growth Entrepreneurship." Cambridge, MA: National Bureau of Economic Research. Working Paper No. 24489. (https://ssrn.com/abstract=3158929).

Babson College Report. 2016. *The State of Small Business in America 2016.* (https://www.babson.edu/media/babson/site-assets/content-assets/images/news/announcements/goldman-10ksb-report-2016.pdf).

Barclays Bank. 2001. *Third Age Entrepreneurs—Profiting from Experience.* (http://www.uk.coop/sites/storage/public/downloads/third_age_entrepreneurs.pdf).

Blum, Arlene. 1980. *Annapurna: A Woman's Place.* New York: Random House.

Blum, Arlene. 2005. *Breaking Trail: A Climbing Life.* New York: Scribner.

Botham, Ron and Andrew Graves. August 2009. *The Grey Economy: How Third Age Entrepreneurs Are Contributing to Growth.* London: NESTA.

Cahill, Kevin E., Michael D. Giandrea, and Joseph F. Quinn. 2013. *New Evidence on Self-employment Transitions Among Older Americans with Career Jobs.* In Working Papers 403. U.S. Department of Labor.

Caliendo, Marco and Steffen Kunn. 2011. "Start-up Subsidies for the Unemployed: Long-term Evidence and Effect Heterogeneity." *Journal of Public Economics* 95(3):311–31. (http://www.iza.org/en/webcontent/publications/papers/viewAbstract?dp_id=4790).

Castellano, Sylvaine, et al. March 22–23, 2016. "Une Analyse des Micro-fondements de la Légitimité des Seniors Entrepreneurs Français." Conférence Micro-fondations des Capacités Dynamiques. Paris.

Duhamel, Marc, et al. 2016. "Senior Entrepreneurship: Empirical Evidence of the Effect of Aging on Entrepreneurial Intent." In 61st International Council for Small Business (ICSB) World Conference, New York.

The Economist. April 26, 2014. "Demography, Growth and Inequality: Age Invaders." Briefing. (https://www.economist.com/briefing/2014/04/26/age-invaders).

Empowering Encore Entrepreneurs Act of 2013. 2013. S.1454, 113th Congress. (https://beta.congress.gov/bill/113th-congress/senate-bill/1454).

Ewing Marion Kauffman Foundation et al. May 1, 2017. "2017 Kauffman Index of Startup Activity: National Trends." (https://ssrn.com/abstract=2974462 or http://dx.doi.org/10.2139/ssrn.2974462).

Gallo, Carmine. February 2018. "New Studies Reveal the Ideal Age to Start a Business, and It's Not in Your 20s." *Inc.* (https://www.inc.com).

Gines, Dell and Elizabeth Isele. August 2019. "Six Steps to Aid Older Rural Entrepreneurs." The Federal Reserve Bank of Kansas City. *Community Connections.* (https://www.kansascityfed.org/publications/community/connections/articles/2019/q12019/senior.%20rural%20entrepreneurs).

The Green Science Policy Institute. N.d. Berkeley, CA. (https://greensciencepolicy.org/).

Hantman, Shira and Eli Gimmon. 2014. "Dare to Dream: New Venture Incubator for Older Adults. *Educational Gerontology* 40(10):737–44.

Hart, Mark, Michael Anyadike-Danes, and Robert Blackburn. 2004. *Spatial Differences in Entrepreneurship: A Comparison of Prime Age and Third Age Cohorts.* In 30th Congress of the International Geographical Union (IGU). Glasgow, UK.

Harvard Health Letter. June 2018. "Working Later in Life Can Pay Off in More Than Just Income." (https://www.health.harvard.edu/staying-healthy/working-later-in-life-can-pay-off-in-more-than-just-income).

Khan, Halima. February 2013. "Five Hours a Day: Systemic Innovation for an Ageing Population." Nesta.org. (https://media.nesta.org.uk/documents/five_hours_a_day_jan13.pdf).

Kibler, Ewald, et al. 2012. *(Work)Life after Work? Older Entrepreneurship in London—Motivations and Barriers*. London: Kingston Business School, Kingston University.

Levitin, Daniel. 2020. *Successful Aging: A Neuroscientist Explores the Power and Potential of Our Lives*. New York: Dutton.

Levitin, Daniel. February 2020. "What Is the Ideal Age to Retire? Never!" Ideas at TED.com. (https://ideas.ted.com/what-is-the-ideal-age-to-retire-never-according-to-a-neuroscientist/).

Maritz, Alex, Roxanne Zolin, Gerrit De Waal, et al. 2015. "Senior Entrepreneurship in Australia: An Exploratory Approach." *International Journal of Organizational Innovation* 30(1):206–21.

Merrill Lynch/Age Wave. 2014. "Work in Retirement: Myths and Motivations/Career Reinventions and the New Retirement Workscape." Merrill Lynch Retirement Study, conducted in partnership with Age Wave. (https://agewave.com/wp-content/uploads/2016/07/2014-ML-AW-Work-in- Retirement_Myths-and-Motivations.pdf).

Northwestern Mutual. 2018. Planning & Progress Study. (https://news.northwesternmutual.com/2018-05-08-1-In-3-Americans-Have-Less-Than-5-000-In-Retirement-Savings).

Pew Research Center. May 2009. *Different Age Groups, Different Recessions*. Social and Demographic Trends Report. Washington, DC. (https://www.pewsocialtrends.org/2009/05/14/different-age-groups-different-recessions/).

Pilkova, Anna, Marian Holienka, and Jan Rehak. April 2014. "Senior Entrepreneurship in the Perspective of European Entrepreneurial Environment." *Procedia Economics and Finance* 12:523–32. (https://doi.org/10.1016/S2212-5671(14)00375-X).

Pilkova, Anna, Jan Rehak, and Zuzana Jancovicova. 2016. "Senior Entrepreneurship in Central and Eastern European Countries: GEM Evidences." Fourth International Conference Innovation Management, Entrepreneurship and Corporate Sustainability. Prague, Czech Republic.

Schøtt, Thomas, et al. 2017. "GEM Special Report on Senior Entrepreneurship 2017." Global Entrepreneurship Research Association. (www.gemconsortium.org).

Shlain, Tiffany and Sawyer Steele. 2016. "The Adaptable Mind." A Let it Ripple Film Studio mini-documentary. YouTube video, 11:02. (https://www.youtube.com/watch?v=937iCwJd3fI).

Straunch, Barbara. 2010. *The Secret Life of the Grown-up Brain: The Surprising Talents of the Middle-aged Mind*. New York: Viking.

Taylor, Chris. January 2012. "Why Boomer Widows Are Financially at Risk." Reuters. (https://www.reuters.com/article/us-widows-financial/why-boomer-widows-are-financially-at-risk-idUSTRE80J1FQ20120120).

Tervo, Hannu. 2014. "Who Turns to Entrepreneurship Later in Life? Push and Pull in Finnish Rural and Urban Areas." In 54th European Congress of the Regional Science Association International. St. Petersburg, Russia.

Understanding America Study (UAS) 165. 2020. "Entrepreneurship and the Understanding America Study: A Research Collaboration among the University of Michigan's Institute for Social Research, the Ross School of Business, and GIEE." Funded by the Ewing Marion Kauffman Foundation (RG-201806-4444).

UPS Store. 2019. "Inside Small Business." Annual survey. (https://www.theupsstore.com/insidesmallbusiness and https://www.theupsstore.com/File%20Library/theupsstore/pr/full-results-isb-survey-2019.pdf).

U.S. Senate, Special Committee on Aging Hearing. February 2014. "In Search of a Second Act: The Challenges and Advantages of Senior Entrepreneurship." (https://www.aging.senate.gov/hearings/watch?hearingid=8DD9C8C7-5056-A032-52B5-5CEC26CDDCDC).

Weller, Christian, et al. 2014. "Increasing Entrepreneurship among Older Americans: Policy Lessons and Recommendations." *Public Policy & Aging Report* 24(4):148–54. (https://doi.org/10.1093/ppar/pru028).

World Health Organization. September 30, 2015. *World Report on Ageing and Health*. Geneva, Switzerland: WHO.

CHAPTER 24

# Older Workers as Volunteers

Doug Dickson

## DEFINING THE TERMS "OLDER ADULT" AND "VOLUNTEER"

First, it is necessary to set some boundaries. Since there is no fixed definition for older adulthood, age thresholds for this stage of life vary widely. AARP famously recruits members beginning at age fifty. The U.S. government sets sixty-five as the age for eligibility in various benefit programs, except when they use sixty, sixty-two, or sixty-seven for specific purposes. Some initiatives set fifty-five as a qualifying age. Researchers and demographers offer no additional clarity, with various studies and surveys tracking many of these thresholds and more. For this chapter and for the sake of simplicity, we will consider an older adult as anyone over the age of fifty, unless specifically stated otherwise.

The language around volunteering is equally problematic. Distinctions are made among *hands-on volunteering* (direct service to people or causes), *skills-based volunteering* (transfer of specific experience gained outside the social sector), *pro bono consulting* (leveraging specialized skills to benefit nonprofits), and *volunteer leadership* (board service, certain interim executives and leadership mentors). There is also episodic or one-day volunteering, like days of service, help with fundraising events, and various one-and-done projects. Many people regularly contribute their time and expertise but don't think of it as volunteering. This might include classroom assistance, coaching youth sports, participating in a faith-based program or activity, or serving on a municipal board or in elective office. Many others informally assist neighbors or other community members on an as-needed basis. While data are not uniformly collected in all categories, our focus will include all these variations.

Finally, we need to define the context for volunteering. While tracking of volunteer activity often focuses on nonprofit organizations, we will expand that to include unpaid positions or internships in (a) health care, educational, religious, community, and advocacy institutions, whether or not they are structured as nonprofits; (b) mission-based businesses; (c) personal or group initiatives operated outside formal organizations; and (d) local, county, state, and federal governments. We also include fellowship and below-market stipend positions meant to serve the needs of social-sector organizations while providing sector exposure and transition experience for older adults. We will refer collectively to these activities as "social-purpose work."

## A BRIEF HISTORY OF OLDER ADULT VOLUNTEER PROGRAMS

Older people have contributed their time and talent to address community needs, either as individuals or in small groups, for as long as we have any record. Indeed, the term "elder" is often used to denote leadership roles based on presumed knowledge and judgment honed by experience. The earliest effort to mobilize the experience of older adults in the modern era began in Delaware in 1953, when a group of retired businessmen gathered to advise small businesses. A decade later, there were fifty such groups scattered across the country, and in 1964, they were consolidated under the Small Business Administration as the Service Corps of Retired Executives (SCORE). Today, SCORE continues to offer free consultation and advice to small-business owners and entrepreneurs with ten thousand volunteer mentors at 364 offices.[1]

Along roughly similar lines, the International Executive Service Corps (IESC) was formed in 1964 as a complement to USAID and the Peace Corps. Led by David Rockefeller, Sol Linowitz, Frank Pace, and others, late-career and retired business leaders offered their "technical and managerial advice" as volunteer consultants to businesses in developing countries.[2] Since then, IESC volunteers have worked in 137 countries on four continents. And, in 1977, the National Executive Service Corps (NESC) was founded in New York City to provide consulting services to nonprofit organizations. Within a decade, the ESC model was replicated in thirty-three locations with five thousand volunteer consultants.[3] Today, ESCs offer an expanded range of services to nonprofits, but the fundamental model of leveraging experienced talent as volunteer consultants remains the same.

Passage of the Older Americans Act in 1965 led to the creation of three new federal programs for older volunteers. The Foster Grandparent Program began as an effort to engage low-income older adults as mentors for exceptional and special-needs children. This was followed by the Senior Companion Program, in which older people provide personal services and companionship to enable others to live independently. The Retired Service Volunteer Program (RSVP) was formalized in 1969 by bringing together private and governmental initiatives that offered community engagement opportunities to older people. Its flexible design allows program participants to serve a variety of local needs, including job training, tutoring, relief services, and aid to community organizations. Today, these programs are united as Senior Corps and run by the Corporation for National and Community Service, the federal agency for volunteering and service.[4]

Experience Corps was conceived by John W. Gardner in 1988 and launched in 1995 by Marc Freedman and Linda Fried as part of Public/Private Ventures, with support from the Corporation for National and Community Service. The program recruits and trains older adults as tutors and mentors to assist public elementary school students who struggle with reading. Experience Corps grew as part of Encore.org (then Civic

Ventures) and since 2015 has been operated by the AARP Foundation.[5] Designed as an intergenerational initiative, it has been studied extensively for its impact on participating children but also on older volunteers.

A small number of forward-thinking businesses have created opportunities for employees approaching retirement to prepare for social-purpose work and volunteering. In 2006, IBM started the Transition to Teaching (T2T) program, supporting long-term employees in their shift to new careers as math and science teachers. This was followed by HP in 2009 and Intel in 2012, who collaborated with Encore.org on an initiative called Encore Fellowships. These part-time, yearlong roles enable retiring employees to transition their experience and skills to specific capacity-building projects in nonprofit organizations. In return, participants receive a stipend and gain valuable experience that leads many to permanent paid or volunteer roles in the social sector.[6] Now in its eleventh year, the program has placed two thousand Encore Fellows in more than fifty cities.

In 2007, the Atlantic Philanthropies funded nine projects around the U.S. designed to engage older people in community solutions to social issues like homelessness, health care access, immigration, and nutrition. Called the Community Experience Partnership, the initiative seeded new programs but also identified promising practices for successfully engaging older adults. Many of these programs continue in one form or another; notable among them is Boomers Leading Change in Denver, which engages people over age fifty in efforts to address health care equity, childhood literacy, homelessness, and hunger.[7]

In addition to programs like these that have led the way, there are numerous governmental and community-based initiatives that engage older people in various ways. The Peace Corps has embraced retirees with flexible arrangements that offer a broader range of choices about location, tenure, and other considerations. Massachusetts has a statewide community service program called Commonwealth Corps that targets older as well as younger adults. The Generation to Generation campaign developed by Encore.org encourages youth-serving organizations to mobilize people over age fifty to help kids thrive. Elders Action Network encourages older adults to address social, economic, and environmental injustice. Ignatian Volunteer Corps and Jesuit Volunteer Corps chapters across the country recruit volunteers age fifty and older to fill meaningful service positions as an expression of their faith. Big Brothers Big Sisters, Boys and Girls Clubs, CASA, the Ys, YearUp, and other mentoring organizations recognize the value of maturity and judgment in creating good mentoring matches.

This history builds a legitimate case for engaging older adults as part of a broad effort to address the social, economic, and environmental issues we face. The question is how many mature adults will join the challenge and how can we encourage more to seize the opportunity to contribute their talent and experience.

## HOW MANY OLDER ADULTS VOLUNTEER?

Determining the number of older volunteers depends on who is measuring and what definitions they use. The Bureau of Labor Statistics (BLS) says that 28 percent of people age forty-five to fifty-four, 25 percent of people age fifty-five to sixty-four, and 23.5 percent of people age sixty-five and over volunteered in 2015. For this count, a volunteer is a person who performed unpaid activities for one or more religious, youth, social, civic, or other community service organizations. As with other counts, women volunteered more than men, whites volunteered more than nonwhites, people with more education volunteered more than those with less, and married people volunteered more than singles. While the rate of volunteering declines as people age, the number of hours performed by each individual goes up. People over age sixty-five made a median contribution of ninety-four hours for the year, while those ages fifty-five to sixty-four put in fifty-six hours and those ages forty-five to fifty-four contributed fifty-two hours. The BLS reports that more than a third volunteered at a religious organization, followed by educational or youth service, social or community service, and hospital or other health service. The most prevalent activities were food collection, preparation, or distribution, followed by fundraising and professional or management support, including board service, tutoring and teaching, and general labor and transportation.[8]

Another perspective is offered by the Corporation for National and Community Service (CNCS) in its 2018 *Volunteering in America Report*. It says that 31 percent of baby boomers (ages fifty-four to seventy-two) volunteered for an organization. The volunteer rate for "silent generation" Americans (ages seventy-three to ninety-three) was 25 percent. As evidence of community service, the report goes on to say that 32 percent of boomers and 34 percent of silents participated in local groups or organizations, and 59 percent of boomers and 55 percent of silents did favors for neighbors.[9] The profile of older volunteers in the CNCS report and the activities they engage in closely parallel what's contained in the BLS data.

There is no available record of how many older volunteers also work, though as we shall see in the next section, there is evidence that the most committed volunteers do so in addition to, not instead of, other activities in their lives. So it is reasonable to expect that, as the number of older workers increases, so will the number who volunteer as well as work.

## WHAT DO WE KNOW ABOUT OLDER VOLUNTEERS?

These numbers suggest that, in general, between a quarter and a half of the U.S. population over age fifty engages in activity that qualifies in some way as volunteering under our broad definition. What do we know about who these people are and what motivates them? In his theory of psychosocial development, Erik Erikson characterized middle age, roughly ages forty to sixty-five, as a time when maturing adults gain a new perspective on the world around them, seeing themselves as caring contributors to the welfare of others. He used the term "generativity" to characterize the urge to participate in activities that have the potential to generate impact and value beyond their own self-interest. Research conducted by Age Wave and Merrill Lynch offers evidence for this idea. Their data show that while retirees make up 31 percent of the U.S. population (as of 2015), they account for 42 percent of charitable donations and 45 percent of volunteer hours.[10]

The Age Wave study also identified the motivation behind this generosity: 81 percent of participants said they want to make a difference in the lives of others, and 61 percent said it offered meaning and purpose in life. Other reasons included staying mentally and physically active (36 percent), nurturing friendships and relationships (36 percent), and expressing or acting upon religious or spiritual beliefs (34 percent). Compared to their parents' generation, boomer retirees say they are more strategic about how they spend their time in volunteer activities, preferring to use the skills and experience they have developed. The study concluded that retirees who volunteer have a stronger sense of purpose and higher self-esteem, and are happier and healthier than their peers.

These findings were mirrored by research from the Stanford Graduate School of Education's Center on Adolescence and Encore.org. The researchers concluded that "the majority of older adults exhibit high levels of pro-social values and behaviors."[11] More than half of those surveyed for this study said they volunteered once or twice a year, and nearly a quarter said they volunteered once a month or more. A majority (65 percent) said they always try to help others.

The study also looked at people who exhibit purpose beyond the self, defined as those who "identify, prioritize, adopt and actively pursue goals that are both personally meaningful and contribute to the greater good."[12] Nearly a third (31 percent) met this definition, saying it was central to their identity and sense of meaning in life. This commitment was consistent across age, income, health status, and geography. The only meaningful difference was that people of color were found to have a higher sense of purpose than whites. The study also found that older people who are purposeful do not sacrifice other aspects of their lives to volunteer. In fact, they were more likely to endorse a view of later life as a time for travel, family, friends, and learning in addition to volunteer activities.

A survey conducted by Penn Schoen Berland and Encore.org compared the motivations of late-career people, still in paid positions, who had either a high or low interest in encore careers (defined as paid or volunteer roles in the social-purpose sector). Not surprisingly, individuals with a high interest in encore careers said these aspects of their work were most important to them: "gives me personal satisfaction," "helps me feel worthwhile," "provides an interest in life," "gives me a feeling of pride in myself and my work," "gives me a chance to demonstrate my skills," and "allows me to pass my knowledge to the next generation."[13] These priorities are also frequently cited by older people as the reasons they seek out and make the transition to social-purpose volunteering.

As late-career workers predisposed to encore careers reach a decision about retiring from their primary careers, those who seek employment as part of their retirement, or decide to reenter the workforce after a break, are likely to seek out purposeful work as well as volunteering. But if social-purpose work is not available, volunteer activity, in concert with other work, may well become the primary outlet for satisfying the needs identified above.

## WHAT ARE THE BENEFITS OF VOLUNTEERING FOR OLDER ADULTS?

If volunteering is a pathway to helping others, it turns out also to have remarkable benefits for those who do it. A study of Experience Corps conducted by Johns Hopkins University researchers documented a significant improvement in the physical health of volunteer tutors. Improvement was measured by increased walking speed, fewer falls, improved strength and balance, and halted or reversed memory decline.[14] Volunteers reported that they made close social connections with children, teachers, and other volunteers. They felt more a part of their community, happier, and more worthwhile and helpful. They also felt more alert and more lively and said they had more energy. And they valued the opportunity to learn and grow in the role.[15]

The Corporation for National and Community Service reported similar outcomes in a study of foster grandparents and senior companions. Volunteers had lower rates of disability, the result of increased physical, mental, and social activity; higher levels of well-being; reduced depression, loneliness, and isolation; a higher sense of purpose; and better ability to manage stressful situations in their lives, like bereavement, unemployment, and retirement transitions. Some of the greatest improvements were shown in individuals with the highest number of risk factors for poor health, which suggests that volunteering not only improves health and well-being, but can actually reverse and stave off poor health outcomes for high-risk individuals.[16]

Several studies have shown that older volunteers actually live longer than nonvolunteers by a range of four to seven years, depending on the study. A meta-analysis of fourteen of these studies concluded that volunteers had a 24 percent reduced risk of mortality compared to others.[17] This longevity effect holds true even when medical history, age, socioeconomic status, social support network, marital status, and physical and emotional health are accounted for. Research at the University of Michigan adds another revealing insight: the greatest health and longevity benefits accrue to older volunteers who are motivated by a desire to help others, compared to more self-interested motivations like getting out of the house, making social connections, and improving skills.[18]

Commitment level also makes a difference. The Center on Aging and Work at Boston College looked at the impact of engagement versus involvement on well-being, with engagement requiring a higher level of commitment and connection to an activity. For older adults who were highly or moderately engaged as volunteers, there was a significant gain in well-being compared to those whose engagement was low or totally absent.[19] This suggests that higher commitment levels heighten the benefits derived from the experience. In other words, it's the more intensive and immersive experience, not just any volunteer activity, that generates the benefits that research has documented.

Backing this up is a preliminary finding from research conducted by the Quality of Life Research Center at Claremont Graduate University and Encore.org. The researchers found that the greater the investment of time in social-purpose activity, the higher the resulting levels of meaning and purpose. Social-purpose activity in this study was work undertaken by high-commitment volunteers (averaging fifteen hours per week) and leaders, which included social entrepreneurs (averaging thirty-three hours per week). This study also found that these older adults felt more relatedness (caring, cooperative, and connection to others), and had higher levels of excitement, energy, concentration, and productivity when engaged in social-purpose activity.[20]

Another study of older people engaged in intensive humanitarian service, like the Peace Corps or disaster relief, also found an elevated sense of meaning from this activity. Participants also said their experience contributed to increased compassion and empathy for others, greater appreciation of cultural differences, expanded social networks, increased closeness to spouses, and a reduced focus on themselves. To achieve these benefits, many had to rise above significant challenges, like adjusting to new situations and cultures, unexpected assignment shifts, and cultural reentry as they returned home following their assignments. But all reported that the benefits outweighed the challenges.[21]

## WHAT IS THE IMPACT OF OLDER ADULTS IN VOLUNTEER ROLES?

The benefits of volunteering for the people who do it is well documented, as noted in the previous section. But what effect does that contribution have on the organizations they work for, either in advancing the mission or building capacity, and on the community more broadly? Encore.org looked at these kinds of impacts in a survey of supervisors who were responsible for the work of older volunteers in a variety of organizations and locations across the country. The results showed strong benefits to communities and organizations when the volunteers were engaged in intensive hands-on or skills-based roles, such as tutoring, mentoring, functional support, or leadership.[22] The survey did not look at lower-intensity volunteering, like intermittent service days and fundraising events, and the results would probably be different for those.

Among the community benefits that supervisors cited were older volunteers' contributions of labor and skills that would not otherwise have been available, and strengthening ties and increasing community satisfaction with the organization's efforts. In terms of organizational impact, supervisors said that volunteers contributed new ideas and approaches to their work, helped scale up mission-related activities, strengthened positioning with funders, improved staff training and development, reduced operating costs, and improved constituent services. In terms of their personal attributes and fit with the organization, older volunteers were found to integrate well with the existing team, building productive relationships and, in some cases, mentoring other team members. They were able to learn new skills, see others' perspectives, bring previous knowledge to the role, and find ways to make change happen quickly.

Experience Corps (the K–3 literacy program staffed by people over age fifty-five) was the subject of a study conducted by the Center for Social Development at Washington University.[23] The results showed that in one year, Experience Corps tutees' reading comprehension and the ability to sound out new words improved 60 percent over a control group's performance. Tutees' grade-level reading skills were 40 percent higher than the other group's. This reading gain was judged to be equivalent to a 40 percent reduction in classroom size. In addition, students were better behaved and teachers were overwhelmingly supportive. Similar results were found in an earlier study by a team from Johns Hopkins University.

For social-purpose organizations seeking to take advantage of specific skills offered by older volunteers, organizations like Bridgespan, Common Good Careers, and Idealist Careers say that communications, management, research, sales and marketing, planning and analysis, operations, and stakeholder relationships translate directly from other sectors to nonprofits. And attributes like adaptability, influence, and working within financial constraints are directly applicable to the social-purpose environment. A case study prepared by the Center on Aging and Work at Boston College for Encore.org bears this out.[24] Not only were individual skills and attributes possessed by the volunteers (in this case, Encore Fellows) directly transferrable to the roles they undertook, but their contributions had lasting impact for the organizations they served. And each of the individuals profiled continues to work in the nonprofit sector, having gained exposure and confidence through their fellowship experience.

A study of the volunteer sector in Massachusetts found that engaging older volunteers was one of five practices most closely correlated to volunteer, organizational, or mission success.[25] The same study revealed that a majority of nonprofits faced challenges in finding enough volunteers possessing the right skills and expertise and with daytime availability. Older adults are a resource ready made to meet each of these needs.

## WHAT ARE BEST PRACTICES FOR RECRUITING OLDER ADULTS?

There are two challenges in engaging older volunteers: finding them and keeping them. Finding older adults sounds easy, but practical experience says otherwise. Volunteer recruitment in most charitable organizations is done in two ways—by word of mouth or through a third party, like a business or university. If an organization has a large volunteer group and an established cohort of older volunteers, then word-of-mouth recruiting can produce results. But if there are just a few positions to fill, other outreach methods will probably be more productive.

Businesses that want their employees to be engaged in the community will often take direct responsibility or hire a vendor to help match interested individuals to nonprofits' needs, relieving the nonprofits of this task. The same holds for students who are recruited through a class where they receive course credit for their volunteer experience or through a university citizenship or community service program. But there are no equivalent third parties for older adults. Senior centers and senior housing facilities typically attract a clientele or residents that skew older, and we know that the older people get, the less likely they are to volunteer. By this older age, those who want to volunteer are already engaged, sometimes by the senior center or housing program they are part of. Religious organizations are also places where some older adults congregate, but many of those operate their own volunteer-led and volunteer-supported programs. The largest number of older volunteers are part of faith-based social programs to which they are justifiably committed and have little bandwidth or interest in engaging elsewhere.

Other community-based programs where older adults can be found include aging-in-community neighborhood organizations, often called villages, and lifelong learning institutes, which are typically associated with universities and libraries. Organizations like these are often absorbed by their own need for volunteers and have shown limited interest in introducing their members to other volunteer opportunities. This requires volunteer engagement managers to recruit older adults one at a time, a "retail" approach that can be time consuming and expensive. It requires information sessions, participation in volunteer fairs and tabling events, advertising, social media promotion, and other community engagement strategies that are less productive than those typically employed to reach students, young adults, or middle-age adults.

Fortunately, there are some approaches that have proven useful in attracting and engaging older volunteers. One is for organizations to make and maintain a connection with people well before they step down from their careers. This has the advantage of providing stability during a transition period that many find difficult or disorienting. Another is to recruit intact groups of people who already have a common bond and want to volunteer with friends, neighbors, or colleagues. This could range from a book group to a club or professional society. People at this stage of life have a renewed focus on social connection, and group volunteering can add a new dimension and reinforce that connection. Finally, using proximity as a strategy has proven successful for many organizations. Geographic proximity or colocation of a school or youth-serving organization with a senior center or housing for older adults can serve as a platform for intergenerational volunteering. Intergenerational community centers, emerging in a growing number of locations, offer opportunities for volunteer roles designed to attract older adults. Schools have always recruited parents in a variety of volunteer roles but less often look to grandparents (or proxy grandparents) living in the area.

Experience Corps has demonstrated the value of intergenerational relationships in the learning process. One study concluded that the best outcomes were highly correlated with the closest relationships between student and mentor. Volunteers who look like, speak the language of, and understand the background of students are often in the strongest position to effectively build a productive relationship. This "cultural" proximity can be a key to recruiting older adults into positions from which they can pay forward their own experience to improve the prospects of the next generation. This may be particularly relevant for immigrant or low-income communities. A related example is a teen parenting program that recruits women who have lived through this experience to offer the benefit and example of their success for young mothers. Proximate skills and interests can also be a basis for attracting and recruiting older adults into volunteer roles. Examples include former teachers as tutors, retired engineers as STEM project advisers, and municipal government veterans as civics coaches. More about this approach can be found in "10 Steps for Engaging Adults 50+" prepared by Encore.org.[26]

Oasis Lifelong Adventure is a program based in St Louis, Missouri, that combines lifelong learning, healthy living, and volunteer engagement in more than twenty cities across the U.S. About a third of participants volunteer in one of Oasis's programs—it runs the largest intergenerational tutoring program in the country—or in other organizations. It has solved the recruiting challenge by combining volunteering with a range of other complementary activities that draw people in and keep them engaged in a holistic set of services known to promote healthy aging. In a similar way, some Experience Corps programs augment the intrinsic health and social value of the volunteer experience by offering health promotion and social activities for participants. These programs build loyalty and generate interest that enhances word-of-mouth and recruiting efforts. They also increase retention, even bridging periods when volunteers must step back because of caregiving, health problems, or other personal needs.

When recruiting and onboarding older adults, it is particularly important to be clear about the requirements of the role, how it fits with the mission of the organization, what kinds of training and support are offered, and what the performance expectations are. Older people often want to see the big picture so they can assess how their personal skills and interests align with those of the organization and role. They are less likely than people of other ages to accept statements at face value, not to challenge them but to fully understand the nature of the commitment. Older adults also want to see themselves reflected in the images used on the website and recruiting materials as well as in the existing team of staff and volunteers. This is also true of the words and messages used to attract people to these roles. The aforementioned "10 Steps for Engaging Adults 50+" provides suggestions for marketing to this population. In addition, the "Gaining Momentum Communications Toolkit" developed by the Frameworks Institute offers guidance about language and messages for appealing to individual motivation while avoiding ageist stereotypes and other age-sensitive pitfalls.[27]

Bringing people over age fifty into organizations, especially at the outset, requires that leaders evaluate the readiness of the team to accept, integrate, and fully engage their talent and experience. Ageist myths and attitudes can interfere with team effectiveness, affecting the ability of both the younger and older team members to make their best contributions. Until an age-friendly culture and policies are in place, organizations risk losing the best that people of all ages can bring to the mission. But organizations with inclusive, multigenerational work teams outperform all others, according to a briefing prepared by the SHRM Foundation and AARP.[28] Age-friendly organizations also adapt their policies to address the needs of older volunteers for reasonable flexibility, remove age-biased language and requirements in position descriptions and applications, and ensure open communications and respect for all in the workplace.

## WHAT ARE BEST PRACTICES FOR RETAINING OLDER ADULTS?

Once older volunteers are in place, the next question is how to keep them. Studies confirm that, on average, older volunteers stay longer than younger ones. The Corporation for National and Community Service says that year-to-year retention of older adults is 70 percent while that of teens and younger adults is about 50 percent. Higher retention is also related to more education, greater number of hours worked (highest is for five hundred or more hours), type of organization (highest is for religious organizations), and type of activity (highest is for professional or managerial roles).[29]

As noted above, older people are much more likely to stay in a role if the culture and policies of the organization align with their needs. Commitment also depends, as it does for most volunteers with extended tenures, on the attention supervisors give to recognition, inclusion, and support. Volunteers leave, according to an article in the *Stanford Social Innovation Review*, when their skills are not well matched with roles, their contributions are not recognized, the value of their work is not measured and reported, there is little or no investment in their training and development, and they feel unsupported by inattentive or uncaring leaders.[30]

Looking at personal factors that influence older volunteer retention, research by the Urban Institute indicates that depression leads people to drop their volunteering by 10 percent and disability by 5 percent. Caregiving responsibilities lead some to drop out; this occurs more often when volunteers are caring for elderly parents than for spouses. Divorce or death of a spouse causes 11 percent to opt out, and, as would be expected, relocation increases the chance that people will discontinue their volunteer activity. People who volunteer the most in terms of years worked and hours committed are the least likely to leave. Those who contributed two hundred hours or more in the previous year were 17 percent less likely to leave than those contributing fifty or fewer hours. And eight-year veterans were 13 percent less likely to leave than those in their second year. Tellingly, the study found that older adults who continued to work for pay found no apparent conflict between the two roles. It also found that people married to a volunteer are more likely to volunteer and to continue volunteering year after year. Conversely, volunteers who remain married to a non-volunteer are 6 percent more likely to leave in a subsequent year, and those who marry a non-volunteer are 29 percent more likely to quit.[31]

We can infer from this last finding that bonds among friends and other close groups, in addition to marriage, can influence either the start or continuation of volunteer activity by older adults. Anecdotal observations support this inference. Many older adults report feeling alienated from friends who don't share their interest in volunteering and relieved upon finding a community of people who do. That community not only reinforces the urge to give back but also provides a supportive environment for sharing opportunities and deepening commitment. Programs like Experience Corps that provide this kind of supportive environment for their older volunteers find that they benefit from high retention and even renewed service following necessary gaps because people feel connected to each other as well as to the work.

Social-purpose organizations too often overlook the need to offer challenge and opportunity to older volunteers as a retention tactic (in addition to achieving optimal value from their skills and experience). As pointed out in "10 Steps to Engaging Adults 50+," volunteers rarely step into high-commitment roles without first passing through stages of increasing engagement—from initial curiosity through casual involvement to increasingly committed roles. Building and strengthening connections is a useful recruiting strategy as well as a path to extended tenure. Creating a ladder of opportunity enables continued learning and growth, which older adults crave as much as any other age group. Highly committed volunteers also become devoted ambassadors for the organization, inspirational recruiters of new talent, regular donors, and credible advocates for the cause.

Volunteering is a proven path to finding paid work and recruiting paid staff. A study by the Corporation for National and Community Service found that volunteering was associated with 27 percent higher odds of employment for job seekers. This association was strongest for those with less than a high school education or living in rural areas but was otherwise consistent across factors like gender, age, race, location, and economic conditions.[32] While not all unemployed men and women find paid work opportunities at the same organization where they volunteer, there are numerous examples involving hiring of skilled volunteers into part-time or full-time paid roles. Some programs, like

Encore Fellowships, offer an opportunity for late-career employees and professionals to gain exposure to the nonprofit sector and to determine if they want to pursue an encore career there. It's also a way for nonprofits to gauge the fit of Encore Fellows who might be candidates for permanent roles. Experience gained through volunteering can also make a candidate from the private sector seem less risky to a nonprofit.

## A LOOK AHEAD

In a variety of surveys, significant numbers of older people say they plan to volunteer as one of their postcareer activities. Yet the number of older volunteers has fallen slightly over the last decade in line with a broader decline in volunteer rates. What stands between the good intentions of people when surveyed and actual results is not clear. It's not easy for older people to find organizations that need their support, nor as discussed earlier, is it easy for organizations to find older people. And some leaders are still blind to the value of older volunteers, as they are to the value of older workers, or are not ready to make the investment needed to create a successful volunteer experience. In addition, older adults may find themselves busier than expected, without an incentive to make volunteering a priority. So what can we expect as the older population continues to grow and as the human capital needs of social-purpose organizations increase alongside this growth?

One likely scenario is that workforce shortages will drive the leaders of organizations to see past their limited capacity and biases to recognize older adults as a human capital solution. This will move them to make necessary investments in recruiting and supporting older people, and they will find new ways to connect with individuals who meet their requirements. Policy changes and other accommodations will likely follow as organizations seek to make themselves more attractive to older volunteers.

Another likely scenario is that health care providers, community and senior centers, and religious and other organizations will increasingly prescribe or promote volunteering as a healthy activity—a source of cognitive, physical, social, and emotional benefits—for older adults. The result of this promotion will be a jump in the number of older people committing their time in volunteer activities. This could help to reset the norm for what older people do in their postcareer years, giving rise to new expectations regarding the nature of retirement.

We are beginning to see improved technology solutions to the challenge of connecting volunteers to organizations, adapting the features of online sites, like Yelp, that offer information sharing, product and service reviews, and reservations, to help people explore and compare volunteer opportunities. Inspiring Service, based in Cincinnati, Ohio, is a pioneer in this space, but others will follow, including the established national platforms, in order to improve the volunteer search experience as well as promote more effective matches. We can also expect more personalized search capabilities, with features geared to the specific needs and interests of older adults, along with other selection criteria. This will enable better targeting of volunteer opportunities based on individual preferences and evolving needs.

We are also seeing community-wide appeals by political, religious, and other leaders for volunteers to step forward to help meet specific community goals, like early childhood education, homelessness, and student housing. Some of these appeals come from communities that are specifically seeking to become age friendly, but more often they arise out of a practical understanding that there is an underutilized resource that can be tapped to address urgent community needs. For example, San Jose and San Diego, California, have engaged older adults in an intergenerational initiative to focus on the needs of children. These and other programs are described in a publication from Encore.org called "Gen2Gen Cities."[33] Appeals like these raise awareness and create a sense that "we're all in this together," making everyone's contribution important to achieving a greater outcome.

Another likely scenario is that greater involvement of older adults in skills-based, hands-on, and board governance roles will lead to a professionalization of high-commitment volunteer activity. As organizations become more selective in "hiring" volunteers, the process will become more competitive and credential driven. This will open the door to education and training programs that prepare people for the transition to these roles and offer certificates or other evidence of qualification. University-based and community college programs will gain momentum in addition to community-based and online programs. Professionalization will also require that organizations pay greater attention to integrating paid and unpaid staff and managing a multigenerational workplace. Nonprofit training programs like Service Enterprise Initiative, offered by Points of Light, will segment older adults as a targeted recruiting market. Finally, the tangled language of volunteering will evolve into much more specific terms that accurately distinguish among the types of unpaid service. This change alone will advance the effort to engage older adults, who will respond to evidence that organizations are taking seriously the knowledge and insight that people with experience have to offer.

Finally, any realistic assessment about the growth and impact potential of older volunteers must also include a note of caution about the likely pace of change. Despite enormous efforts in the U.S. and around the world, we have yet to reach a tipping point either in the engagement of older adults for social good or the acknowledgment by social-purpose organizations that older adults represent a significant opportunity. Change happens slowly, but it can be accelerated by factors both predictable and unexpected. One of the most widely predicted accelerants has been the sheer size of the boomer generation, which may yet have an effect. Another possibility is a crisis of sufficient proportion to swiftly shift both individual and organizational perspectives. But the best long-term hope may be the advent of younger people to this field, whose clear-eyed view of the possibilities helps to surmount the misguided assumptions and missed opportunities that have so far held us back.

## NOTES

1. Service Corps of Retired Executives (SCORE). 2020. "About SCORE: SCORE History." (https://core.score.org/node/147953).

2. International Executive Service Corps (IESC). 2020. "Our Story: History." (https://iesc.org/our-story/history/).

3. National Executive Service Corps (NESC). 2020. "About NESC: History." (http://www.nesc.org/history/252525).

4. Wikipedia. N.d. "Senior Corps." (https://en.wikipedia.org/wiki/Senior_Corps).

5. Wikipedia. N.d. "Experience Corps." (https://en.wikipedia.org/wiki/Experience_Corps).

6. Diane Piktialis et al. October 29, 2014. "Second Acts in Prime Time: Helping Employees Transition to Post-retirement Careers." Conference Board. (https://www.conference-board.org/topics/global-economic-outlook).

7. Boomers Leading Change. 2020. "Our Story: Who We Are." (https://boomersleadingchange.org/who-we-are/our-story/).

8. Bureau of Labor Statistics. 2015. "Volunteering in the United States—2015: News Release." U.S. Department of Labor. (https://www.bls.gov/news.release/pdf/volun.pdf).

9. Corporation for National and Community Service. 2018. *Volunteering in America Report.* (https://www.nationalservice.gov/serve/via).

10. Merrill Lynch/Age Wave. 2016. "Giving in Retirement: America's Longevity Bonus." A Merrill Lynch Retirement Study conducted in partnership with Age Wave. (http://agewave.com/wp-content/uploads/2016/07/2015-ML-AW-Giving-in-Retirement_Americas-Longevity-Bonus.pdf).

11. Pathways to Encore Purpose Project. 2018b. "Help Wanted? Ask Someone 50+." Brief #1. (https://encore.org/wp-content/uploads/2018/03/PEP-Brief-1.pdf).

12. Pathways to Encore Purpose Project. 2018a. "Beyond the Self: 34 Million Older Adults Committed to Common Good." (https://encore.org/wp-content/uploads/2018/03/PEP-Brief-2.pdf).

13. Encore.org. 2015. "Working to Make a Difference: Before and during an Encore." (https://encore.org/wp-content/uploads/2015/07/AttitudesatWorkv5.pdf).

14. George Rebok. 2013. "Baltimore Experience Corps Study." ClinicalTrials.gov. (https://clinicaltrials.gov/ct2/show/NCT00380562).

15. Vijay Varma et al. December 2015. "Experience Corps Baltimore: Exploring the Stressors and Rewards of High-intensity Civic Engagement." *The Gerontologist* 55(6):1038–49. (https://clinicaltrials.gov/ct2/show/NCT00380562).

16. Annie Georges et al. May 2017. "Longitudinal Study of Foster Grandparent and Senior Companion Programs: Service Delivery and Health Benefits Implications to the Volunteers." Corporation for National and Community Service. (https://nationalservice.gov/sites/default/files/evidenceexchange/Longitudinal_Study_of_Foster_Grandparent_and_Senior_Companion_Programs_FINAL_508.pdf).

17. Morris A. Okun, Ellen WanHeung Yeung, and Stephanie Brown. 2013. "Volunteering by Older Adults and Risk of Mortality: A Meta-analysis." PubMed. *Psychology of Aging* 28(2):564–77. (https://www.ncbi.nlm.nih.gov/m/pubmed/23421326/?i=4&from=/2354560).

18. Sara Konrath et al. 2012. "Motives for Volunteering Are Associated with Mortality Risk in Older Adults." *Health Psychology* 31(1):87–96. (https://www.apa.org/pubs/journals/releases/hea-31-1-87.pdf).

19. Jacqueline James et al. 2012. "Engaged as We Age: Just Do It? Maybe Not!" Chestnut Hill, MA: Sloan Center on Aging & Work, Boston College:14. (https://pdfs.semanticscholar.org/d690/afe03d101e46e7d54c93a8034ac15a714595.pdf).

20. Jeanne Nakamura et al. N.d. "Quality of Life in Social-purpose Commitment." Claremont, CA: Quality of Life Research Center, Claremont Graduate University.

21. Kathleen Piercy et al. August 2011. "Challenges and Psychosocial Growth of Older Volunteers Giving Intensive Humanitarian Service." *The Gerontologist* 51(4):550–60. (https://academic.oup.com/gerontologist/article/51/4/550/597576).

22. Jim Emerman and Betsy Werley. 2016. "The Encore Impact Project: A Study of Encore Talent at Work." Encore.org. (https://encore.org/wp-content/uploads/2016/02/ImpactStudy.pdf0.

23. Nancy Morrow-Howell et al. 2009. "Evaluation of Experience Corps: Student Reading Outcomes." *Center for Social Development Report* No. 09-01. St. Louis, MO: Washington University. (https://www.aarp.org/content/dam/aarp/giving_back/volunteering/2012-11/evaluation-of-experience-corps-student-outcomes-aarp.pdf).

24. Jacqueline James. 2016. "Doing Good by Doing Well: Encore Fellows Build Nonprofits' Capacity to Serve Children and Youth." Chestnut Hill, MA: Center for Aging & Work, Boston College. (https://toolkit.encore.org/wp-content/uploads/2016/02/DoingGood.pdf).

25. Christina Matz, Emily Haber, and Lisl Hacker. 2019. "Results of the 2019 Massachusetts Volunteer Sector Study." Chestnut Hill, MA: Boston College School of Social Work for the Massachusetts Service Alliance. Unpublished presentation.

26. Encore.org. 2018. "10 Steps for Engaging Adults 50+: A Guide for Youth-serving Organizations." (https://generationtogeneration.org/10-steps-guide_full/).

27. Frameworks Institute. 2020. "Gaining Momentum: A Frameworks Communications Toolkit." (https://frameworksinstitute.org/toolkits/aging/).

28. Society for Human Resource Management (SHRM) Foundation. 2015. "Leveraging the Value of an Age-diverse Workforce." (https://www.shrm.org/foundation/ourwork/initiatives/the-aging-workforce/Documents/Age-Diverse%20Workforce%20Executive%20Briefing.pdf).

29. Corporation for National and Community Service. 2007. "Issue Brief: Volunteer Retention." (https://www.nationalservice.gov/pdf/VIA/VIA_brief_retention.pdf).

30. David Eisner et al. Winter 2009. "The New Volunteer Workforce." *Stanford Social Innovation Review*. (https://ssir.org/articles/entry/the_new_volunteer_workforce).

31. Barbara Butrica et al. December 2007. "Retaining Older Volunteers Is Key to Meeting Future Volunteer Needs." Perspectives on Productive Aging. Washington, DC: Urban Institute. (https://www.urban.org/sites/default/files/publication/46876/411580-Retaining-Older-Volunteers-Is-Key-to-Meeting-Future-Volunteer-Needs.PDF).

32. Christopher Spera et al. June 2013. "Volunteering as a Pathway to Employment: Does Volunteering Increase the Odds of Finding a Job for the Out of Work?" Corporation for National and Community Service. (https://www.nationalservice.gov/sites/default/files/upload/employment_research_report.pdf).

33. Corita Brown. 2020. "Gen2Gen Cities: A Guide to Intergenerational Strategies for Public Sector Innovators Seeking Solutions to Community Challenges." Encore.org. (https://encore.org/gen2gen-cities/).

## REFERENCES


Boomers Leading Change. 2020. "Our Story: Who We Are." (https://boomersleadingchange.org/who-we-are/our-story/).

Brown, Corita. 2020. "Gen2Gen Cities: A Guide to Intergenerational Strategies for Public Sector Innovators Seeking Solutions to Community Challenges." Encore.org. (https://encore.org/gen2gen-cities/).

Bureau of Labor Statistics. 2015. "Volunteering in the United States—2015: News Release." U.S. Department of Labor. (https://www.bls.gov/news.release/pdf/volun.pdf).

Butrica, Barbara, et al. December 2007. "Retaining Older Volunteers Is Key to Meeting Future Volunteer Needs." Perspectives on Productive Aging. Washington, DC: Urban Institute. (https://www.urban.org/sites/default/files/publication/46876/411580-Retaining-Older-Volunteers-Is-Key-to-Meeting-Future-Volunteer-Needs.PDF).

Corporation for National and Community Service. 2007. "Issue Brief: Volunteer Retention." (https://www.nationalservice.gov/pdf/VIA/VIA_brief_retention.pdf).

Corporation for National and Community Service. 2018. *Volunteering in America Report*. (https://www.nationalservice.gov/serve/via).

Eisner, David, et al. Winter 2009. "The New Volunteer Workforce." *Stanford Social Innovation Review*. (https://ssir.org/articles/entry/the_new_volunteer_workforce).

Emerman, Jim and Betsy Werley. 2016. "The Encore Impact Project: A Study of Encore Talent at Work." Encore.org. (https://encore.org/wp-content/uploads/2016/02/ImpactStudy.pdf).

Encore.org. 2015. "Working to Make a Difference: Before and during an Encore." (https://encore.org/wp-content/uploads/2015/07/AttitudesatWorkv5.pdf).

Encore.org. 2018. "10 Steps for Engaging Adults 50+: A Guide for Youth-serving Organizations." (https://generationtogeneration.org/10-steps-guide_full/).

Frameworks Institute. 2020. "Gaining Momentum: A Frameworks Communications Toolkit." (https://frameworksinstitute.org/toolkits/aging/).

Georges, Annie, et al. May 2017. "Longitudinal Study of Foster Grandparent and Senior Companion Programs: Service Delivery and Health Benefits Implications to the Volunteers." Corporation for National and Community Service. (https://nationalservice.gov/sites/default/files/evidenceexchange/Longitudinal_Study_of_Foster_Grandparent_and_Senior_Companion_Programs_FINAL_508.pdf).

International Executive Service Corps (IESC). 2020. "Our Story: History." (https://iesc.org/our-story/history/).

James, Jacqueline. 2016. "Doing Good by Doing Well: Encore Fellows Build Nonprofits' Capacity to Serve Children and Youth." Chestnut Hill, MA: Center for Aging & Work, Boston College. (https://toolkit.encore.org/wp-content/uploads/2016/02/DoingGood.pdf).

James, Jacqueline, et al. 2012. "Engaged as We Age: Just Do It? Maybe Not!" Chestnut Hill, MA: Sloan Center on Aging & Work, Boston College:14. (https://pdfs.semanticscholar.org/d690/afe03d101e46e7d54c93a8034ac15a714595.pdf).

Konrath, Sara, et al. 2012. "Motives for Volunteering Are Associated with Mortality Risk in Older Adults." *Health Psychology* 31(1):87–96. (https://www.apa.org/pubs/journals/releases/hea-31-1-87.pdf).

Matz, Christina, Emily Haber, and Lisl Hacker. 2019. "Results of the 2019 Massachusetts Volunteer Sector Study." Chestnut Hill, MA: Boston College School of Social Work for the Massachusetts Service Alliance. Unpublished presentation.

Merrill Lynch/Age Wave. 2016. "Giving in Retirement: America's Longevity Bonus." A Merrill Lynch Retirement Study conducted in partnership with Age Wave. (http://agewave.com/wp-content/uploads/2016/07/2015-ML-AW-Giving-in-Retirement_Americas-Longevity-Bonus.pdf).

Morrow-Howell, Nancy, et al. 2009. "Evaluation of Experience Corps: Student Reading Outcomes." *Center for Social Development Report* No. 09-01. St. Louis, MO: Washington University. (https://www.aarp.org/content/dam/aarp/giving_back/volunteering/2012-11/evaluation-of-experience-corps-student-outcomes-aarp.pdf).

Nakamura, Jeanne, et al. N.d. "Quality of Life in Social-purpose Commitment." Claremont, CA: Quality of Life Research Center, Claremont Graduate University.

National Executive Service Corps (NESC). 2020. "About NESC: History." (http://www.nesc.org/history/).

Okun, Morris A., Ellen WanHeung Yeung, and Stephanie Brown. 2013. "Volunteering by Older Adults and Risk of Mortality: A Meta-analysis." PubMed. *Psychology of Aging* 28(2):564–77. (https://www.ncbi.nlm.nih.gov/m/pubmed/23421326/?i=4&from=/2354560).

Pathways to Encore Purpose Project. 2018a. "Beyond the Self: 34 Million Older Adults Committed to Common Good." (https://encore.org/wp-content/uploads/2018/03/PEP-Brief-2.pdf).

Pathways to Encore Purpose Project. 2018b. "Help Wanted? Ask Someone 50+." Brief #1. (https://encore.org/wp-content/uploads/2018/03/PEP-Brief-1.pdf).

Piercy, Kathleen, et al. August 2011. "Challenges and Psychosocial Growth of Older Volunteers Giving Intensive Humanitarian Service." *The Gerontologist* 51(4):550–60. (https://academic.oup.com/gerontologist/article/51/4/550/597576).

Piktialis, Diane, et al. October 29, 2014. "Second Acts in Prime Time: Helping Employees Transition to Post-retirement Careers." Conference Board. (https://www.conference-board.org/topics/global-economic-outlook).

Rebok, George. 2013. "Baltimore Experience Corps Study." ClinicalTrials.gov. (https://clinicaltrials.gov/ct2/show/NCT00380562).

Service Corps of Retired Executives (SCORE). 2020. "About SCORE: SCORE History." (https://core.score.org/node/147953).

Society for Human Resource Management (SHRM) Foundation. 2015. "Leveraging the Value of an Age-diverse Workforce." (https://www.shrm.org/foundation/ourwork/initiatives/the-aging-workforce/Documents/Age-Diverse%20Workforce%20Executive%20Briefing.pdf).

Spera, Christopher, et al. June 2013. "Volunteering as a Pathway to Employment: Does Volunteering Increase the Odds of Finding a Job for the Out of Work?" Corporation for National and Community Service. (https://www.nationalservice.gov/sites/default/files/upload/employment_research_report.pdf).

Varma, Vijay, et al. December 2015. "Experience Corps Baltimore: Exploring the Stressors and Rewards of High-intensity Civic Engagement." *The Gerontologist* 55(6):1038–49. (https://clinicaltrials.gov/ct2/show/NCT00380562).

Wikipedia. N.d. "Experience Corps." (https://en.wikipedia.org/wiki/Experience_Corps).

Wikipedia. N.d. "Senior Corps." (https://en.wikipedia.org/wiki/Senior_Corps).

# PART VI

# SUMMARY AND FUTURE OUTLOOK

CHAPTER 25

# Social Policy and the Older Worker

## An International Perspective

Janet M. Hively and Moira Allan

### SEEING THE POTENTIAL OF THE WORLDWIDE LONGEVITY REVOLUTION

Rapid aging is one of the major twenty-first-century drivers of change, along with new technologies and climate change. Thanks to twentieth-century medical miracles, along with improvements in nutrition and working conditions, more older adults can anticipate twenty extra healthy, active years.

The World Health Organization (WHO) has declared 2020–2030 to be the Decade of Healthy Ageing. WHO's optimistic statement is: "Older people themselves will be at the center of this effort that will bring together all of the stakeholders to improve the lives of older people, their families, and the communities they live in." The WHO action plans are set to develop age-friendly communities, integrated care, and social support. But the WHO plan mentions working later in life in only one line about age-friendly communities: "Promote age diversity, combat ageism and foster inclusion in work."[1]

We need more emphasis on policies to extend work life. Here are four reasons why:

1. Public pension systems around the world are facing shortfalls due to the retirement of post–World War II boomers, now ages fifty-five to seventy-four.
2. Due primarily to low birth rates, the population is shrinking in forty-six countries—including major powers such as Japan, Russia, and most of western Europe—resulting in workforce shortages and reduced pension fund payments.[2]

3. Even countries with stable populations are facing workforce shortages because they have more retirees and fewer workers.
4. Retirees are likely to live beyond their savings and need income.

Then there is a fifth reason to extend work life—the inherent value of productive aging.

## PRODUCTIVE AGING

Studies begun in 1955 by the National Institutes of Health demonstrated that older people with goals and structure have a better chance of living longer.[3] Thus, health supports productivity and productivity supports health. The founding director of the National Institute on Aging, Robert Butler, introduced the term "productive aging" in 1982: "How do we orient our attention toward productivity rather than dependency? . . . I want to stress mobilizing the productive potential of the elders of society."[4] (See also chapters 7, 14, and 21.)

Scott Bass and Francis Caro illustrated "productive potential" when they conducted national productive aging surveys in 1989 and 1992 for the University of Massachusetts Gerontology Institute showing how people ages fifty-five to eighty-four used their time as paid employees, volunteers, and caregivers for the sick and/or disabled and their grandkids.[5] Older adults were heavily engaged in both paid and unpaid work that contributed economic value to the community.

In the twenty-first century, the Blue Zones study of centenarians has shown "what works" for productive aging.[6] In rural areas around the world where there are high percentages of centenarians, there is no word for "retirement." Centenarians have continuing responsibilities that keep them going and often are role models for productivity.

In "Seniors Lead" forums in Minnesota, older adults identified these four core values in relation to their quality of life: self-determination, economic security, social interaction, and meaningful work. They also stressed the importance of combating ageism to ensure recognition and respect for their productivity.[7]

## CHANGING EXPECTATIONS

Presenters at the Milken Institute's Business and the Future of Aging Summit in 2017 argued that the future of aging and the future of work are interrelated. "Our policies are set according to our expectations for ourselves and others. It's time to change our expectations for aging," said Paul Irving, chairman of the Milken Institute's Center for the Future of Aging. "Too few business leaders appreciate that population aging will fundamentally alter the landscape in which they operate." Patricia Milligan, senior partner of the Mercer human resources consulting firm, said that employers need to get over three major categories of unconscious bias: older workers are less productive, cannot learn, and cost too much. And Summit participant Andrew Scott said, "Employers struggle over why or how they should do things for their older employees. What they should do is: revamp recruitment, change retirement policies, and offer more flexible work opportunities."[8]

Social policies are mediators that determine the range of choices and conditions for older adult employment. Ingrained attitudes and expectations about older workers held by employers and other stakeholders influence policies affecting older workers. To make progress, we must reach out and turn stakeholders into partners who understand: (a) the capacities and values of older adults, and (b) how to work with older adults to maximize their productivity.

### Engaging Stakeholders

The stakeholders who influence, generate, and apply older worker policies fall within the following categories:

- Resource centers, think tanks
- Professional associations, research networks
- Older adult/worker advocacy organizations
- Employers, employer associations
- Education organizations
- Government organizations

In every region, the full range of older workers themselves—whether employed or unemployed—should be included in any process of inquiry, education, or planning related to working later in life. Discussing the intersecting topics of aging and work will stimulate engagement in the process of changing expectations and supporting later-life productivity.

## COMPREHENSIVE POLICY PLANNING

### United States Perspective

In 2017, the Special Committee on Aging of the U.S. Senate produced an excellent report called *America's Aging Workforce* that included a history of federal policies and described how aging employees and their employers could work together, but it left the task of prioritizing the issues and taking action to older workers and their employers.[9]

In 2019, the Aspen Institute's Future of Work Initiative produced a *State Policy Agenda* to address the challenges that workers and businesses face due to the changing nature of work in the twenty-first century.[10] Although the study did not focus solely on older workers, its policy recommendations are applicable across generations:

- Four policies would modernize worker benefits and protections: (1) create a system of portable benefits, (2) expand paid leave, (3) limit noncompetes and no-poach agreements, and (4) update unemployment insurance.

- Six policies would build a skilled and resilient workforce: (1) boost incentives for employers to invest in workers, (2) empower workers to invest in their own training, (3) expand access to high-quality training, (4) increase worthwhile apprenticeship opportunities, (5) expand career counseling and reemployment services, and (6) improve state labor market data.

A *Governor's Action Guide to Achieving Good Jobs for All Americans*, published in 2019 by the National Governors Association, offered a toolbox of actions including "Second Acts" to help midcareer workers succeed by

a. expanding access to continuous learning (strengthening partnerships between community colleges and business, initiating continuous learning accounts, offering continuous learning tax credits);
b. promoting seamless job transitions (using a digital badge system to record acquired skills), minimizing barriers created by occupational licensing requirements, and limiting noncompete agreements for workers; and
c. providing holistic support for midcareer workers (access to peer coaching, paid family and medical leave, and improved access to childcare and early education).

The guide suggests another group of actions to empower the rural workforce, including expansion of the digital infrastructure and other networks that support individuals and communities.[11]

## International Perspectives

Countries engaged in comprehensive planning to support active aging include most of the twenty-seven European Union (EU) countries where policy integration is required to maintain the stability of universal health care and a broad collection of free public education and social welfare services. The annual Active Ageing Index (AAI) ranks each of the EU countries and the U.S.[12] In 2018, the U.S., Sweden, Denmark, Ireland, the UK, and the Netherlands rose to the top of the rankings. Women fared worse than men in most countries, and the majority of eastern EU members and Greece ranked at the bottom. Iceland had the highest older worker participation rate in the world—40 percent for ages sixty-five to seventy-four. The AAI covers older people's productivity—not only in terms of paid employment but also unpaid family, social, and cultural contributions and activities that support independent, healthy, and secure living. The assessment has recently been expanded to include China (ranked #7) and Korea (ranked #11). Ideally, the annual AAI would include all countries around the globe.

### CASE STUDY FOR PLANNING: JAPAN

Current demographic information for Japan includes the following:

- Numbers for the country's population, workforce, and pension fund contributors are all shrinking. Now at 28 percent, Japan is the only country with more than 25

percent of its population over age sixty-five. This figure is expected to approach 40 percent by 2060.
- Japan's overall fertility rate was 1.45 in 2015, well below replacement level, and Japan has a no-immigration policy.
- Japan has one of the highest life expectancies in the world, at ninety-one years for females and eighty-five years for males.

The Global Coalition on Aging and the Health and Global Policy Institute have created a summary of areas in need of innovation in Japan and innovations that have already been developed.[13] A few highlights:

- In 2016, 23 percent of people aged sixty-five and older were in the workforce. A survey showed that 66 percent of respondents over age sixty expressed interest in continuing to work beyond age sixty-five. More than half of Japanese companies planned to raise their retirement age.
- Japan had a shortage of 40,000 caregivers in 2015. The shortage is expected to grow to 790,000 by 2035. (Some five thousand nursing care institutions are now testing robots. The market for robots is expected to grow twentyfold by 2025.)
- Plans are underway for compact cities to support "aging in place" featuring dense city centers, transportation connectivity that improves accessibility and keeps older adults mobile, plus information and communications technologies (internet shopping, emergency call systems, etc.). Silver Human Resource Centers connect older adults with short-term jobs serving the daily needs of their local communities.

Cullen Hayashida, cofounder of the Asia-Pacific Active Ageing Consortium, has identified ten strategies to help forestall the workforce shortage crisis in Japan.[14] These policies merit broad discussion by policy makers in other countries preparing for similar workforce pressures:

1. Postpone retirement age.
2. Increase the participation of women in the workforce.
3. Encourage increased births.
4. Increase foreign immigration.
5. Promote emigration of older adults.
6. Promote use of information and communications technologies.
7. Train for active aging.
8. Organize communities to support eldercare.
9. Improve training methods and standards for health care workers.
10. Prevent emigration of young adults.

When and how policy makers in Japan will address these planning options remains unclear. Numerous other countries will soon face similar demographic trends and challenges.

## UNITED NATIONS PLANNING

In 2015, 193 countries approved the seventeen Sustainable Development Goals (SDGs) that comprise the UN's 2030 plan. Each year, at a High Level Political Forum held at the UN building in New York City, member states present their SDG performance reports. The 2019 Stakeholder Group on Ageing (SGA) position paper reported that "the current 962 million people ages 60 and above is projected to rise to 1.4 billion by 2030, with the highest proportional growth in Africa and Asia. Global ageing and growing inequalities must be addressed together. Lifelong learning, decent work and employment opportunities, tackling economic and social inequalities, ending ageism and ensuring equal rights in older age—these are the issues that concern us."[15]

SDG 8 is the primary goal related to older workers: "Promote sustained, inclusive and sustainable economic growth, full and productive employment, and decent work for all." The 2019 SGA Position Paper made four recommendations for specific follow-through:

- Provide social protection and flexible working arrangements in order to facilitate and improve conditions for older persons in the informal and formal labor markets.
- Recognize the specific contributions of older people in both urban and rural settings. This includes paid, unpaid, and volunteer work.
- Remove age-restrictive policies on access to microcredit, loans, and financial investments.
- Enact and enforce national and global anti-age discrimination legislation and review age-related exemptions in existing equality legislation.

The SGA also made two recommendations related to SDG 4 on Lifelong Learning:

- Ensure lifelong learning opportunities that respond to the rights and preferences of older persons. Reskilling, training, and retraining equip older persons to be active agents in a complex and changing world.
- Adapt learning opportunities, content, and methodologies to the interests and preferences of older persons.

Next, the UN's Open-Ended Working Group on Aging (OEWGA) will review and discuss statements from member states and accredited NGOs describing issues and desirable norms for the right to work / access to the labor market in later life. Ultimately, the UN's General Assembly will approve a convention clarifying and protecting the rights of older workers.

# POLICY INNOVATIONS CULTIVATE AND SUPPORT OLDER WORKERS VIA BRIDGES TO EMPLOYMENT

Policy innovations have built bridges to later-life employment through education and training, internships / apprenticeships, and transition guides.

## Education and Training

"The more we define preparation for a career as a private good, the more it becomes an individual's responsibility to figure out how to move ahead. However, education and workforce preparation constitute a public good and require public support," says Richard Kazis, former director of Jobs for the Future.[16] He urges the U.S. to provide robust support for regional systems that invest in human capital. Kazis also emphasizes public accountability for program quality and consumer protection for students.

Located within fifty miles of most Americans, community colleges hold the key for access to higher education and workforce preparation. (See also chapter 18.) They are affordable, accessible, flexible institutions, well positioned to serve residents and employers efficiently. A good example of community stakeholders cooperating to develop win-win opportunities for midcareer and older workers is offered by the Future Skills Centre in Calgary, Canada. The center is investing $7.7 million in ten innovative projects.[17] Some of the projects engage current workers who are at risk of displacement because they lack needed skills. They offer innovative approaches to training and transitions into job opportunities. Other projects are looking at common barriers to successful career transitions and how to improve current skills training with or without involving an educational institution.

In Norway, the right to free lifelong education for adults is guaranteed by law (paid for by a national heritage fund composed of profits from the sale of natural resources). Researchers evaluating the impact of formal education in later life have shown that students beyond age forty are likely to stay in the workforce longer if they have used their right to free study leave.[18]

Singapore has created continuity in its lifespan educational options in the belief that lifelong learning should be the new norm in work and life, enabling workers to enhance themselves professionally and prepare to explore uncharted territory.[19] A Workforce Training Supplement offers low-income workers their choice among various certificated skills-training programs. A National Silver Academy provides five hundred subsidized postsecondary courses, teaching work skills and/or life skills for those aged fifty and above. An opening credit of $500 toward learning and training helps raise awareness and encourages seniors to take courses.

Digital technologies are creating major new opportunities for workers and companies in both advanced and developing economies, but more than half of the world's population is still offline, concentrated in areas where residents are predominantly rural, low income, elderly, illiterate, and female.[20] Those who are less likely to use the internet are also more likely to have difficulties in accessing employment or everyday services. Universal internet access is essential, plus the right of older adults to digital education, training, and capacity-building services basic to self-determination. The Center for Aging and Work at Boston College reported in 2017 that six in ten boomers are extremely or very interested in learning new skills to advance in their careers, and 51 percent are extremely or very interested in training for a completely different type of job.[21] Given the demand, community networks should be cultivated to ensure development of the infrastructure, marketability, and guidance for successful mature worker training programs.

## Fellowships/Internships/Apprenticeships

In 1963, President Lyndon Johnson started Green Thumb, now titled the Senior Community Service Employment Program (SCSEP). (See also chapter 3.) Initiated to help small farmers who were put out of business by industrial farming, the program trains and places participants in paid community service assignments with nonprofit organizations. Successful SCSEP placements turn into ongoing employment for participants or at least cultivate work skills and a go-to network as a foundation for future employment.[22]

As described elsewhere in this handbook (see chapter 24), the Encore Fellows program has matched seasoned professionals with social sector organizations for high-impact, paid assignments in more than fifty metropolitan areas.[23] Similar programs offer the expertise of senior fellows to community service organizations. The Conservation Law Foundation, for example, advertises unpaid one-year senior fellowships that match retiring lawyers, engineers, and scientists in New England to projects based on their interests and relevant expertise.[24]

The Techtonic Group of Colorado has introduced the first Department of Labor–registered apprenticeship program for software developers. Once Techtonic apprentices have billed for one thousand hours, employers can hire them. This "outsourced apprenticeship" model allows employers to take on qualified apprentices of any age for a cheaper rate and with less risk than for new hires.[25]

Internships are typically set up to let young adults sample jobs and gain insight from immersing themselves in a career path; similar opportunities seldom exist for older adults. A new start-up named "Hoppin" offers more than a hundred job-shadowing options for workers of all ages in a range of industries, including tech, venture capital, fashion, and health.[26] And "midternships"[27] create opportunities for older workers to try out their skills in new career pathways and cultivate contacts who can connect them to employment opportunities.

## Transition Guides

Older workers everywhere are encountering a more flexible and collaborative but far less secure world of work. Work transitions after a layoff or retirement can be thwarted by ageism, heavy caregiving responsibilities, or outmoded skills. (See also chapters 12, 15, 18, and 20.) Lynda Smith, a social entrepreneur in South Africa, has created a Skills Bank used by age fifty-plus job seekers.[28] They list their skills, industries, and what they are looking for workwise, and the information is matched with nonprofit and for-profit organizations seeking assistance. And the Institute for Career Transitions at MIT, one of many life/work resource centers and networks for older adults located online or in the metropolitan areas of the U.S., matches age fifty-plus unemployed job seekers with volunteer career coaches and evaluates what does or does not work in their transition process. (See also chapter 16.)

## A WELCOMING WORKPLACE

Research from the European Foundation for the Improvement of Living and Working Conditions shows the importance of goal-oriented motivation for sustainable work outcomes over the life course. Motivated employees have higher levels of work engagement and fewer sick days. "Sustainable" work offers intrinsic motivation, extrinsic motivation, and mutual trust.[29] And to allay concerns that different generations bring to the workplace, it is important to manage open cross-generational conversations among boomers, Gen Xers, and millennials about their hopes and fears for themselves and their organization.[30]

### Inequalities and Discrimination

"Still Working Hard," a study from the Center for Economic and Policy Research, estimates that 10.2 million U.S. workers aged fifty-eight or older were employed either in physically demanding jobs or in jobs with difficult working conditions. These conditions affect high proportions of Latino and African American workers, as well as immigrants and those with poverty-level incomes or low educational levels.[31] The report argues that this information must be considered when public officials weigh recommendations for raising the age for pension eligibility because forcing later-life work would pose a serious hardship to those populations. Right now, many older workers who find it difficult to meet the physical demands of their low-income jobs are struggling to continue long enough to qualify for Medicare at age sixty-five.

Such jobs should be considered for redesign using new technologies. Farmers in the U.S. who need help because of aging or disabilities can turn to Agrability, a national, partially government-funded program that helps them more easily maintain their farms.[32] More than fifteen hundred consultants were sent to individual farms in 2018 to assess need and recommend solutions, including use of assistive technology, different watering or harvesting methods, or additional lighting for better visibility. The biggest single need is related to mobility because of arthritis.

Whereas those in difficult working conditions tend to be low-income workers, discriminatory practices can affect all types of older workers. They may be unemployed and looking for work, happy in their jobs and hoping to stay as long as possible, seeking to advance in their organizations, or wanting to shift from their current jobs to part-time or bridge jobs before retiring completely. In 1967, the U.S. Age Discrimination in Employment Act (ADEA), covering individuals forty years of age and older, outlawed practices such as posting job openings that might bar older workers from applying or forcing older workers to retire at specific ages. However, training opportunities often go to a younger worker because the older worker is not as tech savvy, or an employer denies promotion because the older worker is not expected to be around long. A 2009 Supreme Court ruling made the complaint process more difficult by saying that claimants must prove that discrimination on the basis of age was the sole or overriding factor behind the decision. Then, in 2019, the Seventh U.S. Circuit Court of Appeals ruled that ADEA safeguards only employees, not job applicants. In response, a bill has been introduced in the U.S. Senate known as "The Protecting Older Workers against Discrimination Act," which would restore the pre-2009 standard and reaffirm that workers may use any type of admissible evidence to prove their claims of age bias.[33]

In 2000, the European Union Council approved a Directive for Equal Treatment in Employment and Occupation that could be used to guide the revision of U.S. policies.[34] The directive emphasizes the need to increase older worker participation and diversity in the labor force. It also states that employment and occupation are key elements in guaranteeing equal opportunities for all and contribute strongly to the full participation of citizens in economic, cultural, and social life.

## Benefits/Caregiving

The U.S. Affordable Care Act requires employers to offer affordable, minimum value health care coverage, without exclusions for preexisting conditions, for full-time employees and their children (up to age twenty-six). Health plans must provide coverage for preventive services, including immunizations, screenings, physicals, and certain pharmaceuticals.

Non-employer-sponsored health care options include Medicare for ages sixty-five-plus and for under age sixty-five with disabilities; the Medicaid/CHIP program for low-income families and children, pregnant women, elderly, and people with disabilities; and HealthCare.gov that offers a marketplace for all U.S. citizens or nationals living in the U.S. and not enrolled in Medicare to obtain hospital, medical, and prescription drug coverage.

Nonhealth benefits appropriate for a multigenerational workforce include: work-life balance (flextime, telecommuting, compressed workweek, vacation time, and leave); financial planning, commuter benefits, tuition reimbursement, retirement funding; on-site fitness equipment, free snacks and drinks, casual dress; and personal development/mentoring. Benefits that older employees particularly value include: a dental plan, vision plan, on-site clinic, employee assistance/counseling and support for personal issues, health and fitness programs, ability to work part-time or flex-time, and pre- or post-tax accounts for savings.[35]

Two other benefits being sought through organized advocacy are paid sick leave and paid family leave. Family leave includes not only maternity and paternity leave but also leave for family caregiving. (See also chapter 20.) People caring for family members outside of their full-time jobs experience considerable disruption of their workplace routines.[36] About one in four employed U.S. adults provides informal care for a parent, in-law, or other family member older than sixty-five. The proportion is expected to grow as longevity increases and older workers are retained in the workforce.

Examples of policy proposals addressing caregiving include the following: The National Domestic Workers Association advocates for a Social Insurance Fund for Universal Family Care.[37] The U.S. Administration for Community Living appointed two advisory councils in 2019 established by the Family Caregivers Act and the Supporting Grandparents Raising Grandchildren Act. The councils will recommend effective models of family caregiving and caregiver support, as well as improve coordination across federal programs for older workers trying to balance employment and caregiving responsibilities.[38]

States with a high percentage of older adults and a shortage of caregivers might follow Maine's example. On January 1, 2021, employers must offer up to forty hours of time off each year for paid sick leave that can be used for family emergencies as well as for employee illness. Maine is the only state to allow the time to be used for other than personal illness.[39] A 2017 initiative adopted in Hawaii was designed to keep working family caregivers in the labor force. If they work at least thirty hours a week outside the home, caregivers are eligible for stipends of up to $70 a day to defray the cost of services for their loved ones. Several states are exploring measures to boost pay for health workers who provide long-term care.[40]

## GOOD AND BAD ASPECTS OF WORKPLACE FLEXIBILITY

Workplace flexibility has long been a goal for older workers as well as for millennials and for parents of young children. FlexJobs, a Colorado-based online flexible jobs-listing service with fifty-five career categories, showed that 80 percent of 375 companies surveyed in 2015 offered some sort of work flexibility. Options go beyond traditional formats to include work-from-anywhere jobs, independent contract work, and results-oriented contract jobs. Technology tools such as videoconferencing, shared calendars, computer monitoring, and instant messaging help supervisors track progress.[41] Many older workers prefer to work in a temporary, contract, consulting, or freelance capacity. Once again, however, what may be desirable for skilled workers with entrepreneurial attitudes may turn into involuntary part-time, on-call, precarious employment for low-wage workers. Computer software is too often used by retail businesses to schedule part-time workers hour by hour, day by day, offering no stability or predictability.

Throughout the U.S., the fastest-growing category of new jobs has been "gig" work. A workforce study by Randstad U.S. predicts that by 2025, half of the workforce will be "agile" workers[42] with uncertain income who don't receive any of the benefits provided for full-time employees. Aware of this scenario, the California State Assembly passed the AB5Act, making it harder for companies to label workers as independent contractors instead of employees.[43] The law parallels a California Supreme Court ruling that would use the ABC test to determine worker status. To hire an independent contractor, businesses must prove that the worker: (a) is free from the company's control, (b) is doing work that isn't central to the company's business, and (c) has an independent business in that industry. Absent all three conditions, the worker must be classified as an employee and receive labor protection and benefits. California's legislation provides a model for other states and countries interested in spreading access to economic opportunity and security for all workers.

## EXTENDING WORK LIFE

What social policies would extend work lives without adverse effects on the health or retirement income of disadvantaged workers? In 2018, the International Longevity Center in London reported on outcomes of the EXTEND Project that assessed results of policy initiatives and reforms designed to keep people working longer in five EU member states: Denmark, Finland, Germany, the Netherlands, and the United Kingdom. Europe's significant increases in older workers since 2000 were initially attributed to raising the age at which people become eligible for public pensions. But since none of the policies for raising the retirement age had been implemented in the test countries, EXTEND sought out and identified other factors that likely contributed to the continuing employment of older workers:[44]

- shifting from a welfare state to a work society where paid employment is ideal for all groups;
- shifting from encouraging early exit based on age to signaling that older workers are needed in tight labor markets, that early retirement is expensive for society, and that working enhances quality of life as people age;
- a stable economy encouraging employers to hire, retain, and develop older workers;
- improvement in working conditions and promotion of lifelong learning opportunities;
- explicit attention to the wishes and needs of older women who are less educated and struggling to reconcile longer working lives with caregiving responsibilities; and
- avoiding or eliminating precarious work.

It is not necessarily wrong to link pension age to average life expectancy, but flexibility that accommodates individual needs and interest in working longer benefits the economy as well.

### United States Perspective

How do U.S. retirement policies affect the retention of older workers? The U.S. is gradually moving the age for collecting maximum public pension benefits to seventy but continues to allow workers to collect Social Security benefits as early as age sixty-two, three years before Medicare eligibility. Over half of retirees take their benefits early—often because they don't like their jobs, or they've been laid off or encouraged to retire via incentive programs, or their health is failing. Yet they risk living for twenty-five or more years without a decent income. If they waited until age seventy to make a claim, their benefit would be as much as 76 percent higher and they would have had the chance to save more for the long haul.

Unfortunately, Social Security discourages those who have retired early from returning to the workforce by taxing their earnings by up to 50 percent. That penalty should be eliminated. Similarly, workers who have started collecting maximum benefits at seventy are discouraged from remaining in the workforce because they would have to pay taxes on their higher income *and* the Social Security payroll tax.

Social Security actuaries predict a program deficit over the next seventy-five years, resulting from the slow growth of the labor force and the retirement of the baby boomers, which raises the ratio of retirees to workers. The proposed Social Security 2100 Act would eliminate the deficit by increasing the payroll tax, expanding its application to earnings above $400,000. It would also expand benefits to ensure that workers with years of low earnings do not retire into poverty. It would also lower federal income taxes on benefits for approximately twelve million middle-income adults. A separate Caregivers Credit Act would provide caregivers with Social Security work credits that would expand later benefits.[45]

Several proposals have been presented to expand individual retirement savings plans like the 401(k) plans offered through employers. California launched a state-sponsored retirement program for the private sector, titled CalSavers,[46] requiring all employers with five or more workers to sign on if they do not currently offer their employees a way to save for retirement. The program is expected to give 7.5 million workers an easy way to deduct savings from their paychecks and will bypass setup procedures and investment liabilities for small businesses.

At the federal level, the impending retirement income crisis has spurred bipartisan support for the SECURE Act that would relieve burdens on those working longer by delaying required minimum distribution from 401(k) accounts, allowing workers to contribute to their individual retirement accounts past age seventy, and covering part-time and temporary workers. Automatic enrollment in a savings plan for all paid workers is the likely long-term goal.[47]

The U.S. is fortunate to have a labor market hungry for what older workers tend to prefer—part-time employment and opportunities for entrepreneurial self-employment. (See also chapter 23.) For low-wage workers without savings, several proposals are brewing for new income supplements that would expand economic security. In other countries, however, cries of alarm are being heard because age fifty-plus workers in no-growth, ageist economies face high rates of unemployment as well as disruption caused by digital technologies replacing workers. To develop an employment-friendly ecosystem with emergency measures for long-term unemployed seniors, policy makers will need to come to terms with the cultural assumptions and expectations that are basic determinants for successful retention of older workers.[48]

## THE FUTURE FOR OLDER WORKERS

### Active Aging

In his foreword to *Economic Foundations for Creative Aging Policy*, Richard Adler speaks about two familiar but contrasting scenarios for the future.[49] In the first, governments overpromise a level of old-age benefits that is economically unsustainable so that a gigantic wave of greedy geezers threatens to disenfranchise subsequent generations. In the second, active agers make the most of the "extra years" provided by increased longevity while assuring a worthwhile legacy for future generations. One scenario is win-lose, the other win-win. One is ageist, handing out benefits based on age, while the other promotes "meaningful work, paid or unpaid, through the last breath."

What would it take to realize the active aging vision? The columnist and author Thomas Friedman talks about a hyperconnected "Yes We Can" world in which people who want jobs demonstrate how they can add value better than robots or cheap labor. The skill required to do that requires lifelong learning. Those with more education and capital who can reach global markets will earn much more than others. Friedman says that PQ (passion quotient) and CQ (curiosity quotient) will be as important as IQ (intelligence quotient) because we will need everyone innovating products and services complementary to technology.[50]

In the U.S., the fastest-growing age cohort is eighty-five-plus. In 2018, 4.4 percent of that cohort was employed, twice as many as ten years ago. Noting this same trend, the European Commission funded the Active 80 PLUS research project while developing the Europe 2020 plan for a market economy that is competitive, sustainable, and inclusive.[51] The EU supports detecting and redeveloping the hidden strengths of older adults and encouraging their engagement in meaningful activities, including employment.

An important part of the win-win approach is encouraging older workers *themselves* to propose and/or create innovative models for productive aging over the life course. There are examples in Paris, Hawaii, and Iceland of replicable initiatives developed by older adults who are country liaisons for the Pass It On Network.[52]

- Old'Up is an organization in Paris of volunteers aged seventy-five-plus, founded by Marie-Francoise Fuchs to show that "we can give meaning and utility to our lengthening lives." Old'Up members confront the challenge of being treated as full citizens by participating positively and usefully in society, to be seen as assets, not as burdens. Their efforts include immersive studies in long-term care facilities and teaching old people how to use public transport, museums, and so forth.
- The Hawaii Active Aging Network, led by Cullen Hayashida, is: (a) working with state legislators to urge the State Office on Aging to update its 2013 Active Aging Plan; (b) encouraging public television to showcase active aging role models; (c) meeting with the business community regarding its workforce shortage challenges and how older adults need to be considered as part of their workforce strategy; and (d) pressing for making the state into an "open museum" for economic development around the "now older adult."
- The *Icelandic Mapping Report* has been produced as a model for other European countries. Hans Kristjan Gudmundsson coordinated U3A (Universities of the Third Age) volunteers in collecting information about the assets and activities of Iceland's rapidly aging population and future perspectives in planning for the third age (ages fifty to seventy-plus). Project partners include Iceland's capital city of Reykjavik, multiple labor unions, the National Power Company, and the University of Iceland. The partners both receive and use "best practices" recommended by the report. Some examples follow:
    - Extend the mandatory retirement age from seventy to seventy-two.
    - Allow Reykjavik's municipal employees who have worked for at least ten years to reduce their working hours by 20 percent but still collect a full monthly salary.

- Offer National Power Company employees targeted education and training, temporary reduction of their work time for studies, and transfer between jobs within the company.
- Encourage older employees to take an active part in guiding new employees and to participate in individual study programs and research projects.

The global Pass It On Network connects these and other positive aging advocates so that they can share "what works" for active aging.[53] These examples illustrate the power of older adults themselves to lead systems and influence cultural change. Elders have the passion and curiosity described by Thomas Friedman because they have a vested interest.

## Workplace as Locus for Policy Innovation

The twenty-first-century workplace is an ideal arena for policy innovations. As an illustration, Eurofound issued an "Overview of New Forms of Employment" in 2018 that looked at nine new forms of employment within three categories of innovation: (a) relationships between employers and employees, (b) work patterns that are discontinuous or intermittent or for very limited periods of time, and (c) networking among the self-employed, particularly freelancers. It would be interesting to brainstorm variations in relation to their accommodation of older worker needs. For example, job sharing or collaborative self-employment might be logical opportunities for older workers.

"You can have almost anything you want *IF* you help others get what they want," says Carleen MacKay, a career transition guide based in Hawaii who has walked her talk by posting the latest edition of her "playbook," *New Ways to Work*, as a free download.[54] She describes more than a dozen options for new ways to work, with tools to pursue them—and even offers to show readers how to modify and publish the book with their own local flavor. MacKay thinks of herself in later life as a bartering expert who "has seen the world as it is and not as I was."

The good news is that fostering a multigenerational workplace is an increasingly hot topic. Look for updates at the World Economic Forum's annual meetings in Davos, Switzerland, from the Living, Learning and Earning Longer Collaborative of global employers formed in 2019 to pursue policies and practices that will capitalize on increasing longevity. Discover how AARP is coordinating with knowledge partners that include the Organisation for Economic Co-operation and Development (OECD) and the World Economic Forum.[55]

The issues relevant to "social policy and the older worker" are complex and rapidly changing. Whether just starting out or highly experienced, members of the workforce and their employers should take a strong interest in guiding expectations and practices toward a positive future by shaping policies that empower older workers.

# NOTES

1. World Health Organization. June 12, 2019. *Decade of Healthy Ageing, 2020–2030*. ZERO Draft. Geneva, Switzerland: WHO.

2. Ruchir Sharma. August 18, 2019. "Let's Say Goodbye to Growth." *New York Times*.

3. Nancy Morrow-Howell, James Hinterlong, and Michael Sherraden, eds. 2001. *Productive Aging: Concepts and Challenges.* Baltimore: Johns Hopkins University Press:vii.

4. Robert Butler and Herbert P. Gleason. 1985. *Productive Aging: Enhancing Vitality in Later Life.* New York: Springer.

5. Scott A. Bass, ed. 1995. *Older and Active: How Americans over Age 55 Are Contributing to Society*. New Haven, CT: Yale University Press.

6. Dan Buettner. 2008. *The Blue Zones: Lessons for Living Longer from the People Who've Lived the Longest.* Washington, DC: National Geographic Society.

7. Darlene Schroeder. 1999. *Project 2030: Seniors Lead Forums.* St. Paul: Minnesota Office on Aging, Department of Human Services.

8. Richard Eisenberg. May 9, 2017. "Why Isn't Business Preparing More for the Future of Aging?" *Next Avenue, Aging and Innovation Special Report*.

9. Sen. Susan M. Collins and Sen. Robert P. Casey Jr. December 2017. *America's Aging Workforce: Opportunities and Challenges.* Washington, DC: U.S. Senate, Special Committee on Aging.

10. Aspen Institute Future of Work Initiative. February 2019. *State Policy Agenda.* Washington, DC: Aspen Institute.

11. Steve Bullock. July 2019. *A Governor's Action Guide to Achieving Good Jobs for All Americans.* Washington, DC: National Governors Association.

12. Asghar Zaidi. June 2019. *2018 Active Ageing Index: Analytical Report.* Geneva, Switzerland: United Nations Economic Commission for Europe.

13. Global Coalition on Aging, and Health and Global Policy Institute. 2019. "Ageing and Innovation in Japan: Fact Sheet."

14. Cullen Hayashida. 2019. "Addressing Japan's Eldercare Workforce Shortage Challenges: A Paradigm for a Macro-Methodology." Honolulu. (cullen@hawaii.edu).

15. Stakeholder Group on Ageing. 2019. "Empowering People and Ensuring Inclusiveness and Equality." Position paper submitted to the High Level Political Forum 2019, New York. (www.stakeholdergrouponageing.org/).

16. Jay Walljasper. September 2017. "The Path to Good Jobs for Everyone." Interview with Richard Kazis in *Blue Mountain Center Commons* newsletter. (http://bmccommons.org/the-path-to-good-jobs-for-everyone/).

17. Future Skills Centre. 2019. "Mid-career Workers Innovation Projects." Alberta, Canada: University of Calgary. (https://fsc-ccf.ca/what-we-do/innovation-projects/).

18. Tove Midtundstad and Roy A. Nielsen. 2019. "Lifelong Learning and the Continued Participation of Older Norwegian Adults in Employment." *European Journal of Education* 54:48–59. (https://doi.org/10.1111/ejed.12322).

19. Skills Future Singapore Agency (SG). 2019. "Programmes for You." (www.Skillsfuture.sg/ProgrammesForYou#section3).

20. James Manyika. May 2017. "Technology, Jobs, and the Future of Work." McKinsey Global Institute.

21. Center on Aging and Work. March 13, 2017. *Agework: Fact of the Week.* Chestnut Hill, MA: Boston College. (www.bc.edu/agingandwork).

22. U.S. Department of Labor, Employment and Training Administration. 2018. "Senior Community Services Employment Program." (www.doleta.gov/seniors).

23. See www.encore.org/fellowships.

24. Conservation Law Foundation News. June 10, 2019. "Senior Fellowships, Pro Bono." (www.clf.org/about/employment-opportunities/senior-fellowships-pro-bono/).

25. Working Nation. 2019. "College Alternatives: Faster and Cheaper Pathways to Gain Work-ready Skills for Quality Jobs." (https://workingnation.com/college-alternatives-faster-cheaper/).

26. Future Proof Newsletter. May 2019. "The Startup That Lets You Job Hop." *Forbes*. (www.gohoppin.com).

27. The term "midternships" was used by the SHIFT Network in Minnesota in 2010. Funded by the State of Minnesota, the Midternship program placed mature workers who wanted to change fields into jobs in different vocational pathways for up to three months to try out the field and develop useful contacts for future placements.

28. Lynda Smith. See: Lynda@50plus-skills.co.za.

29. Franz Ferdinand Eiffe. 2018. "The Role of Motivation for Sustainable Work." Working paper. Dublin, Ireland: European Foundation for the Improvement of Living and Working Conditions (Eurofound).

30. Phyllis Weiss Haserot. March 20, 2018. "The Biggest Work Fears of Boomers, Gen Xers, and Millennials." *Next Avenue* (blog). (www.nextavenue.org/work-fears-boomers-genxers-millennials/).

31. Paul Kleyman. March 30, 2016. *Seniors Working Hard for Their Money: 10 Million, Many Ethnic, in Tough Jobs.* New America Media News Report. Washington, DC: Center for Economic and Policy Research.

32. Andrew Soergel. July 20, 2019. "Technology, Temporary Help Keeps Farmers on Job Longer." ABC News. (abcnews.go.com).

33. Sen. Robert P. Casey Jr. 2019. "The Protecting Older Workers against Discrimination Act (POWADA)—S.485." Cosponsors, Sens. Grassley, Leahy, and Collins. For further information, contact Keith_Miller@aging.senate.gov.

34. Council of the European Union. 2000. "Council Directive 2000/78/EC of 27 November 2000." *Official Journal of the European Commission,* L303/16.

35. Sena Meilleur. 2019. "Benefit Considerations for an Aging Workforce." PowerPoint presentation. OneDigital Health and Benefits, Burlington, VT.

36. Matthew A. Andersson. June 2019. "Workers Who Are Unpaid Caregivers of Older Relatives Struggle with Unmet Workplace Needs." News release, Baylor University via EurekAlert.

37. Ai-Jen Poo, with Ariane Conrad. 2015. *The Age of Dignity: Preparing for the Elder Boom in a Changing America.* New York: New Press.

38. U.S. Administration for Community Living. August 7, 2019. "ACL Announces Initial Meetings of Caregiver Advisory Councils." News release, Washington, DC. See councils described at www.ACL.gov/RAISE.

39. Scott Thistle. May 28, 2019. "New Law to Make Maine First State with Paid Sick Time That Covers More Than Getting Sick." *Portland (ME) Press Herald.*

40. Robert Weisman. August 29, 2019. "Costs of Long-term Care Stagger States: Aging Population and Soaring Expenses Force Officials to Hunt for Solutions." *Boston Globe*:A1, A8.

41. Cindy Krischer Goodman. January 4, 2017. "Balancing Act: 2017 Looks Like It Will Be a Big Year for Workplace Flexibility." Reprinted in CapeCodTimes.com.

42. Braulio Pena. 2016. *Workplace 2025 Study.* Atlanta: Randstad U.S.

43. Alexia Fernandez Campbell. May 30, 2019. "California Is Cracking Down on the Gig Economy." Vox.com. (https://www.vox.com/policy-and-politics/2019/5/30/18642535/california-ab5-misclassify-employees-contractors).

44. Brian Beach and Geraldine Bedell. December 2018. *The EXTEND Project: Exploring Pension Reforms, Work, and Inequalities.* London: International Longevity Center.

45. Alicia H. Munnell. February 2019. *This New Social Security Bill Could Make Social Security Even Better.* Chestnut Hill, MA: Center for Retirement Research, Boston College.

46. Margot Roosevelt. July 1, 2019. "Worried about Retiring? California Will Help You Save Money." *Los Angeles Times.*

47. Deborah Carr. May 23, 2019. "The SECURE Act." *Next Avenue* (blog). (www.nextavenue.org).

48. Nicole Legrain and Michel Riquier. December 2014. *Emergency Measures against Unemployment of Seniors and Future Seniors Today and Tomorrow.* Paris: Generations ERIC.

49. Richard Adler. 2015. "The Future of Aging: A Gray Dawn or a Long, Bright Future." Foreword to *Economic Foundations for Creative Aging Policy*:2.

50. Thomas Friedman. February 3, 2013. "It's PQ and CQ as Much as IQ." *Cape Cod Times* (from the *New York Times*):B7.

51. Anita Rappauer and Michael Stadler-Vida. 2015. *Active 80 Plus: Valuing and Valorizing the Knowledge and Skills of People 80+.* Report on Research at European Level. Vienna, Austria: Erasmus+.

52. Contact Moira Allan, international coordinator for the Pass It On Network, at moira@passitonnetwork.org to be introduced to the leaders of these three replicable projects or to others referenced in the chapter.

53. At www.passitonnetwork.org, click on "Pathways" and then on "Work and Economic Security" to find examples of practices in relation to older workers.

54. Carleen MacKay and Phyllis C. Horner. 2019. *New Ways to Work: A Playbook to Make WORK—Work for YOU!* Honolulu, HI: Bill Sager. (www.newworkforcehawaii.com).

55. AARP International. 2020. "Living, Learning and Earning Longer Collaborative." AARP. (https://www.aarpinternational.org/initiatives/future-of-work/living-learning-and-earning-longer).

## REFERENCES


AARP International. 2020. "Living, Learning and Earning Longer Collaborative." AARP. (https://www.aarpinternational.org/initiatives/future-of-work/living-learning-and-earning-longer).

Adler, Richard. 2015. "The Future of Aging: A Gray Dawn or a Long, Bright Future." Foreword to *Economic Foundations for Creative Aging Policy*:2.

Andersson, Matthew A. June 2019. "Workers Who Are Unpaid Caregivers of Older Relatives Struggle with Unmet Workplace Needs." News release, Baylor University via EurekAlert.

Aspen Institute, Future of Work Initiative. February 2019. *State Policy Agenda*. Washington, DC: Aspen Institute.

Bass, Scott A., ed. 1995. *Older and Active: How Americans over Age 55 Are Contributing to Society*. New Haven, CT: Yale University Press.

Beach, Brian and Geraldine Bedell. December 2018. *The EXTEND Project: Exploring Pension Reforms, Work, and Inequalities*. London: International Longevity Center.

Buettner, Dan. 2008. *The Blue Zones: Lessons for Living Longer from the People Who've Lived the Longest*. Washington, DC: National Geographic Society.

Bullock, Steve. July 2019. *A Governor's Action Guide to Achieving Good Jobs for All Americans*. Washington, DC: National Governors Association.

Butler, Robert and Herbert P. Gleason. 1985. *Productive Aging: Enhancing Vitality in Later Life*. New York: Springer.

Campbell, Alexia Fernandez. May 30, 2019. "California Is Cracking Down on the Gig Economy." Vox.com. (https://www.vox.com/policy-and-politics/2019/5/30/18642535/california-ab5-misclassify-employees-contractors).

Carr, Deborah. May 23, 2019. "The SECURE Act." *Next Avenue* (blog). (www.nextavenue.org).

Casey Jr., Sen. Robert P. 2019. "The Protecting Older Workers against Discrimination Act (POWADA)—S.485." Cosponsors, Sens. Grassley, Leahy, and Collins. For further information: Keith_Miller@aging.senate.gov.

Center on Aging and Work. March 13, 2017. *Agework: Fact of the Week*. Chestnut Hill, MA: Boston College. (www.bc.edu/agingandwork).

Collins, Sen. Susan M. and Sen. Robert P. Casey, Jr. December 2017. *America's Aging Workforce: Opportunities and Challenges*. Washington, DC: U.S. Senate, Special Committee on Aging.

Conservation Law Foundation News. June 10, 2019. "Senior Fellowships, Pro Bono." (www.clf.org/about/employment-opportunities/senior-fellowships-pro-bono/).

Council of the European Union. 2000. "Council Directive 2000/78/EC of 27 November 2000." *Official Journal of the European Commission* L303/16.

Eiffe, Franz Ferdinand. 2018. "The Role of Motivation for Sustainable Work." Working paper. Dublin, Ireland: European Foundation for the Improvement of Living and Working Conditions (Eurofound).

Eisenberg, Richard. May 9, 2017. "Why Isn't Business Preparing More for the Future of Aging?" *Next Avenue: Aging and Innovation Special Report*.

Friedman, Thomas. February 3, 2013. "It's PQ and CQ as Much as IQ." *Cape Cod Times* (from the *New York Times*):B7.

Future Proof Newsletter. May 2019. "The Startup That Lets You Job Hop." *Forbes*. (www.gohoppin.com).

Future Skills Centre. 2019. "Mid-career Workers Innovation Projects." Alberta, Canada: University of Calgary. (https://fsc-ccf.ca/what-we-do/innovation-projects/).

Global Coalition on Aging, and Health and Global Policy Institute. 2019. "Ageing and Innovation in Japan: Fact Sheet."

Goodman, Cindy Krischer. January 4, 2017. "Balancing Act: 2017 Looks Like It Will Be a Big Year for Workplace Flexibility." Reprinted in CapeCodTimes.com.

Haserot, Phyllis Weiss. March 20, 2018. "The Biggest Work Fears of Boomers, Gen Xers, and Millennials." *Next Avenue* (blog). (www.nextavenue.org/work-fears-boomers-gensxers-millennials/).

Hayashida, Cullen. 2019. "Addressing Japan's Eldercare Workforce Shortage Challenges: A Paradigm for a Macro-methodology." Honolulu. (cullen@hawaii.edu).

Kleyman, Paul. March 30, 2016. *Seniors Working Hard for Their Money: 10 Million, Many Ethnic, in Tough Jobs.* New America Media News Report. Washington, DC: Center for Economic and Policy Research.

Legrain, Nicole and Michel Riquier. December 2014. *Emergency Measures against Unemployment of Seniors and Future Seniors Today and Tomorrow.* Paris: Generations ERIC.

MacKay, Carleen, and Phyllis C. Horner. 2019. *New Ways to Work: A Playbook to Make WORK—Work for YOU!* Honolulu, HI: Bill Sager. (www.newworkforcehawaii.com).

Manyika, James. May 2017. "Technology, Jobs, and the Future of Work." McKinsey Global Institute.

Meilleur, Sena. 2019. "Benefit Considerations for an Aging Workforce." PowerPoint presentation. OneDigital Health and Benefits, Burlington, VT.

Midtundstad, Tove and Roy A. Nielsen. 2019. "Lifelong Learning and the Continued Participation of Older Norwegian Adults in Employment." *European Journal of Education* 54:48–59. (https://doi.org/10.1111/ejed.12322).

Morrow-Howell, Nancy, James Hinterlong, and Michael Sherraden, eds. 2001. *Productive Aging: Concepts and Challenges.* Baltimore: Johns Hopkins University Press.

Munnell, Alicia H. February 2019. *This New Social Security Bill Could Make Social Security Even Better.* Chestnut Hill, MA: Center for Retirement Research, Boston College.

Pena, Braulio. 2016. *Workplace 2025 Study.* Atlanta: Randstad U.S.

Poo, Ai-Jen, with Ariane Conrad. 2015. *The Age of Dignity: Preparing for the Elder Boom in a Changing America.* New York: New Press.

Rappauer, Anita and Michael Stadler-Vida. 2015. *Active 80 Plus: Valuing and Valorizing the Knowledge and Skills of People 80+.* Report on Research at European Level. Vienna, Austria: Erasmus+.

Roosevelt, Margot. July 1, 2019. "Worried about Retiring? California Will Help You Save Money." *Los Angeles Times.*

Schroeder, Darlene. 1999. *Project 2030: Seniors Lead Forums.* St. Paul: Minnesota Office on Aging, Department of Human Services.

Sharma, Ruchir. August 18, 2019. "Let's Say Goodbye to Growth." *New York Times.*

Skills Future Singapore Agency (SG). 2019. "Programmes for You." (www.Skillsfuture.sg/ProgrammesForYou#section3).

Soergel, Andrew. July 20, 2019. "Technology, Temporary Help Keeps Farmers on Job Longer." ABC News. (abcnews.go.com.)

Stakeholder Group on Ageing. 2019. "Empowering People and Ensuring Inclusiveness and Equality." Position paper submitted to the High Level Political Forum 2019, New York. (www.stakeholdergrouponageing.org/).

Thistle, Scott. May 28, 2019. "New Law to Make Maine First State with Paid Sick Time That Covers More Than Getting Sick." *Portland (ME) Press Herald.*

U.S. Administration for Community Living. August 7, 2019. "ACL Announces Initial Meetings of Caregiver Advisory Councils." News release, Washington, DC. See councils described at www.ACL.gov/RAISE.

U.S. Department of Labor, Employment and Training Administration. 2018. "Senior Community Services Employment Program." (www.doleta.gov/seniors).

Walljasper, Jay. September 2017. "The Path to Good Jobs for Everyone." Interview with Richard Kazis in *Blue Mountain Center Commons* newsletter. (http://bmccommons.org/the-path-to-good-jobs-for-everyone/).

Weisman, Robert. August 29, 2019. "Costs of Long-term Care Stagger States: Aging Population and Soaring Expenses Force Officials to Hunt for Solutions." *Boston Globe*:A1, A8.

Working Nation. 2019. "College Alternatives: Faster and Cheaper Pathways to Gain Work-ready Skills for Quality Jobs." (https://workingnation.com/college-alternatives-faster-cheaper/).

World Health Organization. June 12, 2019. *Decade of Healthy Ageing, 2020–2030*. ZERO Draft. Geneva, Switzerland: WHO.

Zaidi, Asghar. June 2019. *2018 Active Ageing Index: Analytical Report*. Geneva, Switzerland: United Nations Economic Commission for Europe.

CHAPTER 26

# A Portfolio Framework for Extended Work Pathways

## Leveraging the Strengths of Older Workers

Dawn C. Carr, Brittany M. King, and Phyllis Moen

### OVERVIEW

Earlier chapters in this book make it abundantly clear. Older workers have unique skills and abilities that, if leveraged, can play a critical role in the economy, in organizations, and in society more broadly. Since 2008, increasing numbers of older workers have delayed retirement by staying in their jobs longer than planned, transitioning to part-time work, or returning to work after initially retiring. Delays in full Social Security eligibility and eroding safety nets, declines in pensions, recent financial setbacks and accompanying layoffs—these all promise to further blur the lines between work and retirement. Traditional one-way, one-time retirement transitions at ages sixty-two or sixty-five are likely to become increasingly rare.

Despite the preferences and needs of older workers to stay engaged in paid work beyond traditional retirement ages, few work environments have developed formal strategies to utilize their skills and abilities. Companies rarely plan for these kinds of changes, and few have any policies or systems in place to support this career phase. In addition, and in part because there are so few formal arrangements available for those interested in "re-careering" or downshifting in their current position or finding a new job with fewer hours, many older workers do not develop a plan for their extended work lives until they have to find a new job, modify a current one, or return to work after initially retiring or being laid off. (See also chapters 7, 8, 10, and 16.)

For older workers with either the need or the desire to work beyond traditional retirement ages, finding and keeping a job during this phase of the life course can be a serious challenge.[1] Consequently, many older workers cobble together a unique mix of arrangements within particular companies, identifying new lower-skill jobs that are hourly and flexible, taking on self-employment, or using temporary contract-type work to stay employed. In this chapter, we argue that a new, more flexible framework or "portfolio" for later-life work will help both older workers and businesses benefit from extended work lives, thereby leveraging experienced employees' unique skills and abilities.[2] "Portfolio" denotes a series of transitions, a variety of alternative work and non-work pathways throughout adulthood, culminating eventually into full-time retirement.

## FINANCIAL FORCES RESHAPING WORK AND RETIREMENT PATHWAYS

Contemporary older workers are navigating uncharted terrain when it comes to making decisions about how long and in what capacity to stay engaged in paid work and if, when, and how to step into retirement. (See also chapter 21.) In the U.S. today, a growing proportion of older workers relies almost completely on Social Security income because their pensions are inadequate or nonexistent.[3] Prior to the introduction of welfare state systems, retirement was a consequence of health decline and the inability to continue working. And, for those who lived long enough to reach this phase of life, not working typically led to a life of poverty and dependence on family or charities.[4] Over the course of the twentieth century, retirement became normative, accessible to almost all Americans (men), and a time when people from nearly all walks of life found common ground in their ability to step away from the workforce with a reliable pension and Social Security income.

Changes to the American pension system in the 1980s birthed a new system that required workers to plan their own retirement, with little knowledge and in many cases, inadequate resources to carry this out successfully. The first generations of workers that spent their entire careers in jobs that offered almost exclusively defined contribution plans (or no plan at all) reached traditional retirement ages just following the Great Recession in 2008. These dynamics accelerated existing trends that have led to longer work lives, even as eligibility for full Social Security benefits has been delayed and benefit amounts have not kept pace with the cost of living.

This "do-it-yourself retirement savings" structure has not served the average worker well. Although Social Security remains a reliable source of regular income (for now), for many older workers today, the one-third of their income expected to come from a pension to accompany Social Security and maintain a reasonable quality of life in retirement is grossly inadequate or nonexistent. Many older workers can no longer afford to leave the workforce in their early sixties. (See also chapters 2–6.) The consequences have most profoundly affected low-wage, low-skill workers, who make up 44 percent of all workers between the ages of eighteen and sixty-four. These workers have a median yearly income of less than $18,000.[5] More than half of older workers in this category have no plans for retirement (in part because many are in jobs that do not offer retirement benefits), and their employers have little interest in providing training so they can obtain the skills they need for extended work life.[6] Minorities and women are the most economically disadvantaged among them and have the least amount of control over their employment options.[7]

Older workers find themselves needing and / or wanting to work beyond traditional retirement ages, but there are more older workers than at any point in history, given the aging of the large boomer cohort, increased longevity, and reductions in fertility.[8] Nearly one-third of the U.S. workforce is now over age fifty. Shifts in the normative timing and nature of retirement could have significant impacts on the economy, and companies will increasingly need to adapt in ways that utilize the skills and abilities of older workers while offering a portfolio of options and flexible work arrangements to workers of all ages and life stages. In this new risk economy, shaped by mounting demographic, social, health, and financial pressures, the interests, needs, and abilities of older workers are seldom on the radar in boardrooms and human resource departments.[9] Moreover, this portion of the workforce is increasingly at risk of age discrimination, forced early retirement buyouts, and layoffs.

## ALTERNATIVES TO FULL-TIME WORK FOR OLDER WORKERS

Although many older workers are interested in extending the number of years they spend working full-time, others are looking for different kinds of opportunities. The term *unretirement* emerged fairly recently to describe the ways in which an increasing number of older adults return to work after retirement.[10] Unretirement captures the idea of portfolio work and retirement pathways, which may signify a return to a full-time job or some other less-than-full-time arrangement. This can include *bridge* jobs,[11] positions that allow men and women to maintain their participation in the labor force, but in a less intense way, as a transition between career job and retirement.[12] (See also chapter 22.)

In the early 2000s, bridge jobs were a novel concept, with a minority of older workers in jobs that were construed as "bridge" work. But following the 2008 recession and then the COVID-19 economic shock, growing numbers of individuals were seeking bridge employment. More than half of the men and women who left long-term, full-time jobs in 2008 participated in paid work in some capacity before fully departing from the labor force.[13] The shift to portfolio pathways reflects new kinds of financial pressures, a risky economic climate, and cultural as well as policy changes reinforcing working longer as the new normal.

### Encore Careers

In addition to the economic drivers, cultural forces have played an important role in shaping the movement toward alternative work arrangements for older workers. An important example has become known as "encore" jobs. Scholars, thought leaders (like Encore.org CEO Marc Freedman), and nonprofit organizations promote *encore* careers for older workers as a means to bolster purposeful engagement during later life.[14] These types of positions put older workers (typically those fifty-plus) on a different track from their traditional careers, though they typically involve utilizing many of the skills that were cultivated over the course of their careers. The stated purpose of encore placements is to provide less intensive work arrangements that offer opportunities to engage in meaningful activities that meet community needs. (See also chapter 24.)

Several organizations are helping to facilitate transitions to encore careers through training opportunities for workers over fifty. A few notable examples show the impact they are having by redesigning later-life work as a new period of career growth, rather than departure or disengagement. In the mid-2010s, Encore.org partnered with Intel to develop a program for eligible Intel employees interested in spending six months interning at a nonprofit organization to utilize their skills and knowledge in meaningful ways. The purpose is to help them refocus their work lives on a new career (https://encore.org/fellowships/intel/). Stanford University introduced a formal program called the Distinguished Careers Institute, a competitive education and training program targeting workers over fifty interested in changing their career paths. Participants either leverage existing skills or develop new ones and engage in a second phase of their career focused on having a significant impact on society (https://dci.stanford.edu/). And the University of Minnesota was the first public university to launch a lower-cost version of the institute (umac.umn.edu). The fact is, however, that these programs remain financially out of reach for many older workers. Still, there appears to be a trend in the growth of similar programs, some offered by community colleges, which could greatly enhance opportunities for older workers to reimagine their work and their retirement portfolios for the later adult years.[15]

## Self-Employment

Although the majority of workers regardless of age work in and seek out traditional wage and salary positions, *self-employment* is a portfolio option for growing numbers of people. (See also chapter 23.) They may be older individuals who have experienced ageism in organizational policies around recruitment, training, and retention or else mature workers seeking greater customization and flexibility. The percentage of workers who are self-employed increases with chronological age, with nearly a quarter of workers (24 percent) aged 65-plus self-employed relative to only 8 percent of workers who are under fifty.[16] One reason the likelihood of self-employment increases with age is that their eligibility for Social Security and Medicare benefits makes them more financially able to take on part-time work as consultants or contract workers, jobs without health insurance or high wages. Individuals unable to locate wage and salary work that meets their needs may fashion self-employment opportunities as a way to maintain engagement in the labor force.[17]

Self-employed older workers report higher levels of satisfaction with their work[18] and have greater capacity to work part-time, such as in contract work positions, a common type of self-employment in later life.[19] Although the idea of having control over everyday work activities may be enticing, being self-employed in later life often involves significant financial risks.[20] Consequently, self-employment is not an option for all older workers. Those who choose self-employment are more likely to be male, non-Hispanic white, and have higher overall levels of education. In other words, the choice of self-employment is an alternative to wage and salary jobs primarily for more privileged older workers who have the means and the skills to create their own companies or consultancies.

Certain types of self-employment are more successful than others in generating the income older workers need. Being an "independent contractor" can be enticing to some older workers interested in working for companies (often companies that they previously worked for), so long as they can control when, if, and how much they work. Typically, these jobs are project based, lasting a few months or years. Independent contractors are the highest earning of the self-employed. Other types of self-employment offer fewer options and lower pay. For instance, a significant number of older workers engage in "informal work" with a handful of sporadic work hours.[21] Self-employment through participation in multilevel marketing businesses is also on the rise among older workers. (This refers to a business structure or practice by which an individual seller earns commissions from direct sales of a product or service and from the sales of others whom the seller recruits.) Most individuals do not make any money or even lose money when they join these companies, and over half that do make money make about $5,000 per year or less.[22]

## The Gig Economy

Technological innovations have fostered expansion of the *gig economy*, a version of self-employment that includes jobs typically paid based on completion of a particular task (e.g., driving someone to the airport, or contracting for a short-term design project). However, gig jobs typically offer neither job security nor employment benefits. Some gig workers put in full-time hours; others pick up part-time or part-year gig jobs to supplement their income. Research is only beginning to emerge about the involvement of older workers specifically in these kinds of positions,[23] but journalists and popular press coverage on this topic have drawn attention to some important consequences for older workers relying on this type of work.[24] More research is needed to better understand the costs and benefits of these new kinds of work arrangements for older workers, particularly given that regulatory policies are still in development. It is also important to note that older workers may choose gig-type jobs because other options are not available, and participation of older workers in these jobs could be masking the larger problem of later-life underemployment.[25]

## Examples of Emerging Patterns of Portfolio Pathways

Financial, cultural, and structural changes have certainly blurred the lines between full-time careers and retirement, with portfolio pathways increasingly common. Full-time work is lasting longer, as is the transitional period between full-time work and retirement.[26] In general, although a significant number of older workers today do still opt for a traditional retirement exit (i.e., fully departing from full-time work between age sixty-two and sixty-five as shown as figure 26.1, even if it is a delayed traditional retirement path), a growing contingent falls into alternative patterns of later-life work.

As described previously, these individuals are modifying their careers in the later stages to fit their needs—switching to bridge jobs, encore careers, or self-employment (or a mix of these) to provide options for continued engagement in paid work—or else suddenly finding themselves out of work, with few prospects for reemployment.

In figure 26.1 we depict continuing full-time in the unmodified career job as "A" followed by five examples of portfolio pathways—"B" through "F"—selected from the wide variety of pathways that older workers can take (or be channeled into) today as they move between full-time career and retirement. Aside from staying in the full-time career job (A), older adults who are able and willing to remain employed can:

B. remain in their current position but with modified work arrangements;
C. find a new position that is full-time but with preferable work arrangements;
D. transition to a new position that has reduced hours and/or accommodations that are preferred;
E. retire temporarily and return to full- or part-time employment at the same place or a new work environment; or
F. take on one or more short-term contract positions (with varying levels of work participation).

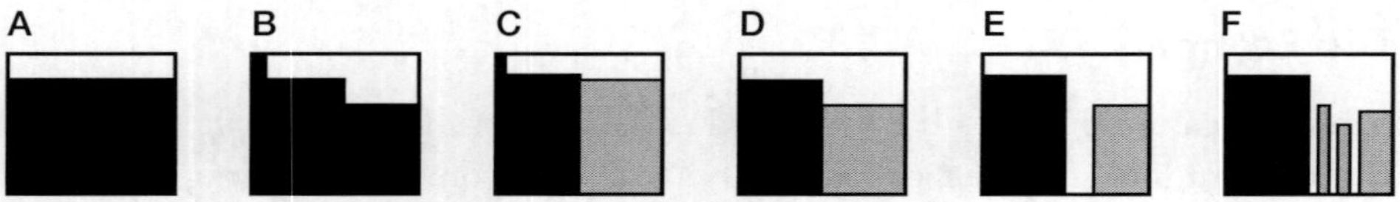


**FIGURE 26.1.** Theoretical Portfolio Pathway Patterns

These figures exemplify the alternative options both available to and desired by older workers today. However, the options vary for workers in different social locations, such as those with a college education versus those with only a high school diploma or less. Moreover, the specific details characterizing each type are likely to vary dramatically. For instance, individuals who take the "B" pathway may slowly decrease their hours of participation over time rather than downshifting to a lower-intensity job. That is, they may work thirty hours the first year, twenty the second, ten the third, and completely leave work during the fourth year after they transition. On the other hand, they may remain working full-time or nearly full-time, but with different kinds of job tasks that target preferred activities like mentoring, training, or developing a new project to lead.

In each situation, the characteristics of alternative work arrangements could be based on jobs older workers seek out and request, or could be a "take it or leave it" situation that does not fit their needs.[27] For instance, someone may determine, due to the expenses of caring for their spouse, that they need to continue working, but they may also need sufficient time to manage their own health and the health of their loved one. However, a job fitting their unique skill set or preferred tasks and activities may not be available, so they might settle for a flexible, part-time job for financial reasons, despite its not being enjoyable or challenging or eliciting a sense of purpose. Still others find themselves altogether unable to work, given the onset of health difficulties, their own or that of a family member. In other words, the larger patterns capture the portfolio pathways older adults are taking, but the factors underlying the specific reasons for one decision or another provide context for whether and how they influence well-being. Barriers that keep older workers from working or from obtaining ideal jobs provide useful insight to this discussion.

## BARRIERS TO ALTERNATIVE PORTFOLIO PATHWAYS

Although different types of later-life work patterns are increasingly common, very few companies have developed intentional work arrangements for older workers seeking non-full-time options. In fact, for most companies, work arrangements for older workers seem to be more reactive than intentional. Several key barriers, described in the following sections, will be addressed in order to cultivate a framework for later-life employment that leverages the strengths of older workers, or indeed the strengths of workers across all life course stages.

### Inadequate Access to Health Insurance

One of the barriers to development of more formal portfolio pathways relates to health insurance. In the absence of a national health care program in the U.S., health care continues to be primarily tied to work, and most companies only offer health care to full-time workers. Given the health risks that come with aging, for older workers who do not yet qualify for Medicare, health insurance is a particularly critical factor influencing work decisions.[28] Although some companies have explored ways to provide health insurance for non-full-time workers,[29] most do not offer it, and lack of access to health insurance remains a key barrier facing many older workers. Other older adults experience "job lock," continuing to work longer because they need the health insurance.[30]

### Inability to Balance Full-Time Work with Caregiving

Growing evidence suggests that providing additional leave time greatly enhances the likelihood that an older worker will remain employed.[31] These preferences relate in part to wanting more "flex time" with age. However, people in their later working years are also increasingly likely to be faced with having a family member or loved one who requires regular care temporarily or for an extended period of time. One of the reasons many older workers leave the workforce early is related to difficulty in balancing care work with a traditional full-time job schedule.[32] (See also chapter 20.) Although there are some programs available within particular companies, the Family and Medical Leave Act is typically inadequate to cover the financial and time needs of caregivers dealing with particularly intensive or lengthy care work. Companies should develop programs that allow for flexible work arrangements when possible, whether in the form of time away from work, the location of work, or the time of day when work is completed. Such measures can greatly relieve caregivers who need to make sure tasks are completed, like getting medications, attending appointments with the doctor, or seeing to the activities of daily living.[33]

## Inadequate Access to Retirement Savings Programs

Retirement savings accounts may also influence the accessibility of formal alternative work arrangements for older workers. Retirement savings accounts were once leveraged to entice workers to remain loyal employees for the duration of their careers by guaranteeing some level of retirement income for life. Given the shift to defined contribution programs, retirement benefits programs today could be used in more flexible ways to support the needs of older workers.

The first problem is access. Not all employers offer retirement savings programs, and this is particularly true for contract workers, contingent workers, and part-time employees. Legally, a company can offer a 401(k) program to employees who work at least one thousand hours per year. And, starting in 2021 as a consequence of the Secure Act, individuals who work at least five hundred hours per year over three years (thus starting in 2024) will be allowed to participate in a 401(k) program (if a company offers it).[34] Should companies begin to make these opportunities available, older workers who desire to continue working in a part-time capacity because they need to accumulate more wealth toward retirement may be able to take on a given work role. This could increase the length of time older workers stay engaged in paid work, even if not full-time, and allow them to transition to a different set of tasks or a different type of postcareer job that is meaningful. On the other hand, a key feature of most retirement savings plans includes an employer match of funds, which is usually unavailable to non-full-time workers.

## Job Insecurity and Age Discrimination

Many older workers find themselves unexpectedly "retired" when offered the choice of taking an early retirement package or facing layoff. Others will be at greater risk of furloughs and layoffs in a post-COVID-19 economy, given that many U.S. firms see older workers as a competitive *dis*advantage.[35] Public policy, and especially the Age Discrimination in Employment Act, are often at odds with age-biased work environments, effectively pushing older workers out the door. In certain industries, having a "young culture" is key to the way businesses market themselves. There is perhaps no better example than the start-up tech industry, in which ageism is particularly well documented.[36] In fact, about two-thirds of workers aged forty-five to seventy-five report having experienced age-related discrimination at work.[37] It is extremely challenging to prove that mistreatment in the work environment is occurring as a consequence of ageism, so few companies are held responsible for this treatment.[38] (See also chapter 12.)

Thus many older workers feel pressured to retire before they are ready.[39] This pressure can come in the form of reduced work hours, reduced pay, and/or deterioration of work conditions such as poorer treatment from supervisors. Consequently, it is not surprising that most firms have not developed strategies to support or retain older workers, and even fewer have developed approaches that seek to utilize the unique skills and abilities of their older workers.[40] (See also chapters 7–10 and 16.) Stereotypes about older workers as slow, unreliable, frequently ill, or untrainable have been proven to be false; buying into those views will prevent companies from effectively leveraging the skills and experience of older people.

### Difficulty with Reemployment in Later Life

Creating formal policies that address ageism will also help address one of the most challenging problems that older workers face, particularly during economic downturns: the challenge of reemployment. Older workers are much less likely to find a new job following job loss or caregiving or health-related exits. Older workers experience greater risks related to becoming unemployed in the first place, and they have a harder time rejoining the labor force after losing a job. During the Great Recession these dynamics were magnified, and workers over age fifty, once unemployed, were much more likely to stay unemployed for six months or longer.[41] It's likely we will see similar or more pronounced effects following the economic downturn related to the COVID-19 pandemic. Extended periods of unemployment have significant consequences for all workers, but older workers have fewer years to bounce back.

Extended years of unemployment and dropping out of the workforce permanently for lack of options are serious problems when it comes to long-term financial security. Older workers who become unemployed often feel forced to dip into their retirement accounts or begin drawing on Social Security sooner than planned.[42] These kinds of decisions have potential to create irreparable damage to financial security during the years when they are likely to experience physical health decline and frailty. With fewer years left to recover, many never accumulate sufficient wealth to live on for the remainder of their lives, and this leaves them at risk of becoming impoverished.[43]

## BENEFITS OF LONGER WORK LIVES

Aside from the financial benefits older workers receive from delaying retirement (either through delayed departure from full-time work or through alternative work trajectories), there is growing evidence that remaining employed can be beneficial to many older people. But there are also benefits to employers.

### An "Ideal" Workforce

Older workers provide added value to their organizations, given their experience, professionalism, interpersonal skills, and problem solving.[44] This points to the importance of considering alternative dimensions of productivity, not simply "hard qualities" but also social skills and reliability.[45] Research suggests that older adults demonstrate more behavioral aspects of productivity and engage in fewer counterproductive activities.[46] Average age-related changes in cognitive function (i.e., decreased information processing speed) rarely have negative impacts on work productivity.[47] In fact, productivity among older workers is more consistent than among younger workers,[48] possibly because older individuals rely on previous life and work experience when they solve problems and complete tasks,[49] and because older workers have better attendance at work than younger workers.[50] They also tend to be first to arrive, remain focused throughout the day, and rarely miss work. This is true even in fast-paced, physically demanding work environments.[51] Thus, older workers are ideal candidates for businesses facing high worker turnover. A recent study found that when controlling for nonrandom sample selection issues, in a large-scale manufacturing plant there were no changes in productivity in association with age.[52]

Intergenerational workplaces are at an advantage in this aging society. Work teams that are age diverse are the most productive, which may relate to having greater diversity of experiences and knowledge to draw from when solving problems. (See chapter 9.) This is particularly true for companies that engage in creative tasks.[53] When companies strategically utilize their older workforce in ways highlighting their talents, skills, and experience, they are likely to be *more* competitive, not less.[54]

## Identity, Purpose, and Meaning

A significant source of individuals' sense of identity derives from work.[55] Paid work can be particularly salient in later career phases as goals change with age, shifting from more future-oriented goals to emotional goals.[56] This is explained in part by socio-emotional selectivity theory, which suggests that as we age, we tend to use attentional resources to solicit positive emotional experiences over negative ones. Consequently, older workers tend to view the purpose and meaning of their work in more complex ways than younger workers.

One way that this shift in focus changes the meaning of work for older people relates to the people with whom they work or the way that work influences the well-being of others. As people age, they become increasingly focused on how their lives influence younger generations. This "generative" drive is a normative part of development in later life and further evidence that older adults are beneficial to the workforce.[57] Work can tap into a drive to give back to other generations, or help individuals feel like the work they are doing can leave a legacy for subsequent generations. This connects one's sense of self with a clearer purpose involving the well-being of others. In other words, for older workers in jobs that allow them to act on a generative drive and maintain meaningful interactions with others, work is not just a functional activity, it is increasingly an emotionally meaningful and purposeful activity that promotes a positive sense of identity.

## Social Relationships

A key reason work is associated with identity, purpose, and meaning in later life relates to social relationships that people develop through work. In most work environments, social interactions are an essential component of everyday activities.[58] A significant body of research demonstrates the strong associations between the quantity and quality of social relationships and health and well-being. These benefits are particularly evident in later life when the cumulative effects of social interactions over the life course are most evident and socially isolated individuals experience accelerated morbidity and mortality trajectories.[59] With age, the size of friendship networks tends to decline and individuals are increasingly likely to live alone or only with a spouse or partner.[60] The work environment can thus be an important locus of social interaction, facilitating the maintenance and development of meaningful social relationships, whereas retirement exit can signal the loss of work-related social interaction, with negative consequences for psychological well-being.[61]

## Health Benefits

Employment in later adulthood can promote financial security, access to health insurance and wellness programs, and lifestyle behaviors associated with physical and cognitive activity. Accordingly, a growing body of research suggests that older adults may be able to maintain, or improve, their overall well-being by remaining in the workforce.[62] (See also chapter 19.) Assessing the extent and nature of the health benefits associated with longer work lives is complicated by the fact that the transition between work and retirement is often related to health. That is, people selectively leave work as a consequence of health problems, and those who continue to work are selectively healthy enough to work.[63] However, scholarship has begun parsing out direct effects from selection effects. And, although part of the health differences between those who continue working and those who retire is related to selection factors, there are direct, beneficial effects of longer work lives on health.[64]

Specifically, with regard to physical health, beyond the associated selection effects, older adults working at least part-time tend to experience a slower accumulation of functional limitations relative to those who are fully retired,[65] and decreased risk for mortality.[66] Similarly, robust results demonstrate that, on average, departure from the labor force is associated with more rapid cognitive losses than continued engagement in paid work.[67] Findings are less clear regarding psychological health; the extent to which individuals experience less depression or loneliness while working relative to retirement is largely contextualized by the type of work, the work environment, and the way the work tasks and activities influence well-being.[68]

## Limitations: Not Everyone Is Likely to Benefit

The challenge to working longer is that not all older individuals are able to do so, given health conditions, the absence of valued skills in a digitalized economy, family caregiving responsibilities, or layoffs. Moreover, any benefits from working longer are highly contextualized by workers' overall health, occupation, job tasks, and the people with whom they work.[69] For instance, an individual who has a very physically demanding job may experience more rapid physical health decline. Professionals and managers are at risk of burnout, unwilling or unable to remain engaged in intensifying work demands and "always on" connectivity expectations as they age.[70]

Recent research also shows that whether cognitive health benefits accumulate from continuing to work depends on the cognitive complexity of the job. Individuals whose jobs are highly cognitively complex do not benefit from continued engagement in paid work because they tend to maintain high levels of cognitive function regardless of whether they work or not. Individuals with jobs that require low levels of cognitive engagement tend to maintain their cognitive function significantly better when they continue working and experience significant declines once they retire.[71]

Finally, individuals who work in jobs that promote high levels of chronic stress experience significant improvements as a consequence of retirement. New technologies ratcheting up work intensity and "always on" expectations can lead to older workers' burnout and emotional distress as well as physical health difficulties.[72] For these individuals, longer work lives are likely to impose a cumulative decline in health and well-being, not an improvement.[73] Workers who report high levels of stress tend to be those with lower levels of autonomy and control over their work activities, individuals who experience chronic discrimination or feel that their work environment places their health and well-being at risk.[74]

## A NEW PORTFOLIO FRAMEWORK FOR EXTENDED WORK PATHWAYS

We are experiencing both an aging society and an aging workforce, in tandem with increasing use of artificial intelligence, automation, and other technological advancements. These transformations are occurring in the context of tremendous global economic and health shocks. The challenge is to reimagine work in ways that leverage the strengths of all workers—younger as well as older. To do so necessitates a new framework of possible portfolio pathways around work and retirement, along with more flexible work arrangements. It also requires recognizing the unique contributions that older workers make and the value of an intergenerational workforce. A new framework must also acknowledge and respond to enduring inequalities, the disparities in skills, health, opportunities, and constraints for disadvantaged subpopulations at every stage of the life course, calling for more innovative and sturdier safety nets.

Multigenerational workforces are the new normal, necessitating both public and corporate policies and practices that recognize the potential for positive outcomes when men and women of all ages work together. (See chapters 8 and 9.) This includes the fact that there are more similarities than differences in the working conditions younger and older workers want or need, and both suffer from uncertainties about their future.[75] The success of our labor force depends on older workers being utilized and acknowledged as essential aspects of a company's image.[76]

Based on the evidence presented throughout this chapter, we identify and briefly describe strategies for businesses to leverage the skills and resources of older adults in three key areas.

### Use New Types of Coaching and Training

The new reality of portfolio pathways around work and retirement necessitates coaching in recognizing and managing the inevitability of change. Plan A is no longer sufficient; older workers, and indeed, workers of all ages, also need plans B, C, and D. Planning in times of hyperchange in technologies and economies is vastly different than in times of stability.

Training also matters. Research shows that workers of all types need a similar *amount* of training, but older workers often need a different type of training, partially because they are at a different stage of their career. In most companies, training focuses on individuals under age thirty-five, with fewer older workers receiving training[77] and a growing proportion reporting that they have been denied access to training because of their age.[78] Normalizing portfolio and contingency planning as well as training regardless of age will offer workers a realistic window into the challenges, risks, and possibilities of twenty-first-century work.

### Develop Policies and Programs for More Flexible Portfolio Work/Retirement Pathways

Companies seeking to harness the skills, abilities, and wisdom of older workers will be more productive than those that facilitate "graceful exits." This approach requires development of formal and informal policies and practices that recognize and reward an intergenerational workforce. These policies should include opportunities for older as well as younger and middle-aged workers to discuss choices about the *structure of their positions*. Contingent on the occupation they are in and the company's needs, business should consider ways to allow workers to modify their current positions based on specific tasks that best utilize their unique abilities, allow them to transition to a job that is lower in intensity, decrease their regular work hours, or move to a project-based / consulting position.

### Develop Policies and Programs for Flexible and Supportive Work Conditions

The coronavirus pandemic is transforming the ways stakeholders think about and are organizing paid work. We doubt that organizations will return to the "old" normal. Creative flexibility regarding working conditions will support older adults, but also workers of all ages.

- Telecommute Options: For a variety of occupations, social distancing requirements associated with COVID-19 provided evidence that many types of workers can be effective when they work from home if they have the resources necessary to do so. Those with health conditions or caregiving responsibilities are especially likely to benefit from partial or full opportunities for voluntary remote work. (See chapter 20.) Not all jobs make this feasible, and not all workers like to telecommute, but it is increasingly evident that telecommuting opportunities can be an important way for certain workers to work longer.[79]
- Flexible Hours: Providing opportunities to have some control over the specific times that an individual is "on the clock" can also help workers stay in the labor force longer.[80] This also includes recognizing and getting rid of low-value work, as well as providing for "heads down" time to focus on specific tasks.[81]
- Unpaid Additional Vacation Time: For many older workers, one of the drawbacks of remaining engaged in paid work past traditional retirement ages is not having enough vacation time to travel or spend time with family living in a different geographic area, or time to take a "sabbatical" from work to refresh and refocus.

Work environments that allow people to apply for extended time away without penalty, regardless of whether they are paid, give people greater freedom to step away temporarily, meet their needs, and return to work ready to be productive, focused, and engaged.[82]

- Lateral Job Transitions: The benefits of work go well beyond the paycheck when the work being performed is meaningful. Some older workers, if given the option, will choose to transition to a job that may have similar (or even lower) pay, but that allows them to focus on specific activities that are more gratifying.[83]
- Promote an Intergenerational Work Culture: In many companies, job activities are intentionally or unintentionally age segregated. That is, workers are often engaged in activities that require interactions primarily with people at a similar career phase, and consequently a similar chronological age. Companies that integrate the skills and abilities of workers across different ages and life stages are more productive, are more innovative, and experience longer-term success.[84] However, this requires organizations to be explicit about their awareness of the value of strategically bringing together intergenerational teams for solving problems.

## CONCLUSION

Age in and of itself tells us little about the skills and abilities of workers.[85] Older workers are an increasingly important component of human capital. Looking to the future, COVID-19 will likely spur greater flexibility regarding where and when work is completed, but increased automation and corresponding downsizing will require workers of all ages to develop new skills. Training, support, and policies that encourage intergenerationally engaged work environments will be able to most effectively leverage the skills and abilities of older workers. Organizations need to develop a new portfolio framework based on celebrating, supporting, and accommodating the skills and abilities of workers across all phases of their career trajectories. Similar to the way building design practitioners have adopted "universal design" strategies that make physical spaces inclusive for people with all levels of abilities, universal design principles can be employed so that workplaces address workers' needs, celebrating and promoting the abilities of workers at all stages.[86]

## NOTES

1. Fengyan Tang and Jeffrey A. Burr. September 2015. "Revisiting the Pathways to Retirement: A Latent Structure Model of the Dynamics of Transition from Work to Retirement." *Ageing and Society* 35(8):1739–70. (https://doi.org/10.1017/S0144686X14000634); Sara Zaniboni. July 1, 2015. "The Interaction between Older Workers' Personal Resources and Perceived Age Discrimination Affects the Desired Retirement Age and the Expected Adjustment." *Work, Aging and Retirement* 1(3):266–73. (https://doi.org/10.1093/workar/wav010).
2. Jen Schramm et al. December 2014. "Preparing for an Aging Workforce." Alexandria, VA: Society for Human Resource Management.
3. Irena Dushi, Howard M. Ians, and Brad Trenkamp. November 7, 2017. "The Importance of Social Security Benefits to the Income of the Aged Population." *Social Security Bulletin* 77(2). (https://www.ssa.gov/policy/docs/ssb/v77n2/v77n2p1.html).

4. Jacob S. Hacker. 2002. *The Divided Welfare State: The Battle over Public and Private Social Benefits in the United States*. New York: Cambridge University Press.

5. Martha Ross and Nicole Bateman. November 2019. "Meet the Low-wage Workforce." Washington, DC: Metropolitan Policy Program at Brookings. (https://www.brookings.edu/wp-content/uploads/2019/11/201911_Brookings-Metro_low-wage-workforce_Ross-Bateman.pdf).

6. Kelly S. Mikelson, Daniel Kuehn, and Ananda Martin-Caughey. April 2017. "Occupational Projections for Low-income Older Workers: Assessing the Skill Gap for Workers Age 50 and Older." Washington, DC: Urban Institute. (https://www.aarp.org/content/dam/aarp/aarp_foundation/2017/pdfs/occupational-projections-for-low-income-older-workers.pdf).

7. Laura Sullivan and Tatjana Meschede. 2016. "Race, Gender, and Senior Economic Wellbeing: How Financial Vulnerability over the Life Course Shapes Retirement for Older Women of Color." *Public Policy & Aging Report* 26(2):58–62. (https://doi.org/10.1093/ppar/prw001); Anna W. Jacobs and Irene Padavic. January 2015. "Hours, Scheduling and Flexibility for Women in the U.S. Low-Wage Labour Force." *Gender, Work & Organization* 22(1):67–86. (https://doi.org/10.1111/gwao.12069).

8. Phyllis Moen. 2016. *Encore Adulthood: Boomers on the Edge of Risk, Renewal, and Purpose*. New York: Oxford University Press.

9. Institute of Leadership & Management. 2015. "Untapped Talent: Can Over 50s Bridge the Leadership Skills Gap?" Tamworth, England: Institute of Leadership & Management. (www.InstituteLM.com/resourceLibrary/UntappedTalent.html).

10. Nicole Maestas. 2010. "Back to Work: Expectations and Realizations of Work after Retirement." *Journal of Human Resources* 45(3):718–48. (https://doi.org/10.3368/jhr.45.3.718).

11. Terry A. Beehr and Misty M. Bennett. January 1, 2015. "Working after Retirement: Features of Bridge Employment and Research Directions." *Work, Aging and Retirement* 1(1):112–28. (https://doi.org/10.1093/workar/wau007).

12. Kevin E. Cahill, Michael D. Giandrea, and Joseph F. Quinn. June 2015. "Retirement Patterns and the Macroeconomy, 1992–2010: The Prevalence and Determinants of Bridge Jobs, Phased Retirement, and Reentry among Three Recent Cohorts of Older Americans." *The Gerontologist* 55(3):384–403. (https://doi.org/10.1093/geront/gnt146).

13. Dawn C. Carr. 2017. "Alternative Retirement Trajectories: The Potential of Part-time Work." Presentation at the Working Longer and Retirement: Applying Research to Help Manage an Aging Workforce Conference. Palo Alto, CA: Stanford Center on Longevity.

14. Philip A. Pizzo. February 4, 2020. "A Prescription for Longevity in the 21st Century: Renewing Purpose, Building and Sustaining Social Engagement, and Embracing a Positive Lifestyle." *JAMA* 323(5):415. (https://doi.org/10.1001/jama.2019.21087); Moen, *Encore Adulthood*.

15. Pizzo, "Prescription for Longevity."

16. David Baer. February 2015. "Older Workers Are More Likely to Be Self-employed." Washington, DC: AARP Public Policy Institute. (https://www.aarp.org/content/dam/aarp/ppi/2015/older-workers-are-more-likely-to-be-self-employed-AARP-ppi.pdf).

17. National Bureau of Economic Research (NBER). 2019. "Self-employment at Older Ages." *NBER Bulletin on Retirement and Disability* 3. (https://www.nber.org/BRD/2019no3/rdrc19-19a.html).

18. Austin O'Connor. February 27, 2018. "Be Your Own Boss, Be Happy." Washington, DC: AARP. (https://www.aarp.org/work/small-business/info-2018/self-employed-numbers-fd.html).

19. NBER. "Self-employment at Older Ages."

20. Susan Ainsworth and Cynthia Hardy. May 2008. "The Enterprising Self: An Unsuitable Job for an Older Worker." *Organization* 15(3):389–405. (https://doi.org/10.1177/1350508408088536).

21. Katharine Abraham, Brad Hershbein, and Susan Houseman. January 2020. "Contract Work at Older Ages." Cambridge, MA: National Bureau of Economic Research. (https://doi.org/10.3386/w26612).

22. AARP Foundation. 2017. "Multilevel Marketing: The Research, Risks and Rewards." Washington, DC: AARP. (https://www.aarp.org/content/dam/aarp/aarp_foundation/2018/pdf/AARPFResearchExecutiveSummaryFINAL101018.pdf).

23. Cody Cook, Rebecca Diamond, and Paul Oyer. May 2019. "Older Workers and the Gig Economy." *AEA Papers and Proceedings* 109:372–76. (https://doi.org/10.1257/pandp.20191042).

24. Aging in Place. "Seniors and the Gig Economy: Updated for 2020." February 27, 2019. AgingInPlace.org. (https://www.aginginplace.org/seniors-and-the-gig-economy/); Amanda Umpierrez. December 2019. "Older Gig Workers Left Hanging without Benefits." *Plansponsor*. (www.plansponsor.com).

25. Retirement Equity Lab, the New School SCEPA. May 1, 2019. "10+ Years of No Wage Growth: The Role of Alternative Jobs and Gig Work." Status of Older Workers Report Series. (www.economicpolicyresearch.org).

26. Richard W. Johnson, Janette Kawachi, and Eric K. Lewis. April 2009. "Older Workers on the Move: Recareering in Later Life." Washington, DC: AARP Public Policy Institute. (https://assets.aarp.org/rgcenter/econ/2009_08_recareering.pdf).

27. Johnson, Kawachi, and Lewis, "Older Workers on the Move."

28. Cheryl Paullin. 2014. "The Aging Workforce: Leveraging the Talents of Mature Employees." Alexandria, VA: Society for Human Resource Management. (https://www.shrm.org/hr-today/trends-and-forecasting/special-reports-and-expert-views/Documents/Aging-Workforce-Talents-Mature-Employees.pdf).

29. Paullin, "Aging Workforce."

30. Xenia Montenegro, Linda Fisher, and Shereen Remez. September 2002. "Staying ahead of the Curve: The AARP Work and Career Study." Washington, DC: AARP. (http://research.aarp.org/econ/multiwork.html); Paullin, "Aging Workforce."

31. Hendrik P. Van Dalen, Kène Henkens, and Joop Schippers. June 4, 2010. "How Do Employers Cope with an Ageing Workforce?: Views from Employers and Employees." *Demographic Research* 22:1015–36. (https://doi.org/10.4054/DemRes.2010.22.32).

32. Emma Dentinger and Marin Clarkberg. October 2002. "Informal Caregiving and Retirement Timing among Men and Women: Gender and Caregiving Relationships in Late Midlife." *Journal of Family Issues* 23(7):857–79. (https://doi.org/10.1177/019251302236598).

33. Gwenith G. Fisher, Dorey S. Chaffee, and Amanda Sonnega. April 2016. "Retirement Timing: A Review and Recommendations for Future Research." *Work, Aging and Retirement* 2(2):230–61. (https://doi.org/10.1093/workar/waw001); Amy Goyer. November 2013. "Balancing Work and Caregiving." Washington, DC: AARP. (https://www.aarp.org/caregiving/life-balance/info-2017/balancing-demands-ag.html); Jody Gastfriend. July 23, 2014. "No One Should Have to Choose Between Caregiving and Work." *Harvard Business Review*. (https://hbr.org/2014/07/no-one-should-have-to-choose-between-caregiving-and-work); Susan M. Collins and Robert P. Casey Jr. December 6, 2017. "America's Aging Workforce: Opportunities and Challenges." Washington, DC: Senate Special Committee on Aging. (https://www.congress.gov/115/crpt/srpt191/CRPT-115srpt191.pdf).

34. Kimbarley A. Williams and Crystal A. Skotedis. January 28, 2020. "9 Ways the SECURE Act Impacts Employer 401(k) Plans and What Companies Need to Do NOW." Boyer & Ritter. (https://www.cpabr.com/9-ways-the-secure-act-impacts-employer-401k-plans-and-what-companies-need-to-do-now/); Stephen Miller. January 20, 2020. "SECURE Act Alters 401(k) Compliance Landscape." Alexandria, VA: Society for Human Resource Management. (https://www.shrm.org/resourcesandtools/hr-topics/benefits/pages/secure-act-alters-401k-compliance-landscape.aspx).

35. Adele Hayutin. 2013. "Demographics of the Aging U.S. Workforce." Palo Alto, CA: Stanford Center on Longevity. (http://162.144.124.243/~longevl0/wp-content/uploads/2017/01/AgingWorkforceProceedings.pdf).

36. Jon Swartz. August 4, 2017. "Ageism Is Forcing Many to Look outside Silicon Valley, but Tech Hubs Offer Little Respite." CNBC. (https://www.cnbc.com/2017/08/04/ageism-is-forcing-many-to-look-outside-silicon-valley-but-tech-hubs-offer-little-respite.html); Joe Kita. December 30, 2019. "Workplace Age Discrimination Still Flourishes in America." Washington, DC: AARP. (https://www.aarp.org/work/working-at-50-plus/info-2019/age-discrimination-in-america.html).

37. Kimberly Palmer. February 20, 2017. "10 Things You Should Know about Age Discrimination." Washington, DC: AARP. (https://www.aarp.org/work/on-the-job/info-2017/age-discrimination-facts.html).

38. Dana Wilkie. May 3, 2018. "Discrimination against Older Workers May Be Common but Hard to Prove." Alexandria, VA: Society for Human Resource Management. (https://www.shrm.org/resourcesandtools/hr-topics/employee-relations/pages/age-discrimination-.aspx).

39. Kenneth Terrell. December 28, 2018. "New Study Finds Many Older Workers Forced Out of Jobs." Washington, DC: AARP. (https://www.aarp.org/work/working-at-50-plus/info-2018/forced-retirement.html).

40. Nicole Maestas et al. 2017. *Working Conditions in the United States: Results of the 2015 American Working Conditions Survey.* Santa Monica, CA: RAND Corporation. (https://doi.org/10.7249/RR2014).

41. Richard W. Johnson and Barbara A. Butrica. May 2012. "Age Disparities in Unemployment and Reemployment during the Great Recession and Recovery." Washington, DC: Urban Institute. (https://www.urban.org/sites/default/files/publication/25431/412574-age-disparities-in-unemployment-and-reemployment-during-the-great-recession-and-recovery.pdf).

42. Sara E. Rix. February 2015. "Long-term Unemployment: Greater Risks and Consequences for Older Workers." Washington, DC: AARP Public Policy Institute. (https://www.aarp.org/content/dam/aarp/ppi/2015-2/AARP953_LongTermUnemployment_FSFeb2v1.pdf).

43. Rix, "Long-term Unemployment."

44. Anna Round. May 2017. "Extending Working Lives: A Devolved, Lifecourse Approach to Enabling Work beyond State Pension Age." IPPR. (http://www.ippr.org/publications/extending-working-lives).

45. Ursula M. Staudinger and Catherine E. Bowen. November 2011. "A Systemic Approach to Aging in the Work Context." *Zeitschrift für ArbeitsmarktForschung* 44(4):295–306. (https://doi.org/10.1007/s12651-011-0086-2).

46. Thomas W. H. Ng and Daniel C. Feldman. 2008. "The Relationship of Age to Ten Dimensions of Job Performance." *Journal of Applied Psychology* 93(2):392–423. (https://doi.org/10.1037/0021-9010.93.2.392).

47. World Health Organization. 2015. *World Report on Ageing and Health.* Geneva, Switzerland: World Health Organization.

48. Jennifer H. Barnett, et al. 2015. "The Paired Associates Learning (PAL) Test: 30 Years of CANTAB Translational Neuroscience from Laboratory to Bedside in Dementia Research." Pp. 449–74 in *Translational Neuropsychopharmacology,* vol. 28, edited by Trevor W. Robbins and Barbara J. Sahakian. Cham, Switzerland: Springer International. (https://doi.org/10.1007/7854_2015_5001).

49. World Health Organization, *World Report on Ageing and Health.*

50. Ruth Finkelstein and Dorian Block. 2014. "10 Advantages of Retaining and Hiring Older Workers: Lessons from NYC Small Businesses." New York: Robert N. Butler Columbia Aging Center. (https://www.mailman.columbia.edu/research/age-smart-employer/advantages-older-workers).

51. Finkelstein and Block, "10 Advantages."

52. Axel Börsch-Supan and Matthias Weiss. April 2016. "Productivity and Age: Evidence from Work Teams at the Assembly Line." *Journal of the Economics of Ageing* 7:30–42. (https://doi.org/10.1016/j.jeoa.2015.12.001).

53. Uschi Backes-Gellner and Stephan Veen. July 2013. "Positive Effects of Ageing and Age Diversity in Innovative Companies—Large-scale Empirical Evidence on Company Productivity: Productivity Effects of Age-diverse Workforces." *Human Resource Management Journal* 23(3):279–95. (https://doi.org/10.1111/1748-8583.12011).

54. Backes-Gellner and Veen, "Positive Effects of Ageing and Age Diversity."

55. Rebecca Riffkin. August 22, 2014. "In U.S., 55% of Workers Get Sense of Identity from Their Job." Gallup. (https://news.gallup.com/poll/175400/workers-sense-identity-job.aspx).

56. Laura L. Carstensen. October 1995. "Evidence for a Life-span Theory of Socioemotional Selectivity." *Current Directions in Psychological Science* 4(5):151–56. (https://doi.org/10.1111/1467-8721.ep11512261).

57. Cheng, Sheung-Tak. 2009. "Generativity in Later Life: Perceived Respect from Younger Generations as a Determinant of Goal Disengagement and Psychological Well-being." *Journals of Gerontology: Series B, Psychological Sciences and Social Sciences* 64B(1):45–54. (https://doi.org/10.1093/geronb/gbn027); John N. Kotre. 1984. *Outliving the Self: Generativity and the Interpretation of Lives.* Baltimore: Johns Hopkins University Press; Johanna C. Malone et al. 2016. "Midlife Eriksonian Psychosocial Development: Setting the Stage for Late-life Cognitive and Emotional Health." *Developmental Psychology* 52(3):496–508. (https://doi.org/10.1037/a0039875).

58. Michel Perreault et al. September 2017. "Employment Status and Mental Health: Mediating Roles of Social Support and Coping Strategies." *Psychiatric Quarterly* 88(3):501–14. (https://doi.org/10.1007/s11126-016-9460-0).

59. Debra Umberson and Jennifer Karas Montez. March 2010. "Social Relationships and Health: A Flashpoint for Health Policy." *Journal of Health and Social Behavior* 51(1)_suppl.:S54–66. (https://doi.org/10.1177/0022146510383501).

60. Cornelia Wrzus et al. 2013. "Social Network Changes and Life Events across the Life Span: A Meta-analysis." *Psychological Bulletin* 139(1):53–80. (https://doi.org/10.1037/a0028601).

61. Ben Lennox Kail and Dawn C. Carr. October 2019. "Structural Social Support and Changes in Depression during the Retirement Transition: 'I Get By with a Little Help from My Friends.'" *Journals of Gerontology: Series B*. (https://doi.org/10.1093/geronb/gbz126).

62. Kevin E. Cahill, Michael D. Giandrea, and Joseph F. Quinn. May 2012. "Older Workers and Short-term Jobs: Patterns and Determinants." Washington, DC: *Monthly Labor Review*; Esteban Calvo. 2006. "Does Working Longer Make People Healthier and Happier?" *SSRN Electronic Journal*. (https://doi.org/10.2139/ssrn.2302705).

63. Cahill, Giandrea, and Quinn, "Older Workers and Short-term Jobs"; Calvo, "Working Longer"; Collins and Casey Jr., "America's Aging Workforce."

64. Kandauda Wickrama et al. March 2013. "Heterogeneity in Multidimensional Health Trajectories of Late Old Years and Socioeconomic Stratification: A Latent Trajectory Class Analysis." *Journals of Gerontology: Series B, Psychological Sciences and Social Sciences* 68(2):290–9. (https://doi.org/10.1093/geronb/gbs111).

65. Kail and Carr, "Structural Social Support"; Dhaval Dave, Inas Rashad, and Jasmina Spasojevic. March 2006. "The Effects of Retirement on Physical and Mental Health Outcomes." NBER Working Paper No. 12123. Cambridge, MA: National Bureau of Economic Research. (https://doi.org/10.3386/w12123).

66. Sander K. R. van Zon et al. May 2019. "Multimorbidity and the Transition Out of Full-time Paid Employment: A Longitudinal Analysis of the Health and Retirement Study." *Journals of Gerontology: Series B*. (https://doi.org/10.1093/geronb/gbz061).

67. Sean A. P. Clouston and Nicole Denier. April 2017. "Mental Retirement and Health Selection: Analyses from the U.S. Health and Retirement Study." *Social Science & Medicine* 178:78–86. (https://doi.org/10.1016/j.socscimed.2017.01.019); Susann Rohwedder and Robert J. Willis. February 2010. "Mental Retirement." *Journal of Economic Perspectives* 24(1):119–38. (https://doi.org/10.1257/jep.24.1.119).

68. Magnus Lindwall et al. September 2017. "Psychological Health in the Retirement Transition: Rationale and First Findings in the Health, Ageing and Retirement Transitions in Sweden (HEARTS) Study." *Frontiers in Psychology* 8:1634. (https://doi.org/10.3389/fpsyg.2017.01634).

69. Birgit Leimer. 2017. "No 'Honeymoon Phase': Whose Health Benefits from Retirement and When." Gutenberg School of Management and Economics & Research Unit "Interdisciplinary Public Policy" Discussion Paper Series No. 1718. *SSRN Electronic Journal*. (https://doi.org/10.2139/ssrn.3068654).

70. Erin L. Kelly and Phyllis Moen. 2020. *Overload: How Good Jobs Went Bad and What We Can Do about It*. Princeton, NJ: Princeton University Press.

71. Dawn C. Carr et al. April 2, 2020. "Alternative Retirement Paths and Cognitive Performance: Exploring the Role of Preretirement Job Complexity." *The Gerontologist* 60(3):460–71. (https://doi.org/10.1093/geront/gnz079).

72. Kelly and Moen, *Overload*.

73. Philip Taylor. March 15, 2019. "Working Longer May Be Good Public Policy, but It Is Not Necessarily Good for Older People." *Journal of Aging & Social Policy* 31(2):99–105. (https://doi.org/10.1080/08959420.2019.1576487).

74. Phyllis Moen et al. July 2016. "Men and Women Expecting to Work Longer: Do Changing Work Conditions Matter?" *Work, Aging and Retirement* 2(3):321–44. (https://doi.org/10.1093/workar/waw018).

75. Phyllis Moen, Erik Kojola, and Kate Schaefers. October 2017. "Organizational Change around an Older Workforce." *The Gerontologist* 57(5):847–56. (https://doi.org/10.1093/geront/gnw048).

76. Finkelstein and Block, "10 Advantages."

77. Maestas et al., *Working Conditions in the United States*.

78. Montenegro, Fisher, and Remez, "Staying ahead of the Curve."

79. Moen et al., "Men and Women Expecting to Work Longer"; Katherine Guyot and Isabel V. Sawhill. April 6, 2020. "Telecommuting Will Likely Continue Long after the Pandemic." Washington, DC: Brookings. (https://www.brookings.edu/blog/up-front/2020/04/06/telecommuting-will-likely-continue-long-after-the-pandemic/); Craig Timberg et al. March 21, 2020. "The New Coronavirus Economy: A Gigantic Experiment Reshaping How We Work and Live." *Washington Post*. (https://www.washingtonpost.com/business/2020/03/21/economy-change-lifestyle-coronavirus/).

80. Roselyn Feinsod, Tom Davenport, and Rich Arthurs. December 2005. "The Business Case for Workers Age 50+: Planning for Tomorrow's Talent Needs in Today's Competitive Environment." Washington, DC: AARP. (https://assets.aarp.org/rgcenter/econ/workers_fifty_plus.pdf).

81. Kelly and Moen, *Overload*.

82. Soulaima Gourani. January 24, 2020. "Why Employers Should Embrace Sabbatical Leave Programs." *Forbes*. (https://www.forbes.com/sites/soulaimagourani/2020/01/24/why-employers-should-embrace-sabbatical-leave-programs/#60d0576e7c05).

83. Johnson, Kawachi, and Lewis, "Older Workers on the Move."

84. Wayne Elsey. September 12, 2018. "How to Maximize the Success of Your Intergenerational Work Team." Forbes Business Development Council. (https://www.forbes.com/sites/forbesbusinessdevelopmentcouncil/2018/09/12/how-to-maximize-the-success-of-your-intergenerational-work-team/#d4050d62b35e).

85. Staudinger and Bowen, "Systemic Approach to Aging."

86. Moen, Kojola, and Schaefers, "Organizational Change around an Older Workforce."

## REFERENCES


AARP Foundation. 2017. "Multilevel Marketing: 'The Research, Risks and Rewards.'" Washington, DC: AARP. (https://www.aarp.org/content/dam/aarp/aarp_foundation/2018/pdf/AARPFResearchExecutiveSummaryFINAL101018.pdf).

Abraham, Katharine, Brad Hershbein, and Susan Houseman. 2020. "Contract Work at Older Ages." Cambridge, MA: National Bureau of Economic Research. (https://doi.org/10.3386/w26612).

Aging in Place. "Seniors and the Gig Economy: Updated for 2020." February 27, 2019. AgingInPlace.Org. (https://www.aginginplace.org/seniors-and-the-gig-economy/).

Ainsworth, Susan and Cynthia Hardy. May 2008. "The Enterprising Self: An Unsuitable Job for an Older Worker." *Organization* 15(3):389–405. (https://doi.org/10.1177/1350508408088536).

Backes-Gellner, Uschi and Stephan Veen. July 2013. "Positive Effects of Ageing and Age Diversity in Innovative Companies—Large-scale Empirical Evidence on Company Productivity: Productivity Effects of Age-diverse Workforces." *Human Resource Management Journal* 23(3):279–95. (https://doi.org/10.1111/1748-8583.12011).

Baer, David. 2015. "Older Workers Are More Likely to Be Self-employed." Washington, DC: AARP Public Policy Institute. (https://www.aarp.org/content/dam/aarp/ppi/2015/older-workers-are-more-likely-to-be-self-employed-AARP-ppi.pdf).

Barnett, Jennifer H., et al. 2015. "The Paired Associates Learning (PAL) Test: 30 Years of CANTAB Translational Neuroscience from Laboratory to Bedside in Dementia Research." Pp. 449–74 in *Translational Neuropsychopharmacology*, vol. 28, edited by Trevor W. Robbins and Barbara J. Sahakian. Cham, Switzerland: Springer International. (https://doi.org/10.1007/7854_2015_5001).

Beehr, Terry A. and Misty M. Bennett. January 1, 2015. "Working after Retirement: Features of Bridge Employment and Research Directions." *Work, Aging and Retirement* 1(1):112–28. (https://doi.org/10.1093/workar/wau007).

Börsch-Supan, Axel and Matthias Weiss. April 2016. "Productivity and Age: Evidence from Work Teams at the Assembly Line." *Journal of the Economics of Ageing* 7:30–42. (https://doi.org/10.1016/j.jeoa.2015.12.001).

Cahill, Kevin E., Michael D. Giandrea, and Joseph F. Quinn. May 2012. "Older Workers and Short-term Jobs: Patterns and Determinants." Washington, DC: *Monthly Labor Review*.

Cahill, Kevin E., Michael D. Giandrea, and Joseph F. Quinn. 2015. "Retirement Patterns and the Macroeconomy, 1992–2010: The Prevalence and Determinants of Bridge Jobs, Phased Retirement, and Reentry among Three Recent Cohorts of Older Americans." *The Gerontologist* 55(3):384–403. (https://doi.org/10.1093/geront/gnt146).

Calvo, Esteban. 2006. "Does Working Longer Make People Healthier and Happier?" *SSRN Electronic Journal*. (https://doi.org/10.2139/ssrn.2302705).

Carr, Dawn C. 2017. "Alternative Retirement Trajectories: The Potential of Part-time Work." Presented at the Working Longer and Retirement: Applying Research to Help Manage an Aging Workforce Conference. Palo Alto, CA: Stanford Center on Longevity.

Carr, Dawn C., et al. April 2, 2020. "Alternative Retirement Paths and Cognitive Performance: Exploring the Role of Preretirement Job Complexity." *The Gerontologist* 60(3):460–71. (https://doi.org/10.1093/geront/gnz079).

Carstensen, Laura L. October 1995. "Evidence for a Life-span Theory of Socioemotional Selectivity." *Current Directions in Psychological Science* 4(5):151–56. (https://doi.org/10.1111/1467-8721.ep11512261).

Cheng, Sheung-Tak. 2009. "Generativity in Later Life: Perceived Respect from Younger Generations as a Determinant of Goal Disengagement and Psychological Well-being." *Journals of Gerontology: Series B, Psychological Sciences and Social Sciences* 64B(1):45–54. (https://doi.org/10.1093/geronb/gbn027).

Clouston, Sean A. P. and Nicole Denier. April 2017. "Mental Retirement and Health Selection: Analyses from the U.S. Health and Retirement Study." *Social Science & Medicine* 178:78–86. (https://doi.org/10.1016/j.socscimed.2017.01.019).

Collins, Susan M. and Robert P. Casey Jr. December 6, 2017. "America's Aging Workforce: Opportunities and Challenges." Washington, DC: Special Committee on Aging. (https://www.congress.gov/115/crpt/srpt191/CRPT-115srpt191.pdf).

Cook, Cody, Rebecca Diamond, and Paul Oyer. May 2019. "Older Workers and the Gig Economy." *AEA Papers and Proceedings* 109:372–76. (https://doi.org/10.1257/pandp.20191042).

Dave, Dhaval, Inas Rashad, and Jasmina Spasojevic. March 2006. "The Effects of Retirement on Physical and Mental Health Outcomes." NBER Working Paper No. 12123. Cambridge, MA: National Bureau of Economic Research. (https://doi.org/10.3386/w12123).

Dentinger, Emma and Marin Clarkberg. October 2002. "Informal Caregiving and Retirement Timing among Men and Women: Gender and Caregiving Relationships in Late Midlife." *Journal of Family Issues* 23(7):857–79. (https://doi.org/10.1177/019251302236598).

Dushi, Irena, Howards M. Ians, and Brad Trenkamp. November 7, 2017. "The Importance of Social Security Benefits to the Income of the Aged Population." *Social Security Bulletin* 77(2). (https://www.ssa.gov/policy/docs/ssb/v77n2/v77n2p1.html).

Elsey, Wayne. September 12, 2018. "How to Maximize the Success of Your Intergenerational Work Team." Forbes Business Development Council. (https://www.forbes.com/sites/forbesbusinessdevelopmentcouncil/2018/09/12/how-to-maximize-the-success-of-your-intergenerational-work-team/#d4050d62b35e).

Feinsod, Roselyn, Tom Davenport, and Rich Arthurs. December 2005. "The Business Case for Workers Age 50+: Planning for Tomorrow's Talent Needs in Today's Competitive Environment." Washington, DC: AARP. (https://assets.aarp.org/rgcenter/econ/workers_fifty_plus.pdf).

Finkelstein, Ruth and Dorian Block. 2014. "10 Advantages of Retaining and Hiring Older Workers: Lessons from NYC Small Businesses." New York: Robert N. Butler Columbia Aging Center. (https://www.mailman.columbia.edu/research/age-smart-employer/advantages-older-workers).

Fisher, Gwenith G., Dorey S. Chaffee, and Amanda Sonnega. April 2016. "Retirement Timing: A Review and Recommendations for Future Research." *Work, Aging and Retirement* 2(2):230–61. (https://doi.org/10.1093/workar/waw001).

Gastfriend, Jody. July 23, 2014. "No One Should Have to Choose between Caregiving and Work." *Harvard Business Review*. (https://hbr.org/2014/07/no-one-should-have-to-choose-between-caregiving-and-work).

Gourani, Soulaima. January 24, 2020. "Why Employers Should Embrace Sabbatical Leave Programs." *Forbes*. (https://www.forbes.com/sites/soulaimagourani/2020/01/24/why-employers-should-embrace-sabbatical-leave-programs/#60d0576e7c05).

Goyer, Amy. November 2013. "Balancing Work and Caregiving." Washington, DC: AARP. (https://www.aarp.org/caregiving/life-balance/info-2017/balancing-demands-ag.html).

Guyot, Katherine and Isabel V. Sawhill. April 6, 2020. "Telecommuting Will Likely Continue Long after the Pandemic." Washington, DC: Brookings. (https://www.brookings.edu/blog/up-front/2020/04/06/telecommuting-will-likely-continue-long-after-the-pandemic/).

Hacker, Jacob S. 2002. *The Divided Welfare State: The Battle over Public and Private Social Benefits in the United States*. New York: Cambridge University Press.

Hayutin, Adele. 2013. "Demographics of the Aging U.S. Workforce." Palo Alto, CA: Stanford Center on Longevity. (http://162.144.124.243/~longevl0/wp-content/uploads/2017/01/AgingWorkforceProceedings.pdf).

Institute of Leadership & Management. 2015. "Untapped Talent: Can Over 50s Bridge the Leadership Skills Gap?" Tamworth, England: Institute of Leadership & Management. (www.InstituteLM.com/resourceLibrary/UntappedTalent.html).

Jacobs, Anna W. and Irene Padavic. 2015. "Hours, Scheduling and Flexibility for Women in the US Low-wage Labour Force." *Gender, Work & Organization* 22(1):67–86. (https://doi.org/10.1111/gwao.12069).

Johnson, Richard W. and Barbara A. Butrica. May 2012. "Age Disparities in Unemployment and Reemployment during the Great Recession and Recovery." Washington, DC: Urban Institute. (https://www.urban.org/sites/default/files/publication/25431/412574-age-disparities-in-unemployment-and-reemployment-during-the-great-recession-and-recovery.pdf).

Johnson, Richard W., Janette Kawachi, and Eric K. Lewis. April 2009. "Older Workers on the Move: Recareering in Later Life." Washington, DC: AARP Public Policy Institute. (https://assets.aarp.org/rgcenter/econ/2009_08_recareering.pdf).

Kail, Ben Lennox and Dawn C. Carr. October 2019. "Structural Social Support and Changes in Depression during the Retirement Transition: 'I Get By with a Little Help from My Friends.'" *Journals of Gerontology: Series B*. (https://doi.org/10.1093/geronb/gbz126).

Kelly, Erin L. and Phyllis Moen. 2020. *Overload: How Good Jobs Went Bad and What We Can Do about It*. Princeton, NJ: Princeton University Press.

Kita, Joe. December 30, 2019. "Workplace Age Discrimination Still Flourishes in America." Washington, DC: AARP. (https://www.aarp.org/work/working-at-50-plus/info-2019/age-discrimination-in-america.html).

Kotre, John N. 1984. *Outliving the Self: Generativity and the Interpretation of Lives*. Baltimore: Johns Hopkins University Press.

Leimer, Birgit. 2017. "No 'Honeymoon Phase': Whose Health Benefits from Retirement and When." Gutenberg School of Management and Economics & Research Unit "Interdisciplinary Public Policy" Discussion Paper Series No. 1718. *SSRN Electronic Journal*. (https://doi.org/10.2139/ssrn.3068654).

Lindwall, Magnus, et al. September 2017. "Psychological Health in the Retirement Transition: Rationale and First Findings in the Health, Ageing and Retirement Transitions in Sweden (HEARTS) Study." *Frontiers in Psychology* 8:1634. (https://doi.org/10.3389/fpsyg.2017.01634).

Maestas, Nicole. 2010. "Back to Work: Expectations and Realizations of Work after Retirement." *Journal of Human Resources* 45(3):718–48. (https://doi.org/10.3368/jhr.45.3.718).

Maestas, Nicole, et al. 2017. *Working Conditions in the United States: Results of the 2015 American Working Conditions Survey*. Santa Monica, CA: RAND Corporation. (https://doi.org/10.7249/RR2014).

Malone, Johanna C., et al. 2016. "Midlife Eriksonian Psychosocial Development: Setting the Stage for Late-life Cognitive and Emotional Health." *Developmental Psychology* 52(3):496–508. (https://doi.org/10.1037/a0039875).

Mikelson, Kelly S., Daniel Kuehn, and Ananda Martin-Caughey. April 2017. "Occupational Projections for Low-income Older Workers: Assessing the Skill Gap for Workers Age 50 and Older." Washington, DC: Urban Institute. (https://www.aarp.org/content/dam/aarp/aarp_foundation/2017/pdfs/occupational-projections-for-low-income-older-workers.pdf).

Miller, Stephen. January 20, 2020. "SECURE Act Alters 401(k) Compliance Landscape." Alexandria, VA: Society for Human Resource Management. (https://www.shrm.org/resourcesandtools/hr-topics/benefits/pages/secure-act-alters-401k-compliance-landscape.aspx).

Moen, Phyllis. 2016. *Encore Adulthood: Boomers on the Edge of Risk, Renewal, and Purpose*. New York: Oxford University Press.

Moen, Phyllis, et al. July 2016. "Men and Women Expecting to Work Longer: Do Changing Work Conditions Matter?" *Work, Aging and Retirement* 2(3):321–44. (https://doi.org/10.1093/workar/waw018).

Moen, Phyllis, Erik Kojola, and Kate Schaefers. October 2017. "Organizational Change around an Older Workforce: Table 1." *The Gerontologist* 57(5):847–56. (https://doi.org/10.1093/geront/gnw048).

Montenegro, Xenia, Linda Fisher, and Shereen Remez. 2002. "Staying ahead of the Curve: The AARP Work and Career Study." Washington, DC: AARP. (http://research.aarp.org/econ/multiwork.html).

National Bureau of Economic Research (NBER). 2019. "Self-employment at Older Ages." *NBER Bulletin on Retirement and Disability* 3. (https://www.nber.org/BRD/2019no3/rdrc19-19a.html).

Ng, Thomas W. H. and Daniel C. Feldman. 2008. "The Relationship of Age to Ten Dimensions of Job Performance." *Journal of Applied Psychology* 93(2):392–423. (https://doi.org/10.1037/0021-9010.93.2.392).

O'Connor, Austin. February 27, 2018. "Be Your Own Boss, Be Happy." Washington, DC: AARP. (https://www.aarp.org/work/small-business/info-2018/self-employed-numbers-fd.html).

Palmer, Kimberly. 2017. "10 Things You Should Know about Age Discrimination." Washington, DC: AARP. (https://www.aarp.org/work/on-the-job/info-2017/age-discrimination-facts.html).

Paullin, Cheryl. 2014. "The Aging Workforce: Leveraging the Talents of Mature Employees." Alexandria, VA: Society for Human Resource Management. (https://www.shrm.org/hr-today/trends-and-forecasting/special-reports-and-expert-views/Documents/Aging-Workforce-Talents-Mature-Employees.pdf).

Perreault, Michel, et al. September 2017. "Employment Status and Mental Health: Mediating Roles of Social Support and Coping Strategies." *Psychiatric Quarterly* 88(3):501–14. (https://doi.org/10.1007/s11126-016-9460-0).

Pizzo, Philip A. 2020. "A Prescription for Longevity in the 21st Century: Renewing Purpose, Building and Sustaining Social Engagement, and Embracing a Positive Lifestyle." *JAMA* 323(5):415. (https://doi.org/10.1001/jama.2019.21087).

Retirement Equity Lab, the New School SCEPA. May 1, 2019. "10+ Years of No Wage Growth: The Role of Alternative Jobs and Gig Work." Status of Older Workers Report Series. (www.economicpolicyresearch.org).

Riffkin, Rebecca. August 22, 2014. "In U.S., 55% of Workers Get Sense of Identity from Their Job." Gallup. (https://news.gallup.com/poll/175400/workers-sense-identity-job.aspx).

Rivers, Caryl and Rosalind C. Barnett. 2016. "Older Workers Can Be More Reliable and Productive Than Their Younger Counterparts." Vox.com. (https://www.vox.com/2016/10/18/12427494/old-aging-high-tech).

Rix, Sara E. February 2015. "Long-term Unemployment: Greater Risks and Consequences for Older Workers." Washington, DC: AARP Public Policy Institute. (https://www.aarp.org/content/dam/aarp/ppi/20152/AARP953_LongTermUnemployment_FSFeb2v1.pdf).

Rohwedder, Susann and Robert J. Willis. February 2010. "Mental Retirement." *Journal of Economic Perspectives* 24(1):119–38. (https://doi.org/10.1257/jep.24.1.119).

Ross, Martha and Nicole Bateman. 2019. "Meet the Low-wage Workforce." Washington, DC: Metropolitan Policy Program at Brookings. (https://www.brookings.edu/wp-content/uploads/2019/11/201911_Brookings-Metro_low-wage-workforce_Ross-Bateman.pdf).

Round, Anna. May 2017. "Extending Working Lives: A Devolved, Lifecourse Approach to Enabling Work beyond State Pension Age." IPPR. (http://www.ippr.org/publications/extending-working-lives).

Schramm, Jen, et al. December 2014. "Preparing for an Aging Workforce." Alexandria, VA: Society for Human Resource Management.

Staudinger, Ursula M. and Catherine E. Bowen. November 2011. "A Systemic Approach to Aging in the Work Context." *Zeitschrift für ArbeitsmarktForschung* 44(4):295–306. (https://doi.org/10.1007/s12651-011-0086-2).

Sullivan, Laura and Tatjana Meschede. 2016. "Race, Gender, and Senior Economic Well-being: How Financial Vulnerability over the Life Course Shapes Retirement for Older Women of Color." *Public Policy & Aging Report* 26(2):58–62. (https://doi.org/10.1093/ppar/prw001).

Swartz, Jon. August 4, 2017. "Ageism Is Forcing Many to Look outside Silicon Valley, but Tech Hubs Offer Little Respite." CNBC. (https://www.cnbc.com/2017/08/04/ageism-is-forcing-many-to-look-outside-silicon-valley-but-tech-hubs-offer-little-respite.html).

Tang, Fengyan and Jeffrey A. Burr. September 2015. "Revisiting the Pathways to Retirement: A Latent Structure Model of the Dynamics of Transition from Work to Retirement." *Ageing and Society* 35(8):1739–70. (https://doi.org/10.1017/S0144686X14000634).

Taylor, Philip. March 15, 2019. "Working Longer May Be Good Public Policy, but It Is Not Necessarily Good for Older People." *Journal of Aging & Social Policy* 31(2):99–105. (https://doi.org/10.1080/08959420.2019.1576487).

Terrell, Kenneth. December 28, 2018. "New Study Finds Many Older Workers Forced Out of Jobs." Washington, DC: AARP. (https://www.aarp.org/work/working-at-50-plus/info-2018/forced-retirement.html).

Timberg, Craig, et al. March 21, 2020. "The New Coronavirus Economy: A Gigantic Experiment Reshaping How We Work and Live." *Washington Post*. (https://www.washingtonpost.com/business/2020/03/21/economy-change-lifestyle-coronavirus/).

Umberson, Debra and Jennifer Karas Montez. March 2010. "Social Relationships and Health: A Flashpoint for Health Policy." *Journal of Health and Social Behavior* 51(1)_suppl.:S54–66. (https://doi.org/10.1177/0022146510383501).

Umpierrez, Amanda. December 2019. "Older Gig Workers Left Hanging without Benefits." *Plansponsor*. (www.plansponsor.com).

Van Dalen, Hendrik P., Kène Henkens, and Joop Schippers. June 2010. "How Do Employers Cope with an Ageing Workforce? Views from Employers and Employees." *Demographic Research* 22:1015–36. (https://doi.org/10.4054/DemRes.2010.22.32).

van Zon, Sander K. R. May 2019. "Multimorbidity and the Transition Out of Full-time Paid Employment: A Longitudinal Analysis of the Health and Retirement Study." *Journals of Gerontology: Series B*. (https://doi.org/10.1093/geronb/gbz061).

Wickrama, Kandauda, et al. March 2013. "Heterogeneity in Multidimensional Health Trajectories of Late Old Years and Socioeconomic Stratification: A Latent Trajectory Class Analysis." *Journals of Gerontology: Series B, Psychological Sciences and Social Sciences* 68(2):290–97. (https://doi.org/10.1093/geronb/gbs111).

Wilkie, Dana. May 3, 2018. "Discrimination against Older Workers May Be Common but Hard to Prove." Alexandria, VA: Society for Human Resource Management. (https://www.shrm.org/resourcesandtools/hr-topics/employee-relations/pages/age-discrimination-.aspx).

Williams, Kimbarley A. and Crystal A. Skotedis. January 28, 2020. "9 Ways the SECURE Act Impacts Employer 401(k) Plans and What Companies Need to Do NOW." Boyer & Ritter. (https://www.cpabr.com/9-ways-the-secure-act-impacts-employer-401k-plans-and-what-companies-need-to-do-now/).

World Health Organization. 2015. *World Report on Ageing and Health*. Geneva, Switzerland: World Health Organization.

Wrzus, Cornelia, et al. 2013. "Social Network Changes and Life Events across the Life Span: A Meta-analysis." *Psychological Bulletin* 139(1):53–80. (https://doi.org/10.1037/a0028601).

Zaniboni, Sara. July 1, 2015. "The Interaction between Older Workers' Personal Resources and Perceived Age Discrimination Affects the Desired Retirement Age and the Expected Adjustment." *Work, Aging and Retirement* 1(3):266–73. (https://doi.org/10.1093/workar/wav010).

# Index

*Note*: Page numbers in italic type refer to figures or tables.


AARP, 398, 441, 443, 475
ableism, 54
Abrams, Dominic, 215
Ackerman, Phillip L., 159
Active Ageing Index, 464
active aging. *See* productive aging
activity complement theory, 253
activity substitution theory, 253, 256
Adams, Gary A., 197, 417
Adler, Richard, 473
Administration for Community Living, 43
adult education and adult learners, 332–40; community colleges' role in, 336–40; comparison of younger and older, 337–40; functions of, 332; graduation rates of, 338–40; international comparisons of, 333–35, *334*, *335*; momentum of, 339–40; motivations for return to school, 337–38; participation in, 334–35, *335*. *See also* learning, upskilling, and retraining
Aerospace Corporation, 399
Affordable Care Act (Obamacare), 42, 78, 435, 470
Aftel, Mandy, 430
AFW. *See* age-friendly workplace
age: chronological, 232, 269; cohort proportions and median age by industry, *172*; defining, 232–33, 353–54; diverse effects of, 308–9; functional, 232, 270; generational, 150, 232–33, 271; lifespan orientation to, 271–72; organizational approach to, 271; psychology of work perspective on, 272; psychosocial, 270; stereotypes related to, 133; subjective, 232, 357–58; workplace responses to, 4
the aged. *See* older adults
Age Discrimination in Employment Act, 40, 78–79, 152, 180, 269, 353, 393, 469–70
age-diverse workforce: advantages of, 4, 6, 119–21, 174–75, 490; as antidote to ageism, 217; attitudes toward people, tasks, and organizations in, 153–60, *154*; generational differences as consideration for, 150–53; knowledge transfer in, 119; management of, 4–5, 119–22, 131–39, 149–62; promotion of, 121, 494; psychological benefits of, 120; stability and turnover in, 119–20, 137; teamwork in, 5, 120–22, 136–37, 149–62; work design considerations in, 135
age-friendly workplaces (AFWs), 191, 193–204; barriers to implementation, 199–200; characteristics of, 194; flexible arrangements in, 196–203; future of, 203–4; opportunities and challenges for, 197–99; organizational axis of, 196; organizational factors in, 195–96; studying and creating, 194–97, 217–19; worker orientation axis of, 196
ageism: age-diverse workforce as antidote to, 217; COVID-19's effect on, 437; culture-based, 53–54, 58; defined, 211; effects of, 54, 211, 213–16; and employer policies and practices, 173; internalized, 5, 37, 40, 54, 211, 214–17, 219, 234–35, 358; interpersonal manifestations of, 213; interventions to address, 217–19; job satisfaction lowered by, 38, 120, 214, 215; and leadership, 212–13; learning/upskilling/retraining opportunities hindered by, 135, 193, 213; as obstacle to extended work life, 37–39, 75–76, 174, 193, 212–13; older women as targets of, 76, 79, 115; overview of, 37; productivity losses due to, 6, 37, 134; race/ethnicity and, 38; recruitment/hiring and, 122, 134–35, 174, 212, 234, 236; retirement decisions motivated by, 213, 393, 395, 488; social policy and, 469–70; and stereotype threat, 214–17, 234–35; structural, 54; workplace-related, 5, 37–39, 54, 78–79, 111, 115, 133–34, 174, 211–19, 393, 462, 488. *See also* stereotypes, age-related

Age Smart Employers Award, 204
Aging Workforce Research Initiative, 181
Agrability, 469
Alden, Elaine, 199
Allen, Natalie J., 158
Allport, Gordon, 160
alternatives to full-time work, 483–87. *See also* bridge employment; encore careers; gig economy; part-time work; senior entrepreneurship; unretirement
alternative work. *See* informal work
American Academy of Social Work and Social Welfare Grand Challenges Initiative, 41
American College of Occupational and Environmental Medicine, 194
American Society on Aging (ASA), 1–2
Americans with Disabilities Act, 79, 238
Angelou, Maya, 431
Aronson, Louise, 394
artificial intelligence (AI), 315–16
Aspen Institute Future of Work Initiative, 463–64
Atewologun, Doyin, 217
Atkinson, Carol, 199, 203
Atlantic Philanthropies, 443
attitudes: organization-oriented, 158–60; people-oriented, 153, 155–56; summary of, *154*; task-oriented, 156–58
automation, 313–14, 331–32
autonomy and self-determination, 55, 75, 288, 311, 359
Azevedo, Vanessa, 290

Babson College, 435
Bacon, Francis, 434
Bahr, Peter Riley, 336
Baltes, Paul, 293
Bargh, John A., 219
Bass, Scott, 250, 462
Behaviors from Intergroup Affect and Stereotypes, 213
Beier, Margaret E., 197
Belbase, Anek, 332
belonging, 120, 155, 275, 352, 355–56
Berntsen, Dorthe, 232
Big Brothers Big Sisters, 443
Blanco, Luisa, 91, 92
Blum, Arlene, 436
bona fide occupational qualification (BFOQ), 269–70
boomers: gig work by, 117–18; labor force participation of, 112; lifetime earnings of, 19–21; race/ethnicity of, 17; retirement incomes of, 21–26; retirement security of, 16, 26–29
Boomers Leading Change, 443
Boston College, 182, 271, 394, 446, 448, 467. *See also* Sloan Center on Aging and Work
Bouchard, Lauren, 351
Bowen, Catherine E., 353
Boys and Girls Clubs, 443
bracero program, 90
Bratter, Bernice, 394
bridge employment: antecedents of, 413–15; defining, 412; outcomes of, 415–16; overview of, 411–12; prevalence of, 179, 267, 307, 411; research suggestions on, 416–17; as retirement alternative, 8, 372, 411–17, 483; self-management and, 280; theories related to, 412–13. *See also* phased retirement
Bridgespan, 447
Brkljacic, Tihana, 232
Brooks, David, 401
Brough, Paula, 355
Brown, Kirk Warren, 218
Bryant, Jacqueline, 215
Bureau of Labor Statistics, 182
Burr, Jeffrey A., 254
Butler, Robert, 250, 462. *See also* Robert N. Butler Aging Center, Columbia University
Butrica, Barbara, 253

California Paid Family Leave Program, 378
Calvo, Rocio, 61
career change. *See* re-careering
career development theory, 159
Caregivers Credit Act, 473
caregiving, 371–81; balancing work with, 8, 372–75, 377, 487; company policies for supporting, 177; costs and benefits of, 373–74, 378; demographics of, 36; extended work life affected by, 8, 36–37, 40, 59–60, 74, 193, 255–58, 372–75, 377, 380, 487; flexible work arrangements and, 487; gendering of, 36–37, 74, 257–58, 374–76, 380; policies and practices for supporting, 377–79, 470–71; as productive aging, 254–56; race/ethnicity as factor in, 376, 380–81; recipients of, 255; research suggestions on, 379–81; "sandwich," 59, 372, 379, 380; socioeconomic status as factor in, 377; types of, 372–73; unpaid status of, 59–60, 74, 78, 80; for veterans, 181; well-being affected by, 257, 374. *See also* grandparenting
Carnevale, Anthony P., 336
Caro, Frances, 462
Caro, Francis, 250, 254
Carstensen, Laura L., 159, 361
CASA, 443

Center for Retirement Research, Boston College, 182
Center on Aging and Work. *See* Sloan Center on Aging and Work
Centers for Disease Control and Prevention, 182
Certified Age Friendly Employer, 204
Certified Professional Retirement Coach program, 398
Chalofsky, Neal, 359
Chang, E-Shien, 54
Chen, Yiwei, 218
Chen, Yung-Ping, 250
choice, work-related, 55–58, 62, 73, 75, 273, 355
chronological age, 269
Civic Ventures, 442–43
Civil Service Retirement System, 181
cognitive abilities, 132, 151, 215, 236, 277–78, 491
cognitive load, 235
collaboration. *See* teamwork
Collins, Susan, 435
Colquitt, Jason A., 160
commitment to work, 158–59, 414. *See also* engagement; productive aging
Common Good Careers, 447
Commonwealth Corps, 443
communion striving, 414
community, 275, *276*
community colleges, 336, 467
Community Experience Partnership, 443
compensatory theory, 257
competence, 6, 267–73, 276–79. *See also* job performance
Congressional Research Service, 182
Conservation Law Foundation, 468
contact hypothesis, 160
Contarello, Alberta, 358
contextual performance, 235, 237
continuity theory, 356, 411–12, 413
contract work, 117
Cook, Sarah K., 376
Cornell Radio Guild, 429
corporate policies, on retirement, 395–96
Corporation for National and Community Service, 442, 444, 446
counterproductive work behaviors (CWBs), 235, 237
COVID-19 pandemic: economic effects of, 69, 80; effects of, on older adults, 58; effects of, on older workers, 62; effects of, on retirement, 401–2; effects of, on women, 80; essential work during, 78; flexible work arrangements as result of, 493, 494; labor market effects of, 2, 74; and older women's employment chances, 69, 77, 80; reemployment after, 489; and senior entrepreneurship, 437; societal effects of, 10
crowdfunding, 427
crystallized intelligence, 151, 236
Csikszentmihalyi, Mihaly, 289
cultural responsiveness, 60–61
Cummins, Phyllis A., 336
cumulative inequality and dis/advantage, 38–39, 42–43
Curavic, Marko, 428–29

Daniels, Kevin, 297
DB pensions. *See* defined benefit (DB) pensions
Decade of Healthy Ageing, 461
defined benefit (DB) pensions, 16, 17, 23–24, *24*, 70, 93, 192, 279, 482
defined contribution (DC) plans, 23, 70, 93, 279, 482, 488
de Lange, Annet H., 286, 288, 289, 294
demographics: retirement security and, 17–19; and senior entrepreneurship, 426–27; technology in relation to, 307–8; workforce management in response to, 4, 111–13, 121–22, 131, 149, 249
Dennis, Helen, 173, 394
Díaz-Valdes, Antonia, 60
digital skills, 331
Dingemans, Ellen, 415
Directive for Equal Treatment in Employment and Occupation (European Union), 470
disability, effects on work of, 277
disability accommodations, 70, 79, 176–77, 238
discouraged workers, 115
discrimination: laws against, 39–40; multiple forms of, 37–38; sexual orientation or gender identity as basis for, 57, 64n27; social policy and, 469–70. *See also* ageism
diversity and inclusion practices, 120, 121
Dominican University Venture Greenhouse, 434
Doron, Israel, 194, 196
dyadic leadership, 296
dyads, collaborative, 155, 157–60
Dychtwald, Ken, 394
dyscompetence, 269

Earl, Catherine, 200, 201
Earle, Alison, 60
educational attainment: of Hispanic populations, 89–90; of older adults, 17–18, *18*, 114; social policy on, 330, 467
elder abuse, 354
eldercare, 59–60

elder orphans, 400–401
Elders Action Network, 443
Eller, Anja, 215
email, 312–13
emotions as social information, 153
Employee Retirement Income Security Act (ERISA), 180
employers. *See* workforce management
encore careers, 53, 307, 394, 397–98, 445, 483–84
Encore Fellowships, 443, 452, 468
Encore.org, 394, 442–43, 445–49, 453, 483–84
engagement, 6; age-diverse workforce linked to, 120; ageism as obstacle to, 152, 153, 214–15, 234; career development opportunities linked to, 159; caregiving as, 254–56; defined, 97; encore careers as means of, 483; flexible work arrangements linked to, 178, 200; patterns of social, 356; policies and practices promoting, 251; self-employment as means of, 484; volunteering as, 252–54, 451; well-being linked to, 446. *See also* commitment to work; productive aging
entrepreneurship. *See* senior entrepreneurship
Eppler-Hattab, Raphael, 194, 196, 197, 217–18
Erikson, Erik H., 360, 394, 444
Eschtruth, Andrew D., 332
esteem, 356–59
Eurofund, 475
Ewing Marion Kauffman Foundation, 435
Experience Corps, 42, 442–43, 445–47, 447, 449, 451
experience/wisdom of older adults, 2, 9, 119, 137
extended work life: business benefits of, 118–19, 174; caregiving's effect on, 8, 36–37, 40, 59–60, 74, 193, 255–58, 372–75, 377, 380, 487; challenges for, 36–39, 42–43, 53–63, 193; constrained choices concerning, 55–58; COVID-19's effect on, 58, 62; disability accommodations and, 238; employees' experiences in, 119–21, 171–74; employer-controlled factors in, 73; factors influencing, 15–16, 36, 43, 54, 73, 192, 251, 276–79, 327, 396–98, 461–62, 471; financial issues associated with, 15–30, 113, 180–81, 279, 482–83; gender as factor in, 74, 76–77; health effects of, 428, 462, 491–92; Hispanic populations and, 88, 97; international contexts for, 70–72, 371, 464–75; lifespan development relevant to, 132; needs fulfillment and, 354–60; negative outcomes of, 491–92; neoliberal factors influencing, 70–71, 80; personal benefits of, 15, 35, 490–91; protective factors for, 39–42; resentment of, by younger workers, 216; retirement security as factor in, 4, 16, 29, 251, 395, 429, 482–83; societal benefits of, 15, 35, 489–90; societal expectations for, 36, 69–72, 76–77, 80, 87, 472–73; stakeholders in, 463; underemployment in, 61. *See also* ageism; older adults; older women; older workers; social policy
EXTEND Project, 472

Fair Employment Protection Act, 39–40
Fair Labor Standards Act, 181
*familismo*, 91–92
Family and Medical Insurance Leave Act, 41, 378
Family and Medical Leave Act (FMLA), 40, 78, 177, 378, 487
Family Caregivers Act, 471
Farfán, Jesús, 358
Federal Employees Flexible and Comparable Work Schedules, 41
Federal Employees' Retirement System, 181
Feldman, Daniel C., 235
financial issues: benefits of extended employment, 15; extended work life affected by, 15–30, 113, 180–81, 279, 482–83; literacy about, 178–79; of older women, 4; retirement decisions influenced by, 4. *See also* retirement security
Finkelstein, Lisa M., 234
flexible work arrangements: in age-friendly workplaces, 196–203; attractiveness of, 197; business benefits of, 198; and caregiving responsibilities, 487; for federal employees, 181; line managers' implementation of, 201–3; negative aspects of, 311–13, 471; policies encouraging, 70, 73; prevalence of, 41; productivity resulting from, 203; technology's role in, 202, 311–12; and transition to retirement, 73, 118–19, 122, 179, 203; types of, 198–99, 239; as workforce management strategy, 5, 122, 178, 239, 471, 493
flextime, 198
fluid intelligence, 151
Foster Grandparent Program, 442
framework of work motivation, 159
Freedman, Marc, 397, 442, 483
Frey, Carl Benedikt, 331
Fried, Linda, 442
Friedman, Thomas, 474, 475
Fuchs, Marie-Francoise, 474
full retirement age, 15–16, 22, 71, 76, 87, 93, 125n38, 327, 353–54, 394, 472

full-time work, alternatives to. *See* alternatives to full-time work
functional age, 270
Furunes, Trude, 297
Future Skills Centre, Calgary, Canada, 467

Gailliard, Bernadette M., 199
Gardner, John W., 442
Geber, Sarah Zeff, 401
gender: and caregiving responsibilities, 36–37, 74, 257–58, 374–76, 380; discrimination based on, 57, 64n27; earning power affected by, 76–77; as factor in extended work life, 74, 76–77; as factor in life course, 69, 74; of labor force participation, 328. *See also* LGBT+ population; men; older women; transgender adults; women
generational age, 150, 232–33, 271
Generation to Generation, 443
generativity, 360, 394, 414, 416–17, 444, 490
Gen Xers: lifetime earnings of, 19–21; race/ethnicity of, 17; retirement incomes of, 21–26; retirement security of, 16, 26–29
Ghilarducci, Teresa, 2
Gibson, Bryan, 219
GIEE. *See* Global Institute of Experienced Entrepreneurship
gig economy, 62, 72, 117–18, 399, 427, 471, 485
Ginsberg, Ruth Bader, 267
Global Coalition on Aging, 465
Global Entrepreneurship Monitor (GEM), 435
Global Institute of Experienced Entrepreneurship (GIEE), 425–29, 432–35
goal orientation, 132
Gonzales, Ernest, 253
good enough jobs, 75
Government Accountability Office, 182
grandparenting, 59–60, 255
Gray, Robert, 429–30
Great Recession (2008–2009), 25, 72, 76, 77, 87, 112, 115–16, 330, 401, 482, 483, 489
Green Science Policy Institute, 436
Green Thumb, 468
grit, 120
Grosch, James W., 196
Gudmundsson, Hans Kristjan, 474
Guterres, António, 436

Hall, G. Stanley, 9, 11n1; *Senescence*, 1–2
Hao, Yanni, 254
happiness: bridge employment and, 415; of Hispanic populations, 97; job satisfaction linked to, 7; retirement and, 415. *See also* well-being
Hart-Cellar Act, 90
Hawaii Active Aging Network, 474
Hayashida, Cullen, 465, 474
health: bridge employment and, 415; company injury prevention practices, 176–77; extended work life's effect on, 428, 462, 491–92; of Hispanic populations, 97; leadership in relation to, 297–98; in lifespan development, 132–33; as obstacle to extended work life, 193, 277; in older vs. younger workers, 236–37; productive aging linked to, 462; retirement in relation to, 97–98; volunteering as contributor to, 446; as workforce management concern, 136, 176–77. *See also* well-being
Health and Global Policy Institute, 465
HealthCare.gov, 470
health insurance: as enticement for employment, 78, 175–76, 487; Hispanic populations and, 93, 94; lack of retiree benefits, 16; legislation mandating, 470
health-promoting leadership, 297–98
healthy worker effect, 133
Henry, Julie D., 215
Hewlett-Packard (HP), 41, 443
Heymann, Jody, 60
Hijzen, Alexander, 332
Hinterlong, James, 250
hiring. *See* recruitment and hiring
Hirschfeld, Robert R., 213
Hirschi, Andreas, 357
Hispanic happiness paradox, 97
Hispanic health paradox, 97
Hispanic populations: caregiving responsibilities of, 60; culturally-responsive approaches to, 60–61; educational attainment of, 89–90; and extended work life, 4, 88, 97; family/group orientation of, 91–92; impact of, on United States' population, 88–90; migration history and work-related factors of, 88–90; outcomes of retirement in, 98; productive aging framework applied to, 97–98; retirement planning in, 91–94; retirement security of, 88, 93–94; retirement timing in, 94–95, *95*, *96*, 97; undocumented individuals, 89, 90, 94
Holman, Halsted, 288
HP. *See* Hewlett-Packard
human resources (HR). *See* workforce management
Hunter, Woodrow, 398

IBM, 443
*Icelandic Mapping Report*, 474
Idealist Careers, 447
Ignatian Volunteer Corps, 443

income security, 2, *28*
independence. *See* autonomy and self-determination
independent contractors, 485
informal work, 62, 330, 485
injury, older workers' susceptibility to, 176, 193, 237
injury prevention, 176–77
innovation, 430–31
input-mediator-outcome-input model, 161
Inspiring Service, 452
Institute for Career Transitions, MIT, 468
Intel, 443, 484
intelligence. *See* cognitive abilities; crystallized intelligence; fluid intelligence
intelligent agents, 315
interaction. *See* social relationships and interaction, work-related
intergenerational teamwork, 5, 120–22, 136–37, 149–62. *See also* age-diverse workforce
intergroup contact hypothesis, 40
International Executive Service Corps (IESC), 442
intersectionality, 61–62, 75–76, 193
Irving, Paul, 462
Isabella, Lynn A., 356

James, Jaquelyn B., 200
Japan, extended work life in, 464–65
Jesuit Volunteer Corps, 443
job analysis, 272–73
job crafting, 157–58, 196, 293, 357
Job Demand Model of Performance, *268*
job demands, 36, 157, 193, 195, *268*, 280, 289, 292–94, 311, 318
job displacement, 116–17
job performance: age-related reception of reviews of, 136; competence/dyscompetence and, 268–69; feedback on, 136, 270; measures of, 235–36; motivation in relation to, 238; of older adults, 6, 231–39; stereotypes' effect on, 6, 215, 234–35. *See also* competence
job resources, 157–58, 239, 289–90, 292–95, 311–12, 318
job satisfaction: in age-diverse workforce, 157; ageism lowers, 38, 120, 214, 215; bridge employment linked to, 414; life course changes in, 153; life satisfaction linked to, 7; of older women, 155; self-employment and, 484; variability of, 153
Johnson, Lyndon, 468
Johnson, Richard W., 197
Johnston, Claire S., 357

Kaliterna, Ljiljana, 232
Kalokerinos, Elise K., 215
Kanfer, Ruth, 159
Katz, Lawrence F., 330
Kazis, Richard, 467
Kell, Harrison J., 235
Kenny, Glen P., 237
Kerttula, Jill, 432
King, Eden B., 234
knowledge transfer, 119
Komp, Kathrin, 256
Kooij, Dorien T. A. M., 197, 286, 293, 294, 360–61, 413
Kowske, Brenda J., 233
Kram, Kathy E., 356
Krueger, Alan B., 330

labor force participation: by age group, *72*; factors influencing, 113–15; gendering of, 328; international comparisons of, 328, *328*, *329*, 371–72; of older adults, 112–15, 251, 286, *287*, 327–28, *328*, 371–72; of older women, 112, 328, *329*, 400; reentry to, 117, 179, 489; of women, 19, 22; of younger workers, 112–13
Lachman, Margie E., 357
Lahaie, Claudia, 60
Lancee, Bram, 253
Larsen, Zrjezdana P., 232
Lawton, M. Powell, 268
leader-member exchange, 155, 296
leadership, 136, 156, 212–13, 296–98
learning, upskilling, and retraining, 7; ageism as obstacle to, 135, 193, 213; attitudes toward, 330; community colleges' role in, 336, 467; considerations for older workers, 133, 135, 177–78, 215, 237, 278–79, 314, 319, 492–93; international perspective on, 467–68; motivation of older adults for, 133, 151–53, 309; self-management and, 299–300; social policy on, 181; technological affordances as source of, 314–15, 467; technology as subject of, 237, 308–9, 314, 319, 331; as workforce management strategy, 123, 177–78, 278–79. *See also* adult education and adult learners
Levitin, Daniel, 431
Levy, Becca R., 234
LGBT+ population, 381, 400. *See also* transgender adults
life course: defined, 290; gendered trajectories in, 69, 74; Hispanic populations and, 88–90; self-management and, 290–92; stereotypes and biases developed in, 40

life events: and bridge employment, 413, 415, 416; self-management and, 290–92
life expectancy, 17, 113, 192, 327
lifelong learning. *See* adult education and adult learners
life planning, 398
life satisfaction. *See* happiness
lifespan developmental perspective, 132, 138, 151–60, 195, 271–72, 279
lifetime earnings, 19–21
line managers, and flexible work arrangements, 200–203
Linowitz, Sol, 442
literacy, 333–34, *334*
Living, Learning and Earning Longer Collaborative, 475
location flexibility, 198–99, 202, 239, 493
Loeppke, Ronald R., 194
Lorig, Kate R., 288
love, 355–56
low-income workers, 53–63
Lueke, Adam, 219
Lumina Foundation, 330

MacKay, Carleen, 475
Macmillan, Ross, 290
Maestas, Nicole, 200
Maia, Angela, 290
mandatory retirement, 76, 181, 192, 270
Manning, Lydia K., 351
marginalized populations, 53–63
marginally attached workers, 115
marital status, 18–19, *19*
marriage, *275*
Martins, Carla, 290
Maslow, Abraham, 7, 352, 354–60
Matz-Costa, Christina, 256
McCaskill, Claire, 429
McNamara, Tay K., 253
meaningfulness of work, 42, 75, 97, 132, 195, 196, 297–98, 357, 359–60, 490
Medicaid, 94, 470
Medicare, 16, 94, 279, 470
meditation, 218–19
men: as caregivers, 374–76, 380; median annual earnings of, 20, *21*
mentoring, 119, 159, 161, 360, 443
Meshoulam, Ilan, 194, 196
metastereotypes, 233–35
Meyer, John P., 158
midternships, 468, 476n27
Milken Institute Center for the Future of Aging, 3
Milligan, Patricia, 462
mindfulness, 218–19
Montepare, Joann M., 357
Morrow-Howell, Nancy, 250, 251
motivation, generational expressions of, 133, 151–53, 238, 309, 357. *See also* rewards, intrinsic vs. extrinsic
Motowidlo, Stephan J., 235
Munnell, Alicia H., 330
Mutchler, Jan E., 253, 254
Myers, Karen K., 199
Myles, John, 80

Nagarajan, N., 195
Nagy, Noemi, 357
Nahemow, Lucille, 268
National Center for Productive Aging and Work, 182, 195
National Domestic Workers Association, 470
National Endowment for Financial Education, 398
National Executive Service Corps (NESC), 442
National Governors Association, 464
National Institute on Aging, 182
National Institute on Occupational Safety and Health (NIOSH), 182, 194–95
National Institutes of Health, 462
needs, Maslow's hierarchy of, 352, 354–60
neoliberalism, 70, 80
neuroscience, 431
Ng, Thomas W. H., 235
Nielsen, Karina, 297
NIOSH. *See* National Institute on Occupational Safety and Health
Noack, C. Martin G., 353
Norheim, Kristoffer, 237
not good enough jobs, 75

Oasis Lifelong Adventure, 449
Obama, Barack, 78
occupational change, 118
OECD. *See* Organisation for Economic Co-operation and Development
Okun, Morris A., 257
older adults: alternatives to full-time work for, 483–87; caregiving responsibilities of, 36–37, 40, 59–60; defining, 441; increased employment of, 15; labor force participation of, 112–15, 251, 286, *287*, 327–28, 371–72; proficiency levels of, 333–34; theories about, 1; work denied to, 1–2; workplace policies and practices for, 5, 121–23, 134–38, 171–80, *175*, 191–204, 239, 280–81, 395, 470, 475, 493–94. *See also* adult education and adult learners; ageism;

extended work life; older women; older workers; social policy
Older Americans Act, 39, 42–43, 353, 442
older women: ageism experienced by, 76, 79, 115; caregiving duties of, 74; COVID-19's effect on, 69, 76–77, 80; as entrepreneurs, 431–33; extended work life of, 69–80; factors in work life of, 74–76; financial situations of, 4; intersectional hardships afflicting, 79; job satisfaction of, 155; labor force participation of, 112, 328, *329*, 400; labor market disadvantages of, 74; precariously employed, 4, 72–73; varied work experiences of, 69–70, 75
older workers, defining, 269–73, 353–54
Old'Up, 474
optimal distinctiveness theory, 155
Organisation for Economic Co-operation and Development (OECD), 41, 192, 197, 286, 328, 333, 371, 475; employment rates for older workers, *287*
organizational citizenship behaviors (OCBs), 235, 237
organizational culture, 174–75, 217–18
organization-oriented attitudes, 158–60
Osborne, Michael, 331
Osler, William, 393
out-group homogeneity, 233

Pace, Frank, 442
paid family leave (PFL), 40–41, 78, 177, 181, 378, 470
Pak, Karen, 290, 294
participative leadership, 136, 156
part-time work, 61–62, 118–19
Pass It On Network, 474–75
Patient Protection and Affordable Care Act. *See* Affordable Care Act
Pavlova, Maria K., 254, 257
Paycheck Fairness Act, 42
Peace Corps, 443
Pension Protection Act, 181
pensions. *See* defined benefit (DB) pensions
people-oriented attitudes, 153, 155–56
Perry, Jane, 197
personality characteristics, 132
personal relationships, *275*
person-job fit, 157, 268–69, 286, 290, 361
PFL. *See* paid family leave
phased retirement, 8, 73, 111, 118–19, 122, 179, 203, 251, 279, 372, 395–96. *See also* bridge employment
physical labor, 75, 78, 133, 192, 195, 236–37, 313, 315, 329, 469
physiological needs, 354
Pitt-Catsouphes, Marcie, 200, 201, 271
Points of Light, 453
portfolio pathways, 9, 482, 483, 485–89, 492–94
positive psychology, 289–92, 352
Potočnik, Kristina, 254
poverty, adults below poverty level at age 70, *28*
Powell, Jerome H., 2
pre-boomers: lifetime earnings of, 19–21; race/ethnicity of, 17; retirement incomes of, 21–26; retirement security of, 16, 26–29
precarious employment: and caregiving responsibilities, 379; older women and, 4; secure versus, 72–73
primary control, 293
productive aging, 249–58; age-friendly workplaces for, 193–204; caregiving as component of, 254–56; concept of, 35–36, 193–94, 249–51; engaging activities in, 252–56; health linked to, 462; Hispanic populations and, 97–98; ideological function of concept of, 53, 54, 80; models of aging at variance with, 53, 54, 97; neuroscience and, 431; process model of, 413; social policy for promoting, 473–75; societal benefits of, 249–50, 252; volunteering as component of, 252–54. *See also* commitment to work; engagement
productive engagement, 35
Program for the International Assessment of Adult Competencies (PIAAC), 333
Program of Comprehensive Assistance for Family Caregivers, 181
Protecting Older Workers against Discrimination Act, 39–40, 470
psychology of work, 272
psychosocial age, 270
public policy. *See* social policy
Public/Privates Ventures, 442
PulpWorks, 434
Putnam, Linda L., 199, 202

Quality of Life Research Center, Claremont Graduate University, 446

race/ethnicity: ageism and, 38; caregiving experience affected by, 376, 380–81; composition of age 70; population by birth cohort, 17, *17*
Radl, Jonas, 253
Radpour, Siavash, 2
Rasch, Rena, 233
Rau, Barbara L., 197, 417
re-careering, 118, 251
Recognize, Assist, Include, Support, and Engage (RAISE) Family Caregivers Act, 378

recruitment and hiring: ageism as concern in, 122, 134–35, 174, 212, 234, 236; self-management tips related to, 299–300; technology's role in, 122, 316–17, 319; for volunteer programs, 448–50, 452–53
reemployment, 117, 489
reentry, to labor force, 117, 179, 489
relationships. *See* personal relationships; social relationships and interaction, work-related
Renewment, 394
replacement rate, of preretirement earnings, 26–27, *27*
research suggestions, 10–11, 43, 63, 98, 138, 150, 161–62, 182, 318–19, *318*, 379–81, 416–17, 435
resilience: as component of self-management, 289, 299–300; defined, 351; development of, 351; against discrimination, 40; as factor contributing to well-being, 7
Retired Service Volunteer Program, 442
retirement: ageism as factor in decisions about, 213, 393, 395, 488; changing conditions of, 8, 192, 393–402; corporate policies on, 395–96; defining, 394; delay of, 36, 69–72, 76–77, 80, 87, 396–98, 472–73 (*see also* extended work life); factors influencing, 8, 395–98; financial feasibility of, 4, 395; fluid patterns of, 8, 73; future of, 401–2; happiness in relation to, 97–98; health outcomes in relation to, 97–98; history of, 393–94; incentives for early, 396; mandatory, 76, 181, 192, 270; as new life stage, 394–95; outcomes of, in Hispanic populations, 98; personal priorities in, 399; push/pull factors in, 396; skill and income levels as effects on, 4; transition to, 8, 73, 111, 118–19, 122, 179, 203, 251, 279, 372, 395–96, 411 (*see also* bridge employment; phased retirement); use of time in, 398–99, *399*; work undertaken during, 399
retirement coaching, 398
retirement incomes, 21–26; housing and financial wealth outside of retirement accounts, 25–26, *25*; median income at age 70, *26*; pensions, 23–24; Social Security, 21–23; total of, 26
RetirementJobs.com, 204
retirement planning: bridge employment linked (negatively) to, 414; company counseling on, 178–79; evolution of, 398–401; family/group orientation as influence on, 91–92; in Hispanic populations, 91–94; personal relationships and, 275. *See also* life planning
retirement savings programs, 488
retirement security: culturally-responsive approaches to, 60–61; demographic shifts and, 17–19; educational attainment as influence on, 17–18; evaluation of, 26–28; extended work life in relation to, 4, 16, 29, 251, 395, 429, 482–83; of Hispanic populations, 88, 93–94; individual responsibility for, 36, 70; lifetime earnings as influence on, 19–21; nontraditional employment as obstacle to, 330; precarity of, 87, 482, 489; projections and outlook for, 28–30; public opinion on, 401; retirement incomes and, 21–26; senior entrepreneurship as means to, 429; unemployment and, 489
retirement timing: effective age of retirement, 76, 94–95, *96*; expected age of retirement, 71, *71*, 94, *96*; in Hispanic populations, 92, 94–95, *95*, *96*, 97
retraining. *See* learning, upskilling, and retraining
rewards, intrinsic vs. extrinsic, 151, 156–57, 238, 357, 415–17. *See also* motivation, generational expressions of
Richman, Karen, 91
Rix, Sara E., 203
Robert N. Butler Aging Center, Columbia University, 204
Robinson, Marilynne, 11
robots, 313, 315–16
Rockefeller, David, 442
Rodríguez-Cifuentes, Francisco, 358
role accumulation theory, 254
role enhancement, 255
role strain, 255
role theory, 412–13
Romaioli, Diego, 358
Rubin, David C., 232
Rudolph, Cort W., 2
Ryan, Katherine M., 234
Ryan, Richard M., 218

safety needs, 354–55
Salthouse, Timothy A., 236
Sandiford, Peter, 199, 203
Sanzenbacher, Geoffrey T., 330
satisfaction. *See* happiness; job satisfaction
Scharn, Micky, 396
schedules. *See* flexible work arrangements
Schedules That Work Act, 40, 41
Scherbov, Sergei, 426
Schnell, Tatjana, 359
Scholl, Juliann C., 195, 196, 197
Schwellnus, Cyrille, 332
Scott, Andrew, 462–63

secondary control, 293
SECURE Act, 473, 488
selection, optimization, and compensation strategies, 132, 136, 138, 293, 294, 361, 416
self-actualization, 359–60
self-concept, 273–74, *274*
self-determination. *See* autonomy and self-determination
self-efficacy, 288, 289, 300, 309, 414
self-employment, 117–18, 484–85
self-esteem, 356–59
self-management, 6–7; and competence/performance issues, 267–81; psychological perspective on, 289–92; and retraining, 299–300; skills and capabilities involved in, 288–89, 299–300; and sustainable employability, 285–300; unemployment and, 298–99; at work, 288–89; work-related interventions to aid, 292–98
self-reflection, 289, 299
Seligman, Martin, 289
Senior Community Service Employment Program (SCSEP), 39, 42, 181, 468
Senior Companion Program, 442
Senior Corps, 42, 442
senior entrepreneurship, 425–37; advocacy and policy related to, 435; assets provided by, 426, 427, 430–31, 436; COVID-19 and, 437; demographic shifts and, 426–27; education programs for, 434, 438n31; encouragement of, 433–34; growth in, 426–27, 429–30; impact of, 427–29; in international settings, 428; motivations for, 429; neuroscience and, 431; older women and, 431–33; overview of, 8; research suggestions on, 435; as retirement alternative, 280, 307, 397
Senior Entrepreneurship Works, 425
Service Corps of Retired Executives (SCORE), 442
Service Enterprise Initiative, 453
Sewdas, Ranu, 356
Shanahan, Michael, 290
Sheldon, Karen, 432–33
Sherraden, Michael, 250
Shlain, Tiffany, 430–31
Silbereisen, Rainer K., 254, 257
skill level, as effect on extended work life, 114–15, *298*, 331
Sloan Center on Aging and Work, 200, 257, 271, 446, 448, 467
Sloan Foundation, 5, 204; Program on Working Longer, 199–200
Smeaton, Deborah, 197
Smith, Lynda, 468
Smyer, Michael, 271
Sobal, Jeffery, 55
social capital, 42
Social Insurance Fund for University Family Care, 470
social policy, 9; bridges to employment in, 467–68; and caregiving, 377–79, 470–71; educational attainment encouraged by, 330, 467; extended work life/delayed retirement encouraged by, 70, 76–77, 80, 192; international perspective on, 464–75; productive aging promoted by, 473–75; and senior entrepreneurship, 435; in United States, 3, 180–81, 192, 463–64, 472–73; on workplace conditions, 469–71. *See also* Social Security
social relationships and interaction, work-related, 151, 160, 234, 239, 293, 312, 355–56, 414, 416–17, 490–91
Social Security: calculation of benefits, 354; earnings limit set by, 125n38, 125n39; financial health of, 16, 21–22, 27, 87, 279, 473; Hispanic populations' knowledge of, 93; life expectancy pressures on, 17; retirement income from, 21–23, *23*; rule changes (retirement age) for, 15–16, 71, 76, 279, 394, 472
Social Security 2100 Act, 473
Social Security Act, 279, 393
Social Security Administration, 182
Social Security Caregiver Credit Act, 40, 41
Society for Human Resource Management (SHRM), 6, 191, 198
socioeconomic status, and caregiving, 377
socioemotional experience, 132, 151
socioemotional selectivity theory, 135, 136, 151, 155, 159, 308, 416, 490
solo agers, 401
Sonnentag, Sabine, 254
stability, employee, 119–20, 137
Stanford Center on Longevity, 394
Stanford Graduate School of Education Center on Adolescence, 445
Stanford University Distinguished Careers Institute, 484
state government policies, 181
Staudinger, Ursula M., 353
stereotypes, age-related, 40, 133–34, 152–53, 211–19, 233–35, 270–71, 314, 353, 425
stereotype threat, 214–17, 234–35
Straunch, Barbara, 431
stress, in the workplace, 280
subjective age, 232, 357–58
successful aging. *See* productive aging
succession planning, 203, 216
Sun, Xiaomin, 212

Super, Donald E., 159
supervisors, and flexible work arrangements, 200–203
Supporting Grandparents Raising Grandchildren Act, 471
Sustainable Development Goals, 466
sustainable employability, 285–300
Sweet, Stephen, 200

talent management, 120, 122
Tang, Fengyan, 253, 254
task-oriented attitudes, 156–58
task performance, 235
Tasner, Paul, 434
Taylor, Philip, 200, 201
teamwork: dyads, 155, 157–60; intergenerational, 5, 120–22, 136–37, 149–62; leadership styles and, 136, 156; organization-oriented attitudes and, 159–60; people-oriented attitudes and, 155–56; task-oriented attitudes and, 157–58
technology, 7, 307–19; age-related attitudes toward, 317; as assistance to older workers, 278–79; automation afforded by, 313–14, 331–32; characteristics and affordances of emerging, 309, *310*, 311–17; communication concerns arising from, 318–19; demographic shifts and, 307–8; digital skills, 331; flexible work arrangements associated with, 202, 311–12; future impact of, 307–8; interaction, adaptation, and feedback afforded by, 314–15; as learning/upskilling/retraining tool, 314–15, 467; physical labor mitigated by, 133, 237; as recruitment and hiring tool, 122, 316–17, 319; research suggestions on, 318–19, *318*; training of older workers in, 237, 308–9, 314, 319, 331; ubiquitous, 309, 311–13
Techtonic Group of Colorado, 468
telecommuting. *See* location flexibility
temporary work, 117
Thomas, Christopher H., 213
Thomas, Kathryn, 173
Thomas, William, 394
Thorsen, Sannie, 213
Tilburg, Theo Van, 256
time flexibility, 198, 239, 493
time perspective, 361
Title V, Older Americans Act, 39, 42–43
"too old for" (TOF) narratives, 358
Topa, Gabriela, 358
Tormala, Zakary, 212
Trafford, Abigail, 394
training. *See* learning, upskilling, and retraining
transcendence, 359
transformational leadership, 137, 156, 296–97
transgender adults, 57, 61–62. *See also* LGBT+ population
Transition to Teaching, 443
Tripartite Alliance for Fair and Progressive Employment Practices, 218
Tri-State Learning Collaborative on Aging, 181
Trump, Donald, 78
Truxillo, Donald M., 157
turnover, employee, 119–20, 137

ubiquitous computing, 309, 311–13
underemployment, 61–62, 77
undocumented immigrants, 62, 89, 90, 94
unemployment: effects of, 116; job displacement as cause of, 116–17; long-term, 115–19; occupational change and, 118; reentry issues and, 117, 179, 489; self-management and, 298–99. *See also* underemployment
unified theory of acceptance and use of technology, 317
United Nations: Open-Ended Working Group on Aging, 466; Sustainable Development Goals, 466
University of Michigan, 446; Institute for Social Research, 435; Ross School of Business, 435
University of Minnesota, 484
unpaid work, caregiving as, 59–60, 74, 78, 80
unretirement, 37, 42, 179, 203, 372, 397, 414, 472, 483
untagging, 298, 299
upskilling. *See* learning, upskilling, and retraining
U.S. Administration for Community Living, 470–71
U.S. Department of Labor, 181, 468
US Department of Labor, 39
U.S. Department of Veterans Affairs, 181
U.S. Federal Reserve Bank, 435
U.S. Fish and Wildlife Service, 181
U.S. Senate: Small Business and Entrepreneurship Committee, 435; Special Committee on Aging, 180, 435, 463

vacation, 493
Van der Mark-Reeuwijk, Kerstin G., 295
Van Groenou, Marjolein Broese, 256
Van Willigen, Marieke, 257
Verhaegen, Paul, 236
Vickerstaff, Sarah A., 199
vitamin model, 312

volunteering, 441–53; age of participants in, 256–57; characteristics of participants in, 444–45; contexts for, 441–42; defining, 441; future of, 452–53; motivations for, 444–45; as path to employment, 451; personal benefits of, 256–57, 445–46; prevalence of, 443–44, 452; as productive aging, 252–54; professionalization of, 453; programs for, 442–43; recruiting for, 448–50, 452–53; retention of older adults for, 450–52; in retirement, 399; social capital earned by, 42; societal benefits provided by, 9, 447–48; work in relation to, 253
Von Hippel, Courtney, 215

Walters, Abigail N., 330
Wang, Emily, 331
Wang, Yi, 251
Wansink, Brian, 55
Ward-Griffin, Catherine, 292
wealth, outside of retirement accounts, 25–26, *25*
well-being, 7–8; caregiving's effect on, 257, 374; eudemonic, 352, 360; as goal state, 352; hedonic, 352; Maslow's hierarchy of needs and, 352, 354–60; in older vs. younger workers, 236; retirement in relation to, 97–98; self-determination as factor in, 55, 75; volunteering as contributor to, 254, 446; work as source of, 352, 354–61; as workforce management concern, 176. *See also* happiness; health
Wiley, Jack, 233
wisdom. *See* experience/wisdom of older adults
women: caregiving by, 36–37, 74, 257–58, 374–76; labor force participation of, 19, 22; median annual earnings, 20–21, *20*; Social Security benefits for, *22*; Xennial, 20–22. *See also* older women

work: barriers to older adults in, 2; constrained choices concerning, 55–58; diverse influences on, 274–75, *274*; meanings of, 43; secure versus precarious, 72–73. *See also* extended work life
work design, 135, 292–93, 469
workforce management: of age-diverse workforce, 4–5, 119–22, 131–39, 149–62; demographic shifts and, 4, 111–13, 121–22, 131, 149, 249; extended work life considerations for, 119–21, 171–74; interventions to aid self-management, 294–95, *295*; policies and practices for older adults, 5, 121–23, 134–38, 171–80, *175*, 191–204, 239, 280–81, 395, 470, 471, 475, 493–94; recruitment as aspect of, 122, 134–35; technology-related, 316–17. *See also* age-friendly workplaces
work-life balance, 41, 178, 218
work-life fit, 361
workplace age discrimination scale (WADS), 37–38
work satisfaction. *See* job satisfaction
work schedules. *See* flexible work arrangements
World Economic Forum, 475
World Health Organization, 217, 461

Xennials: lifetime earnings of, 19–21; race/ethnicity of, 17; retirement incomes of, 21–26; retirement security of, 16, 26–29; Social Security benefits for, 22

YearUp, 443
YMCA/YWCA, 443
younger workers: labor force participation of, 112–13; stereotypes about, 14, 133, 152–53, 212

Zacher, Hannes, 197, 286

# About the Contributors

**Moira Allan** is the Paris-based cofounder and international coordinator of the global Pass It On Network of positive aging advocates from sixty-five countries.

**Takashi Amano** is an assistant professor of social work at Rutgers University, Newark, whose research interests are physical, social, and intellectual activity engagements; cognitive impairment and dementia; and long-term support and services in later life.

**Andrew Arche**, a senior double majoring in psychology and cognitive science at the University of Michigan, is interested in the negative mental health effects of informal caregiving.

**Peter Riley Bahr** is an associate professor in the Center for the Study of Higher and Postsecondary Education at the University of Michigan who studies pathways into and through community colleges or career and technical centers, leading to the workforce or four-year institutions.

**Margaret E. Beier** is associate professor of psychological sciences at Rice University whose research concentrates on the intersection of aging, lifelong learning and development, and work.

**Melissa Brown** is a part-time faculty member at the Boston College School of Social Work and a consultant to organizations promoting social inclusion for individuals with disabilities.

**Anne-Marije Buckens** is the founder and owner of 50 Company, a career agency for older workers in the Netherlands.

**Dawn C. Carr** is associate professor of sociology at Florida State University and faculty associate at the Pepper Institute for Aging and Public Policy.

**Kara A. Carter** is a doctoral student at the University of Iowa School of Social Work with clinical experience in medical social work and end-of-life care.

**Damir Cosic** is a senior research associate at the Urban Institute whose research focuses on income distribution and labor market experience of older Americans, and their transition into retirement.

**Phyllis A. Cummins**, senior research scholar at Scripps Gerontology Center, Miami University, Ohio, investigates education and training for older workers, the role of community colleges, skill development over the life course, and economic security in retirement.

**Meghan K. Davenport**, a graduate student in psychological sciences at Rice University, studies workplace aging, training, motivation, transitions in and out of the workforce, and the influence of individual differences on these processes.

**Helen Dennis**, a nationally recognized leader on issues of aging, employment, and the new retirement, is an editor, an author of more than one hundred articles, a weekly syndicated columnist, and a PBS/Next Avenue "Top Influencer in Aging."

**Antonia Díaz-Valdés I.**, a data analyst and teacher at the Society & Health Research Center in Santiago, Chile, and at Boston College, focuses on understanding the retirement intentions and behaviors of Hispanic older adults and the impact on health and well-being of retirement timing.

**Doug Dickson** cofounded the Encore Network and is board chair of Encore Boston Network, a cross-sector coalition dedicated to engaging the talent of people over fifty.

**Elizabeth F. Fideler**, editor of Rowman & Littlefield's *Handbook on Aging and Work*, is a founding member of the Sloan Research Network on Aging & Work at Boston College and author of three books on older workers.

**Trude Furunes**, professor of organization and leadership at University of Stavanger, Norway, and visiting professor at HAN University of Applied Sciences, the Netherlands, studies the aging workforce, human resource management (HRM), health promoting leadership, and hospitality management.

**Ernest Gonzales**, assistant professor at NYU's Silver School of Social Work, contributes to the development of knowledge on policies and programs shaping health among individuals and benefiting communities and society.

**Janet M. Hively** is an international consultant and cofounder of several networks that support productive aging, including the Pass It On Network.

**Elizabeth Isele** is the founder and CEO of the Global Institute for Experienced Entrepreneurship and a PBS/Next Avenue "Top Influencer in Aging."

**Richard W. Johnson** is a senior fellow in the Income and Benefits Policy Center at the Urban Institute, where he directs the Program on Retirement Policy.

**Brian Kaskie** is a professor of health management and policy at the University of Iowa whose primary research interest concerns the intersection of public policies and older Americans.

**Brittany M. King** is a doctoral student in sociology at Florida State University whose work addresses the bidirectional association social support has with health and how it can be influenced by later-life transitions.

**Katherine D. King** is a licensed clinical psychologist and assistant professor of psychology and member of the geropsychology concentration faculty at William James College.

**Annet de Lange** is professor of human resource management at HAN University of Applied Sciences, the Netherlands, and professor at the Open University, Heerlen, the Netherlands, as well as visiting professor at University of Stavanger, Norway.

**Áine Ní Léime**, senior researcher at the Irish Centre for Social Gerontology, National University of Ireland, Galway, has led several cross-national research projects focused on gender, older workers, and extended working life, using a life course perspective.

**Kelly Ann Marnfeldt** first studied social connection and purpose across the life course at the USC Leonard Davis School of Gerontology and continues at USC's Secure Old Age Lab, focusing on strategies for preventing elder mistreatment and neglect as well as alleviating caregiver burden.

**Christina Matz** is an associate professor in the Boston College School of Social Work, chair of the Older Adults & Families concentration, director of the Spier Fellows in Aging program, and member of the research faculty at BC's Center on Aging & Work.

**Phyllis Moen** directs the Life Course Center at University of Minnesota where she holds the McKnight Presidential Chair in Sociology and investigates retirement, labor market, organizational, family, and life course changes as they intersect with health, well-being, age, gender, and other dimensions of social disadvantage.

**Karen Pak**, assistant professor of strategic human resource management at Radboud University, Nijmegen, the Netherlands, focuses on the job characteristics, HR practices, and major life events that influence the extension of working lives.

**Jensine Paoletti** is a PhD student at Rice University studying industrial-organizational psychology, particularly leadership and teamwork and idiosyncrasies in age-diverse work contexts.

**Sarah E. Patterson** is a National Institute on Aging postdoctoral fellow concerned with enduring norms and expectations of family functioning across domains: aging, health, and the life course; intergenerational inequality; and gender inequality at the work and family nexus.

**Georgina Randsley de Moura** is professor of social and organizational psychology at University of Kent, England, with research interests focused on areas of leadership and innovation, particularly how individuals, groups, and organizations identify and react to leadership potential.

**Michael P. Robinson** is a master's student at Liberty University working toward a degree in industrial-organizational psychology.

**Hannah Rochford** is a third-year PhD student within the University of Iowa's Health Services and Policy Research program.

**Cort W. Rudolph**, assistant professor of industrial-organizational psychology at Saint Louis University, studies a variety of issues related to the aging workforce, including application of a lifespan development perspective, well-being and work longevity, and ageism.

**Eduardo Salas**, Allyn R. & Gladys M. Cline professor and chair of the Psychological Sciences Department at Rice University, has coauthored more than 450 journal articles and book chapters and has coedited thirty-three books and authored one book on team training.

**Jennifer Schramm** is a senior strategic policy adviser for labor market issues at the AARP Public Policy Institute, where she focuses on identifying challenges and opportunities related to workers and job seekers ages fifty and above.

**Christine Rutledge Smith** is completing doctoral studies in clinical psychology at William James College, with interests in gender dynamics in the workplace, middle- and later-life career transitions, geropsychology, psychotherapy, and psychological assessment.

**Karen E. Smith** is a senior fellow in the Income and Benefits Policy Center at the Urban Institute, where as an internationally recognized expert in microsimulation she has played a lead role in the development of the dynamic simulation of income model.

**Amanda Sonnega** is an associate research scientist at the University of Michigan's Institute for Social Research program in Social Environment and Health, where she is responsible for integrating communication, outreach, and education efforts for the Health and Retirement Study.

**Ben Steeden** is a social psychology researcher and associate lecturer at the University of Kent, England, whose research focuses on evaluations of leadership potential, ageism in the workplace, and well-being at work.

**Sarah Michelle Steeley** received her master's degree in geriatric social work from NYU in 2020 and currently works at a nursing home in Manhattan, serving New York City's elderly population.

**Anthony A. Sterns**, CEO of iRxReminder LLC in Cleveland and adjunct professor of business management and leadership at CUNY's School of Professional Studies, is a recognized expert in gerontechnology and a pioneer in the use of smartphones for improving the quality of life for individuals living with chronic illness.

**Harvey L. Sterns** is professor emeritus of psychology and director and senior fellow of the Institute for Life-Span Development and Gerontology at the University of Akron, and research professor of gerontology in Family and Community Medicine at Northeast Ohio Medical University.

**Debra Street**, professor of sociology at SUNY Buffalo, conducts research in social gerontology centered around public policies that promote health and well-being among older people.

**Hannah J. Swift** is a social psychologist at the University of Kent, England, whose research explores issues of ageism, equality, prejudice, and discrimination in international journals and reports.

**Elora C. Voyles**, an assistant professor of industrial-organizational psychology at Southern Illinois University, Edwardsville, researches interpersonal perceptions and factors (such as stereotypes and metastereotypes) that enable or limit success at work.

**Mo Wang** holds the Lanzillotti-McKethan Eminent Scholar Chair at the Warrington College of Business, University of Florida, was editor of the *Oxford Handbook of Retirement*, and currently serves as the editor in chief for the journal *Work, Aging and Retirement*.

**Yi Wang** is an assistant professor of social work at the University of Iowa with research interests in productive engagement, social and environmental determinants of health disparities, and age-friendly communities.

**Ruilin Wu**, a graduate of Rice University with a major in psychology, is interested in research on personality, teams, and well-being at work.

**Takashi Yamashita** is an associate professor of sociology and faculty member in the gerontology PhD program at University of Maryland, Baltimore County, interested in lifelong learning, social determinants of health and well-being, health literacy, gerontology education, and social statistics education.

**Hannes Zacher**, professor of work and organizational psychology at Leipzig University in Germany, investigates aging at work, career development, and occupational well-being; proactivity, innovation, leadership, and entrepreneurship; and pro-environmental employee behavior.